THE TRIUMPH OF THE

MIDDLE CLASSES

THE TRIUMPH OF THE MIDDLE CLASSES

BY CHARLES MORAZÉ

ANCHOR BOOKS

DOUBLEDAY & COMPANY, INC.

GARDEN CITY, NEW YORK

CONTENTS

BOOK TWO:
THE BOURGEOIS REVOLUTIONS, 1780–1840

BOOK THREE:
CAPITALIST AND INDUSTRIAL EUROPE,
1840–80

CONCLUSION

FOREWORD

The year 1900 was a wonderful one, when men were proud to be middle-class, and to be Europeans. The fate of the whole world was decided around green baize-covered tables in London, Paris or Berlin. Rubber trees from the Amazons were shipped to Malaya, the vast coal seams of the Upper Hwang-Ho were being exploited at the expense of the wretched labourers, and in the north of the Upper Vaal a mining city sprang up in a few short weeks. Mobilized by steam, the planet's riches were being shifted 'from one side of the world to the other', to quote *Le Bateau Ivre*, on orders flashed by telegraph in two or three minutes. Decisions reached by boards of directors in London, Paris or Berlin affected the lives of millions of human beings who did not suspect that their right to happiness depended on quotations scribbled on blackboards in three noisy exchanges built like temples, in which raged the battles of unbridled financial ambition. Not a single detail escaped the notice of Europe's financial capitals: they fixed the price of a tram ticket in Rio de Janeiro, and the working hours of a coolie in Hong Kong. So much power had never before been concentrated in so few hands within so small an area of the globe. It was the age of triumph of the European middle classes. This book sets out to explain how this power was built up.

In 1780 the ancient civilizations of the world, whether Chinese or Indian, of the Crescent or of the Cross, existed side by side on an almost equal footing. Yet almost all were showing signs of increasing age, and especially in the rigid, undeviating routine which characterized rural life and labour. The Far East could, it was true, boast cities far bigger than London or Paris, but it had no parallel to the urban development of Western Europe—a unique phenomenon springing from the surge and ferment of new ideas around the shores of the North Sea. Curiosity, a desire for novelty, boldness, a zest for gain—these were the qualities which stimulated the progress of science and the development of trade, the great achievements of the nineteenth century. We shall attempt to recapture something of the curiosity experienced by travellers in this age of progress, in order to see the world of 1780 through the young and confident eyes of London or Paris, mutual rivals, yet each on the threshold of a great and epoch-making future. These vivid descriptions, accounts and reminiscences of Europeans fascinated by the exotic and the cosmopolitan emerge very vividly from the dusty volumes. We hope to be forgiven for devoting a hundred pages to these descriptions of a young Europe confronted with ancient civilizations (Book One, pp. 1–101).

The stage was set, the play about to begin. Proud of their science and their law, and buoyed up by their newly acquired wealth, the middle classes emerged from the old social framework and became the champions of action in the service of method: banks and blast furnaces, harbours and highways, changed the geography of Western Europe, a Western Europe which now extended as far as Berlin. With considerable difficulty, and at the cost of several revolutions, they were to achieve their political ambitions—the destruction of the old, conservative monarchies, the proclamation of freedom of enterprise and control over as much of public administration as needed to be preserved. Never had the times appeared so rich in hope, nor human destiny so malleable. Artists and poets, thinkers and statesmen were anxious or elated: Romanticism discovered history and the power of evolution. From Europe the movement spread to America, not only to North America where that Republic so dear to the radical thinkers was being created, but to South America too, where new nations were coming into being on the European pattern. Even the East was stirring. Sixty years of passion and tumult, of injustice and innovation from 1780 to 1840, saw these middle-class 'revolutions' (Book Two, pp. 103–262).

From the 1840s onward the battles of the European middle class were waged with renewed vigour; the victors had a new weapon at their disposal—steam—which made ships ten times more powerful, and pulled the coaches of the new railways. The innovations of 1800 were soon out of date: scarcely were the first blast furnaces perfected before they became old-fashioned and were superseded by more powerful ones. The banks increased their services tenfold. Yet for a time the middle classes were uncertain and afraid: in 1848 the people of Paris made their bid to dominate progress, but without success. The hour of socialism had not yet struck, and it was an arrogant capitalism which established Napoleon III and Bismarck in power. Both these men were eager to equal and surpass England, and competed with each other to achieve this the sooner, projecting the rivalry of big business onto a national scale. Thus London, Paris and Berlin became the great controllers of world progress, because it was they who had been the builders of 'capitalist and industrial Europe' (Book Three, pp. 263–378).

Yet even before this European process was completed, the middle classes of Europe had harnessed their commercial, financial and industrial skills to conquer the world. They thrust their ruthless way across every continent, bringing wars in their train, inciting revolts, but everywhere triumphant. We shall review this 'world conquest' (Book Four, pp. 379–521) in which, without even bothering to exploit the whole of their own continent (see p. 477) the middle classes of Europe forged ahead, transforming Japan, stirring up the southern hemisphere, and shaking Asia from its torpor. Ships, roads, telegraphs and railways opened up the way for a thousand schemes of rural and urban development. Everywhere, the past remnants of age-old civilizations crumbled away under the picks of labour squads snatched from their old rural villages, and everywhere buildings and factories appeared, brought from or inspired by Europe. These were the victories and triumphs of industry.

Yet victory was by no means complete. The vast expanse of China, wretchedly poor but still very much alive, refused to be brought under the yoke. And though the huge, patient mass of India assimilated technical progress, its surface was merely grazed by the still fragile structures of capitalism. The African, inured to slavery, might well have been an easy prey, yet Africa, that giant land of rock and water, of blazing sun and towering vegetation, cost Europe an exhausting effort. In America, the success was too great, for within fifty years it had become the leading industrial power in the world.

A wonderful year indeed was 1900: to the European middle classes, proud of their struggles and successes, proud at having mastered the world with so little loss and with only a modicum of heroic sacrifice, the future seemed secure. Yet 1900 was the eve of those apocalyptic wars in which neighbouring European powers destroyed each other, the eve of a proletarian revolution as wide as a continent, the eve of a spiritual revolution less obvious but even more significant for the future since, going far beyond anything that European individualism could have foreseen, it removed the very foundations of what had been the science of the middle-class era. At the very height of its triumph, cracks were starting in its fabric, and they eventually led to its decay (see Conclusion, pp. 523–51).

This is the epic of a middle class, an epic of science, good fortune, and world-wide influence, but also of ignorance, selfishness and chauvinism. The details of this century are already fading, although it was claimed that in it alone was achieved as much as in the whole of recorded time put together. The present book is simply an attempt to understand it, and it is meant for those who wish to do the same. The writer does not sit in judgement on the dead; his sympathies, on the contrary, are warm and human. The study of the past is not sad but salutary. The middle classes of nineteenth-century Europe conquered the world not because they were middle class or European, but because they were more capable than their predecessors, or than leaders in other parts of the world, of exploiting the technical weapons put into men's hands by the progress of science. For a century and a half, science and progress claimed the European middle classes. Science and progress choose those who serve them best.

BOOK ONE

YOUNG EUROPE—
OLD WORLDS
1780

1

Europe Rises in the West

WE are not beginning with the usual description of Europe on the eve of the French Revolution for the simple reason that it obviously never occurred to the Londoners, Viennese, Parisians or Romans of the day that they *were* 'on the eve of the French Revolution'. Their main aim was to be happy. It may be objected that every age wants happiness, but this is not true. There are times when it is fashionable to die for the sake of honour or mystic love, when 'grand passions' are all the rage, but not even in the Germany of the *Sturm und Drang*, nor in the sentimental dramas of Diderot, nor even in Rousseau's appeals for a new education, did passion reach such a pitch of intensity that it excluded gaiety, a delight in the miniature or the dainty trinket, or the love of music and intellectual amusements. Between two intensely serious ages, that of the serious Romantics and the serious middle classes, the climate of the 1780s may be summed up in the word *esprit*, by which was meant not the Spirit of the Trinity, nor the questing spirit of knowledge, the sacred guardian of progress, but 'spirit' as Voltaire defined it in his *Dictionnaire Philosophique*—'ingenious reason'. It meant, too, the subtle pleasures of society people who implied more than they said and preferred to leave as much as they could to the imagination.

In 1785, then, society's chief diversion lay not in the fact that it was divided into three Orders, but in discovering in the first temperate *salons*, and in the delightful new coffee-houses, some ingenious novelty, some fresh source of trifling pleasure. Yet we ourselves must not be carried away, as they were, by this passion for baubles and trinkets which at the time made Matthew Boulton's for-

tune, and which a few years later led to the downfall
of Cousin Pons. It is unlikely that we shall be, at least if
we have the genuine feel of the period; for the fashionable
toy of 1785 had none of the sheer prettiness, the drawing-
room appeal, of its successors or of its predecessors. It
represented tremendous and quite recent achievements.
There was the mechanical clock, a triumph of the new
technique of clock-making, or the geometrical object
which ingeniously took to pieces and bore witness to the
astounding new discoveries made by mathematicians;
there was Chinese jade, now at long last beginning to be
distinguished from jasper. These objects revealed a gentle
revolution in domestic habits, and one which introduced
into the daily life of Europe both scientific skill and an
eagerly cosmopolitan outlook. The European discovered
the Indian and the Inca, the Huran and the Chinaman, a
whole vast planet that the man-about-town could now
draw on for a host of minor pleasures, stuffing his pipe
with tobacco, and making his own cocoa (unless, copying
Africa and Asia rather than America, he preferred tea or
coffee).

It was an age which perfected the art of living, which
gave to Greuze's portraits a smile utterly different from
that found in Da Vinci's, and a charm not untouched by
sensuality. It was a delightful age when, after two centuries of strife and stormy seas, the European citizen was
beginning to feel that the whole wide world was working
exclusively for his pleasure. Voltaire called it 'the iron
age', a strange epithet to us who are acquainted with the
real iron age of blast furnaces and Bessemer converters.
But we must go further in our attempt to think ourselves
back into the atmosphere of the period which forms the
start of our study.

The men of 1780 were certainly not living in hourly
expectation of the Revolution. They neither wanted it,
nor were afraid of it; in fact no one gave a thought to it,
in spite of contemporary historians who profess to discover signs to the contrary even in La Bruyère's *Caractères*. What really interested those men of 1780 was the
progress of science. Very few could really understand it—

but the building of the Academy was almost as dear to Berliners as the King's Palace—and Parisians were already beginning to realize that the centre of their world was no longer at Versailles, but in the workshops, botanical gardens, and libraries which every day revealed something new to arouse their curiosity. Londoners out for a Sunday stroll made for the newly-built docks in the port, went to see the first steam mill, admired the first iron barge; others flocked to the lecture-halls of the Royal Society. They combined their love of science with a curiosity about technical processes which budding inventors made even more fashionable by lively expositions of the complicated procedures for measuring the earth, or observing the stars; or of the ingenuity which made hot-air balloons rise into the sky of their own accord. Aristocrats thumbed the Encyclopaedia in search of recipes for cosmetics or rare delicacies. Plates illustrating mechanics or human anatomy were studied with interest. Yet curiosity was not merely bookish and academic; it ranged far and wide. Travel had never been so popular nor inspired such a lively literature, in the tradition of Laurence Sterne.

In 1786 Goethe left Carlsbad secretly, because he wished to travel alone. He set off, like so many of his contemporaries, in search of Italy, Rome and its ruins. It is generally stated that not until Valmy did Goethe declare that 'a new era was dawning'. It was in fact on his arrival in Rome that he wrote: 'I shall live in peace and quiet here for the rest of my days. A new life is opening out before me.' The truth was that in the ruins of an empire he had just become aware of a new human dimension. When Europe discovered the ancient world of Herculaneum and Pompeii it discovered also the vast perspectives of history itself. Winckelmann, in his work on the classification of Roman remains, had fired the imagination of scholars with his theory about the various periods of ancient art; fashion too, first in England and then in France, stealthily consigned to the attic, piece by piece, any furniture and fittings that were baroque or rococo, and replaced them by the 'antique'. The antique brought into house interiors its colonnades and pilasters, its decorations in grisaille with their delicate lines, and its Pompeian style; antique ruins invaded parks and gardens. Within a few short years the 'antiquity' of Horace and Virgil took on a new meaning. Their books were no longer regarded as immortal decrees of fate, as well-tried guides to the poetic art, or as a compendium of prophecies. They acquired a date and were given their place in this new classification of time and space. They assumed a historical picturesqueness, the finer shades of which were more readily appreciated because men had discovered the geographical fascination of America, China and India. There was a new art of living, a new art of feeling and thinking, an eager, impressionable curiosity which swept over the whole of Europe from the fogs of London and Paris to the lights of Rome. Thus was cosmopolitanism born.

Yet this was also the age of patriotism, a new kind of patriotism. 'Patriotism' and 'nationalism' were not new concepts in 1785, but although a sense of honour was still comparatively strong, it was linked more with the idea of self-respect *à la Voltaire* than with respect for race or royalty. Voltaire showed himself aware of this in his comment on the line from Corneille: *Fille de Scipion et, pour dire encore plus, romaine*. He regarded it as a wretched piece of affectation. But how do wars and treaties and the European balance of power fit into the picture? Naturally the entire political set-up, all the indispensable machinery of government, continued unchanged, although it occupied a far more modest place in public opinion then than it does in many modern history books which claim to give a faithful picture of the age. Vergennes' cabinet may have regarded the victorious sea-warfare being waged against England on the Western Atlantic seaboard as a revenge for the defeats suffered in the Indian Ocean, and honoured Suffren accordingly; yet it was not this policy of theirs which aroused enthusiasm, but the birth of a new agricultural republic on the shores of the New World, and the public's real hero was La Fayette, who had gone there as a *franc-tireur* on a temporary commission; and perhaps also Beaumarchais, who was none too scrupulous in furnishing arms to the colonists.

The enthusiasm with which men of culture welcomed the birth of the United States completely stifled the few expressions of regret in France at the loss of Canada and India. The partition of Poland caused little stir, and did little to diminish the prestige of the two monarchs responsible for it. Louis XVI, philosopher king, reformer of agriculture and industry, patron of the arts and sciences, and his accomplice Catherine the Great, Empress of Russia, and 'Semiramis of the North'.

How could land cultivation be improved? How could industry be made more prosperous? How could people be made happier? These were the chief preoccupations which we would now call patriotic or national. Happiness is writ large, in a place of honour, in the American Constitution.

It is not, however, our intention to embark on a sterile exposition of European politics in the 1780s, but rather to recall certain vital facts which will help to place the following chapters more firmly in their context. In the course of three centuries the Atlantic had become the central trade area, a great battlefield far more important than the sleepy Mediterranean. For two hundred years skilled sailors had brought wealth across the Atlantic and the adjacent Indian and Pacific Oceans, to the shores of Europe; and fortunes, which previously had been amassed by pillage and conquest, were now made by traders using wily and cunning tactics, diplomacy, forcefulness and powers of persuasion; and these traders were less interested in gold and silver than in a wide new range of products from all over the world on which European fashion had set a high price. The age of enlightenment was essentially and primarily the age of trade, and trade so profitable that it was able to make many and varied demands on politics as well. It was trade which gave England its economic, financial and monetary institutions, its banks and insurance companies, its credit and business codes. It was trade which dictated to England its political institutions, its Board of Trade and its costly interventions in diplomacy and war. And it was trade which imposed on the European nations a social structure of its own choosing, a society in which 'all other obligations took second place to those of debtors to creditors', in which the landowner must curb his political privileges, and was only forgiven for being wealthy provided he tried to bring down the price of farm commodities, and opened his fields to potential mine-owners and his parks to town-builders. The country labourer was forgiven for being poor (and poor at the expense of his parish) provided he would work for next to nothing in the shops, or better still in the new factories owned by prosperous business-men. This was a society, in short, where the new hero was the man who risked his money to make still more, and who, if he failed, became a victim of the harsh commercial laws, a bankrupt without hope and with no future but a debtor's prison.

In all this activity, industry was merely the handmaid of business. It was still far from being as profitable as trade, and very far from gaining complete control over economic life. Furthermore industry had not as yet made more than limited contacts with a science still in its infancy and too young, in fact, to be of use to it. Relying on the initiative of bold *entrepreneurs*, it had to do the best it could with techniques which had been taken over from the old trade guilds with hardly any adaptation or improvement. There was no such thing as an industrial revolution in 1780; it had not yet evolved from the revolution in social customs.

This, then, was the great age of commerce, and particularly of that most important of all its branches, maritime trade. In this sphere England's superiority was incontestable: English trade outstripped Amsterdam, overwhelmed and shaken as it was by yearly financial crises; and it outstripped Nantes, Bordeaux or Lyons, although they were as prosperous as Liverpool, Bristol or Birmingham, and rather more elegant, since their prosperity had a longer urban tradition behind it. But this very tradition was liable to hamper the new maritime trade to an extent that only later became apparent. The success of London may be measured in addition by the prosperity of Frankfurt and Hamburg, which in some respects were its outposts.

The winds of fortune blowing in from the Atlantic penetrated, though not at once, to the inland heart of Europe. Danzig, first and foremost, maintained its old prosperity; Berlin was gradually improving its position. Princes and princelings of Eastern Europe, too, were attempting to set up maritime companies for trade with the Indies. There were maritime companies in Copenhagen, which was understandable, in Berlin, which was surprising, and even in Dresden, Vienna and Munich—and the Russians, too, were endeavouring to gain a foothold on the Baltic, while the old inland fairs were beginning to organize their widespread inland trade on 'maritime' lines. But these inland 'maritime companies' had a hard struggle. Eventually the princely exchequers grew tired of heaping subsidy upon subsidy. A maritime destiny is not for the asking! It is tempting to assert that from east to west across Europe there was a wide range of political and social institutions, from society on the English model to ancient feudalism, and that each different type adapted itself to an economic structure which took into account the increasing difficulties of trading companies from London to Nijni-Novgorod. This might be correct if it were not for the monarchies, whose inflexible traditions upset this neat arrangement. The monarchs, whether great or small, may have acknowledged and envied the great success of maritime trade, and may have been favourably disposed to listen to the suggestions made to them by their middle-class subjects, who wanted to lay their hands on some of the wealth pouring in from the sea and hoped to carry out on their own estates some of the improvements made by the great landowners. But these same monarchs were usually very determined to live in a royal style themselves, and not in the new tradition set up by the English kings. They wanted the heavy pomp and splendour of traditions inherited from Louis xiv.

Every German sovereign had his Versailles, and there were more architects building castles and more landscape gardeners designing parks in eighteenth-century Germany than had ever before been known in Europe. And all these rulers were looking for a Colbert to direct their trading ventures, unwillingly taking a hand themselves when the minister they hoped for failed to emerge from the ranks of their counsellors. The less beribboned the dress the greater the freedom of speech and of action; but there were endless royal fêtes in the style of the court of France; and this imitation of both France and England, more or less influenced by justifications drawn from the philosophical dictionaries, made up what was known as enlightened despotism.

Thus the economic progress which in Western Europe laid the foundations of political liberalism and created a vigorous public opinion, served in the German states to increase the lavish ostentation of the princes and often their absolutism as well. East of the Rhine there were, it is true, varying degrees of despotism. Frederick II naturally had every intention of being his own chief minister (in the French manner), in sole control of the governmental machine. On the other hand, in Saxony, one of the oldest 'nations' in Germany, the Elector had followed English precedent in granting a moderately free hand to his Lutheran subjects in the discussion of and decisions on public affairs, since he feared that they would take offence at his alacrity in being converted to the Catholic Royal House of Poland. Joseph II, blindly trusting in the reason extolled by the *Encyclopédie*, made changes, carried out reforms, codified laws and produced such an excess of order that he brought a whirlwind about his own head.

It is not, however, our purpose to analyse the political mechanism of Europe in the 1780s. It would tell us practically nothing that we need to know for an understanding of how the Europe of the late eighteenth century became the Europe of 1900. In 1900 there were still, of course, many of the same family traditions, the same frontiers, the same parks, castles and administrative habits which had existed in the previous century, but in the nineteenth century, the princes, good or bad, saw the future of their countries taken out of their hands; and in that respect too, the French Revolution, spectacular though it was, was only one manifestation of that great whirlwind of change which was beginning to blow across Europe. It was a storm which raged, not simply from 1789 to 1815, but from 1780 to 1900.

But in 1780 it was as yet no more than a stiff breeze which had its source not in the secret diplomacy of cabinets, in military discipline, in religious fanaticism or what remained of them, but in the very search for modest pleasures, the zest for new things and the curiosity about science and the world, its geography and history. It was fanned by trade, and by the novelties turned out by craftsmen who were making China fashionable everywhere in European society. This fresh wind blowing through society seemed at first to carry no threat to the old political organism whose gnarled trunks, apparently so sturdy, were rooted deep in feudal traditions. Yet when the breeze became a hurricane they were blown down, and though restored here and there in the nineteenth century, fell once and for all in the early twentieth.

What features of the 1780s are essential to a knowledge of Europe? They are to be found, undoubtedly, not in political organisms, but in the soil of Europe, in its peoples, its countryside, its towns, its rural landscapes, its ports and factories; in the myriad activities which, pursued with toil and effort, were to change the very nature of its labours. These were more important even than the Eastern question, or the Polish question, or any financial questions. We propose now to set out on a journey, a sentimental journey in the manner of Sterne, and to travel with deliberate nonchalance the roads along which the postillions of Goethe, Euler, Maupertuis, Diderot, Haydn and Mozart trotted in 1780. We shall not pay particular attention to the big things, but confine ourselves to the small and the insignificant, and try to form an impression of everyday life which though so unchanging in appearance was of endless variety beneath the surface. It was an upheaval in this everyday life which was soon to shake the history of the nineteenth century; the explosion started in Europe but was to change the whole world.

LONDON-BERLIN: A CONTRAST

It is impossible to study here every detail of the life of Europe, which was divided into numerous countries all jealous of their individuality, at a time when patriotism extended very little farther than the parish pump. Nevertheless so important are the differences between the countries directly exposed to Atlantic influences and those still on the periphery that we may be permitted to dwell on them at the outset.

Modernism in England

Every merchant in Frankfurt or Amsterdam, every philosopher in quest of happiness and world prosperity, every sailor waiting for the wind in the tall-masted sailing-ships which scoured the globe, would have urged us to start our world tour with London. Either you liked it or you did not, this upstart city with its thriving business and swirling fog, but it set a magnificent example of the prosperity achieved by a small people, one of the least numerous in Europe, yet the most influential of all because of the irresistible power of its trade and its banking institutions. Its public buildings could not compete with the architectural masterpieces that were the pride of more aristocratic cities; indeed the interest of London lay not in buildings, but in the city itself—the city as a whole, which set a new fashion in urban comfort. We shall not spend too long in visiting the many new churches which had sprung from the fertile brain of Sir Christopher Wren after the Great Fire of the previous century: London's St Paul's was, after all, little more than an imitation of St Peter's in Rome. Let us instead look first at the streets, at traffic hurtling down the Strand at breakneck speed, or along the endless reaches of Holborn. New paving stones kept the roadway clean and level, and since it was fashionable to walk from one place to another in town, the pavements were wide, with railing along the outer edge to protect pedestrians from the throng of carriages. From wooden posts hung lanterns for use in the evenings, and the old watchmen who called the hours all through the night were scarcely needed now, at least in the city centre, since the city was so orderly, and clocks and watches were already in general use. Though there were coffee-houses all over Europe, none could compete with those of London. Only six hundred yards from Westminster were the Ranelagh Gardens with their famous Rotunda, more than sixty yards in diameter. In the middle, in a fireplace surrounded by columns, an enormous brazier supplied heat and light. Strains of music floated down from a raised dais, and for a crown you could buy, with rye bread and butter, those brand-new beverages coffee, tea or chocolate. For those who preferred it the rival establishment at Vauxhall could boast a rotunda in the same style, only a little smaller, but surrounded by even more spacious gardens which at night were lit by over a thousand oil lamps. A band played in the open air, visitors flocked there in their thousands, and numerous pavilions in Chinese style combined a homely welcome with the thrills of the exotic.

England also set a fashion in good living, and in home life, in what Englishmen called 'comfort' and everyone else was to call 'confort'. English private houses had lofty ceilings, spacious staircases, and their brick walls were panelled in light-painted wood, and decorated with graceful garlands. New houses were going up all over London; the builders did not always own the land on which they built; they leased it for sixty years and built lightly, to avoid having to hand over a still valuable house to the landowner. There were, therefore, many new houses side by side with dilapidated ones. Moreover they were uniform in style; behind those façades, miniature reproductions of Hampton Court, there were tiny houses crowded together, but also great buildings, especially in the centre of the city. The nobility had moved out of the city, deserting their town houses which were turned into business premises. Lord Montagu, for instance, installed the British Museum in his mansion. In the parks of the aristocracy middle-class houses were often built around small squares, an arrangement which combined privacy with a love of nature dear to inhabitants still new to city life. London was no longer the sprawling wooden township of Stuart times; it was already a solidly built city ready and waiting for the overcharged elaborations of the Victorian style. But English comfort implied more than a pleasant home life; it meant also clear Hertfordshire water piped and distributed through Sir Hugh Middleton's new canal; better still it meant water pumped under steam pressure through lead pipes; and heating in well-constructed fireplaces with coal, which was more convenient and less costly than wood and had only one disadvantage: it intensified the fog and even—it is said—affected the sun.

Hard work was the order of the day. The penny-post system for letters and parcels catered for correspondence in this enormous city of 800,000 inhabitants. At its heart was the Pool of London near which rose the colossal Customs House, almost as big as the Bank. Around them was built the City, replacing the old administration from Westminster. Innumerable small barges plied to and fro on the Thames below London Bridge, among the ships whose masts were like a swaying forest, branches of a commercial network whose roots tapped the world. Everything could be bought there. Everything was sold, even security. Nowhere else in the world was it so easy to insure oneself, for so modest a sum, against the hazards of the sea and the fluctuations of trade. To keep pace with this entirely new activity, colleges were founded for further education. The leading scholars of the day were brought into contact with a wide public in the amphitheatres of the Royal Society. But above all, this whirl of activity inexorably shaped society. The rich families left the City when it was taken over by business and commerce, and created a new fashionable neighbourhood at St James. Meanwhile the common people crowded into the East End: around Newgate with its prison, and the stench of the meat markets. Already a wretched prole-

tariat was herded together there, their poverty increased
by middle-class prosperity and by the great and continuing wealth of the nobility.

It was not easy to get out of the city, so great was the
throng of carriages. Even Frenchmen were left speechless
at the way the coachmen hurtled along roads which were
often indifferent, narrow, and continually in need of repair. Nowhere else in Europe was there such a busy round
of traffic as that which connected London with its countryside and with other towns and cities. Once this bustle
had been left behind, there was the green English countryside, with its meadows and valleys, its cottages tucked
away amongst trees, its small estates hidden behind
hedges. These estates were not over-large but were prosperous because they were never smaller than a hundred
acres, and were well stocked with cattle which were the
admiration of every landowner in Europe; the cattle win-
tered indoors, were put out to grass in summer, and provided London with the finest meat in the world. Stock-
breeding had not, however, entirely supplanted corn. In
good years England had surplus corn to sell to Portugal
and Spain and sometimes even to France. Outside London it was still a predominantly rural country. There were
still large pockets of land in England given over to the old
systems of mixed cultivation which had supported the
freeholders, small tenant-farmers who had been the backbone of Cromwellian England. But almost everywhere
new crops, new farming methods, and new social groups
were beginning to efface them.

England was still proud of its landed gentry, who had
stopped taking up arms against the court after their abor-
tive attempt to seize power in the seventeenth century,
and had destroyed the old régime by economic innovations instead. Indeed, the success of the agricultural
reformer, Townshend, contributed to that of his brother-
in-law, Walpole, who was for long master of London.
In return the London merchant helped the agriculturist.
Parliament continually passed bills authorizing the split-
ting up of common lands, a process which completed the
ruin of the poor whilst making the fortune of the average

or large landowners. Townshend, then, was one of a number who, on retiring from public life, set the fashion for studying agriculture, and made stockbreeding as important a business as the composition of a ministry. Nowhere else in Europe, Young assures us, were there such well-tended fields and such a comfortable country life. Seventy per cent of the population was still rural—a high proportion by twentieth-century standards, but small in the eighteenth century by comparison with the rest of Europe. It was large enough, however, to produce abundant crops of rye, oats and barley and the widest range of vegetables, while continuing to breed fine long-haired sheep, a tradition inherited from the Middle Ages. Yet it was hardly the golden age of country life. In the midst of this prosperity, English travellers had a good deal to say about the extreme poverty of the country people; not only were there vagrants, driven from the countryside by the disappearance of common lands and enclosures who were starting to drift towards city suburbs, but there was poverty on poor lands untouched by the reforms. In these particularly poor areas, philanthropists even did their best to keep alive some of the wise traditions of former days, by reintroducing pig-farming and poultry-keeping, small rural sidelines which had gone out of fashion. Poor countrymen had such a struggle to make ends meet that it was no wonder they were attracted when merchants offered to lease them a hand-loom, and held out the possibility of piece-work. Many middle-class 'merchants', of country stock and new to trade, made their fortunes in this way. One of the first was Sir Robert Peel's ancestor, who started a small cotton mill on his farm and employed his own family as well as the poor from neighbouring cottages, thus paving the way for the next generation's exodus to the nearby town. Such was the rise of one of the foremost families in England.

London was not the only town that made a great urban blot on the green landscape of southern England. Near the Pennines, black, sprawling patches revealed the spread of towns and mills. Though the ancient port of Bristol was still the second largest city in the country, and though development of colonial trade enabled it to maintain its position during the first half of the century, its supremacy had recently begun to be threatened by new towns which had sprung up from nowhere. They might not rival Bristol in size, but their progress was meteoric; Liverpool, Manchester, Birmingham and Sheffield soon outgrew the older centres of Leeds and Bradford. The old privileges of the trade guilds had disappeared, and those of the trading companies were broken or rather worn down by economic practice and new commercial concepts which the Law Courts, backed by public opinion, gradually came to confirm. The East India Company, for instance, was incapable of exercising its monopoly alone, and had to agree to a sub-contract in exchange for an indemnity. This indemnity, however, gradually decreased, opening the way for numerous rival companies and shipowners eager to engage in so profitable a trade. The Elizabethan guild rules, though they had never been very strictly observed, were invoked more and more rarely and then only for use against crying abuses, such as the disasters caused by the blundering ambition of would-be businessmen who took advantage of the powerlessness of the workers to put their new schemes through more quickly. But the injustice had to be exceptionally harsh, and had sometimes to end in riot, before the corporative régime was again invoked. The new political religion held that profit was the source, as well as the just reward, of creative activity.

So water-wheels soon appeared along the rivers, working the forge-bellows and grindstones of cutlery works. Ironmongers no longer manufactured their wares. Ancient villages were rudely jolted awake. Spinning-jennies, or spinning-frames, invaded the countryside in the wake of the looms, before being concentrated in certain city suburbs, in vast mills run by water-power; and steam-power was soon to follow. So factories hummed busily in places where poor country folk had settled with their meagre belongings when driven out of their small-holdings. Sometimes the small landowner became the small mill-owner. But more often than not he was pulled down to the poverty-stricken proletarian mass on which the manufacturer drew for whatever labour he needed. For this labour he paid practically nothing, and it enabled him to sell his goods at enormous profit in the city markets, and even more in country markets, where hawkers' packs were everywhere in evidence on fair-days.

All this economic activity creates the impression of a kind of vast industrial republic. Yet dominating it all was some 'prince' or, as the saying ran later, some 'king of industry'. There was Boulton of Birmingham, for instance, living in his brand-new mansion, surrounded by a veritable court of artists, poets and inventors (it was with the support of this wealthy patron that James Watt perfected his steam-engine). Boulton was the aristocratic-ironmonger who was to be associated with Wedgwood in an alliance so powerful that it obtained from Pitt's Government, along with the revision of excise duties, freer access to international exchange. Boulton went to Europe in search of artistic inspiration for his products, his knick-knacks. He made cheap reproductions of the marble statues being discovered in Italy, whilst Wedgwood drew on the arts of antiquity for designs for his pottery, ceramics and porcelain. Thanks to them, every middle-class sideboard had its china made from the local clay of the Potteries, and every middle-class kitchen boasted utensils made from the new iron. For Wilkinson, another king of industry, erected furnaces on the banks of the Severn. This iron king had been the first to put smelting and iron puddling on an industrial basis. He had ventured to span the Severn with the first iron bridge. He presented the citizens of London with an extravagant toy in the shape of a boat, made entirely of iron, floating on the Thames.

The rôle of these kings of industry should not, however, be exaggerated; though they caught the imagination of their contemporaries, they were insignificant in comparison with the powerful figures which were to arise in industry a century later. Moreover, they were very few and far between. They reflected a society in process of evolution but which, taken by and large, still kept fairly close to its classical structure. We have seen that the common people, when driven to it by the energy born of despair, could invoke the old guild rules and rely on them to force from the new masters certain improvements in wages. But the masters themselves often used these rules to check dangerous competition. The Government, and even Parliament, hesitated to do away completely with the old laws and principles. In any case they continued to accept the obligation of king, county and parish to ensure that the poor had bread and work. They were still reluctant to compel beggars to work in the workhouses, and the English state, although it soon became the model of the indifferent liberal state, was at that point still a welfare state. The Government opened workshops, particularly in London, tried to ensure that apprentices had a good training, and improved the status of journeymen, for whom they endeavoured, though unsuccessfully, to ensure a decent livelihood. The example of the early masters of industry was more potent than state initiative. Such vast fortunes so speedily amassed were an incentive to ambition. There was naturally the fear of bankruptcy, which so often resulted from rashness, but to stay idle in that rapidly changing society was to run the risk of swelling the ranks of the paupers. So every river in England became the scene of industrial activity much admired by travellers. The gap widened between the prosperous countryside and its burdensome poor, and around the new country houses there surged a tide of change which threatened to engulf the last remnants of the old, merry England.

Tradition in Germany

We move, now, from one end of Europe to the other: to the roads stretching endlessly over the monotonous plains of the Weser and the Spree. Imagine a traveller riding into Berlin in one of those light travelling-coaches, 'berlines', so swift and well-sprung that they were soon to become popular with the middle classes all over Europe. He would have to cross the barriers surrounding the city.

A sightseer would be more likely to be attracted by some famous buildings (the Prince's palace, the King's palace, the building of the Academy) than by the city as a whole. Around these places, Berlin was an overgrown village with a population less than one-eighth of that of London. True, it could boast many factories, each consisting of a central workshop with a large number of home workers, often run by masters with French names. They turned out porcelain and woollen goods, particularly the famous red and blue cloth, and of course silks, all imitated from the French. They also made cotton using English processes, and—a great novelty—made a first attempt at running a sugar refinery.

But Berlin was not a workers' city, it was first and foremost a city of soldiers. The Prussian soldier was different from other soldiers: in Berlin he lived at home with his family, and so made up almost a third of the city's population. In Potsdam, nearby, there was a school which provided the rudiments of education for five thousand soldiers' children. If there were more than the army required, they were given a few crowns and sent to live with peasants who brought them up and gave them work until they were old enough for military service and were needed by the Prussian army. In England it was the merchant's way of life that threw light on the real social forces at work in the country, whereas in Germany it was the soldier who held the key to progress. In Berlin the soldier was employed in the factories in peacetime, and when he was not on manoeuvres. He took what employment he could find and was welcomed by numerous industrial establishments financed by the Royal Treasury as well as by private firms. Outside Berlin, in the country, he worked on the land, leaving it from April to May and going back for the harvest in July. We should bear in mind the type of eighteenth-century warfare in which Frederick II distinguished himself. There were no frontier battles, but heavy raids into Russia or similar expeditions thrusting deep into the heart of the country. The army might be, in fact had to be, everywhere. The sword lay beside the plough. As with the ordinary soldier, so it was with the officer. The country squire, the small country landowner of good old stock, so proud of his Teutonic past, was the best captain in the royal army. The king called him up for his wars, but also saw that he was given good seed to sow, credits for draining his marshes, and sound advice from the Berlin Academy which not only produced brilliant mathematicians, but acted as a kind of vast agricultural college, concentrating on concrete techniques of value to the economy rather than on abstract speculation. Thus soldiers and captains worked shoulder to shoulder on the farm as well as in the army. Such was the origin of Prussian solidarity. Agriculture fed the people, and filled the royal granaries. It supplied rural and urban markets, but also filled the stores of the commissariat. Industry, on which the king kept a watchful eye, provided clothing for the middle classes, but also for the army; and it was designed for manufacturing weapons as well as tools. Frederick II built up his country on the lines of a vast entrenched camp.

There were some exceptions to this general view of Prussia. There was, for instance, Breslau which it had recently acquired; the flax and hemp grown on its surrounding terraces produced magnificent linen, perhaps the finest in Europe, and a great loss to Maria Theresa; and fine woollen cloth came from the neighbouring mountains, and from the ports. But the chemical industry was a product of this double activity; with state encouragement, it made a start with the new vitriol works, bleaching mills and explosives factories.

The age-old search for yellow amber still went on along the seashore, but every month saw the opening of new glass, china and textile factories in Koenigsberg or Memel. The king encouraged it all, to enrich his country and his treasury, and sustain his policy—whether pacific or military.

The Prussian ports deserve a detailed description. Memel, the old Hanseatic town at which only seventy ships put in at the middle of the century, was loading more than seven hundred round about 1785. Stettin, the fortified town, was the storehouse for all the countries along the Oder, and handled large imports of foodstuffs and exports of timber. Amidst these growing ports, Koenigsberg was struggling to hold its own all the more creditably since the technical facilities of its old harbour were proving more and more inadequate. To keep going at all it had to send a large number of ships to its outport Pillau. The ruler of Prussia realized how useful these ports were to him; he was keen to see shipowners and merchants group together and form royal companies, and he always afforded them his protection. At Danzig (a great commercial city which was already becoming a problem to Europe's diplomatists) Frederick II had just handed over all sea-borne trade exclusively to the ancient citizens of the town, leaving the newly-arrived Prussians the quasi-privilege of trading freely on land, from east to west, and throughout Pomerania, which until recently had been part of Poland.

The rising state of Prussia gradually awoke to life and order, taking its place in Germany as a whole. Germany, while retaining its traditional political character, was nevertheless, in its turn, becoming increasingly active. A detailed description would reveal its infinite variety: in Munich industry was reminiscent of Paris; there was a great factory making Gobelin tapestries, and textile mills turning out cloth inspired by French fashion. The industry of Nuremberg continued to show that its economic roots were deep in the Renaissance; its brass, copper, silver ware and woodwork were exported all over Europe. Then there was Mainz, its cellars stocked with Rhenish wines, and Dresden, famed for its furniture, its fine shops filled with saxe-blue cloth. Each of these cities was actually the centre of a small state, whose prince, after erecting all the buildings needed, lived on the income from its customs duties, and even, when hard up, on hiring out to more affluent princes soldiers who were soon famous throughout Europe for their discipline and their cheapness. Each city was therefore the seat of a small court, often outmoded and pretentious in its way of life, but with a certain provincial charm, with its own poets, painters and philosophers, and of course its inevitable *Hofmusiker*, who was conductor, composer and orchestral manager all in one. From one end of Germany to the other, the *Bruderschaft* movement encouraged young people to indulge their passion for long rambles on which they sang together and marched in step, especially on Sundays, returning in the evening to the local concert hall where they listened to orchestral music or joined in community singing. There was a general atmosphere of *gemütlichkeit*, liveliness and good fellowship.

It should not, however, be thought that these small German capitals were hide-bound in their routines. The staid citizen, his wig tied with a butterfly bow, his long-tailed coat flapping round his thighs, who wanted nothing more novel than a clay pipe and the beerhouse, might perhaps give that impression; but German youth was already being disturbed by the turmoil of *Sturm und Drang*. The day was over when, at Jena, the great Saxon University which had been the home of the Lutheran tradition, the students commissioned J. S. Bach to write a cantata, celebrating in mythological style the praises of one of their revered professors. A small, intellectual revolutionary movement was evidence of a youth impatient and eager for emancipation. Goethe, with the complicity of the Duke, shocked the Court of Weimar with his farces; and above all Schiller, having stirred up the University of Stuttgart, was soon reduced to tramping the roads of Germany pursued by the myrmidons of the Duke of Württemberg from whose army he had deserted. He lived hunted and wretched, existing on potatoes which were rotting in his drawer, but writing *Die Räuber*, that haunting play which proclaimed that the law could never create great men, that routine and discipline only led to degradation, that liberty alone could foster genius. This eccentric poet gained a following among young people all over the land. At Mannheim he was fêted like a conqueror and even the well-bred Goethe was eventually captivated by the poverty-stricken rebel. They were more-over brought together by their mutual enthusiasm for the recent discoveries of science, since one of their first friendly contacts took place as they came out of a lecture in Jena on the progress of biology.

The origins of this revolt of German youth, a revolt which a generation later was to inspire Fichte, Grillparzer and Père Jahn, lay, certainly not in economic ambitions, but in a violent need to break up the old-fashioned framework of their narrow urban civilization, that very framework which was also hampering economic development. In any case those were years during which the entire youth of Germany travelled widely—the *Wanderjahre*. They moved from country to country, and got to know each other; without settling down in any one place, they travelled throughout Germany. Sometimes criticism of municipal life led them to the delighted discovery of nature, and, like Goethe, they identified themselves with Werther. Or else they turned plebeian with Schiller and, less eager to enjoy nature, wished to begin by destroying those 'nests of pestilence' the courts of princes: from the inevitable and bitter struggle between intrigue and love was to emerge a prosperous Germany which would have made Sparta look like a nunnery.

These young people certainly despised the middle classes for being too submissive to the prince. But the Germany of their dreams was actually taking shape before their eyes in the form of timid experiments which brought fresh vigour to old institutions: the Leipzig fairs took on a new lease of life and exhibited Bohemian glass, Silesian linen, Augsburg silverware, Hungarian leather, Dutch swords, and fashionable French novelties. There were also the Frankfurt fairs at which merchants from Italy, Holland, France and Switzerland argued over big deals near the obscure ghetto where Nathan de Rothschild was keeping a wary eye on his fluctuating fortune as he dealt in old clothes and sold carefully selected antiques cheaply to neighbouring princelings.

Most important of all these commercial cities was Hamburg, now a large city of more than 100,000 inhabitants (not counting the Jewish population). It was built in the Dutch style, and a notable feature of the enlargement carried out in 1785 was the completion of the *Herrengraben*, a new canal which cut through the ramparts and enabled more ships to reach the centre of the city. Hamburg was famous for its vigorous maritime trade which was both envied and protected by the Baltic and North Sea merchants, and neither the reviving shipping of Denmark, nor that of Sweden, which had leapt into sudden prosperity, was as yet in a position to compete with it. Moreover, this city was not only growing more beautiful, it was also acquiring entirely new industries. It already prided itself on the quality of its sugar, which was even more famous than its beer, and on the variety of its textiles. Its flourishing trade, its banks, its numerous laboratories and workshops grouped around the old sixteenth-century municipal bank, won for the city and its finances such a high reputation that its coinage, the Mark, stamped with the city arms, was valid throughout the length and breadth of Europe.

Elsewhere in Central Europe

It is impossible to pursue this economic pilgrimage, in detail, through the whole of Central Europe. We can only refer in passing to Prague, one of the most modern cities so far as its economic reputation is concerned and one of the oldest in the charm of its architecture, to the steel works of the Tyrol, to the iron foundries of Innsbruck, and particularly to Vienna—the threshold of the East, with its suburbs inhabited by Turks and Armenians who came to sell their country produce and buy ironware (scythes and sickles) and cloth. Vienna was the capital of one of the oldest monarchies and the place where the best gold braid in Europe was made.

Yet this long list of cities should not mislead us. Apart from these small capitals, Central Europe consisted of countryside of the most primitive kind. Serfdom was almost universal and had its roots deep in the soil. Just beyond the Rhine was to be found the age-old division of the land into plots cultivated on a three-course rotation, bordered by communal lands and forest—the old agricultural system which had supported the European peasantry in the Middle Ages. Whether or not the system was Germanic in origin, it was certainly Germanic in the eighteenth century. This agricultural picture naturally varied in character in every area of Central Europe, from the manorial system in the West (*Grund-herrschaft*) to feudal land-ownership in the East (*Gutherrenschaft*). In Brisgau and Austrian Swabia serfdom had disappeared as early as the sixteenth century. In the West, generally speaking, feudal rights had been somewhat relaxed and were sometimes replaced by gifts in money and kind granted to the peasants by the lord of the manor for the tasks they did for their master; and slowly the village community was breaking up. In fact, if not in law, the lot of the Rhineland peasants was probably not very different from that of peasants on the Meuse.

In the East, on the other hand, in spite of the rigorous efforts of Joseph II, the restrictions under which the serf laboured were still very oppressive. Peasants were even to be found working on their own lands by night because their days had been taken up with work for the noble-man's benefit. The use of the term 'peasants' lands' does not even imply that there was a régime of individual ownership, since the peasant lands belonged to the village, which managed them in common. And beyond the Elbe the farther we penetrate into Poland and the vast stretches of Russia, the more firmly we find this communal peasant system established, assuming an almost geographical inevitability. The nobleman was not so much a landowner as an owner of men. If he wished to mobilize soldiers, he ordered his villagers to provide them. If he needed workmen for a factory he intended to open on his own estate, he selected the smartest of his subjects and transported them to the site of the building. If he needed servants he took young people from the village to be trained and educated for his household. The village community had no option but to ensure the survival of its members through the bitter winter as best it could. Work on the land, the management of the village inter-ests as a whole, were conducted according to routines of very ancient origin, going back to neolithic times.

Under this curious system the wealth of a country was reckoned not in the produce of the land, but in manpower. When Catherine II opened a money-lending establishment in St Petersburg in order to make available to the nobles of her country credit facilities which would enable them to adapt themselves to the new trends in economic life, it was human souls which were pledged as security, the number of souls owned by each nobleman being determined by a census held every five years. It was a Russian system, but also a Transylvanian one, and with few modifications it extended as far as the banks of the Elbe. Throughout these regions governed by a rigid system of land tenure, there were naturally variations in economic structure between one area and another. In Eastern Germany there were peasant holdings: individual farms, the remnants of West German medieval colonization in Slav territory. Most important of all, and particularly from the beginning of the century, great streams of trade began to flow along the old routes, and corn was collected in the villages for the nobleman's bailiffs to sell in Danzig, so that he could buy with the proceeds those luxury goods hitherto unheard of by the lords of Poland or St Petersburg. In this way the latest fashions from the great Western capitals penetrated to the most backward society in Europe. German princes, Russian and Polish nobility came to inherit the splendour of Versailles. But this circulation of goods was not always easy: the roads were in bad repair, and sometimes petered out in the fields. The roads of Eastern Europe could not be compared with French roads, nor its countryside with the English countryside.

In order to keep their merchants, so useful if the supply of luxury goods was to be maintained, the nobility and princes granted them extraordinary privileges, frequently extended to Jews, the most active of them all. This was the case not only in the maritime republics of Germany: in Russia Catherine issued a decree placing them above the middle classes but below the nobility, and excepting them entirely from all the restrictions to which the common people were subject. In Sweden, the merchant was respected. In Poland he quietly pursued his own interests amidst the quarrels of the great. The merchant may have still been incapable, even in Sweden, of exerting any permanent influence on political life, but he was gradually gaining possession of the centres of communication to which the ruling class was beginning to attach increasing importance. He started a great movement which gradually tried to dominate industrial production, not yet, of course, in great factories, but in the home industries carried on by peasants in their cottages.

Thus, under the direct rule of Frederick and of Catherine, or the indirect authority of Joseph II, there was a noticeable enlargement of the trade arteries which spread their network through the old feudal country areas. Here indeed, unlike England, there was little direct connection between the landowner devoted to the improvement of agriculture and the merchant in the city. The growth of commerce was protected chiefly by the prince, overlord of the landed gentry. In London trade was created by liberty, in Berlin and Paris by despotism. In Poland the wealthy aristocrat and his innumerable train of poor dependants paid no heed to this basic difference and wore themselves out in paying lip-service to the word liberty only to fall more easily under the autocracy of Russia or Prussia; whilst in the lands of the House of Austria, from the Low Countries to Hungary, the people mutinied against Joseph II's reforms, because they were too radical or too ruthless.

For the closing years of the eighteenth century already showed the paradoxical features of an evolution which dominated Europe right up to our own day; in the East, progress and despotism; in the West, progress and parliamentarianism. Nor were the results interchangeable. For in the West the merchant gained control of power, whereas in the East the nobility remained in power and merely sanctioned his activities. It was to be the same with industry, for though it was more robust than commerce in its first vigorous growth, it soon fell into the same rigid pattern.

PARIS BETWEEN TWO WORLDS

There are two Europes, one of the sea, the other of the continent. Between the two lies France. Where did it stand at this juncture? Was it caught up in the whirl of economic innovations which were beginning to give England its Victorian characteristics or was it still a backward country, bogged down in feudalism, into which new ideas could be injected only by the authority of the monarch? The France of Louis XVI saw many travellers: the majority, first of all, naturally, were French, but there were also Germans, English, Italians, and many of them have left detailed accounts of their travels. Yet it is difficult to gain any clear impression from them. A splenetic Italian paints too dark a picture whilst the gentle Franklin is more indulgent. A German praises everything he sees in the highest terms, with one exception—the exceedingly slipshod way in which the soldiers march. But what of Young, the inquisitive, accurate, and ruthless Young? He is by turns enthusiastic and indignant. He saw foul cesspools and splendid cities, delightful stretches of countryside and others so poverty-stricken that they were a standing reproach to the despotic régime which had caused them. Unfortunately these opinions frequently give contradictory versions of the same phenomenon. A manufacturing city in Flanders, for example, might be considered either a busy hive of industry or a wretched hell; a farm in Caux might be called a mud heap or a quaint cottage which only needed whitewashing to be better than English cottages. How is it possible to form an accurate picture when faced with such an accumulation of conflicting opinions?

It would be simple to state that France was a land of contrasts. But there were contrasts in England between the Downs and the new industrial countryside, and in Germany between the Pomeranian peasant and the Hamburg citizen. Yet if the word contrast could be applied to any one country in particular it was undoubtedly the France of 1780. It was a combination of the civilization which created the commercial supremacy of England and the feudalism which typified the endless plains of Eastern Europe. France was the country of the past and of the future. The royal apartments at Versailles, once the jewelled shrine of kingly omnipotence, illustrate the extent to which France lived in the past. Petitioners certainly still flocked there, and in the Hall of Mirrors beggars rubbed shoulders with bourgeois dressed in serge and noblemen glittering with decorations, especially at one o'clock on Sundays, the hour of the Royal Mass. The most unwashed of scoundrels could even gain access to the king's chamber, in the crowd which swept past the Swiss Guard in the ante-chamber to the Great Hall (the Oeil-de-Boeuf). The king himself used to retire to his attic, where he enjoyed working with his hands as a locksmith, and (like any middle-class father) he loved to relax with his family in the queen's private apartments. Louis XVI, the plump adolescent, behaved like a school-boy in the midst of a ceremonial to which the valets adhered more rigidly than their masters. He was a figure-head issuing orders, a mere symbol of authority. Around him the courtiers most crippled with debt were often the most extravagant: rebuilding *châteaux*, erecting follies in a few weeks to be used for a fête lasting a single evening. In the most famous park in the world, the queen played the farmer's wife. The royal family had lost its majesty. They even turned a pilgrimage to the tomb of poor Jean-Jacques Rousseau into a fête and went in fancy dress. In a Louis XIV setting, they lived in the manner approved by Diderot.

Paris itself showed the same contrasts. In the northern and eastern quarters, the streets unpaved and unlit, there were sewers piled with offal and rubbish thrown from the houses, whose overhanging fronts made the narrow streets gloomy. The dark shops were pervaded by the sour smell of poverty. Already, around the Hôtel-Dieu and Notre Dame there was growing up a strange and poverty-stricken quarter into which honest people hesitated to venture. But at the opposite extreme were the glittering splendours of the city of cities—the Place Louis xv and its colonnades, the gardens of the Palais-Royal, its arcades, its kiosk, its gay and lively throng, the Boulevard des Capucines with its broad belt of trees amongst which rose the pagodas of the Chinese baths. There was the Temple and its famous fête; and a copy of London's Vauxhall competing with the Café de Foy and the Café Italien; all were furnished in silks, velvets, mirrors, and gave the Parisians the illusion that they were living like kings. Yet, after all, such crude contrasts have been a feature of every city, whether ancient or modern.

More detailed facts are available. An ordinary person living on bread and cheese nevertheless ate off china plates, used a knife and fork, and had a four-poster bed. It is difficult to find out how his budget was balanced. Though much is heard of incredibly meagre meals, they were almost always washed down with wine. Even outside the cities, country folk normally in rags would put on finery for High Mass on Sundays. There is Rousseau's story of the peasant who looked so poor but, on being assured that his visitor was not a tax-collector, offered him the comparative riches of his larder. In any case, the wealth of the peasant seemed to have no connection with that of the soil. Young found what he called mud huts in Normandy, and stone houses too fine to be called cottages in Quercy. This astonishment may simply be that of a man accustomed to brick buildings and confronted with the splendours of stone architecture. But, in the same vein, it was Gilbert who claimed that poverty in France followed 'industry and the wealth of the soil'. In a rich countryside, a poor peasantry; in a poor countryside, a well-to-do peasantry. The population tended to accumulate in places where the hope of a livelihood was greater. And the rich country areas were also those containing industrial towns; hand-looms were installed in the peasant farms which the merchant from the town kept going with orders carried out at cheap rates.

Yet poor though the country districts were, they were gradually shedding all traces of serfdom. The law limited the right of mortmain, a right which made the landowner complete master of the peasant's person and reduced him to the status of a serf. In the eighteenth century, French people were beginning to think this went too far. Beyond the Rhine, and certainly beyond the Elbe, it was a fact as well as a right; in England it was no longer either fact or law; in France, if the law still existed, it was not applied. Although Louis XVI had suppressed the law of mortmain in his domains as long ago as 1774, he had made it clear that he could not abolish it from the lands of his subjects without encroaching on the right of ownership. The royal Treasury, in any case, could not possibly pay the landowners the 'just' indemnity which would enable this last vestige of slavery to be banished for ever. The law courts and the high judicial courts made a practice of limiting the consequences of this right. In many estates it disappeared of its own accord, and in others famous law-suits showed how difficult it was for the lord of the manor to produce the requisite proofs from his archives when challenged. About 1781, a landowner in Franche-Comté lost a law-suit he felt certain of winning: a vital bundle of papers proving his rights, many of them going back two hundred years, were of no use to him at all. A few formal objections disposed of them; the law was feudal, but practice was liberal.

But to return to our travellers: the Russian Karamsin found country districts poorer than those of the Neva, the Austrian Hartig affirms that the Champenois were living on cooked clover, yet the severely critical Young rated Bordeaux higher than Liverpool. North of the wide Garonne the merchants' town houses, the crescent curving around the king's statue, the lovely theatre, made a harmonious group unique in the world. And Nantes was as impressive as Bordeaux. Both hummed with activity. The many ships and the importance of their cargoes were evidence of the strength of French maritime trade. Yet nothing could be more wretched than the poverty of the Landes or the Vendée.

By-passing Clermont, which Arthur Young dismissed summarily as 'carved out of a dunghill', we move on to Lyons, one of the most famous cities on the Continent. Its 200,000 inhabitants lived packed into a small area around the finest town-hall in Europe, a seventeenth-century building repaired in 1702 by Mansart after the fire of 1674. At any rate the people of Lyons thought their town-hall superior to that of Amsterdam. The eighteenth century saw the peak of its prosperity; never before had so many looms clattered at the foot of the Croix-Rousse, never such a busy hum of trade, from the Place Bellecour (then the Place Louis-le-Grand) to the Terreaux. For the previous twenty-five years goods leaving Lyons had been exempt from local customs duties, which had brought about a phenomenal increase in trade. Its most famous products were silks, and cloth of gold, and braids, which almost rivalled those of Vienna, and in recent years new products from the dye-works, soap factories and drug-factories which made the Vitriolerie quarter one of the world's finest centres of the chemical industry. The town expanded by imposing an increasingly heavy burden of taxation; the engineer Perrache embanked the Rhone and imprisoned it between great stone quays. In the new quarters with their streets intersecting at right angles Lyons was beginning to assume the aspect of a capital city; it was proud of its academies, its palaces and even its governor Villeroi, whose wildly extravagant way of life was the envy of many an imperial prince.

Such then was France, with its powerful and prosperous cities set in a countryside in which opposition to change seemed to increase in proportion to the richness of the land. Such a dogmatic assertion calls for further elaboration. Young, indeed, is a reliable guide, and he declares that the improvement in agricultural techniques was far from being as thorough in France as across the Channel. The reason for this lay in the different system of land ownership. In England the small estate had vanished. In France, on the other hand, it was so deeply rooted that the trend towards larger farms encouraged by the new technical improvements had only limited effects. We are told that many farms which were too small were broken up, particularly when their farmhouses fell into ruins because they were too costly to repair, and were leased in small plots to neighbouring farmers. But this did not mean that they ploughed more land or increased their livestock, and if their yields improved slightly in quality, production as a whole sometimes decreased. There was, of course, Rochefoucauld-Liancourt, who made a name for himself by modernizing great estates on English lines, but his example was not followed by the majority. The small farmer stuck to his old ways. For one thing, he could not read. There was therefore little likelihood that he would ever be affected by the pleas and the advice of agronomists, who were great publishers of treatises; this sort of treatise was read much more widely in the towns than in the country. There were, it is true, a large number of agricultural societies in which well-meaning people expressed pious hopes and were particularly anxious that each village should have its resident adviser capable of instructing the peasant population— a praiseworthy intention but of no practical significance. In such conditions, the work of progressive administrators often ran counter to the aims proposed. For instance, to improve stock-breeding the use of studs was extended throughout France, and these were given special protection, notably by forbidding breeding in the countryside. These studs were the admiration of travellers. Nevertheless they did harm to French livestock, which decreased so sharply in twenty years that in 1785 there was talk of suppressing them: there were not enough horses for the cavalry and Spain could no longer buy mules. It seemed far better, on the whole, to have less highly-bred animals and more of them. In consequence, because the government could not carry its precepts right into the heart of the country, its effects were crippling in spite of its good intentions. It is true that the royal *château* at Rambouillet was renowned throughout Europe for its achievements— particularly in breeding merinos; but its example was followed abroad more than in France. Botanical gardens were all the rage, royal gardens by which the government set such store that it even opened one in Louisiana in order to introduce American plants into France (cotton was tried out in the south and in Corsica); but if these royal gardens were a tremendous help to the new study of natural history, they were of little use to agriculture. The King might guide the plough, the Queen turn dairymaid; but the villein's yearly routine continued unchanged.

Similarly, French cities owed their beauty to an architectural tradition which was far more monarchical than bourgeois. The hastily built London houses may have looked less attractive, but they were the result of a surge of individual wealth and of trade, while the superb avenues in Paris and the provinces were the work of the government. The Bordeaux bourgeois, the future Girondist, was indeed rich, but the splendid layout of his city was not of his planning though he helped to pay for it. The same applied to industrial life. Wagons from Lorraine, workers from the Auvergne massifs converged at Le Creusot, and blast-furnaces were built under the active supervision of English iron-founders, particularly Wilkinson. France was making its first successful attempt at smelting with coke, but the chief shareholder was the King. Similarly, the chief shareholder in the nearby glassworks was Queen Marie-Antoinette; and again in the new mines at Anzin. Were there *any* great ventures not financed by royal capital? The Duke of Orleans worked wonders, and was a great builder of shops, houses and apartments around his royal palace. He was patron and shareholder in Central Canals, and created several industries, but it was all made possible by his royal fortune. This did not mean that the bourgeoisie were unhappy or poor—craftsmen's shops had probably never done such a thriving trade, or been so quick to carry out orders for more and more utensils for even the poorest kitchens— but it was hardly possible to find a single powerful, middle-class company creating big capital. Associations of capital did exist, those of the Partisans. The success of the Paris brothers and the fortune of Lavoisier are famous: but again, this accumulation of wealth and this organization of capital were made through royal financial channels in the service of the Treasury and derived from taxation.

Public opinion, formed by popular books extolling liberty, had no use for the Court and courtiers, yet it was just as definitely in favour of the progress brought about by the royal administration and even by the aristocracy. What conclusion can the historian draw from such a paradox? If we examine the texts of the period we find that all echo a common satisfaction in having had the good fortune to be born under an enlightened king whose youthful reign gave promise of both progress and liberty.

This hope was to persist as long as the illusion lasted that the king could be at one and the same time dictatorial enough to impose reforms and compliant enough to live like a bourgeois. The artisan, the merchant, the shipowner, who had made a fortune but had not been able to gain control of credit, looked to the king to give them what they had not been able to take for themselves. This meant in effect that they were expecting the Bourbon locksmith to create in ten years economic institutions which it had taken England two hundred years to perfect. They were expecting him to be as enlightened as Frederick II, but in a country where the middle classes, already exceedingly active, had no longer any intention of bowing down to despotism.

DECLINE OF THE SOUTH

If the Atlantic trade played such an important part in the comparative transformation of London and Berlin, it did so at the expense of the Mediterranean, which until recently had been Europe's main gateway to the world. Formerly the highways of civilization, the peninsulas were now no more than its museums.

Revival in Spain

Let us turn to Spain. It was a land corroded by the floods of gold and silver which had been sweeping across it ever since the New World was first plundered and drained dry by the victorious adventurers following the routes opened up by Christopher Columbus. The land was deserted by its sturdy peasants who had been conscripted long years ago and torn from the soil to man ships, and had left their vital work in Europe to follow the mirage in America. It was a land neglected by a people indoctrinated by hordes of monks and priests who relied on the authority of the all-powerful Inquisition to discourage every worldly enterprise of any magnitude. A land, in short, ravaged by the 'American sickness'. There are writers and philosophers in plenty who hold Spain up to a virtuous Europe as the most appalling example of what despotism can produce when it is founded on slavery and encouraged by fanaticism. They describe the ragged soldier with no thought in his head but desertion, the arrogant beggar soliciting alms with pride and receiving them with condescension, the haughty, impoverished nobleman looking to adventure for a living he will not earn by daily toil.

But Spain has its defenders as well. They show the other side of the picture, the virtuous and enlightened Charles III, setting an ideal example of economic restoration to the courts of Europe: the Inquisition curbed, the ambition of the Church restrained, economic affairs put on a sound basis, restrictions in trade removed, the currency strengthened by the creation of the St Charles bank—and even a model army, the only one in the world which cared for its veterans, and guaranteed them an adequate retirement pension. In any case, in matters of finance and commerce, the Spaniard had a sound reputation for honest dealing, and was so scrupulous in honouring his commitments that 'the whole of Europe entrusted him with its assets, and had no cause to complain'.

It was an attractive country, defying description. Everywhere, in its wealth as well as in its poverty, Spain's outlook made itself felt. And what of the countryside? There was Valencia, an outer province and one of the richest—the Orient of Spain. It produced silks, rice, oils, wine, currants, dates and palm trees. It was like a survival of the gardens of the great Arabian civilization, existing side by side with a Nordic agriculture: hemp and flax brought trade to city shops and country homes. In the central provinces of Estremadura, in Navarre, and even in Castile, there were oases of cultivation threatened by the invasion of the sheep. Indeed the Spanish sheep crossed with the Maghreb ram had a European reputation, and was highly prized in England since it produced the finest wool in the world. Yet it cost Spain dear. The enormous flocks of greedy animals, tearing up the roots as well as the stems as they grazed, ravaged the countryside as they moved ceaselessly over the land. The association of wool producers, the famous Mesta, made a fortune from these products in the Segovia market, but resisted all reforms, since it could show that tens of millions were brought in by breeding. At last, to fight this harmful monopoly, the Friends of the City had been formed, a young association or rather group of associations encouraged by the king whose aim was to revive small farming and populate waste lands lying between the large towns, too far apart from each other, in which hordes of the poor and needy were congregating. But as yet all these efforts had met with little success. It had not escaped notice that not far from Madrid good, fertile land had been broken up for the exploitation of nitrebeds, though it was appreciated that these provided the saltpetre vital to Madrid's powder-magazines, the largest in the world, relics of an age in which trade was conducted by the musket.

In this country of barely ten million inhabitants, Charles III worked miracles in raising the general income, doubling it in a few years, and making more efficient use of taxation, thanks to the land register that he instituted; yet the impression persisted that Spain was still the base for world conquest.

Foremost among Spanish cities was Madrid, an artificial city. It was, of course, admirably planned around its Plaza Mayor, a vast square surrounded by identical five-storey houses with identical balconies, and which set a pattern for every city in the Spanish New World. It was there that the famous bullfights were held. Madrid was a beautiful city, but its streets were dirty and its ways and habits seemed expressly designed to amaze the English;

houses were let without window-panes, and every tenant had to bring his own when he moved in; the first floor of each house belonged to the king, and enquiries about renting them were addressed to his officials. Yet this artificial capital was also a great commercial capital. The *Deputación de los Cincos Gremios Mayores* of Madrid, which included all merchants trading in textiles, jewellery, spices and drugs, not only directed the city's economic activity but had a large stake in the trade of Cadiz, owned the largest factories in Valencia and managed others all over Spain, and its ships, for trade with the New World, continued to be the safest means of transit available to European merchants. This great commercial organization even encouraged a luxury glass-making craft long famous and which at that time made mirrors reputed to be the finest in the world.

Yet another surprise was the curious city of Cadiz, built on an island; it was a lovely town with paved streets and tall houses, its artificial character as a commercial centre emphasized by the high cost of living; its castle protected by precipitous rocks and a system of forts, was a reminder of the privileges enjoyed by the Spanish Crown in overseas trade. It was a town packed with foreigners—French, English, Dutch, and Italians—who knew that over and above their legitimate profits they could make good money from smuggling; even the court guards themselves were accomplices when silver ingots and bundles of merchandise were illicitly passed through the posterns at night, to be shipped off on the high seas as quickly as possible. And smuggling was a necessity in Cadiz, if the goods from Europe were to be paid for. In Cadiz, reputed to have the best harbour in Europe, and the most envied, the flotillas bound for America anchored —approximately eighty ships which sailed each year bearing the iron-ware, wines, cloths and oils contributed by every manufacturer in Europe. They came back laden with precious metals, raw wool, copper, tin, and cocoa.

Another port carrying on a brisk trade with the New World was the old Roman port on the Corunna peninsula. It exported to Havana, Buenos Aires and the Philippines the same merchandise as Cadiz, and received gold and silver in exchange, as well as sugar, tobacco, and raw hides. Bilbao, the pretty capital of Biscay, had taken on a new lease of life, and was beginning to feel the advantages of the expansion of sea-trade, and of the freedom granted by Charles III to his subjects to trade with the Empire. Its longstanding trade in Spanish wool and in fish (dried cod from Newfoundland and Norway) was now supplemented by trade with America.

Barcelona was an attractive city built in a semi-circle at the foot of the hills, on the coastal plain which had been the objective of so many recent battles: a new fort had just been built for it on the Monjuich, but the main sea defence of its splendid harbour consisted of a long seawall. The exports of Barcelona were oils, alcohols, and the most famous of all Catalonia's industrial products—fabrics. Every year more than twelve million silk handkerchiefs were turned out by its factories to meet the demands of shops all over Europe. Silk and cotton stockings and wool velvets were equally in demand. The city had an air of prosperity, with its wide, paved streets radiating out from the Plaza San Michele, dominated by the vast cathedral. Barcelona was also a busy ship-building centre and its huge yards were said to be the finest in Europe. They served as a reminder to Spain that, in addition to its Atlantic trade, there was still wealth to be exploited in the Mediterranean basin.

We cannot leave Spain without seeing what insight Goya, the most perceptive of its painters, can give us into its enigmas. In 1785, when he was almost forty, he settled in Madrid after travels and adventures in Italy. He was adopted by Mengs, an official with an official style, and became court painter to the Bourbons. He filled this role with such candid realism that it must always arouse wonder. Charles III's honesty is no less admirable; Goya's portrait of him makes no attempt at flattery, though it has captured his witty, cynical expression, rather reminiscent of Voltaire. And what of Goya himself? His is the swarthy face just visible behind the handsome Count of Floridablanca—the skeleton of truth behind the tinsel trappings of the court. Goya was commissioned to paint sketches for tapestries, and dismayed the tapestry-weavers by the minuteness of detail he put into the vintagers and harvesters, the games of pelota and blind-man's buff, and all the sturdy, muscular, animal peasant life which contrasted so strongly with the foppish affectation of the lace-bedecked landowner. He portrayed the decadence and cynicism of the royal family in his studies of the Cardinal Infanta's suite—and the smug ugliness in the face of Maria Luisa, soon to be queen. He was equally ruthless in his treatment of the wild-eyed stupidity of the litanists in St Ignatius. Of three hundred years of past greatness, Spain in its decadence had retained but one noble quality—courage in facing up to the truth. The political façades had crumbled away; what remained was the fierce, tenacious solidity of human nature reduced to its essentials.

Some mention must be made of Portugal, which political thinkers in the West were studying with considerable interest. This little country was said to be rich, for it imported what was left of the gold of Africa and Brazil. It was also said to be deeply in debt, losing the greater part of its colonial gold to England to pay for a crippling import trade. It was said to be enlightened because of the general admiration felt for the famous Pombal, who cut down the number of religious foundations and encouraged secular education. Nevertheless Catholicism was the only religion tolerated, and clerics still represented more than fifteen per cent of the population. Pombal encouraged agriculture, yet three-quarters of the corn consumed in Portugal had to be imported. He did his best to discourage the exclusive production of a single wine, highly prized in England, yet wine remained the country's chief export. At all events, it seems that he infused new life into various industries, particularly textiles, which had collapsed under the competition from England to which his predecessor Methuen had exposed them. All economic progress was utterly dependent on English shipping, and the English were the real masters of Portuguese colonial trade; Portuguese banks were working even harder for London than for Lisbon, which was only just beginning to recover from the terrible earthquake of 1755.

Italian Autumn

In Italy the evenings were more serene and men could relax and enjoy the enduring charm of its dead past. Let us accompany the cultured men of the day who journeyed there to search for treasures in the old palaces of the mother of the arts.

Many travellers went to explore Venice in this age when educated people were beginning to reflect on the history of nations. It was a source of wonder that so magnificent a city could have originated with a few wretched groups of men who had sought refuge in the islands of the lagoon during the Gothic invasions. Venice was the queen of the seas which were its very foundation. From whichever side one approached, it seemed to be surrounded by a forest of masts, large vessels between which slipped a swarm of small boats. The city itself was built on piles, which were driven deep into the waters of the canal to strengthen the low-lying foundations. Four hundred bridges connected the islands with each other and added a final touch to the artifice of a city which, as its people proudly asserted, would remain the mistress of the gods just as Rome had made herself mistress of men. Its natural defences were moreover so strong that Venice had no need of fortresses and gates to guard its treasures. But land was so scarce that the inhabitants were in constant danger of falling off the narrow quays into the five feet of water of the smaller canals. As for the Grand Canal, the widest and deepest, it cut the city in two and was spanned only by the famous Rialto Bridge. This meant that people had to use 'barques and galleys' all the time. There were no carriages in Venice, but enormous crowds of pedestrians jostling each other in the narrow squares, too cramped for the city's 200,000 odd inhabitants and their gay and lively social round, the envy of Europe, which lasted from the Carnivals (which began at Christmas) to the Wedding of the Doge and the Sea on Ascension Day.

Very few realistic paintings of these Venetian carnivals exist and the tiny figures of Canaletto and Guardi no more than hint at their bustle and movement; but the spirit of Venice still survives in a painter whose warm humanity scaled the heights of genius: Tiepolo, the last representative of the Mediterranean movement that still has a profound influence in Europe. But Tiepolo died leaving no successor and with him Venetian painting came to an end.

The Palace of St Mark—with its chapel, the famous church—was the political centre of the Republic. The Doge was still the incarnation of its power, but he did not exercise it. Montesquieu singled out Venice as the model of an aristocratic republic; in fact magistrates were chosen by lot or by election from among the two thousand noble families in a procedure in some ways reminiscent of the Ecclesia of Athens or the Roman Conclave. This hierarchy of consuls settled all affairs, but by good sense rather than by force. When there was any uncertainty the majority fell back upon a compromise—to the despair of leaders and ambassadors. The power of Venice had greatly decreased since the days when it was mistress of the Eastern Mediterranean. In 1780 its only troops were Dalmatian. It still guarded the Adriatic ports, but Tunis held out against the small permanent fleet it maintained to keep down piracy. Its trade still reflected something of past glories, encouraged by the exports of lace, cloth of gold and silk, mirrors and glass; and it still maintained a form of monopoly over Levantine drugs and Russian leather. Venice, the converging point for Alpine valleys and the southern outlet for textiles from Holland and Germany, remained prosperous at a time when the once great cities of Mediterranean Europe were falling into decadence and apathy.

Venice had most cause to fear the power and influence of Rome. It banished all ecclesiastics from its councils and forbade its dignitaries to accept any Roman benefice except that of cardinal, since this only carried authority in Rome.

Yet Rome too was awakening to new life and was the meeting-place for thinkers and artists from all corners of the world. It was there that Goethe and Mozart and David and Goya and the celebrated sculptor Canova first made each other's acquaintance. The road from Venice to Rome leads us in any case to a city about which educated men throughout Europe were talking—Bologna. They cited as a model of modernization (and of physiocracy) the *chirografo di nostro signore papa Pio VI, nel quale si ordine et stabilise il regolamento de la publica economia de Bologna.* In this theocracy the Papal letter was law, replacing the old complicated system of taxation embodied in a tangle of rigid decrees issued by the Bolognese Senate and confirmed by the Popes. The letter provided a new system favoring neither the urban middle class nor the impoverished nobility, to which were added the families of each fresh Pope; it was a law which, though it did not set the peasant free, and gave very little more to eat to those who existed mainly on chestnuts, did at least clarify the many heavy taxes and duties, delivered the state from a crushing debt, and above all freed the circulation of corn and imposed taxes on the swarms of clerics inhabiting the city, and on the convents perched on every surrounding hill.

Let us continue our journey. According to contemporaries, poverty was rife in the Roman countryside, the land was deserted, and beggars lined the roads and crowded around the doors of inns; yet food was not expensive. There was much idleness and despondency in the factories, yet there was an enormous number of well-endowed almshouses.

Where did the wealth come from that subsidized all this idleness and poverty? Over and above the revenue from his states, the Pope received a substantial additional income from the Christian world. Spain alone contributed one-fifth of the expenses of the Roman budget, but this budget, which showed an excess on its ordinary expenditure (the army was quite small), had a constant deficit if extraordinary expenditure was included. Extraordinary expenditure included the embellishment of churches (the new sacristy of St Peter's had to be rebuilt three times because of the architects' negligence), subsidies to Malta and the battle against the infidel, and above all purchases of corn from outside, in accordance with the ancient tradition of the *annona*, to give cheap food to all those who lived by going in processions. The deficit was made up by *cédula*, a curious papal currency. These notes were issued in theory against the security of gold reserves deposited in the Castel Sant' Angelo, but they were so inordinately in excess of the reserves that this paper money would have been quite worthless if the Romans had possessed any of the critical acumen which in those parts seemed to be the exclusive attribute of the foreigner. In Rome nothing was ever finally settled. An excess of Pontifical goodwill, for instance, compelled the judges to give detailed reasons for their judgements, and allowed the unsuccessful plaintiff to refer the case indefinitely from one court to another: no lawsuit was ever concluded. Everything was casual and easy-going, and in this patriarchal, indulgent atmosphere, inexhaustible patience was required in face of the endless delays. Aided and abetted by the climate, the people lived on next to nothing, and the nobleman lived like a king on a mere pittance. The Church provided food, the Church organized festivals both sacred and profane; there were theatres run by clerics in every part of Italy. The trusting nature of its citizens and the generosity of foreigners brought some equilibrium to this strangely unbalanced situation. From conclave to conclave the *status quo* was maintained and prolonged, in the hope that the draining of the Pontine marshes, which had started a long time before but still dragged on, would eventually revive a neglected agriculture. And trade was slack, thanks to customs dues which were crippling but easier to evade, if need be, than anywhere else in Europe. Nothing was manufactured in Rome, everything was bought in the port at Civita-Vecchia, the outlet of the states of the Church, and paid for out of the resources of Christendom. The population of Rome was declining so slowly that there were still 125,000 inhabitants building their houses with stones dug out of the ground during excavations made in the hope of finding valuable antiques which would fetch a good price. Mediocre architects made a living out of repairing the countless small palaces. Coachmen and hotelkeepers grew rich on pilgrims and visitors. Rome lived solely on its past and on its present position as the Head of Christendom.

In fact the largest city in Italy was not Rome but Naples, a sprawling monster of nearly 500,000 inhabitants and one of the biggest cities in the world. The soil, on its basis of lava, was so fertile that anything would grow, pomegranates, oranges and figs, and costly produce could be sold—flax, oil, wines and saffron. Salt and sulphur were available nearby, from which were made vitriol and soap. The harbour was enormous, consisting of the whole bay protected by a small breakwater. Yet trade was slack and the magnificent bay sheltered an almost non-existent royal fleet. The Bourbon king lived like a bourgeois in his enormous palace: his luxury, like that of the beggars and the swarms of monks, was the beauty of the earth. Taxation was arbitrary, and fluctuated according to privileges and benefices, the multiplicity of privileged lands, and the idle ingenuity of collectors who fleeced the poor peasant right and left.

We cannot leave the south without a glance at Sicily, so rich in arable land, with its marble quarries, its precious stones, and the coral from its coasts. Sicily even harboured scoundrels who had the right of asylum in the convents which enjoyed so many commercial privileges that they virtually controlled business in Messina and Palermo. Palermo, famous for its silk gloves, regarded itself as the capital, with its 90,000 inhabitants, many of them impoverished noblemen, with its gardens, palaces and fountains; whilst Messina was only just recovering from the terrible earthquake of 1783, in which it was reduced to a mass of rubble and then swept by a dreadful fire.

The Venetian Republic, the Papal States, the Kingdom of the Two-Sicilies, these were the backbone of the old Italy. But this group was rounded off to the north by widely differing states. One of them, Bourbon Tuscany, was just entering upon a phase of activity and almost of wealth. Here a scattered agriculture produced unusual crops—saffron, flax, broad beans, kidney beans—and competed with industry, which made fabrics and table linen, porcelain and china. It was encouraged by a shrewd and enlightened despot who was to bring fame to Leghorn, the famous free port whose ever-increasing population watched without astonishment as Greeks, Americans and Turks freely practised their own religions, whilst even the Jews had their own synagogue. All this intermingling of races was not just the living sign of a widespread Mediterranean trade flourishing at the expense of Venice and Genoa. Farther north were the rich Milanese. Milan may have been rather dull and only moderately busy around its cathedral and its famous library, but its soil was among the most fertile in Italy, well irrigated and rich in corn and rice. The Hapsburgs could have worked wonders with it if they had had any other ideas beyond crushing it with taxes. These were taxes, moreover, from which the officials raked off so much *en passant* that a bare twentieth ever reached the Court of Vienna. Piedmont still formed part of Italy, a rough mountain kingdom whose ruler was excessively ambitious and burdened his land with taxes which were borne with equanimity since they affected nobles as well as the common people. A scanty, laborious agriculture supported Turin, a clean, bright town, an arsenal, and a military as well as a commercial centre, where one could buy the silk cultivated in northern Italy. Then there was honest, poor, industrious Nice, a tiny fortress-town, enclosed within a narrow space, and with only vast ruins on the outskirts to bear witness to its ancient dignity. The countryside was only sparsely populated in a region where everything was considered in terms of strategy; and the ruler of the rock of Monaco, that tiny citadel, now depended for his living on France after having formerly been dependent on Spain.

This was Italy, then, a wonderful much-envied land whose store of ancient treasures was being heedlessly exhausted. It had no unity as a country; the military tradition of order and hard work survived only in Piedmont, a harsh state on the mountain perimeter which acted as a fragile barrier between northern Europe and the easy-going life of the south.

2

Progress Crosses the Atlantic

IN 1780 it was almost three hundred years since the West had discovered that the earth was round and had ventured to cross the oceans; the Mediterranean, the China Sea, the Indonesian seas, like the Atlantic, were, so to speak, opened by these voyages round the world. The daring of sailors destroyed the prosperous overland trade which formerly linked China with Europe through Constantinople and Central Asia. Even in the eighteenth century, two spectacular results were apparent: the Arab worlds, which had controlled the land routes, were collapsing in ruins, and the Mediterranean itself seemed to have relapsed into slumber. In contrast the Atlantic and Pacific were rewarding the bold foresight of those who had plotted the movements of the stars and built ports in every bay of the new worlds.

In this chapter we shall deal in turn with the decline of the Mediterranean and the progress of the Atlantic, leaving the Pacific for a later chapter.

What exactly was understood by Europe? Where did it end? In the Urals in the east, and on the Bosphorus in the south-east? Eighteenth-century geographers were cautious men and generally gave Asia as the eastern boundary of Europe. So Catherine II may have been a European princess, but it is by no means certain that the Sultan of Turkey deserved a similar honour. He was generally regarded as an Asiatic despot. On the other hand, could the Greeks be excluded from Europe? Some were in Athens, a little city at that time part of the Ottoman Empire and numbering no more than 15,000 inhabitants, and some were in Constantinople where they formed the most important commercial core of the city. A host of glorious memories made it imperative for enlightened Western minds to claim them as their own. On the other hand, the Serbians, the Rascians who spoke only Slavonian, were they too to be classed as Europeans?

MEDITERRANEAN RUINS

The territories which the maps grouped together under the name of the Ottoman Empire included parts of both Europe and Asia. The old régime very sensibly ignored the requirements of our modern geographical definitions.

The Ottoman Camp

The Ottoman Empire was little more than a vast army encamped on the lands seized by the successors of the Osmans. Christians, whether they were Greeks or more occasionally Latins, belonged to Europe, whereas Muslims, even if they were Serbians, belonged to Asia.

The Turks, like the Arabs, hardly ever persecuted the Christians as such; they 'protected' them for a financial consideration. In the first place, they made them pay a heavy poll-tax, and officials armed with gauges measured their children's skulls to see whether they had grown big enough to be liable for it. Merchants and craftsmen in addition paid excise duties, dues which (on the advice of Villeneuve, the French Ambassador) had just been reinforced by heavy customs duties. The majority of the subjects of the Ottoman Empire had to contribute the equivalent of one-tenth of their produce, but the whole skill of the tax-collector went into the assessment of this tenth; the fisherman returning to harbour with one hundred fish often had to hand over the ten biggest fish, the equivalent of half his profit. As for the well-dressed merchants and the religious dignitaries, it went ill with them if their voluntary contributions were not adequate. For the Ottoman had unexpected ways and means of making them pay up. He would immediately confer on them some honorary post, which made them direct subjects of the Sultan, who could then exercise his discretionary powers of life and death.

The Ottoman pretended to have nothing whatever to do with the affairs of these protected subjects. He put judges and executioners at their disposal, and at heart preferred the Christians to manage their own affairs; except for levying a special tax on any village where a crime had been committed, he would take no further interest in the criminal. If, however, the victim's family appealed for a Turkish trial, the executioner in attendance tied the culprit's wrists together, and led him to the place of execution through the motley crowd in the market place and the streets, without the spectacle arousing any particular attention. On the way, the plaintiffs were free to continue their negotiations and discuss with the condemned man the price of his ransom. If agreement was reached, the accused was at once handed back to the Christians. If poor or obstinate, the guilty man walked on to his death, chatting with his executioner if he felt like it.

It is almost impossible to enumerate here the extremely wide range of occupations engaged in by the indigenous inhabitants of the Empire; it would involve a geographical study of the whole of Balkan Europe and Asia Minor. But one feature was outstanding—the utter and universal poverty of the peasant. In Syria, when times were good, he lived on dura bread, onions and lentils; and when times were bad, on acorns. There was no question of seed selection or stock-rearing. Little donkeys drew a plough, more often than not the old-fashioned swing-plough made from a tree branch cut below the fork; the corn was scarcely ripe before it was cut and stored away in caves: every possible device was used to outwit the bands of Arab robbers who came up from the desert. Owing to its precarious food supply, Palestine itself had barely more than 100,000 inhabitants. Syria proper had perhaps two million.

A few great cities, amongst them Damascus, were more favoured. Bread cost less there than in the surrounding countryside, chiefly owing to the requisitions of the pashas who were anxious to maintain peace in the unruly bazaars. When there was famine, old remedies were applied:

it was forbidden to take corn out, provisions were collected in the city and every wagon that tried to escape was handed over to the Arab robbers by order of the pasha. In this way activities absorbing large numbers of people were maintained in the urban centres. Money was minted, damask cloth was woven, silks figured, glass blown, and the brightly coloured ceramic tiles which decorated every mosque in the Empire were made. There were charming little palaces, their clustered domes built around exquisite gardens, modelled on the pious foundations erected for the use of pilgrims journeying to the Holy Places, since Damascus was still one of the most famous halts on the road to Jerusalem and Mecca.

Yet though several cities continued to flourish, the population of the lowlands was decreasing. Syrians, Greeks and Armenians were endeavouring to escape from the casual despotism of the Turks. They set out towards Persia, and even towards Africa and Europe. Large numbers made for Russia, often taking with them the Jews who were their partners in trade.

All along the Mediterranean coast, the Franks had enjoyed long-standing privileges, of which the French in particular reaped benefits in the form of low customs duties and the special protection of the Turkish administration. In return for these, they exhorted the Christians to patience. They brought sugar from the West Indies, coffee and cochineal from Cadiz, and cloth from Languedoc, and they shipped bales of cotton and cloth, copper and silks. This was the famous Levantine trade. These Levantine ports were in a sad state of decay: they were small roadsteads with scarcely any shelter, their ancient defences repaired with stones dragged from nearby ruins; the sea-walls were strengthened and supported by the shafts of pillars taken from ancient temples or Latin churches. The harbours were often choked up with mud and sand. Acre and Tripoli were in this state of dilapidation. Nevertheless mule-trains still came down to them from Aleppo or Ramleh (at that time a French trading post). Throughout European Turkey the English merchants were active, especially at Salonica, where tooled leather, skins, and the famous carpets were on sale. Yet just as much, if not more, of this trade from European Turkey went overland to Austria, extending the Asiatic trading quarter on the outskirts of Vienna, already described.

The Turkish military machine was kept going by these remaining traces of agricultural, industrial and commercial splendour. The Ottoman Empire was little more than the indefinite prolongation of a state of siege declared by a conqueror who had never advanced beyond a military administration for the simple reason that he was not interested in adapting himself to the complexities of civil administration. Besides his privy purse, the Sultan was especially anxious to keep the coffers of the public Treasury as full as possible, since the bulk of this money was earmarked for the upkeep of an enormous military machine. But what was left of the power that Machiavelli praised so highly? Did it still number the half-a-million men referred to in the European chancelleries? It did still include a great variety of formations; the most famous corps of all still being the Janissaries, the sons of Christians, to whom were added contingents from every country in Asia. The army on campaign was a mobile state: there were crowds of Jews and merchants, representatives of every trade guild in the Empire, and the whole ministry, under the orders of the Grand Vizier (when not of the Sultan in person), accompanied, naturally, by the entire Chancellery. It was a vast, cumbersome assemblage of heavy wagons and draught animals, and in the wars against Vienna it was reputed to have numbered as many as 8,000 wagons and 5,000 camels. This moving horde had to be fed—and well fed. It was accompanied by as many as 10,000 oxen, the same number of buffalo, 100,000 hogsheads of fruit and provisions, and always by the Treasury itself, a weighty strong-box covered with vivid carpets.

Yet this vast army was not really organized; it had achieved the golden age of chaos. Between the moment when the Grand Vizier reviewed it and the moment it began to march, deserters reduced its fighting strength by one-third; the finest artillery guns in the world (the copper and tin came not only from Asia but also from Holland

and England) were heavy and of varying calibre, and inadequately provided with ammunition. Moreover, shock troops were too eager for battle to wait for the artillery to prepare the way, and the latter, according to Tott, was of very little use except to sound the sunset cannon when the army was encamped for the night, which apparently cost no less per salvo than 54,000 pounds of powder, and to no purpose other than making an infernal din. This armed horde could not move about regardless of the time of year. It had to have grass for its horses and cattle. In short, even if it had still been disciplined as in Machiavelli's day, it would have been utterly unsuited to the requirements of swift, light, modern strategy. The Turkish army and its organization were the exact opposite of those of Frederick II and the enlightened despots, and this accounted for its many defeats.

In theory the fleet at least was strong, made up as it was by all the contingents contributed by Africa and Asia, but the Bosphorus itself was hardly suited to the manoeuvres of great sailing ships, and in the far Mediterranean, the Russians, taught by the English, wiped out the Ottoman fleet at Chesme. In effect, the naval strength of the Porte was reduced to a few small ships of seventy guns.

The Sultan, moreover, was not merely a military leader and a feudal overlord; he was also a religious leader, accepting advice only from the Grand Mufti who enjoyed the inestimable privilege of kissing his master's shoulder, and not only, like his other subjects, the hem of his robe. Moreover, the submission of the Mufti was maintained by tradition; even up to 1787 there was kept in the harem the symbolical mortar on which this same Mufti could be ground to powder if ever he was guilty of treason. The authority of the Ulémas, a college interpreting the law, had been worn away in dissension and vain ambitions. Therefore the Sultan was theoretically the secular and religious head of the hundred local lords who, from the Caucasus to the Atlantic, professed the religion of Mahomet. Yet the faith, like the army, had lost confidence in itself.

The military weakness and the religious shortcomings of the Ottoman Empire enabled Russia to dispute its suzerainty over the Crimea and Georgia where considerable political and religious confusion continued to prevail right up to the end of the century.

Arab Ruins

The state of independence existing in Africa was undoubtedly as serious. Egypt was the habitual refuge of every dethroned Bey living on plunder in the mountains. The Sultan's envoys dared not venture far from their palace. The Pasha paid even less homage to the Sultan than he received from his own subjects. In practice he relied on the Arabs to keep order. The Arab officer guarding Cairo was greatly feared, whether he ruthlessly enforced the law and put to death everyone remotely suspected of theft, or whether he accepted bribes and protected the powerful brigands. And under this corrupt and indecisive rule the fellah eked out a bare existence, living on barley broth, and producing just enough corn to feed the caravans passing through on their annual journey to Mecca. In this Egypt the European trader endeavoured to get a footing. Merchants from Marseilles intrigued on the spot to get a passage through to India. Sometimes the idea of Sesostris' canal was brought up again.

For although Alexandria had fallen into decadence, in spite of its harbour, Cairo, the great creation of the Arabs, was still a dream city in western eyes. Saladin's palace still stood on the hill—a group of palaces, with gardens approached by the gigantic staircase which even camels could climb. Marble and columns were everywhere, and in the centre rose the beautiful mosque. This 'heavenly city' was served by an aqueduct of more than five hundred arches—or rather had been, for it was falling into decay along with the three-storey well where oxen harnessed in circles hauled the water up from landing to landing. Lastly, there was the wonder of the city, its central lake; for eight months of the year water carnivals were held on it with gondolas and fireworks, and for the remaining four months it was turned into a garden gay with shrubs and flowers. Cairo was still one of the cross-roads of the world.

The Latin Christian and the Copt rubbed shoulders with the Arab and the Jew. Asia and Africa sold their own people, along with their best incense, their aloes, their aigrettes, lacquer and ivories. Something like 100,000 inhabitants milled around the great bazaars in this famous city, a survival from the past.

Farther from Constantinople, and even prouder of its autonomy, was Barbary. Tripoli had become a desert where hardly a single passing caravan was to be seen, and where the Arabs, abandoning the remnants of the cloth and saffron trade to the Jews, lived on piracy in small city-fortresses built near the coastal water-cisterns. At Tunis linen cloth reported to be the best in Africa was woven by the lake, and there were still faintly perceptible traces of Arab civilization between the low houses covered with balconies and the gardens which surrounded the city; but inside the old ramparts, no longer kept in repair, the population was content to live on piracy. No thought was given to the hygiene of the city, swamps were allowed to foul the air and rainwater tanks were badly infected. In spite of so many risks, French merchants had gained a footing in the city, which tolerated their presence because they bought the produce of its plunder. These French merchants were beginning to ensure some measure of coastal trade, and soon Tunis became a kind of international receiver of stolen goods: even the English and the Dutch infiltrated into it. The Moorish Bey had overthrown the Turkish Bey. Even more than Tunis, Algiers was the capital *par excellence* of plunder, and the largest urban centre in Africa next to Cairo. Indeed, the luxury of some of its houses and their gardens was evidence of the success of the world's biggest venture in piracy, and attracted French and English merchants; Jews from Leghorn opened several banks there. The English even opened Gibraltar to the pirates. The French from Marseilles installed at La Calle a precarious bastion where coral fishing was carried on. As the citizens of Algiers were rich and could pay, people were beginning to trade hardware, sugar and coffee to them. But this wealth was not lasting. The price of cargoes was going down.

Finally, in the West, the 'King' of Morocco had just left his old fortress of Marrakesh to take up residence in Meknes. This was still the country of the nomad Adouans ruled by marabouts and caïds, the country of caravans which journeyed twelve hundred and fifty miles, five hundred of them across the desert, to bring what remained of Guinea's gold. This Sudanese gold seems to have aroused little interest in Europe. In 1750 a company was formed in Copenhagen to trade with Marrakesh. But the Portuguese had lost interest and abandoned Mazagan in 1767, for even though it was well provided with harbours, by 1780 preference was being given to Mogador. And anyway the same thing was happening in Morocco as in the whole of Barbary; the foolish local chiefs, flattered by the competing European traders, were too easily persuaded to grant trading privileges, and since piracy was given a free hand the large number of buyers soon put up the selling prices.

Constantinople

Constantinople was perhaps an even more important centre than London or Paris; its population was in the region of a million, consisting for the most part of Greeks and Armenians, but also of subjects drawn from every corner of the Empire and, of course, of Turks. It was a strange city on the beautiful site of the new Rome. The old city was built around the incomparable church of St Sophia, whose bold and extravagant style had been frequently imitated and improved upon by the Turks. They were proud of their large, airy mosques, even bigger than the church of Justinian, although they kept to the same architectural pattern of one great dome resting on four pillars. The harbour, the famous Golden Horn, still attracted ships from every point of the compass and merchants from all over the world. In the upper town, behind the mosque of Eyoub, the covered bazaar was a centre for merchandise from three continents. Nearby was the slave market: an enclosure for the men, a covered bazaar for the women; Jews bought lovely Georgian girls in order to teach them elegance and to sell them again at a high price. High on the other side of the harbour was the noble suburb of Pera, with its embassy gardens and palaces; lower down, in the suburb of Galata, a dense cosmopolitan crowd of sailors and adventurers milled around shops licensed to sell wine, which even attracted a few Turks. Dominating Galata was a tall fire tower, which unfortunately did not prevent the terrible fire of 1782 from devastating two-thirds of this wooden suburb with its dirty, winding streets so riddled with vermin that even the fire did not exterminate them. More dangerous even than fire were epidemics, like the plague which killed off thousands of victims every year, and which was responsible for more deaths than the earthquakes. Yet Constantinople remained a hub of the world. This was not because of the harem, a monument to the vulgar and cosmopolitan taste of the Sultans, where the Sultans walked in the shady gardens among countless little Byzantine or Chinese pavilions. Nor was it because of the pretentious fortifications of the Sublime Porte, but because of the ferment of trade, peoples, customs and religions, on the shores of the narrow Bosphorus, where the history of the world seemed to be rotting away.

ATLANTIC ACHIEVEMENTS

Servile Africa

Ocean trade, however, was still a comparatively new phenomenon, a novelty which more than two hundred years of slavery had made extremely profitable.

The whole Atlantic coast of Africa, with the exception of the Barbary coast and the desert seaboard, was known vaguely as Guinea. It was one of the busiest coasts in the world, chiefly because it was on the route to the Cape of Good Hope, and the Cape Verde Islands had become one of the most famous ports of call; but it was also the centre of an enormous trade, the trade in Negroes. Compared with this inexhaustible supply of saleable humanity, and the profits it brought in, all other branches of the

African trade—pepper and gold dust or ivory and Benin bronzes—seemed insignificant. Many were the battles, and bitter the rivalry, to control the traffic in Negroes. The treaties throw little light on the problem of who controlled the innumerable fortified points on the coast. Hardly had the island of Fernando-Po been wrenched from the Portuguese by the Spaniards than it was abandoned. The Dutch were more prudent and only imposed a substantial duty on the Portuguese of the Gold Coast. Yet ships from Recife managed to evade it by bringing their vessels alongside spots not mentioned in the original agreement. The French were more methodical and built a harbour, but an English ship massacred the men working on it, though no state of war had been declared. The Danes obtained permission to erect huts and stalls, but never succeeded in making use of them. Moreover, about 1755, slaves were becoming scarcer and slave-masters more choosy: it was no longer a buyer's but a seller's market, and the seller preferred to lead his files of captives towards harbours frequented by international shipping, where he could obtain a better price because of the competition. Hence the extreme complexity of what may be called the commercial geography of this strange traffic, always on the move, ever changing, not only because it dealt in men, but because of the varying rate of flow of the tidal currents at the mouths of certain harbours, the silting up of river mouths and periodic outbreaks of fever which made some ports unusable.

Nevertheless the trade was still very profitable. Great Britain sent out hundreds of ships mainly from Liverpool but also from Bristol and London, laden with ironware, glassware, guns, and printed cottons from Eastern bazaars or manufactured in the new English mills. These were Africa's main imports, and every European country tried to align its trade with that of England.

This trade, however, was not only conducted by barter, and in the closing years of the eighteenth century an oriental shell was still in use. It was a curious currency and varied in value from one country to another. The price of an African was reckoned in shells. The white man, moreover, did not go direct to the villages for Negroes; the business was done by local chiefs, minor chiefs of small tribes, who were half sorcerers, half family men; or by the more powerful potentates of Juda or Benin, pale replicas of the famous Monomotapa. It is true that at first the native chieftains sold only Negroes condemned by tribal law, but as printed calico became more fashionable and more expensive, so the tribal law became proportionately stricter. In the regions most favourably situated for the trade, the quota provided by the law was soon increased by the supply from war, and even by the abduction of the ruler's own subjects. This business of slave catching was a dangerous one, and the bodyguards of the Negro kings liked to try their hand at it. But sometimes the villagers would band together to resist and go to the king himself to complain, and then it was the bodyguard who was sent into slavery, as the king did not want to be the loser all round.

Yet the coastal native adapted himself to the situation, preferring to sell rather than be sold. Gradually the melancholy columns came from farther and farther inland. The captive's neck was imprisoned in a wooden fork, the handle of which rested on the shoulder of the man in front. This chain of slaves could neither sit down nor lie down except all together and on the orders of the man holding the first fork. It was an interminable journey. In order to keep Gorée supplied the French undertook journeys which might last for months. The traders complained that slaves had doubled in price in the African markets, but they had to be sold at four times the price in American markets. Luckily the price remained low in the south of Zaïr—the Congo—which was a great advantage to the Portuguese of Brazil, who had retained their possessions on the coast of Angola while they gradually abandoned the ports in the north. Sometimes a bold spirit tried to substitute some new trade for this traffic, which was beginning to be disliked even in Europe, but it was not easy to penetrate into those central African kingdoms of which such miraculous tales were told. It was said in particular that gold was washed down in the mountain streams and was even to be found in the mud in which the natives paddled; but as yet no-one had managed to get a footing there and organize the collection of the gold efficiently enough to offset the enormous cost of transporting it. The heart of Africa was, in fact, unknown. Of that vast continent, only its capes, estuaries and coastline were known.

At the extreme tips of the continent were a few good natural harbours, and there was a flourishing settlement at the Cape of Good Hope. This was a port of call on the long voyage to the Indies, and it had been admirably laid out by the Dutch; their company had successfully discouraged rival English agents who were weary of doing battle and preferred St Helena. At the Cape, ships willingly paid a high price for fresh supplies of water, vegetables and fruit, the more so as the Dutch had succeeded in creating extensive gardens and the fruit was renowned for its quality throughout the Ocean. Carefully selected seeds and plants from an experimental garden were sold to the settlers, who cleared all the surrounding land. These settlers came from every city in Europe, and only one condition was imposed—they had to be Protestant. French settlers who came after the revocation of the Edict of Nantes did well there and consequently attracted numerous Germans. The whole of this microcosm of Europe stretched for a radius of a hundred and fifty miles and there were about 15,000 settlers in all. They were dissatisfied because the company, having distributed land free, actually had the audacity to subject them to an ownership tax, although it was already making a large profit from trade in the port. Nevertheless, the company had the forethought to build an admirable hospital, which was all the more appreciated since the agents of the great maritime companies were often paid according to the number of sailors they succeeded in bringing back to Europe alive.

Work on the land had never attracted the native Hottentot. At first, diseases brought from Europe had decimated the local tribes. Those who survived went inland hastily, retreating as the white man advanced. It was said that one Hottentot had gone to settle in the Indies where he had made a modest fortune, and then, shedding his clothes and his Western luxury simultaneously, had returned to the indolent nakedness of his fathers. The assimilation of black nations was not easy, and the story of the Hottentot was one good reason for not troubling too much about it. In 1785 the chief concern of the people of the Cape was not to assimilate the native, but to know whether or not the European settler would have the right to trade direct with ships which anchored in the ports or whether this was to remain a company monopoly.

There is no need to pursue in detail our voyage along the eastern coast of Africa. Everywhere there was a general desire to imitate the prosperity of the Cape. In the Ile Bourbon, or Réunion, were to be found horticulture and agriculture, which through the efforts of 'one of the King's botanists' were nearly as good as the Dutch plantations. There were several thousands of French people on the island who had fled there from Madagascar where the natives from the interior would make sudden descents on the coast and murder over-adventurous Frenchmen who were too anxious to get rich. These massacres of white men were sometimes led by a handful of Arabs who had lived in proximity to the natives for hundreds of years and resented European competition. Farther north, the east coast of Africa was considered even more uninviting and unprofitable: it was dominated by the Banian, the sea-faring Indian of the Persian Gulf, and the Sultan of Zanzibar.

If proselytizing Muslims penetrated as far as Madagascar, Prester John could be claimed as a glorious victory for Christianity, except that it was the Egyptian Copts who converted the Abyssinians. They stubbornly refused to listen to the Roman missionaries who attempted to prove that Christ was not only God, but also man; the Negus, who would don a crown of thorns before putting on his royal crown, punished this 'heresy' by death. A few Dutchmen, perhaps the only ones to do so, managed to settle in Abyssinia, because they were less interested in dogma than in a modest trade in ivory and spices, which did little to enliven the dreary capital of Gondar, a mud town abandoned by its population in the dry season for the comfort of tents and the freedom of the steppes.

Accustomed as we are to the amazing advance of progress on the American continent, we have to make an effort of imagination to realize what America was like in 1785, and how it appeared to an inhabitant of Europe. People were not even entirely sure where its natural frontiers were, the continent was so vast. The expedition of a group of scholars who undertook to measure the earth by triangulations taken from Peru was a most hazardous venture. Equally heroic was a Jesuit father who vanished without trace in California where he had taken his telescope to get a better view of the stars. There was much argument about the exact configuration of the north-west coast of the continent: many well-informed people were expecting an influx of Chinese into America and believed that North America was attached to the Asian continent. Almost nothing was known of the interior of this vast continent, either to the north or the south. People may have read between the lines of the more or less fanciful stories told by travellers who collected trappers' tales and believed that great Indian civilizations, prosperous but unknown, peopled the north-east of the continent. As for the great southern mountain range, there was considerable doubt as to the whereabouts of the kingdoms of Toupinambas, so fashionable in Europe. The high Cordilleras of the Andes were better known than the great range of the Rockies though certain of its peaks had been given picturesque names by French-Canadian trappers.

A further surprise for the twentieth-century reader is that economically the West Indies by themselves were as important as all the rest of the continent put together. Moreover it was only the immense popularity of the independent English colonies which prevented the whole continent from being regarded as Spanish. Brazil and England, in fact, occupied only a few scattered border strips here and there, while Spain controlled the Panama isthmus, and consequently the safest route to the Pacific coast, and might be said to have gripped the New World by the waist. Carolina could well have been French; it was English only because the Spanish had so many other possessions that they despised these sandy wastes. Throughout the New World places which are now the greatest human townships on the face of the earth were then only small settlements; taken all together, they would not have equalled the population of a single one of the great cities of Asia. In short, though the Europeans had gained a foothold on the continent and conquered the Indian cities, they had scarcely begun the economic conquest of the continent.

The Awakening of Spanish America

What remained of the fabulous Spanish Empire? It can best be assessed from its physical centre—Panama. The passage round the Magellan Straits was much feared by sailors, and merchant ships greatly preferred the route across central America. The town of Panama, rebuilt after the lootings of the late seventeenth century, was the capital of the Kingdom of Terra Firma—a pretentious name which concealed a disappointing reality: a country without culture, with only mediocre fisheries and a few pearls. Yet great wealth flowed across this poverty-stricken land, as cargoes from Europe were unloaded at the Panama docks and transported either by mule or in large barques to Porto Bello on the Pacific. Outside the trading season it was a small town with an unhealthy climate. The garrison was made up of one hundred soldiers who came to take up their stations there at the opening of the commercial campaigns. For several days merchants from Spain mingled with those from America. There was amazing bustle and activity. Under the supervision of the commander of the convoy the price of merchandise was hammered out. The Americans brought their precious metals, and Europe its manufactured goods which the Creoles were eager to buy. The market had been famous for the scrupulously fair dealing which characterized it, but by the time we are speaking of this great Panamanian trade was on the decline. We know that the Treaty of Utrecht gave the English the right to bring slaves and goods to this market in the so-called 'permit ship' (which was followed by numerous others which kept it constantly supplied). What with English competition, the unhealthy site, and especially improved techniques of navigating around the continent, the Panama trade was declining and did not recover until the famous canal was opened in 1914. Meanwhile there was a long period of trade depression in central America, although it fluctuated over the continent as a whole.

Up to the mid-eighteenth century the voyage from Callao to the Pacific coast of Chile had taken six months, following the indentations of a dangerous and broken coastline. The first captain to venture into the open sea instead of keeping to the coast did the round trip in a month and was nearly condemned for witchcraft. Nevertheless his daring marked the opening of a new era: the Panama isthmus lost its trading monopoly. The round voyage benefited Chile and its inland capital Santiago, and even more Valparaiso, which of all the harbours formerly in use was the only one to expand, because it was the nearest. In 1783 peace reigned in Chile, and white people from all over the coast were coming to settle there. There was a plentiful supply of cheap timber for building, and the peace-loving Indian (when he was not drunk on European alcohol) sold his cattle and even his children for a good price. Adequate farming was developing on the plateaux, and the mines were still stirring men's imaginations as well as contributing to trade. Sea communications drained off the coastal trade as far as Panama, whilst other trade routes brought goods through the snows and over the precipices of the Corderillas of the Andes, and from as far away as Buenos Aires. It was this latter route which was followed by the mules loaded with tallow, leather, maté tea and sometimes a few slaves who reached their new masters in much fresher condition than those taking the northern routes. In the opposite direction from Chile to La Plata caravans wound their way loaded with ponchos, wool for making cloth, whisky, and even a little gold. The country farthest away from Spain,

Chile, was also the first to profit by the trade concessions which Madrid granted to all Spaniards in 1778, and Valparaiso expanded as a result.

Whilst Chile was growing in importance at the edge of the known world, new life was stirring in 'Paraguay', a vast region with vaguely defined frontiers between Brazil and the endless plains of the south. It was known chiefly for its central region and what was left there of the Jesuit missions now run by monks of various other orders. We know how successful the Jesuits were in assembling 100,-000 peaceful and trustworthy Indians in villages, regulating everything by and for the Society. The Spanish merchants of Santa Fé and Cordoba, and the Portuguese merchants of Sacramento could hardly be expected to tolerate an empire which defied the principles of economic freedom and private interests in search for lands, cheap labour, and easy business. Once the missions had been destroyed, the economy of La Plata was dominated entirely by stock-breeding. The mountain stretch of the route to Santiago was hazardous, but it could not have been easier in the plains. Everywhere there was magnificent grassland, and in some places there were even cultivated fields. Thanks to its sturdy mules, the already prosperous stock-breeding industry was sure of a good market, especially in Buenos Aires. The city's wide streets were lined with low houses and small gardens, riotous with flowers, which stretched as far as Santa Fé. Nearer the city centre whitewashed brick houses were already replacing those made of earth. Its 30,000 inhabitants could boast several brand new public buildings, yet Buenos Aires had still not extended as far as the river, and was ten leagues away from its port, La Enceñada, an unreliable harbour bordered with huts. No one, in fact, had yet discovered the secret of building an adequate port on the treacherous banks of the muddy estuary of La Plata, often swollen by storms and continually blocked by shallows. The attempts made at Montevideo to construct a similar, rival, port were by no means completely successful. The barques going down river managed quite well, but sea-going ships almost invariably ran aground. La Plata faced inland, rather than to the sea.

Lima was the centre of Spanish rule. Peru had once been the treasure-house of America, but was now in decline; even Lima had been destroyed by the 1746 earthquake, like all the coastal settlements. At Callao, a tidal wave had completed the destruction of the town. But a magnificent competition in rivalry achieved the rebuilding not only of the port but of the capital as well, which emerged even finer than before. True, the old Incas were sceptical when they saw the Spaniards digging deep foundations for their stone houses. 'They are digging their graves', they said. Nevertheless, the whole of European Peru was being built to last, the display of luxury was a sign of its confidence. The corridor leading to the Viceroy's hall was paved with silver. They flaunted their wealth, although the result was disturbing: the mines were being exhausted. The cities in the high mountains were still there: Cuzco, the old Inca city, was the greatest. Its ancient buildings had overawed the European invaders at first, though they later affected to despise them. Its new baroque churches softened the heavy background of the natural landscape. It still had 25,000 inhabitants. Potosi had almost as many, La Paz fewer. Small towns atrophied in the high mountains where the air was rarefied, life hard and short; where workers' riots were violent and managers alternated between extremes of benevolence and cruelty. In these high lands, where a living was hard to come by, the day had passed when the Incas could pick up at will huge nuggets of gold from which they made vases and jewellery, when on up-rooting a tree a hunk of silver could be found at ground level, when a few shovelfuls of earth uncovered veins of metal which could be chipped out with a chisel. As late as 1730, a nugget weighing forty-five pounds was discovered near La Plata. Fifty years later there was no longer any hope of such discoveries. The trenches gaped open, useless: pits were deepened in vain and extend by wooded galleries, and only with difficulty kept free from flooding. The raw metal had to be treated with mercury (of which Peru fortunately had several rich deposits), and yields and profits were so seriously on the wane that many preferred to invest their capital in agriculture and in the few industries vital to the inhabitants of these cities. In any case by that time gold and silver were no longer the country's sole source of wealth. Llamas and pacos came down from the mountains loaded with chunks of minerals less rare but now more marketable: copper, tin, sulphur and even platinum. It was the closing period of colonialism in Peru; the creoles of Chile and La Plata were beginning to turn away, relying on their own efforts to bring them wealth. They were no longer so willing to submit to the out-dated authority wielded from the effete Spanish palaces in Lima.

In the north, in New Granada, the King of Spain had gained nothing by relaxing his restrictions, and scarcely managed to maintain the dwindling trade between Quito and the mountain towns scattered throughout this wild, rough countryside. And the Caracas Company in Venezuela only managed to survive, when ships of the Spanish fleets were no longer compelled to put in at ports along the coasts, by conceiving the idea of lending capital to agriculturists and having the interest paid in agricultural produce. Within two or three years the port of Puerto Cabello revived and La Guaira became prosperous. Caracas also found itself in an excellent position in the middle of an area producing cocoa, as well as indigo, which fetched a high price in every market in the world; but the Caracas Company was short-lived. About 1780 an economic crisis made American merchants cautious. The old organizations disintegrated, and people relied on individual initiative to take the place of the failing business concerns which could no longer be directed all the way from San Sebastian.

Mexico had a similar history. Most of the country was separated from its Atlantic port by wild mountains. On the Pacific side it sloped down more broadly and gradually stretched towards Acapulco. Its territories northwards spread over half the North American continent, where its frontiers petered out beyond Santa Fé, the tiny capital of New Mexico. If this vast area alone brought Spain as much income as all the rest of its American continental possessions put together, it was chiefly because of the silver and gold from its mines, which were being worked again. In the south of the Oaxaca country the Indian, under the whip of Spanish merchants, grew cochineal, which was in great demand for textile industries all over the world; in Los Angeles and its surrounding villages small local industry produced ribbons and textiles of every kind and improved the quality of its output by copying materials from Europe. These communities, tiny islands of new activity, were not to be compared with the great cities of the past, with the bold towers of Puebla's vast cathedral, and particularly with Mexico City. Surrounded by floating islands, overgrown with grass and trees, on its mountain lakes, Mexico City was the pearl of America. In the days of Montezuma it boasted more than 200,000 inhabitants; but even now, with its 60,000 souls, it was still in 1780 the first city in the whole of America. Its majestic square in the Madrid style was bordered by sumptuous palaces, and by a huge cathedral built on the ruins of an old Indian temple. All around were the crowded quarters of the poor, where the police were constantly on the watch; there was frequent danger of riots, especially when the Indians had drunk too freely of their beloved *pulca*, an alcohol made from the same agave-aloe which supplied him with textiles and foods. Everywhere canals were built to drain a soil liable to flooding in the rainy season. Sumptuous carriages decorated with gold patterns bowled along the streets. As in every Spanish American city, the population was mixed. Europeans were in a minority, making up barely a sixth of the population of Mexico. The rest consisted of African Negroes, half-castes of every colour, and especially Indians, who retained traces of the unusual qualities that led to the construction of the strange pre-Colombian buildings around Mexico and Yucatan, and which are beginning to attract interest and attention again after a long period of neglect.

The formation of a united Brazil was to be one of the wonders of the nineteenth century. Towards 1785, in fact, that vast country gave no signs of being a unified empire, but seemed to consist of a multiplicity of mutually suspicious and rival cities, inadequately linked with one other, and each attempting to exploit for itself the immense resources of the interior.

The Brazilians occasionally allowed their small and remote capital to mediate in local conflicts, provided it did not annex power at the expense of local interests. Moreover, the whole of the south was still uncertain of its true nationality, and had not decided whether Spanish or Portuguese was to be its mother tongue. The fine natural harbour of Bahia de Todos os Santos had no adequate deepwater connection with the interior, which was cut off by high mountains, and there was no way of unifying this huge country in which the north, proud of its longstanding wealth and prosperous sugar refineries, was acting independently. Bahia had to give pride of place to Rio de Janeiro, a more convenient outlet for the centre of the country. In these central regions were precious metals; the gold-seekers who had been trying to make a way through the hostile forests for two hundred years, at last discovered the precious veins of metal. Sumptuous baroque churches plated with gold were erected near the mines. Towns sprang up in the desert where the workers alternated between extravagant festivals and feverish labour; the subsoil was already getting worked out at the time of which we are speaking and was soon exhausted. To the task of retaining a monopoly in this wealth, the riches of Minas-Geraes, Portugal devoted all its remaining energies. Its policy towards Minas was one of unremitting severity, though it was lax enough elsewhere; it led to the martyrdom of the hero Tiradentes in 1789 as he was addressing a meeting at Ouropreto on the liberal examples of North America and France. Pieces of his body were exhibited in all the surrounding towns. The mule-tracks which led by laborious stages from the interior to the coast would soon carry less gold; but by then landed proprietors of the interior were reaching an agreement. Their efforts at land clearance were being helped by the development of the mining towns, and the merchants of the coast. These two middle-class groups, both proud of their authentic Brazilian roots, were to unite in a mistrust of foreigners that soon developed into hatred, and they persuaded their customers to feel the same.

Free Anglo-Saxon America

The Spaniards made their settlements around former Indian sites in the south and centre, but the English-speaking peoples who created the small cities in the north had proceeded quite differently. Consequently these small North American cities had neither the wealth nor the population of their Spanish rivals. New York, which still occupied only the southern part of its Manhattan peninsula, had scarcely more than 25,000 inhabitants. It had a fine Anglican church and its French, Dutch, and German chapels, but had previously been regarded merely as a fortress. Nevertheless, its people were beginning to build stone houses, with fine English fronts, and a new town hall, which was intended to be the most remarkable in America, was nearing completion. It had one of the finest natural harbours in the world, and trade with England had flourished, especially during the War of Independence: it was therefore with reluctance that New York took part in the discussions in Philadelphia which defined the new federal Republic. For Philadelphia, with its 35,000 inhabitants, was assuming the rôle of a capital and even superseding Boston, the first city of them all, the birth-place of freedom, and the first place to make a stand against England.

The admirers of the young federal Republic had nothing but praise for Philadelphia, a small gay city where living was cheap, with delightful small houses along the banks of the Delaware and its tributary, which was spanned by a fine bridge; its market-place, raised on pillars and bordered with brick arches, was particularly famous. The whole city was organized around this centre, dominated by the town hall which had its windows framed in marble, an unusual luxury in this new agricultural Republic. Philadelphia was famous also for its numerous freshwater fountains, and its tree-shaded walks stretching away into innumerable orchards. In 1785 the small inns of this potential capital were full; it was not that the delegates of the thirteen states were very assiduous in attending the Congress, but the city was crowded with petitioners. Amongst them were large numbers of demobilized officers, a threat to the new state. They had in fact formed an association of 'Cincinnati', protesting that those who had laid the foundations of their country's freedom were entitled to greater consideration, and that it might perhaps be their duty to take the destinies of the young country into their own hands. They sent their Cincinnati badge to all their friends on the continent, and particularly to the French. Every liberal-minded person in Europe followed the debate which was to give power either to the new civilians or to yesterday's heroes. The soldiers were anxious, and so were the merchants, whose safes had been crammed with paper money which had been issued for the war but was beginning to depreciate.

The newly born Republic was an object of concern to every honest soul in Europe. People dreamed of emigrating. Jefferson proposed that entry should be forbidden, and Franklin, in Paris, explained at length the difficulties and risks involved in land clearance: America was far from being the land of ready-made happiness. Philosophers and theoreticians in Europe, and especially in Paris, paid no heed: they overwhelmed the Congress with good advice. Have a fleet, said some; give up commerce and trade, said others, and concentrate instead on the virtues of agriculture. Be a democracy, said Mably. You will progress only under the leadership of an aristocracy, replied Morvilliers. It was no use! The 3,500,000 new Americans paid not the slightest attention to this flood of solicitous literature. They cultivated their land, attacked the forest, attempted to irrigate their sandy soil, worked in small workshops beside rivers and harbours, traded in the small markets which were set up at road junctions, with only one idea in their minds, to buy as little as possible; hence the falling-off of trade which would—the English hoped—lead the young Republic to regret secession. But the spirit of independence was strong: there was eager competition for the news-sheets published in Philadelphia, New York or Boston, which played up to their readers by protesting against the excessive taxes to which the war had given rise.

America, then, at that date was not industrial. The tar factories which were stripping the forests in the Carolinas could hardly be called industries; nor could the state-controlled tobacco drying plants in Maryland or Virginia, or the boat and barque building yards in Boston. During the war country families had been obliged to spin and weave, though the cloth they made was only coarse in quality. The great majority of American farmers, eager above all to devote themselves to their lands, were waiting till goods could be imported from Europe again. On the other hand, there was great variety of agricultural produce. Jefferson had interminable lists of them drawn up, the largest, naturally, being for Virginia. In the south, the warm, moist summers set a premium on possession of slaves. Was the high-minded Republic going to tolerate them? Public opinion was beginning to take notice of the not wholly disinterested protests from England. Though the state of Virginia had, for its own part, decided to forbid trading in slaves, it did not forbid the use of them. Charleston continued to be a busy port for the slave trade. Close by the southern states were islands which had remained European, and had an enormous Negro population, so that they needed to export men and import foodstuffs; consequently an easy profit in the slave trade could be made by the southern farmers. Public opinion in the north was wavering, and the feeling against slavery filtered through from London to Boston. This was a city almost like London in miniature, built like an amphitheatre around the Bay of Massachusetts, studded with fertile islands and fruitful orchards. The city with ten churches of all denominations in the style of Wren, its English-looking houses and streets, espoused the ideology of the capital against which it had revolted.

As for the west, it was a controversial topic. Briefly, these virgin lands were to be set apart for the creation of new states. It would have been condoning too great an inequality between the old colonies to allow that some of them should be hemmed in by their neighbours, whilst others, open to the west, would develop unhindered. By undertaking to create these new states the Confederation had suddenly increased in power and significance and was confirmed in it by the new state of Kentucky, formed about the wonderfully rich grasslands of the western slopes of the Alleghanies. The vast west was still no more than the perilous domain of trappers whose tracks followed the Great Lakes and the rivers. These trappers were almost all French, as the English preferred to remain near the coastal areas, even in Canada, where they settled.

About 1780, Acadia became Nova Scotia: in face of the advancing English, the French had followed the land routes towards New France, and were soon replaced by English Royalists who were themselves refugees from the United States. A few thousand families, scattered here and there, they were not particularly anxious to embark on the great adventure into the interior. As for the French on the St Lawrence, they were, so to speak, shut in on their tiny citadel of Quebec, and evolved on the surrounding plains a peasant population like that of France. They were more reconciled to separation from the mother country when they learned, through its priests, that a wave of moral laxity and irreligion was sweeping over Paris. The French court had, as we know, taken very little interest in the problem of America because, for continental Europe at least, the real centre of interest so far as America was concerned was the wonderful chain of islands which formed the West Indies, the pearls of the Atlantic. To give them their true place in the economy of the late eighteenth century would mean devoting more pages to them than to the United States itself. It was towards the West Indies that most of the slave convoys made their way. There was good money to be made from growing coffee, cocoa and tobacco in the sheltered valleys, as long as they were not too swampy, and in laying out enormous plantations of sugar cane. Mule convoys converged on the small harbours, selling the produce of the land in return for riches brought by ship; amongst these the precious metals from Mexico were most highly prized. The islanders' greatest problem was not to yield to the seductions of a climate which Europeans found delightful, but on the contrary to get rich quick by making slaves do the work. The buccaneers had learnt from experience. When they were unable to get a plot of land, they kept shops in the small towns in order to sell as dearly as possible to the planters the goods for which there was such competition when the ships tied up at the quays. The one subject of all their Sunday arguments and weekday dreams was how to get back quickly to Europe with a substantial fortune. This was especially true perhaps in the French West Indies: the Dutch were more loyal to Curaçao, and the Spanish to San Domingo. It was they who had introduced cattle-breeding, much appreciated by the French consumers who held the other part of the great island. But in the French possessions the day of the adventurers was over. These former members of the minor aristocracy had achieved marvels at the beginning of the century by pacifying the pirates whose interests they defended against the voracious India Company.

This powerful and hated company showed, moreover, how ill it rewarded the services of its settlers. There still lingered the memory of Law's bankruptcy; he paid the settlers out in valueless paper notes, so that when the poor wretches landed on the French coast they learned that they were utterly ruined. The company certainly put up a good defence: the West Indies offered an excellent opportunity for trade, and European businessmen from every capital in Europe were no less eager to increase their profits than the Creoles were to get rich quick. But although the great ocean trade remained in the hands of Europeans, their ships did not linger unduly along the island coasts, which retained the monopoly in coastal and inland trade. This island trade sent its boats plying from island to island, and tried to expand as far as the American continent; it gradually created a network of interests increasingly capable of holding their own against the demands of the distant capital. The old governors' palaces often changed masters and sometimes flags as well. The settlers paid no heed, learning from experience that it was easier to make money in an open town, where troops of all nations were always welcome provided they paid up, than in fortified towns which were destroyed and ravaged by each fresh war. They held aloof from Europe's quarrels: they protected themselves against European competition, and exploited the Negro. In San Domingo there were already more than 300,000 slaves; the death-rate was exceedingly high, but a constant supply from Africa was guaranteed. Once Europeans had been converted to anti-slavery there was of course a decrease in the traffic; this caused the settlers some anxiety, so that they tended to keep their slaves, rather than free them as before, even though they knew that this fresh severity could lead to sudden revolts in their territories.

Thus from north to south the vast American continent was everywhere breaking its links with Europe. The break was made in the north. It was being prepared in the south and centre. The Atlantic, which had been the vital means of Europe's hold over America, was in process of becoming the instrument of American independence.

3

The Call of Asia

ALL through the Middle Ages contacts had existed between China and Europe, although they were indirect: it had taken months, even years, to accomplish the journey overland and had involved innumerable ship crossings, which almost always included the Indian Ocean. Now, during the eighteenth century, European ships established direct contacts. These direct contacts brought a revelation to everyone in the Western ports and cities in the eighteenth century, as they had done to a small group of adventurers in the sixteenth century. The products of Oriental craftsmanship, Oriental agriculture, and the manners and customs of these enchanting civilizations revolutionized European taste. In addition, the powerful European merchants penetrated deeply into several Eastern countries, and in order to exploit Western fashions they strove to transform the economic structures of the East: successfully in India, with greater difficulty in China. As for Central Asia, it was beginning to be a depressed area both economically and culturally. Its unsettled state attracted neighbouring peoples and gave them the excuse and the opportunity to intervene. The beneficiary this time was not a sea power. It was a land power, familiar with the slow rhythm of life of continental peoples: it was, in fact, Russia.

THE DISCOVERY OF INDIA

Every wealthy mansion in Paris (and of course in London, as well as its counterparts in Germany), had at least one 'Indian' drawing-room, in which, inset in the Western panelling, botanical, zoological or human scenes imitated from India were portrayed. India was just as popular as China in cultured circles, with perhaps this slight difference, that its philosophy was not quite so admired; nevertheless it probably exerted an even stronger influence on public taste. If India was less often admired in Paris than China, this may have been due to a lingering bitterness at the loss of an empire which Suffren's efforts had failed to defend against English ambitions. A more likely reason was that Indian civilization was alien to the Frenchman. It was a world at once more secret and more subtle; the improved communications had brought it closer physically, but it was as far away as ever mentally, for its passive organization remained incomprehensible to Western minds.

Eighteenth-century European thinkers found India quite inscrutable. On the one hand they were dazzled by the splendour of such potentates as Aurangzeb, the Louis XIV of India, last representative of a dynasty of kings which had enhanced the old Hindu arts with the refinements of Persia. People still remembered his throne 'encrusted with diamonds, decorated with vine-branches made of pure gold, their leaves enamelled in natural colours, the grapes being of emerald, ruby and garnet'. The famous throne had, in fact, disappeared, carried off in 1738 during a Persian raid. Yet Agra remained a vast capital city, with some million inhabitants, which a man on horseback could scarcely ride round in a single day; it boasted eight hundred bridges, a hundred caravanserai, innumerable mosques, and twenty magnificent baronial castles, so arranged that they appeared to be paying homage to the King of Castles, that of the Moghul, whose harem alone contained twelve hundred women. Merchants from all over the world seemed to meet in Agra, for not only was the finest indigo to be obtained there, but also all the produce of Central Asia and India. The nearby town of Delhi, in which the Moghul had also lived for a long time, was easily outclassed by Agra. Delhi itself was quieter than Agra, but the Prince's palace was even more dazzling, especially on high festivals when elephants bore the imperial processions in state.

Yet at the time we are considering little was left of the power of the Moghuls. The one reigning in Delhi had no longer any authority. A rival and perhaps legitimate claimant lived on a pension paid him by the East India Company, which also ensured him a refuge in Bengal and gave him military protection against the attacks of his enemy, for the finest province in India had become almost the private property of merchants.

The Ganges was in the hands of foreigners; not the kind of foreigner who swept down in one fierce raid to loot and plunder a territory for a season, and then withdrew to his distant lands; nor was it the foreigners who had come over the last hundred years to settle on islands in river estuaries, or in the mouths of harbour channels, where they awaited their moment to steal some of India's wealth. This time the foreigner who had India in his power was a methodical exploiter who intended not only to reimburse himself as quickly as possible for the enormous capital expended on its conquest (a conquest at first directed less against the Indians than against his European competitors) but also to organize a permanent administration of India which should be to his own advantage.

In 1785, this corner of the world presented a series of violent contrasts. Here was the shrine of Juggernaut, the most famous temple in Asia, home of the great Brahmin. Its enormous idol was covered with diamonds and drenched with perfume, and it was surrounded by attendant idols reputed to be carved in gold. From the farthest reaches of the peninsula it continued to attract pilgrims who came on their knees to cleanse themselves in the Ganges after having paid, each according to his means—but even the poorest of them generously—for the right to enter the sacred city. The most fanatical threw themselves under the wheels of the chariot in which the idol was carried. And in the middle of this milling mass of humanity were a few passive commissioners, tall, lean, fair-haired representatives of a different race, who disliked any excesses and carefully respected the natural order of things. They assessed taxes, obliged puppet princes to sign laws and regulations, and by the offer of moderate rewards or through pressure exerted by local chiefs recruited thousands of Indians whom they intended to train as workers in the factories they were opening on the coasts. They emptied the coffers of former tax-collectors, and enrolled disaffected soldiers in their own regiments, officered by Europeans. They built cities: Calcutta, the most important, was an insignificant mud-town on the river Hooghly, but it grew at such speed that, in spite of the putrid vapours rising from the swamps which only now were beginning to be drained, it was soon a great city. Yet this artificial city was to impede the development of all its rivals, Indian as well as European. The merchants' tents gradually left the old traditional capitals, cut off from their hinterland by the new frontier created by the Company. Thus the development of the old Chandernagor, built Indian-fashion on piles, was artificially halted, and the city became fossilized in its outmoded Franco-Indian form. Calcutta was already the ruling city in a country where obedience had never been regarded as dishonourable.

On the other hand, the position held by the English Company in Bengal should not be exaggerated. The transformation of India by England was far from being completed. The English themselves were not agreed about the future of the country. While Warren Hastings was strongly pursuing the Company's interests by taking advantage of the passivity of the Indian population and the uncertainty of its masters, in the House of Commons in London Fox thundered out his protests against the Company's scandalous exactions and its criminal negligence in allowing some millions of men to die; in 1784 the Commons ordered Hastings to be impeached and to render an account of his stewardship before the Lords. Pitt struggled to induce the Lords to agree to a reform of the Company embodied in the famous India Bill, which received a stormy passage through the Commons, culminating in the suicide of Clive, victor of Lally-Tollendal, and the overbearing leader of this new conquest.

Whilst London discussed their fate, the Indian peasants were aware of the changed situation only through the presence of new officials who appeared in their villages

from time to time. The majority of Indians remained indifferent to the disastrous transactions which marked the
end of the old imperial India and added considerably to
the hardship of their lot, which for centuries had been
steadily deteriorating. This passivity of the common people was perhaps the result of their religion, which inculcated a respect for order; by degrees this had transformed
the old social structure and consolidated the caste system, and may even have paved the way for the country's
downfall. Certainly, at the time of which we are writing,
this passivity was the country's most noticeable characteristic.

Caste did not however exclude freedom, at least in principle. It split freedom into separate compartments, as it
split the whole country. The fact was that everywhere the
old Indian community still existed; we have noted the
survival in Eastern Europe of this communal life, which
gave rise to the intellectual myth of a common Indo-
European civilization. In the village the assembly settled
everything, and its duty was to ensure a livelihood for
all. It may have been to protect these villages that the
former conquerors had guaranteed that soldiers would not
enter them, and had imposed a similar obligation on the
armies to ensure that they respected the educated classes.
In any case, at the end of the eighteenth century, the educated *élite*, the soldiers, and the peasants, were three
worlds functioning in water-tight compartments, separated
from each other by an ever widening gulf: there was no
mutual social contact, no sharing of even an occasional
meal, and certainly no intermarriage between these various
worlds. And following their example the infinite variety
of artisans formed themselves into trade groups which in
turn were grouped into castes, the frontiers of which were
no less rigidly fixed, although difficult to define. Originally,
in the days when this structure was more general than
tyrannical, the individual had the right to abandon his
caste, to become an outcast, with greater freedom. But
later, when the structure became fossilized, the outcast's
lot was disastrous, and he was rejected on every side. Certain trades came to be considered unclean or degrading

(that of scavengers, for instance), and this added a new rigidity and increased the number of untouchables, the slightest contact with whom necessitated purification.

Religion in India never developed a moral conscience capable of overcoming the appalling inequalities of the caste system. Buddhism retained its admirers among the literate, and its teaching was propagated everywhere, including southern India, where it was more strictly observed than elsewhere. It did not eradicate the primitive animism of the common people which compels an Indian to remove every living, moving thing carefully from the patch of earth on which he is about to sit, saying, to God: 'I have spared the ant, Lord, do Thou put it down to my account'. And belief in the transmigration of souls also led to a respect for the order of nature: in a new life the good will attain a higher caste, but the bad may descend to the vilest of animal forms. Thus every living creature had to be respected in the eyes of the Hindi sage.

The Muslim religion also spread from the north, brought in by each fresh wave of conquerors; but even in Kashmir and Nepal where the Koran was widely disseminated it did not succeed in effacing old customs. It was propagated throughout the peninsula by merchants and craftsmen, but only served to strengthen respect for the old beliefs. Indeed, its most notable effect was to induce in those who resisted it a heightened fanaticism in the observance of the old customs. To each wave of Islamism, the peasant replied with new fervour for Hinduism.

So from generation to generation the community villages retained their differing patterns of toil, varying from one end of the country to the other, but always true to themselves. The village produced barely enough to feed itself, after handing over to other castes and to the lords their due share of rice, fruit, curds and milk, and leather. Certain castes forbade the eating of meat, others held the cow sacred, but consented to eat the ox; others would touch neither leeks nor onions 'which grow out of impure things'. To satisfy all these different diets, the peasant watched for the arrival of the monsoons, which were first spotted from the top of the Ghats, for he was afraid of floods except in specified places where they could be controlled. It should be noted that the English victory in India brought them control of a crop which was a highly profitable economic proposition: the poppy, which already grew widely in Bengal, and produced opium of a medium quality.

As for craftsmanship, its infinite variety defies description, whether in the realm of small useful articles or in skilled luxury trades, such as jewellery. Indian goods, particularly cottons, were very popular in Europe, and this popularity proved fatal for India. European trading companies were no longer content to buy ready-made produce; they wanted to develop it to order, pledging in advance enormous capital sums in order to buy raw materials, pay wages, and train workers, of whom they intended to have only the very best. Around every European settlement grew up zones of industrial activity, attracting population, the craftsmen seeking work or peasants threatened with famine: and these forces most probably accounted for the prodigious new cities of India—European settlements founded on unhealthy islands or barren sandy wastes.

Bombay, Buon Baya (in Portuguese 'good bay'), was nothing but 'a filthy islet' when the Portuguese presented it as a wedding-present to Charles II. At the end of the eighteenth century it was a new city of nearly 200,000 inhabitants, the capital of yet another principality belonging to the East India Company, and already powerful enough to send troops into the interior to conquer new lands and cities. It gradually extended itself inland, by judicious payments of gold, by negotiation or by treachery. Relying on small contingents of several hundred armed men (later increased in number), it expanded its settlements and tried to carve out a new Bengal in the west of the country. But it soon faced the solid feudal régimes of the Mahrattas. Madras, in the east, was built on a sandy, uninspiring site, with an inadequate supply of drinking water. Gossips maintained that the Englishman who settled there did so only in order to be near his Portuguese mistress who lived in the neighbouring colony of Saint Thomé. But Madras, however difficult its site, was admirably placed to attract to itself all the trade of the rival settlements on the Coromandel Coast, and had the added protection of the powerful British fleet.

This Coromandel Coast had lost the former glories of its maritime empire which had stretched as far as the Sunda Islands and across Indo-China. But it could not escape the consequences of its geographical conditions: it had two monsoons in regular succession, great ocean currents and a whole chain of suitable harbours. The Dutch, Portuguese, French and English had disputed over the bases of this ancient maritime coast, in a costly struggle which gave birth to great feats of arms, miracles of political juggling and an infinity of stories. The mastery of India could only be won from the sea; this was obvious enough, and Suffren had continually repeated it, but Clive was the first to prove it. He used the stretches of the River Ganges to effect what Dupleix with his land policy had not been able to achieve permanently in the Deccan. The interior of the Indian peninsula, together with the north-west, still formed in 1785 an island of land resistance against the maritime inroads of the East India Company, whereas the wide northern delta allowed it to push far inland.

This was India. Its weakness in the eighteenth century was that it never expected attack from the sea. There had been a few stubborn 'pirates' on the coasts of Rajputana, who had long been a source of uneasiness to the Moghuls and had attacked the sea-routes and disorganized the European and particularly the English fleets. But the Mahrattas were almost as concerned as the English to destroy this 'nest of disorder'. And although India possessed good ship-builders it was content to let them work for the Company. As for sailors, the skill of the famous Malabars is legendary. The most enlightened of the Moghuls from Central Asia had never had any great liking for seafaring activity: there was no sailor caste and no curiosity about modern improvements in navigation, any more than there was a caste for the new developments in metallurgy and armaments. The haughty Aurangzeb himself was quite content to leave to the despised foreigners the task of scouring the seas. The Moghuls must have smiled to see those down-at-heel emperors whom the Portuguese set up on the Malabar coast in order to make sure of getting their services cheap, at the cost only of a little flattery.

So it was that the old caste-divided India, though still defending itself in the centre of its vast peninsula, saw its coasts encircled by the English who had already sailed up the Ganges and were now threatening the capital itself.

It was the sea that conquered India, the sea and the ships from Europe. On each side of the Indian peninsula there had formerly existed two great sea empires. These soon fell, but were not fully supplanted by the advances of Western trade. In the west, the Moslem and Banian ships had apparently remained in control of trade along the East African coast as far as Madagascar. They were also masters of what little trade was still carried on in the Arabian Sea, and remained so until the Mediterranean trade broke through Suez and destroyed the last vestiges of this old and decaying maritime civilization. Little remained of the famous Ormuz, a huge treasure-house which still stirred dreams of adventure in any imaginative Western mind. It had been the most flourishing of the ocean ports where the loveliest of Asian slaves and the produce of the world's most cultured civilizations were to be found. But from Albuquerque to Shah Abbas war on land and sea had ravaged the dream island, and with a decadent Persia turning away from the sea, the centre of activity shifted to Basra. Basra was part of the mainland ruled by the Arabs, a rich fertile country which yielded acres of the finest corn. Shepherds from the interior came there to offer butter, leather, and above all camels in exchange for the coffee and tobacco they loved, and also for opium. All these precious commodities, which were also produced in the rich fertile lands of Arabia, aroused the envy of the desert tribes and provoked them to savage raids on the caravans bound for Damascus or Mecca. The routes from Aden and Mokha were in most respects safer, and European interests were already infiltrating along them.

But Europeans had found an easier conquest in Eastern waters, where navigators were continually making fresh discoveries; the Spaniards, for example, were busy exploring the Philippines with the help of the strange long-haired black natives who until then had been chiefly engaged in continual inter-tribal warfare in Manila. The Spaniards had succeeded in settling on the coast and had introduced European cattle, which were doing well there; and there were also ample local resources to be exploited: trees which bore abundant fruit, gold-nuggets in the rivers, and the skill of Hindus, Chinese and innumerable half-castes.

Batavia was the Queen of the Eastern Seas; its deep harbour thrusting far inland made it the finest port of the East: hence the fantastic growth of that swarming city, built on mud. Every country in the world had, at some time of the year, ships in Batavia. It was the great port of call between the New World and the Far East. This commercial wealth was based on extraordinarily rich agricultural resources. The soil was fertile when irrigated (and so much water had been taken from the river for irrigation that in 1780 its estuary was nothing but a sandbank). It produced rice, coffee, spices, and food in sufficient quantities not only for crews of ships anchored in the bay, but also for several islands in the Pacific, and sometimes supplied places as far afield as Mexico. The island of Java sold much and bought little: most goods, English hardware, for instance, had to make a long journey to get there. As a result, Batavia had acquired vast wealth in gold, which was administered by the Resident General of the Amsterdam Company.

The Dutch, who had driven out their European rivals, had no great difficulty in dominating the small local kings, or in subduing the betel-chewing, opium-smoking, feudal society which kept in its service armies of slaves, easily obtainable in the Celebes or the Moluccas; and Holland saw to it that the market was always well stocked. Close watch was kept on the labour gangs bent double over the ground, but who only a few years previously had shown the degree of violence to which they could carry their revolt. Free trade was practised by Chinese or Indians who got rich on the side and where possible sent their profits to their families at home. The Company kept as tight a watch on this illicit traffic as it did on the gangs of slaves. The Dutch might confer coveted honours on the local chieftains, and respect the Muslim religion (mixed up as it was with survivals of the old paganism), but they made it clear that all the gold must go to Amsterdam. So these islands—where so much of the work was done by slaves, these busy yet depressing cities in which innumerable small ships were built for the Pacific trade, where every type of dress, every way of life known to Asia has intermingled—constituted one of the most envied commercial sites in the world. By sheer hard work gold was extracted from the Batavian mud, just as not long before, and for the same reasons, it had been dredged from the mud of the Lower Rhineland.

CHINA REMAINS ALOOF

The end of the eighteenth century marked one of the most splendid periods in the history of China—but it probably appeared even finer in the missionaries' tales that were read in Europe. These remarkable Jesuits had been expelled from France by Louis xv in 1763, under the joint pressure of fanatics and Jansenists, and in 1773 the whole order was condemned by the Pope under the combined pressure of the 'enlightened' monarchs. Nevertheless, Father Verbiest had enjoyed immense authority in China in the previous century, and so did his successor Father Gerbillon. In 1715 the latter had even succeeded in persuading the proud Emperor of China to write to Rome, defending the Jesuits' tolerant attitude to ancestor worship, which the Emperor represented to the Pope as being a simple, pious tradition. But the Son of Heaven had pleaded in vain, and his failure must have rankled. Christianity was thus forbidden in China—but the Jesuits themselves remained in favour. People remembered that they had reformed the calendar, repaired the old wooden cannons, cast new ones, and rebuilt the ruined citadels.

One of the last of the Peking Jesuits, Father Ventavon, wrote in 1764 that the Emperor and noblemen of China agreed that the Roman religion was good, 'but if they opposed that which was preached, it was from fear lest, under the pretext of religion, we should conceal some ulterior motive. They had heard of the conquests made by Europeans in India.'

The exceptional position of these few Jesuits, most of whom were at the Imperial Court of Peking, should not blind us to an extraordinary fact: the immense Chinese Empire which the Manchus had restored in Tibet, Kashgaria, Chungaria, Mongolia and Southern China, making it as great as it had been during the most glorious Han period, this Empire which was the largest in the world, bigger than the whole of Europe and yet united under one single prince, was closed completely and effectively to Europeans. The few occasional caravans which the Russians, after endless journeying across the steppes, managed to get through to Peking could hardly be reckoned as contacts; nor could the insignificant coastal trade for which the English, Portuguese and Dutch competed along the great estuaries under the amused and scornful eyes of minor officials and Chinese merchants. The Chinese extracted every possible advantage from the rivalry and hesitations of the Europeans: when it was a foreigner who was being robbed, there was surely some excuse for violating the teachings of Confucius on the subject of honesty in business.

European philosophers read the books of the condemned Jesuits with profound pleasure, and from this reading there suddenly grew a realization of the vastness of the Chinese civilization. In the light of this momentous discovery, China ceased to be an obscure and distant example of despotism. After Quesnay, the greatest and wisest government in the world was universally praised throughout the cultured society of Europe, and particularly in Paris. Its supporters claimed that it was based on the evidence of natural rights and enlightened reason. Let us attempt to sum up what was written, and what is known today, about one of the most admirable periods of Chinese history.

'It was an attractive sight, the fertile countryside where land was never fallow, where even the mountains were cultivated on their highest slopes, built up by a hundred terraces; such mountains elsewhere would have produced nothing but brambles and bushes but here they made a delightfully fertile scene and bore three harvests a year.' Obviously China was not all one endless garden, but in the writings of the period everything came in for admiration, the forests of pine and oaks, of palms and cedars, and the many trees unknown in Europe, the *ram mu* with its everlasting wood, the rosewood with its lovely black grain, and the ironwood, so hard that ships' anchors were said to be made of it. There was an infinite variety of fruits, and herbs with a thousand virtues; and bamboo was used for every purpose. The Chinese peasant was poor, certainly, but at least he appeared to be free. The Emperor's close concern with agriculture was particularly praised. It was recalled that one of the emperors was himself a ploughman, and there was enthusiasm for the celebration of the spring festivals which in every village was presided over by the Mandarin, or by the oldest and most respected sage.

Although the Chinese peasant was obliged to hand over almost half his harvest to the state, and although he lived frugally on a little rice, oil and tea, it was quite true that the Manchu emperors in power since 1644 had done what they could by dividing hereditary estates, and trying to combine the smallholdings of three hectares; it was these smallholdings which turned three-quarters of the Chinese peasantry into small landowners, given over to agriculture and the cultivation of their land, which they fertilized skilfully with the manure that was essential if the ground was not to be exhausted by three harvests a year. The Manchu dynasty, to make its power secure, supported the slaves against their masters. Slavery had probably never been so harsh as under the rule of the Mings; slaves and servants were beaten to death without the administration making any attempt to intervene. From that time onwards, however, the brutal master risked deportation or flogging, and after several generations the farmer was regarded as the owner of at least a part of the land he had been cultivating. This was a feature of which the Western philosophers approved.

Of all the products of Chinese industry, none was more famous in Europe than the porcelain—so famous in fact that Dutch factories tried to imitate the best Chinese pieces in order to heighten the value of their own wares. In China, vast industrial centres were made up of a conglomeration of small factories organized in guilds. In Kiangsi there was Kingteh, where it was estimated that more than 500 kilns and a million workmen were grouped together, and where the finest paste in the whole Empire was made; at least, the European merchants thought it was superior to that of Peking. As for the Canton porcelains, well known in Europe under the name of *Indian porcelain*, they were apparently made simply because the Chinese believed that European merchants had very poor taste and they were far inferior in quality to those of the interior. At all events this seems to have been one of the really great periods of Chinese ceramics; there was monochrome, *sang de bœuf* or sapphire blue, as in the eighteenth century, to which had been added what was known as the *famille rose*, and the *mille fleurs* pattern on a rose-pink background, the finest flowering of a thousand-year-old art.

As for silk, even Europeans recognized that it was very unevenly spun and that fabrics were not always in the best of taste. Yet certain of these silks were admired and eagerly sought after, chiefly because of their unparalleled whiteness. These smooth silks attracted foreigners much more than the brocades, which were already being made more efficiently in Europe: the Chinese never seem to have taken the trouble to spin gold and silver thread properly, and they decorated their material with gilded paper. On the other hand, the green and red dyes they produced were so good that contemporary Europeans could congratulate themselves if they could improve on them.

In China, of course, nothing was known of the mechanization which was being introduced in Europe. Nevertheless a few Chinese, so skilled at every kind of manual work, tried their hand at applying some of these new techniques; they succeeded in manufacturing watches and guns—but these were isolated attempts which did not give rise to any real industry. Chinese civilization remained in a pre-mechanized stage. The population was so numerous that flour mills were very often turned by human labour; water-wheels and windmills were known, but were in general too widely scattered and too expensive to deal adequately with the nation's requirements.

This predominance of manual work did not prevent China from maintaining vast cities. They were usually square in shape, surrounded by high walls with towers at each corner supported by flying-buttresses. These large towers, often hexagonal, were also to be found in the centre of the cities, close to the temples and the gateways rather like our triumphal arches, and they were a distinctive feature of old pictures of China. The population swarmed around low-ceilinged shops piled high with silks and porcelain and all kinds of glazed pottery. These represented high-class trade, since the small trader did not need a shop: the barber strolled about, with a chair on his back, in search of a customer. In the same way, most craftsmen worked only to order in the actual homes of those who had placed the commission. The bath merchant carried hot water to the house. The strolling players had no theatre: they simply used the big market places, transporting their troupe from town to town. And there were certainly plenty of towns. Father Lecomte wrote: 'I have seen seven or eight cities all bigger than Paris, not to mention several others which I have not visited. There are more than eighty cities of the first rank, comparable to Lyons or Bordeaux. There are more than one hundred like Orleans and more than six hundred like La Rochelle or Dijon.' In all, there were more than four thousand walled cities. All were linked by roads or canals, though these sounded more impressive than they actually were to Europeans who thought in terms of their own royal highways or stone-banked canals. The artificial rivers attracted special attention, particularly the Grand Imperial Canal from Canton to Peking. The Europeans at once imagined seven hundred and fifty miles of waterway bordered with stone embankments and avenues of trees. The different branches of this canal must in fact have varied a good deal, and probably included several overland sections across which boats had to be dragged over the clay soil. Another wonder of China was its daring bridges spanning embanked valleys or broad rivers; and the pontoon bridges, which opened to let boats through. The whole empire gave the impression of a vast fair, bustle and animation prevailing everywhere.

Peking, a capital beautified by the Mings, had been burnt down when the dynasty fell in the seventeenth century. But the city had been restored, and once again the traveller could admire the golden river and the marble gates, the palaces with gilded roofs arranged according to the order of the Cosmos, and all the glittering framework of the Imperial religion. In the last years of the century the Garden of Spring and the Garden of the Round Light were completed, to form what is known as the Summer Palace. French *salons* were decorated in Chinese style, but French missionaries in China were also appreciated for their skill as painters. One of them, Father Attiret, has caught the charm of these pleasant man-made valleys, watered by streams channelled from the mountains, with pillared façades supporting the gilded and lacquered structure, made of cedar-wood brought from twelve hundred and fifty miles away. In the middle of the great lake, on a rock, rose the small central palace, from which all these wonders were clearly visible.

Yet it was not only the material civilization of China which Europeans praised. Chinese medicine, in so far as it was known, aroused the admiration of many Western doctors. At a time when Western medicine consisted essentially of the application of ideas which the Arabs had taken as much from the Far East as from the Greeks, the skill of the Chinese at detecting minute variations of the pulse won them high esteem. In philosophy, too, Chinese civilization had produced achievements to equal the elegance of its lovely houses, and the size of its urban settlements.

In theory, every educated man was a nobleman, and in theory too, there had to be a school for every twenty-five houses. But in fact, if the privileges of birth had no sanction in law, they were recognized in reality, since it was difficult to achieve the Red Girdle unless one was born into a cultured family. But also, and the liberal-minded traveller consoled himself with this thought, the precious Yellow Girdle reserved for members of the Imperial families could sometimes be worn by beggars legitimately, for the Imperial families remained prolific, even after suffering the most disastrous vicissitudes of fate. In any case nobility was acquired, and maintained, by the study of texts. Children were taught the thousand sentences of the Santseking, adults the wisdom of Confucius and his commentaries. The man of letters could give a brilliant performance when called upon to make one of the traditional public speeches that were dedicated once a fortnight to some fresh virtue. Good servant that he was to the Empire and the Emperor, the man of letters could earn some of those greatly envied titles of nobility which were transmitted not to his descendants but to his forbears, and went so many generations back in proportion to the degree of magnanimity shown by the Emperor. For, side by side with Confucianism, ancestor worship was so deeply rooted that it could well seem more than just the filial piety of which the Pope had been so suspicious. The dead were laid in a richly decorated coffin and given the most elaborate funeral rites. An altar in every home was consecrated to the ancestors. For the rest the people relied on a higher power—the Tien—of which every person in authority was an emanation, the Emperor first and foremost.

China was undoubtedly tolerant. She may have feared the Christianity of the barbarous West, yet the most varied superstitions were allowed to spread. Buddhism introduced the human figure of Buddha, which was soon followed by innumerable idols installed in equally innumerable pagodas in which the clergy lived comfortably and well. Not only did the people regard them with awe and reverence, but scholars went there to meditate on the transmigration of souls, a doctrine which they came to accept. All these sects intermingled with each other and were constantly being revised. There was a continual ferment of religious enquiry and each man furnished the shrine of his conscience as best pleased him. All these differing creeds had one observance in common, the obligation to preserve, at all times, that extreme politeness whose subtle delicacy was mistakenly interpreted by Europeans as dissimulation. This politeness and its rituals arose from a great desire for goodness and wisdom, since the gesture and attitude were to control the conscience from without. The Chinaman with a barren wife was free to take a concubine, but it was his legitimate wife whom the resulting children had to regard as their mother, for the complicated marriage rites were intended to safeguard the future of the family.

The stories about these rites brought back from their long journeys by European merchants were often no more than caricatures of the real thing, for they could really know little about China. Their experiences were confined to a few sea-ports, notably Canton and Ning Po. Canton, they said, had a million inhabitants, and the influx of merchandise was immense. The river was covered with an amazing number of great ships. In fact, the draught of water was so shallow that European ships had to stay in the marshy roadsteads which were studded with islands and more than three miles from Canton. One of these islands was well populated, well provisioned; it was reserved for the French who were not a little proud of it, since the Portuguese, English and Dutch had to make do with more barren ones. Commercial rivalry was fierce between these islands. The most famous was that of Macao, but its activity was not increasing; ships were turning away from it, a sad ending to Portugal's ambitious schemes. And no one could have forecast the amazing future of Hong Kong, a stony islet at which ships from England were beginning to anchor in increasing numbers. European trade was attracted by silks and porcelain, but it was not wholly uninterested in gold either. The Chinese preferred silver, Europeans gold: hence the origin of a trade which would have been extremely profitable but for the hazards of the long journey. The English and the Portuguese went in for it on the largest scale. A certain Frenchman, too, made a handsome fortune by bringing silver from Mexican mines to the Pacific port of Acapulco, and after putting in at the Philippines, exchanging it for Chinese gold.

The Chinese scorned maritime trade. It is true, Chinese ships made for Japan, Manila, Batavia, Tongking or Cochin China. But it was only small-scale coastal shipping, the lingering survival of the old coastal trading and the empire of the seas which had been the refuge of the last of the Mings, and of the pirate Koxinga who for twenty years had successfully disputed possession of Formosa with the invaders from the north. Yet its importance should not be underestimated; it was to lay the foundations not only of the outer China which had already played such an important rôle in the national resistance to the conquerors of the land but also of the offshore China which later was to transform the Pacific Ocean. On the other hand, the Chinese kept a closer watch on the vast continental masses of which their country was part. Of the 800,000 men under arms (this figure included the whole number, even local militia, which were of very unequal value) the sections not guarding the interior of the country were massed along the famous wall, built of stone and brick, from which they sallied forth on expeditions intended to preserve peace and goodwill among friendly and neighbouring merchants, and to keep within the Chinese *orbis* the unsettled regions of Tartary and Tibet. In the course of these operations China encountered the Russian caravans. (These Chinese expeditions did not penetrate very far across the steppes of Central Asia along the route of the old silk trade towards the West but they helped to create a new route along which went rhubarb and tea.) In the eighteenth century they had the right to bring goods which were traded in Peking itself, under the eyes of the sovereign. But this privilege was often contested, since a strong faction at court accused them of abusing it. The

Russians succeeded, nevertheless, in keeping the imperial privilege of maintaining a trading post in Peking.

But during the period of Manchu or, as it is more often called by Europeans, Tartar splendour, China despised these land barbarians as thoroughly as those who came by sea. These men with their strange white skins and fair hair (a characteristic of the demons of popular imagery) seemed alien to them. In reality, these European traders, like tiny insects, had done no more than touch the vast body of China with the minute antennae of their remote ambitions.

THE STRUGGLE FOR CENTRAL ASIA

Beyond the Tian-Shan and the Altai, beyond the Himalayas and as far as the frozen sea in the north and the Atlantic in the west, sprawled an enormous continent intersected with forests and mountains, furrowed by rivers and huge lakes, with seas stagnating in the hollows of low-lying land. Did this vast region stretching from Kamchatka to the Baltic belong to Europe or to Asia? The eighteenth-century Westerner had become accustomed to looking on Sweden, Poland and Russia as a part of his world, whilst Persia belonged to the East, to Asia. But when we come to survey this vast region as it was in 1780, we shall be dealing with it as an integral whole, and as part of the East.

We have seen how Western maritime trade reached the shores of Asia and began to penetrate to India and Indonesia. These sea-routes were relatively new: for ten centuries China's trade with Europe had been carried overland across this same, huge continent. The land trade had carved out economic channels too deep to vanish without trace, and which remained important since they were the channels along which Russian history began to infiltrate in the nineteenth century. What was the position at the time of Catherine the Great?

The routes from Asia to Europe were a succession of halts, post-stages precariously established and widely spaced, for the use of the great caravans whose journeys lasted many months. These routes seem to have followed three natural directions. The most famous and most direct, the 'silk route', after following the oases of the Tarim Valley, took the shortest cut across Central Asia and emerged at the end of the Mediterranean. This, generally speaking, was the route followed by the Turkish invasion; it enabled them to take over Constantinople, and it was still the backbone of their power. Persia and Afghanistan were enclosed within mountains, as if in natural fortresses, between China and India and between Turkey and Russia.

Russia was gradually establishing itself along two other great continental axes, which might perhaps be called the tea routes; the China tea transported over dry land was considered superior to any tea that had been shaken about in the damp holds of ships. Naturally, just as many other commodities besides silk travelled along the silk route, so the tea routes were also used for lambs' wool, tallow, rice and spices of every kind. These goods, on leaving Turkestan, went towards Astrakhan and the Caspian, or Archangel and the White Sea, or Gotland, Hansa and the Baltic. The first route followed the Siberian rivers, ideal for descending traffic. On these endless journeys small ships had to be made which were destroyed or left behind when the time came to leave the rivers and resume the overland trek. The building of these boats presented no problem because of the inexhaustible supply of timber in the surrounding forests. Boats had to be built for the second route also where it crossed the Caspian, and here the forests of Kazan were equally useful. The English, as we know, had tried to take advantage of both routes through Moscow to Central Asia in the heroic days of the first Muscovite Company. They still held an important position in this two-way traffic. There were English agents in Astrakhan, but that strange city built at the mouth of the Volga was also frequented by the Swedes and the Dutch, and of course by Mongols, Turks and Jews. Large numbers of Armenians were also active throughout this whole region. The curious city of Astrakhan lived on fishing in the Caspian between the two peak seasons of its commercial traffic: winter, when the sledges glided over the frozen Volga, and summer when the unfrozen waters were no longer a danger to shipping.

Three routes, then, led Europe towards China. It is difficult to imagine what this traffic must have been like, and what were the conditions of the areas through which it passed. There were tales of Tartars, and Mongols, of unarmed caravans being attacked by dangerous robbers, incidents which Borodin was to evoke so vividly in music.

In fact the status of the whole area, extending over several hundred miles north of the seas, was politically ambiguous, situated as it was between the old, solid Moscow and the domination of the Turks: there stretched undefined territories which for centuries had been a refuge for serfs escaping from Russia, for the politically persecuted, and the heterodox of all religions: it was these areas which made up the Ukraine in the west, and which extended as far as Persia. They were frontier lands where man had no rights other than those he was capable of defending. And the real rulers were the Cossacks. We know how the Ukrainian Cossacks had first offered their services to Poland against Russia, and had then entered Russian service against Poland. Pushkin has told us the history of the great revolt of Pugachev, who gathered together tens of thousands of rebels about 1773; they gained control of the Don, and threatened Moscow itself, where a section of the people were waiting for them, seeing in Pugachev the true Tsar Peter III. By the time Pugachev was captured at Tsaritsyn and drawn and quartered by order of Catherine, the Cossacks had laid waste a huge area to the east, before seeking refuge with the Turks beyond Kuban. Yet even in Pugachev's time, most of the frontier Cossacks had eventually accepted Russian authority and, in return for their autonomy of government, were getting used to their rôle as zealous servants of the autocracy. They provided troops for the army, and became involved in all Russia's military ventures, against the Poles as much as against Prussians and Swedes, while still retaining a predominant rôle in the military structure of the south. It was their detachments which accompanied the slow-moving caravans as they penetrated into the high

Caucasian valleys towards Tiflis and Armenia, or into the trans-Caspian deserts, towards the valley of Syr Daria, and the ancient cities of Samarkand and Bokhara. The atmosphere of these caravans has also been described by Pushkin, and a few years later Tolstoy portrayed the life of the Cossacks which had hardly changed since the eighteenth century. The Cossack was half-soldier, half-peasant. For his work and service he received for cultivation thirty deciatins of the land which his slow conquests were acquiring for Russia, and whose cultivation, apart from producing a much-needed food supply, helped on the work of land clearance, opened up the forests, and thus made it easier to keep an eye on troublesome local tribes who retreated as their natural defences were destroyed.

The Russian army was Asiatic; it was a versatile army which adapted itself to all these different tasks. In the north and north-west it operated in European style, disciplining itself to fight the Swedes, fortifying St Petersburg, and opening up Russia's path to the west; but in the south-west it remained a vigorous, largely disorganized affair, holding off the Turkish raids or moving in a compact body to thrust out spearheads towards Constantinople. In the south-east a cavalry army was always on the alert, and sometimes ventured into Tartar territory to demolish a fort or break up a village of Central Asian bandits. The bandits would rebuild their village farther away, constructing their flimsy dwellings from the time-worn débris of the ancient Mogul capitals. Finally, to the east, merchants and peasants had created Russia's Siberian empire.

Samoyeds, Tunguzes and Gakuts passively accepted this domination without realizing its true extent. They kept their Muslim or pagan traditions under the guise of a conversion to the Orthodox Church, which was all the more sincere for being less enlightened. The Russian merchants, whether they settled down or journeyed over this immense country, caused little inconvenience to the original inhabitants, who were glad to sell, even cheaply, sable and fox skins, precious stones and foodstuffs of every kind. Moreover, the chancery of Tobolsk had scarcely any means of controlling life in the countryside. It had only the roughest idea of the position of each small wooden township, and was barely able to keep in touch with its faraway assistant-governor at Ienisseisk.

Russia was lucky enough to have no eastern neighbour. It had been able to seize Kamchatka without offending anyone at all. As for the south, nothing now remained of the brilliant medieval capitals but ruins. The irrigation canals, the marvellous oases of former days, had silted up, forming a level uninhabited battleground on which robber bands were continually at each other's throats. Central Asia was nothing but a breeding-ground of legends, which made it no easier to conquer. The Russians tried to intervene, in particular in Persia. In the previous century the cultured public of Europe had read Montesquieu's account of the admirable Persian civilization, but now it was torn apart by incessant civil wars between Ispahan and Teheran, extending from Mazanderan to the frontiers of Baluchistan. The Russians protected first one claimant and then another in the wars, and sided first with Turkey and then against it; nor did they escape without reverses, for the Persian theatre of operations was too far from Russian urban centres, and the small bands of troops who ventured there were generally cruelly defeated, decimated, and the remnants led off to slavery. Unsuccessful in Persia, the Russians fared very little better with the brilliant Emir of Bokhara. Yet if Russia failed to conquer Central Asia (and it was not in fact one of its major objectives at that time) it had, at all events, nothing to fear from that quarter. It trained armies there and drained away the remnants of its wealth. Russia, strengthened by its eastern and southern marches, could display its full strength in the west and south-west. Politically it came into collision with two states whose military power had become legendary: Poland and Turkey, two major powers which opposed each other in the mid-seventeenth century with something of the enthusiasm of Crusaders. But as we have seen, the Turkish government was no longer in complete control of its own subjects. It could terrorize them, but it no longer governed them. Much the same situation existed in Poland, whose elected king was powerless against his over-powerful vassals. In both countries the Russians found richer and more profitable battlefields than in Asia. In that part of the world at least conquest had some point: the countryside was well populated with industrious serfs and the towns were busy centres of trade. Consequently the Russian troops, with their experience of frontier fighting, felt that victory was worth achieving. They took advantage of the frequent disturbances, inevitable in a country combining so many races and religions, which jeopardized the established authority and provided ample pretexts for intervention. Russians backed Orthodox against Muslim, Lutheran against Catholic, insinuating themselves everywhere, assuming authority in Warsaw and almost in Constantinople itself. In this way Russia began the astounding drive towards the west and the sea. To the amusement of England, it succeeded in sailing a fleet all the way from the Gulf of Finland to the eastern Mediterranean to destroy the remnants of the famous Turkish navy at Chesme.

There was a profound difference between the situation in Poland and in Russia towards the end of the eighteenth century. The great Catholic kingdom of yesterday was collapsing. Muscovy, taking a lesson from Byzantium, acquired a belt of territory stretching westward for two hundred miles. Nevertheless there was no difference in structure between Poland and Russia; both had the same social pattern of peasants tied to the land, chattels in the hands of their master (though conditions were perhaps a little less harsh in the west than in the east), and the same comparative absence of a middle class, which gave excellent opportunities to the Germans and Jews settling in Warsaw as well as in St Petersburg, Moscow or Nijni-Novgorod. They had the same nobility—a strange group composed of powerful lords with genuinely old hereditary titles and rich princes making money out of thousands of enslaved souls and maintaining a swarm of poverty-stricken nobles. These nobles were of doubtful descent, but ever ready to form a guard of honour when some looting expedition was afoot. The Tsars watched this nobility with jealous eyes and carefully supported the ambitions of the most humble against the over-powerful. Up to the time of Catherine II, coteries of noblemen and their quarrels proved almost as dangerous to the throne of Russia as to that of Poland. But Poland suffered the crucial disadvantage of having to defend herself on every frontier, while Russia could exert her full weight in the west.

In this winning game, Russia wore down Turkey and established itself on the Black Sea, the Sea of Azov, and in the Crimea. It assumed a right which the Turks were quite powerless to challenge: Russian ships, laden with corn, were already crossing the Bosphorus and new settlements were already foreshadowing the future prosperity of Odessa.

Russia was like a vast living organism, a composite biological structure, and the special skill of Catherine II lay in allowing herself to be carried along by that intense stream of life and riding its triumphant forward surge; she had no military knowledge but she knew how to select the right men capable of diverting those breaking waves to her advantage, of subduing Pugachev and the Turk, of allowing the stream of colonizers to roll on unhindered towards the limitless east, and of leading the battalions recruited from this flood of rough, primitive peoples against the weakening states which separated them from the solid continent.

BOOK TWO

THE BOURGEOIS REVOLUTIONS
1780–1840

4

The West and its Tools

WITHIN fifty years, from 1785 to 1835, the face of Europe was transformed—but what of its political structure? A comparison of the political mechanisms in Europe at these two dates would throw very little light on the upheavals it underwent from 1789 to 1815. The disappearance of Poland was implicit in the agreement reached at St Petersburg in 1772. The modification of the imperial title (Austria instead of Germany) was a logical consequence of Joseph's policy, and the adoption by Bourbon France of institutions on the English model might also have been regarded as a predictable outcome of the trends of French opinion at the accession of Louis xvi. A politician of 1780 would not have been unduly bewildered at the picture presented by Europe in 1835; a moralist would have noted that on the whole ways of life in Germany and Eastern Europe were not so very different in 1835 from what they had been fifty years earlier.

But in Western Europe, particularly in France and England, there had been immense changes in society and habits, and a vast upheaval of what is known as 'human' geography. New blast furnaces were springing up all over industrial England, and the industrialization of France had begun. The appearance of the countryside had undergone a change, and that of the cities an even greater one. Was this the industrial revolution? This label, which we were unwilling to apply to the economic and social movements of the late eighteenth century, might well be appropriate here, if there were not to be more revolutionary changes taking place in Europe from 1840 to 1855, from 1885 to 1900, and above all in the twentieth century. It might be wiser to postpone the use of the phrase still further, with a caution induced by the vastness of the changes taking place today before our very eyes. Nevertheless, during the fifty years which included the French Revolution it would be true to say that a great new force took root in Europe and that the extraordinary surge of developments in the following century was no more than its natural flowering. There was more than a difference in degree between the slow rhythm of evolution which characterized the Western peoples from the fourteenth to the eighteenth century, and the suddenly quickened pace which gripped them in the nineteenth—there was a difference in kind. If the changes effected by the generations from 1780 to 1840 were less spectacular than those of the following century, it is nevertheless true to say that they contained the embryo of all future changes throughout Europe and the world. A turning-point had been reached in the world's history where a slow advance was to be superseded by a headlong rush, and it is this turning-point that we shall attempt to describe, and the causes of which we shall endeavour to ascertain.

Was there any outward change in the physical appearance of Western man from 1780 to 1835? There has certainly been a measurable change from 1850 to 1950, so that the question is justified. But the answer is quite definitely in the negative. From works on anatomy, from the teachings of medicine and the plastic arts, it is obvious that the human physique underwent no change, either in Germany or even in England; there was the same build amongst the well-to-do, the same bodily structure, and such physical deformities as were to be seen amongst countrymen and suburban alike could be attributed to the wretched lot of the poor in both periods. Looking at the poorest classes in the new industrial societies, one might even wonder whether the poor of 1840 were in fact worse physical specimens than their ancestors.

If it were possible at all to speak of progress in this period, it might be apparent not so much in the individual as in the masses. Amongst them it was quite obvious in Western Europe at least that a change of some kind had taken place in the lives of collective human groups, a change so decisive that from henceforward it was to dominate the whole history of the world. The revolution could be summed up in four words: man was living longer.

Whether or not this was a biological change, if not of individual man, at least of mankind in the mass, its effects were profoundly important: since he lived longer, man could make better use of his brains and the result was a sudden and prodigious enriching of his mental equipment. The combination of these two changes brought with it a complete structural reshaping of societies, which we shall discuss at the end of the threefold study which is to be the subject of this chapter.

MAN

Man was living longer, so much was evident from the statistics. In the early years of the nineteenth century in France the number of deaths was approximately 28 per 1,000 inhabitants; in the third decade the ratio fell to 25. To give a more detailed picture, in 1814 the death rate was very high, which was understandable in view of the war raging in France; yet the same was true in 1802, the year of the Peace of Amiens, which makes it uncertain whether or not the war was a decisive factor. The decrease in the death rate from 28 per 1,000 under the Empire to 26 per 1,000 under the Restoration was perhaps not wholly due to the fact that Europe was at peace. Under Louis-Philippe the average was still falling, in spite of a very heavy increase in the death rate at the time of the cholera epidemic (1832) and during the economic crisis of 1837, since they were balanced by years when the rate was exceedingly low (22 per 1,000 in 1835). Outside France the English, if not the Irish, enjoyed an even longer expectation of life, whereas in the whole of Eastern Europe the death rate hardly ever fell below 38 per 1,000. Thus the contrasts between Western and Eastern Europe, so much in evidence in the late eighteenth century, were reflected as soon as the mechanism of statistics enabled them to be recorded in a change in the balance of life.

This decline in the death rate was reflected also in an increase in population in the first half of the nineteenth century. It was nearly as high as 13 per 1,000 in England, though it fell to less than 2 per 1,000 in Ireland and less than 4 per 1,000 in Württemburg, and was even lower in Hungary. Moreover there was not the same geographical regularity here as in the incidence of the death rate. Some Eastern countries showed a marked increase, and not only Prussia (which was almost on a level with England in rate of development), but also Saxony and Russia who surpassed it very noticeably. The population increase in France, on the other hand, was hardly more than in Württemburg. Thus the variation in the death rate was far from being the only factor in the growth of population. It meant that Prussia, for instance, had a fertility rate higher than that of England and much higher than that of France, which brings us face to face with one of the most delicate problems in this human evolution of Europe. One cannot be too cautious in interpreting these complex results from West to East. In England, after 1740, the death rate declined very appreciably. But there was also a slight decline in the birth rate, fairly adequately balanced by an increased longevity, so that taken as a whole the population did not stop increasing. This general trend, which was becoming evident in the second half of the eighteenth century, became very marked in the nineteenth century. The number of inhabitants in Great Britain and Ireland rose from sixteen to twenty-five million between 1800 and 1830, a striking increase in comparison with Europe as a whole, where the growth during the same period was only from one hundred and seventy-five to two hundred and five million inhabitants.

In France there was a decline both in the death rate and in the birth rate, with a slight time-lag in comparison with England. But up to 1830 the total population increased less, as the French birth rate dropped more quickly than the English, and the death rate fell more slowly. In Prussia the death rate remained really high;

but it was balanced by a fairly high birth rate which increased the population by nearly fifty per cent, a rate comparable to that of England. It was almost the same in Austria. We have seen above that the incidence of low mortality towards 1820 was linked geographically with the establishment of major sea-trading concerns about 1780. We can now add that the birth rate around 1820 was high for those countries which in 1780 had what might be called a strongly defined political structure, as for instance English liberalism, or enlightened Prussian despotism; whereas the political vacillations in France were linked with a relative sterility in 1820.

The fall in the death rate, as a physiological phenomenon, spread as the middle classes became richer; it only affected the working classes where they were caught up in the new tide of prosperity. This was partly because changes in the birth rate had psychological causes: it rose when the social group remained relatively stable, but fell where there was high social mobility.

The new longevity is sometimes attributed to improvements in medicine, such as the discovery of vaccine. The Englishman Jenner is credited with this though it had long been practised in Asia and was probably imported to London from Constantinople. In any case, Jenner's first inoculation took place only in 1796 whereas the longer life of the population had already been obvious twenty years earlier. The science of medicine was scarcely more advanced in the eighteenth century than in the time of Molière. It is true that some diseases which today are not defined with anything like the same wealth of detail (particularly the melancholias) were treated with some success, and this gave rise to endless comments on the closeness of the ties between mind and body. And eighteenth-century doctors paid great attention to the minute variations in the pulse and based an elaborate system of classification on them. The treatment of the humours always entailed bleeding, clysters, and a variety of potions. The list of curious practices has come to include the most fantastic remedies, which were still recommended in mid-century treatises, like the 'water of a thousand flowers' made from decoctions of fresh cow-dung (the poor ate this exceedingly economical *materia medica* raw to save money); it was used as an antipleuritic. Macquart gives a really staggering list of the remedies used in his day, but had already reached the sound conclusion that they should be avoided, particularly the drinking of various urines, a custom which was still very widespread.

By the eighteenth century, however, though medicine was not very advanced, problems of food and diet had begun to be studied. Plants and meats, milk and spices were boiled and dissected, and from these studies some very sensible conclusions were drawn. 'Cures' became 'diets', which was a step in the right direction. People no longer believed that alcohol was an elixir which ensured long life, or that white meat was dangerous. Similar researches were being pursued in cooking, and cooks, though quite unaware of the new trends in medicine, were influenced by their customers' new tastes; they too were moving towards simpler recipes in which spices were much less frequently used. They aimed more at satisfying the appetite without blunting it than at tickling the palate by a sometimes dangerous search for new sensations. Our cooking, said one of them, must become chemical; in other words, its sole aim must be physiological efficiency.

Changes in cooking led to improvements in hygiene. It was not that anyone suspected the existence of microbes and their dangers, but more fastidious tastes and habits induced people to wash more frequently: they were less in awe of water, made greater use of soap and changed their linen more frequently. Over-elaborate clothes, tapestries, curtains and hangings, and heavy bed curtains, formerly thought to be effective in the battle against epidemics, were going out of fashion. The result was an improvement in living standards, of which the well-to-do were the first to feel the benefit, but which soon made itself felt over a widening area of the population, and if the new fashions spread much more rapidly in the towns than in the country, the latter nevertheless benefited from urban progress, which had already made considerable strides in the eighteenth century.

At the beginning of the nineteenth century, people were becoming interested in the spread of the precepts of medicine and hygiene: Louis XVIII founded the Academy of Medicine, and Bichat refused to read the 'black books' inherited from his predecessors. A thorough knowledge of anatomy became the rule among his associates. By a quite natural reaction the new school, founded by his pupil Broussais, ignored the nervous system and concentrated on repairing changes in tissues. He still overemphasized the importance of the digestive system as the source of disease; and consequently continued to use old prescriptions. It did not matter much! The pathological school was making progress and soon Laënnec's auscultation was to triumph over observations of the pulse. After 1820 clinical observations became more searching, and statistics enabled a finer distinction to be drawn between the various fevers and the diseases which had previously been mistaken for them. Schelling's abstract philosophy would hardly allow any differentiation between them, but they were to be fully classified in the first thirty years of the nineteenth century, starting with the pathological and functional disturbances of the organs, thanks to Laënnec's research on the lungs, Bouillaud's work on the heart and Bright's on the kidney. The way had been prepared for the decisive experiments of Claude Bernard.

Medicine then, was by no means a negligible factor. We shall study the general improvement in economic life later in more detail, and shall then discuss the food resources made available to mankind in the first decades of the century, the improved yield of cereal crops, the production of fine maize harvests, and the advances made in sugar beet and the sugar industry, as well as the introduction of plainer and cheaper clothes, and more widespread laundering: all these factors were even more decisive than in the previous century in contributing to the progress of mankind. Hence the explanation of the paradox: in the cities the working classes were penned like cattle in the slums and ravaged by a fearfully high death rate, but the greater luxury in the well-built areas more than balanced this appalling poverty. And the city, too, influenced the economy of the countryside from which it drew its food supply; it speeded up progress, and so helped to lengthen expectation of life. The growth and development of the city meant the increase of man's life-span.

On the other hand it carried with it a decline in the birth rate. The growing family, caught up in the rising tide of middle-class prosperity, was thrifty. Not to feed useless mouths—Malthus' great preoccupation—was also a general preoccupation of the new society. They counted their pence, planned their budget and calculated, and could do all this the more accurately since the family had begun to break up and to change its proportions. It had still been a vast collective group at the end of the old régime, and still opened its doors to newly married couples. They had their place at the common table. Several generations and innumerable families of cousins lived happily together under one and the same roof. In these conditions it was impossible to calculate the cost of a baby. Under this God-will-provide-for-the-family régime, lack of forethought was a positive virtue, the corollary of the virtue of Christian charity. It was even the cardinal virtue of the old Christian family. The change of habits which took place in the last decade of the eighteenth century led young married couples to set up their own homes. They wished to live in their own houses and to keep themselves. The large number of well-paid jobs opened to them by the widening of social life encouraged this process. The new family broke away from its own folk. It now consisted of the limited group—father, mother, child. A careful housekeeping budget was now not only possible, but essential: the newly married couple would have felt ashamed to ask their elders for help. The obligation of honour in this respect completely changed its meaning between 1780 and 1820. Since responsibility fell more and more on the individual, since each man felt master of his own destiny and responsible for his own children, young couples had to calculate their resources very carefully, and not be in too much of a hurry to start a family. The obvious result was a decline in the birth rate.

Thus the progress of urban civilization, which meant essentially an increased expectation of life, was also the cause of a decline in the birth rate. This progress in urban civilization was bound up with the development of a more individual way of life, characterized by a new pride in living. In spite of the falling birth rate, the population of England continued to increase because its general economic and social condition was at once more stable and more prosperous. France, although aware of this new pride in living, was developing in uncertain conditions, swept by the violent upheavals of the Revolution and the Empire; French parents were cautious, and the fall in the birth rate occurred even more rapidly than the increase in expectation of life. In Germany, urban civilization made only slow progress and people clung tenaciously to the old family traditions. Germans remained loyal to the old, dignified way of life and this had a greater effect on the population figures than increasing longevity, which was anyway not very noticeable.

Among the fascinating details of this new way of life let us stress only one essential point: from London to Dresden men were living longer. One consequence was that a bigger place could be found for education, and it was a wise father who urged his children—when there were not too many of them—to acquire the intellectual equipment needed to establish them in life as soon as possible on their own account. This father of a small family, looking to his own and his children's future, saved as much as he could and invested his money to the best advantage; so this rise in population had two main effects: an advance in education and increased demand for credit. We shall deal with these two problems in turn.

SCIENCE

Now that most families were attempting to provide for themselves it was no longer appropriate to trust to Providence for food and shelter. That sort of faith and resignation was only appropriate for the very poor, to whom the English philosophers were attempting to preach the necessity of birth control. Even a modicum of wealth creates duties.

The French Encyclopaedists made bitter attacks on the traditional teaching of the Church. The man who was creating science, measuring the earth and the heavens, opened up new avenues of technique, and producing comfort and luxury, surely had the right to be angry with those who opted out of the common tasks—for instance those beggar monks detested by Voltaire. Side by side with the new responsibility assumed by the head of the family, went a new reliance on science and technology.

European man in 1840 was no longer as he had been in 1780. In sixty years a profound change had taken place. Even in the eighteenth century the Westerner would not venture to affirm his superiority over India or China. From the beginning of the nineteenth he no longer had any doubts about it. However, he did not consider himself a race apart. Innumerable representatives of the white Western peoples scattered over the face of the globe, and particularly the Portuguese, proved abundantly that they could inter-breed prolifically with the other human races. There was at that time no racial problem in the biological meaning of the phrase. Perhaps one cannot state that heredity played no part in the formation of the intellectual equipment of the new Westerner; but in the present state of our knowledge, it is as impossible to define its rôle as to prove it.

It can hardly be denied that the general way of life prevailing in Europe's new cities was superior to the customs still followed in the East; and as a result the material wealth of Europe was growing at the expense of the rest of the world. We shall not probe too deeply into religion or the arts, where values are so imponderable, nor into manual skills, for the eighteenth century craze for *chinoiserie*—maxims, trinkets, landscape and customs—was beginning to lose a little of its fascination, though it still served as a reminder of the Oriental's greater skill in this sphere. The real reason for European superiority lay in the equipment used, and in the respective mental processes of each type of mind. Brilliant though Chinese civilization was, fertile though its endless experiments were, resulting in many effective new techniques, they had hardly anything to do with what today we call 'science'. One essential element was missing—the art of proof by logical reasoning.

Christopher Columbus, before becoming a courageous navigator, had to prove to all the commissions which had opposed his plans that he had an accurate knowledge of the works of Eratosthenes, of Greek reasoning and Alexandrian mathematics. Even so he relied on persuasion more than on logical reasoning. It was during the two following centuries that Europe rediscovered the Greek art of proof by reason. This new procedure was in its infancy even at the time of D'Alembert. But at last the certainty conferred by reasoning was felt, and tested, and although it was used indiscriminately for arithmetical problems or parlour games, it nevertheless fixed, from the time of Fermat and Pascal, the rigid standards by which all knowledge was to be judged.

At the beginning of the nineteenth century these mental processes which had been developing in isolation for two hundred years, began to be linked together, and the basis was laid for modern scientific method—a revolution confined to the countries of the West.

The new mathematical reasoning made it possible to see a common basis for all the experimental results which had previously been contradictory and scattered, but which now became systematic, co-ordinated, and organized around a few major principles. The system around which all human knowledge crystallized bore the name of the most illustrious of its promoters. Newton's thought, his reasoning and his calculations dominated almost the whole of the nineteenth century as they had dominated the eighteenth. In this respect Newton was synonymous with the West, and we shall see that the time when his theories were attacked at their foundation was also the moment at which European domination over the rest of the world began to slip—the end of the nineteenth century.

Newton, to the majority of the educated public, was the inventor of the theory of universal gravitation, which was popularized in France by Voltaire and his friend Madame du Châtelet. But Newton's more narrowly scientific work, known only to a small circle of genuine scholars, was much more influential than his popular theories. He condensed into a few formulae the immense body of calculations which astronomers had been accumulating for a century past (Kepler's contribution alone was enormous). These Newtonian formulae remained valid throughout the whole of the eighteenth century and for most of the nineteenth. The real superiority of Western man, as Lucien Febvre makes clear in his book *Pensées et croyances d'Occident*, undoubtedly lay in his attempt to create a synthesis which reduced everything to a single, simple whole, rejected the vague juxtapositions characteristic of Eastern thinking, and eliminated from the 'definitive' result everything which might possibly be based on instinctive intuition alone. So the attempt was made to integrate all the natural sciences in a small body of Newtonian principles around astronomy, the oldest and most rewarding subject of man's research.

Having paid due homage to the founder of modern science we can pass on to Descartes. His geometry had been just as valuable to Newton as the observations of Kepler or Galileo. For although the object of Newton's study had been astronomy, the instrument he had used in his systematizing, verifying and proving was mathematics: and Cartesian analysis in particular, which had resulted from the creative fusion of arithmetic, algebra and geometry. Let us, however, keep to the history of principles.

No period had ever been so rich in scholars as the one we are about to study, from 1785 to 1840. It is impossible to do justice to them all, or even to name them. But all envied, admired and used Newton. 'A system of the Cosmos can only be established once', declared Lagrange, who, in one of his characteristic moments of depression added, 'The mine is almost too deep already. . . . Sooner or later it will have to be abandoned.' This idea that the last word had been said in mathematics haunted the minds of that generation. In a few years' time, in Germany, Gauss and his brilliant associates were indeed to discover new lines of enquiry, but in the 1800s the Newtonian system had reached the peak of its authority.

In England, surprisingly enough, Oxford and Cambridge were inactive, and the famous Royal Society was focusing its attention on the sea. Under the influence of the current English mania for ocean travel, it was more interested in studying the surface of the earth than in speculating about mechanics. The awakening was to come in England around the year 1840 with Dalton and Faraday. The scientific method had already been introduced in Germany with the work of Gauss. But in 1800 it was the Institut de France which gave a lead to Western science, or more particularly the Académie des Sciences, whose papers were the most widely read. The Institut established the reputation of every brilliant young scientist in Europe; and Europe to all intents and purposes meant the world. It was in fact two Frenchmen who developed Newton's system to the highest degree of perfection, Lagrange and Laplace. The first, in many respects, was the more likeable. A gentle, serious, reserved genius, who was to die at 76, a few days before the collapse of the Empire, Lagrange was a true citizen of the cosmopolitan Europe of 1785. He had worked in Turin and Berlin before rejoining his famous old patron D'Alembert in Paris. Later, though sickened by the excesses of the Revolution, he nevertheless presided from 1791 to 1799 over the commission for the Reform of Weights and Measures, out of which emerged the decimal system. He was one of the first to note the limitations of the old algebra, by proving that equations of the fifth degree cannot be reduced to a resolvent equation of lower degree. He was to leave to his pupil Cauchy ('You see this young fellow? He will surpass us all') the distinction of overcoming this difficulty. He himself at twenty-three had conceived the theory of analytical mechanics: when he committed it to paper he did so almost hesitantly, with a modest disclaimer of his own work; but it was staggering in its implications. From Newton onwards, everyone was preoccupied with the problem of motion. Maupertuis had made it out to be a product of speed and distance. Lagrange made it the space integral of the amount of movement, and starting from that point, evolved a complete treatise of all the problems of mechanics. This was the end-product of Galileo's old intuitions, now translated into the language of certainty. Starting from Galileo's simple experiment of a ball rolling down an inclined plane, a tool of thought had been evolved over the next two centuries; a simple definition had resulted in an infinity of rigorous corollaries with far-reaching applications. Newtonian mechanics in its entirety was reduced to a perfect whole, the single centre of which rested on this definition of motion; and this mechanics was adequate to account for all the scientific discoveries made up to that date.

At about the same time, applying these principles to astronomy, Laplace, a Norman peasant, a son of the Revolution and an admirer of Napoleon (who made him Minister of the Interior), and who finally gratified his childhood ambition by becoming a Marquis under the Restoration, not only re-examined and co-ordinated the old problem of probabilities, but earned the title of the French Newton for his work in elucidating some of the most subtle and difficult points in the *Principia*. Newton had postulated the interference of God in establishing order among the planets disturbed by comets. Lagrange pursued his calculations further and God was done away with. Thus the mechanism of the heavenly bodies gave the system its final precision. 'God?' Laplace said one day to Napoleon, 'I need no such hypothesis.' And his certainty of mind might well be summed up in these terms: 'A mind which knew all the elements existing in the world today would know the future.' After Laplace, the impetus given to research within the framework of the Newtonian *Principia* was to continue, but the system had already begun to be disproved and attacked at various points.

The great importance of the series of discoveries which started with Kepler and proceeded by way of Descartes and Newton to Laplace was its attempt to embody in a few simple formulae, strictly deduced one from the other, the whole of man's knowledge of the heavens. Its finest achievement, to which Galileo, Descartes, Newton and

Lagrange all contributed, lay in the formulation of mechanics, an instrument of extreme accuracy which was henceforth to be used by scholars working in the most varied fields of experimental research. It gave them a number of exact definitions on which the precision of mathematical reasoning could rely. As a result, analytical calculations could be amazingly effective in observations of the phenomena of heat, electricity and the composition of matter. Their effect was to translate all observations into terms of mass, motion and force, the three keys of this new mental equipment.

It is not therefore surprising that the heyday of the Newtonian system coincided with an amazing outburst of scientific activity which in a very short time was to change the state of experimental research, and to create modern physics and chemistry. All this may almost be said to have originated between 1785 and 1840, although we must give due credit to certain outstanding predecessors. In these years the new sciences, now expressed in a mathematical form common to all, became interdependent. It was rare for an experiment performed by one branch of science not to benefit all almost equally. The historian's chief difficulty lies in deciding with which of these experiments to begin in order to make his point clear.

For the sake of convenience, let us take the problem of fire. If the worldly philosophers of the eighteenth century were a little too prone arbitrarily to confuse lightning, combustion and light, it was because the experimenters of 1780 were working in separate compartments. The ascent of paper balloons filled with hot air was certainly spectacular, and seemed to confirm the Aristotelian theory of an 'essentially' light fluid, fire, which contemporary chemistry called phlogiston. In a few years, however, phlogiston went completely out of fashion since it put forward only a superficial explanation and one which could not be verified. And it was the idea of mass, apparently so far removed from that of fire, which made sense of combustion. It is a strange story.

There is no need to describe Lavoisier's experiments in detail; let us go straight to his conclusion: 'Combustion does not change the weight or the mass of the bodies which are its agents.' This has been summed up in the famous phrase: 'Nothing is lost, nothing is created.' Thus the permanence of mass, Newton's basic principle, made its official entry into the study of combustion and created chemistry. For a hundred years substances had been weighed in order to verify the *Principia*. They were to go on being weighed for another hundred years, but now in the interests of chemistry. It was a problem which engaged the attention of every scientist, Dalton and Berzelius, Avogadro and Gay-Lussac, as well as the solitary recluse, Ampère. Gases combine in volumes which bear a simple relation to each other: hence the idea of mass led to that of the atom, an old word, but a new concept. The list of simple substances grew longer; with the help of probability theory Mendeleyev compiled a long list towards the middle of the century, not only of those which had been successfully isolated by experiment, but also of those likely to be discovered. Calculus aided in the analysis of matter. With the help of mathematics, the science of chemistry began its triumphant and irresistible course.

Lavoisier, working on combustion in relation to mass, may have abandoned the study of fire, but this in turn was taken up by mathematicians. First, fire was treated as a fluid, a caloric, and as such raised once more questions of mechanics applicable to gases. Count Rumford, a restless traveller who came from America and ended as a baron of the Holy Roman Empire, suggested the idea of a relationship between heat and work. The taciturn Fourier, a friend of Napoleon and a member of the Egyptian expedition, and later Prefect of Grenoble, devoted his spare time to the translation into mathematical terms of well-established experiments, eventually arriving at the analytical theory of heat which was to permit the perfecting of Dalton's calculations. Another Englishman, Hamilton, studying the kinetic energy of gases, confirmed the heat-work equivalence which was to be most clearly expounded in the treatise by the German Helmholtz in 1847. And the idea of work, a mechanical idea which had originated from Galileo's experiments and Newton's principles, began to dominate the science of fire, or rather the new physics.

This new triumph of mechanics was still incomplete when another phenomenon emerged under its laws—electricity. The first essential in the preliminary stages was to make qualitative distinctions between substances which were conductors, non-conductors or insulators. In 1780 this knowledge had been acquired. By 1800 all cultured Europe was waxing enthusiastic about an amazing novelty. Static electricity, produced in the famous Leyden jars, had been known for a long time, but no-one had succeeded in producing a continuous current. Then came the day when Galvani made frogs' muscles move with brand-new electricity obtained by the contact of separate substances. Carrying this experiment further, Volta set up the first 'pile'—by piling up alternate plates made of two metals. Thus electro-statics were followed by electro-dynamics. Next the pile was observed to present a whole series of chemical phenomena. The fact that the new electric current was useful in making analyses of substances, particularly of water, served to confirm Dalton's theory, and added to the list of simple substances. The next step was obviously an attempt to determine the quantity of electricity proportionate to the mass of simple substances which it isolated. In this way chemistry furthered electricity, and so repaid its debt: electricity became measurable, and in its turn came within the scope of calculation and mechanics.

One of the problems which had preoccupied Newton, and many less brilliant thinkers after him, was that of the mutual attraction between masses of matter. In order to measure the mutual attraction of two bodies, the French engineer Coulomb had invented a small but extremely sensitive balance, consisting of an axis suspended on twisted threads. The balance had been most effective in measuring magnetism. Using this highly sensitive balance, Oerstedt in Copenhagen observed that an electric current acted on the magnetic needle. Magnetism, incredible though this might seem, came within the sphere of electricity. Ampère in France and Faraday in England took up the problem again, and the result was the magnificent series of definitions which enabled mechanical mathematics to define the relations between the two phenomena more accurately. The work of Joule and, particularly, of Gauss soon made it possible to define magnetism and electricity either in terms of heat or in terms of work. When Faraday came to review the whole problem he realized with rare insight first that electricity was not unconnected with the atomic conception of matter, and secondly that like magnetism it defined 'fields' which might easily explain with greater accuracy the notion of distant attraction, which had been suggested by Newton in the eighteenth century.

There remained the problem of light. Newton had conceived the idea of particles moving in a straight line. But Young and Fresnel showed that light behaved like a wave mechanism. These ideas were very confused, and the question was not cleared up until Maxwell discovered that the ether indispensable to the wave mechanism was linked with the fields of electricity and magnetism. Although this was not discovered in the first half of the century, the first steps towards this brilliant conclusion had been taken.

To sum up: towards 1850, with the addition of mass (and the atom) and the magnetic field, all the experimental sciences came within the province of general mechanics of which Lagrange had been the greatest exponent. The laws of mechanics had first been applied to the field of astronomy, and every year they led to new discoveries (Leverrier's detection of Neptune is one example), so that by now they dominated scientific knowledge.

Naturally the mathematician of 1840, who was expected to work in so many and such varied fields, was very different from his counterpart in 1800. If this chapter began with the name of Lagrange, it can end only with that of Gauss, his near contemporary. Gauss was probably the most formidable mathematician of any time. Grandson of a gardener, and son of a Brunswick workman, he discovered at the age of ten, on his school slate and entirely by himself, the laws of arithmetical progressions. Poor and lonely, pathetically devoted to his prince who was defeated and wounded at Jena, Gauss was a man of genuinely simple heart; but his achievements are difficult to summarize, since they cover so wide a field. He discovered the meanings of complex numbers and at the same time of Euclidian geometry. Fermat's theorems were mere child's play to him and he discovered congruence. He had made his name by solving a most forbidding calculation, that of the irritating planet Ceres, which disconcerted astronomers by the difficulty of its trajectory. Gauss was also universally known for his contribution to the study of electricity. He was, in fact, the very incarnation of the mathematician of 1854. Lagrange had been afraid in 1780 that the sciences might have reached the end of the road: Gauss gave them new life, with consequences which we shall study later.

The members of the French Institut and of the Royal Society, and the professors of the new German universities, were not all physicists or chemists. In Paris Cuvier was the permanent secretary of the Académie des Sciences. And indeed biology, like medicine, was far from being swallowed up by the all-powerful mechanics. It was not until the end of the century that the chemist Pasteur broke through the old discredited science of medicine, and Mendel was to die without seeing the triumphant conclusion of his observations and calculations. Yet we should not be misled: although general mechanics and the new mathematics did not fully invade the field of biology, it is still true that some attempts were being made to subject medicine and biology to mathematical disciplines.

Voltaire declared that 'it would be very odd if laws which governed the universe made an exception of man, that minute inhabitant of a planet'; and this dictum seemed to inspire the great discoveries of 1785. Linnaeus, in his system of nature, classified man as a primate along with all other living beings. Buffon had demurred on this point, but the idea had gained ground. Gall still surrounded his curious phrenological observations with a mass of doubtful hypotheses, but Muller discovered the specificity of the nerves, and Marshall Hall proved, on the whole conclusively, that a whole area of human physiology acted in accordance with automatic reflexes. La Mettrie and his extraordinary machine-man had little effect on medicine, which had already reached the threshold of the experimental stage.

The mechanistic influence penetrated gradually into the study, not of man as a whole, but of his component parts. Bichat had already declared that the body was merely the sum total of its component tissues. Soon Van Beer showed that the egg was not the adult being in miniature, but an original mechanism from which must be developed every kind of tissue. From then on biology was no longer limited to natural history: the study of the cell became its chief preoccupation. Certainly, the study of the substance of the egg and of the cell was not yet free from the vitalist principles which had permeated eighteenth-century biology, much as phlogiston had in the realm of physics. Nevertheless, biological experimentation was already moving towards the principle of the conservation of energy, which was fairly generally recognized in that field after 1850.

Above all, biology was in many ways already penetrated by the important new study of chemistry. From 1828 an organic substance, urea, was obtained by mechanical synthesis. The work first of Priestley in the eighteenth century, then later of Saussure, and finally in 1830 of Liebig, led to the discovery of the carbon cycle, showing how chlorophyll used solar energy to return to the ground the carbon extracted from it by living organisms. Lavoisier's discovery is an instance of a biological process present everywhere in nature which conditions, if not defines, life itself on the face of the earth.

The earth and the globe themselves became the subjects of experiment. As early as the eighteenth century an English geologist had stated that the process which had formed the earth's crust was still going on, and that the geological strata to be seen in quarries originated solely from the deposits laid down in marshes, lakes and seas. At the same time, in Lyell's *Principles of Geology* (1830), fossils were no longer treated as freaks of nature but as evidence of the world's history; and it was not long before the ice ages were identified (1840).

It was precisely this study of fossils which was to make the reputation of Civier, a thorough man who reorganized the classification of the whole animal kingdom 'arranged according to its organization'. Attempts were made to calculate the age of the earth. Lamarck was already suggesting the possibility of evolutionary development and Malthus was outlining the struggle for survival; biological science was approaching Darwin's great mechanical synthesis. Finally, statistical method was starting to be used in anthropology, following the lead of the Belgian Quetelet; the average height of French conscripts, and the head measurements of Scots, were registered on graphs drawn up according to Gauss's probability theory.

Now comes an important question. All this preoccupation with mechanics in fact concerned only very few men in Europe. Can they legitimately be credited with a power equal to that of the businessman, the soldier, the European adventurer who was making his way all over the face of the globe? All this science which had accumulated in a few generations round the turn of the century was to be transformed in the second half of the nineteenth century into a new and formidable industrial force; but in what way were industry and the already vigorous economic activities of Europe in 1800 indebted to it?

There is no simple answer. The best we can give here is that the new industry and the rapid growth of Europe in 1785 both had the same sources as mechanical science. They developed simultaneously and each helped the other.

A few examples will show how this came about. James Cook opened up a new outlet for European activity, the world of the Pacific Ocean. He charted it accurately, and his charts were more reliable than those of Bougainville. But he was only able to do this because he possessed the balanced chronometer which one of his contemporaries had invented in 1761; because Newton's system had definitely fixed the positions of the heavenly bodies; because magnetic phenomena were more clearly understood; and because he discovered the cause of scurvy and its cure. Most significant of all was the point of origin of these great maritime discoveries; the Royal Society sponsored an expedition, not to find new lands, but to observe a conjunction of Venus and the sun: so it was an attempt to apply Newton's *Principia* which led to the discovery of a new world.

Humboldt's career is equally revealing. A German by birth, he was drawn to Paris because it was the capital of the sciences, and became the pupil of Gay-Lussac. He climbed the Andes to study decreases in temperature and magnetic variations, and by drawing up isothermic charts he revealed the conditions which gave rise to tropical storms. In this way he originated the science of cartography. Humboldt applied it to biology and showed the distribution of living beings over the earth; Darwin, still a young man, was to do the same on the *Beagle*, chartered in 1831 on behalf of the Royal Society, in order to establish a chain of chronological measurements. In 1848 Huxley carried out similar work in Australia; man discovered the world in the course of verifying his scientific hypotheses.

The physical and natural sciences were advanced in the course of astronomical research, and every collation of findings in the astronomical, physical and biological sciences made the voyages of merchant ships and warships less hazardous. The spirit of experiment which resulted in scientific achievement in the field of general mechanics also furthered industry by sending Europeans over all the oceans of the world.

Yet it was not only through the direct contact of scientific research and the techniques of navigation that science contributed to the rise of industry. It did so by inspiring all human activity with a kind of mechanical certainty which aroused a spirit of enterprise and spurred Europeans along the path of profit-making and industrial power. We shall not go as far back as Locke, the doctor and experimenter, who extolled liberty because it would encourage the establishment all over the land of a vast system of individual economic experiments. England may have left theories and mathematics to the French, but from 1785 onwards it became a major field of industrial experiment.

Many works on metaphysics systematizing ideas taken from England and France were produced in Germany in the late eighteenth century. Kant's syntheses had barely been completed before they were surpassed. The extension of the sphere of mathematical reasoning and the certainty of logical proof considerably reduced the field of intuitive imagination. From Leibnitz to Kant, the metaphysicians had been allowed a wide range of territory, but after Hegel their right to it was abruptly disputed, because science believed it could provide more conclusive proof than metaphysics of the efficacy of Western intellectual tools. On the ruins of its metaphysics, Germany was to erect the finest group of laboratories the world had yet known.

French theory, English experiments, and the sudden new developments in Germany brought about a revolution in the mental equipment of Western man. Young people in Europe were learning less Latin and Greek: new engineering schools, new or rejuvenated universities, and mechanical workshops offered an education in keeping with the modern trends. Public lectures and specialized periodicals enjoyed an unprecedented popularity. It was no longer only scholars and men of letters who were socially acceptable, but engineers, for it was they who created wealth. In order to make their task easier new rules of property and credit were drawn up and to these we must now turn our attention.

THE LAW

'*Quid leges sine moribus.*' The question of the relationship between law and customs in late eighteenth-century Europe lends itself to an infinite variety of treatment. There is certainly no lack of material. French writers of the day filled volumes with their ideas on this great problem. The English too, though more reserved, had never before dis-

cussed at such lengths law and individual rights, freedom
of opinion, the suppression of slavery, and the possibility
of improving the law to bring about an improved way of
life. It is all too easy to be swept away by this tide of
polemic and discussion; the main points must be kept
clearly in mind.

The first essential to bear in mind is that 'civilization',
a word newly coined at that time, was almost synonymous
with ordered customs and good laws. The noun 'civilization' was new but the verb 'to civilize' had long been in
use and meant to judge in the civil courts a case first
brought before the criminal courts. The advantage of the
civil procedure over the criminal was, in Europe and particularly in France, considerable: one prohibited torture,
the other allowed it. We know the horror aroused among
eighteenth-century thinkers by the question of torture, and
its ghastly instruments; a decree of 1670 had limited the
use of these methods but only to the extent that a man
due to be executed in public was not to be killed in the
secrecy of the torture chamber. English law had already
abandoned this barbarous custom, and Catherine II had
followed this good example, at least in her declarations.
Louis XVI finally abolished torture in France. Civilization
was making headway, and civilization meant first and
foremost sound justice and good laws.

Voltaire, as we know, praised English law, which,
though doubtless harsh, was at least applicable to all
alike. Now the basis of this equality was *Habeas Corpus*.
Every imprisoned person could obtain from the High
Court of Justice the right to be brought at once before
his judges; they released him if the reason for his arrest
seemed insufficient, and the person responsible for his
arrest was punished, even if he was a minister. England,
therefore, did not acknowledge the separation of powers
advocated by Montesquieu. The executive was subject to
the judiciary, the highest political authority in England.
As for the law, it was made by Parliament, which in certain exceptional cases could even suspend *Habeas Corpus*, as it did for instance during the revolutionary wars.
But when this suspension came to an end in 1801, a law

of indemnity, retrospectively applied, brought to book those officials and ministers who might possibly have abused it. England's fine example was not followed by any other European government; on the continent preventive detention remained almost discretionary and, above all, the agents of the state could not, whatever happened, be summoned before the ordinary tribunals. In all that concerned their administration, they had the privilege of a special jurisdiction and of administrative tribunals. This special jurisdiction meant that some remnants of the privileges of absolute monarchy survived into the nineteenth and even the twentieth century, under cover of the separation of powers. It created, side by side with the law, administrative law.

Thus in England an ancient practice ensured equality and liberty for every citizen. Those two words were interconnected not only in the theory of power but in the popular conscience. And the power of these two ideas, closely linked with each other and with the practice of *Habeas Corpus*, can well be imagined. Whenever there was a forbidden meeting or a discussion in the press, any sanction taken against an opponent might, at the request of any citizen, lead to a public enquiry before judges. Public opinion could make itself felt not only through Parliamentary elections, but also through the citizen's permanent right of appeal to judges who could themselves be tried for flagrant injustice. Every debate on the interpretation of the law made Parliament more careful to draft its laws clearly. Nowhere else in the late eighteenth century did public opinion have this power. In England anyone who knew how to wield it had a power capable of challenging that of the Government itself. It was in this way that the opposition to Lord North's cabinet had so brilliantly made itself felt, and because of this, too, many famous politicians were enabled to begin their careers. One of the most remarkable was Wilberforce (from 1780 to 1833), who brought about the abolition of slavery in 1807; he was a private individual but a powerful leader of the Englishman's conscience. This broadening of public opinion did much to regularize justice, and to secure its uniform application throughout the country.

Legal practice and jurisprudence were progressively made more explicit and available to all. In other words, the problem of a code of laws was hardly ever posed in England, and certainly if it had been it would have presented very great difficulties. For the laws, even the oldest of them, remained on the Statute Book, and accumulated in increasing numbers even when they contradicted one another. Only very rarely did Parliament deliberately repeal them. This was not important, since it was the judges rather than the executive who were responsible for administering this varied and contradictory body of laws, and the judge was guided and supported by public opinion which in this way continually created laws though a subtle interplay of institutions. It is easy to imagine how difficult European jurists, and particularly the French, found it to analyse this situation. In general they admired its results and to produce a similar régime in France, the Constituent Assembly determined to create an elected judiciary power emanating directly from the nation.

But it required long practice to give this type of legal system any semblance of uniformity in dealing with the innumerable customs, letters patent and statutes; and new laws made by the elected legislative power were continually being added. In default of such practice the central power had necessarily to take the initiative in coordinating and systematizing the collective body of laws, so that the role played by *Habeas Corpus* in England was taken over on the continent, though in a very different way, by the legal code. The code was in effect an attempt to reduce the laws to order; it had to provide the courts with a practical instrument, indispensable if judgements were to be uniform throughout the country; this instrument defined obligations accurately, and unconditionally annulled former decrees, at least in so far as they affected matters which had been duly codified. In this way, however, the legislature gained the upper hand over the judiciary then being organized.

The legislature was predominant, at least in France,

from 1790 to 1800. For the code was probably considered as a mere collection of ancient laws rather than as a new law in itself. It was regarded at the time as a kind of editing process, a putting in order, a popularization. From this point of view it could be regarded as the work of the executive. A code which would throw light on a legal dispute was obviously needed everywhere in Europe, and often it worked out to the advantage of monarchical authority—a point on which there is more to be said.

One need only recall the authority which Justinian, Theodosus and Tribonian acquired from their efforts to draw up practical collections of laws. Colbert, in his attempt to introduce a little order into state subsidies, grants, the navy, civil statutes and, with the help of Savary, into commerce, had created separate codes for each, though these were still referred to as statutes in *Parlement*. In this respect Colbert was a worthy successor of Marillac, and a predecessor of Pontchartrain. But the codes grew too numerous. In Lorraine the existence of a Leopold code did not prevent the town of Nancy from having one of its own. Codes were fashionable throughout the whole of Europe: Charles of Sicily, Frederick of Prussia, Catherine of Russia, to mention only the most famous, set to work compilers who, as they could not co-ordinate laws and customs in common use or choose between conflicting ones, left the courts bewildered. It was to bring order into the law that the revolutionary assemblies undertook in committees the mammoth task of logical clarification which was to result in the first systematic code, and to endow words with a new meaning and significance.

Voltaire had complained that in travelling one changed laws as frequently as horses. The influence of Roman law and of legal bodies had not superseded local customs. Doing the best they could, jurists commented on existing fact and dealt out exhortation and advice, as did Pothier in his treatises. Consequently, in the constituent and legislative assemblies of Europe the jurists were becoming masters of the law. The Convention decided to tackle the problem forthwith. It initiated the great undertaking entrusted to Cambacérès. When he became Consul it was Tronchet, president of the new Court of Appeal (*Cour de Cassation*), who directed the work. Their chief aim was to produce a clear result and one which would take into account traditions (even canonical traditions) and the laws of the Revolution, as well as the opinions of Bonaparte.

In spite of warnings like those expressed by Savigny, the compilers tended strongly towards the practical; they reproduced rather than innovated, co-ordinated as best they could, drew on southern law for matters relating to the dowry, and relied on Pothier's precautions for the law of contracts. Above all they were selective. Once the Civil Code was drawn up, the famous law of the year XII repealed Roman laws, regulations, decrees and local usages—everything in short which might hinder its working. The judges, suddenly delivered from the burden of innumerable ancient records, wielded the same instrument from one end of France to the other.

The basic inspiration of the new code is to be found not so much in the introductory remarks of Portalis as in the code itself, and if after so many centuries of effort it was comparatively easy to draw up, this was because property and ownership could at last, and for the first time, be accurately defined in simple terms. Quit-rents, revenues, and feudal dues had been swept away, and with them went a thousand doubtful points which had complicated the labours of eighteenth-century judges. Details are unimportant: the crux of the matter is contained in one phrase: property was unfettered and free. Property still meant real estate, for the definition of personal property remained obscure: France's industrial and financial experience was still too brief to have produced effective legislation. In spite of this gap, the improvement was remarkable. The vast procedural machinery and its paralysing delays were abolished. That 'every man should know the law' could become a concrete reality. Economic activity was at long last freed from the dead weight of the old legal procedures, although in time new and unwieldy legislation grew up around the interpretation of its clauses.

Most important of all, no sooner had the French code been promulgated than it conquered Europe. The Empire introduced it into Italy and Holland, and it was adopted in Frankfurt, Danzig, the reconstructed Poland and Illyria, Westphalia and the Swiss Cantons. After the fall of the Empire, many countries which had adopted it recast it, though such a process involved great difficulties, especially in Holland and Germany. Meanwhile, a *Revue de droit français* was published in Mannheim throughout the century, and the decrees of the French Court of Appeal were followed by half Europe. In this way the French code was introduced into Rumania, Italy, Louisiana, Argentina and Uruguay. If it was not universally adopted, it was at least imitated in principle. In Saxony an attempt was made to clarify the old Germanic law; Spain endeavored to overcome the particularism of the *fueros*; the new American republics followed the fashion, while in Russia Nicholas eventually fulfilled Alexander's ambition by publishing his own compilation.

The success of the French commercial code of 1807 was less marked, for though the Revolution had settled the question of property, it had made little progress in solving the new problems created by commerce. The French commercial code, therefore, remained bound up with the old cautious precepts of Colbert; and the rest of Europe was understandably reluctant to adopt it. After 1870 France acknowledged the superiority of the German-inspired commercial code.

The real significance of the French attempts at codification is not easy to define. It was not really weakened by the vagueness of its enactments on personal property and commerce, since its chief value lay in its insistence on the uniformity of the national law. Person and property were no longer differently defined according to whether they were inside or outside a town's gates, or on opposite banks of the same river or of any of the other innumerable divisions which had existed for centuries on the land. If the code did not fully succeed in being really European, it did at least stimulate every nation in Europe into drawing up its own national code. It thus strengthened the national unity of a divided Europe; it also showed the advantages of a complete revision of legal traditions, and opened the way for the great reforms necessitated by the new economic structure.

Land was now free, and its produce belonged to its owner, who felt every personal incentive to improve its yield and to extend his business. Uniform contracts meant that men in different parts of the land could group together for a co-ordinated effort. Now that people were free of local restrictions they could be mobilized within the nation in the service of a better economy. The restrictions imposed by out-dated traditions on present-day activity were finally lifted. If a clause proved to be harmful, it could be abolished by the legislative power and replaced by another without overtaxing the scruples of the judge or the uncertainty of the plaintiff. Thus, by degrees, continental Europe was catching up with England; public opinion, stimulated by economic progress, demanded that authority be as flexible as in England in adapting the law to everyday needs. Political changes, the appeal to constitutions, the revolutions in nineteenth-century Europe, were all results of this need for a flexible and continually renewed code. The people of western Europe had entered an age of major industrial development and had now acquired the means to free themselves from the restricting effects of past traditions. The living had to free themselves from the dead.

This attempt at codification, a new characteristic in Europe at that time, was not confined to the law. Weights and measures varied to an extent that seems as strange to the modern mind as the variation of the old laws from town to town, and from province to province. There were as many 'leagues' and 'pounds' as there were domains and manors, in fact more: a measure needed only to be registered and published for its use to become legal. Furthermore, peasants and craftsmen often cared very little whether the measures they continued to use were registered or not. The skill of the merchant and the trader was based on a knowledge of the innumerable and deceptive differences, and the question was still being asked quite seriously in the eighteenth century what use the trader would be, and to what would his skill be reduced, if measures were unified. But it was obvious that most Englishmen found quite enough risks and worries in trade without the addition of this particular hazard. By a slow process initiated in the eighteenth century and concluded in 1767, England had reduced and co-ordinated its system, keeping two pounds (one of which was a troy pound for precious metals), one mile, one quarter. The subdivisions of these measures still remained fairly complicated, the ordinary pound consisting of sixteen ounces, the troy pound of twelve.

A similar process was slowly being carried out in continental Europe but it was far less advanced than in England, and in that sphere too French logic tried to speed things up. The Constituent Assembly was the first to set up a commission for the unification of weights and measures, with its members drawn from the leading mathematicians of the day. First they rejected sub-multiples of 12 (and 244 and 976) or 4 (and 16 and 512) in favour of division by 10 and the power of 10. Enumeration had proved the superiority of this 10 basis. Why, asked Legendre, try to push an hexagonal tenon into a pentagonal mortise? Then they looked around for a basic unit of measurement—the metre. Their first idea was to fix it by the length of a pendulum beating once per second at zero altitude in latitude 45°. This was a typical physicists' idea, and it would certainly have facilitated the many calculations of mass which, as we have seen, were so important. This, however, seemed too daring to the majority of the commission. It chose a fraction of the earth's meridian, though there is not the least connection between it, a Great Circle of the earth (a very uncertain quantity in any case) and the current system of length or weight; but it was one way of keeping close to the earth. After the decimal division and the metre, the entire system of weights and measures was founded, and usage was very greatly simplified.

Unfortunately, the old usage persisted and the law

sanctioned it by assimilating the fathom to two metres, the pound to half a kilo, and so on. The metric system nevertheless replaced a number of provincial measures which could be fitted in to the new measures. However, though it became legal in France in 1801, it was not made compulsory until 1840. Its success in Europe was linked with the adoption of the code, but was more lasting and on the whole more widespread. The German Empire adopted it in 1872, Europe and South America followed suit. In 1864 it was even legalized—though little used—in England, and then in the United States: it had made its way round the world.

This adoption of a system that rejected any concrete meaning of the units of measurement in favour of simplicity of calculation represented an intellectual advance as important as the transformation of the legal code. In this case too the new system was divorced from the original connections with man (*pouce, pied, coudée*, etc.), from the requirements of agricultural work (*journal, ouvrée*) and from historical traditions. The metre and its combinations are purely mental concepts. The abstract measure was widely adopted; trade was simplified and was based throughout the world on two major systems.

After the reform of measures came the successful introduction of the decimal system into money transactions and coinage; and in France francs, décimes and centimes were soon tied to a fixed weight of silver with a definite standard. This freed commerce from all the old apparatus of money-changers, and left the merchant free to concentrate on the quality of his goods, and the banker on the quality of credit.

Credit was now the important issue. Commercial good faith could no longer be concealed behind a jingle of weights, measures and coinage. Administrative and commercial accounting had everywhere abandoned Roman figures and the use of tokens in favour of Arab numerals and written transactions, so the new units of measurement could now deal accurately and clearly with everything that could possibly be written down in precise figures. The old ways of assessing were replaced by the single question of how much trust one could place in the signatory of a contract. The problem of confidence, or what is now called credit, could at least be limited and defined even though it could not be completely abolished.

The metric system was a guarantee against numerical error, and the code against legal error; but no government department, and no system of law or of measures could define the *economic* value of an undertaking and its owner. It was in this sphere of credit that the speculations and risks of private initiative had full play.

One remark in conclusion: from now on, the rough and tumble of competition was to be between individuals and not between families. The old Christian family group, the *gens*, which in our study of population we saw breaking up, was, as we can now see more clearly, being replaced by individuals personally responsible for their debts and contracts. Civil affairs were removed from Church jurisdiction and made the sole concern of public administration, not just from a wish to secularize, nor because a desire for progress had arisen to complement and supplant the desire for God; nor was it merely because the state was more anxious to watch over its citizens who would furnish its armies and elect its organs of government; it was also because the concepts involved in the code and in the new forms of financial transactions dealt primarily with the individual, and so the individual had to be identified beyond all shadow of doubt. A man giving credit was no longer satisfied for his debtor to be designated merely by his Christian name; this now became just a forename to avoid the confusion that it had created, even when accompanied by indications of trade, or place, or by various nicknames. Each child of course had its Christian name, but each must now have its proper surname and each citizen his civil status. Already in the eighteenth century the use of the family name had spread from the nobility to a few commoners. Now it became general and compulsory for all, though the more accurate date of birth was preferred to the date of christening, and the birth certificate to the baptismal certificate. This finally put into effect the aim of theorists who had advocated credit and attributed the failure of the law to the casual, unbusinesslike methods of the *ancien régime*. No obligation, whether family, religious or social, could now supplant that of debtor to creditor. While science encouraged the development of a philosophy and a moral outlook independent of God, whose effects on family and population have already been noted, the law now recorded, and safeguarded, the individual's new position in the economic society.

Now at last we can embark upon a study of the new man at work, and observe his vicissitudes and his reverses.

new port in the Spanish Empire, there was a strengthening of the credit system and capitalism which formed the centre of England's economic life. At its peak about 1786, it was ready to enter into competition with France by a reciprocal lowering of customs duties. This step was not without risk, since France in 1785 could boast a production quantitatively superior to that of England in almost every sphere and particularly in what is known as heavy industry. In the luxury trades the superiority of Paris was overwhelming.

At that time England held the lead, not in industry, but in agriculture. There again, it was the result of two hundred years of agricultural effort following the secularization at the time of the Reformation. Between 1780 and 1830 this effort was at its height. Young noted it with pride. Young's forty-five volumes of the *Annals of Agriculture* were the favourite reading of kings, lords and gentlemen farmers from 1784 onwards. It was also the time of the wholesale passing of Enclosure Acts which changed the entire landscape of central and western England. At much the same time techniques of specialized stock-breeding on a large scale were perfected, by men such as Bakewell, whose horned cattle were at first the object of ridicule (it was said that they were too dear to buy, too fat to eat). Lastly, tuberculosis was finally stamped out from cattle in the most fertile areas of England.

Towards the close of the eighteenth century this meant the end of numerous small farms whose tenants lived on the produce of their own fields and on the general widespread use of common land. The smallholder had either to raise the money needed to increase his holding by purchasing common lands and the plots of his poor neighbours and enclosing them, or to renounce his independence and get out to the town, driven from a countryside where stock-breeding required an ever-decreasing labour force. The yeoman of earlier days was in an even worse position. Possession of a house in the old countryside with its common lands had meant, if not wealth, at least a secure livelihood. When there were no more common lands the yeoman too had to make for the town. The English countryside was emptying, and the era of medium or large estates began. A property of one hundred acres was considered small, one of three hundred average. This gives some indication of the size of the English estate in contrast with the minute plots on the Continent, which still bore the mark of the old feudal system. These large estates were regarded by Arthur Young as the chief sign of his country's agricultural progress.

The segregation of rich and poor on English soil was also aggravated by circumstances arising from wars with France and the rest of Europe. The disappearance of the small farm, with its pigs and cows, its farmyard and its kitchen garden, brought about a change in diet and made it necessary to rely on foreign aid; and this coincided with a time when imports from Europe became more difficult and costly. It was, of course, impossible to bring butter, eggs and milk from America. Prices went up. In 1785 corn was two shillings a pound; this was thought expensive, yet it reached four shillings in 1805 and six shillings in 1811. The fortunate victor of the battle of the enclosures found himself comfortably off, and never before had he earned so much money. Good land quadrupled in price between 1780 and 1800. In such conditions the struggles for power in the villages (and eventually in the House of Commons) to obtain bills of enclosure became more numerous.

Yet these high prices worsened the situation of the poor. It was no use cutting down on food, going without meat, and eating nothing but porridge and whey; the poor were haunted by famine. There was no longer any question of beer, not even the home-brewed ale which masters used to serve at the common table in the good old days of collective living, when there were freeholders and the agricultural worker was a companion rather than a paid employee.

Under the old régime it had been considered one of the essential duties of a lord to feed his dependants. In the new régime of *laissez-faire* the landowner no longer had any such obligations towards his employees. He en-

gaged them if he needed them, and dismissed them when
he had no use for them. Nevertheless in England old
tradition was revived in face of the rising tide of poverty.
The period 1785–1840 was to see the great debates on
the Poor Laws, which vacillated between strictness and
leniency and revealed the country's fear of infection by a
Jacobite revolution if poverty was too rife, and the feelings of pity aroused in the minds of philanthropists. We
shall only outline the essentials: Pitt at the start favoured a broad interpretation of the tradition; the parishes
were to feed the poor without requiring them to enter
workhouses. The poor, driven from the land, sometimes
wandered from parish to parish in search of work. When
the French Revolution was at its height in 1785, Berk-
shire affirmed the right of the poor to a minimum of food,
and its decision was confirmed by a law. This minimum
was to be found from local taxation, and employers in
town and country took immediate advantage of this to
lower wages, deducting the amount contributed by the
parish.

From this point Malthus's gloomy predictions began
to be fulfilled. The poor man, thus encouraged, would
have every incentive to relapse into indolence; if he was
married he would have swarms of children; humanity
would be wrecked on the shoals of poverty. The big
landed proprietors who paid the taxes protested against
this relief, asserting that agriculture provided it for the
benefit of industry; parishes which agreed to feed their
own poor now turned away those of neighbouring parishes. So from law to law, from restriction to restriction,
the lot of the non-producer became increasingly hard. In
order to earn a living the poor had to work in the notorious workhouses, grim places which took husbands from
wives, mothers from their children, gave only a minimum
of food and imposed a harsh discipline. Schemes were
devised to turn people away from country workhouses
and to thrust them into the industrial towns, so as to
lighten the burden of taxation and bring down the birth
rate. Meanwhile, various worthy souls urged the rural
poor to resume the traditional tasks of gardening and

small farming. Cobden, in direct contrast to Young, reckoned a country's wealth by the number of pigs he saw wandering around a cottage.

Two distinct classes were beginning to emerge from the agricultural revolution: first that of the landowners, most of whom adopted the way of life of the upper classes. They had top-boots, guns, comfortable furniture and even the new-fangled piano in their country houses. Their sons and daughters dressed like children of the nobility and sometimes even succeeded in getting into the same schools. The classes who benefited from agrarian change were drawing closer together around the land-owning country gentleman, a process clearly illustrated in sentimental English novels of the early nineteenth century: young ladies of modest birth could marry lords' sons and aristocratic daughters went so far as to marry well-dressed commoners. The local vicar conducted these ceremonies with some emotion and, if he was a young man, sometimes turned his own thoughts in that direction. These were the impressionable, romantic years of the new rural England, described by Mary Webb. Everything seemed to be blending together and fusing into one common society. The heart could concentrate on its own problems with all the more interest and emotion because social barriers were frailer. But a considerable barrier still separated landowners from farmers, even if they were well-to-do and farmed in a big way.

The real poor ended up in the overcrowded city suburbs and the filthy slums. They and their wives and children worked in cotton mills, mines, foundries, and for a mere pittance with the terrible threat of unemployment always hanging over them. There was unemployment with every crisis—whenever the supply of cotton from overseas was held up, when the market was saturated, or when the mill owner was refused the overdraft he asked for from the local bank. If he then hastened in his carriage to London and met with a second refusal justified by a rise in the discount rate at the Bank of England, his factory would close down and the resulting poverty was frightful. But there was also unemployment when the em-

ployer's business was going so well that he started getting
rid of his old plant and replacing it by mechanical looms
driven by water and steam. So far as the worker was concerned there was nothing to choose between unemployment due to prosperity and that due to a crisis. The poor,
the common people, became as it were a reservoir on
which industry drew according to its needs—human raw
material.

There was plenty of it: in 1790 Manchester had 50,000
inhabitants, and in 1830 it had almost 250,000. Many
other cities and towns (Glasgow, Birmingham and Liverpool) were increasing at a similar rate. The rural world
was being drawn into these privileged centres: contingents of Irishmen, rough and stout-hearted, came to swell
the migration. A few cities, it is true, were developing
more slowly; Bristol, a former great port, was beginning
to lose its relative pre-eminence, as were the old centres
of the wool trade. On the other hand, London was in-
contestably the most powerful city in the world. It can
be estimated that at the beginning of the nineteenth century only twenty-eight per cent of English families were
living on agriculture. Even if country craftsmen, those
who had village workshops or worked in their own homes
for city manufacturers are included, the rural population
figures barely reached fifty per cent. It was more than a
century before France was to achieve the same proportions. The figures indicate the extent of the English industrial revolution.

Let us examine the technical aspects of this revolution:
we have discussed the many remarkable inventions produced in the eighteenth century—power-driven looms and
spinning jennies, coke smelting, the growing use of hydraulic power, and the first steam engine. Though these
various inventions had proved their worth and had been
applied here and there, to the general admiration, by the
end of the eighteenth century they had not yet been
brought together into great industrial concerns. Ten years
later the position was very different.

The first large textile establishment equipped with
steam-driven machinery was opened in Manchester in

1806. There were fifteen of the same type in 1818. In 1823 there were probably 10,000 mechanical looms in the country. In 1830 this figure had risen to 50,000, although there still remained 250,000 hand-looms in use in town and country. These were weaving cotton, a product for which mechanization was particularly suitable. Wool kept closer to tradition, and carpets were all woven by hand up to 1850. In 1830 the power-driven woollen loom was still an exception. The setting up of the mechanized silk industry apparently dated from the 1820s in Manchester, though it was not systematized until the end of the century. Fulling by hydraulic press was introduced only at the very end of the eighteenth century and reached Dundee in the 1820s. The application of chemical processes, following on the discoveries of Berthollet, was first tried out on the industrial scale in Scotland in 1814.

Similarly, there are few signs of a revolution in the metal industry before 1825. In 1789 one-quarter of the production was still dependent on charcoal. The war of course gave it a formidable impetus. Until 1820 all foundries made guns. Production stepped up from 70,000 tons in 1789 to 260,000 in 1806, and 700,000 in 1830. Puddling was not introduced before 1793 and did not penetrate to Scotland until 1830. As for steel, people were still complaining in 1830 that far too much was being imported from country mills in Germany or Sweden. The use of steam-engines was being extended at the same period. It is true that in 1786 Watt himself had built the plant of the London Mills (the Albion Mills), and soon afterwards a steam-engine was working the pumps used for London's water supply. But the greatest novelty of all dated from 1816, when *The Times* was printed by steam, and other newspapers were soon to follow suit. In 1831 Glasgow could boast 328 steam-engines, of which 60 were on ships anchored in the Clyde.

In agriculture, there were no harvesters before 1850, but from the late eighteenth century threshing machines were becoming widely used and a few of the great landowners even had steam-driven ones in 1820. At about the same date a mechanical haymaking machine proved fairly successful.

In short, the beginning of the industrial revolution in England, too often attributed to the previous century, coincided with the Revolution and the Empire in France, and the first cycle of the changes it brought about was to continue until after 1840. The statistics of external trade confirm this view: foreign trade rose from 500,000 tons about the mid-eighteenth century to a million just before 1789; but it reached five millions in 1800 and continued to increase at the same rate up to the middle of the nineteenth century.

It had been trade which, in the eighteenth century, had brought greater flexibility to English institutions on the eve of the capitalist revolution. Trade profited greatly by the resulting changes and in turn stimulated more change. The old corporate medieval practices disappeared, and in particular the fairs. Sturbsidge or Stirbitch vanished, and in his place appeared the new figure of the commercial traveller with his order book and his samples. In the cities wholesale warehouses sprang up claiming that they offered the whole year round the prices that prevailed at the fairs: the result was a change in the habits of the customer (who no longer confined his purchases to certain seasons, but spread them out over the whole year), and fresh scope was provided for exchanges and bank credits had to be increased.

New banks were continually founded. In London there were sixty-nine in 1797, and about seventy-seven in 1808; the secretary of the Local Bankers' Association reported two hundred and thirty country banks in 1797 and almost five hundred in 1804. At that time there were three banks for the 4,500 inhabitants of Abingdon and six for the 7,000 of Boston in Yorkshire. The numbers continued to grow; in 1810 there was a total of eight hundred local banks. There was competition for custom in the small towns. Banking found its way even into the most remote country districts. In the cities banking houses controlled the fortunes or ruin of businessmen. Everyone applied for credit. During the 1810 crisis Baring told a parliamentary committee that the bank had granted credits of five to ten million pounds to humble folk, even to work-people who had broken their contracts and gone into business on their own accounts and who 'had scarcely a hundred pounds to their names'. Moreover in spite of the war metric currency was still in circulation, India and China were ceasing to be sellers and becoming buyers, and money which had formerly moved from West to East was beginning to move in the reverse direction. The East India Company asked the Bank of England to buy as much as £100,000 worth of silver in 1803. The circulation of Bank of London notes increased continually. It rose from £11 million in 1790 to almost £18 million in 1804, and these figures give only a faint idea of the total circulation of notes issued by all the banks. Indiscriminate advances to the Government had forced Pitt to suspend convertibility in 1797 and the suppression lasted through varying fortunes until 1820. Not only Treasury Bonds, but many other kinds of notes increased the circulation of paper money still further.

It is easy to see how the cautious Mollien in France could simultaneously admire the English Government's good fortune in having so much money available without an adequate basis of precious metal, and also speculate on the weakness of the English system. One of its strong points, however, was the wisdom of the Government which, after the unfortunate experience of 1797 (and learning from the contemporary experience of France), steadfastly refused to borrow too much from the Bank. However excessive British circulation may have seemed, it was deliberate, justified by trade and by the briskness of business.

Crises were inevitable in this young economy, and the periodic recurrence in ten-yearly cycles was already making itself felt. In 1783 the first great wave of change began, and in 1804 the English were forced to sue for peace; they were uneasy about the future of the Nordic trade, since the Scandinavians and Russians seemed to be favouring France. The most serious crisis broke in 1811, caused by the blockade set up by Napoleon at the far end of the Baltic in one of the most vulnerable areas of English trade: he had control of Danzig, the source of corn and wood. In England the price of provisions rose violently, the war with the United States made maritime trade precarious, stacks of unsaleable goods piled up in the London warehouses, and merchants faced with ruin went from bank to bank begging for credit which was refused them even at the highest rates of interest. Finally the excessive boom of the preceding years and the over-sanguine hopes raised by the opening of Rio de Janeiro to English trade had given birth to so many dubious ventures that a cleaning-up operation was inevitable. It occurred quite spontaneously, but brought widespread poverty and wretchedness in its train. Napoleon's defeat in Moscow and Wellington's advance through the Iberian Peninsula restored hope and confidence in business; but the crisis was slow to resolve itself and was indeed intensified in 1815 when supplies were no longer needed for the army and the allies. One can understand Thackeray's disillusionment and moralizing tone in describing *Vanity Fair*, that society in which fortunes were quickly made and as quickly lost, so that middle-class families were ruined just as they seemed about to succeed on the social ladder to the aristocracy.

But although the role of *entrepreneur* was hazardous and required qualities of daring and courage, the real sufferers in these crises were the common people. Up to 1815 England lived in dread of popular revolts on the Jacobite model. Once Napoleon had been defeated, riots broke out in London and Manchester, and Wellington's armies were called out to fire on the people. These were not the first revolts bred of poverty (they had already occurred at the end of the eighteenth century): the Luddites, the machine-breakers, banded themselves together, threatened factories and burned down mills. Ruin and despondency followed these explosive outbursts, though usually they did not last long. Yet the Government feared they might become widespread, which accounted for the mistrust of workmen's associations like that of the muslin and cutlery operatives in Glasgow in 1787. In

1797 (in the name of *laissez-faire*) a law had been passed against workers' coalitions, though associations of employers were tolerated if not encouraged. The only resort left to the workers was the old corporative law, the *ancien régime* tradition of protecting the poor, which it became increasingly difficult to evoke.

Yet it is worth noting that however tragic these crises were in England they never seriously threatened the English economy. They gave an astonishing character to certain great parliamentary debates: in 1811, for example, the party favouring the re-establishment of convertibility opposed those who wished to maintain the Restriction Act of 1797. Ricardo and the orthodox economists pointed to the depreciation of the pound, which had lost forty per cent on gold, fourteen per cent on the franc, and seven per cent on the Dutch florin; and they urged the Government to submit to the discipline of the gold standard. But to do so would have meant slowing down the borrowing drive and the war effort, and might possibly have meant making peace with Napoleon. Patriotism must prevail; each man must exert himself to the full so that England might successfully balance on the tightrope between popular revolts brought on by the crisis, the threat of overloaded credit, and the danger of relaxing the war effort. Thus while European countries were counting soldiers and cannon, the English in their island were counting pounds sterling, credits and gold reserves. The crises of 1785–1815 were revolutionary, but in different ways on opposite sides of the channel. In England they were economic, in France political; in England social, in France military.

When peace had been restored, the English crises continued to recur in a ten-yearly rhythm which began to intrigue economists, and soon became the chief object of their study. And these crises became increasingly serious as capitalism became more firmly established. The 1825 crisis was regarded as a catastrophe comparable to the great fire of London. Nevertheless, the growth in volume of American trade, particularly with the new nations of the south, the prospects of a rich trade in the eastern seas, and the considerable profits made by the new English factories had at first provoked a feverish activity in the 1820s; new mills were being opened everywhere. In order to amass the necessary capital, appeals were made to a public eager to buy shares and bonds even from the Government. This speculation soon led to inflation of their currency; the price of consumer goods rose, the drain of gold began, the Bank reserves were endangered: in short there was a sudden tightening up of a credit, a rise in the discount rate, and notes of all kinds were suspended. The bold speculator had to sell; immediately prices fell by more than thirty per cent; a vast wave of bankrupts engulfed England. This provoked an equally grave disaster in the United States, which were linked to England by the cotton trade.

Once this cruel cleaning-up operation had been completed, life was resumed again, and there was a cautious return of initiative. So as to give credit a wider range a new law freed the issue of credit entirely except within a sixty-five mile radius of London, where the privilege of the Bank was maintained. In 1836 there were 670 private banks in England. Industrial opinion remained vocal about the weakness of its representation in Parliament. There were only fifty businessmen out of six hundred MPs. The clubs embarked on a campaign, the press increased its circulation by demanding electoral reform, workmen let themselves be persuaded by the organizers that reform would mean cheaper bread and free beer. In 1825 Huskisson put through a bill making workers' associations legal and setting up a scale of customs' duties which lowered the price of imported foodstuffs and raw materials. Finally, in 1832, under threat of a popular revolt to which the memory of recent events in Paris lent an added terror, Parliament passed the electoral reform which opened its ranks to representatives of the new industrial cities. The electorate was not greatly increased, rising from 650,000 to 800,000, but this was enough to create an atmosphere favourable to a number of social reforms.

These reforms had not been fully assimilated when a

fresh crisis arose, a complicated one which recurred in successive waves from 1836 to 1839. There was a scramble for gold between England, where speculation surpassed even its peak period of the 1820s, the continent, where industrial progress was just beginning, and the United States where reconstruction on a vast scale was in progress to the accompaniment of violent convulsions in the cotton market. At one moment it was in America that there was a shortage of gold, and seven hundred banks suspended payments; the next was in England, which had to obtain as much specie as possible from Hamburg. In 1833 the problem of the renewal of the monopoly of the Bank of England had arisen. Finally, in 1844, Peel's famous Bank Charter Act separated the banking and issuing departments of the Bank of England so that it should be protected from financial crises even at the risk of an excessive limitation of credit.

In 1844 such strict measures harmed no-one, so great was the degree of prosperity which had returned, but in 1846 signs of a fresh storm began to appear; we shall return to this, since it marked the beginning of a new age. We should just note here that all these crises, though particularly dramatic in England, affected the rest of the world too and particularly the countries of continental Europe, where they resulted not in discreet forms of credit but in violent popular or military revolutions.

GOVERNMENT IN FRANCE

It is curious that when so much historical research has been done on the closing years of the old régime there should still be so few reliable analyses of the mechanisms which unleashed the Revolution. Graphs of prices show a crisis linked to the drop in the price of corn, which reached its lowest points in 1777, 1785 and 1786. Yet England had gone through similar crises, and had shown no trace of revolutionary symptoms beyond a few popular agitations from which the capitalist régime had emerged even stronger than before. It is true to say that the economic crises which swept over the West during the period of 1780–95 proved fatal to only one political régime—that of Versailles. They shook Austria, but did not overthrow it. They in no way undermined the Prussian monarchy, and actually strengthened the English system. The reasons for the destruction of the old régime must then be sought in the régime itself; the economic crisis merely provided a climate which fostered their violence.

The monarchy of Louis xv had benefited from the expanding economy of the eighteenth century. It had been an unusually prosperous period for France as well as for England. Agricultural methods had improved and industry had expanded; new goods were produced (cheap cottons, loom-woven silks, porcelain and glass), maritime trade increased, making Nantes and Bordeaux the major sugar ports and Marseilles the chief Mediterranean port; all this brought France new growth and prosperity. But the old monarchy, prosperous enough in years of calm, had lost the power of producing remedies for times of stress. England, as we have seen, drew on credit for resources to meet the strain, but there was nothing comparable in France. Was it the fault of Louis xv or Louis xvi? The unfortunate Louis xvi at all events could no more be blamed for this deficiency than he could be given credit for the prosperity which marked the early years of his reign. It was not the king nor yet the court which proved incapable of erecting the structure of credit which was essential if economic crises were to be surmounted: it was the whole of society.

French society was still constructed on an archaic pattern, its only resource in time of crisis being (as it had shown in its reactions to seventeenth- and eighteenth-century crises) to make new rules, whereas since Cromwell's time England had dealt with crises by creating liberty. French society, if it had been alone in Europe, might possibly have been able to survive by the rule-making procedures of a previous age. But the machinery for making these regulations was too cumbersome and inflexible to keep pace with the fierce international competition which the expansion of commerce had brought about in maritime trade since Utrecht, and in overland trade since the trade treaty of 1786.

Louis XVI's enlightened ministers and the lords at his court who were interested in industry attempted to introduce into France the economic techniques of English society, though by so doing they rendered the old French monarchic procedures effete. Thus Louis XVI was by turns too orthodox in a progressive France or too progressive in an orthodox France. The revolutionary ferment spread without difficulty through the monarchical body, which had lost its old, protective shell and had not yet acquired a new one.

The English remedy for the 1785 crisis was credit. Why was there no equally effective credit in France? The reason was that French society, unlike that of England, was so constructed as to restrict its own credit. First it had no bank. The very word 'bank' was forbidden. When some Swiss financiers adapted an idea originally proposed by a Protestant group backed by the speculator Panchaud, and opened the *Caisse d'Escompte*, they did not dare call it a bank. Its title was confirmed when Necker took over the ministry. This bank, as if ashamed of itself, was so careful not to fall into the same errors as the Scottish financier Law that it managed its credits with excessive caution, limited its clientèle, stood out against Calonne who was expecting it to contribute too much to state finances, defended itself even against Necker, and by dint of remaining in the background managed to keep going until the introduction of the *assignats*. But France had no state bank. This *Caisse* neither could be, nor wished to be, the leaven of French modernization.

Of course there were shipowners, industrialists and merchants in some French cities and particularly in the ports who ran a credit bureau in connection with their business. But French middle-class businessmen were basically against credit. They had no confidence in the banknote. They wanted gold, and the premium they placed on it (as Colbert would have wished) led to a result which surpassed the wildest dreams of the mercantile fraternity. France was draining gold from the rest of the world. By 1785 she had become the gold reservoir of the world. It was in order to pay for this gold that she had rejected the financial advantages offered by paper currency.

Bank credit has become so familiar to us since the nineteenth century that its full social importance is sometimes overlooked. If a collective group is to be trusted to put notes into circulation, to use them to give support to businesses in process of reconstruction, to expanding industries, or to businessmen in temporary difficulty, it is essential that every member of that group, or at least the majority of them, should feel a sense of solidarity and should play the credit game without cheating. In France in 1789 nothing could have been further from this position. La Rochefoucauld transformed his estates at Liancourt and turned them into a modern farm, finer probably than any in England; but he did this out of his private income. The model farm at Rambouillet was created out of the king's privy purse. The Duke of Orleans may have founded textile factories, porcelain or pottery works, and opened his royal palace to merchants, but this again was done without borrowing and out of his own resources. The same applied to the industries launched by a few great aristocrats. When the Azin mines were finally opened up, when Le Creusot was smelting with coal and Indret forging steel by English methods, and when textile mills and metal works appeared all over France—in each case it was done with ready money, accumulated from landed property, and without resorting to credit. Of course the innumerable small craftsmen who continued to make articles to order in their own homes, with a partner and two or three apprentices in a shop at the back of the house, had not the remotest idea what credit was. They had no stock. The protection afforded the craftsman by the corporate system, the guarantee it gave him against competition, meant that he had no need of credit.

Although there existed in France influential merchants like those in England, they were not clearly distinguishable from tradesmen. The name financier was more often used for those people who were exclusive experts in matters of credit, who met to discuss the price of stocks and shares in the Hôtel de Soissons, the first exchange. This was not merely a question of nomenclature. The financier drew his resources from administration of the royal taxation. It was from the state and the authority he derived from his administrative office that he derived his power, and not from private credit. English credit, on the other hand, was sufficient unto itself without any kind of outside help.

In fact the French financier, so despised since the days of La Bruyère, had some excuse: not only did the government turn to him in its difficulties, but it was on him that the Treasury itself usually relied for most of its ordinary resources; moreover whenever the middle classes had a little money to invest, it was to the king and the government that they entrusted it, in preference to banks or merchants. They bought not only government stock, but also those posts which sometimes, before 1789, carried a title and conferred nobility on the holder. A vast swarm of solicitors, attorneys and recorders throve on lawsuits which proliferated under the corporate régime, and the most shrewd and go-ahead members of the bourgeoisie became lawyers. The centralizing monarchy, originally established to see that justice was done, had created for itself a bourgeois society in its own image; it was more concerned with dictating the law than with creating banking.

A society of this kind could hardly therefore expect to display financial flexibility when faced with a crisis. A few powerful industries directed by aristocrats and financiers, a few bourgeois merchants practising financial self-help, living on their own resources and never entirely without landed property, could afford to await better days and prepare a few timid reforms in their industrial methods. But the industrious lower middle class was strangled by the inelasticity of the currency based on gold; and the excessively zealous government refused to debase the alloy used for the gold. In time of crisis, there was no possible way of escaping a deficit.

This social economy based on metal was controlled by

archaic governmental methods—in other words by restrictions, controls and regulations. When gold ceased to circulate, it was essential to stop goods from circulating too. Turgot had had a bitter experience of this: by an over-hasty relaxing of control over the circulation of goods he had set in motion a wave of bankruptcies. Every crisis in the old structure inevitably called forth the old remedies: hence the economic significance of the feudal reaction which was evoked whenever economic activity was threatened. The threat itself almost always came from the land, from a bad harvest.

A bad harvest meant an impoverished peasantry, dearer bread, craftsmen without orders, industry without credit or work, workers without pay: at such times as these, the weight of rents and of taxes was a grievous burden, so heavy that it killed taxable assets. The treasury emptied; and as a final resort launched loans which no one took up. In the general unrest and mounting poverty, the privileged aristocrat (or cleric, or wealthy bourgeois), whose landed property enabled him to finance himself, won on every count. He could expand his business and his estates by exploiting the downfall of others; he alone had reserves of wealth on which to draw, and it was to this man of influence that the government had to turn for help for its own treasury, before it could even begin to think of asking for help for the nation's strangled economy.

The eighteenth century had seen the appearance and growth of a generally enlightened public opinion; but it had had no possible opportunity of acquiring financial techniques. Although the salons and cafés, the aristocrats of the court or of industry greatly enjoyed discussing tools and methods of agriculture or industry, they knew nothing at all about banking. They were content with a sound currency and a pure metal coinage. When poverty and unrest increased, it was not therefore lack of credit which was blamed, but the king, the court, or the regulations. English liberty was praised everywhere, not because it was seen as the basis of credit, but as a symbol of increasing prosperity which was believed to be due solely to its political virtues. The American experience had failed to educate public opinion on this point. It was to political liberty in itself that people gave their votes, and not to the financial apparatus it supported.

The argument as to whether the French economy in 1785 was rich or poor has continued from Michelet to Jaurès, but no definite conclusion has been reached. Economic activity apparently throve when times were good and slumped when times were bad. France appeared flourishing or wretched in turns, and although people managed occasionally in periods of prosperity to put something aside for a rainy day, they were never in a position in times of adversity to call on credit or to draw cheques on the future. The result was a series of lean years, when savings were exhausted and the country was reduced to hopeless misery. The government, with its treasury empty, could act only as it was authorized to, whilst the worried artisan from sheer force of habit looked solely to the king to solve all his difficulties. It was on this colossal note of misunderstanding that the Estates-General met in 1789.

The government learned during the nineteenth century that only a strong issue of paper currency could save the country in these grave crises. England had learned this from experience. Louis XVI, on the contrary, gave honest Necker his head, and Necker's honesty was the only thing in which the bourgeoisie had any confidence at all. The lawyers of France gathered in the Salle des Menus Plaisirs at Versailles, with a mandate from the Third Estate to defend honesty and integrity. The government talked finance, the Third Estate replied in terms of virtue; no real exchange of views was possible. The Revolution grew out of the most fruitless arguments at the very moment when, as we have seen, England was meeting the crisis by developing its banks.

The monarchy foundered because of its inability to organize credit in France, because it summoned the Estates-General who were no wiser on the subject, and because it doubled the representation of the Third Estate without acquiring a single additional financier in the process. The greater the number of members associated with the deliberations of the Third Estate, the more lawyers they included. These eminent lawyers were entrenched in the routines of everyday procedure; they had been brought up on Montesquieu's reflections and Voltaire's sarcasm (though Voltaire had strongly suspected that there must be some great economic force at work beneath the law, which he had never been able to identify); they were stirred by Rousseau's sentimental outpourings; they dreamed of a strong society built for virtue by virtue. It was all very abstract; what France needed was accountants, while what she had was lawyers: instead of counting acres of land, the length of roads, bales of wool or cotton, they discussed the rights of man and of the citizen. The treasury was empty, the assembly filled it with a constitution. It revived all the points raised in France in the impassioned discussions on American independence. The masterpiece was drawn up, and the great principles of 1789 were laid down; and indeed it *was* a masterpiece, for in the world of that day it would have been almost impossible to find an assembly more competent or better prepared for the task. Its members were well matched from the start, since they shared a common education and long years of common practice.

The assembly was crystal clear when it came to translating into legal terms two centuries of experience. The 'claims of citizens' must be based on simple and incontestable principles. It was an attitude of mind reminiscent of general mechanics; and it reflected the spirit of deduction which had created philosophical speculation in France, to the detriment of the old Christian faith. For long years the French *parlements* had been twisting the law they were charged to apply in order to foster liberty, property ownership and security. In corporate lawsuits they had done their utmost to protect the inventor and the innovator: decrees which conformed too closely to tradition were bitterly criticized by enlightened society, attacks on the liberty of conscience were condemned, and judges who applied the royal laws strictly were pilloried by opinion. Landowners arriving with carriages full of dossiers to support their ancient rights had been dismissed summarily, to the delight of all Paris, and backed by the honours list of the *Encyclopédie*. In order to condemn the Jesuits, the progressivists had made them appear ridiculous. It was this whole century of struggle and controversy that was summed up in the final song of victory celebrating the natural and inalienable rights of man; and it gave to the *Déclaration* the strength of its style and structure. Moreover, the cosmopolitan culture of 1789 had left its mark on these French texts, which drew on the lessons of English or American political experiments; there were also reflections inspired by the virtuous Chinese emperors who were depicted climbing to the top of a hill to proclaim their good intentions before the supreme being. It was this cosmopolitanism also which gave the *Déclaration* its universal appeal.

It would be difficult, therefore, to overestimate the power and the effectiveness of the enormous intellectual achievement which emerged from the commissions of the revolutionary assemblies. They shaped the development of the new era of European and world thought and gave Europe the tools which were to help it assert itself. In all that concerned ideas and intellectual concepts—law and the code, the fixing of measures, the metric system—the revolutionary assemblies did magnificent work, but they failed signally on the vital practical problem of the organization of money for purposes of credit.

For all these masterpieces of intellect had no practical significance when it came to monetary and credit techniques. Eventually, of course, after a great many speeches, they had to tackle this fundamental problem which had formerly been the province of the monarchy but had now to be dealt with by the assembly which had taken over the monarchy's responsibilities. Though desperate appeals were made to it, it fell into the most fantastic error: there were in the Constituent Assembly a few rare economists like Condorcet, a few practical men like Talleyrand, and a few (far too few) experienced bankers like the farmer-general Lavoisier, or the outstanding Dupont de Nemours. All urged the assembly to think long and hard about Law's fiasco. Law had tried to sell his colonial companies in banknotes; the assembly was contemplating selling Church lands in the same currency. How was such a mistake in monetary technique possible? First, because all the reserves which had supported the French economy through the crises of the eighteenth century had been derived from landed property; but more particularly because the vast majority of the assembly consisted of lawyers; they were convinced that the fundamental difference between Law's disaster, still fresh in memory, and the new experiment was embodied in a new legal statute which would be an adequate safeguard: such an innovation would in itself be enough to validate, in 1790, what had been disastrous in 1718. We quoted above the anonymous preface to Law's *Money and Trade Considered*, laying down the conditions of sound currency. It went on to say that these conditions existed between persons equally subject to the law, and that credit thus meant simply trusting in the laws themselves. This may be a legal theorist's view of the economy; it would hardly be that of a banker or a technical expert. From lack of experience, France, unfortunately, was about to embark once more on the same adventure. From 1791, there were two prices in France, one in cash, the other in *assignats*. In a country accustomed to gold, there should have been twice as many psychological precautions taken to ensure that a correct relationship was maintained between the note and gold. In actual fact far fewer precautions were taken in France than in England.

Thus this magnificent assembly of lawyers, deservedly immortal for its work of codification, was about to plunge the country into a series of regularly recurring catastrophes, the effects of which were evident right up to the mid-twentieth century. Yet the real responsibility lay not so much with the assembly as with the whole of French thought and French society, which rated legal expertise higher than understanding of credit. The basic lack of this credit, which the assembly dismissed as a minor issue, was soon to split the whole of society, and bring to the scaffold most of those who, far-sighted or otherwise, had been connected with this fatal blunder.

The crisis of 1789 necessitated a widespread recourse to credit. Far from organizing this remedy, the constitutional monarchy which was evolving in France actually destroyed the financial framework of the old régime. The break-up of the court and the departure of the great noble families and financiers (apart from one of the wealthiest, the Prince of Orleans, who stayed in Paris to watch over his own concerns) destroyed the classic consumers' market at the same time as it emptied the treasury. The *Caisse d'Escompte* disappeared, engulfed by the assignats before being officially suppressed in 1793. An immense floating population of unemployed emerged from the suburbs in search of non-existent bread. There was looting in the countryside and rioting in the towns. The panic did not create a climate favourable to credit. The old economic masonry of the old régime was crumbling. The unemployed, instead of seeking bread from the factory, the exchange and the bank, shouted for it under the windows of the town hall. French society was too dependent on the land, and on landed property; the sale of national property encouraged this tendency still further; capital either went underground, or was used for speculating on the price of land. Industry came to a standstill. The Anzin mines were paralysed, and the blast furnaces at Le Creusot went out. The economy was dying—in fact it was dead.

Two important events showed its passing. First the rise of a socialist government on the ruins of legal liberalism, and second the success of mass-recruiting for the army.

In fact only a socialist-minded government could maintain an economy without credit, and the Committee of Public Safety, under the guidance of Robespierre, actually rushed full speed ahead towards the steep and slippery slope. Credit was dead, so the whole credit structure, not only the *Caisse d'Escompte* but the trading companies, the capitalist groups and the *bourse*, might as well be destroyed. Banking operations, in the estimation of all good members of the Constituent Assembly, were deals in stocks, no more and no less. Trade in merchandise was speculation or monopoly pure and simple. So death to stock-jobbers, speculators and monopolists! Thus the liberal economy, hounded from its very last strongholds, was replaced by the vast and improvised machinery of a planned economy: requisitioning, maximum prices, maximum wages, and maximum everything. Yet the decrees of Ventôse were beginning to tackle the problem of a redistribution of land in favour of the poor. Although the value of the assignat was low, the terror checked its further depreciation. It did not matter whether the note was covered by gold or not, or what its real value was. Any citizen who was dishonest about its value was obviously a bad patriot, a suspect, and a case for the dreaded terror. It was not for gain, or handsome profits, that the factories kept going, or reopened in the worst possible economic conditions in every French canton administered by Paris; it was not for profit, nor from fear of a ruthless government that saltpetre was raked from the cellars, or that Monge drew up plans for fortresses and guns; it was from politic belief in the threatened mother-country.

A patriotic dictatorship was substituted for a liberal banking system; influential merchants, theorists, or lawyers who had come up from the Gironde to Paris to establish the government of their dreams, had a rude awakening: they either perished on the scaffold, or were proscribed, or were relentlessly hunted down. This continued as long as the Committee of Public Safety was able to equip its armies by requisitioning, to the sound of the *Marseillaise*, and to ensure fairly adequate food supplies to the cities by the compulsory mobilization of all available resources.

Yet one man, Danton, saw the position clearly. Before making a dangerous deal with the speculators, he had advised the republican armies not to hesitate to seek in the liberated countries a livelihood which the Republic itself could hardly provide. The army was the great outlet for the working people, particularly in towns, where they were thrilled by the great patriotic adventure planned in factories now deserted by their customers. Mass conscription became inevitable with the destruction of the economy even before it was ordered by the famous decree. Thus the towns with a reduced population stopped feeding the troops of the sections. As the national army increased in size so the revolutionary troops diminished, and the more successful the regular army, the more precarious became the position of the Committee of Public Safety which had brought it into being. The well-known phrase 'victories swooped down on Robespierre like furies' is a most apt description of the position in which that extraordinary moving spirit of this epic now found himself. It seemed to him that the Republic was lost and the brigands triumphant. By brigands he meant the financiers, merchants and commissaries.

However formidable the work accomplished by the Committee of Public Safety it could not succeed. It had aimed at a lasting reform of society, but it could not possibly hope to build the permanent apparatus of a vast controlled economy with no monetary basis. Monge, a fine geometrician, had had no training in economics. No-one in the country really believed in the permanence of reforms which were called 'revolutionary' precisely because they were exceptional and temporary. Men and capital went into hiding, waiting for the return of a bourgeois peace, while the very fact that France was the gold reservoir of Europe meant that capital was all the easier to conceal. It needed only a slight shift of majority in the Convention, engineered by men who resented Robespierre's enquiries into the affairs of those who were doing well out of the régime, for gold to reappear once Robespierre was overthrown. It was even being squandered openly by dandies and spendthrifts. It set up a new economic current which galvanized the old society into new life, and led the Convention, in spite of itself, towards the re-establishment of the bourgeois economy. Then the strange world of the Directory came into being, a motley crowd made up of speculators in national lands, businessmen from the old régime, who had been living hidden away in little back shops, experts in the mobilization of military production, and foreigners whose alien status offered them a certain security against the Tribunal and who could take advantage of the stable currencies of their own countries. There were marvellous business openings for the Swiss, a subject on which Benjamin Constant dwelt at length in his diary. Beside, or above this financial *élite* which now emerged from its hide-out, were the revolutionary leaders who had managed to avoid both the guillotine of Fouquier-Tinville and the 'dry guillotine' which followed it. They had succeeded in keeping their posts by the adroit game of co-operation, first under the Convention, and then under the assemblies, councils and ministries of the Directory. They were to attempt to take their place in the revival of business.

Between the two groups, financial and political, it was not always easy to achieve agreement. The wealthy bourgeoisie mistrusted the Jacobins. But the political group was equally suspicious of the old hands who had toadied, first to Pichegru, then to Sieyès, and finally to Bonaparte. It also mistrusted the whole political see-saw of the Directory, whose chief aim under the fiendishly clever direction of the superb intellect of Citizen Barras was to keep Thermidorians in key positions at all costs. It was a policy furtively plotted in governmental councils, at parties and at the famous balls given at the Palais du Luxembourg, all spick and span for the occasion, or in the glittering, recently opened Hôtel de Salm, around the petticoats of Madame Tallien, Madame Récamier and Josephine de Beauharnais.

But the well-to-do remained suspicious. The *assignat,* whose depreciation had been checked by the terror, fell in value until it was a worthless piece of paper. The *mandat territorial* which replaced it was no more successful. Credit was not restored. Nevertheless, the conditions in which it could be restored were gradually being established; the political situation of 1790 was more stable, and new economic measures took into account the bitter experience of the past years. The Constitution of the year III made property ownership and liberalism secure: the legal, bourgeois revolution was an accomplished fact. The Constitution abolished everything that went beyond the

bourgeois revolution towards socialism and recreated a
kind of court life. Relief at the ending of the terror
brought artisans' shops back to life. Orders poured in for
fabrics, furniture, building work, house decoration and
knick-knacks, and there was less fear of unemployment;
this lasted as long as the armies remained on a war footing and were mainly stationed beyond the frontiers, since
they could be maintained there without placing any strain
on the country's precarious economic revival. The stubborn patience of the peasants, of the *Pères Goriot*, was
rewarded, and they enlarged their farms with national
property. The peasantry again enjoyed a secure livelihood, and again began to invest its money. The *Caisse
d'Escompte* reopened under the name of the *Caisse des
Comptes courants*.

Who protected this newly emerging credit? Who was
on the council of this new bank of issue, a bank which
still did not venture to disclose its name? There was Le
Couteux, a Rouen manufacturer, a former deputy, cautious and self-effacing. There was Casimir Périer of the
famous Grenoble family of cloth manufacturers, who
bought the Château de Vizille and a block of shares in
the Anzin mines for next to nothing. There was Per-
régaux, a Swiss banker, who had adroitly survived the
vicissitudes of the Revolution, along with other fellow-
countrymen like Mallet, Hottinger and Delessert—the
whole circle which revolved around Madame Récamier.
For the benefit of a carefully selected group of known
and trusted industrialists and merchants, a sound note
based on sound credit was brought cautiously into circulation, but there was no intention of putting it at the
service of the Directory. The great number of *mandats
territoriaux*, printed by the Directory itself, were exploited for their rapid loss in value.

It was in this divided and ill-assorted society, protected
from foreign invasion by a now disciplined army, that the
destiny of the régime was to be decided. The Directory
held its ground so long as Barras remained in power, as
he kept with him the other politicians who had survived
the Revolution. But once the peasants felt secure, and

the craftsmen had work, they tended to push to the fore at elections men quite out of sympathy with the members of the former Convention. Barras, aging, disillusioned and overworked, planned to retire to his great estates, to round off a most successful career in a philosophic calm worthy of the eighteenth century. Mutual uneasiness in face of the unknown future, whether too royalist or too Jacobin, drew politicians and financiers together in a common desire to safeguard the system of co-optation which had proved so successful in government as well as in banking during the previous four years. This rapprochement, engineered by Sieyès, was aimed at dividing the spoils as they were—banking for bankers; good, permanent senatorships for the politicians; and power for Sieyès himself, who would use the army to protect the whole arrangement. Two factors were omitted from their reasoning. The first was the army, which had to be kept mobilized away from the cities and even, if possible, from the frontiers, while the second was Bonaparte, shocked at the realization that the ultimate end of this arrangement was the enrichment and consolidation of a privileged few, solidly united among themselves.

Bonaparte, it is true, was an ambitious general, but when all was said and done, no more dedicated, meticulous or loyal individual had ever come up against Barras. He could turn his hand to any task, small or large, private or public. Guglielmo Ferrero has rightly stressed the submissive and sometimes beseeching tone of his letters to the Directory during the Italian campaign: after all, his first victories (whose significance was not yet apparent, as they followed six years of victories) could barely serve as sufficient explanation to the republican Government for the major changes that the General, brought by the exigencies of war from Italy, sought to introduce in the Directory's plan.

Bonaparte had already done some hard thinking in prison. Hoche had been removed from the same army of Italy, and but for Thermidor might have suffered the same fate as Custine. But Bonaparte, with that singular patience he was so often to display during his married life

with Josephine, bided his time, like the true soldier he
was; and soon the fact that Sieyès' associates were by no
means disinterested began to attract attention. Bonaparte
may have hesitated to throw grenadiers into the assembly,
but he had no hesitation whatever in relegating Sieyès to
the presidency of the Senate in order to assume complete
power himself in a matter for which, after all, he bore the
full responsibility.

But the first consul could not change the pact concluded between politicians and financiers. The former
were comfortably ensconced in the Senate with a permanent income. The financiers had their bank, the *Banque
de France*, in which they held magnificent directorships
enabling them to keep the advantages of credit exclusively to themselves and to their friends; these advantages
had cautiously been kept secret because the bankers
refused, at first uncompromisingly, to take charge of the
French economy. Parisians all, they were interested only
in Paris, their Parisian friends and a few provincial notables. Above all a magnificent concession had been made
to the bankers: the *Banque de France* was to take over
the *Caisse des Comptes courants*. This had been dissolved, and the bank's working capital, which was vital
for a large circulation of paper money, would have to be
much more substantial than that of the *Caisse*. Thirty
millions were needed, of which the bankers had put up
only two millions. The state alone could provide the rest.
In England the financiers of the bank had lent to the
state, but in France the state lent to the financiers of the
bank. The bank's cash balance, in fact, was ensured by
realizable assets, by the securities of the Treasury's
Receivers-General, by receipts from tolls and duties and
by the proceeds of the state lottery: this was a return to
the financial techniques of the old régime, basing credit
on the cycle of taxation. Thus, the society of the Consulate had much in common with that of the old régime:
dynasties reappeared, dynasties of senators, only too
pleased for the Consul to adopt the hereditary principle
for his office, since they were eager to establish it on their
own account; and dynasties of financiers unobtrusively

introducing their own hereditary succession into the governing body of the *Banque de France*. Both dynasties were content to see the Consul aspiring to the Empire, since they were delighted at the opportunity it would give them to sport the finery of counts, dukes and princes.

Mollien, however, rightly denounced the narrow-mindedness of these 'fifteen heads of business houses who brought to the bank only a concern for their own affairs, and who assessed the future of the bank only in terms of their own personal fortune'. No great skill was needed to make credit available to industrialists out of the state's money and the proceeds of taxation. It was no more than had been done by the financiers of Louis xv, in fact by all those of the old régime, from Jacques Coeur onwards. It would have been better to choose other men with a wider outlook, but perhaps they had emigrated to Italy or England. At any rate they were not to be found in that 'arid, sandy waste', which was how Bonaparte described French society in 1800. It was the very mediocrity of these *parvenus* which eventually led to the curtailment of their ill-earned privileges after the crisis of the 'united merchants' in 1805. A governor of the *Banque de France*, Deprez, had persuaded the bank to pay good notes for the promised Mexican piastres, which never got safely across the sea because of the battle of Trafalgar. The new franc was again subject to the risks of Law's system: Napoleon imposed a governor of his own choice on the bank and ordered it to open branch banks. In short it was to follow a policy which would serve imperial France more effectively and the interests of the governors less exclusively.

Although the basis of the new French financial credit was restricted, it was fairly sound. This time the technical as well as the legal conditions of the Code were fulfilled, since Mollien had taken a lesson from England and safeguarded them effectively. This newly found credit developed all the better because the army, founded in the crisis at the end of the eighteenth century, was not disbanded and in the course of its military advance through Europe introduced into the French, that is the Parisian, market something of the economy of continental countries. Napoleon was only a soldier; he brought military solutions to the problem and those military solutions were accepted by civilians whose business concerns they affected. A peaceful Empire would have been quite inconceivable in 1805.

Neither the mediocre Sieyès nor the detested Talleyrand could possibly have organized the immense changes involved in bringing back the enormous numbers of soldiers under arms into the factories, mills and countryside. We know how severely the 1785 crisis had hit France because it had developed so late compared with England, and because it had a surplus population which ended up in the army rather than in industry. In 1805 it was even further behind. Had the *Banque de France* been founded in 1720 at about the same time as the Bank of England (although this was of course inconceivable at the time), its credit would possibly have been enough to stave off the French political crisis. In 1800, it came too late to repair in a few years the results of a hundred years' time lag. The French economy needed the war, with its expedients and its blockade, in order to take advantage of a continental market even more backward than its own was compared with England. It could not have existed in a framework of European liberty, which was the real reason why no serious protest was ever made against the Napoleonic adventures. The Emperor could play about with his soldiers just as he pleased, since no-one in France would have known what to do with them if they had been returned to civilian life.

Thanks, however, to the providential blockade, French activity awoke from the lethargy of the Revolution. It experienced some periods of brilliant success and dominated the rest of the continent. It would be all too easy at this point to pour out floods of statistics. We know that Napoleon liked to keep an inventory of the civilian population as he did of his troops. He naïvely assumed that a prefect could state how many citizens were at work, and what kind of work they were doing, just as a general can account for his soldiers, his ammunition, and the uses to which they are being put. He sent out questionnaires and demanded replies within a fortnight—only just about time to put a few approximate figures on paper. It was less risky for a prefect to over-estimate his Department than for a general to over-estimate his resources.

The career of a typical industrialist will illustrate the rapid growth which followed the blockade. Charles Ballot gives the main facts about the life of Ternaux. He was the son of a Sedan wool manufacturer, a man unfortunate in business who had been set on his feet again by Guillaume Louis to such good purpose that, even in 1789, he employed more than three thousand workers, some concentrated in the town itself, but a large number dispersed throughout the surrounding districts. Though he supported the legal revolution enthusiastically at first, in 1792 Ternaux protested against the treatment meted out to the king, and left France in some haste in order to escape the fate of his colleagues of the municipality who perished on the scaffold for taking the same attitude. He contrived to liquidate his assets on fairly good terms, and was apparently able to get most of his capital out of the country in gold. At any rate, he opened a business house at Leghorn in order to sell German cloth in Italy, a not unprofitable venture. He visited Germany and England, where he observed the new mechanization. He returned to France under the Directory and tried to restart his business, although in somewhat desultory fashion. Under the Consulate he increased his fortune, especially in Sedan, and made his business one of the finest in France. From Sedan he turned his attention to Rheims, where he took two people into partnership, for he needed the high-class cloth which was made only in the city. In the Rheims area, all the work was done in the countryside. Ternaux and his partners regrouped the workers into a huge new factory in the city and provided them with English looms. Then began a period of outstanding success furthered by the blockade. He bought a secularized convent here, an abandoned warehouse there, or a whole plant which was rusting away. In Paris he and his brother opened a large joint business-house, which was the nucleus of the whole concern. In short, from Sedan to Louviers, from Verviers to Leghorn, all the wool in continental Europe came in the sphere of influence of this brilliant French businessman. In a former convent in the rue Mouffetard he proceeded at vast expense to try out machinery made by Douglas or Cockerill. With the help of several ingenious colleagues, he himself invented an apparatus for dyeing. With considerable daring he ordered fleeces by the land route from central Asia for super-luxury goods. He secured tools and workmen from Spain for bleaching merino wool, which had only just been introduced into France. He acted as adviser to the imperial administration which showered medals upon him. He recommended everywhere the machines he had proved successful. He was the first to try out great concentrations of workers, which were still considered rather risky. He had fifteen hundred workers at Ensival, and five or six thousand in Rheims (and the number was increasing); he expanded his business from Leghorn towards Genoa and Naples and from Bayonne to Lisbon. He controlled Germany, visited Russia, and opened a mill in St Petersburg. It should be noted that the shrewd Ternaux made widespread use of what was to be known as a trust eighty years later; theoretically independent businesses were created, each with its own commercial reason for existing, and in which Ternaux did not figure by name; but in reality he directed them because he controlled their capital. The establishment in Paris only had a small number of employees but inevitably became the centre of this vast network with its ramifications throughout Europe. It was in Paris that the markets, and more important still, the credits, were shared out; it was both a bank and an exchange whose existence was closely linked with that of the continent. This immense structure of industry and credit was solid enough to withstand political crisis. Ternaux continued to be the model industrialist under the Restoration, and in the closing years of his life, under Louis-Philippe, the aged Rouget de Lisle, still a prolific hymn-writer, composed for him the *Chant des Industriels*.

There were under the Empire a few other businesses similar to Ternaux's, such as those of Bauwens and Richard Lenoir, but their numbers were fewer than in England. It should be added that Ternaux, being a wool merchant, was in a privileged position. Cotton merchants had had no difficulty in dominating the continent, imposing high prices forced on them by a blockade which cut off their supplies of raw material. Then, before they had completed the courageous process of converting their plant from cotton to wool, the fall of the Empire brought a drop in prices so that the return of free cotton ruined them. Ternaux himself had had some experience of the limitations and dangers of imperial protection; his business in St Petersburg and Lisbon collapsed even before the end of the Empire. Richard Lenoir's bankruptcy was complete and total.

Nevertheless, the temporary success of very large business enterprises led to great innovations, especially in the introduction of steam-engines. The first great factory was that of Périer's, built on the hill at Chaillot near the steam-pump which had been supplying the western quarters of Paris with water since the early years of Louis XVI's reign. The mills at Chaillot made not only heavy plant, but mining equipment (which replaced the armies of horses previously used) or rolling-mills and even parts for organ-builders; but these mills almost went bankrupt during the Revolution. Orders had flowed in from the revolutionary government (especially for guns), but instead of the half million in cash they had been promised, they were merely entered in the great debt book for three per cent stock! There again it was the Empire, its protectionist policy, its blockade and its credit (the state bills were discounted by the *Banque de France*), which at Chaillot and elsewhere in France saved Périer's various enterprises. Other flourishing businesses were started in Lyons and Digoin, and it was claimed that French steam-engines were even better than those of Watt.

Strangely enough, the French metal industry did not share the trend of progress in textiles or in the use of steam. Le Creusot, the outstanding success of the old régime, made no innovations until about 1830, and France made no move to introduce coke smelting. 'Those who so glibly suggest the substitution of mineral fuel for vegetable coal', wrote a metallurgist in 1814, 'seem to have no idea that it will involve an almost total reconstruction of the blast furnaces, refineries, machinery, and workshops . . .' This was a task obviously beyond the means of French industrial credit, so that France's metal industry continued to operate on the old lines with very little cast steel and almost everything in wrought iron, forged in tiny foundries scattered all over France. The price of this iron, which was in great demand and produced in small quantities, rose in France as much as it dropped in England. The products were no better, and the ironmasters were no richer, since wood was dear and came from forests that had been over-exploited, and capital resources were too closely bound up with the land. This landed capital brought in large returns only at the cost of deforestation, and was thus self-destructive.

Dearer cotton and dearer iron were two factors which explained the dissatisfaction of ambitious industrialists. The consumer had to protest against the high prices resulting from the economy of the blockade. In Europe as a whole and even in France industry was becoming strong enough in 1812 to stand up to English competition in textiles, and obviously had more to gain than to lose from a resumption of liberal economic relations across the North Sea. Napoleon was well aware that he was helping to keep the malcontents quiet by allowing so many infringements of his blockade, but these breaths of fresh air were by no means enough to satisfy an economy which was becoming increasingly self-confident. The point at issue was the system itself: was it worth while to conscript all those thousands of men into the army when industry could perhaps make good use of them? People said that the blockade, all things considered, was doing more harm than good. They were getting tired of the war and felt confident (sometimes rather blindly) in the possibilities of an economic peace, especially since France also experienced the crisis of 1811–13; as usual, the severity of the crisis was attributed more to the political régime than to the actual structure of expanding capitalism.

Thus the very notables who had summoned General Bonaparte, thrust him into a position of power for life and then made his position hereditary, were now beginning to complain about the ogre. They plotted and barely concealed their impatience after the *débâcle* of Moscow. They were ready for a change, and for a return to the political situation as it had been, provided of course that their property, their code, and their place in the social hierarchy was guaranteed, and that the privileged few were allowed to retain their hereditary titles.

It was this that made the return of Louis XVIII very much simpler. The monopoly of the Bank was to be confirmed and even extended, the governor once more becoming the tool of the directors, while the provincial branch-banks (which Paris regarded as costly and almost useless) were to be suppressed; the imperial Senate would move up en bloc to the House of Peers, and the King would then be able to settle into the usurper's chair without undue dislocation of the economy. The return of the Eagle was a bad business, the Bank refused to cooperate, credit went underground and the great ones fled. The officers on half-pay and a group of liberal-minded patriots did, it is true, attempt to create a new constitution, but they could no longer rely on the powerful conspirators of 1799. In the House of Peers, established again after Waterloo, it was the former conspirators who were the most ruthless at the time of Ney's trial.

All things considered, those who had done well out of the economy had been right not to fear peace and the return of Anglo-European collaboration. From 1815 to 1820 French industry was in better shape than that of England. Lyons, Lille (and the mining towns of Roubaix and Tourcoing, which were growing as rapidly as Manchester), Normandy, and of course all the ports, took on an air of modern prosperity. In Paris there was speculation in everything, including patterned fabrics, perfumery, luxury materials, corn and iron. A great wooden shed was hastily erected to deal with the sale of Stock Ex-

change securities and state funds, into which, in response
to the appeal launched by the Rothschilds and Laffitte,
flowed the savings which had accumulated during the
blockade. The shops were lit up at night, to the delight
of foreigners who were always fascinated by that exquisite French taste which made the fortune of the merchants. Though heavy industry developed only slowly,
merchants were rapidly growing rich. In peasant workshops in Auvergne they collected cloths and fabrics woven
by employees in their own homes from the raw materials
with which the merchants had supplied them, and they
operated on the same system in Flanders and Cambrésis. Skilfully exploiting the cheapness of rural labour
to bring down prices in the big factories, the merchants
then made these the excuse for lowering the country
worker's wages still more, so that the poor man soon had
to set his entire family to work long hours in order to
make his old loom produce the money needed to supple-
ment the income from his inadequate little field. In Paris,
in the cities and in the trading ports, however, the middle-
class businessman was thriving, and displayed his luxurious possessions in the sumptuous mansions which former
aristocrats, who had now been ruined, let out in flats or
sold to speculators.

With the coming of peace, the consumers' markets
were greatly expanded. Officials, clerks and a whole lower
middle class of artisans, shopkeepers, officials and employees bought specially treated cotton or Calais linen so
that they looked as if they dressed in silk. Stendhal
rightly noted in France what Carlyle noted in England:
a transformation of society the like of which had not
been seen for four hundred years. Among the lower
classes, there were growing up innumerable families who
managed to imitate the aristocratic way of life in some
way or other.

Nothing is so persistent as a nation's taste. The France
of 1820 still remained true to the impeccable taste which
for two hundred years had characterized the Louvre and
Versailles. The label 'quality' was applied to both noble
blood and to good merchandise. Work done by hand in

a craftsman's shop or in a family workshop, even when the articles concerned were only cheap, were regarded as very superior to shoddy English trash, turned out by some anonymous machine. The shopkeeper, who shared this attitude, encouraged the natural trend to hand-made goods. This in turn reinforced the lack of enterprise of the industrialists, who were in no hurry to change their way of doing things. The lesson of Colbert had been too thoroughly learned to be really understood. France produced luxury goods for the lower middle classes, as she had formerly produced them for the courts of Europe.

These 'luxury goods', however, had to fall in price all the time if they were to be produced in ever-increasing quantities. More and more workmen were being absorbed by the small artisans' workshops; wages were very low, and very little trouble was taken to give the workmen a thorough training. In spite of this, in the absence of a courageous policy of mechanization these cheap luxury goods were much dearer than the corresponding English article. Though some might sell in London where fashion and snobbery made them popular, they could barely hold their own, even in France, against English products. This explains why the chief aim of French economists was to protect French 'quality' against the unfair competition of English mechanization. The apprehensive demands of the old corporate spirit had been transferred to a national scale; and they were soon translated into a systematic protectionist policy.

Under the Revolution and the Empire, protectionism had been introduced under the guise of patriotism and had brought wealth to the new middle class. After the Restoration it assumed the prestige of tradition. At first d'Artois did indeed try to re-establish international commercial exchanges, but from 1816 to 1826 customs duties were imposed and increased. Both the aristocrat who sold timber from his forests and the owner of a small iron-foundry were anxious to impose duties amounting to 120 per cent on iron smelted in English coal blast-furnaces. Duties on coal were lower, since France got very little from the Loire and Anzin mines, but they were high enough to ensure colliery profits and slow down the progress of iron-smelting with coal. The superiority of French silk was assured: consequently there were no restrictions, but cotton fabrics were absolutely prohibited.

Thus under the Restoration the state was still the indispensable protector of industry, just as the king had been the protector of the guilds. The whole administrative machine invented by the old régime and rebuilt by the Empire continued its role of promoting and controlling industrial activity. Civil engineers, mining engineers, foresters and surveyors trained by the polytechnics and the mining schools (including that of St Etienne) inspected, granted or refused permission for new installations, drew up reports for the government on measures of a general nature, and brought useful inventions to the notice of their ministers. In short they kept an eye on activities in general and based their recommendations on their conscientiously compiled statistics and on the battery of forms so dear to the administrative mind. Meanwhile the courts based their judgements on the Civil Code, which as we have seen was better at dealing with questions of landed property than of industry; and in any lawsuit almost always pronounced in favour of the owner of the field or meadow against the industrialist who wished to use water from the river for his mill. Provided the French middle classes could control the state, they were content to see it clamp down with all its authority on progress.

But now in 1828 the ruling aristocracy wanted to put noblemen in all the high administrative posts. The great feudal landowners wanted to take over all the responsibilities of the monarchy. The administration even drew up a liberal scale of tariffs on the pretext of bringing down internal prices. It was obviously a favourable moment for the landed nobility who had been untouched by the crisis which was now sweeping over France just as it had swept over England earlier; but a bad one for the lower middle classes who were feeling its effects. They began to complain of tyranny. Old feuds flared up between the merchant and the aristocrat, between the shopkeeper and the court. The young journalist Thiers rapidly made a name for himself in politics. The elections went against the king, who was anxious that the trade licence of an industrialist or merchant should no longer count as a qualification for the electoral roll, a proposal embodied in the Third Ordinance which was one of the causes of the revolution of 1830.

When the progressive Thiers came to power he tried in vain to introduce into France industrial freedom on English lines, and particularly freedom of trade, the lowering of tariffs and the stimulus of economic competition. Some of his reforms were accepted; for instance, after the rapid development of cotton weaving it became possible to import cotton warp; but within a very short time strong coalitions of interests again brought together the protectionist allies of 1820, the landed proprietors, metallurgists, shopkeepers and artisans. The English crisis of 1840 was even more fatal to Thiers in the sphere of economics than of politics. Guizot reassured industry and France went back to the guardian state which meant peace and security—or did until the crisis which began in 1846. The new government thought of lowering protective tariffs, and steps were taken to bring this about in 1847, but only tentatively, since the monarchy of Louis-Philippe fell before it could be carried through.

Beneath these changes of régime, the increasing cohesion of the administration was maintained. The administration sent out questionnaires, collected important information about English methods and practice, and made every effort to disseminate them in all earnestness. It gave particular encouragement to the early attempts at coke smelting and to the use of coal in iron foundries. It organized exhibitions with the collaboration of the chambers of trade and the Society for the Promotion of National Industry. It continued, in short, to control activity throughout France, that curious country which rebelled so bitterly against political authority only to fall the more readily under the sway of administrators. Not that the latter were without merit. They had the finest mathematical training in the world, they built many new schools, they encouraged initiative by the offer of prizes and developed educational facilities in the academies in Paris and Lyons at a time when England had not a single school of engineering; they carried out experiments the results of which, in a typically French way, were studied with a view to acquiring a clearer grasp of the theory that lay behind them.

It is understandable that in such conditions the problem of credit was solved in ways entirely different from those adopted in England. The bank expanded very little. The first move the *Banque de France* made under the Restoration was to close its provincial branches, and it was with something approaching reluctance that it re-opened fifteen of them after 1836, driven to do so by the rapid progress of the large iron and textile areas. Its policy, nevertheless, remained extremely rigid, in striking contrast to the freedom with which notes of all kinds were allowed to circulate in England. In France, parallel with the issuing bank, there were the influential private banks in Paris, run by a handful of aristocrats and great landowners, which are still known today as *la haute banque*. These were at one and the same time stimulating and cautious. They included a considerable number of newcomers: Jews, Swiss and English, and did very little business in the provinces. There, small capitalists, solicitors, landowners, merchants, and sometimes industrialists formed associations to provide the necessary floating capital. But there could be no question of very big deals. It was not until the thirties that industrial concerns like Le Creusot, technically well equipped since the end of Louis xvi's reign, could emerge from the grim series of bankruptcies which in France affected even excellent English technicians between 1780 and 1830. Even the mines in the north of France emerged only by a miracle from a series of financial difficulties, which explains their desire for inflexible customs duties.

Whilst in England appeal for capital by joint-stock companies had met with great success, this system was almost unknown in France. A joint-stock company could be founded only after three favourable reports by a commission specially selected by the Council of State and the Minister of the Interior. Almost always, where the best businesses were concerned, major arguments were produced to prevent the company from being set up. In moderately important businesses, resort was made to the old procedure of the *commenda* already laid down by Savary and Colbert. This was the method by which a joint-stock company had to be set up.

There had also been surprisingly little development in insurance in France; life and fire insurance had existed in England and Germany since the beginning of the eighteenth century. In France a tentative attempt had been made to introduce them on the eve of the French Revolution, but had failed. It was not until the end of the Restoration that insurance really began to take root in France, and even then only because a great number of foreign companies had established themselves in the country to exploit the French market. On the other hand, the French system of government stock was brilliantly successful. People like Balzac's '*Père Grandet*' bought stock. The Paris *bourse* speculated particularly in stock. Thus roads and canals were not built, as in England, by private initiative; in France they could be constructed only by the *Ponts-et-Chaussées*, which was financed from the state budget.

This was the paradoxical situation in France; it was continually changing its government, and was continually critical of fiscal arrangements but nevertheless put its sole trust in the administration and state credit. This was in fact a prolongation into the mid-nineteenth century of the situation we noted in 1780, a country at the meeting place of two great economic systems: that of England, dominated by public opinion, and that of Germany, where economic power preserved a despotic structure.

Nevertheless new equipment and methods were introduced into France in spite of all these procrastinations; industry emerged in a stronger position from each of the economic crises which took the form of political revolutions in France. Modern methods of iron-smelting were introduced in the forties, particularly around the Massif

Central, in the east and the north. Many small family concerns had to close down in face of the competition from the new blast-furnaces and rolling-mills. Similarly vast concentrations of textile industries sprang up around new centres like Roubaix and Tourcoing. Mulhouse was an excellent example of creative effort, comparable to the most ambitious of English ventures. In 1828 Charles x called Mulhouse the capital of French industry and in 1846 Heilmann's carding-machine attracted the attention of manufacturers all over the world to Mulhouse. It was near the newly awakening Germany but was separated from it by such rigid customs barriers that a Western manufacturer declared it was easier for a camel to pass through the eye of a needle than for a needle to get into France.

That gives an indication of the extent of French protectionist policy and of the unifying role of the administration. The raw materials essential for industry in Alsace had to be brought by long hauls from Le Havre, rather than from the nearby Rhine. The difficulties which French geography put in the way of the co-ordination of industry were one reason for the severity of protectionism and French bureaucracy. The extent of these impositions could be judged by the number of wagon convoys making their way across the country; France was huge by the European standards of the time, but gained little help from its contours and its rivers.

Hence the importance of the construction of the railways, which were to reshape the economic map of Europe. Some were started in the forties, and opened up a completely new age just as decisively as they had done in England, perhaps even more so.

FEUDALISM IN GERMANY

In 1785, as we have seen, a new Prussia emerged, centred on Berlin. It was to undergo many vicissitudes before its eventual triumph: for although the central European economy had been brilliant in the gay days of the old Nuremberg, the variety and importance of its resources at the opening of the nineteenth century had hardly affected its archaic structure. Its map, even more than that of France and England, bore the imprint of history. The whole of the Rhine valley with its attractive scenery, its village fêtes, its vineyards and its trade, was reminiscent of France. Beyond the Elbe and the Oder, the forest which fringed the cultivated zones was a reminder of the comparatively recent date of the agricultural settlements on the edge of the Slavonic clearings. In the north, polders and dikes, pumps and windmills and village houses, strung out in line according to the exigencies of irrigation, showed the influence of Holland. In the centre, the vast stretch of open country, with its clustered villages and its strips of land divided up in accordance with the old tradition of three-year rotation of crops, betrayed the persistence of the forms of collective agriculture that have left their traces also in Lorraine.

There was not one but several Germanies. Not that the political states which shared out these plains and varied uplands so unevenly between them made any attempt to conform to the boundaries of this economic maze. It was rather that each state included within its borders both urban and rural traditions, as well as a variety of landscape; as if each one had enlarged its old Germanic core with conquests to east or west and with settlements on newly colonized lands. This was even more pronounced in the east than in the west, where a more western structure preserved the independence of traditions and increased the number of compact little states, duchies, free towns and ecclesiastical principalities. In Prussia the fragmentary structure of the lands inherited by the German dynasties could be seen in miniature, and the variety of domains that ensued seemed better protected in the east by the protective and paternal Empire than in the west. Germany as a whole showed little sign of the progress that Arthur Young admired. It seemed as if it was still too enmeshed in past history to be ready to enter the industrial era.

The combined population of the twelve largest cities in Germany barely equalled that of London or Paris. Almost eighty per cent of the German people were, it is true, dispersed over the countryside. Urban development was hampered by the rural structure, for just as each village formed a compact group in the centre of the lands for whose collective cultivation it was responsible, so too many cities such as Berlin were primarily composed of farms exploiting the surrounding lands. It would not give the right impression to say that German cities were large country towns. To a Frenchman a country town is a commercial rather than an agricultural entity; the produce of the land is sold there, it is true, and rural progress is given a certain stimulus; but the French country town is not the collective owner of the land. Almost everywhere in Germany the bonds uniting the small town with the surrounding countryside were very close; they formed a single community for which tradition, strengthened by the laws of the princes, fixed in detail the class and occupation of each inhabitant. The peasant could not set up a shop in the town, nor the craftsman from the town take up agriculture. Each given community had its fixed quota of bakers, butchers, harness-makers and blacksmiths. The peasant belonged to the peasant class and the artisan was immutably fixed in his artisan class. Private ownership rarely succeeded in breaking into this closely knit society of rigid traditions. The capitalist merchant made little headway except in the largest urban centres, and even there he had to worm his way in between the innumerable corporate regulations and privileges which kept each man in his place, forbade competition and prevented centralization.

Ever since the eighteenth century many princes had tried to encourage individual ownership—an easy task both in the extreme east and the extreme west, but for opposite reasons. In the east, the conquest of the Slav lands had benefited those, like the country squires of Frederick II, who not only owned the lowland serfs but also ruled the towns; and it had especially benefited the direct owners of fairly large estates which they were gradually learning to farm in the English way. In the west the smallness of the states which were stimulated by com petition with the Rhineland or Hanover, and their ready access to information because each minor prince had his industrial advisers (Hanover was directly influenced by London), had contributed to the prosperity of the merchants and of the owners of medium or large farms, which were also worked by modern methods. The task was not so simple in the small courts of Saxony and the south, particularly in Bavaria, where the old system of small country estates persisted, a régime which, though less profitable, was equally tenacious. But though the agriculture of the old Germany had some westernized enclaves, industry had not yet felt the impact of the West.

The metal industry of the Westphalian countryside which became so famous at the end of the century was still being carried on in conditions similar to those under which craftsmen were working in Paris and the provinces. At Solingen knives were made by the dozen, but only to order. The metal did not come in bulk from blast-furnaces, but was smelted at home, by charcoal of course. When orders were scarce, the blacksmith in his leather jacket worked in his fields. In the east, especially in country districts, the Saxon and Silesian cloth industries had only very old-fashioned looms scattered all over the region, dependent on a few merchants in the towns (the forerunners of the great twentieth-century merchants) who drove around the flat countryside in covered carts distributing raw material and order-sheets, and collecting the goods when manufactured. Often, in those 'extremely progressive' regions, which were almost entirely free from the old constraints of class, the peasant could have a loom, and stabilize his income by working through the winter.

There was no sign that the Industrial Revolution was at hand, and no hint of changes like those taking place in England. Even the crisis of 1785–95 stifled the Colbertian attempts of Frederick II and the enlightened despots by forcing a return to the old ways.

Not that the cities were uninterested in progress. In 1798 the works of Albrecht Thaer, who purported to explain the methods of English agriculture to his fellow

countrymen, met with some success. The great landowners derived some benefits from it. Soon this body of
information was circulating in the universities (Thaer
was professor in the University of Berlin from 1809 to
1812). Ministers were influenced by his teaching, and
they not only proposed the marling of sandy soils, the
advantages of potatoes or beetroot, and the careful
selection of stock in breeding cattle and sheep, but also
the legal reform of the law about land.

It was into this curious medieval Germany that the
French revolutionary forces erupted. Once the army of
the princes was disbanded, since Austria was powerless
and Prussia remained hesitant, Hoche, Moreau and Napoleon swept from victory to victory. The west was able
to put up a stouter resistance because of the solidity of
its urban organization, as Custine learned to his cost,
but once that dike had been breached, the troops spread
out where they wished, even as far as the plains of Poland.
Moreover in the towns the common people eagerly welcomed the popular revolutions, while in the rural principalities the frightened and apathetic princes were taken
by surprise.

Once victory was achieved the French occupation in
western Germany found an economy sufficiently like that
of France to ensure the triumph of the new administration and the new Code. All along the Rhine French pre-
fects or the king of Westphalia built admirable roads in
networks graded like those of France. They introduced
the new legal system, and freed the peasant from the
lingering remnants of feudalism. They applied the Cartesian principles of the French officials to municipal administration. The prestige of French currency and credit
was all that was then needed to modernize the Rhineland,
since it was ripe for these changes. Farther east the situation was not the same. Whether the princes in their anxiety hastened to join the French alliance, even to the extent of furnishing contingents of troops, or whether they
passively waited for the victors to impose their terms,
the old social structure baffled the imperial administrators, who could not, in fact, do without the local dynas

ties if they were to conduct business at all. Thus Prussia could be dismembered and lose the outlying western possessions which were too far from the centre, but she could not be suppressed. Napoleon, east of the Elbe, could act only in accordance with the old feudal system: he was forced to abandon all thought of direct rule.

Nevertheless, in those areas which were not affected by French activity, French ideas still made a certain impact, backed as they were by the prestige of brilliant victories. Moreover in Bavaria, Swabia, Saxony, and especially in Prussia, the advantages of private ownership, free enterprise and codes abolishing serfdom appeared all the more attractive since the French legal system facilitated the introduction of technical improvements learnt from England. This marked the beginning of the slow, difficult and spasmodic emancipation of the German peasants. In fact, the French Code had succeeded in France, and partially succeeded in western Germany, only because its way had been prepared by much past history, and by a hundred years of progress of which it was merely the culminating point. Elsewhere, even in anglicized Hanover, any ruler who might have wished to follow in the footsteps of Joseph II would have been similarly disillusioned. Reforms were not introduced into Hanover until 1831. Elsewhere there were quarrels, discussions of principle and interminable debates; in Brandenberg, for example, Marwitz was torn between his fear of exposing the defenceless peasant to violent capitalist competition and his desire to bring new vigour to the state.

This was the climate that prepared the way for the cautious Prussian legislation of 1807 and 1808, and explained the courageous attempts and the disappointments of liberal ministers and the difficulties and evasions of the dynasties in southern Germany. It explained, too, the fragmentary and incomplete character of the reforms attempted in 1807, 1808, 1811 and 1821, but not carried out until 1860. It was the colonized lands in the east, where the authority of the Junkers was paramount (based both on ownership of private lands and on authority over the serfs of the communal villages) which made the easiest transition from the old régime to the new capitalist régime. This explains the relative modernity of Prussia compared with the small states of central Germany.

The liberation of the peasants was not achieved without hardship on their part. The traditionalist country squire made extensive use of his rights to induce the serf to work on his land, which the latter was the more ready to do since the squire continued to supply him with certain commodities which had otherwise to be bought commercially, or protected him against war and above all against famine. The squire exacted from his peasant not gold, which was extremely rare, but provisions in kind of a sort which would not upset the economic balance of the village. Reformers who were familiar with conditions in France and England realized the advantages of a redistribution of land which involved suppressing the common lands, and breaking up the collective villages. It enabled them to enlarge and enclose their own estates and carry out improvements which increased German agricultural returns by more than five per cent from 1800 to 1815 and by more than fifty per cent from 1785 to 1850.

Thus the land began to produce bigger harvests after 1820. Stretches of waste land were cleared and marshes were drained and methodically farmed. Above all two new crops, potatoes and sugar beet, made astonishing progress. Merino sheep were an outstanding success; by 1830 Saxony was breeding more than any other country, surpassing the France of Rambouillet and even Spain. There were fewer horned cattle but more good meat and good leather. The population increased. This increase, already apparent even before 1830, presented the old Germany with unexpected problems. The squire, of course, the new large-scale landowner, used paid labour, but not in sufficient numbers to provide a steady livelihood for all these extra people who were no longer protected by the old paternal feudal traditions. The surplus population had to build up its life outside the old class barriers, and was to form the nucleus of the new industrial force.

Here and there industry showed fresh signs of life, in places where it already had deep historical roots, especially in Silesia. It was a prosperous time for the merchants, who sold good wool-cloths not only throughout the whole of Germany but also in the external markets which they were gradually penetrating. This trade formed the basis for the great commercial capitalism of nineteenth-century Germany; its origins were modest but it soon grew in importance. Westphalian industry felt the repercussions of this extension of markets and surplus manpower. In 1821 the Prussian Government set up a *Gewerbe Institut*, the counterpart of France's *Conservatoire des Arts-et-Métiers*, to spread the new industrial techniques. It attempted to extend the original French road system from one end of the monarchy to the other, and succeeded in doing so in the western half. The problem of capital was a difficult one: nevertheless, after 1830 prosperity stimulated a remarkable accumulation of capital in the towns.

In 1830 Borsig, a former pupil of the *Gewerbe Institut*, opened a foundry in Berlin: by 1847 he was already employing 1,300 workers. In the Rhineland, at Ruhrort and Oberhausen at about the same date, ventures on a similar scale introduced smelting by coke using English methods, and made Westphalian steel famous for its high quality. Sometimes peasants who had previously been blacksmiths became paid workers. At Essen the foundations of Krupp's fortune were being laid. A more sensible way of mining coal was already being adopted: in 1793 each coal mine employed on an average three to five workmen, then larger concentrations developed, and the total number of miners in Germany quadrupled between 1837 and 1845. The output of these men gradually increased as more steam-engines came into use. Finally, since capital attracts capital, the success of the metal industry attracted to the Rhineland the textile industry, which had already established itself at Elberfeld and Crefeld by 1845.

We saw that Frederick II attempted, in the eighteenth century, to imitate Colbert. With this impetus, Germany continued to advance until the opening of the nineteenth century, and in the next half-century the founding of a western system of land-ownership and liberalism replaced mercantilism.

This was the background of the German revolution of 1830: a liberal constitution introduced representatives of commerce and industry into the princes' governments; above all, throughout the whole of Germany, the development of modern activity led to an increased circulation of goods, with a wider appeal to more extensive markets.

But to go back to 1815: trade was at that time hampered by the multiplicity of customs barriers. So long as the economy had remained crystallized around small towns living in an almost closed system, this multiplicity of duties strengthened the authority of the princes and justified the fragmentation of the country: each princely family, often divided into several branches, administered its state as a landowner does his estate. But Prussia, because she was really a state, had been the first to realize the need for customs reform. This could not be achieved independently in Prussia since it was split up by so many tiny independent principalities; in particular the main body of Prussia was separated from those possessions on the Rhine which had been granted it by the Congress of Vienna.

Then began Prussia's historic struggle to achieve a customs' union in northern Germany. At first the princes stood out against it. Their tiny enclaves which refused to be integrated into the Prussian customs system, and which relied on the Diet and the authority of Austria to defend their liberty, were then transformed into a veritable smugglers' paradise within the Prussian economy. The three *anhalts* in particular made a handsome fortune out of the Elbe, and it took twelve years of patient effort on Prussia's part to persuade the princes, one after the other, of the advantages of a common administration: the minor dukes only allowed themselves to be persuaded after having been granted exorbitant advantages. Nevertheless, gradually, the idea of a customs' unions gained ground. In opposition to it, however, another system of unification extending from Hamburg to Saxony cut it into two while at the same time, in southern Germany, Bavaria and Württemburg had united in a common organization orientated towards Austria.

The task on which the Prussian ministers were engaged called for the greatest patience; they tried to take advantage of every trifling difficulty experienced by the princely régimes. Whenever a crisis started in England and then touched off a political revolution or a ministerial crisis in France, it also led to structural modifications in the German economy and presented yet another opportunity to the advocates of union with Prussia. Soon the south was drawn into the Prussian system and the cohesion of the centre began to break down. From 1840, just as the development of railways was about to begin, Prussia's leading position in the customs system was no longer in dispute.

6

The Man of 1830

IN 1830 Europe was shaken by a series of revolutions. They brought about no fundamental change in the political structure of the Continent, but they revealed the profound modifications which had already taken place after half a century of technical progress. The social hierarchy was no longer a stable reality fixed by an immutable decree of providence. It was a turmoil of ambitions, failures and successes, which were undermining the old *élites* in order to make way for the new ones. This rapidity of change was such a new phenomenon that thinkers and artists became fascinated by the strange problem of progress. They no longer saw it as an abstract idea so cherished by the Encyclopaedists, but as a concrete reality which could be expressed and exploited. The concept of time took on a new meaning, and people rediscovered their history, began to be aware of their individuality.

This individuality was apparent in every sphere, in family as in social life, in poetry and history as well as in music and painting. The new awareness of time had less immediate effect on peoples who for long years had been accustomed to the Cartesian logic of space; those who, on the other hand, were less governed by reason, escaped into this new dimension opened up to the imagination. The French were cautious but the Germans gave way to their enthusiasm. For the rest, a new spirit was everywhere abroad.

DEVELOPING SOCIETIES

Society in 1830—the very words conjure up portraits by Ingres, caricatures by Daumier, noisy theatrical first nights, the flashy successes of worldly musicians and also the easily provoked revolutions in which Alexandre Dumas covered himself with glory. It was a tolerant and fanciful age, passionately searching for happiness; from 1815 to 1870, the arts profited from the long period of peace.

Yet this picture is too dated and unlike Paris as it actually was in the 1830s. There was in fact, no such thing as *a* society of 1830, any more than there had been a single *ancien régime* society from Dresden to Rome or from Prague to London in the heyday of cosmopolitanism. If one cannot point to a uniform society in the eighteenth century, it is even more difficult to do so in 1830. There was not *one* society, but a multiplicity of societies, looking for common ground but coming into conflict in the arena of experiment and experience that Europe had become in its transition from the traditional age of the past to the industrial age of the future. There were different rural societies from east to west, and the capitalist societies varied from city to city, and from nation to nation; and each of these separate societies was divided within itself into watertight compartments, mutually ignorant of each other. Cobbett's England may have seemed modern, but here and there were country districts in the north and east where small landed gentry still made their own beer and bread, and spun and wove their own cloth just as they did in feudal Germany. It is equally difficult to make an accurate assessment of rural society either in the France of François le Champi, in Germany or in Europe as a whole. About 1830, in a journey from west to east, from north to south, one would encounter in turn a fine modernized farm around its manor house subscribing to the *Annals of Agriculture*, and the most wretched peasant hovel owned by a serf in fact or law; and in the same place we may see a small well-to-do landowner, already sporting a white cravat. All this world was moving slowly, but it was moving. The very small farm had almost disappeared from England at the very moment when it was becoming more firmly established in France, while Germany from its feudal tradition was evolving the beginnings of the medium-sized farm. Old and young alike were beginning to take an interest in the outside world, and the newspaper was beginning to reach a country public where groups met together to read it in common.

It is difficult to assess the moral basis of the society of the old régime. According to Montesquieu it was honour, a conception which lost its appeal at the end of the eighteenth century and changed its meaning in the nineteenth. It could hardly have been loyalty to God, loyalty to the king or loyalty to an eternal moral law, for these sentiments would not have been thought 'intelligent', and 'intelligent' was the fashionable adjective of the day. 'This age', wrote Carlyle, 'is neither heroic, nor philosophical, nor religious, nor moral. It is, more than any other, the mechanical age.' This tendency was evident throughout spiritual as well as material life; in other words the mechanistic conception which science was evolving had affected moral life. It was best shown in Bentham, who meticulously calculated pleasures and pains in order to prove to his own satisfaction that the balance was favourable to virtue, by which he meant wisdom applied to work. Ure went on to say that Providence has assigned to man the glorious function of immensely improving on the products of nature by skilful initiative. In this way a link was established between moral and industrial mechanics and between moral and commercial book-keeping.

In this world where industry and commerce were already being personified everywhere as allegorical figures, proudly displayed on the façades of great new buildings and on the front pages of newspapers, and referred to in the edifying proclamations of private and public men, the universal criterion soon became the mutual trust which could be established between businessmen. This trust was based as much on business ability as on the honouring of a contract which was legally binding for the parties concerned. In England a man was said to be worth £1,000, £10,000, or £100,000. In France he was a man of first-rate or third-rate credit, a grading which determined his social career, his opportunities of accumulating capital, and his chance of getting a good discount. And side by side with the traditional organs of justice new institutions grew up; boards of directors of large business concerns, governing bodies of banks, and most important of all, the board of directors of the bank of issue. If a request for credit could surmount all these obstacles and be favourably received by the highest authority, the phrase used of a merchant that 'his word is worth its weight in gold' was literally true, since his request for credit ended in the issue of paper money which was everywhere accepted as the equivalent of gold. The new ambition was to have sound, reliable credit, and the new dream was to hold a directorship in one of the most influential companies.

A man with credit could enlist the wealth of others in addition to his own wealth. He could then be in the main stream of business: buying, selling, and increasing his capital. He borrowed to enlarge his sphere of action. He employed 100, 1,500, then 3,000 workmen. What was more difficult and even more praiseworthy, he commanded a market in which prices were aligned on those of the shrewdest dealer. It was up to him to choose carefully the nature of his business, the quality of his raw materials, his equipment and his partners. Steadily he climbed the ladder of the new aristocracy, that of industrial power. The grandfather was a peasant, the grandson was educated at a public school and ended by becoming a baron and a member of important councils; such, with various origins and vicissitudes, was the career of the Peels, the Radcliffes, the Cobdens and all the rest of that influential and vigorous English society. This was also the *cursus honorum* of several ancestors of the great French textile families. They were successful because they followed the stream of progress: they were prepared to abandon the old traditional agriculture when necessary, they ordered handlooms, they settled in the centre of the towns when mechanized industry, especially cotton, was concentrating there; and they aimed at a national and then an international market.

There was, however, a fundamental difference in this respect between France and England. Ever since the disastrous days of the Stuarts, who had misused their absolute power to confer upon themselves any number of financial privileges, English merchants had done their utmost to put their banks beyond the reach of royal greed. Democracy, according to Bentham, was necessary to reconcile the individual interests of the sovereign and the corporate interests of the financial aristocracy. Pitt (as we have seen) came to regret his excessive recourse to bank credit. The parliamentary régime was meticulously careful in respecting the free play of credit institutions. Gladstone refused to be a member of a commission on railways which he himself had urged should be set up, because his in-laws had powerful interests in railways.

In France the picture was quite different. The Bank, created just when the established power of the financiers balanced the rising power of Bonaparte, soon grew accustomed to a certain measure of subjection to the Emperor. In addition the successive changes in régime—republican, consular, imperial, monarchist, imperial again and finally parliamentary, first under a Bourbon and then under an Orleans prince—put the ruling aristocracy in a very unusual situation: there was always the fear that a revolution or a *coup d'état* might at any moment endanger its position. Virtue, in its eyes, consisted not in preserving as rigidly as possible the separation between political and economic power but, on the contrary, in maintaining the most rigid control of both at the same time. It would, naturally, be absurd to think that all the privileged people and all the politicians in England were as scrupulous as Gladstone, but the difference between English integrity and French shrewdness had so many consequences that it must be stressed.

It was Chateaubriand who said: 'Just as you can tell

a stag's age by the branches on its antlers, so today you can tell how many places a man holds by the number of oaths he has taken.' After 1830 the stag's antlers sprouted more branches than ever. In 1835, Talleyrand remarked: 'Yesterday there were only six of us in the House of Peers . . . we were all former members of the National Assembly, and we were more than eighty years old.' On the governing body of the Bank, founders, or the descendants of founders, were in control. It was a demonstration of the superb skill and shrewdness of a small body of men who had succeeded in weathering every storm simply because they had happened to be present at every successive debate and every council which had selected the ruling powers of the various régimes. And this group brought to the parliamentary life of the 1830s the lessons of the republican, imperial, and monarchist years. No matter of moment could be put through without close agreement between political and industrial power, which the small body of men at the top were best placed to bring about. Credit was dispensed by the middle classes, but always with considerable assistance from taxation. If sometimes the state asked the Bank for too much, it was because the Bank had always asked for a great deal from the state. The best instance was to be afforded by the railways, financed by the state and run by private companies whose profits were guaranteed by the state. This arrangement was a survival of the liberal régime, as well as of habits of mind and traditions of work inherited from the old régime. It took England more than a century to free itself from its old ways and establish the credit of its currency and of its Bank on a relatively independent foundation; France, building up its parliamentary and bourgeois system in haste, had to use such materials as were left over from the monarchy and the style of the building was affected accordingly.

Each generation, of course, added new blood to the direct heirs of the old régime (now greatly aging), but it was easier in France to make a career in politics than in business. In England the parliamentary leaders had first proved their mettle in industrial life. The middle classes grew up in the shadow of power before actually crossing its threshold, and fame, esteem, and an effective hold over public opinion was sometimes achieved by men who remained outside all public office. The best example was probably the amazing Wilberforce, who could have made a brilliant career in Parliament, and who might well have been prime minister, had he not chosen to remain a private individual in order to launch his formidable and successful campaign against the slave trade and slavery. This initiated a magnificent movement of national unity, and converted innumerable English consuls who had formerly been procuring slaves into apostles of the freedom of labour; and this was at a time when there was an emigration movement of whites who were not at all anxious to enter into competition with the negro. The career of a Decazes, a Guizot or a Thiers in France, is in sharp contrast to this, since they first made their name in politics, and consolidated their fame by a term of office before they plunged so advantageously into the economic stream. Decazes achieved a dukedom before he built Decazeville. Those who, like the Périers and Laffittes, made their name in credit and industry before achieving political fame were far smaller in number. Even so, their early beginnings were closely connected with the opportunities for profit offered by the good old days of the *assignats* and national property. Whilst in England the origins of the influential families of the 1830s have to be sought much earlier than the eighteenth century, in France the new Gouin concerns, still very insecure in 1848, were an isolated instance of success achieved by a family already engaged in business in the provinces under the old régime. It is not exaggerating the contrast to say that the great French bourgeois rose to power within thirty years, and that they looked like *nouveaux riches* beside the English middle-class gentlemen whose fortunes had taken one hundred and fifty years to make. The roots of the new society were planted deep in the hothouses of imperial protection. The French economic tree did not take kindly to the open air. Just when Cobden was risking his fortune to ensure the triumph of free trade in England,

French industrialists were fiercely protectionist. This was how Mimerel, a northern deputy, addressed the House: 'I like to think', he said, 'that it is not the Government's intention to disturb the nation's industry in its possession (*sic!*) of the country's custom.'

Obviously these habits were also the result of a difference in standards between English and French produce, though the latter had been superior to its rival even under Louis XVI. Then, too, as late as the middle of the nineteenth century, the consequences of customs of the old régime, whereby the bourgeoisie used law and jurisprudence to establish itself in France, were still operating; in England, however, it was almost in spite of the law that the middle classes were established. Of course the contrast with the English outlook was far more marked the farther east and the farther away from the Atlantic one went; ever since the sixteenth century the Atlantic had been bringing commercial and economic novelties to Europe. In Germany the real bankers were still the princes; they dominated with all the weight of their treasury the activities of any institutions which issued banknotes. Apart from a few business centres, Hamburg, or Frankfurt, private credit remained hesitant and every enterprising businessman had first to take the road to the court. It was quite hopeless for the bourgeoisie to dream of breaking free from these restraints in 1848. Germany had, it was true, a growing number of small manufacturers who were to achieve great wealth. These were like the Verlegers, whom Gerhart Hauptmann describes in his moving tragedy, *Die Weber*. The Verlegers went round distributing work to country mills just as English merchants had done in the seventeenth century, and others in the eighteenth. But whereas in France and particularly in England this type of middle-class merchant tended to disappear and make way for large-scale banking and industry, in Germany he still remained the only conspicuously active element in the economy of the 1840s. What was achieved from 1785 to 1899 in France and other nations with new middle-class dynasties, only came about in 1840–6 in Germany. There is an obvious paradox here, but one which a little thought will explain. The more revolutionary the origins of the bourgeoisie, the greater the dependence of industry on the state.

These differences between the various middle classes also throw light on the differing social problems. In Germany there was not, properly speaking, a labour problem before 1848; this does not mean to say that there was no poverty among the working classes. There was still the poverty characteristic of the old régime, which looked, sometimes with justification, to the old-style feudal overlord who was in honour bound to protect and feed the poor. In France and England the problem was different in kind. The bourgeois state held aloof in principle from any intervention in social problems, the regulation of which must be left to the natural course of events. But while in England political power, perhaps because it was relatively independent of economic power, had never entirely shed its feudal obligations (laws for the protection of the poor and old guild rules, for instance), in France the political power, which was closely linked with middle-class interests, became much more radical in the application of *laissez-faire*. The point is worth examining in greater detail.

At the beginning of the nineteenth century English workers could still invoke the Elizabethan Long Law, which by organizing the guilds had given their members and apprentices a certain protection. This law had never been repealed. In France it would have been quite unthinkable, after the Constituent Assembly had passed the radical measure introduced by Le Chapelier, for the workers to appeal to regulations laid down by Henry IV though they were contemporaneous and almost identical with the Long Law of Elizabethan England. In London there existed a body which, though more limited in its application than the French national workshops of 1848, could have been regarded as socialist in character had it not been inherited from the old régime. It was the Corporation of the Poor of the City of London, whose workshops dated from the seventeenth century and had increased during the eighteenth century in the great urban centres.

In 1832 there were more than sixty-seven corporations of this type, the Gilbert Incorporations. Of course, industrialists frequently attacked the disadvantages of the system and the idleness which was said to prevail, in the workhouse at Oxford for instance. Nevertheless, it did represent a living foundation, based on tradition and law, on which social legislation could build more easily, and it prevented the growth of socialist ideologies, and the temptation to experiment, in which for centuries England has indulged only with moderation and restraint. At first people's fears were aroused by the Malthusian doctrine and workhouse life was made into the dreadful caricature of charity denounced by Dickens in *Oliver Twist*. But eventually philanthropists raised their protests, not only in a private capacity, as Robert Owen was to do, but even openly in Parliament itself by people such as Lord Ashley and his friends, with the result that England was a century in advance of France in the foundation and application of labour laws.

Dickens had begun to stir up a great wave of sympathy for the victims of industry and a materialist civilization; he praised the nobleman who protected the people and his philanthropic friends in the middle classes, such as Pickwick; he violently and scornfully condemned the rest of the middle classes, for whom business was merely business, and thus helped to create a parliamentary opinion in favour of improving the lot of the worker. At this time the landed aristocrat himself, worried by the manufacturers' propaganda in favour of free trade which was threatening the price of his produce and especially of his corn, and worried by the railways which were cutting across private property and whose profits threatened road and canal shares, developed a lively enthusiasm for everything that might restrict the extortionate profits of industry, and advocated particularly a rise in the cost of labour. He supported the formation of corporations and clubs which protected the interests of specialist workmen. All this ended in the recognition of trade unions, the control of female and child employment, and the legal ten-hour working day. Greville vividly described the

curious nature of these debates about workers, in which
the ruling classes who held the reins of power were disturbed by the great wind of reform which was blowing
from the Conservative side, disconcerting the Liberals
and investing the Tory party with a youthful and reforming role. He wrote in his diary that he did not remember
ever seeing anything like the scene which followed the
ten-hour bill of Lord Ashley; some voters did not know
how they should vote, and simply voted with their friends;
the whole affair was awkward and unpleasant.

In contemporary France on the other hand, a large
majority, untroubled by doubts or distress of any kind,
were whole-heartedly behind the government in its ruthless suppression of the workers' riots in Paris and Lyons.
Even stranger were the comments of d'Argout, Minister
of Trade: 'Whatever the worker's lot may be,' he wrote,
'it is not the manufacturer's business to improve it. . . .
There is no law compelling a scale of wages to be fixed
for any particular industry. If there are contracts, they
affect only those who have signed them, and the government is not only powerless to insist on their observance
but positively cannot interfere in the matter. If the boards
of arbitration let themselves be drawn into the affair, the
court of appeal will quash the case.'

Thus the French bourgeoisie of 1830 was solidly united
in its demands for state aid for itself in the name of the
nation, but refused similar assistance to the workers in
the name of liberty. The aristocrats who had not rallied
round the new bourgeois order were driven out of the
House of Peers, electoral pressure kept them out of the
Chamber of Deputies, and the obligation to take the oath
kept them from the higher administrative offices. Thus,
although urbanization, industrialization and banking
were much less advanced in France than in England, the
people in power were exclusively middle-class. They were
so firmly entrenched that there was no possibility of a
new policy based on the charitable tradition of the old
régime.

The English working class had never lost faith in the
possibilities of the parliamentary system. However half-

hearted and long delayed electoral reforms might be, it remained confident, organizing itself to struggle within the framework of established institutions for right of entry into the legislative councils. The first signs of socialism did not appear in a struggle against the state, nor in legal battles, but in practical issues of everyday life. In France, however, the entire legislative body presented a united front against working-class hopes. A solution along the lines of co-operation or philanthropy was never a practical possibility at any stage. The bourgeois state in its entirety would have to be dismembered, along with legislative and administrative machinery closely integrated with it. Socialism took refuge in revolutionary theory. Substitution of a social republic for parliamentary machinery was the most moderate of its demands. Idealists called for the total suppression of the state, which offered to the workers nothing but the bayonets of the soldiers and the prosecutions of its police.

The importance of these differing legal outlooks between France and England cannot be too strongly emphasized. In England a body of traditions inherited from a previous age was powerful enough to influence conduct and affect legislation, and thus inhibit any solution which was too radically middle-class. In France the revolutionary tradition, which caused workers and bourgeois alike to rise up against anything reminiscent of the old system, enabled this newly emerging middle class, which really controlled the state, to consolidate its position. Neither the workers nor their supporters fully understood the fundamental explanation until Marxism came forward with a new and radical solution, and one which was this time radically anti-bourgeois; that was the idea of the inevitable class struggle. It was the result of the legal rationalism in which French socialism originated, rather than the consequence of actual material conditions of middle- and working-class life. So the people's new *Marseillaise*, the *Internationale*, gained ground in France. It was yet another instance of the stubborn persistence of the theoretical turn of mind in France, which already in 1789 had preferred the abstract theories of right to the realism of credit, and now in 1830 preferred the abstraction of parliamentary government to the reality of industrial experiment.

It is important to note that working-class poverty was no less appalling in England than in France. It might even be argued that it was worse. We hear of the hardships endured at Cambrésis by workers living on starvation wages, for which an entire family had to work for ten to twelve hours a day, and of the scandalous state of degradation of the 'dangerous class', mostly made up of the unemployed who 'squatted' in the ruins of filthy dwellings in the heart of Paris, where the pickpockets and depraved murderers emerged at nightfall, and where the descriptions in Eugène Sue's novel are not at all overdrawn. But Dickens gives us ample proof that the horrors in the slums of London and Manchester were every whit as dreadful as those of Paris; this urban poverty was probably even more widespread geographically on the other side of the Channel where industry expanded more rapidly and more extensively than in the French countryside. French philanthropists were unanimously of the opinion that in the south and west the old cities devoted to trade and agriculture remained clean and tidy, sometimes even welcoming the poor, and did not develop the horrors of the industrial and particularly the textile cities of the north.

England had her Benthamite theorists at the beginning of the century, but by 1830 their popularity was on the wane, to the advantage of pragmatism. Middle-class France remained devoted to theory, the attitude of Thiers and Guizot. This bourgeois theory was opposed by a rigid and uncompromising working-class theory—socialism.

French socialism originated at one and the same time from the great hopes which mechanization had aroused in the mind of Saint-Simon and the doubts it awakened in Sismondi. Saint-Simon proposed a reorganization of society which was to take advantage of the railway to establish universal peace, and use technical progress to banish a useless aristocracy and abolish landed property, since the idle rich frittered away the income from this in empty pleasure. In any case he placed the magnates of industry or banking at the top of the hierarchy. In contrast, Sismondi, struck chiefly by the squalor of working-class slums, blamed technical progress and even suggested that research laboratories should be closed. The disciples of Saint-Simon, after the riots and revolutions of 1830, blamed the idle industrialists and bankers for all this poverty. Bazard demanded that the tax paid by labour to capital should be suppressed.

The basic idea of a profound transformation of society was clearly stated: there must be an end to the exploitation of man by man; it must be replaced by a collective or communist structure, ensuring a fair distribution of labour and property. Opinions varied on this point too; Proudhon insisted on the logical conclusion, 'property is theft'; he wanted to do away with any kind of state. Louis Blanc, on the other hand, hoped that universal suffrage and the establishment of a republic would result in socialized factories and workshops being organized by the state.

In England, Owen tried at first to put socialist experiments into practice and almost succeeded, in 1830, in grouping the workers' syndicates (authorized from 1822) into a vast trade union, and so virtually founding a labour party. And although he failed, it was nevertheless on these lines that the English working-class movement was to be organized fifty years later.

French socialism, on the contrary, provided an essential political content to the philosophy of Hegel and Feuerbach which had a formative influence on Karl Marx in Germany; and Engels helped his friend to a better understanding of socialist Saint-Simonism. Even Leroux contributed to the German theory of the irreversible tide of history which leads from capitalism to socialism by the gradual dwindling of profits. Later observation of English industrialism was to round off Marx's thinking. From a French seed, socialism grew into a European tree—the brotherhood envisaged by Gracchus Babeuf, revived on modern lines, in revolt against the injustice which enabled the idle rich to profit from other peoples' labour; socialism prepares to call on the workers of the world to unite.

THE AESTHETICS OF PROGRESS

It has been said that the man of 1830 was by temperament a Romantic; we shall try to clarify the meaning of this new feeling by suggesting that the Romantics had discovered history, and that their new perception was an awareness of time.

Gently, almost imperceptibly, this new spirit had been evolving since the middle of the eighteenth century. Greek perfection had, of course, been studied for centuries, discussed, held up as an example, and judged far superior to the moderns, but now this admiration for the antique took a new turn. Lebeau's fine description of the house of Caylus will serve as an illustration. 'The hall of his house was reminiscent of ancient Egypt. The first thing you saw was a handsome Egyptian statue five feet five inches high. The staircase was decorated with medallions and curios from China and America. In the house itself you were surrounded by Egyptian, Etruscan, Greek and Roman gods and priests and magistrates, amongst which a few Gallic figures hardly dared show themselves.' He had casts made in Malta of two Phoenician inscriptions, the deciphering of which led to much competition. He founded a prize in the *Académie des Belles Lettres* to encourage the study of the customs of ancient peoples, and to prevent artists from making mistakes through ignorance of historical costume.

This new passion for antiquity seized the whole of cultured Europe when news of the excavations at Herculaneum and Pompeii were made known, and received a further impetus when Champollion deciphered the hieroglyphics. German universities opened numerous centres for historical studies, and philology replaced the old aesthetic appreciation in classical studies. In short, cultured emphasis shifted from beauty to historical truth.

We have already had occasion to mention the love of antiquity which gave a new fascination to Rome in 1780

and filled first English and then European interiors with
a whole new range of ornaments and knick-knacks. It had
an astounding success in England, where the fashion began, especially in country houses. It was the age of Chip-
pendale, which represented the modern manner of the
early industrial era. It seemed as though the middle classes
wished to evolve their own interpretation of antiquity.
Middle-class taste tended first of all to adopt 'perfect'
lines imitated from Greek and Roman models. The design of antique bowls, vases and jars, the lines of folds
and drapery were carefully studied and copied by many
European craftsmen, particularly those working in England under the direction of the potter Wedgwood, or the
iron-founder Matthew Boulton. The same influence was
apparent in the delicate scroll-work which decorate Adam
interiors in England; in the small and delicate pieces of
furniture carved by Riesener for connoisseurs at the
French court. Marie-Antoinette in particular loved Riesener's skilful work. The same influence can be seen in
the modifications—made during the course of building—
to several charming German palaces, especially in Potsdam, so as to insert a few straight lines into the elaborate
rococo which was suddenly discovered to be too servile
an imitation of French taste. It was this same taste for
classical decoration and furnishing, though in a very un-
adorned and humanized form, which developed into the
Biedermeyer style in Germany and Austria. This taste for
the antique, which originated in the first half of the
eighteenth century in Rome, where it was passionately
debated by artists of varying talents and of all nationalities,
was made fashionable in Germany by Winckelmann and
later by Goethe himself. It was a fashion which commended itself to the new middle-class families all the more
readily since the decoration and type of furniture it inspired was simpler to make and less costly to reproduce
in the workshops of the master cabinet-makers and car-
penters than the extravagant fancies of late baroque. The
middle classes, first of England and then of France, persuaded Europe to abandon complicated and delicate ve-
neering and fussy motifs and use full-grained woods, par-

ticularly the new mahogany. This English taste, which combined classical form with middle-class simplicity, took a firm hold on Europe, remained in favour during the time of the Empire, and found its full expression in the Louis-Philippe style. The triumph of the Pompeian style in Parisian decoration was apparently complete at the time of the Directory when even women's fashions were inspired by what was believed to be Roman. Talma and Josephine de Beauharnais built their mansions around classical marble patios. It was not only in the minor arts that the Roman style was successful; the fashion affected everything.

In 1780 David electrified artistic circles in Rome with his three Horatii, proud and resolute, their faces expressing the courage and military virtues of Rome. The painting shows three arched porticoes, three women, three swords and three heroes; the perfect symmetry of their attitudes was intended as an expression of Roman discipline. In David's art antiquity was not yet a history lesson. It was an attempt to convey an eternal virtue by means of a noble style, bold design and unequivocal colours. In his studio, David, as we know, preserved a rigid discipline. This pageant-master of the revolutionary festivals and painter of the rising imperial fame was indeed convinced of the absolute value of his art and when his days of activity and fame were over he passed on his aesthetic certainty to Ingres. We have only to compare his early portraits with the famous *Madame Morel* in the Louvre. But Ingres was a pupil with ideas of his own, as we can see by comparing the *Danse de Léonidas aux Thermopyles* with *Thétis suppliant Jupiter*. Even in later life David was still fascinated by the depiction of movement, in painting as a means of expressing courage, manliness and the doing of great deeds. The majesty of Jupiter, on the other hand, is conveyed by his immobility and by the sculptured lines of his throne, while Thetis, sinuous to the point of distortion, foreshadows in the young artist the aging painter of the voluptuous Odalisques of a later date. Antiquity was no longer a reservoir of controversial subjects for vast canvases or a source of all the virtues, as it had been at the time of the Revolution. With Ingres, classical perfection turned middle class.

Long orations in classical style had been much in vogue in the Revolutionary assemblies. The use of Greek and Roman first names, which had persisted so long in other Latin countries, only went out in France with the return of the most Christian kings: it persists to this day in the south. This taste for things classical reached its peak with the style known as the 'return from Egypt', which was to the lower middle classes what mansions built on Pompeian lines were to the rich and fashionable. They chose Jacob furniture in their houses and admired the triumphal arches of Percier and Fontaine. This style symbolized the destiny of the middle classes, who were unable to reorganize the economy which the Revolution had destroyed and suffered the Empire until the moment of defeat.

The taste for antiquity had created not only English kick-knacks and the Louis XVI and Empire styles but also a new outlook; it focused attention on the dimension of time which the eighteenth century had hardly noticed. The problem of time had, it is true, obsessed Pascal and religious thinkers, and led to mysticism, but it also led many great minds to irreligion. Men shrank from its mystery. After 1780, however, the notion of time became more human. It was no longer linked with metaphysics but with nostalgia and history. First the English, then the French, put ruins in their parks, where fine old trees were preferred to model plantations. The death of a young woman left them inconsolable, their grief was lifelong, and Chateaubriand's description of the funeral of *Atala* set a fashion in literature. The love of history was mingled with melancholy at the irrevocability of life, for which neither divine goodness nor unbridled orgies could afford consolation any longer; when the old poetic forms were revived in the poems of André Chénier, melancholy was their predominant theme. All intensity or delicacy of feeling was submerged in the vague, undefined concept of evolution, a reflection of the great tide of life itself.

When Jouffroy delivered his lectures to an enraptured

student audience at the *Collège de France* in 1825, his subject was 'The Problem of Human Destiny'; and when Christianity became fashionable again, it was supported not by arguments from the Word of God or from Holy Scripture, but from the history of the early days of Christianity.

Even before the triumph of economic individualism and the rights of freedom, men were trying to read their destiny in history. Poetry, the theatre and philosophy no longer shrank away from the problem of time, while the middle classes were no longer afraid of it since they realized that it was on their side. Every businessman, every family which had left the countryside to build up the new urban civilization, was acutely aware of it. The middle-class economist too, continually proclaimed it, or demonstrated it by theorem and corollary in the manner of Bentham. However harsh and unjust the industrial society might appear to be in its ruthless treatment of the poor, it was its stubborn determination to fit itself for its task which in the end relieved the wretchedness it had caused everywhere in its earlier stages. Time would bring redress provided man held fast to the idea of freedom.

Time as it was experienced by the artist or studied by the philosopher and the historian and which distinguished human beings from each other even more than space—this was the theme of romanticism. In its treatment by Stendhal, Michelet or Edgar Quinet it was a great theme, for it dealt with the history of individual man and the history of mankind.

A comparison of the same Napoleonic story seen through the eyes first of David then of Gros (Bonaparte visiting the plague-victims at Jaffa or the battlefield at Eylau) reveals the effort that was being made to seize the historical moment and to derive emotion not so much from the majesty of the whole as from the realism of detail. There was as yet no sureness of touch in the realism: corpses were piled on top of each other or, in Géricault's paintings, starving wretches writhed in agony on a raft. It was a realism in which carefully built up detail, as with David, and only later, with Daumier, captured a vivid, fleeting impression. Géricault was not content simply to ask his friend Delacroix to act as his model for the men on the raft, but actually went to the Hôpital Beaujon to paint the dead and the dying.

It is often said that romantic painting, like the new history, was revolutionary or, to use the then fashionable word, liberal. True, when we admire the vast canvases of the time on the walls of the Louvre it is not easy to distinguish the conservative from the liberal. Already in 1819 Delescluzes was protesting against this over-simplified conception of art which interpreted paintings in the light of political ideas. But this conception did reflect the novelty of this new trend and the dangers it held for the traditionalists. It is perhaps absurd to see in the *Raft of the Medusa* nothing more than a devastating criticism of the Minister of Marine. The Minister himself was most tactful; he commissioned a picture from Géricault as acknowledgement of his genius, but the subject was to be the *Sacré Cœur*. Géricault, disappointed, declined the offer and left for England.

Time cannot be expressed on canvas as easily as space. The French Romantics, as we know, owed much to the English painter Bonington. He showed them how to capture, in a rapid sketch, a single fleeting mood of the landscape he was painting, or a burst of sunlight on a passing cloud. The effects of light achieved by Constable and especially by Turner were truly remarkable: the fact was that painters who had been seeking to express feeling through line since Watteau's time had at last discovered colour at the very time when chemistry was enriching the artist's palette. Decamps was a chemist and Delacroix kept his palettes as he did his sketches. It was through an interplay of colour, as Goethe had foreseen even before Chevreul, that the surface of the picture might be made to evoke time, which was now the most important element in human feeling.

Géricault was undoubtedly the first great French painter to use the new English methods. His *Horse Stopped by Slaves*, painted in Rome as early as 1816, did aim to show movement by the play of muscles, using colours typical of Michelangelo, but in *Racing at Epsom* in 1821 it is the colouring of the sky and the ground which gives an illusion of speed.

Another painter who was feeling his way simultaneously towards realism and the use of colour, trying always to make the surface of his canvas express time, was Delacroix. He had begun by trying his hand at historical subjects (*The Massacre of Chios,* 1824), before turning history into the symbol of the victorious advance of the Revolution (*Portrait of Liberty,* 1830). Now art concentrated passionately on movement; but barely had the great victory been won, when it seemed as if inspiration had suddenly run out. This happened at a time when society was becoming more orderly; Casimir Périer was selected for office rather than Laffitte, before the choice finally settled on Guizot. All this intense effort at synthesis, which had led painters to exalt time with a simultaneous use of history, colour and realistic detail, began to slacken and become diffused, as if exhausted by its own success. Finally Delaroche, Isabey and Decamps achieved little more than cold, anecdotal history, foreshadowing the worst banalities of the following generation. Dupré and Théodore Rousseau also limited themselves to the delights of colour in landscapes in the manner of de Cuyp; and even in Africa Delacroix did not discover the splendid scenes which had inspired the 'Orientales' of a previous generation, but an opportunity for accurate descriptive painting.

From the end of the eighteenth century German literature had also rebelled against the French models of the age of Louis XIV, and had substituted praise of the transitory and ephemeral for their ideal of unchanging man. This too was an attempt to bring time into art. In 1767, Lessing, meditating on Winckelmann's discoveries, was fired with enthusiasm for a group of classical sculpture (a late example) and wrote a book on the Laocoon. The plastic arts may have found difficulty in conveying an impression of time, but poetry was the natural medium for its expression. It was at Goethe's suggestion, as an act of self-discipline, that Schiller immersed himself in historical studies. He read everything that had been written about the revolt of the Swiss cantons, and the result was *William Tell* written in one draft and performed a few months before the premature death of the man whom Wagner considered the finest representative of the 'young Germany'. It is worth considering Schiller's career more closely: before achieving *William Tell* with its masterly analysis of events and character, Schiller had been experimenting and was first carried away by political idealism (a phase in which he wrote the mediocre *History of the Netherlands* and the play *Don Carlos*); then, gaining in power and self-confidence with his studies of seventeenth-century Germany, he wrote his *History of the Thirty Years War,* which led on to the fine *Wallenstein* trilogy. In this he already reached a level of objectivity which he proudly announced to Goethe as a victory. 'Wallenstein does not interest me', he wrote. 'He does not seem to me to be noble in any of his deeds.' In his *Maid of Orleans* he altered the tragic ending and idealized the harsh reality in a last revolt of his artistic temperament; it was his last historical failure, for then came *William Tell,* which was acknowledged in Germany as his finest dramatic masterpiece.

Faced with the extraordinary intellectual career of this German poet, whose dominating interest was history, it is interesting to reflect on the progress achieved since the tentative rationalizations of Corneille. Schiller had thought deeply over the outline of philosophy which Emmanuel Kant had at first entitled *Prolegomena to all Future Metaphysics* before he confronted the human mind with his two famous *Kritiken.* In his philosophy time was a prerequisite of feeling. Schiller held that man's destiny could be fulfilled in the harmonious combination of instinct and morality, and though he never learned Greek, the Greek world, as it appeared through the admiring eyes of poets and tragedians of his day, seemed to him as dangerous as the Kantian rigidity. Thus it was that Schiller opened the door wide to German Romanticism. Goethe held out longer than any of the rest against this assertion of instinct. His Greek tragedies, though separated from Racine's by a hundred years, have all their consummate art.

Just as French Romanticism originated when the classical art of David and Ingres was in its prime, so German poetry too experienced this simultaneous tendency towards classicism and romanticism. But though Goethe was more successful with classical style than Schiller, he too shared Schiller's preoccupation with history, as witness his *Egmont* and *Torquato Tasso*. He also had a great sense of the reality of daily life and succeeded in giving it nobility in *Hermann and Dorothea*. His long life span enabled him to be a contemporary of David, Gros, Géricault and Delacroix, and he expressed in his poetry everything they had attempted to capture in their painting—the flow of history and the sense of realism; and his verse had both music and the brilliance of colour to evoke the destiny of man. This was achieved most successfully in *Faust*. *Faust* is no incarnation of liberty. The most classical, the most antique of the German poets mistrusted to the very end this idealization, this abstraction which was so characteristically French. But *Faust* is a poem in praise of movement, and of man's genius for seeking happiness, which he finds only in creative action, in the creation of material wealth.

This juxtaposition of French painting and German poetry is an extreme over-simplification of the essential characteristics of romanticism. France had her poets too. Vigny, the aristocrat, also defended the concept of truth in art, though more concisely than Schiller (a plebeian) had done in the *Maid*. He held that truth enables a man to achieve self-mastery when he is in danger of being ruled by his instincts. The brief sketches in his *Servitudes et grandeurs militaires* contain more realism even than Goethe's *Dichtung und Wahrheit*. Nevertheless, French dramatic poetry developed late in comparison with that of Germany. When the historical plays of Victor Hugo were raising storms of protest on the Parisian stage, Schiller, who had profoundly shocked the theatres at Mannheim, Stuttgart and Dresden in his youth, had been dead for twenty years. Germany was probably more responsive than France to this new exciting awareness of time.

Above all Germany was a century in advance of

France in music, an art which is probably more concerned with time than any other. We cannot attempt a summary of that period of musical history which included all the greatest geniuses. We shall merely note the contrast: at a time when Mozart had been dead for more than twenty years; when Haydn had just died and been mourned in Germany and in England as the greatest musical genius of all time; and when Beethoven was at the height of his fame, it was Rossini who was drawing the fashionable crowds in Paris. In 1810 it was Rossini who conquered the French capital and made the fortune of the *Théâtre des Italiens*. It is understandable that the *Barber of Seville* should be preferred to Mozart's *Marriage of Figaro*, although it was composed in a fortnight, so enchanting is Rossini's airy lightness; but a great many inferior imitators were also successful. It could only be the poor taste of the French public that made them prefer Donizetti and Bellini and later Auber, Hérold, Offenbach and other Cherubinis. Kreutzer, solo violin at the *Théâtre des Italiens*, whose admirable technique was learnt from Viotti, never played the sonata which Beethoven dedicated to him, and this is the only reason the idolized composer of *Lodoïska* and *Aristippe Ipsiboé* has been saved from oblivion.

The French looked for flourishes, lightness, charm and grace in music and above all not too much emotion. They certainly did not want the torrent of feeling that was sweeping through German music at that time.

The difference was not one of national temperament but of psychological and social climate. This can be illustrated by two parallel careers: Meyerbeer, born in Berlin of a rich family of Jewish bankers, made money in Vienna out of Italian music, and later had a great success in Paris where he found in Scribe a librettist worthy of him; and he enriched French opera with the *Huguenots* and the *Prophet*. This 'nobody', as Wagner called him, stifled the early career of Berlioz. Mendelssohn, born in Hamburg of a rich Jewish banking family, was lucky enough to please Goethe and to be influenced by Johann-Sebastian Bach. He was a tremendous success in London, and later in Leipzig and Dresden. He founded the Dresden academy which became the musical centre of the new Germany, and supported and encouraged Schumann there.

While France was content with light music which copied the technique of the eighteenth-century Italians, and even ignored the lessons learned from Gluck, Germany was experiencing an extraordinary musical development. The eighteenth century had defined the scale, and the orchestral instruments. With Haydn the structure of symphonies and sonatas marked a distinct departure from the old *Suites* and the new and classical architecture of composition was introduced. Mozart, a master of emotion as well as of the keyboard, surprised and disconcerted his contemporaries by the unexpected daring of his phrases and musical confessions. But he still belonged to a generation which travelled cosmopolitan Europe. He had made a tour of the capitals: Munich, Vienna, Brussels, Paris, Milan, Rome, and Naples. He could almost be said to have composed to the trotting of horses. Austria, however, was more open to European influence than Bach's Thuringia. The new feeling for German concentration, its enrichment and its diffusion by and through Europe originated from Vienna and from the palace of the Esterhazys. They were the great patrons first of Haydn and later of Beethoven.

At the turn of the eighteenth century the final improvements were being made to the pianoforte, which was gradually replacing the harpsichord. The piano with hammers did not need a double keyboard to modify its *forte* and its tones, and it inspired Beethoven to write one of his most magnificent sonatas. But with Beethoven the era of cosmopolitanism was at an end. He was no great traveller, for his life was lived on an inner plane and his geography was purely musical. Like his masters, Beethoven at first avoided the expression of personal feelings in his music. But, even though he could no longer hear it, music became his only outlet for self-expression after 1810; his physical handicap shut him in upon himself completely, so that at the end of his life the only way in which he could express himself was by scribbling on scraps of paper and above all by pouring all his deepest emotions into his compositions. Almost as soon as it had been defined, musical form was enlarged and altered by this tremendous revelation, which amazed and shocked well-to the young Mendelssohn. The great movement in space bred society and even disturbed Goethe, as he confided which had characterized the generation of 1780 was followed by this passionate exploration in time.

The new generation in German music began where Beethoven had left it. The changes in the design of instruments led to a vast improvement in the technique of instrumentalists and made possible a great delicacy of touch. After Clementi the outstanding pianists were Moscheles and Clara Wieck, who became Schumann's wife, and Paganini became the leading violinist. Music had reached the point where it could express every feeling from the outpourings, joys and sorrows of Schubert to the passions, violent emotions, leaping enthusiasm and melancholy of Robert Schumann.

This flood of music from Germany and the Rhine was received with enthusiasm by the rest of Europe, except by France. Wagner was then in his adolescence. This music was brilliant at expressing the inexpressible; it was beyond the sphere of poetry and conveyed the passage of inner time. It burst upon the theatre, giving romantic drama a power which the artificiality of opera in general and Italian opera in particular had never been able to achieve. Beethoven's *Fidelio* and *Egmont,* even more than Mozart's *Don Juan,* gave added depth to feelings which the words had done no more than state. Musical drama burst into new fields with Weber's *Freischutz.* Only music could express all that magic and witchcraft, and give dramatic life to the dialogue between man and Satan which stretches human stature from heaven to hell. The psychological destiny of human history was once more rooted in the Middle Ages which the eighteenth century had so little understood. Their seething unrest found even stronger expression in romantic music than in the drawings or the poetry of Victor Hugo, and provoked an even more violent emotional reaction than did the pseudo Ossian revivals.

This age of emotion which ignored the boundaries of reason and argument found its finest expression in music, thanks to the daring new combinations of sound. Eventually even France proved receptive to the new art with Delacroix in the 1840s. The circle of admirers surrounding the young Chopin, who was supported, tyrannized, cared for and overwhelmed by the impetuous George Sand, was still small, but it was very enthusiastic. The Pole's rival, Liszt, was a virtuoso as well as a composer, and his liaison with Madame d'Agoult shocked polite society. One of the most amazing representatives of all this passionate young generation was Berlioz. The composer of *Benvenuto Cellini* never became wealthy, for his work was too unlike the popular Italian operas filling the theatres, but he was an important symbol of what was to come. His life, like that of the Brontës, was spent in the imaginative creation of tremendous passions, although in reality he indulged in little more than moderately sentimental adventure. His *Symphonie fantastique* was an attempt to portray the history of his love and he used music to convey his deepest feelings. In his search for self-expression he included in his music the drums of an execution, the *Dies irae* of the Gregorian liturgy, and a witches' sabbath. The man was, indeed, a symbol of the great gulf between a society which was a hundred years behind the times in matters of taste and a young generation which suddenly and brutally erupted with its *Sturm und Drang*.

It may be true that France was a hundred years ahead of Germany scientifically and probably politically, but its sensitivity at that time seemed blunted. French painting had never been so brilliant, but it was sixty years since Lessing had shown that painting could not be made to express time. Time was poetry and music; it invaded German metaphysics, and broke out in the sufferings of the young Goethe and of Schiller fifty years earlier than in Victor Hugo's *Légende des Siècles*. It poured out in German music sixty years before it brought unhappiness to

Berlioz and, even then, was surrounded by a society still unwilling to listen to him.

The French power of rational thought had been fruitful, especially in the technical field, but it was closely linked with a love of order. After 1840 it was through a wave of disorder that the face of Europe was transformed; it was swept along by great storms, and a wild speeding up of time. The result was the age of romanticism and, later, a new realism which destroyed the old economic structures. The most striking concrete expression of this was the railway.

THE CALL OF THE PEOPLES

In the nineteenth century Europe was undergoing major political changes, in which the railways played a considerable rôle. They were not always the organ of progress, however. The countries which were already almost united in 1830 were consolidated by the coming of the railway in 1870, but those still unprepared saw new bands of steel, forged by the old empires, tightening around them. In other words Germany and Italy on the one hand, and the Austrian Empire on the other, emerged from the railway revolution in a stronger position. The principle of nationalism won the day across the Alps and the Rhine, but was unsuccessful among the Slav peoples. In order to understand this fact properly we must think ourselves back to the eve of 1830. It was as if every possible nation was hastening to proclaim its right to exist before the railways were built, so that it might be acknowledged as a nation by the transport system which defined the political boundaries of Europe for over a century.

The reasons for this strange situation must be sought in the increasing speed of means of communication which preceded the building of railways and made them popular. The comparative ease of travel, the improvement in postal services and the optical telegraph (as well as the marches of campaigning armies) passed ideas from one end of Europe to the other. These ideas aroused the interest of the uneducated and unsophisticated mass of the people. As we know, catchwords and slogans can generate currents of enthusiasm: for instance, Victor Hugo's magnificent metaphors acquire their full meaning in the context of this Europe of 1830. He called the theatre a point of focus for the poet and a resounding echo. Hence specific phrases or lines of dialogue drew an eagerly responsive public whenever they were spoken on the stage.

Let us consider only three words: firstly the word *race*. Hitherto its meaning had always been very aristocratic or possibly even feudal. It was used by the nobleman to describe his ancestral descent. Used by a royal line, the word took on a special majesty; the Bourbons for example were 'the third race'. But the revolutions had placed these titles of nobility within the reach of other social groups. True, the newly-rich bourgeois of 1830 would probably have been mocked had he spoken of his 'race'. But used collectively, to refer to a whole people, the word race now conferred a kind of ennobling dignity. Already Sieyès, in his defence of the Third Estate, had laid the foundations of his popularity by attacking Boulainvilliers, who had claimed that the French nobility were descended from Germanic conquerors and held their privileges by right of conquest. If that were so, said Sieyès, the Gallic people must drive them out and exact a military revenge. The dubious proceedings of the terror might thus be justified by being called a military operation. Augustin Thierry later adopted this strange theory, and based his *Histoire* on the principle of racial conflict.

Doubtless the young intellectuals living, learning and loving in nineteenth-century Paris were sometimes suspicious of this concept, charged as it was with a suspect mysticism. Michelet and Quinet forcibly condemned the very idea of race. Yet neither of them was insensitive to the new dignity of the *people*; they were proud to be identified with barbarians, and the new status the word conferred, for it was after all the people who should be the rulers and not the kings. The time was now ripe. Chateaubriand hesitated to claim that race carried all the essential values; he cited Christianity and Jerusalem. To this

Bible Michelet was to answer with the *Bible de l'humanité*:
the people achieved their highest dignity not in the Church,
but in universal brotherhood on earth. This revival of the
concept of inheritance and traditions necessitated wide
reading. Philosophy came first with the admirable lectures
of Jouffroy at the *Collège de France*; then history, which
resulted in the discovery of claims to nobility not of sover-
eigns as in the past, but of previously little-known collective groups now quite suddenly invested with importance.
In this search the French people naturally earned the
gratitude of humanity; for they graciously acknowledged
the claims of many peoples besides themselves. Edgar
Quinet pursued German studies and as the son-in-law of
a Rumanian poet also studied the 'eight million men who
are knocking imploringly at the threshold of our Western
societies'. A chair of Slavonic language and literature
was founded at the *Collège de France* and offered to the
famous Pole Mickiewicz, who was a poet, conspirator,
philologist and crusader of the emigration, as well as
being inevitably an inseparable comrade-in-arms of Quinet
and Michelet.

If 'the people' in the singular retained its prestige in the
twentieth century (for reasons connected as much with
the industrial socialism which followed on the railways as
with the feelings of 1830), the peoples, in the plural, were
still regarded with a certain suspicion at that date. This
was probably because of the sense in which the word had
been used by the monarchy (royal or imperial), when
'our peoples' suggested the art of dividing to rule. Avoiding the use of 'peoples' in the plural, nationalists preferred
to say 'nations'. The 'nation' had acquired the glory of
the Revolution, and the word had marched round Europe
covered with victorious standards. The two words 'country' and 'nation' enabled every man to cherish his belief
in the essential goodwill of others. At the moment when
the outburst of German patriotism was causing uneasiness
in France, Quinet himself was trying to rescue the basic
idea from excesses.

The man who best expressed the idea of nationhood
was probably Mazzini, the remarkable moving spirit of

'Young Italy', a secret society which began the struggle for the unity, liberty and independence of its country. Nations could be defined in terms of geography, history or language, but Mazzini discovered a hidden force of faith in one's country. This was the heyday of 'nationalism', when the word was first introduced and meant an alliance of peaceful peoples. Not that Mazzini refrained from action. He was the heart and soul of every plot, and the force behind every riot. He not only constituted the rallying point for Italians eager to free themselves from Austria, but also united the Swiss of the regeneration and courageous Poles in his Young Europe movement.

In every country in Europe the new words and the impressive demonstrations which accompanied them met with extraordinary success. The princes were incredibly indulgent to these movements. University professors famous for their devotion to their country were honoured. Historical studies and the old traditions of folk culture were held in high esteem. At the same time the cult of the national language took on a new meaning.

In Germany, German had been the major language for the last fifty years, thanks to Lessing, Goethe and Schiller. But it seemed as if the long eclipse of German by the French of monarchic society was now provoking a widespread reaction, based on the new and omnipotent philology led by Fichte, with his *Discourse to the German Nation*. A political ideal was beginning to form in Germany, though it was only conceived in general terms at that date. Fichte was not the only successor of Kant to play an important part in its development: soon Hegel was preaching the idealization of the state. The historical and particularly the philological schools made rapid strides: they lauded Alexander for regrouping cities into an Empire, they began to discover a kind of grand march of history from India to Europe, in which the nineteenth-century Germans were to be the torch-bearers. Congresses were held at which the doctrine and dogma of Germanism were discovered; they were tentative and isolated at first but soon grew in number until a great organization was formed covering all the universities and giving strength to the new nationalism.

There was perhaps less eagerness in Italy than in Germany to make claims on history. During his ambassadorship Chateaubriand had, in 1829, diagnosed the real significance of the Italian *mal du siècle* as a need of national brotherhood. Austrian rule was more unbearable in the peninsula than in the small German states, for in Italy the Austrian really was a foreigner and a barbarian. The people of Italy, energetic but without staying power, expected great results from acts of bravery which too often ended in abrupt defeat.

In Poland hopes of a new spiritual country lingered on even in 1830. The King of Prussia had allowed Polish to be used alongside German in administrative documents. Through the indulgent goodwill of Alexander and the liberalism of Grand Duke Constantin Czartoryski, the University of Vilna attracted a brilliant group of Germans and Poles, while in Warsaw Linde was drawing up a great Polish dictionary. All this activity was alas brought to an end by the catastrophe of 1830. Whilst the 'pilgrims' relapsed into mysticism, the Polish fatherland was stifled by Russianization. The Prussian part of Poland was spared for several years. All the remaining intellectuals and conspirators took refuge in Germany to become a source of great uneasiness to Nicholas, and soon to the King of Prussia himself, until William IV finally expelled the suspects. But of all the masters of Poland, Metternich was the harshest; when Galicia was rebellious, he allowed the peasants to be incited against the nobles in a terrible medieval rising, and a price of ten florins was paid for every nobleman's head. Then many Poles gave up all hope of salvation for Poland, except through the salvation of all Slavs, and resigned themselves to the idea of a Russia which would protect the Slavs against the Germans.

This Slav feeling is very marked in Kollar's work. Czechoslovakia, in fact, lies at a remarkable crossroads; the Czechs are neighbours of the Poles, but also understand the aspirations of the Austrian Slavs, an ocean of related peoples with Hungary like an isolated island in the middle. And although Prague was surrounded by German influences it was protected by its mountain shield. It was affected by the great philological and literary movement which swept through the German universities; the works of Herder were eagerly welcomed, translated and expanded. Szafarzik published his *Slavonic Ethnography* in 1842. It was estimated that the European Slavs, numbering approximately eighty millions, were divided into fewer groupings than the Germans, although they were more numerous than the latter. The old peaceful virtues and the civilizing influence of the Slavs, which had already been praised by Herder, were remembered. The old traditions had to be honoured once more and the Slav languages allowed to enrich each other in order to strengthen racial unity. The list of great men who contributed to this task is too long to quote, but their names are to be found on the pedestals of statues in almost every east European capital. Serbian and Bulgarian histories were written, grammars were compiled and old legends revived, while a whole spate of poetry resulted from this revival of the ancient unity of the Slav peoples. But Latin was still often the only common language between one people and another, and the Hungarians, who oppressed the Slavs dependent on Pest all the more ruthlessly as their own national pride became stronger ('a Slav is not a man'), put Croat deputies into difficulties when they forbade them the use of Latin in Pressburg. It was in vain that enlightened Hungarians feared the explosion of wrath of so many subject peoples; Kossuth, the very incarnation of Hungarian patriotism, was the most intractable defender of Magyarization.

Thus the Slavs were not particularly united in spite of Kollar's affirmation; it was no light task to create for them a common language, and the presence of the Rumanians did not simplify it.

These divisions made the shrewd policy of the Austrian Empire all too easy. Prussia had succeeded in uniting the Prussian country squire and his peasant in one patriotic movement. In Austria, the Magyar or German commander was in charge of Croat soldiers and could count on the old loyalties of the local men. Thus, in face of the irresistible movement of German nationalism, Slavonic nationalism could not succeed soon enough, before the coming of the railways reinforced the framework of the Austrian administration for another hundred years. Its structure became stronger than in the days of the Holy Roman Empire, although Vienna had to lose control of both Germany and Italy at the same time, because of the railway.

Germany in particular benefited from the system of ideas which bound together the concepts of race, nation, country and language. The philosophy of Kant's followers first set Marx thinking, but it exerted an even more active influence through Engels, thanks to the innumerable chairs of philosophy which were springing up like mushrooms in Germany. These new teachings revealed affinities between the agrarian civilizations of eastern Europe, the German agrarian civilizations and all the communal civilizations of India about which little was known in detail but whose originality was being studied with the greatest interest. These teachings also revealed similarities between the roots of German vocabulary and those of Asian dialects; Aryanism was on the move throughout the vast Indo-European world. It ignored anything which did not fit into its system. With the conception of race, it idealized this vast community of peoples; and with the concept of nationhood it exalted the two finest incarnations of its age-old traditions—the German fatherland and the German language. The German scholar was soon proud of having been the first to express the inexpressible quality of historical stories, and made a religion out of the movement for German unity which was fostered by the railways. He was soon ready to sacrifice the French type of liberty and fraternity, and freedom and brotherhood on the English model, to his new god, Germanism. Grillparzer had become the champion of this new Germanism by exalting the victory of Hermann the Teuton over Augustus the Latin in the woods of Teutoburg.

7

The European Worlds

MEANWHILE the map of the world was being radically altered. In 1770 America belonged to Europe, and the legal traditions of what was known as the Colonial Pact kept the New World in a state of subjection. Fifty years later, Europe had almost entirely lost its hold on the New World. Yet America was shaping and moulding itself in the image of Europe. It was in order to be Europeans in the fullest sense of the word, and to enjoy all the privileges of that distinguished title, that America defended the rights of its citizens and established its rights as a nation. European trade reaped a handsome reward. What the old monarchies lost, the new middle-class business circles gained. A new conception of power came into being, less legal and military but more economic and financial. It enabled the seafaring peoples, and particularly the English, to continue their successful advance into Asia. This proceeded easily in India, but with greater difficulty in China where the continental mass provided a stronger resistance to seaborne ventures. Russia continued its conquest of central Asia; and France was extending its influence to the southern shore of the Mediterranean and Africa.

THE WEST IMITATES EUROPE

Napoleon had attempted to subdue sea-power by land-power. It was certainly easier to keep a fairly accurate reckoning of the strength of armies on the march than to estimate the power of millions of tons of shipping sailing the seas of the world, and the Emperor as a result had underestimated English sea-power just as he underestimated the power of English credit. It was very difficult for him to gauge its size, since even in the seas of Europe he could not see the real currents of the English economy. He had no feeling for a sea-based economy. Napoleon's political and administrative ideas came to him from his entourage of newly-rich, already described. These continental Swiss, brought to power by the Revolution, had not known the old seafaring military or mercantile aristocracy. The Revolutionary blockade followed by the continental blockade of the Empire had ruined the maritime tradition, which was a very much more serious loss than the purely material one of the fleet. Even at that time, in spite of Cugnot, Jouffroy d'Abbans or even Fulton, steam-powered ships were no more than useless toys, and the sailing-ship still reigned supreme. Ships could be built with comparative ease, so the construction of a great fleet took only a few months, and there were plenty of sailors along the French coasts; but the trained officers for these ships were lacking; thus no sound appreciation of naval affairs reached the Tuileries, especially after the critical affair of Deprez and the United Merchants.

England First

Meanwhile, the English and American fleets were acquiring mastery of the seas. The English navy had been rapidly enlarged until the whole of coastal England was familiar with the heavy wooden ships. They ceaselessly patrolled the North Sea, and kept a day and night watch, strengthened after the setting up of the camp at Boulogne, and continued until Napoleon had fallen. All naval shipyards were building at great speed, so that in 1815, 20,000 ships sailed over the routes of this new sea-empire. Naturally vast quantities of wood were required for the building programme, since for each warship four thousand fine oaks had to be felled. For a considerable time English forests had been devastated by the requirements of the fleet. It was slow and costly to bring wood from America. Therefore England began to consider the enormous forests of northern Europe near at hand; the key to England's freedom was to be found where supplies

of wood could be obtained, from Norway, Sweden, and
the vast forests of Finland. England had to keep the passage through the Danish straits open at all costs, for in
addition to wood it obtained corn and meat by the same
route.

Napoleon's destiny, however, led him towards the
Mediterranean, and his rashness ended in the disaster of
Aboukir Bay, although at that very time any hostile move
by the Nordic neutrals was enough to cause England
alarm. When there was a possibility that these neutrals
might gain Russian support, England was so terrified of
seeing the roots of its naval power cut off that it was
constrained to make peace, at the Treaty of Amiens in
1802. In the story of Bonaparte's love affairs we may
have possibly the microcosm of the Empire's fate. We
know that before the young and brilliant officer made
love to Josephine in order to please Barras, he had
turned away from Désirée Clary after a brief and idyllic
affair. Désirée later became Queen of Sweden as wife of
Bernadotte, who re-entered Paris as victor in 1815. Napoleon had taken no interest in these Nordic states. Even
in Holland he had failed to benefit from the lessons that
the clever and adaptable Louis had learned from his
subjects. He never attempted to conquer Denmark. It is
true that when the Grand Army camped in Poland in
1811 and found itself in direct control of the eastern
Baltic, England's position was made even more critical.
But this was not a deliberate move in a systematic policy
of intervention designed to harm Britain's northern trade,
and Napoleon never exploited the advantage it gave him.
He was pursuing a continental policy which came to grief
in the wastes of Russia and perished in the flames of
Moscow just in time to save England.

So England remained certain of receiving regular supplies of wood and could continue to build its fleet unhindered. The only source of competition that might cause
anxiety was in its former American colonies. There, too,
shipbuilding yards were buzzing with activity and there
was no shortage of wood, of course. Within a few years
the fleet of this newly-born nation amounted to more

than half the English tonnage, and took its place as the second in the world. In 1792 the Americans landed in Japan, where they successfully disputed the trading rights of the Dutch in 1797. This was a success without a future, but it forged a first link, and turned the United States from the coasts of England, whose superiority was still manifest in the 1812 wars against Washington.

Nevertheless, from 1780 to 1850 Suffren's country was still devoting immense thought, calculation and ingenuity to the improvement of sailing-ships, in seeking to lighten the wooden hulls, and to make the greatest possible use of the frame. When the British navy made its last sailing-ships in about 1830, it copied French models. However, it is true that the United States also benefited considerably from French improvements; with a daring use of capital provided by brand-new shipbuilders, they produced the clippers which were the most extraordinary sailing ships in the history of the sea. These ships had long, narrow lines, carrying an immense area of sail (more than forty times that of the hull) and sailed so fast that between 1825 and 1850 they had reduced the North Atlantic crossing from 25 days to less than 10, with 3,000 tons of cargo. This was swifter and much cheaper transport than was provided by the first steamships.

Every expansion of the maritime economy favoured the commercial activity of London. The blockade certainly harmed England's markets in Central Europe, but it also forced England to exploit its sea-power more fully and the more distant markets which England had already begun to exploit after the Treaty of Utrecht were still bringing in profit. From this point of view the Emperor's intervention in the Iberian peninsula forced the two American monarchies to play the English game. When the court of Lisbon was threatened by Junot it had turned with some hesitation to its 'natural protectors' the English. While Braganza was crossing from Portugal to Brazil, the English admiral had ample time to indoctrinate his protégé and to wrest a firm trade treaty from him. When the stocks of English manufacturers threatened the economy of the capital, as much as possible was dumped on the quays of Rio de Janeiro; the taste for English luxury goods soon spread in the old colonial city thanks to the relative cheapness of these surplus products. Not only the Portuguese courtier, but the native Brazilian had small palaces built, furnishing and decorating them in the same style as he adopted for his carriages, his finery and his fêtes; in this way this new court consoled itself for its exile. In exchange the English ships brought to London precious metals, Brazil-wood (a dye product still widely used) and several raw materials in the way of metals. English banks arranged credits for the Brazilians and supported the founding of a state bank in Rio de Janeiro.

Although English pressure on Brazil was heavy and sometimes tactless, it was more effective than the exhibitions of impatience staged by British admirals in the Spanish ports and especially in Buenos Aires, where Beresford and Whitelock failed to stir up public opinion in spite of the weakness of the Spanish Viceroy. The outcome benefited only Deliniers, who boasted of his victories to Napoleon (1807–8). Nevertheless Napoleon's invasion of Spain, the cheapness of English foodstuffs which the great agricultural countries eagerly demanded, and the example of French and American ideas, led to a wide revolutionary movement which started in 1810; its effect was to detach Spanish America from its European court and draw it more and more into English economic channels.

But before dealing with this English economic victory in Spanish America, let us pause to describe the changes taking place in the United States. The example of their prosperity, following on their independence, had important repercussions on the whole of the continent.

The United States Governed by the South

The thirteen colonies were far from being the largest state in either population or size immediately after achieving their independence, but their subsequent transformation was the quickest history has ever known. In less than seventy years the Americans had, as it were, exploded all over the continent; the area they occupied rose from one to eight million square miles while the population grew to about fifty millions.

By the peace treaty, England had given up to the victors not only their own lands but all English territories from the Alleghanies to the Mississippi. Thus when the constitution of the new federal republic came to be drawn up the colonists had to decide in whose hands the authority over so many new lands should lie. The states opening on to the west and in particular Virginia wished to extend their own authority in that direction. On the other hand, the states shut in on the Atlantic seaboard, who were restricted by old frontiers which cut them off from the west, feared the excessive expansion of their rivals and intended the unoccupied lands to be used for the creation of new states. They proposed that for the time being they should be governed by the Federal Government. Winning their point in this matter, the small but often highly developed states ensured the authority of a central government which the bigger states, particularly the less developed ones of the south, did not accept without reservation. The political destiny of the United States could be seen in their constitutions; the means at their disposal looked less promising at first sight. They had achieved incredible results in the great open country, but the means they had used were imported directly from Europe at that date. For the first fifty years there was nothing unusual about the American economy. The north-eastern states still remained more maritime than industrial, while their harbours were first fishing-ports and then shipyards, building those beautifully designed ships which were to become the models of the world's last sailing fleet. If industry was progressing, it was still at the craftsman stage, since so much English equipment had to be imported. In the south, more and more cotton was being grown; it soon replaced Indian cotton in the European market because it was produced cheaply on virgin lands and it was processed better than the cotton of the Old World, and because Whitney had already invented the picking machine. Finally, the triumphant westward advance of the settlers passed the Alleghanies and moved on towards the rich lands of the Mississippi. This unceasing conquest of new territories gave American families an almost boundless faith in the resources of their lands. The birth rate was high and the death rate relatively low in a population which closely followed all the medical and hygienic precepts of the most up-to-date Europeans. The native population increased and trebled in fifty years.

This process was of course helped by immigration, though this remained moderate; over this same period it accounted in all for less than half-a-million Europeans and Negroes. There were many Anglo-Saxons who felt quite at home in this new England which had adopted the customs of the old country; and the Irish already realized that cultivation of the land was more rewarding in this expanding economy than in their own island. Large numbers of Germans made their way from the plains of the Rhineland to Hamburg, and then sailed via England to the shores of America, particularly to Pennsylvania and Maryland. They were welcomed there by fellow countrymen who still remembered their own language, but they soon learned to speak nothing but English so that they could merge as soon as possible into a new country which they adopted so wholeheartedly that they often even changed their surnames.

The Negroes were still being dragged there in droves in almost as great numbers as before independence. Several states had, it is true, adopted a free constitution, forbidding slavery. Pennsylvania in particular had proclaimed the right of free birth: the children of slaves were to be freed. The slave trade had been condemned by the Congress of Vienna and the English, who had been the greatest dealers in black ivory during the previous century, were now the most fanatical in spreading the ideas of Wilberforce and keeping a watch on the seas. But it could not be denied that cotton was a lucrative crop, thanks almost entirely to the Negroes. The slave trade enabled shipowners, even those from the north, to make handsome profits. Nearby Cuba was a prolific slave-market and one in which there was very little risk. In short, the Negro population continued to grow, all the more since they had large families. In 1808 the Federal Government condemned the slave trade in principle, but it was another twelve years before the measures which were slowly enforced began to restrict it. After 1820 the trade continued, but under cover and at increasing cost; it became, in fact, so expensive that it was finally abandoned—although not until 1830.

The increasing production of cotton, tied to this forced importation of Negro labour, was probably the outstanding feature of American life at this date; however swift the westward advance of northern agriculturists, it was more than equalled by the expansionist policy of the southern farmers. The advance towards the Mississippi in the south was also a much easier proposition. At first it came up against the frontiers of France and Spain, but both readily relinquished their claims, one in 1803 and the other in 1819. New Orleans entered the Union, but what was most important was that all the lands from the Mississippi to the Pacific ceased to be legally French and were opened to the triumphant advance of American farmers. Southern expansion extended to Florida and the north of the Gulf of Mexico as well.

This first phase of American history was an age of good relationships. Quarrels between the supporters of Hamilton or Jefferson died down, and a measure of balance was achieved between those who wished the centre of gravity of the Union to be kept on the Atlantic sea-board and consequently advocated political, administrative and monetary centralization, and those who wished all efforts to be concentrated on the new lands of the west and south. As the number of inhabitants in the interior grew, however, their claims acquired greater weight and led to changes in the American structure radical enough to provoke the upheavals which followed in the time of Jackson.

This southern hero, victorious general of the Florida

war, had offered himself as candidate in the Presidential election at the head of a new party called the Democrats, whose policy was to defend the interests of western farmers against the industrial and traditionally commercial east. Once elected, he reorganized the administration from top to bottom, suppressed the central control of the bank, circulated easy credit, and issued a great variety of banknotes, sometimes barely covered by local banks whose policy was often exceedingly reckless. This transformation in the structure of credit was the American equivalent of Europe's 1830 revolutions and was caused, moreover, by the same economic crisis.

The Mississippi became the great economic artery, navigated by the first steamboats which brought to New Orleans a volume of traffic greater than that of New York. A few years later, the shores of the lakes proved to be ideal sites for industry and towns, especially as all this constructive effort gave a marked impetus to mining activities to the north of the Alleghanies in Pennsylvania, which turned out to be rich in raw materials such as iron and coal, and soon became a great producer of steel.

In the meantime, the old rivalry of north and south continued. The north's economic successes had perhaps a more solid foundation, but those of the south were very real, and in any case more spectacular: with their enormous lands and magnificent horses, the aristocrats of the south were the real rulers of the newly acquired territories. They dominated the political life of the United States in practice, following a militant policy at this period. Their determination to conquer added almost two million square miles to the Union, through the annexation of vast Mexican territories. In fact, in the thirties large numbers of planters had crossed the Mexican frontier and settled in Texas with their slaves and their cotton. Mexico was barely in control of such a vast and remote land any longer. The agitation kept up by the new settlers (which gave some Frenchmen the illusion that they might be able to stage a come-back in America) soon ended in the foundation of the free State of Texas in 1835; and the new republic lost no time in requesting admission to the Union in 1840. The causes of the ensuing war are somewhat obscure and complicated, but the ease with which the Mexican was defeated immeasurably heightened the self-confidence of the gallant Southerners. American troops even marched as far as Mexico and imposed their own peace terms. This war was the expression in the United States of the European crisis of 1848, and was brought on by the same economic depression.

The duality of America assumed a more serious aspect after that date. The quarrels between the industrial Northerners and the cotton-planters of the South with their immense territories had been kept in check for some time while both sides were so prosperous. But strife recurred on a grand scale when the vast state of Texas was colonized by slavery. In 1820, with the entry of Missouri as a state supporting slavery, the South had undertaken to confine the penetration of slavery to latitude 36° 60'. But in 1850, the Southerners were talking like masters, and regarded themselves as the embodiment of triumphant patriotism, and the new chivalry. From the ranks of their aristocracy came the best orators, the most convinced and the most convincing politicians. The new Democrats, in the name of the Patriotic Union, persuaded a majority of Northern electors to adopt the conciliatory attitude which was vital if the Union was to be preserved. In 1850, the Northern states consented to pursue runaway slaves on their lands in order to return them to their Southern owners.

Despite the Southern progress, the North was often said to hold the upper hand. Between these two old antagonists of North and South, the West, which had also continued to grow, was to play the part of umpire.

In the 1840s in fact, the advance towards the West was all the more rapid since the lands on the right bank of the Mississippi were the richest in the Union. This was the black earth zone, whose fertility soon became legendary. Bridges were thrown across the wide river, and ships provided excellent transport for agricultural machinery and heavy sacks of corn and maize. The industrial Mid-

dle West had a strong vested interest in this cultivation
of virgin lands, since it manufactured the ploughs, har-
rows and a whole range of implements for the new country. These products were continually being improved, and
the revolutionary new harvesting machines caused a
sensation when they were displayed at exhibitions in Europe. As the Americans penetrated beyond the banks of
the Mississippi, they began to realize the immense resources of the Rocky Mountain area. The feeling gained
ground that a country that was so rich and so free must
be a new earthly paradise, and great religious movements
swept the country: Methodism became a little more tolerant, opening its ranks to Episcopalianism and Angli-
canism, and everywhere there was a strange respect for
any form of religion; the most curious new doctrines were
widely accepted and credence was given to the most
disconcerting manifestations of religious eccentricity.
There was the curious story of the Mormons who discovered a new bible written on leaves of gold, and announcing an American Messianism: all who followed the
word of Smith belonged to the chosen people. The pe-
culiarity of this doctrine and of its polygamous way of
life stirred up such harsh persecution of the Mormons
that they fled to the rich alluvial lands on the shores of
the Salt Lake, protected by wide stretches of desert and
rock in what was later called Utah. In the Salt Lake they
discovered a new Dead Sea, into which flowed the little
Jordans of a new Promised Land.

Such, then, was the vast and complex experiment in
which the rival doctrines of the chivalrous, victoriou
aristocracy of the South, the hard-working and industria
middle classes of the North, and the conquering peasantry
of the virgin lands of the West, carried away from tim
to time by great whirlwinds of Messianic mysticism, wer
being pitted against each other on a chess board the siz
of a continent. In the second half of the century, befor
they became united around the railroads, the Unite
States went through an appalling civil war. But well be
fore the middle of the century, the miracle of their terr
torial, economic and demographic expansion attracte

the attention of the other Americas which now aspired to independence in their turn.

America for the Americans

We have described the relative importance of the cities of the Spanish Empire; and they were also the crucible in which a very unequal society was being forged. Their population consisted of small traders, creoles, and sailors, grouped around ports whose equipment was provided by the government and whose activity depended upon trade, stimulated by the liberal measures proclaimed by Charles III. Their new-found prosperity was based on trade between the agricultural hinterland and industrial Europe. From 1810 onwards, it was clear that industrial Europe meant first and foremost England. All this mass of ordinary people living in the port cities were in no sense an *élite*, but it was they who kept the shops and streets busy and provided the contingents of volunteers who were called on to deal with each new political crisis. The new nationalism was beginning to develop out of these recurring political upheavals.

Above this urban population the aristocracy fell into three major groups. First there were poor creoles of humble birth who had made a large fortune out of trade or the exploitation of lands surrounding the towns. They were beginning to emerge as leaders and figureheads for the new patriotism which had nationalism as one of its chief ideals. Side by side with them were many aristocrats who had only recently arrived in the colony, but who were firmly settled there and began to rear families; they continued to exert a great influence by their personal conduct although their official duties imposed by Madrid were coming to an end and they were increasingly tending towards local patriotism.

Finally there were the officials, every one a Spaniard and essentially a monarchist at heart, who were there only to fill the lucrative posts dispensed by the capital. They looked down on the creoles, and even on those of their predecessors who had finally opted for the New

World. The more local patriotism developed the further they were driven into isolation, and they soon became suspect. This minority had at its disposal troops and income from the Treasury which consisted chiefly of customs receipts, and was bitterly resented by the merchants. In a short time the officials found that the creole and half-caste peoples, most of the middle classes and some of the aristocrats were solidly turned against them.

As English merchandise and the prosperity which accompanied it increased in the ports, the conflict between nationalists and Spaniards became more intense, and before long it was spreading to the interior. Planters and stockbreeders could obviously not be expected to have any very clear ideas about politics, but they were loyal to a few leaders, most of whom were great landowners won over to the defence of local interests. Soon the clergy itself was drawn into the conflict. The half-castes saw the struggle as a chance to bring out into the open all the bitterness and uneasiness they felt at the presence of the Spaniard. All these factors combined to create an atmosphere of seething unrest which resulted in the collapse of the old Viceregal administration. For a time the re-establishment of the legitimate monarchy in Spain calmed tempers, but the old Christian interests loyal to the monarchy carried the day only because of their hopes that Madrid might reform the viceroys and open the doors of the government to local interests on the spot. However, Madrid, which was wholly taken up with plans for restoration in Europe, had little interest in these overseas territories except for the income they brought in by taxation. Consequently in 1818 and 1820 uprisings broke out everywhere.

From Mexico to Chile all was unrest and upheaval, although the outbreaks were not sufficiently large or uniform to engulf the whole of Spanish America at once. It was a case of each city defending its own patriotism, and involving only its own hinterland in its activities. There were innumerable independent rebel centres which leaders like San Martino or the 'polytechnician' Bolivar could not succeed in linking together. Iturbide's Mexico formed an isolated group at one end of the Empire, and the Rio de la Plata republic of Buenos Aires at the other end. In between there was no uniformity in the string of capitals from Santiago to Guatemala, although everything was happening in them simultaneously. This excessive fragmentation, which did not prevent Spain from being defeated, militated against the setting up of a creole empire. San Martino, discouraged, left his America to end his days in the calm retreat of Boulogne-sur-Mer. Similarly Bolivar and Iturbide failed in their later attempts at empire-building. The economics and the politics of Spanish America remained enclosed within small states, each constructed around its own city.

Inside these states none of the political or social problems had been solved by the defeat of Spain. The rural population who lacked any economic or political education continued to be the devoted soldiers of inland leaders and of the great landed proprietors. These two groups, anxious to remain masters of their own fate, had to defend a very lax federal law against the centralizing tendencies of the small capitals which were the seat of the government in each new republic. The landowner-captains were always ready to fight, and could in a few days improvise a formidable cavalry which was raised on their own estates where there was an abundant supply of horses, servants and retainers. They wanted to dictate their own law to the city. The city, for its part, relied on its population of merchants who were now in control of the ports, the market and customs revenue; and it could always find from among the conflicting groups a leader who could count on enough popular support to raise infantry. This leader then built fortifications, and exploited the lack of unity of the country leaders; with a mixture of daring and diplomacy, using money from trade and weapons from Europe, he then tried to impose the authority of the city on the countryside. Thus, even after the break-up of Spanish America, each republic had its quarrel between city unionists and country federalists. The quarrel was to persist throughout the nineteenth century, and its effects are still evident in the twentieth.

This was not a quarrel of ideas; any catch-phrase borrowed from the political and legal disputes of Europe was only used to disguise the respective claims of town and country interests. The more important the part played by the port and the city, the greater was the success of the unionist party. It was this which enabled Rosas to establish his famous dictatorship in Buenos Aires which endured for a quarter of a century; he built up the Argentine during that time but finally encountered the resistance of the city of Montevideo. The interminable struggle between Buenos Aires and Montevideo ended in a partition of lands and interests on both sides of the Rio de la Plata, and led to the creation of the new country of Uruguay.

Only one region succeeded in avoiding the general pattern of urban and rural enmity because it was too remote in the interior and still too loyal to its organization of tiny villages carved out of the forest. This was Paraguay where an Indian majority preserved its autonomy in the face of two Spanish states.

These three examples will be enough. It is not necessary to enlarge on the theory of the system of European settlement in Peru, whose capital was cut off from the vast lands it controlled and which had now to be content with the old Indian territory enclosed within its ancient frontiers. It would also be too complicated to attempt to explain in a few lines the strange destiny of Mexico and of various states in Central America, where the poor white, the Indian and the half-caste formed an alliance against the aristocracy loyal to Spain.

Let us next consider the origins of Brazil. The country had given asylum to the Portuguese royal family, and when John VI of Braganza returned to Europe, he made a secret agreement with his son Pedro advising him to proclaim independence on his own initiative if the yoke of Lisbon seemed too heavy for the Brazilians; for they had also felt the stirrings of nationalism and were claiming that only men born in the country had the right to make its laws. At all events, the wise policy of the Braganzas succeeded in preserving the unity of this vast land where revolts in north and south did not result in final separation since each side always accepted in the end the flexible and easy-going rule, undemanding and always open to reform, which was exercised from the palaces of Rio de Janeiro. Pedro I was proclaimed constitutional Emperor in 1822. He abdicated in favour of his son Pedro II after the crisis of 1830, and a ten-year regency followed.

Africa Not for the Africans

South Africa had been in a state of flux since 1780, and especially since the beginning of the nineteenth century when the Dutch governors, with their rigid and restrictive administration, handed over the Cape to English rule. The white settlers, who were Dutch and French at the time of the Netherlands Company, loaded their *trekken* and set out for the northern plains in defiance of the official ban on such adventures, under the tolerant eyes of their new masters. In this movement, the migrants came up first against the Hottentots and then against the Kaffirs. The Negroes, who were themselves conquerors coming southward in search of independence, at first retreated before this invasion from the sea. Some allowed themselves to be won over and once more found themselves slaves; indeed slavery was abolished only in 1834, when there were more than 30,000.

While the old population was spreading out over the northern plains, new arrivals were landing on the coasts; the English were now settling at Port Elizabeth before succumbing in their turn to the call of the interior. Two races, two languages and two legal systems, both from Europe, were struggling for influence. Sometimes the Englishman imposed his ways and sometimes he respected his Dutch neighbour, who nevertheless acted as the African had done before him. The Dutch fled from the new conqueror, set out across the plains, passed the Orange river, reached the Vaal river, and crossed it in 1837, disputing the land with the Africans the more stubbornly the farther they moved away from the ports where they had landed, the more so since the English anti-slavery movement was affecting their traditional colonial economy. The Kaffirs, threatened in their retreats, turned to large-scale reprisals, burning lands and destroying the white man's herds in a merciless battle which dominated the mid-nineteenth century. But when the English army intervened on the side of the settlers, the Kaffirs embarked on a gigantic programme of suicide; in a paroxysm of mystic frenzy, they destroyed their own herds and their own farms, and by this act of collective folly laid the country wide open to the invaders.

With the Kaffirs subdued, the Dutch could press on to the territory of the Zulus, when there were fresh battles, and fresh victories won at a cruel cost.

EUROPEAN PENETRATION OF ASIA

The new Latin-American states were an opportunity for England. In each there were cities to be built, ports to be improved and agriculture to be modernized. English technique, English material and English capital found profitable investments, although these were not always completely secure, for each economic crisis brought disaster to the most adventurous business concerns. Through large-scale buying of brazil-wood at a time when artificial dyeing was already being introduced, the Rothschild Bank suffered several losses; and the Barings invested too heavily in Argentina. But on the whole the fields opened up to England's merchant shipping and trade still seemed limitless. Obviously in this rapidly increasing trade, British businessmen realized the prodigious benefits they stood to gain from free trade from 1840 onwards. If there were no customs duties to pay, the new overseas nations would choose London as the site of their financial, commercial and industrial companies. Every improvement in technique strengthened the position of the London market.

The English had also to reckon with competition from the United States, which was already showing signs of a lively ambition, especially since the Americans still feared an invasion by England. The Monroe doctrine had an economic significance: it was designed to dispute with London the task of providing America with the equipment necessary for its development. But the United States had its hands full already with its own lands in the west, and economically Buenos Aires, Rio de Janeiro or Callao proved to be closer to London than to New York. Moreover, England had the great good fortune to possess enormous advantages not only in the Atlantic Ocean but increasingly in the Pacific and Indian Oceans. In 1825 Tasmanian fishermen settled at Portland. In 1836 a settler went to live at the place on the Australian coast which later grew into Melbourne. In 1830 a company was formed to exploit the south coast which distributed lands to many colonization societies. In 1835 Adelaide was founded and named after the wife of William IV. The rapid growth of India was the most important of all.

Capitalism in India

In India, in the nineteenth century, English capitalism was trying to encompass one of the oldest of Eastern civilizations. Nowhere else was there such a direct and ruthless clash between two worlds, two ways of feeling and of reasoning, and two ways of life, between an invader equipped with every available industrial tool and peoples nourished by traditions laid down like alluvial deposits by tides of invasion through the centuries from every part of Eurasia. It is difficult to describe this vast encounter between Europe and Asia in a few words and we must leave out a great many aspects of it, although to an Indian philosopher the truth could only be arrived at through a study of every single aspect.

It is tempting to confine our attention to military history. In that realm Western superiority was so overwhelming that our traditional historical studies concentrate on it with a thoroughness which at least has the merit of being obvious. Wellesley's battle against the Mahrattas, and the bitter struggles to seize the remains of the Mogul Empire after the capture of Seringapatam, the occupation of the Punjab, the control of the routes to Afghanistan and Persia, the conquest of the Gurkhas, and the subduing of the Rajputs in 1789–1823, are well known. However, the details of this story would reveal ways of fighting very different from those of European armies at the same period; much of it was a continuation of the eighteenth century conflicts and in many respects it was also a battle against the remnants of the French experiment. But although the Directory confirmed the winding up of the French East India Company in 1796, many French officers stayed on to become advisers to Hindu princes, with an authority heightened by the brilliant victories of Napoleon. The English learned a great deal from the struggle. They had to face resistance which, although unskilled, was liable to break out at any time, and had also to deal with a disconcerting subtlety in negotiation. The cruellest Indians showed themselves to be the most loyal once they had been defeated, while the smooth-tongued were the most dangerous in peacetime, since every term of a treaty had to be endlessly re-discussed, re-negotiated and enforced. The last blow struck by Indian resistance was the famous revolt of the Sepoys, whose notorious massacres provoked a bloody reprisal.

The English learned to take advantage not only of the religious rivalry between Muslims and Hindus, but also of the infinite number of conflicting interests which divided princes and empires; and to exploit the myriad local rivalries which could sway potentates from one policy to another. All these eventually ensured the dominance of the merchants who, though few in number, were in close touch with each other through the new techniques of communication, particularly the optical telegraph; they were also bound together by a community of spirit and feeling born of their belief in the superiority of European civilization.

England continued with the conquest of India and installed fortified posts in the frontier regions. At the same time it changed the structure of its Indian policy. The commercial privileges of the Company came to an end in 1813, although it was to continue to administer the country until 1865. Above all, English civilization modified the structure of this huge country's institutions.

When it first occupied Bengal, the Company's great task had been to fix and collect the land dues in spite of a punctilious but intermittent supervision by parliament in London. It took a lesson from the experiences of the Moghuls, and retained the services of the *zamindars*, a kind of farmers-general who were responsible for the land tax on a contractual basis. Gradually, however, their functions were divested of all the traditional subtleties which had made them so flexible; the *zamindars* then became landowners in the European style, possessing gigantic estates of which they were merely the tax-collectors. The peasants, who had previously been subjects of the Treasury, became tenants with a precarious tenure. This system had every kind of advantage for the Company. It spared it the trouble of going into Indian affairs in detail, and gave security to its allies (an unheard-of legal gift) since they had become its accomplices in the exploitation of the country. Thus the system of large estates was able to spread southward as far as the presidency of Madras.

However, there were quick reactions against this brutal irruption of property rights into a civilization which knew nothing of all the rigours of land-ownership in Europe. The most far-sighted Indians persuaded the English administration that if the right of property was to be adapted to an Indian economy, its beneficiaries would have to be more carefully selected from the complex hierarchy of rural society. The farmer and the *rayat* were obviously more suitable to assume this rôle of landowner than the faraway and indifferent tax-collector of former times. The *Rayat-wari* system was therefore developed after 1830 and was particularly strong in the centre and south of the peninsula; or was re-established in Madras and penetrated as far as Bombay. The occupant of the field became its owner. On the other hand, of course, it was on him that the full burden of heavily assessed taxation fell, although it was revised every thirty years. This dual system of ownership, by *zamindars* and *rayats*, created two classes on European lines in a proud society in which previously the honorary rank of the castes had been only incidentally based on wealth. There had been great landowners, particularly in the north, and average landowners more frequently in the south. However, both gradually became aware of the enormous advantages of the European system of property rights. This *laissez-faire* economy absolved the landowners from all obligation to care for their tenants, once the rent assessment had been discussed and then fixed for a long time to come. Even the *rayat* soon became a person of property since he farmed out his land to one or more peasants without rights. It was these peasants who had ultimately to bear the full weight of the new money-based social pyramid.

A further innovation was that the landowner, whether great or small, paid the land tax in money, and consequently exacted his rents in cash. This marked the end of the era of transactions in kind, when the whole collective life of a community had centred around the distributions of food, organized in the centre of the village. Reforms which were so profoundly revolutionary did not penetrate easily into all the country districts of India.

The old communal rules persisted in the south, where the village groups supervised the distribution of the monsoon rainwater collectively; this was then stored in innumerable artificial cisterns and rationed out on the lands during the dry season. The same continuity of tradition persisted in certain northern regions, particularly in Kashmir, where a marvellous network of canals distributed the waters from the Himalayas. Proud traditions were also preserved elsewhere in the regions not subject to European rule. In these incompletely assimilated areas, governmental power was hardly represented except by commissioners or residents stationed near the local ruler, whether he was a powerful prince or a village chief. These commissioners had full power in theory, but were in fact reduced to incessant negotiations and endless palavers. Gradually a *modus vivendi* was reached in these areas, sanctioned by the central government; it tended to establish uniform practices and thus to set up an Indian law, but it did not succeed in eliminating the many varied local traditions.

Naturally the English tried to establish civil and criminal codes of law on the Western pattern, and to create some unity in the legal system. They had to be satisfied with laying down clear rules which took no account of the caste system although they did allow Europeans to have a special legal system of their own. They had to give up all idea of geographical uniformity; there were laws rather than one universal law, and although the principle of ownership was recognized in some districts, it was far from being generally accepted. However, it was widespread enough to have brought in its train an extensive circulation of money, which in turn created new relationships between men. Many landowners, and even more tenant-farmers, had to borrow from a money-lender, whose importance in rural society thus increased considerably. In many cases the peasant's subjection was closer and harsher under the régime of mortgage and money-lending than under the old communal village system, even when the latter was at the mercy of great and powerful feudal lords. It is difficult to say whether this new Western system of ownership can prove lasting. To-day as formerly, numerous cases are quoted where whole villages disappeared as a result of political disturbances, vanishing into the forests and hiding there for long periods, awaiting a suitable moment to return. They would reappear twenty or thirty years later, rebuild their villages on the old site and according to the old rules, and resume their communal life of work and mutual assistance.

However precarious these new social structures which Europeans were initiating in India may have seemed, they did nevertheless show concrete results about the middle of the century. Of course, much fairly fertile land remained fallow. The English occupation, which was almost comically small in number, did not include any settlers anxious to clear great stretches of land since manual work was considered beneath the dignity of the European. The half-castes were no more anxious to undertake it; as for the Indian, the very idea of leaving his ancestral land was repugnant to him. Consequently there was very little radical clearance of land. In general the old crops continued to be grown by the old methods, which were often quite efficient and brought in several harvests a year on the rich lands of the Delta.

The various kinds of rice were carefully cultivated, since they formed the basis of the local diet. The villages tried to sell a surplus, especially since under the new system they needed to have money. As rice sold well, the poor in India lived on millet, sorghum and all kinds of minor cereals. In addition to cereals, the pulses—there were as many different kinds of peas as there were districts—and the oil-crops which mainly consisted of flaxes or sesames for which there were innumerable uses in a village community, sometimes sold fairly well in the market. Lastly the traditional cotton attempted to compete successfully with its new rival from the United States, at least for internal consumption.

The End of the Celestial Mandate in China

China remained a vast besieged fortress. In the previous century Kien-Lung had ensured the autonomy of the Middle Empire; of the previous Christian population he retained only a few isolated Jesuits (for example the president of the Court of Mathematics) and a few Western technicians, mainly artillerymen. He felt powerful enough to exact tribute from foreigners, and admitted the Portuguese, who had been in Macao for two hundred years, only as Chinese subjects. But the seventeenth son of Kien-Lung, his successor, Kia-King, was not left in peace; for the first twenty years of the century, he had continually to dismiss foreign embassies from Russia, America, England and Japan which came to request commercial privileges. The English were particularly persistent. In 1808, for instance, after Admiral Drury had been expelled from Macao he hit upon the idea of going up to Canton, where he was met with a stiff cannonade and turned back; this added one more rebuff to the many administered to those who had been trying to get through to Peking and the Summer Palace for twenty years. For a time the Westerners hesitated. The Dutch abandoned the attempt in the face of Kia-King's obduracy, while the Spaniards were content to slip in under cover of Portuguese privileges; the Russians sent embassies and gifts brought by caravans in even greater numbers than before, but without much success, while the King of Sweden relinquished his privileges to the Göteborg Company. France kept up the illusion of protecting the Catholic missionaries who were forbidden by the Empire but were tolerated by the local potentates fairly generously.

There was another reason for the restlessness of Kia-King's reign. Conspiracy seemed to be rife in every district of China and the time to proclaim the end of the dynasty's rule appeared ripe. Secret societies flourished; that of the Water Lily, for instance, even managed to get a footing inside the Peking Palace. This unrest became even more widespread under Kia-King's successors and the period of the great troubles began. Arrests and executions did not prevent the spread of the secret societies in Canton or Honan. The court was overwhelmed with alarmist reports; it was thought that the Society of the Dryads of Heaven and Earth had been exterminated, but its cells proliferated all over the country and its members incited what was later known as the Taiping rebellion. Religious quarrels, too, grew more bitter, in particular the conflicts between Muslims and Chinese. In Kashgaria a descendant of the prophet tried to remodel the state to his own advantage and evoked the law in the name of the Sultan of Constantinople. Everywhere the Muslim population was becoming stirred by the great news of progress from India and the West, and resented Chinese obstinacy.

In this disturbed atmosphere the persistence of the English paid dividends. Even after the previous stinging rebuffs, Lord Napier attempted to get through to the Emperor in 1833 but died of exhaustion. In 1839, the Guild of Canton Merchants, acting on orders from Peking, pitched 21,000 cases of opium from India into the sea. Rarely had a spectacular gesture such sound moral justification, although China itself had long been growing the poppy. But it was a direct blow at the Indian economy and a threat to the rapid development of that vast empire which the English were having some difficulty in controlling. This time England despatched fifty ships and five thousand men, instituted the blockade of Canton and sailed up the Pearl River. The court at Peking grew worried and there was a hasty treaty. Canton, Amoy, Foochow, Ningpo and Shanghai were opened up to British trade and consuls were established there. The Chinese had to pay a high price for the opium which had been destroyed, as well as the entire cost of the war. Above all, the English obtained possession of the small island of Hong Kong, facing the Sino-Portuguese settlement of Macao. The small squadron quickly established a station, a port and a resident there. The port became thronged with English and American ships. The town of Victoria was begun in a hastily-chosen creek that proved to be often devastated by typhoons. Macao declined in importance and the ungrateful Spaniards left it for Amoy, soon taking with them the Portuguese themselves. Canton lost some of its trade to the new English harbour, which was soon fitted out with European equipment. True to the liberalism which had already brought such rich returns to the capital, the English Government declared Victoria a free port. Following in England's footsteps the whole of Europe now tried to get a footing in the Chu-kiang estuary. In 1845 France obtained privileges and had her right to protect missionaries confirmed. Then the United States made a treaty, followed by Belgium, Norway and Sweden.

So the vast land of China was beginning to lose its coasts to the seafaring activity of the West, led by England, with the United States following in its wake. Of all the old powers, Russia alone resisted the lure of the sea.

The Steppes of Central Asia

If Catherine II had created the illusion of being an enlightened despot thanks to the philosophers, it was with Alexander I that Western institutions began to creep in. The French Revolution held no terrors for him in its early stages, but on the contrary showed him how powerful ideas of reform could be. Passionately devoted to new ideas, he tried to spread education, opened grammar schools—where Pushkin was educated for instance—encouraged an almost free press, and no longer used banishment as a way of dealing with his political opponents. He delighted in the company of Speransky, a man of humble birth and a son of a Greek Orthodox priest, whom he made his private adviser. This mathematics teacher dreamed of setting Russia on the road to liberty. He secretly admired the new developments in France and drew up plans for a reform of the legislature and administration for the Tsar (the only republican in his Empire). At the Ministry of Justice and later as privy counsellor and secretary to the Imperial Council, he tried to apply these reforms, but their effect was shattered by the French invasion, which revived the old Russian patriotism and caused the reformer to be exiled to Perm.

After his victory, the aging Alexander was disillusioned. He professed liberalism in Paris and recalled Speransky to St Petersburg, but lacked the courage of his convictions. He veered from one doctrine to another as the mood took him, promised the Poles liberties he failed to grant, and detested Metternich but nevertheless aligned his policy on that of Austria. His fine proud nationalism turned gradually to mysticism. When the Tsar hesitated, all Russia hesitated too, and this indecision continued under the reign of Nicholas I. Nicholas brutally suppressed the liberal decembrist movement which had hoped to take advantage of his accession to impose its reforms but he defended Greek liberty against Turkey and the Holy Alliance. In 1830, political uncertainty drove the Tsar into a suspicious autocracy. Education was closely supervised and the press spied upon and stifled; Poland was annexed after its unsuccessful revolt. The prevailing feeling in Russia was one of danger. It was obvious that maritime Europe, after breaching the Mediterranean and India, was now threatening central Asia by penetrating and settling there. Russia's counter-attack led her to the Crimean war.

This political vacillation on the part of Russia sprang from the dual nature of this vast land, which bordered Asia on the marshes of Kazan and shared a common frontier with Europe in the west. At each swing of the pendulum, however, Russia was drawing closer to the West. Nicholas I had entrusted to Speransky the drafting of a code, which was in itself a typically French approach, although the forty-eight volumes of this gigantic general collection of laws could be little more than a codification of the old ukases, treatises and manifestoes. They were followed by a more systematic résumé in fifteen volumes, intended to guide judges, but not to tie them down. Alexander II made a treaty with the allies of the Crimea and abandoned Persia to English influence, a move dictated by the fact that Russia's internal problems had demanded his full attention.

Russia was on the move. It was a huge country which defied all statistics and disconcerted the observer by the apparent uniformity of its peasant countryside, although this impression concealed subtle differences. Great changes took place in its population from time to time. At the end of the eighteenth century it had something like thirty million inhabitants. By the mid-nineteenth century the number had more than doubled. In Moscow and its neighbourhood, the birth rate at that time was probably the highest in Europe and perhaps in the world. It is true that expectation of life was little more than twenty-four years; Russia's infant mortality was twice that of France and more than three times that of Norway. Yet the population not only increased, owing to the birth rate, but shifted from one region to another in numerous internal migrations driven hither and thither by famine and attracted by lands which were reputed to be more fertile, and of which wonderful tales were told. This was especially true of lands in the east, and the starving peasants were dazzled by these rumours of imaginary paradises. The urban centres, although there were not many of them yet, were already attracting the peasant.

In spite of Boris Godunov's old decree, Russia had only very few towns of more than 100,000 inhabitants in the middle of the nineteenth century. There were to be six in 1870 and ten or so at the end of the century. Mills were built. From the eighteenth century onwards, the nobles had been regrouping some of their serfs into factories, which were vast compounds often in the country where the families lived together, each in its *isba*, and worked with rudimentary looms. Mills like those in England were introduced only very slowly, chiefly for cotton. Concentration in the mines took place more quickly. From 1816 something like a thousand tons of gold had been extracted from the gold-bearing sands of the Urals. In the Altai, in Transbaikalia, they were working silver-bearing lead, coal, and soon, beyond the Caucasus, naphtha, which was already very valuable.

It was perhaps a little too early to claim this as an industrial awakening in the first half of the nineteenth century. The migrations originating in the country districts in Russia were similar to those in western Europe. But although some led to the towns in the same way, others led more often to other regions, to the vast empty lands bordering the old Russia and to the vast stretches of Asia. Here the old traditional activities had been affected by England's seagoing trade and were dying out, so that the old economic centres in the heart of the country were decaying and consequently being left wide open to Russian expansion.

The Russian world was a strange one for the Westerner to understand. Its economy, compared with that of France or England, seemed static and backward and yet was continually growing. Like the American world it was surrounded to east and south by an enormous area over which it was free to expand. There was nothing unusual in whole villages and bands of peasants leaving their homes because of an epidemic or an economic crisis, or simply in pursuit of a mirage, at the call of a preacher announcing the promised land. It was more through this voluntary movement than through transportations, although these, as we know, played an important part, that Siberia was peopled by Russians. In addition the frontier nations on her borders continually protected, controlled and assimilated these advancing elements of Russian civilization. The continual extension of Russian territory, whether by migration or by political infiltration and conquest which was considerable even in the eighteenth century, reached astounding proportions.

This dynamism was perhaps precisely the result of the apparent confusion characteristic of everything Russian. Property had no clearly defined boundaries nor the law, religion or the country itself, except in the west where it met the German Empire. Imperceptibly one passed from Russia proper to 'marches'. where the peasant was still a soldier as well and was obliged to answer the call of military leaders. But the soldier who had come from the interior also wanted land so that he could become a peasant. Those who had been unfortunate in the land they had received arranged matters between themselves and set up a *mir*. Officers and high-ranking leaders received a fairly large portion on which they settled as lords or middle-class landowners. In every case the Russian Empire acquired new lands. Life in these marches was always turbulent, although it was not so wild as it had been: in the west Poland had been conquered, the Ukraine had lost the last remnants of its military organization, and its Cossacks no longer fought except at folk festivals. Turkey, too, had lost its aggressive power and no longer disputed possession of the Black Sea, and there was no longer any danger from Persia. There were no more bitter struggles for the narrow passes leading into the closed river basins of central Asia which had made it for a time the fortress of Eurasia. Persia remained inactive between her two new rivals; the Russians were threatening it from the west while there was the English menace from the south. English shipping enabled Afghanistan to continue to keep order in this part of the world, just as the Bactrians had done in former times.

There was one main reason for the decline in the land power of the great Hakemite Empire of the noble Bactrians, which was still strong enough to defeat an English force. This was the inevitable decline of the great trade currents which had run from Asia to the Mediterranean and from India to Scandinavia, for it had been under their influence that these river basins of the Balkash, the Aral, and the Caspian had become the trade centres of the old continent. Every city was decaying and almost in ruins. Thus the old civilization was collapsing and the old empires were crumbling from the Black Sea to the great mountains of Tianshan. The vast mass of Russia was expanding continuously, not only towards the primitive Siberia offered to Boris Godunov, but equally towards the lands of the Muslim Empire.

It is true that the Russian drive southward was in quite a different category. The Scythian, Byzantine and Muslim civilizations had left much more decisive traces of their passage, and the population retained certain habits of work and of trading, while sometimes even a military discipline and some remnants of political organization remained, although its extent naturally varied from one region to another. From the end of the eighteenth century Russian penetration spread out through the Caucasus; at the beginning of the nineteenth century the mountain barrier was crossed and Tiflis was reached. The Russian stream then flowed easily down the depression towards the Black Sea and the Caspian and spread southward unchecked until it met resistance from Turkey which defended the Euphrates, or from Persia. The Russians then turned towards the northern chain and cleared the valleys of all remaining pockets of resistance. It was an easy conquest, owing partly, perhaps, to the fact that the Muslim overlord was disliked by the native population, and the Christian welcomed the orthodox soldier as a liberator, since they both practised a rite inherited from Byzantium.

At the time of the conquest, the Turks had decimated

the handsome Georgian races which had been the pride of the slave-dealers in Constantinople. Afterwards they had massacred as many Russians as possible, whether venturesome soldiers or incautious settlers, and had reduced the rest to slavery. Slaves and sons of slaves were therefore awaiting the arrival of the liberators. Once they had conquered Erivan and Mount Ararat, the Russians controlled the holy places of Armenian Christianity, which they treated with a respect which was all the more effective politically because it was genuine. The news of the restoration of the famous monastery spread throughout Turkey as far as Constantinople, where the Armenians controlled trade. The Tsar was considered as protector and saviour by all the Greek Orthodox Christians and he had no choice but to assume the title. The Armenian merchant preferred to remain where his business was, but the poor man and the peasant often left Turkish Armenia to breathe the free air of the new Russian Armenia. It is difficult to judge the extent of these movements of peoples, since they were offset by a gradual return of Muslims from Transcaucasia towards lands which had remained politically Turkish, but the military frontier soon became also the ethnic and religious frontier.

Russian civilization was nevertheless advancing in the wake of its small armies. To consolidate his authority, the Tsar confirmed the great lords in their possessions, and even granted them lands when they had none of their own, but on the slightest suspicion they were confiscated and redistributed to soldiers and officers. Russian peasants in their turn crossed the mountains and obtained plots of land which they quickly organized into *mirs*. Finally the boatmen of the Black Sea and Caspian brought to the gates of Baku and Batum the promise of increased trade.

THE CROSSING OF THE MEDITERRANEAN

The eastern opulence which had characterized the Mediterranean during the Middle Ages had been brought by the rich traffic from China, through Persia to Egypt. It had launched wave after wave of prosperity throughout North Africa. The real reason for the decadence of the southern Mediterranean lay in the decline of central Asia. The advance of Russia and the inactivity of Turkey led to the independence of Egypt, and left the states north of the Atlas Mountains to their own devices. They had to make the best use they could of such maritime traditions as were left to them by resorting to piracy on the high seas.

At the same time Atlantic traffic was entering the Mediterranean through the English Straits of Gibraltar. In this case, however, it was not English maritime trade which replaced the old economic system of the continent; this time it was French settlers who crossed from one shore of the sea to the other, from Europe to Africa.

Nationalism versus Islam

In 1779 Persia had selected Teheran as its new capital. It was a strategic move to enable more effective mobilization so that Georgia might be saved from the Russian threat. However, the move proved useless, since Persia, which had remained a feudal empire, could not put up any resistance to the Russian campaigns of 1804–13 and 1826–8. The diplomacy of Abbas Kajar attempted to play off the English against the Russians in vain. The English had allowed themselves to be beaten in Afghanistan by troops whom the Persians had often dominated in the past. The Persians could hardly hope for aid from France. The imperial victories had indeed made a deep impression throughout Asia, but there were no French troops available on that immense continent. The only Frenchmen there were archaeologists and scholars, although they were made very welcome. Consequently Persia had to accept the Russian advance. But a nationalist *élite* which was coming into being intended to place responsibility for the defeat on the outmoded traditional education, and the old Islamic religion, which was paralysed by sterile disputations. A new Persia was developing, and the old Persian rock began to emerge through the sedimentary deposits laid down by Islam.

The same process was apparent at about the same time in Turkey after the loss of the Crimea, when the Khan had embarked too late on essential reforms and the Sultan Mahmud II dissolved his janissaries. An admirer of Napoleon, he tried to remodel his army on modern lines. This plan was thwarted by the joint action of France and England at Navarino in 1827—a repetition of Chesme. Fortunately the French wrecked Western plans by supporting Mehemet Ali in Egypt. Turkey succeeded in using diplomacy where Persia had failed; its leaders succeeded in holding out and even tried to follow up military reforms by administrative reforms which gave the Turks some redress against the old, rigid practices of Islam. Sultan Mejid's readiness to reform led to a reconciliation with Mehemet Ali, who was quite content to be a life-ruler of Egypt.

Istanbul was now developing into the capital of Turkey rather than the centre of Islam as it had been previously. Like Persia in the east, Egypt in the west was striving to become a nation, but the fellaheen were far from being a people in the modern sense of the term. After having massacred the Mamelukes systematically, Mehemet Ali, a Turkish official of Albanian stock, appealed to all men of ambition in the Mediterranean world including Lebanese, Greeks, Jews, Albanians and even French, to set up an Egyptian aristocracy. He needed a language which could be mutually understood by so many different peoples; the choice was a kind if composite Arabic which the fellah was slow to learn.

He sent 120 students to Paris, while he encouraged trade, developed cotton-growing, built villages and developed the towns. From 1800 to 1845 Egypt's population trebled. A new nation was breaking through the rigid structure of the old Islam.

At about the same time, the Moroccan empire was deprived of its most important source of wealth and prestige. The Moroccans had taken a great part in the continental activity of the African slave trade. It was they who had recruited supplies for the great Turkish and Indian markets, which had profited the Sultan of Zanzibar in particular; and they reaped further advantages later by directing this traffic from central Africa towards the west and the growing market on the Atlantic coast. The suppression of the Negro trade, at first in theory by the Congress of Vienna and later in fact, robbed them of this source of gain, while at the same time allowing the Westerners who had set foot on African soil to appear as liberators; this obviously acted to the detriment of the race and religion of the lords of Islam. The growing power of Western naval resources was also restricting the income from Atlantic piracy, especially that of the notorious Salé pirates; thus Morocco gradually lost one of the sources of revenue which came up from the Niger towards the Mediterranean.

Through its geographical position between eastern Islam, cut off from its Arab and Turkish bases, and a western Islam cut off from black Africa, Algeria became a wide corridor wide open to the claims of the north.

The Birth of French Africa

France certainly cannot claim a place on the high seas comparable with that of England; but she made good use of the Mediterranean. In 1789 Marseilles had 100,000 inhabitants; by 1816, after the ups and downs of the Revolution, the figure was the same. Thirty years later the population had doubled, while numerous minor industries were beginning to grow up around the port. Shipping in Marseilles increased in the first half of the century from 400,000 to 2,000,000 tons. The old and inadequate harbour had to be doubled in size by the addition of two large new docks in 1844. Marseilles became the largest commercial port after London and Liverpool; there was competition from the Italian ports and from Austrian Trieste, but they never seriously challenged Marseilles. This was partly because it was a vital stage on the quick post route from London to Calcutta. The overland route was preferable since the horse was still quicker than the sailing-ship; the journey was made first across France and then across the Asian isthmus, so that the only part for which sea travel was necessary was from Marseilles to Cairo.

However, the supremacy of Marseilles was assured because it became a French bridge-head to Algiers. The capture of Algiers in 1830 might well have seemed an achievement of naval power, and England viewed it with misgiving. After a few years it became clear that the Barbary Coast was now nothing but a position in which the remaining wretched chiefs, corrupted by plunder, lived out their lives. They died out because the seas were more efficiently patrolled *à l'anglaise*. Beyond this coast the continent still had to be conquered, however, and there was only one army available for the task. It exacted a high price for its services. It was the French army, forged in the Emperor's wars, and tired of resting on its laurels for fifteen years; it was still tenacious enough to transform this French expansion southward into a national epic. What neither Charles x nor Louis-Philippe had foreseen soon became a reality. Algiers could not be conquered by sailors, but had to be defeated by land. Thirty years of warfare costing six thousand million francs with hundreds of thousands of men lost in battles that were always hard and often frightful, put Algiers between the Seine and the Rhine and between Paris and Brussels, as Lamartine remarked in 1846. France, thrust out of northeast Europe by the treaties of Vienna, was advancing southward on a wide front.

First came soldiers and soon after them the settlers. Frenchmen were hesitant about crossing the sea. In 1831 the authorities had to enlist 4,500 Parisians 'whom the misfortunes of the time made permanently available to the hands of agitators', to constitute a first contingent of volunteers. The Spanish, Italians, Maltese and other peoples from the old Mediterranean regions were readier to volunteer. The protection of Bugeaud's military police afforded them in Algeria a way of life which differed little from that to which they were accustomed in their own countries. The racial and other tensions to which this immigration might have given rise were quickly absorbed by the common problems; the immigrants were assimilated under the authority of the French government; although it sent the least dependable and sometimes the least valuable of its officials to these 'remote eastern lands', nevertheless it implanted French laws, decrees, and administrative traditions in the population. It is true that there were soon rumours of incidents here and there in which both sides were guilty of cruelty, where the French thrust the Arabs back into the desert as the Arabs had thrust the Berbers into the mountains, but this was soon brought to an end. The native population enjoyed the same administrative rules as the new settlers. The structure of European bourgeois land ownership was imposed as well as it could be on tribes which were three parts nomad. The African was 'assimilated' without any real thought and probably out of sheer lack of imagination; the policy was partially successful in time, by dint of ignoring the difficulties. The French government succeeded in achieving there what had failed in Italy, Württemburg and Holland. Reassured by the presence of this government, which was strong just because it was completely unaware of the difficulties, French immigrants grew accustomed to the idea of crossing to Algiers, and African France was born.

North Africa returned to what was really its natural geographical role at this time; it became once more a part of the West, after having been an extension of the East for so long. The English, who took fifty years to realize what was happening, and the Turks, who did not care, made no move. Algiers became the first city of North Africa after Cairo and Algeria was the first region of European Africa after the Cape. Thus there were to be two Mediterraneans: the French Mediterranean in the west, Turkey's in the east; England sanctioned this situation as long as she could enjoy free access to both currents of trade which led to the Red Sea and the Persian Gulf via Gibraltar and Malta.

At that date Saint-Simon was considering the possibility of a reconciliation of peoples, and the title he gave to his reflections was 'the Mediterranean System'. In do-ing so he may have over-emphasized the connections between the destiny of the Mediterranean and that of the world in general and he may have considered the planet on too small a scale, but he believed, perhaps rightly, that mankind was witnessing a tentative revival of what the *pax romana* had been eighteen centuries earlier.

BOOK THREE

CAPITALIST AND INDUSTRIAL EUROPE 1840–80

The Victory of Industry

A VARIETY of fates, covering in all a period of some two hundred years, have been allotted to the industrial revolution by different historians. At all events, it was the revolution of 1848 which marked the triumph of industry. Technique and industry are not synonymous. The establishment of great industrial concerns presupposes a general effort on the part of the people, with migrations of workers, the construction of towns, the digging of canals, and the surfacing of roads. In short: a whole new organization of labour affecting millions of men is necessary and this profound transformation lasted all through the nineteenth century. If that is what is meant by the industrial revolution, it is premature to apply the term to the inventions of the eighteenth century. But there was a crucial period in the nineteenth century, 1845–55. Railway building had been started all over Europe, but the work had to be interrupted everywhere since the effort was too great for the means available. It was this interruption, the unemployment it led to and the helplessness of societies whose ambitions outran their means which provoked the revolutions of 1848. These were the decisive battles in which capitalist industry was at stake. It was at this point that railways became the most powerful weapons of the new economy, and thus ensured the triumph of the new capitalist structure.

THE RAILWAYS—CATALYST OF THE INDUSTRIAL REVOLUTION

The improvements in industry and agriculture during the 1830s had profound repercussions on the circulation of goods. This was the golden age of canals and stage-coaches. England already had a network of roads which covered most of the country, although their quality was not very good. They were famous for the density of their traffic and for the jolting they gave to the traveller. The new surfacing invented by Macadam did not improve them to any marked degree; the dressing of tar did not become general until the second half of the century, and meanwhile the weight of traffic, especially of coal and iron, pitted the surface with ruts and holes. These English roads were, moreover, private property, and the tolls had to cover not only capital expenditure but continual upkeep which was cheap only because of the cheapness of labour. The swing-gates along these toll roads were at that time one of the most familiar features of the English countryside. In France the road system continued to be maintained by the state which had reorganized the *Corps des Ponts et Chaussées* for this purpose in Louis xv's reign. This road system, extended by the great road-builder Napoleon, continued to grow after the Bourbons had been restored to power; the flow of traffic was centred around Paris, so that the cities and frontiers could be served by direct roads; there were passes for crossing into Italy, Spain or Switzerland. But the quality of the roads was still very mediocre. The metalling was very shallow, and after a few weeks of bad weather the road could often not be found, since it disappeared into the fields.

On the rest of the continent the years were marked by a parallel development: in Austria roads were built radiating around Vienna while in Italy the French and Austrian roads were carried on over the Alps towards Brindisi. The Prussian Government, in particular, had expended vast efforts and great expense to link Berlin with the Westphalian network. In the new western provinces, it came across the sections of road laid down by the French Government. Because it was most anxious to complete this sector, Prussia postponed the construction of a road system in its eastern provinces, which explains the still archaic nature of those roads or rathe tracks, which are almost impassable in wet weather, especially in swampy areas. All the German states energetically competed with each other in trying to ensure better communications, especially with the great international artery, the aorta of German trade, the Rhine.

On all roads traffic was beginning to be controlled by powerful coaching companies; this was a novelty in contrast to the general pattern of individual transport in the previous century. Two famous companies were operating in France: in one, the banker Laffitte had interests (Caillard, Laffitte and Co.), and the other was that of the *Messageries Générales*, the very wealthy successors of the former *Messageries Royales* created by Turgot. There was a new fashion for travel which kept the post-stages busy; it was illustrated in engraving, and celebrated in the popular theatre, poetry and music. The new stage-coach caused quite a sensation, with its touching departures, its eagerly awaited arrivals, and its bustling journeys. It sometimes met with tragedy when the route lay through forests barely opened up, where bands of highwaymen still lay in wait. It employed a large number of stable-hands and managers and drained the surrounding countryside of manpower and horses; horse-breeding had never before been so lucrative. Obviously the means used for travelling in 1830 were not very different from those of preceding centuries. Nevertheless the quality of the roads, the excellence of the organization and the relative comfort of well-sprung, light-wheeled carriages enabled postillions to drive coaches at high speed; the psychological love of speed has its first origins in this development in road traffic.

The canals were being developed as rapidly as the roads. Every river in Europe in 1830 carried those famous tow-barges which seem so strange to us. Although less popular than the new stage-coaches, they were greatly favoured by the new tourist, because they were more comfortable, travel was more picturesque and safer, and finally because of the accommodation on board, which sensitive souls preferred to overcrowded stage-coaches. On the great rivers there were numerous ports and inns, some of which were well kept. The slowness of the trip was enlivened by entertainments on the boat and on the river-banks. The Loire was famous for its tourist attractions, but the Rhône was rather frightening, providing the traveller with many a thrilling tale, especially when it was swollen with flood water, so that the boats had to shoot between the piers of the bridges.

In order to connect these rivers with each other, canals had been dug everywhere, and were even more comfortable to sail on than the rivers. Michel Chevalier had cause to complain, in 1838, that France's rivers were not worthy of her canals.

France possessed a fine system of waterways and the Canal des Deux-Mers with its large dock at Béziers was no longer the finest. France's Central Canals, which had been begun under the *ancien régime*, were improved during the Restoration, when work in the north was resumed and the length of waterways was doubled. Under Louis-Philippe, whose family had always had extensive interests in the building and leasing of canals, effort was concentrated in the north and east, and again the network was doubled: the Marne was connected with the Rhine, the Rhine with the Rhône and the Aisne with the Marne. All of this was made possible by the tolls levied on the boats which used them, bringing good profits to contractors and farmers.

In England, private enterprise had achieved an improvement in transport comparable to that effected by the *Ponts et Chaussées* in France. This early part of the nineteenth century was a time of great expansion and progress, and was known as 'the age of canals'. Nevertheless, the most ambitious projects, particularly the Caledonian Canal opened in 1831, had not fulfilled the hopes of their constructors, and in spite of heavy governmental subsidies could never pay the interest on the heavy debts incurred, thus discouraging shareholders. On the contrary, numerous small canals and all river transport brought in handsome profits, especially where they enabled the coastal trading ships to penetrate inland.

In Germany the great preoccupation at this time was

to make the Rhine, which was already used by large ships, more suitable for navigation below Ludwigshaven. The Elbe and the Oder naturally carried a great deal of traffic. There was some talk of canals, though very little work was done on them. The great transport problem facing Germany was an administrative and political one; how to reduce the multiplicity of controls and customs at each frontier, since each state, however tiny, regarded itself as the exclusive owner of its waterways.

In 1830 a technical revolution took place on the rivers. Barges were still often towed by horses, but already the slow boats hugging the banks were being outdistanced by the new steamboats, which could travel in mid-stream. Some of the old bridges over the Loire had had to be reshaped and sometimes replaced by light iron footbridges to give room for the funnels of these new boats. Steam made boats less subject to the uncertainties of wind, currents and sandbanks. In Germany the crossing of the Baltic Straits was made by steamboats which penetrated into the very heart of the continent without any transfer of cargo. In France and England steam shipping was developing, so that the same ships could be used for sea and inland transport. The great English ironmaster Aaron Manby, who later transferred to Charenton and then to Le Creusot, had built his own iron steamship in 1822. It was greatly admired by the Parisians, and he professed to prefer it to all other means of transport for the journey from London to France. In 1832 a small iron steamship, the *Alburkah*, performed a great feat by sailing up the Niger.

This sudden expansion of trade on roads and canals gave a great impetus to economic growth within each country and throughout the whole of Europe, while the invention of the optical telegraph encouraged it still further. The great wooden arms invented by Chappe during the Revolution and first used exclusively by the state had soon begun working for trade. They topped every tower and height in Europe. In bad weather they stopped, showing that there was bad visibility at some point on the route. The Berliners, strolling through the city, could tell

when bad weather was on the way by the breakdown of
the Western telegraph.

Thus in 1806 there were indications that the countries
of Europe were drawing closer together, and that a greater
solidarity was developing between provinces and between
nations. Following the telegraph came cargoes of goods,
and then credit began to spread from town to town and
from capital to capital. The *Banque de France*, which
had resisted the opening of provincial branches for so
long, had to establish many under Louis-Philippe and had
to compete with the provincial banks of issue by setting
up branches in the chief cities of France. In England the
spread of local banks was too strong to be checked by
the development of these London banks. In Scotland in
about 1830 there was a sudden increase of issuing banks,
which even went so far as to put one-pound notes in
circulation. Peel was incensed but neither governmental
pressure nor crises were able to make the Scots see
reason. Yet the note and credit of the Bank of England,
and particularly of the London Bank, were going from
strength to strength. In any case, the influence of the
City extended as far as the highlands, where it played the
rôle of supreme regulator. The fluctuations of market
prices could be followed in detail from one end of the
continent to the other, so that people risked their capital farther and farther over the frontiers. They used the
already existing banking networks, consisting of the
Rothschild, Baring and Hope banks, from London to
Paris, Amsterdam, Frankfurt, Berlin, Vienna and Naples,
widening their scope and consolidating them. It was in
this way that European solidarity was created; it enabled
the *Banque de France* to lend part of its gold reserves to
support the Bank of England in a crisis on several occasions, in 1825, 1839 and 1847. In the same way, the Bank
of England opened its discount system widely to French
paper money. English capital was invested throughout
the whole of Europe, encouraging local money to come
out of its hiding places and swell the credit put at the
disposal of the great industrial concerns; a new era was

opening up to European industry. It was then that the railway really came into its own.

Once more the French were theoretical and systematic, for they planned before they acted. They had a railway system before any railways. There was the well-known Saint-Simonist movement, which was a curious intellectual group where logic merged into mysticism. Its promoters dreamed of a vast Mediterranean railway system as the forerunner of a world system, which would ensure the brotherhood of nations and universal peace for all eternity; the more generous their estimates of the advantages and benefits to be reaped by business concerns from swifter and safer transport, the more persuasive their arguments became. It is true that this splendid theory was adopted only by a small *élite*, chiefly in Paris, but it was a most influential *élite* consisting of Jewish and Protestant bankers, although also including a few solid directors of the *Banque de France*. It was an *élite* of engineers and also of polytechnicians who were to ensure a fine future for the pupils of their school for generations to come; senior ministry officials were also involved. Enfantin was not just a quaint mystic who wore his waistcoats buttoned down the back, for as a polytechnician he had the entrée into banks, ministers' bureaux and the yards of contractors engaged on public works, and was on familiar terms with old school friends of the *École Polytechnique*. This small enlightened *élite*, confident, ambitious and eager, exerted the greatest possible pressure on the French Government, and tried to convince the outside world. It almost succeeded in a series of missions in Italy, Spain and Egypt, where it was already busy with a project for a canal between the two seas.

But Saint-Simonism should not lead us to overlook the importance of Leipzig, another centre of thought where Frederick List was trying to get new ideas adopted in Germany. List's liberalism and unionism had brought misfortune on him, but had also led him to evolve a national system of political economy. When he was freed from prison and exiled, he travelled in America and France; he returned convinced of the necessity of a customs union and a railway system. He preached his message from Augsburg to Magdeburg, lectured to businessmen, and made his name as a journalist. He was soon influential enough to have a say in the formation of governments and in particular that of Prussia. Of course, List's activity came several years after that of the Saint-Simonists, but it had more speedy results, for the German railways were built before the French.

The English had no famous schools of engineers, and lacked theorists. But they went one better and set a practical example. Since the eighteenth century English coal-mines had been making use of railways, and the cost of maintaining roads and transport was saved by installing small trucks on rails running from the mine to the river or the coast. In France, Anzin copied this method, and so did a number of small metallurgical and mining centres all over the continent but especially in Belgium. Thus the English posed the problem of the railways on a wider scale, for it was now a case of providing them not simply for an industrial firm but for a whole industrial area.

The decisive step forward in the progress of railways was the replacement of the horse by the locomotive. George Stephenson, a clock-maker, believed he had discovered the secret of perpetual motion at twenty-five. Then one of those English farmers whose social status was peculiar to England, as we have seen, taught him enough mathematics and physics to enable him to become director of a coalmine, whose owner helped him to perfect a steam-engine which drew the coal-trucks. Having taken out a patent, Stephenson founded a locomotive works near Newcastle. In 1829 he won the competition organized by the Manchester-Liverpool Railway Company with the *Rocket*. In 1834 the Newcastle-Carlisle Company still kept up its stables, but in the following year it bought an engine from the firm of Stephenson and Company. Parliament approved. In 1835 the victory of the locomotive was assured for in March of that year the three coaches *Expedition*, *Social* and *Prospect* were drawn by the Stephenson *Rapid* from Blaydon to Hexham.

The railways had won the day and the countryside was transformed almost overnight. English metallurgists were working at full pressure and new blast furnaces, gigantic for that time and producing a hundred tons a week, sprang up everywhere, but especially in the Midlands, and in Scotland where there was formidable industrial development round Glasgow. By 1830 England was turning out two thousand tons of iron per working day, and rolling it by steam-power, for steam-engines were gradually replacing water mills. This iron made the safest rails in the world. New companies were busy snapping up capital and credit to make trucks and engines. Others hastened to obtain parliamentary sanction for the creation of new lines, in a frantic rivalry which led to fierce arguments about sites for stations in the towns and in country areas about the routes for lines. Astonished countrymen first saw surveyors, followed by gangs of navvies, invading their fields and meadows, digging and building, bridging rivers, and constructing lines along the sides of hills and mountains. A terrific fever seized the country, and technicians succeeded in stepping up production to such a degree that it exceeded local consumption and left a good surplus for export to the continent in a few short years. The great railway fever lasted forty years, and changed Europe and the world.

Naturally, in the early stages things did not always go smoothly and there were many difficulties. It sometimes took a long time to obtain credit. In order to attract it, innumerable construction companies put forward magnificent plans which were reasonably economical on the surface. Barely had the company been formed than technical progress and more accurate calculations forced an increase in the weight of rails and the solidity of rolling stock, while at the same time the law imposed more numerous precautions affecting brakes and signalling; the cost of labour was continually increasing and the salaries of technicians rose rather than went down, so that a company's actual outlay was always more than had been foreseen in the original estimates. Public opinion was disturbed, and canal and toll-road owners organized great campaigns against the railways, inveighing against their dangers and the ruin they would bring to rash investors. They lobbied Parliament with their objections to this unnatural craze, which would ruin the solid, safe transport of former times and drag the whole country down with it to disaster.

Moreover, the navvies scattered all over the countryside sometimes broke down fences, and robbed farms and cottages. It was said that no good could come out of this wild, beer-swilling mob. In 1839, a parliamentary committee was told that the railways were a calamity, but the railways replied to these protests by increasing their capital, strengthening their safety measures, and declaring their faith in ultimate success.

The gradual opening of railways along the classic routes of coaches and canals was a tremendous boost for the new mode of transport. Above all, the few great noblemen who dominated conservative opinion began to use the railway for their own journeys. This desertion of the canal and the road by the kings of public opinion was a notable event. It must be admitted that great efforts were made to make the stations comfortable. They were equipped with handsome waiting-rooms with a buffet in the middle where the staff were instructed to refuse tips. It was thought that the railway would drain away travellers, but would leave goods for the roads and canals. Up to the middle of the century a famous glass manufacturer had transported his fragile wares by water, but from about 1835 goods were piling up in the stations, and more trucks had to be built hurriedly. The great metal and mining concerns had their own rolling-stock which they used on the railway companies' lines by mutual agreement. Meanwhile the dividends paid by the inland waterway companies and the toll-roads decreased sharply. On the Birmingham Canal they fell by eighty per cent between 1825 and 1838. There was also a change in the method of calculating railway costs and fares. The railway charges had been previously based on the old traffic on the canals and roads, but after a few years the new traffic was found to be much higher than had been foreseen for the railways were now attracting a new type of customer.

Many people who had not been in the habit of travelling were now fired with a longing to see what a train journey was like, and very soon acquired the habit. Crowds of third-class passengers who had never travelled before invaded the stations and trains. Merchandise also seemed to be attracted by stations. There was naturally a corresponding decline in road traffic, although this only affected the main highways. On the minor roads serving the area around the stations there was such an increase that the organization of road transport and the administration of road maintenance and construction had to be overhauled completely. But the canals themselves survived in these widespread changes. In high society, and even among humbler folk, the railway craze was so strong that it left its mark on the country's whole way of life. It affected language too, and it was fashionable to talk of matters being 'in train', or of 'steaming ahead'. The phrases were used first of business but then even of one's love affairs, for the Victorian age truly came into being around an iron cradle.

England's transformation was soon followed by that of Europe, although the English economic methods could not be exported very easily. The power of British capital, allied to the easy circulation of money and credit, meant that the new economy could develop without intervention from the state. Parliament, torn by conflicting arguments, usually approved the creation of new companies without discussion. General laws, debated at great length, obliged companies to take more technical and financial precautions, compelled them to keep their prices down, and insisted on reductions for soldiers and officers, or Sunday trips for city workers. In fact these laws aroused the opposition of the railways, who were encouraged by Cobden and his associates to proclaim their rights of ownership as vehemently as their opponents proclaimed the rights of the nation in matters which went beyond individual ownership. For some months Parliament gave a committee something approaching plenary powers over the railways.

This Committee of Five (known as the 'five kings') achieved very little, for it was swept along by the current; the most stubborn aristocrats ended by being appointed to the governing bodies of the railways, and the Government reduced intervention to the minimum among so much intense competition.

This English pattern could not be reproduced on the continent. It was the new state of Belgium which set the decisive example here. Almost as soon as it came into existence, the Belgians made it a point of honour to prove the vitality of their new state by constructing a network of railways which was the best co-ordinated in the world. They planned a junction at Mechlin, connecting Antwerp with France and Ostend with Germany. After brief discussions in 1834 Parliament voted by acclamation that these national enterprises should be undertaken by the state. Within two years Brussels was connected with Antwerp and within ten years the plan was completed and the system flourishing. Soon other lines were added although they were privately owned. The Belgians had almost caught up with England by methods which were a model for their neighbours.

The history of French railways began with the small mining railway connecting Saint-Etienne with Andrézieux, which was first drawn by horses and oxen and then by engines; it was to this little railway that Vigny referred so slightingly in his *Maison du Berger*. This entire industrial civilization seemed unaesthetic, dangerous and inhuman to a public brought up to the slow trot of stagecoaches. Thiers' sceptical sallies are well-known. But the Pereires and Rothschilds persisted in their battle, supported by a troop of Saint-Simonists and by many people who came back from a journey to England praising the advantages of this new form of travel. Small companies sprang up on all sides while Government and Parliament willingly granted permits which appeared to affect only suburbs and industrial areas.

However, in the offices and councils of the financiers a general plan was being worked out. The small line from Paris to Saint-Germain was built by Pereire in 1835, not as an amusement for Parisians but as the fore-runner of a great section running along the Seine to Le Havre. English investors had barely regained their outlay from their own country's railway development when they began to take an interest in French lines, particularly the one between Amiens and Boulogne; it was this that obliged the Rothschilds to acquire the Paris-Lille line with all haste. In 1842, just when the Belgian network had proved its worth, agreement was reached on a great general plan. From Paris lines were to go the Channel and Belgium, to Nancy and Strasbourg and to Lyons and the Mediterranean, and there were to be two lines to the Pyrenees, one through Toulouse and the other through Bordeaux.

It was all the more important that the Saint-Simonists had won the battle of principle and law, since in the private ventures that had been started the small companies were doing very badly, using poor quality material and spending their efforts in a search for illusory profits which the suburban lines could not bring in. The view that the state should take over the railways, following the Belgian example in every way, was widely held. The protagonists of free ownership fought back and tried to keep profits and initiative in their own hands. The result was an uneasy compromise with the state meeting the very heavy cost of the substructure, as it had done for the roads; the *Ponts et Chaussées* laid the bed of the track and were responsible for excavations and embankments, bridges and tunnels. This substructure was to be given with substantial credits to the companies who were to lay the rails and purchase the necessary rolling-stock. For a number of the most profitable lines, notably that between Paris and Lille which was backed by the Rothschilds, a purchaser was easily found. The deal provoked the first quarrels between the Rothschilds and the Pereires. For other lines, the state built the substructure before knowing whether companies would be found to buy them from it so that progress was very slow and very unequal, according to the part of the country concerned.

But eventually, about the middle of the century, the system was beginning to work; Paris was connected to

Belgium, the Channel and the Loire, and tracks were already being laid towards Troyes and Dijon. Certain venturesome spirits embarked on the manufacture of rolling-stock. On his return from a study trip to England, Gouin, the banker's son, opened a construction centre at the Batignolles, getting men from the *Compagnie du Nord* and various bankers together on his board of directors. Using English methods, he built locomotives and coaches in works that occupied the present site of the *Gare Saint-Lazare*. The metal industry was gradually developing Le Creusot which had been practically inactive since the days of the Constituent Assembly; it restarted its furnaces after 1834, and rapidly developed under the initiative of the Schneiders its new owners. This metal industry made full use of English technique, and sometimes of English technicians. At Creil a powerful industry developed, backed by the *Compagnie du Nord*, although rails and plant still had to be imported from England. There was very little rivalry with the canals and roads, for agreements had been reached with the large coaching companies. In fact in the heroic days of the Parisian railway the bodies of the stage-coach were taken off their wheels and, with their passengers still inside, were lifted by crane and put with their axles on the rails! The rivalry with canals and rivers did not become apparent until the triumph of the railway was a foregone conclusion.

While French railways were developing, plans were also going ahead in Germany. The exhortations and predictions of List were producing results. In Leipzig in 1833, he had published his pamphlet advocating a Saxon railway which would be the first section of a German railway, for in his opinion the centre of the whole German railway system must be Berlin. The company building the first sector from Leipzig to Dresden in 1839 received help from the Saxon Government. It was not quite completed when a second line was laid down in the suburbs of Nuremberg and the King of Bavaria prided himself on having inaugurated the first railway in Germany.

People wondered whether the kings of southern Germany, the teachings of List, the enthusiasm of Rhenish manufacturers and even the progress of the *Zollverein* were to overcome the hesitations of Prussia. There was no lack of medical men to declare that the speed of the trains would make passengers ill and even mad, or that a journey through a tunnel would give rise to immorality. Nevertheless, the iron fetters were about to close on Werther's poor, beloved Germany. Although the Prussian authorities were worried at not having completed the Western road network, and although the roads in the Pomeranian east had not even been started, they were persuaded by the wildly enthusiastic Crown Prince Frederick William IV and sanctioned the Leipzig-Magdeburg line and the development of plans for a wide network linking the Rhine, Berlin and Magdeburg. In 1842 work was proceeding all over the country; the Prussian Government adopted a vast plan for the whole of Germany and, above all, agreed to ensure a minimum rate of interest for the companies constructing these various lines.

Numerous central German states constructed their own internal lines on their own account. Bavaria abandoned private enterprise in order to progress more quickly. Towards the middle of the nineteenth century, Munich was linked with Berlin and Stettin with Hamburg, and railroads penetrated to the heart of Prussia from the Rhine. At the same time in Vienna, the state, realizing the political importance of a rail network which would draw together the unequal members of the old monarchy, had already linked Prague and Cracow with Vienna in a line which ran on southward to the Dalmatian coast through the difficult Alpine terrain. By 1848 the railways in Germany and Austria covered twice the mileage of the French railways. In order to make it one of the most formidable in Europe, the German network now needed only the line from Mainz to Bonn along the historic Rhineland gap, and the link with Berlin around the Black Mountains.

These German railways were cheap, and rapidly fitted out, and it was soon clear that they were the most efficient and would bring excellent returns. In central Germany land and labour were cheap, and the terrain not difficult enough to need great engineering skill. Here, as in America, the railway often preceded the road and the canal. The demand for raw materials, rails, sleepers and rolling-stock increased rapidly, and was no longer met by imports from England. Prices rose and the potential profits spurred on the Westphalians, Silesians, and contractors from every industrial area in Germany. The Siemens firm in Berlin was one of the first to exploit the situation. Schemes were undertaken which would meet the demands. The age of prosperity seemed as if it would never end. When the customs barriers were opened in 1834 a vast number of wagons was waiting near the old frontiers for the day when transport would be cheaper; as soon as the breach was opened the railways moved in.

Towns were changed and expanded and the old rural industries were now being concentrated in the capitals. People were so eager to invest money in railways that they started undertakings (as at Frankfurt) which were even more rash than the most imprudent of English schemes. Blast furnaces were started and steel works expanded their rolling-mills; a kind of industrial nationalism was aroused, and people believed that German steel was the finest in the world. The urban proletariat, which was building up at the expense of the countryside, volunteered for these new industries, and for the food and sugar industries which were soon added to the list. In a few years this industrial upheaval radically altered the meaning of the *Zollverein*.

The first aim of the *Zollverein* had been to decrease the customs duties levied on goods and to allow Germany to profit by the cheapness of new products, particularly from England. The aim now, which List had foreseen and advocated, was to raise the duties, not at the internal frontiers, but at the external boundaries of the German zone, so as to protect the newly-emerging local industries. Cheap sugar was brought down the Rhine from Holland, and the commercial towns had been pleased to get it; but ten years later they were objecting to the *Zollverein's* policy of low prices. The Prussian Government took note of their protests and raised the tariffs, and the towns applauded the measure; thus the new sugar industries were protected. It was now raw materials and not manufactured goods which were being unloaded from the clumsy barges along the Rhine, while trucks loaded with refined sugar were travelling in the opposite direction from before, going from south to north and even trying to get into Holland.

This sudden change in the economic significance of the *Zollverein* and the comparative flexibility shown by the Prussian Government increased the effectiveness of measures still further. Inside the new economic frontiers industrial growth was phenomenal and capital everywhere was wildly stimulated. The *Gewerbe Institut* developed its researches in industrial chemistry. What had been the land of craftsmen and peasants was now becoming that of a substantial chemical industry. The cultivation of sugar-beet and potatoes opened up a vast market for the new manures and for the products of distillation. In ten years Germany changed from medieval agriculture to modern industrialism.

Here we must leave the railways for the time being. In the rest of Europe, by the middle of the nineteenth century Italy still had only a very few lines. American railways will be discussed elsewhere. A further general point must be made: the development of communications by water and by road was linked with that of the optical telegraph as we have seen, and the development of the railways brought another innovation, the electric telegraph.

Gauss had linked his observatory at Göttingen with his physics laboratory by an electric wire. He offered his invention to the railways in Saxony but they could see no particular use for it. The idea was taken up in England however, and was soon a great success. From station to station the electric wire announced the trains, and ensured the smooth and continuous flow of traffic. The procedure was then adopted in Germany as well as in Belgium and France, and all the European railways took up this convenient method of signalling. England was the first to extend the use of this railway telegraph to the general public, and thanks to the alphabet invented by the American Morse, the system was already very popular with the public in 1846. In 1848 the Siemens firm experimented with a submarine cable at the bottom of Kiel harbour, and in London there was soon talk of a telegraph which would link Europe with the continent and New York.

VICTORY IN 1848

We have noted that economic crises recurred every ten years, affecting England in particular. One of the crises in this cycle occurred in 1846. England dealt with it in its usual fashion, reforming the economic structure in the midst of a wave of bankruptcies, while the continent was swept by the famous revolutions of 1848.

It is first important to note that prices had been decreasing continually, slowly but steadily, from 1815 to 1848, with only brief upward trends. Agricultural and industrial wages had followed the same graph closely and life was hard for the poor. Poverty sometimes exploded into revolts, especially in England and France, although they were easily suppressed by the state, which was responsible for the maintenance of order. It was seen as normal to respect freedom in all disputes about wages, as long as they remained on the economic plane and were thus favourable to the industrialist. It was regarded as equally normal for the government to bring maximum pressure to bear to prevent these impoverished men from making too violent an appeal to public opinion.

But the continuous drop in prices was no less upsetting to businessmen. They paid a little less for their labour and raw materials, but the economic advantage thus gained was largely offset by the difficulty they had in selling their goods; nobody would buy except at very low prices. The more widely they resorted to credit and drew cheques on the future, the more embarrassed their finances became so that they were soon on the verge of bankruptcy. They had to make continual appeals for funds to the shareholders and in the enormous surge of activity the smallest monetary resources played their part in bolstering up credit. This was to be seen in the ruthless manner in which the bank rate was raised on the eve of a crisis. In England, where the structure of banking organizations was particularly hazardous, these spectacular rises ruined several local banks and their clients with them. However, this brutal eliminating process did ensure the vigour, the *savoir-faire* and the market-sense of those enterprises which survived; after every crisis they proceeded to grow rich on the spoils of the vanquished. The *Banque de France* had come to the help of the London Bank and French gold helped England to find security for its credit, which the English based less on gold than on industrial activity. In a time of crisis the English capitalist structure called on France's more orthodox system to nurse it through the growing pains caused by these fundamental changes.

A further interesting point which must be stressed was the efficiency of the circulatory system in England. From an industrial or rural area ruined by the crisis, both middle and working classes could move away to a more prosperous district fairly easily. Thus although it entailed hardship the economic balance of the country was effectively established. It is therefore easy to see why the crises did not seriously shatter the public's confidence in economic freedom. Public opinion supported the ruthless measures taken against agitators who threatened economic liberty. Thus there was little outcry against the terrible verdict passed in London on the agricultural workers who had marched on the capital demanding a minimum wage; two were hanged while 420 were deported to Australia. But ships leaving English ports for overseas at this date did not carry convicts. A growing number of immigrants were fleeing from the poverty at home, especially from Ireland, but also from Scotland, Wales and the more backward areas of England. Emigration increased from 2,000 a year in 1830 to 30,000 in 1850. These emigrants went to settle in Canada, New Zealand, and Australia. Thus, by force of circumstances, and thanks to improved communications, England achieved greater internal stability after each upheaval and populated her Empire at the same time.

It would be inaccurate to claim that the English Government paid no heed to the nation's economic interests, for indeed they were the subject of endless debate in Parliament and the heated passions aroused by the Corn Laws were a matter of common knowledge. At a time when the whole English tariff system was moving towards considerable reductions in duties and the abolition of restrictions, imported corn was subject to excessively high rates of duty. This meant dearer bread in the towns, but it also meant that the landed interests of the aristocracy were firmly protected. It was not so much the workers as the industrialists who protested, for they were eager to grasp at anything which would justify a drop in wages and would thus extend their security margin and their capital. Eventually in 1846, after long hesitation, Sir Robert Peel accepted a gradual reduction in the duties on corn with a view to their eventual abandonment. This victory for urban interests was made possible only by the growing weight given to the towns in the electoral reform bill of 1832.

In any case, England had an economy which was flexible enough and credit which was firm enough to bear the gradual slight decline, which characterized these years of industrial development, without too much harm. On the continent the same decline acted on an economy that was still more rural than industrial, and thus delayed the start of industrialization; for people hesitated to invest their money in view of the risks being run by credit. If the *Banque de France* was so ready to lend money to England at a time of crisis, it was because it granted credits with extreme caution and watched its reserves jealously. The industrialists followed rather than initiated progress, clinging to the protection of the state rather than dissuading it from intervention in economic life. Apart from certain industrial areas of Prussia, the same attitude was prevalent over the whole of the Continent.

Let us now examine the effects of the crisis to west and east of the Channel. The collapse of credit in 1846 appeared at first sight to resemble preceding crises. Ten years of successful speculation had thrown doubtful securities onto the market and they had to be eliminated. But the great difference now was that credit was largely tied up in the railways and metal industries. Thus bankruptcies were particularly numerous and spectacular. The help given by the *Banque de France* did not prevent the Bank of England from acceding to Cobden's request that its cautious policy be abandoned and separating the departments of credit and issue. It thus repudiated Peel's Act of 1844, because a large number of notes was needed in circulation. The extension of paper currency and credit accompanied the huge rise in the bank rate which was to go up to twelve per cent for the general public. Moreover, the effects of the passing of the Corn Laws were only superficial. In fact, while the price of wine was falling, that of corn was very high, even outside England; in England itself the bad harvest of 1846 was followed by the good one of 1847, but throughout the rest of the world there was a succession of bad harvests, especially in America. In Danzig, which was the Chicago of that period, prices reached fearful heights. At the same time the potato harvest was disastrous, for in 1845 the plants were damaged by a disease which spread from Ireland to Holland, from northern to southern France, and affected Germany and Italy. The peasants were ruined and famine ravaged both town and country. The combination of low industrial prices and high agricultural prices could not possibly have been worse.

In England the unrest grew. The Working Men's Association drew up its People's Charter and demanded annual elections based on universal suffrage. Orators travelled the country while meetings and strikes increased. O'Connor proclaimed the need for an armed rising. It was in this atmosphere that Marx and Engels conceived the idea of the class struggle. But gradually the movement petered out ending in 1852 in the absurdity of a monster petition which proved to have far too many fictitious names. The safety devices of the English economy came into action and good business recovered at the expense of indifferent business, giving a renewed impetus to concentration. Great numbers of people left their homes by rail or by sea, and many emigrants left for the colonies or the United States. Good harvests all over the world ensured the country's food supplies from 1852 onwards, for foodstuffs were now being imported on a large scale. Soon newly discovered gold in America was available to give security for notes courageously increased by credit. The bank rate came down to a reasonable figure, and the Act of 1844 was re-established. Once more the crisis had strengthened British capitalism and the conservatives returned to power. *Tout va très bien, Madame l'Angleterre.*

On the continent, the picture was very different. In 1847 agrarian unrest created by bad harvests spread throughout country districts everywhere, from Holland to Sicily and from Berry to Poland. In Italy peasants met in the villages, camped out all night in public squares and cheered emissaries who came from the cities to address them on such subjects as freedom, republic and union. Sometimes they demonstrated under the very windows of the princes' palaces, demanding constitutions in the belief that these were synonymous with prosperity. All over Europe police posts were attacked, and a succession of riots stirred up the regions affected by the food crisis. These revolts assumed a national character in Galicia and Cracow. In Germany there was acclaim for the Union and for the liberalism of Frederick William in granting a *Landtag*. Metternich was afraid of being overwhelmed, but during the winter of 1847–8 the princes thought of going back on their concessions.

In France the workmen had demanded bread and in Lille had plundered the bakeries, for instance. They had been severely censured, had pleaded guilty and shown themselves repentant. Calm returned when the summer harvests reached the markets. But although bread could be bought again, credit still remained just as rare and just as expensive.

The lower middle classes persisted in their demands for

reform, which may perhaps have been inspired to some extent by political ambition, but which were also rooted in anxiety. Financial worries were common to small businessmen with falling incomes, to small capitalists whose company dividends were poor or non-existent, to shareholders whose plight was similar and to whom the railway companies continued to appeal for fresh capital even though they had paid no dividends, and lastly to small shopkeepers who were finding customers few and far between and the wholesale merchant ever more exacting. This fear turned to anger at the sight of the new power wielded by the privileged few of the Bank, of industry, and of the railways, for the state drew largely on receipts from taxation to build the substructure of railways and support big business. The lower middle classes wished to have a share in these great concerns protected by the Exchequer. First they wished to have their own representatives, men like themselves, in Parliament. They persisted in this campaign, supported at innumerable dinners where the privileged few of the régime were condemned in speeches and song. They demanded reform, sometimes by the light of Chinese lanterns, so that the lower middle classes added fuel to the flames of popular discontent.

The two anxieties merged into one, and at the first opportunity they exploded. It needed only an incident under the windows of Minister Guizot, whose stubborn and Anglophile ideas convinced him that his Government would be strengthened by riding out the storm unmoved. But France was still only half aware of the laws governing the new liberal economy which tended to reduce the rôle of the State. The National Guard cold-shouldered the king of the opportunists.

French chartism was at first less exacting in its demands than that of England, but it soon began to move towards socialism. First it demanded universal suffrage and then drew up varied and wide-embracing plans for a reformation of society although there was little agreement between the members of *La Réforme* and those of the *National* on that subject. The bourgeoisie paused for reflection. The suburban workers, whose opinion carried great weight with the man in the street, went boldly ahead. They listened to those who came to address them, and delivered inflammatory speeches in squares and clubs. They were no longer demanding only universal suffrage under the windows of the *Hôtel de Ville*, for they wanted bread, guarantees of work, a social republic and the red flag. The bourgeoisie realized with astonishment that they had opened the door to a social revolution.

The provisional government in Paris was torn between those who respected property and the Code, and those who wished to set up the socialist state, open national workshops, initiate a large-scale enquiry into the condition of the working class and discuss the workers' lot in a commission meeting in the Luxemburg. The monetary crisis was getting worse. The *Banque de France* had to be forced to issue a large quantity of notes, and even in small denominations. Proudhon would have liked credit to be free; it was obvious that it must at least be easy to obtain. An attempt was made to open discount banks in every administrative area. There was also an attempt to set up branch banks to benefit the great trade corporations. Notes and money were in wide circulation again, and although this tended to raise prices debts were settled and the bourgeois were now anxious for a different reason. They were no longer alarmed by bankruptcy, but rather by economic communism, and at elections and in clubs and newspapers they began to call for order at all costs. At first their hero was General Cavaignac, who savagely suppressed the Parisian workers as they protested against the closure of the national workshops, but the days of June 1848 witnessed ghastly reprisals. Then the providential man of order appeared in the shape of Prince Louis-Napoléon Bonaparte, nephew of the great Emperor. The peasants, impelled by fear of communism, rushed to support the winning side, and Louis-Napoléon was elected President of the Republic.

There was socialist agitation, a great deal of disorder and too much bloodshed, but the real result lay chiefly in the new credit and in the new and large circulation of banknotes. The banks set up by the Republic, which was anxious to have a social policy, were to be separate from the state. They were only to survive if they could live off their own capital. The task of supporting the national, communal, and departmental budgets was taken from them, especially when the moderate majority insisted on a reduction in public expenditure. Thus the institutions with socialist tendencies avoided state control and passed into the hands of liberal capitalism.

In Europe the news of the February Revolution in France stirred up political unrest. Metternich fled from Vienna while republics were proclaimed in Budapest and in Rome. In Turin Charles Albert was only able to canalize the agitation by declaring war against Austria. In Berlin, King Frederick William IV summoned a *Landtag* and declared himself ready to assume the leadership of German unity. However, parliamentarians of all the states were making for Frankfurt, where a German parliament was eager to bring about national unity. As we know, this enthusiasm was short-lived. The Russian army, coming to the support of its 'faithful and loyal' ally the Austrian army, was soon victorious over the Hungarian rebels, and this enabled the Austrians to defeat the Italians. The Prussian army dispersed the remnants of the Frankfurt parliament. There again, order was restored. The new and lasting outcome of all this unrest was that the order which had been restored was not the old order. First, a new step had been taken towards the abolition of serfdom: in Austria for instance the young Kudlish, the only peasant deputy in Europe, took advantage of the short-lived parliament elected by universal suffrage to put through the abolition of serfdom as well as a whole series of agrarian measures which soon had their effect in the most highly-developed regions of Austria. The peasant had to buy back his rights, for ownership was respected, but his eventual status was that of unquestioned owner of the land. In 1848 Austria took the step taken by France in 1789, with middle-class approval. When the Emperor was restored to full possession of his political rights, he revoked every political concession except this one profound social reform. In Munich, Stuttgart and Berlin far-reaching agrarian measures were adopted in the same way. No doubt serfdom had been abolished there in theory but many steps had still to be taken before abolition became a reality. The German peasantry did not emerge from the events of 1848 with the same status as its counterpart in England or France, but very important concessions in line with the French laws of property and ownership had been made and not even the most reactionary régimes dared to withdraw them subsequently.

Thus the revolts of 1848 were an explosion of liberal nationalism which failed, although their effect was to shake the feudal structure so thoroughly that it gave place to a capitalist and bourgeois law, supporting individual ownership, based on a code like that of France. The year 1848 saw the last ineffectual flicker of Romanticism and the first great victory for capitalism.

Eastern Europe then became middle class and shed its tenacious traditions, its feudalism, castes, trade guilds and time-honoured ways of life. It entered the age of codified law, which was kept well up to date by great elected assemblies, and guaranteed the owner his land and the industrialist his credit. In Frankfurt, Rome or Paris there had been little mention of railways, but it was they which had broken up the rigid framework of credit based on personal estate; and by their demands a new monetary and financial world was created, enabling the railways to expand into new areas. The agricultural crisis activated a revolution in the urban industrial economy. Order was re-established in Europe as in England, for gold from the New World no longer enriched either an antiquated feudalism or a radical socialism, but rather strengthened the financial economy imposed by the railways, which gave its shape to capitalism.

ITS EFFECTS ON CAPITALISM

The 1848 revolution saw the definitive failure of socialism. French theorists who had severely criticized middle-class indifference to poverty as being barely concealed under an affectation of charitable virtue, could not seize power in spite of the vehement eloquence of Proudhon, who dominated the debates in the republican assemblies; they could not even prevent the disastrous failure of the national workshops which were a caricature of the dreams of the first socialist age. Outside France, English chartism collapsed in ridicule, for the worker across the Channel was definitely no revolutionary. In Germany, Marx and his friends had tried to take advantage of the revolutionary movement to win support for their own brand of socialism. After having launched their celebrated manifesto in Paris, they had gone back to Cologne to replace the too liberal *Kölnische Zeitung*, on which Marx had been a collaborator some years earlier, by the *Neue Kölnische Zeitung*. But Marx was expelled in 1849. The crisis of 1846–8 deprived English landlords of the precious Corn Laws and the feudal lords of eastern Germany of the gangs of serf labour and Austria of serfdom itself. Middle-class capitalism was the great victor. From 1850 onwards it was to flourish with extraordinary vigour with the new supplies of American and Australian gold.

It was in February 1848 that Captain Sutter discovered several grains of gold dust at the foot of a waterfall in the Californian mountains. In a few weeks thousands of men rushed in from all over the Union. San Francisco, which had just been a village in March 1848 when the treaty whereby Mexico handed over California to the United States was signed there, rapidly became a town buzzing with activity, and with huts being built at top speed. Immigrants flocked in from Europe and China, attracted by the prospect of the sudden and fabulous fortunes which a few lucky placers had made. After 1850, systematic exploitation of the mines led to the installation of more efficient plant. Gold flowed over the American continent and soon over Europe.

At about the same time gold was discovered in the alluvial deposits in the colony of Victoria in Australia, then in the quartz itself. Although less spectacular, the effects were similar to those of the American finds. In the ten years following 1850, the world production of gold was ten times greater than in the ten preceding years. As is well known, the French had always preferred metal currency, and welcomed the gold with a special enthusiasm; the state struck an impressive quantity of coins, striking five hundred million in 1845, for the world's gold found its way more readily to France where it fetched the highest price. The circulation of gold increased in other European countries also, and the banks of issue, in particular, filled their vaults. In this gold rush the English were more cautious after their long acquaintance with problems of values, and the upheaval in the gold market brought hardly any changes in the prices of the metal there. It is true England also minted new coins, but took advantage of it chiefly to establish her banking system more firmly. The influx of gold, which was exclusively Australian, had at first little effect on the prices of goods, but it developed credit with a paper currency. The minting of this money increased England's metallic circulation by almost fifty per cent, but the use of the banknote and especially of the cheque increased by a far higher proportion. The use of the cheque became so widespread in England that shopkeepers and farmers adopted it as the only possible way of doing business although it was almost unknown on the continent. Cheques were often used for amounts of less than two pounds. Even if he had an income of only fifty pounds a year, the Englishman immediately opened a bank account. In 1885, payments in metal currency represented only one per cent of the London Bank payments and six per cent of those in Manchester.

The Act of 1826 granted complete freedom of issue, except in an area of twenty-six miles around London, where the privilege of the Bank was absolute. There was a good deal of argument about the exact meaning of this privilege; for example the question arose as to whether provincial banks could open an office in London, the main centre of business, without losing their rights of issue. When it was ruled that they could not, many banks nevertheless settled in London and forfeited their privilege of printing. Only the Scottish banks put up a firmer resistance to this extension of the privileges of the Bank of

England. On the other hand, the right of issue was losing much of its significance, since the remarkable development of payment by cheque meant that there was less resort to the note. Settlements between the great deposit banks were made neither in metal nor in notes, but were transacted in the accounts of a clearing house, which dealt with transactions amounting to several hundreds of thousands of pounds every year.

The London and Westminster Bank, one of the most important of the English private deposit banks, soon became a model for every bank in Europe, for it had a reserve capital of less than three million pounds, and held approximately twenty-two million in deposits. Such influential private banks, established as joint stock companies, had to resort to the Bank of England only rarely, so the latter did not need to be unduly anxious about its insignificant gold reserves which were barely one-third of those held by the *Banque de France*. The privilege of issuing paper money, a relic of the royal right of minting money, was therefore by-passed to all intents and purposes by the gradual improvement of English banking procedure. At the same time the Bank of England enjoyed a monopoly of issue which it was in process of acquiring without the intervention of the state, since the development of banking led all the provincial banks to settle in London, near the clearing house. It was a masterpiece of liberalism to co-ordinate the free activity of the English economy in the capital without any pressure from the political power. In this way financial centralization was achieved purely by private initiative once the need for it had become apparent.

French banking evolved on very different lines. In order to meet the credit crisis, the provisional government had recommended the establishment of departmental banks and of trade credit societies when it was reforming the *Banque de France*. Most of these establishments, whose capital was to be provided partly by the state and the departments, were stillborn, while others lingered on for a month or two before wasting away. On the other hand, the *Comptoir d'Escompte de la Seine* became a private concern, and flourished under the name of the *Comptoir National d'Escompte de Paris*. The *Banque du Département du Nord*, which became the *Crédit du Nord*, was equally fortunate, as were several trade banks, particularly that of the *Entrepreneurs de Travaux Publics*. The unusual feature about the composition of the *Comptoir National d'Escompte* was that the Council of State had allowed it to set up as a joint stock company. Within a few years the *Crédit Mobilier*, the *Crédit Industriel et Commercial*, the *Société Générale*, the *Société des Dépôtes et Comptes Courants*, and other companies were established to benefit from this new way of accumulating capital.

Not all these new banks were as prudent as their English counterparts by any means and this point is worth dwelling on. After 1848 the *Banque de France* had the monopoly of issuing notes for the whole of France, because the local issuing banks created by Napoleon I and Louis-Philippe had been absorbed by the *Banque de France*, whose notes were the only ones in circulation. It was the state which had made this decision and had settled the problem of monetary unity by authoritarian measures. A few bankers, under the Second Empire, protested against the right of monopoly exercised by the *Banque de France*, which had been imposed on the whole of the country by the state. Very little use was made of payment by cheque, and compensation was meagre. The wide circulation of metal currency was a sign of a restricted paper currency, but this meant that credit was scarce and was based entirely on the *Banque de France*. The latter, taking no risks, consequently piled up in its coffers considerable reserves of precious metals, proud of the fact that it could now maintain a steady discount rate more easily than England. It also gained great satisfaction from being the gold-controller of Europe. Whenever a sudden drastic rise in the English bank rate sent businessmen, and even the Bank of England itself, as we have seen, hastening to Paris in search of precious metals, it was to the *Banque de France* that they turned. Although it was attacked by those who accused it of stifling credit, on the other hand it was defended by those who found its caution reassuring.

It was a difference of opinion which further enlivened the quarrel between the Pereires and the Rothschilds.

As we know, Jewish bankers played a vital part in the building of the railways. Pereire, a railway enthusiast, and Rothschild, the largest holder of free capital in France, had at first been prepared to undertake the great task in complete agreement. Rothschild, content with holding the *Nord* and the English connections, was one of the directors whose word carried most weight in the *Banque de France,* while the Pereire brothers, their heads still full of Saint-Simonist projects, were interested in vast plans covering Austria, Spain and the Mediterranean. They financed the great development of the economy of the south although even so they were obliged to open a credit institution, the well-known *Crédit Mobilier.* But because they could not use it for the issue of paper notes, and had tied up the funds entrusted to them too quickly, the Pereires embarked on a struggle to deprive the Bank of its privilege of issue. They believed that the mere right of minting money would enable them to possess the wide credit necessary for the bold financial policy on which they were launching out. It so happened that when Savoy was annexed to France, the *Banque de Chambéry* brought its banknotes and its privileges within French frontiers. The Pereires and their friends seized the shares of this bank and tried to turn its notes into rivals of those of the central bank. The *Banque de France* then asserted its rights, Chambéry lost its rights of issue, and soon afterwards the *Crédit Mobilier* went into liquidation.

This incident occasioned a great quarrel between theorists for or against privilege; it was above all a demonstration of the solidity of the rights the Bank had acquired, while no-one doubted the right of the state to confirm its privileges any longer. This situation was all the more paradoxical since the state was in the hands of Napoleon III who was a firm supporter of the Pereires and the *Crédit Mobilier.* The underlying cause of this paradox lay in French scepticism about cheques, for the development of bank money lagged more than half a century behind England. It was to be chiefly the work of Henri Germain,

founder of the *Crédit Lyonnais*. His patron of 1863 was
mainly anxious to attract large deposits by guaranteeing
them against theft and fire so that he insisted on the effective help the Bank could give industrialists and merchants
by insuring their cash service itself. By making wise use of
these deposits and by a cautious policy, the *Crédit Lyonnais* was able to open branches in Paris and Marseilles,
so that it was soon as powerful as the *Crédit Industriel et
Commercial* and then outstripped it. It even surpassed the
Comptoir d'Escompte, and soon the *Crédit Lyonnais* became the leading French deposit bank. From 1860 it was
the major bank to introduce cheques.

But there is little reason for surprise in the difficulties
encountered by the cheque between 1860 and 1870.
The *Banque de France* was regarded as the most reliable
of all issuing authorities, and French specie reserves as
the most powerful stock of gold in the world; between
notes and gold as the two methods of payment, there
was very little room for the cheque. It is difficult to believe
that France's reserves could not have kept the deposit
banks generously supplied, perhaps as much as, and even
more than, the English reserves. But it kept a good part
of its cash-balance in gold, which held up the full development of French credit institutions until the closing
years of the nineteenth century.

In England there was security and in France hesitation,
but in Germany there was an irresistible wave of enthusiasm which led to the rapid growth of credit institutions
from 1840. There were a great many note-issuing banks
in the Germany of the confederation, because each prince
had his own currency. Hamburg had one of the soundest
banks of issue, whose *marc banco* was esteemed throughout Europe and served as a standard for the whole of
Germany. Nuremberg still had its old seventeenth-century
bank and its florin, while a large number of private establishments were also manufacturing notes with a restricted
circulation. In this scheme of things the Bank of Prussia
held a pre-eminent position which was strengthened by
the place Prussia had assumed in the *Zollverein*, but it
still could not contest the superiority of Hamburg. In

short, the legal position of the German banks was similar to that of the English, in that there was plurality of issue. Bank money, and banknotes, increased in competition with each other, and the future of the four great and famous banks which were to dominate the destiny of capitalist Germany after 1880 had already begun to take shape. The *Dresdner Bank* was connected with the progress of the iron industry in the Rhineland, and particularly of Essen and Krupps. The *Deutsche Bank* operated in the countries of central Europe. The *Darmstädter Bank* and the *Disconto Gesellschaft* carved out a place for themselves; indeed bills on the latter increased from six to forty million marks between 1855 and 1862.

In spite of the confusion of currencies which brought the southern florin into conflict with the northern thaler, whose rivalry was sharpened by that of Prussia and Austria, and despite the difficulties encountered by the Union thaler which Prussia tried to circulate through the economic channels of the *Zollverein*, and the difficulties experienced by the Congress of 1861 in defining a mark, the German public, which hitherto had been so cautious, had the greatest confidence in the banks and unhesitatingly supported credit. One example will serve to illustrate this. An old soldier, Friedrich-Wilhelm Raiffeisen, was Burgomaster of a Rhineland village; he was anxious to help the peasants, and launched a corporate movement of agricultural banks, after the famine of 1847. Schulze-Delitzsch, a Prussian judge, took the lead in a parallel move to help the artisans in the towns. From 1860 there was a widespread development of mutual credit societies, with unlimited liability, which granted loans to their members. They met with tremendous success and their offices sprang up all over the country. By the time the Empire was an accomplished fact, every large village and naturally every town had its bank. The *Raiffeisen* and *Delitzsch* banks helped each other. In one generation the practice of credit had penetrated every layer of society, for the bank attracted savings and could grant extensive credits. Almost a quarter of the German peasants were affiliated to a credit society. The situation, though not exactly similar, was comparable to that in England, and radically different from that in France.

France appeared to be a conservative and routine-loving country in its loyalty to gold, but this continued dependence on gold could be regarded as misplaced loyalty to an outdated rural structure. In 1852 Napoleon III tried to mobilize rural savings by founding the *Crédit Foncier*. It was the state which took the initiative here again, although misguidedly, since the *Crédit Foncier* was used to finance the transformation of the towns and to speculate in urban land in the main, while playing a very minor part in rural improvement. This example fully confirms the impression that France was hanging back between two rapidly developing countries in the general development of capitalist institutions between 1850 and 1880.

The development of new financial structures was rapid throughout Europe. Belgium had a substructure of credit on the Anglo-German model, and from 1848 there was unity of issue as in France. This derived from the merging of the Bank of Belgium and the *Société Générale*. Italy had so large a number of note-issuing establishments in 1848 that there were more banks than there were states, since the number was increased by several private banks, but nevertheless there was no easy development of credit there. If there was a move in favour of unity, the Sardinian Government brought pressure to bear on the banks of Turin and Genoa and even restricted, although it did not suppress, the privilege of the southern banks after victory had been won. If there was a desire to encourage agricultural savings the government of the new Italy proclaimed freedom of issue, but failed to create any of the necessary institutions. In Spain the situation was similar to that in Italy. The southern limits of the great capitalist thrust passed just south of Vienna, included the plain of the Po and Barcelona, but extended no farther, while the northern limit of this European capitalism was Stockholm.

Naturally enough this picture of monetary Europe is almost the same as that of financial Europe. Long-term credit found its ideal vehicle in the joint stock company which was already widespread in England and it soon began to appear on the continent. In Belgium there were about one hundred in 1850, and almost three hundred in 1860. Contemporary France was still loyal to the limited joint stock company; although each company could be established only by a special law in each individual case. In this way banks and railway companies came into being, but finally a general law was promulgated in 1867. Eighty societies were established in 1868 and two hundred and twenty-three followed in 1870. Prussia continued to authorize them in the French way, although the Hansa towns had been legalizing their joint stock companies on the English system ever since 1843. Apparently over Germany as a whole limited liability companies were by no means rare, and in the excessive division of power characteristic of confederate Germany even the system of authorization itself had not prevented a fairly substantial rise in the number of joint-stock companies. When a long and detailed decree was issued on the subject in 1884 under the Empire, several thousand societies already in existence hastened to conform to it. Everywhere the banks made sure that newly-issued shares were taken up.

In England practice preceded legislation but in France the law came first and imposed the economic structure. In Germany the economic system came into being of its own accord, preceding the law.

We have said that on the continent the 1848 crisis was the result of the inadequacy of capitalist equipment, and the weakness of banking institutions. From 1850 onward this inadequacy was overcome, and consequently the railway programme could be resumed on a grand and imposing scale after a few months of stagnation. From 1850 to 1870 the length of track in Great Britain went up from 6,000 to 15,000 miles, that in France from 2,000 to 12,-000, while German track rose from 4,000 to 12,000 and Italy's railways increased from 500 to 4,000 miles. By 1870 Europe's railway system was almost completed.

Capitalism and railways developed together. Nevertheless, relations between the state and the railway concerns were not entirely compatible with the varied credit structures we have observed. Once again in the case of the railways the political geography of Europe in 1870 played an important part. It ranged from English liberalism to eastern state control and the French structure seemed like a hinge between the two. For whereas in England the companies were free and controlled by the interplay of competition, in France the system was very curious; the companies were free, but sought help from the state, which granted it only by imposing its own control. The imperial regulations made many private companies link up into large networks which prevented them from competing with each other in practice. In fact, the tendency of French companies to resort to the state always seems to have been strengthened by economic necessity and by the difficulty of obtaining substantial credits. In Germany it was different, for the Prussian Government was interested in the railways for military reasons and constructed strategic lines. It was also concerned for political reasons and thus acquired the Hanover, Hesse–Cassel and Hesse–Nassau lines. The southern states were in search of a free port on the international Rhine, but Prussia seized the Rhineland traffic, thus vitiating the king of Bavaria's efforts to defend his own railway system. The private companies, which appear to have done good business until about 1880 at least, since their mileage then was three times larger than that of the Prussian state, were soon bought back by the German Government.

The telegraph remained quite independent of geographical differences, because it was in state hands all over Europe after 1870, only America remaining loyal to the principle of private industry. In England, telegraph systems were in the hands of the railway companies until 1870, but this was an arrangement which proved most inconvenient in practice, so the English Government bought the lines and entirely reorganized the system. In Germany from 1849, the year in which Berlin was linked up with Frankfurt, there was great activity. Soon all the cities in Germany were connected by a system of electronic wires which belonged to the state until they came under a federal ministry in 1871. In France Napoleon III was passionately interested in the development of the telegraph system. From 1851 to 1854, he had all the Paris prefectures interconnected; for political reasons he made this service available to the public in 1851, so as not to increase the budget and antagonize French middle-class public opinion.

Here then was capitalist Europe equipped with powerful means of communication in the railways and the telegraph. This iron framework was a great support for the newly developing industries, particularly the iron and electrical industries. It also brought about a new imbalance between town and country: banks, railways, and telegraphs opened up a new era in the history of the development of the Western countries. However, at this point we have to cease to consider Europe as a whole. A glance at the map of the telegraph system reveals how it reinforced the importance of the capitals and of national frontiers, for although capitalism triumphed from one end of Europe to the other, it sometimes acted as a spur to national rivalries.

9

Industrial Nationalism

ONCE victorious, the industrial revolution transformed the political structure of Europe. First it strengthened the power of England, which had been shaped by commercial liberalism and big business for more than a century and a half. Every new achievement in industrial and financial techniques was initially an English victory in the nineteenth century. It was therefore with fervour that the subjects of Queen Victoria supported economic liberalism and its technical apparatus. Germany had only narrow outlets to the sea, but possessed such rich mines that in a few years she became a first-rate power. The railways united Germany and enabled it to consolidate its position and spread out over the continent before turning its attention to the sea. It annexed a piece of France. France was a maritime power, although less well equipped for this rôle than England and was also a continental power, but was less well endowed than Germany. Thus it was uncertainty about its future which made France hesitate between the maritime world and the continent of Europe, concentrating on each in turn, only to win and then to lose what it had wanted in both spheres. The French had their railway but had lost Lorraine and Alsace; they had lost the coveted Mexico as well, but were now firmly entrenched in Asia and Africa.

ENGLISH STEEL—MASTER OF THE SEAS

In England the 1846–8 crisis was simply one of those ten-yearly crises which had already occurred in 1825 and in 1836–7, and which returned in 1857, 1867 and 1874. The financial outlook remained the same. The joint-stock banks, pressed by their customers in difficulties, turned to the London Bank, which increased its discount rate to protect its relatively small reserves. Although it was normally at two and a half per cent, it could rise as high as ten per cent. When credit reached this exorbitant figure, a number of over-adventurous businesses had to give up the struggle and go into liquidation. Production and trade adjusted themselves, the demand for credit became less urgent and the bank rate fell to its normal level. Life went on as before.

There were two almost immediate signs of recovery: plant and equipment improved greatly and the geographical distribution of industry changed, at least until 1880. Between 1830 and 1850 for instance, blast furnaces were already forty-eight feet high; these iron monsters leapt up even higher in the following generation and reached eighty feet or so. In 1880 they were to be one hundred and ten feet high, and were then able to turn out the enormous quantity of three hundred tons a day. Up to 1850, the great geographical innovation was the development of iron-smelting in west Scotland, where the comparatively limited supply of ore was soon exhausted. In the following years the industry opened up, first in Wales and then at Middlesbrough in Yorkshire, so that in a very short time the modern products of these ironworks were providing tools and implements for Lincolnshire.

During the same period old blast furnaces were closed down and dismantled, because their capacity was too limited; and to compete in price mass production was necessary, since it alone enabled valuable by-products to be recovered and ore and fuel to be used more sensibly. In spite of improvements in coking (in France and particularly in Belgium, which discovered how to recover the gases long before England), Durham alone must have wasted 45,000 tons of sulphur a year up to 1880. But English industry could afford this technical wastage because of the excellence of its commercial organization.

England was the first to make use of one technical advance, however: the substitution of steel for iron, the outstanding event of this period. From 1850 to 1860, the production of iron rose from three to four million tons; it fell to half this figure in 1880, because steel from England was just starting to conquer the world. For many years previously, Durham and Staffordshire had been making steel by the puddling process, and one big railway company, the North-Eastern Railway, had gone over to the new metal, which was more durable although more expensive. The English admired and envied the machines for mechanical puddling which were already in use in Cincinnati in the United States. In 1856 Bessemer made the startling announcement that he had discovered the possibility of converting iron into steel without the use of fuel, and by a speedy process. This was the famous 'converter'. At first this unexpected step forward left ironfounders sceptical and uncertain, but at the 1862 exhibition Bessemer was able to show tools and weapons made from his steel. The customer was convinced, and gradually iron was replaced by steel. Once again the example was set by the North-Eastern Railway, which substituted Bessemer's cheap steel for expensive puddled steel. This move was soon followed by all the companies. Rails were cast in steel, and were so strong that they largely compensated for the extra cost incurred. First railway engines were made of steel, ship's engines and their new propellers came next, until finally the ships themselves were steel built. In 1870 225,000 tons from a total output of 240,000 tons of steel were made by the Bessemer process. In 1883 more than 500,000 tons of Bessemer steel were turned out; this was its peak production period, for there was already competition from a new source—Martin steel.

Bessemer's process certainly had several drawbacks, the chief of which was that it required ores of specially high quality. These had to be imported from Sweden and Germany, so that some English mine workings had to be abandoned. The solution of the problem was discovered by two cousins, a Welsh chemist, named Gilchrist, and an official of the Thames Police court, called Thomas. Both of them were passionately interested in metallurgy, and realized that if the converter was lined with basic materials the phosphorous ores could be used as well. Throughout Europe the new patent was rapidly adopted.

The period 1850–80 was the heyday of English steel. Steel was made into flat plates and in 1854 the *Clytemnestra*, a steel ship, triumphantly weathered a cyclone off Calcutta. In 1868 Lloyds began to question the safety of iron ships, and by 1885 iron had disappeared from the British navy. This success speeded up the disappearance of wooden ships and sailing-ships, since steel could be adapted to all the new improved techniques and was ideal for parts subjected to great strain. The main shafts of ships driven by propellers, and the crankshafts of steam-engines (particularly the new double-expansion steam-engines which needed longer axles) are examples.

The rapid growth in the use of steel emphasized the importance of standardization as an invaluable commercial necessity. The idea was first tried out by Whitworth in his own mill and was soon adopted by the Admiralty, shipowners and of course the artillery services. Engine parts, screws and bolts, ship's propellers and tools in general had to be reduced to a few main types, so that spare parts could be stored in readiness in arsenals and ports of call. Any mechanical damage could now be repaired quickly, whereas it was slow and costly to forge a replacement for a broken part.

In about 1880 the supremacy of English steel was such that the English had understandably neglected certain aspects of their industrial development, as we have already seen in connection with the use of coke. English coalmines were soon surpassed by those of the Borinage in swifter and more efficient cutting and better lifts, safer pit props and more efficient ventilation. Soon even the French mines were accusing their English rivals of holding human safety cheap in order to bring down running costs and so conquer markets, although the reproach was not entirely justified, since the geological siting of the English pits made them much easier to work and less dangerous, and thus less expensive.

We shall not dwell on the growth of the textile industry except to say that the number of spinning-frames rose in thirty years from 200 to 245,000 while the output of each machine had almost doubled. The output from the looms more than doubled, although their numbers had increased by barely fifteen per cent. All this showed a vitality that was still unique in the world. But nothing was comparable to England's triumph in the manufacture of steel. Undoubtedly it was steel that held the key role, just as cotton had done almost a century earlier. In conclusion, we shall mention the success of machine-made cement, for it was a discovery which held great things for the future. At the end of the eighteenth century a Kentish labourer, following the fashion, had given the name of Roman cement to the 'plaster' he got from the clayey chalk of Kent, which 'took' far more quickly than the traditional hydraulic limestone. In 1824, Joseph Aspdin of Yorkshire achieved exactly the right mixture of sandstone and clay in a cement that he named Portland, and after 1870 cement was made on an industrial scale.

With steel for ships and engines, coal for steam and cement for harbours, England had all the essentials needed to keep and strengthen its economic domination of the seas. In 1845 many wooden sailing-ships were still being built in England after French models, particularly the famous *Sans Pareil*. Out of a total of 3,400,000 tons, the English fleet contained only 170,000 tons of iron shipping, but it had performed miracles from 1855 to 1860, cutting down the time for a voyage to Australia from eighty-three to seventy-eight days. But it was still too long a voyage, since the American clippers were already faster. But within half a century, steel accounted for ninety per cent of England's tonnage, which had trebled in the meantime; this vast substitution had obviously had its problems. Cunard had been one of the first to go over to iron and steam, but it was unwise at that early stage to move too quickly. This could be seen in the notorious *Great Eastern*, which was 692 feet long and sixteen times as big as the biggest other ship afloat; it was so huge, requiring as it did a coal reserve of 12,000 tons, that it was never able to find enough freight and passengers to cover the cost of the North Atlantic crossing. It was turned into a collier and then a trawler, but always ran at a loss; the ship ended its career as a cable-layer, but the only person to make money out of it was its last purchaser, who had it broken up. This lesson in caution was not forgotten and the subsequent progress of the steamship was irresistible just because it had been carefully planned. The steel steamship was the invincible weapon of British commercial imperialism.

The English certainly used it with courage and boldness, and with a breadth of outlook rarely found on the continent. In England, it was accepted without question that it was unwise to attempt to protect the nation's industries, according to John Stuart Mill. He went on to say that in normal business dealings foreign goods were hardly ever imported except when it was in the national interest. He believed that it was absurd to base a general political system on the obviously unlikely possibility that war might be waged against every nation in the world at once and on the assumption that a country could be blockaded like a city if weak in sea power. In short, Stuart Mill admits that the state may intervene to protect a new and weak industry, but only as a purely temporary measure, and only in so far as this industry gives proof that it is vital to the nation.

These were not only Mill's opinions, but those of the great majority of English people, who were convinced of the benefits of free trade at least as far as England was concerned. We have already spoken of the importance of Peel's repeal of the Corn Laws in the late 1840s. The consequences were not long delayed, for from 1850 onwards a quarter of the population of England was living on foreign bread; this was an adventurous policy for that time, although it made the fortune of the Rouen mills. The imports of cattle doubled between 1850 and 1853, while butter was brought from Ireland and Brittany and even from Portugal, Holland and Denmark. If the Admiralty still felt a lingering uneasiness at the thought that half the wood used in England came from Scandinavia and tried to protect local forests in consequence, its anxiety was short-lived. England naturally imported wool from its

colonies, but also well-made Saxon cloth from Germany
England imported all its cotton and imports of ores ex
ceeded exports; this trend became more and more pro
nounced as time went on. Exports of coal rose steadil
on the other hand. Iron exports rose from 200,000 ton
in 1839 to 600,000 tons in 1849 and reached 1,300,000
tons in 1853.

The likeliest source of rivalry to England lay in America
The United States were past-masters in the preparation o
wool; their Singer sewing-machines were unrivalled eve
in England, their agricultural tools were widely used i
the English countryside, and the competition of Scottis
products was still very largely ineffective. England cease
to compete in certain areas; wooden articles, for example
could never be made as cheaply or as attractively as thos
from Germany and English children loved the Germa
toys. The English could never hope to make clocks bette
than the French, or watches comparable to the marvellou
products from Switzerland, while it was impossible t
compete with certain French luxury fabrics such as silk
or fine woollens from Roubaix or Saint-Quentin, o
leather and skin boots and gloves, although Mancheste
tried to compete with French silks in the English marke
through the efforts of Huskisson, Jacquard's rival. Th
Lister loom, too, tried to produce woollen goods to equa
those of the famous Heilmann of Mulhouse. An attemp
was made to process English glass for light-house lamps
for the manufacture of which France had enjoyed
monopoly until that time.

Businessmen in London were sometimes impatient a
the exclusiveness with which France shut herself behin
customs barriers and resisted the entry of English good
iron and coal in particular, although other markets offere
British trade ample compensation for this restriction.

Since English products sold well, England had littl
need to expend her energy in making objects it was mor
convenient to buy from its neighbours, especially as a
transport benefited the merchant navy, and any de
helped its market. In the absence of customs' duties, trans
via Liverpool or London did not add to the cost of good

significantly, so that in consequence these great English commercial centres became the nuclei of world trade. As the years went by the English improved their sales technique, for whether it was a question of presenting samples, guaranteeing the quality of a consignment or fixing a fair price, their word was law, and they made the most of their skill. But since it was also to the advantage of the continental merchants to make use of this same skill, profitable transactions continued to increase. Cobden was right, for England became the commercial centre of the world.

The English were great handlers of money as well as dealers in goods, since they were the best informed and the most skilled in taking advantage of financial opportunities. There was always someone in a good position to suggest to Argentina, Brazil or Peru, and obviously even more easily to Canada or India, a plan for building a railway, a harbour, or a lighthouse, or for opening up a market. From 1850 to 1880 England invested one thousand million pounds in the world, or more than one-tenth of all the capital invested in Great Britain itself. This capital brought in orders for English industry, including more than £160,000,000 worth for railway material alone during the same period. Of course, not all these investments were sound. More than £3,000,000 were lost in rather risky ventures in Confederate territory during the American Civil War, although weapons made of the new British steel were effective on both sides. But when the fluctuations of markets beyond its control caused Britain anxiety, it could always fall back on its imperial markets; for instance, investments in India between 1870 and 1880 rose from forty to two hundred million pounds sterling.

All this capital brought in good returns, and the English could afford to see their import figures surpass those of their exports without undue alarm, because the revenue from capital, added to profits from freight, insurance and brokerage, more than made up the trade deficit. England had been the great trading nation of the eighteenth century and became the great industrial nation of the nineteenth century because industry was used to further trade, which explains how it brought such rich rewards. The wealth of England's economy came from a combination of genius for trade and flair for business, even more than from the steel on which industrial power was based.

This was important in shaping English politics; England never experienced the shattering upheavals of the 1848 revolution. It was not that it escaped the agricultural crises which brought famine to Europe and impelled the peasantry and the growing urban proletariat out of their traditional submission. Ireland in particular was badly affected. The financial crises of the time also affected England and indeed were more dangerous there than in any other country. The ravages of unemployment which inevitably accompanied the closing of mills were more widespread in England than elsewhere, and resulted in the structural reorganizations which were such an important feature of England's economic life every ten years, as we have seen. However the mass of human beings whom the agricultural and financial crises drove into the public squares was quickly absorbed by English trade, English railways and English ships, so that before they had the chance to foment serious political troubles they had embarked for parts of the world where labour was needed. It was this fact which, in retrospect, gives its real meaning to the success of the anti-slavery campaign in a nation which had profited so much from the slave trade in the previous century. In 1849, emigrants from the British Isles to the United States numbered 300,000, of whom two-thirds or more were Irish. Australia, too, absorbed a good number, particularly for work in the gold mines. This emigration was essential if the social balance of the home country was not to be destroyed. Thus each period of crisis was also a period of mass exodus and more than two and a half million emigrants must have left between 1832 and 1880. They were all the more willing to go since they often found at their destination centres of English activity prepared by English capital and equipped with English material.

The crises which led to political unrest or even revolution in continental Europe worked to the advantage of an England equipped with powerful steel ships, and actually increased its world commitments in the prevailing atmosphere of free trade. Moreover this vast emigration was not left to look after itself since the philanthropic associations, which on the continent were concerned with finding bread and work for the down-and-out, devoted their energies in England to finding them a place on a ship which was leaving. The administrators of the Poor Law slowly awoke to the implications of this new solution, but many emigration societies were set up as well, including a Female Middle-Class Emigration Society in 1861. All this activity was co-ordinated by the Colonial Land and Emigration Commissioners, who alone sent more than one hundred and twenty ships to Australia and never ceased to work for the improvement of conditions aboard, for conditions in the early stages were tragic and deplorable.

Thanks to this effective safety-valve, the social and political evolution of England continued without too much upheaval. From over a million, the number of poor kept by the parishes in workhouses fell by half in 1880. This lightened the poor-rate, which had been very heavy at first, and soon the excessive strictness of the rules was relaxed and the poor were allowed to work outside the workhouses. The growth of savings banks, soon to be followed by the establishment of the Post Office Savings Bank, the co-operative societies and the mutual aid societies proved useful to the *élite* of a proletariat not too weighed down by poverty. The dangerous class had been reabsorbed by emigration.

The middle classes in power were less uneasy at the prospect of 'educated' workmen organizing their own clubs and unions. Those who gave the lead were the luxury-trade unions like publishing and they were followed by the Mechanics Union, which soon became the most wealthy union, and by the Union of Building Workers. A fairly high membership fee enabled them to provide reading-rooms and schools, to undertake large-scale investigations and to publish journals. Thus the workers played their part in educating public opinion, which was very important in England, as we have seen, and which enabled a middle-class public to acquire at least some knowledge about the problems of the people. In 1871 these unions, which had long been recognized in fact, were recognized in law, and were allowed to consult together and to organize strikes. The power of the unions then became dependent on the size of their membership rather than on their resources, so that subscriptions were lowered to allow the inclusion of non-specialist members; the Miners' Federation in the 1880s increased its membership from 36,000 to 200,000, for example.

Tolerance was the outstanding political quality of the English middle-class business community. Self-confident and proud of the benefits it had reaped from the triumph of free trade, it welcomed the continued political successes of the Liberal Party, which had come into power at the time of the repeal of the Corn Laws, and had remained in office without too much difficulty until 1867. The type of man admired by this liberal middle class is typified by two leading politicians of the day. Palmerston, or Dear Old Palm, as he was called, is the first. His background was beyond reproach, for he was educated at Harrow, Edinburgh and Cambridge; he had entered Parliament as a Tory in 1808, and had held office in the Ministry of War. As a young man he had viewed the continent with a somewhat supercilious nationalism, but was soon won over by the commercial and industrial middle class. While the Tories had been greatly disturbed by the revolutions in France, Palmerston saw in them the sign of England's supremacy. Soon his enthusiasm for the new England took him over to the Whigs, and as Foreign Secretary he found it easy enough to deal with Guizot and Thiers. He supported free trade from 1846, and had so clear a conception of continental politics and of England's opportunities that Peel recognized in him a potential statesman. This Whig, who had become one because he realized the rôle played by economic affairs in the destiny of peoples, supported and admired Louis-Napoleon Bonaparte: preferring that Saint-Simonist to the man he called 'that scatterbrained windbag de Tocqueville'. Such bold views brought him into conflict with public opinion, which was less ready to shed its traditional opinions in the matter of liberal policy and slower to understand the bonds which bound liberalism to industrial progress. Palmerston had to withdraw from power for a time, but on his return in 1852 he threw himself into the military alliance with Napoleon against Russia. He himself regretted this rashness, for although it ended in the common victory of the Crimea it had involved the country in a war which was not only unprofitable but possibly even harmful. He blamed Napoleon III for the Crimean war even more than for his uncoordinated policy in Italy and said to him in 1861, 'Between you and me all is over'. Nevertheless, he successfully negotiated the trade treaty opening up France to English goods. As he grew older, Palmerston continued to take an interest in armaments, especially in the navy, but by that time the star of Gladstone was already rising.

Gladstone, too, had received a very upper-class education at Eton and Oxford, and had also started as a Tory exercising his administrative talents at the Board of Trade, in conjunction with Robert Peel. In 1842 he had the courage to introduce a tax on income, while in the great debate centred around the Corn Laws Gladstone had first hesitated and then announced his conversion to liberalism. During the Crimean war, he rallied to the defence of Palmerston, whose successor he eventually became. As Chancellor of the Exchequer and leader of the Whigs from 1865, he remained the leading exponent of English liberalism, opposed to every war and to every constraint, even when exercised by England in Ireland. From a burning religious conviction he derived a political doctrine which advocated unwavering support for the peaceful conquest of markets. So solid were England's economic bonds with the world that it could easily afford to renounce its army as an aid to maintaining its international position for all that was needed was to preach liberalism. Gladstone maintained that it was necessary to grant Canada and Australia freedom to govern themselves, while rejecting all military intervention in South Africa, and on the continent in 1870-1. He ended his career in a supreme struggle to win for Ireland the Home

Rule which English opinion refused and stood firmly by his convictions, even though it meant a breach in the Liberal Party.

The history of the great English Liberal Party hinges on these two careers. In Palmerston's day it still believed in the need for armed intervention and played a risky diplomatic game on the international chess board, but under Gladstone it was concerned only with England's moral position, neglected diplomatic and military procedure, and relied entirely on England's immense material success. It was an approach which left a wide field for manoeuvre open to the Conservatives, which Disraeli did his best to exploit. He was a negotiator of consummate skill, and sought to carry on the great imperial tradition, which was revived by the Imperial Federation League in 1884 at a time when international competition was beginning to threaten English supremacy and was jeopardizing the future of liberalism. It was this new Conservative spirit which refused Home Rule to Ireland, strengthened British naval power, intervened in South Africa and in the world at large, when the golden age of Bessemer steel and the financial and human pre-eminence of England had passed its peak.

The country's internal affairs, too, reflected its economic development. New men went into Parliament on the wave of the industrial success achieved by the new middle classes. The electorate was enlarged by fresh classes of the population, who were given schooling in the growing towns, and the result was the reforms of 1867 which appreciably enlarged the electoral body. Thus England symbolized the power given to the Westerner by his commercial, industrial and banking tools.

PRUSSIAN STEEL—MASTER OF EUROPE

Of all the countries of Europe, the 1848 Revolution was most successful in Germany. Traditional historians usually maintain the opposite, because attempts at the political unification of Germany failed in 1848. It is true that in a country where feudal traditions were still so strong these first seeds of liberalism fell on stony ground: a brief uprising that was quickly checked left its supporters full of bitterness, disheartened those who had planned it and led the philosophers to doubt idealism. However, the shock of 1848 did eradicate the remnants of feudalism and prepared the ground in Germany for the new harvests of capitalism.

In Prussia laws had been passed in 1816 and 1821 to liberate the peasants wherever the provincial states wished to take advantage of the measure. The events of 1848 in Prussia are easy to interpret: archaic legislation led to popular uprisings and Manteuffel granted the farm-labourers (*spannfähig*) the right to claim their freedom. There were no longer any of the intermediate powers to bridge the gap between state and people as Montesquieu had advised; and the monarchic state profited from the economic progress of the people. The remnants of serfdom were soon eradicated from Württemberg and Bavaria too. In 1847 German agriculture was in fact still enslaved, whereas by 1870 it was free practically everywhere. This emancipation worked to the advantage of the well-to-do peasants. In a few years, the laws applying to land tenure in Germany became similar to those in England and France, but the social structure of German agriculture was closer to the English model, which, as we have already remarked, was more suited to the rapid adoption of modern methods. It is true that there were still differences between Bavaria, where half the lands were divided into tiny holdings of something like twenty-five acres, and Mecklenburg where sixty per cent of the lands consisted of estates larger than 250 acres; but even in Bavaria *métayage* was disappearing fairly rapidly, and the average peasant farm was soon larger than fifty acres.

Up to 1850 there had been some division of common lands, but though the local lord took his share individual peasant farms hardly ever benefited by it; the village's portion remained, in fact, undivided. It was only very gradually, as the country's industrialization progressed, that the German peasantry went over entirely to individual ownership. The result of this evolution was that communal holdings were not divided into lots, but leased out *en bloc*, which greatly facilitated attempts at redistribution. Germany differed most from France (and even from England) in the way in which the peasants left the countryside; the exodus of the poor peasants happened at a time when the railways were already in existence. The new proletariat, instead of collecting in great numbers near the nearest towns, could choose areas where industry was already flourishing or go directly to one of the great ports from which they embarked for America—generally for the United States. From 33,000 in 1844, German emigration rose to 250,000 a year in 1854; the trend was strong enough to attract the most underprivileged workers from the east, those of the 1810 *Gesinde Ordnung*. This decree gave to the employer (but not the worker) the right to break a contract and thus gave him the means of imposing pitiless discipline. The German emigrant was soon replaced by the Polish immigrant in these power levels of rural life.

German production improved as that of England had done a hundred years earlier, and at first this progress helped to strengthen the exporting position of Danzig, still a great European supply port in the middle of the century. Twenty years later the situation was reversed, and Germany became an importer. This reversal of commercial trends took place in a single generation there, whereas in England it had taken almost a century. It proved how quickly German agriculture had adapted itself to the new resources of rail-borne trade, which meant that any country need produce only what it could grow cheaply and at a substantial profit. Yields of corn at the end of the century were to reach twenty-five hundredweight to the acre in Mecklenburg, far surpassing those of France. Potato crops grew in size too and production went up to forty million tons a year, six times that of England. Such decisive progress was not achieved without good technicians. The first problem tackled by the German school of chemistry was that of the land. In the 1850s specialist schools began to appear in the small towns, and at Hildesheim for instance there were twenty-two peasant schools in 1870. Obviously the food industries also benefited from these new methods; sugar production rose from two hundred thousand tons to a million between 1860 and 1885.

From 1850 to 1880 the proportion of Prussia's rural population fell from seventy-two to sixty-four per cent, and the change in Saxony was even more rapid. The cause lay largely in the increase in coal production over the same period; it went up by eighty per cent in England, but almost quadrupled in Germany, and the number of mines more than doubled. From 1860 to 1875 Germany's iron production quadrupled (in France it doubled). Steel production in 1880 was higher than in France, and half that of England, which it surpassed in 1900. This progress was due also to the high concentration of the new German concerns. Foreigners were amazed to find that each German coalmine employed on an average eight hundred workers. Through the influence of the joint-stock companies, the number of big concerns in the Ruhr was reduced from three hundred in 1858 to fewer than two hundred in 1870. Naturally, work processes were continually being improved, and more modern methods adopted. In 1840, ninety per cent of Prussian iron was being smelted by wood; by 1860, eighty-eight per cent was produced by the use of coke: that was the real significance of the 1848 revolution in Germany.

Germany had, of course, bought a good deal of plant and equipment abroad, though only what was absolutely essential: in the 1840s its production was almost equal to the needs of consumption; in 1857 it could supply no more than sixty-six per cent of them; ten years later Germany began exporting. Berlin's coal consumption from 1840 to 1870 went up from 30,000 to 800,000 tons. Here again, progress was the result of cooperation between research and industry. In 1858 a mines committee of the Ruhr brought together fifty companies and embarked on a programme of extensive research. This committee organized production and opened a rail factory at Dusseldorf in 1850, a zinc works in Upper Silesia in 1860, and a tin works at Cologne. In this way Germany continually had new groups of producers systematically studying markets and techniques. Borsig was still one of the leaders of Berlin in 1860, and later came the *Hörder Verein*. These industrial 'general-staffs' formed a nucleus for the great cartels, as for instance the famous Westphalian cartel of 1876 which was soon called on to control half of Germany's production.

This modernization was not brought about without suffering and poverty. In 1850 there were more than 200,000 peasants in Prussia who were spinning and weaving flax. During the 1848 crisis they had suffered terrible hardships, dying by thousands; and the organization of the flax industry was achieved only at the cost of these painful social changes. About 1850 there were still 250,000 hand-spinning frames in Germany. There were no more than 30,000 in 1882, and these remaining weavers were to prove far harder to get rid of. But the brutality and poverty of those years were the price that had to be paid for the progress of the new textile industry: in 1846 Germany exported nearly all its raw wool, but twenty-five years later German mills were using all the raw wool of the country and more was being imported. This coincided with developments in American stockbreeding which were already making cheap wool available. In Germany, cotton did not—as in England and France—act as a spur to the textile industry: there was very little of it in Germany in 1850. The fact was that Germany was forging ahead at tremendous speed. She did not suffer too much in the process: Elberfeld, Stuttgart and Breslau began to import cotton. In 1866 almost 70,000 tons of raw cotton were already being imported, and ten years later, owing to the incorporation of Alsatian industry, the quantity had almost doubled. Elberfeld and Crefeld, encouraged by this success, were even competing with London in the world silk market.

Finally, when we come to consider German trade, it is important to remember that the late development of German industry in comparison with England and France led to a much more rapid rate of progress. Germany profited from the example of Western Europe in particular. As

Germany depended on manufactured goods or on machines for rapid modernization, it imported them in better conditions from countries whose great desire was to sell, and so to lower their prices. When Germany bought rails for its railways before making its own, when it selected the best foreign workmen before its own were trained, or when it used the best available machine-tools before manufacturing them for itself, it did so cheaply. These useful transactions were made easier because the commercial and customs systems were fairly flexible. After the 1848 crisis, German industry was first protectionist, in order to defend its production against foreign invasion; then, when Germany wished to speed up its modernization programme, which was already well under way, and to begin exporting, it went over to free trade. In 1880 List's prophecies came true: Germany had become an industrial country. Like all industrial countries at that time, it then reverted to protection. Here, as in England, there were three phases, and here too they closely followed the chronology of politics. Let us see how they did so.

In France the freedom of individual initiative had been proclaimed by the Revolution of 1789; in Germany the old corporative way of life collapsed in 1848, together with the last traditions of serfdom. It is impossible to go into all the details of the economic liberation which was achieved in very different circumstances from one state of the confederation to another; but everywhere it was hastened on by the anxiety of each not to be outdone by its neighbour. Thus all the old, small seigniorial capitals with their carefree way of life which had lasted until the middle of the nineteenth century, were turned into economic centres in the modern style in the space of one generation in this general stampede.

Between 1854 and 1859 factory chimneys appeared all over the country. Since the liberal movement gained strength in Germany there had been a marked increase in credit, which enabled the new industry to benefit from the habits of mutual aid and trust inherited from the corporate methods of former days. This movement of credit was as strong in the country as in the towns, and depended on the fairly large class of average landowners, so that it only developed where employment increased. Commercial companies were organized around the new railways from Liège to Bremen and Hamburg and along the first great trunk lines serving Cologne, Crefeld and Dortmund, which were the centres of gravity of the new Westphalian iron industry. In the east the Berlin-Magdeburg-Leipzig triangle covered the areas of traditional Saxon craftsmanship. The south was less well provided for, except perhaps in the region around Baden along the Rhine. Prussia was already moving towards free trade, whilst Bavaria and Württemberg were protectionist. Inside the *Zollverein* there was incessant quarrelling between the two groups. In the north, the metal industry became independent between 1854 and 1864. Imports of iron went down from 125,000 to 100,000 tons, while the output of iron rose from 400,000 to 900,000 tons. The time of high protective tariffs was over. The produce had to be marketed and foodstuffs had to be bought cheaply to feed the new working class. In short, tariffs had to be lowered. In the south, however, industrialization was slower, and to adopt low tariffs would have meant disrupting Germanic economic solidarity in favour of Prussia. Prussia furthermore refused to modify the heavy transit dues on German wines exported by Bavaria and Württemberg. The Austrian Government realized that the new industrial development of Prussia threatened to tip the balance to the north, especially if Germany bought foodstuffs from other countries instead of from Bavaria. Austria itself was forced to adopt protectionist policy, since it was at the start of its own economic expansion. After the 1848 crisis Austria was able to impose its customs policy on Hungary (which naturally favoured free trade since it exported a great deal of corn); and since Austria also aimed at controlling the German market, it posed as the protector of the southern states.

There were disputes within the *Zollverein* as well as within Germany as a whole, but as public opinion gradually began to take shape, fostered by the new press and by the progress of credit and trade, the change of outlook began to tell in favour of the north. The Association of Economists was founded at this period and a union of German industrialists was on the way. All these new bodies favoured a progressive policy which advocated the lowering of tariffs and the development of trade. Prussia was already in a similar position to England's as an importer of raw materials and foodstuffs, and an exporter of manufactured goods. The commercial and financial structure of Prussia was sound, particularly since the reorganization of the currency (which was increased and readapted to the new circulation of money). A new commercial code was carefully worked out, and measures were taken to help the workers (*Gewerbe Freiheit*), although nothing would help them more than cheap bread.

The Austrians in their turn, under the leadership of Brucke, were attempting to profit from the new railway junction with Trieste. This had now been completed after many setbacks, and it was hoped to use it to revive the Mediterranean trade and to serve all central Europe; but it proved impossible to divert to Trieste the route from India for which Marseilles, Genoa and even Brindisi were competing. Support was given to the trading companies (the Lloyd-Triestino), a loan society on real estate was set up (the *Hypotheken Bank*) and, most important of all, the famous *Oesterreichische Kredit Anstalt* was founded with the assistance of the Rothschilds. Eventually Austrian currency was reformed. Encouraged by this advance, Brucke tried to intervene in Germany's customs disputes in order to gain some advantage for himself, but without success.

In fact although progress in Austria was rapid between 1850 and 1860, it was less than in most countries. Bremen, Hamburg and the Baltic ports profited from the growth of Atlantic trade. Hamburg opened trading centres in east and west Africa. The Hansa traded with Zanzibar, and Bremen's connections with the United States were strong enough to bring the *Nord Deutscher Lloyd* into being. The *Berliner Handels-Gesellschaft* was founded in Berlin and the *Disconto Gesellschaft* was adapted to large-scale international trade. Trade on this scale led almost inevitably to free trade. Even Switzerland lowered its tariffs and after the Crimean War Russia began to send corn across Germany, to the great advantage of Nordic trade. Above all, France had just signed the famous treaty of 1860 with England and a similar one with Belgium, and had also made overtures to Berlin.

The threat of a commercial treaty between Berlin and Paris was very disturbing to Austria. At that time Austria had just lost the war with Italy. Napoleon III, indeed, had not managed to secure the total victory for which he had hoped, but he had disrupted the Austrian economy, and was apparently aware that by inviting Prussia to sign a commercial treaty involving a lowering of tariffs he could further its expansion at the expense of its Austrian rival. The damage to Austria was all the greater since it put the countries of southern Germany in a great difficulty. The old *Zollverein* admitted all the German states on an equal footing, and the *Zollverein* council could proceed only by a unanimous vote; a single veto blocked every resolution, as the dispute of the 1850s had abundantly shown. All Prussia's proposals had been systematically blocked by Bavaria and the council hardly met again after 1850. In 1858 Bismarck denounced what he regarded as sabotage and advised the ministers to withdraw from the *Zollverein*. In signing a trade treaty with France, Prussia knew it was running the risk of breaking up the union if Bavaria should reject the new customs policy. It was a reasonable risk to take, since Austria could not offer the southern states any economic openings as good as the natural outlets to the north.

The Austro-Prussian economic battle began in 1862. Brucke had died in disgrace. Hamburg had sold itself to the highest bidder and was now an ally of Prussia. Bavaria tried in vain to keep opposition to the Prussian plan alive by seeking to arouse greater German enthusiasm for a Germanic union including Austria. A plan for a Franco-Prussian treaty put an end to this once and for all. Economic requirements are the most compelling of all. The

Zollverein, including Bavaria, had to give in. Bismarck granted Austria most-favoured-nation treatment: this was not a great concession in the circumstances since Austria was economically cut off from Germany.

Prussia's victory was all the more significant since in the course of the negotiations on the treaty with Paris, the *liberum veto* was not used. The legal rights of Bavaria and Württemberg became meaningless once Prussia could threaten to dissolve the *Zollverein*, on which both were economically dependent. Prussia controlled the outlets to the sea which were essential to the economy of southern Germany. In a few months the old constitution of the *Zollverein* was replaced by a new one in which each country was represented by a number of votes proportionate to its population, and a customs parliament was to make decisions according to majority vote. This move in 1867 made Prussia the master of Germany.

As Clapham aptly remarked, Bismarck achieved German unity not so much by blood and iron as by coal and iron. Prussia's vast industry won the greatest victory of the nineteenth century in the field of economics. When Prussian troops defeated the Austrians at Sadowa, and when later the customs parliament was created, the foundations of the new Prussian Empire were laid several years before the ceremony at Versailles. The fierce economic competition in the 1860s placed Prussia in an invulnerable position.

After Sadowa, Bismarck only demanded economic concessions from the defeated Austrians who were forced out of the English and French markets to make way for the German economy. This was in spite of opposition from the trading states of the north, which were still anxious about this southward deflection of trade currents. This demand of Bismarck's had serious consequences for Austria; since the Austrian customs régime could no longer be imposed on Hungary. The latter, an agricultural country, accepted the autonomy decree of 1867 which destroyed the economic unity of the old monarchy.

Let us return to Bismarck in 1868. The economic and military victory over Austria turned a difficult internal situation to his advantage. He had only been called to power in 1862 because William I despaired of getting a parliament dominated by merchants and industrialists (particularly by Schulze-Delitzsch) to approve the credits needed for the reorganization of the Prussian army proposed by Roon. Bismarck's success was therefore a double one, since by opening up unlimited prospects to German finance he rallied the industrial opposition. All the currents of public opinion that had been against the *Zollverein's liberum veto* were now, at the instigation of the economists and influential merchants, transformed into a patriotic campaign which even infected Bavaria. It brought about unanimity in Germany which Bismarck was able to exploit against Napoleon III by enticing this ill-starred man into the diplomatic and military traps which he and Moltke had prepared for him.

In any case, Bismarck could hardly have been caught unawares in his struggle against the liberals, for he had been watching the progress of the German working-class movement and its growing opposition to the middle-class programme since 1862. When the unfortunate Lassalle, who had fought for the unity of the working class, was killed in 1864, he was less regretted by Marx (who accused him of collaborating with the middle classes and of putting his trust in such middle-class institutions as universal suffrage), than by Bismarck, who later adopted some of his theses. Bismarck had probably intended to harness this working-class power against the middle classes if the latter had continued to impede the military measures desired by the king of Prussia. After the victory of 1870–1, however, Bismarck no longer needed to woo the German worker's party, since he had the support of the merchants and industrialists. On the contrary, now that the workers were becoming united under Bebel's leadership into a social democratic party they had become increasingly dangerous and Bismarck was soon to think of fighting them.

In 1871, Bismarck saw not only the last states enter the *Zollverein*, but the customs parliament, previously only an economic organization, become the Parliament of the Empire and a political entity. The king of Bavaria was now personally in favour of the Empire and was carrying public opinion in south Germany along with him. He himself suggested that the imperial crown be offered to William.

Then a new phase opened. The unassuming Delbruck, that model official who had presided over the destinies of the Customs Union and remained true to the policy of liberalism, was compelled to leave his post in 1877, defeated by the new crises and by the new needs of the economic empire. Bismarck, now Imperial Chancellor, was putting through emergency laws against socialism and inaugurated the protectionist *Realpolitik* which opened a new phase of German history. Once unity was achieved and strengthened by modernization of the economy, Germany's main requirement was to orientate industrial production towards those world markets which were still free —those of central Europe. The great German banks then concentrated on an intensive exploration of central European markets, and were already turning their attention to Turkey (it was perhaps significant here that Roon was a geographer and Moltke had been military adviser to the Sultan). The steady progress of the German economy opened up to it the European routes across the Mediterranean; Austria had failed to create an outlet to the Mediterranean via Trieste, but now German credit was attempting to obtain one through Constantinople.

Now that Prussia had conquered Germany it intended to dominate all central Europe, and eventually to be the head of a great continental empire.

FRANCE BETWEEN TWO EMPIRES

In 1848 France had been the focal point of the revolution; in February of that year France had again stirred up the waves of unrest which appeared to have died down in southern and eastern Europe. But by 1849 order was restored in France. Whilst revolutions or wars continued to shake southern and eastern Europe, France, through the mouth of Lamartine, was already counselling calmness and restraint and preaching reconciliation. Then the new Republic adopted a constitution with a monarchical executive power, and elected neither the poet Lamartine nor the Republican General Cavaignac, but a prince with the magical name of Louis-Napoleon. The revolution was an urban phenomenon caused by the weakness of French credit institutions which suddenly collapsed under the weight of the railways. The restoration of order appeared to be a rural achievement, since universal suffrage gave the peasants a greater voice in the nation's affairs. This is worth considering in more detail.

In 1848 French peasants were still not very different from what they had been in 1800. There had of course been some technical advances as we noted throughout the first half of the century, but there had been little structural change and no appreciable transformation of rural society. In 1862 France still had 2,400,000 farms of less than twenty-five acres, and in practice even the large holdings were no bigger than a hundred acres; only just over 150,000 farms were larger than a hundred acres. Compared to the English or German country estate in the middle of the century the French estate remained small. Consequently the number of small landowning farmers was still enormous, more than two million. There were almost as many gentleman farmers as agricultural workers, and the latter, too, often possessed small plots of their own. We shall not reconsider at this point the legal importance of the civil code, but merely emphasize that the agricultural scene of 1850 in France was not basically different from that of the eighteenth century.

The result was that however marked the urban development of France might be, it did not play as decisive a role as urban development in England or Germany. There were twenty-seven cities with more than 20,000 inhabitants in 1800; there would be at the close of the century forty of more than 40,000 inhabitants. France's rural population was still seventy-eight per cent of the total population in 1866; this proportion was higher than in Prussia, or in Germany which was in other respects still so close to feudalism. Whilst France's cities, with their enlightened and progressive *élite*, had brought out their civil code for the world to copy fifty years earlier, launched Proudhonian socialism ten years earlier, and had recently welcomed the manifesto of Karl Marx, the French countryside was still the most conservative in the world. The roots of a land-owning peasantry went very deep, for as Marc Bloch has so clearly shown, they were already vigorous under Louis XII. It is not easy to estimate how much agricultural equipment was being used on French farms. The number of ploughs seems tremendous, simply because it included even the wooden swing-ploughs which twentieth-century geographers found still in use only a few years ago. On the other hand there were very few hay-making and mowing machines, and mechanical threshing machines were possessed by only a very few great landowners. The rural world, even that of the well-to-do, was by no means over-enthusiastic about the American or Scottish techniques so popular in England and even in Germany.

Indeed, this dominance of the countryside enabled France to produce all the corn that was needed in good years and to be self-sufficient in food supplies; this had been Colbert's aim and was the chief goal both for the monarchy of the old régime and for Napoleon I. The price of bread was still taxed as before. Agricultural societies existed in great numbers, and many of them appear to have been half a century old, but their effectiveness had increased hardly at all. The Restoration had encouraged agricultural shows and Napoleon III was to take an even greater interest in them. Fortunately, Flaubert used one of them as a setting for a famous episode in *Madame Bovary*: the rustic pictures he gives of rich, progressive Normandy would not have displeased Young, but Young had been dead for nearly fifty years.

On the big farms, farmers continued to try out improvements in sheepbreeding. French merinos tried to compete with the sheep of Spain, and even more with those of Saxony and England. But there were no startling changes in French cattle: their numbers rose only from twelve million to thirteen million, whilst those of sheep actually went down from thirty-two million to thirty million. For agriculture was advancing very slowly indeed. Throughout this period the vine was a basic element of the rural economy; except in years when the crops were affected by mildew, France produced ample wine, the consumption of which had risen by fifty per cent between 1840 and 1870. The area sown with wheat increased by thirty-three per cent between 1850 and 1870. The production of sugar was developing slowly, and in 1870 it was not a quarter of that of Germany. The cultivation of beet, however, made the fortune of several modern-minded landowners, one of whom was Morny. The area sown to corn and beet was apparently increased, mainly at the expense of fallow ground. This was excellent, but the increase in production was not accompanied by an improvement in quality: French yields were barely half those of Belgium and Holland, and were fifty per cent lower than those of England and Germany.

In these circumstances, it is surprising to find that the reign of Napoleon III has acquired such a high reputation in the field of economics. In actual fact, all the effervescence of this period hardly affected more than one-third of the total population. The Prince declared on the ninth of October 1852: 'We have vast uncultivated lands waiting to be cleared.' An absurdly small credit had indeed just been granted for the development and improvement of Sologne, and several rural areas hoped to receive a similar life-restoring gift. In reality the Sologne credits went to a small railway. The most memorable part of this famous speech, in which occurred the phrase 'the Empire and peace are one', was the sentence: 'There are roads to be opened up, harbours to be dug, canals to be finished, our railway network to be completed.'

The credit crisis which had overthrown Louis-Philippe arose from the massive demands for capital put forward by the railways. There were half-finished excavations for tunnels and embankments, and ballast was waiting for the rails; lines already laid down were waiting for their rolling stock; stations were half-built in Paris and other cities. All these projects had to be completed.

This was the period when efforts were being made throughout Europe to attract all possible trade and business to the ports and towns along the great transport routes, so as to gain a few months' lead over competitors and create habits which would hold good for the future. Austria, as we have seen, was improving Trieste. The Lloyd-Triestino line already possessed financial resources and a fleet of ships which were superior to those of all French or Italian competitors. It now needed to establish a flow of trade from Amsterdam or Antwerp to Trieste that would be powerful enough to divert the English traffic to India which had previously gone via France. In order to retain its geographical advantages France needed to secure the Paris–Marseilles link as quickly as possible. Neither north nor south of Lyons was there as yet the least idea how the companies were to be organized. There were urgent problems in west France too: Bremen and Hamburg were starting a regular service with America modelled on the English services, and Le Havre and Rouen were not yet in any position to compete.

The capitalism of Louis-Philippe had failed. A socialist programme had been sketched out by the provisional government, but had met with no success. Acting at top speed, the republican Government had at once given work to the many thousands of unemployed who had been left stranded beside the half-finished tracks on which work had been interrupted through the financial embarrassment of the railway companies. Thousands of building workers were still wandering idly about Paris. State control, and socialism were suggested by a very small group of economists. There were bitter arguments on political theory in the clubs of the young Republic, but they were all overruled by one grim, inescapable reality: the Government could not procure the necessary resources, for if the French investor had previously been reluctant to lend his money to the railway companies, he was not now going to hand it over to the Treasury of the social republic.

We have seen how in 1848 suggestions had been put forward for a tentative reform of credit, which became the basis of the new French capitalism. The shortage of money which had lasted since 1846 ended in 1850 and as a result the position of private enterprise, and especially of the railway companies, improved. As a rebuttal of socialism, Thiers had hastily thrown together *Propriété*, a curious and childish book, a collection of platitudes, in which he defended landed property without giving any detailed answer to Proudhon's claims on the subject of credit. But capitalism was making such fair weather that everything, even Thiers' lightweight performance, combined to speed it on its way. The Constituent Assembly had already decided to respect the companies' privileges. Then the task of the executive gradually became clear: Louis-Napoleon Bonaparte, who had been elected by countrymen, or in other words by landed property, used the authority bestowed on him by this rural majority to extend credit based on personal estate (*crédit mobilier*). Once they had been given power the companies, in order to get the capital they lacked, launched preference shares of small amounts which could be taken up by a wide public, even in country districts. The state guaranteed these shares, in other words it exerted all the power of its institutions to push their sale. In addition the state decreased its budgetary charges as much as possible so that taxation could be lowered and all available financial resources could be concentrated on private enterprises. Thanks to this situation, which had been imposed on him by events, Louis-Napoleon appeared as the saviour of both town and country. The workers resigned themselves to the situation, and the capitalists accepted the Prince's authority.

We have spoken of Palmerston's sympathy for Napoleon III; it was now to have practical results. England's railways were much more advanced than those of France, and had already reached the stage when all the essential lines had been built and were fully operative, so that any further projects would be of only minor importance. As a result, English investors were looking around for new schemes for their capital—and where could better opportunities be found than in France? After all, the British Empire's great natural routes led from the Channel (through the Parisian basin and the Rhone Valley) to the Mediterranean and on to India. Soon ships crossing the Channel were bringing France material, rails, and above all capital, more even than the considerable amounts imported under Louis-Philippe. The capital was carefully followed up and watched by English businessmen sitting on French boards of directors. It was clear that the companies were entitled to better contracts with the state than those of the 1842 law, and the Government had agreed to grant them. But in negotiating these additional concessions, the Government took the opportunity to ask the companies owning the best lines to take on in addition branch lines which were more difficult to place. Thus France's great network of railways came into being. This solution of the problem of the railway-building crisis of 1847–8 was natural and inevitable, but credit for it was given to the head of the executive who in consequence was able to proclaim himself Emperor without appreciable opposition.

Actually, in so far as any clear economic opinions can be attributed to Napoleon III, they would have led rather to a kind of state socialism. But the author of *Extinction du Paupérisme* was making the middle classes uneasy. Napoleon III gained power only because he had renounced the application of his own principles. True the officials of the *Ponts et Chaussées*, who were polytechnicians and consequently Colbertians and inherited a tradition going back to the old régime, were only half satisfied with a solution which gave to engineers of private companies a responsibility and an authority which they felt belonged only to themselves. Their engineers took good care of the roads, but the roads now took second place to the railways. The canals, at all events, would have to be publicly administered, since they represented the only means of transport capable, it was said, of moderating the high fares exacted by the new railway companies. But a great canal scheme was hardly feasible. Already in 1852 the Midi Canal had had to be handed over to the *Compagnie des Chemins de Fer du Midi*. Plans were drawn up, but to be carried out they would have needed much more money than Napoleon III could raise, since he had done all he could to stimulate investment in private initiative. Moreover, the legislative body was most watchful, and within a few years it placed the disillusioned Emperor in an untenable position.

At first the wave of optimism was general; the railway programme absorbed all the vagrant unemployed and continued to attract workers away from country districts. Towns grew at the same time as shares rose on the exchange. Shares were taken up so readily that it was necessary to apply for double the amount desired in order to get any at all. The new banks made handsome profits from the sale of all this paper and increased the number of their customers. Satisfaction was widespread in England. Austria was defeated in the race to the Mediterranean. Prussia was just as successful in its efforts to push German trade in the direction of the North Sea, but this prospect still caused no uneasiness in France. Paris was in holiday mood. The Emperor took his full share in these rejoicings; this was the brilliant life he had dreamed of. Millions, millions, *châteaux*, a civil list, wrote Victor Hugo, who added: 'I have been down into the cellars at Lille. I have seen those black tombs.' It could not be denied that not all branches of industry derived equal benefit from the new developments and the contrast they afford deserves examination.

Surrounded by the luxury of his court and the riches of the *parvenus*, Napoleon soon forgot his intention of stamping out poverty, which was still acute, particularly in the textile areas. Spinning and weaving had flourished during the Restoration and the July Monarchy but their economic prosperity was achieved mainly at the expense of the workers (what a magnificent field of observation for Marx!). A good deal of the work was still being done in the countryside, and since many French weavers often owned a small field (unlike their English counterparts), they could afford to accept the continual drop in prices imposed by the merchant who brought their raw material and orders. But the fall in wages was more disastrous for the wretched city workers, crowded into cellars or, in Lyons, in hovels built into the hillside.

The requirements of French fashion, ever-changing, which sought to give each buyer the impression that he was acquiring 'a unique article' which would earn him a reputation for originality anywhere in the world, prevented the large-scale use of modern looms. Fine, detailed work of this kind was ideally suited to the sweating system. The isolated worker suffered severely from the luxury character and the renowned high 'quality' of French textile productions.

The home cutlers were a little more fortunate than the weavers, particularly in Auvergne, but also in Poitou and Champagne; they kept alive an outmoded commercial and industrial structure which nevertheless succeeded in exporting to European markets because of the originality of its craftsmanship.

In heavy industry, on the other hand, everything had to be sacrificed to mass production. At the end of Louis-Philippe's reign, coal seams were discovered to the south of Lille. Working began when the companies took advantage of the new credit, after 1850. Then pits opened at Lescarpelles, Courrières, Lens, Loos, Béthune and Saint-Omer. In twenty years production rose from five to thirteen million tons. The production of the north and the Pas-de-Calais alone almost equalled the total output of the old mines dug out of the periphery of the Massif Central. Mining in France had to contend with difficulties unknown in England, and consequently French prices were thirty per cent higher, but there was a good French market for coal and so production was easily absorbed. From 1851 iron output reached the 1846 figure of 600,000 tons, and then it was trebled in twenty years. The steel output was soaring, but could by no means compare with that of England, though Napoleon III had done his best to attract Bessemer to France and to appoint him adviser to numerous ironmasters. At Le Creusot and Hayange converters appeared after 1863. There was a geographical displacement just as there had been in England, particularly towards Denain and Anzin. Large concentrations of industry were taking shape in the centre and east. Under the direction of Schneider there were 10,000 workmen at Le

Creusot, which thus ranked as one of the major industrial centres of the world. At Rive-de-Gier under the direction of Pétin-Gaudet there were 6,000 workers, and 5,000 under Wendel at Hayange. The price of rails dropped by half, but the French still preferred iron rails to steel and became as a result the second largest producers of iron in the world after England. Old centres like Commentry, Fourchamboult and many others remained busy, and by 1850 seemed assured of the same future as the industrial areas of England. In comparison with the swiftness of change in Germany, French industry made only moderate progress, and Paris remained stubbornly attached to individual craftsmanship right up to 1878.

Napoleon III was an observer of this industrial scene rather than its instigator. Yet it was only natural that he should believe in his great destiny, for this dreamer came to power at the very moment when gold re-established a credit system and he appeared as the country's saviour. Nevertheless his inactivity irked him. He thought himself called on to realize the most grandiose projects of the Saint-Simon school, particularly the Mediterranean system. A new edition of de Tocqueville was a sign of the revived popularity of the United States in France. It was the fashion to compare England and America. The Anglo-French industrial bloc was envisaged as playing a similar rôle in Europe to that of the Atlantic seaboard on the American continent, in which case central Europe would assume the rôle of the great central American plains. The Chicago of Europe was to be Constantinople. The westward expansion of the United States must have its counterpart in Europe in a great economic conquest reaching out towards Asia. Shipping companies were started on the Mediterranean. At first the French lines were far inferior to the Lloyd-Triestino, but soon the *Messageries Maritimes* won for France, with English consent and capital, a supremacy all the more easily achieved since Algeria was a French outpost in 'the East'. Palmerston, seeing in Napoleon III something of the qualities which attracted him in the great English industrialists, gave his support to the Black Sea adventure. The French battalions in Rumania and the Expeditionary Force in Crimea were the pioneers who were to take large-scale trade and industrialization eastward in their wake. The French negotiated the building of railways in Greece and the digging of the Suez Canal in Egypt. Syria could provide Europe with an even better supply of horses than Kentucky!

The dearly-bought victory of Sebastopol gave England cause for thought. Trade was less attractive if it was going to involve war. The dangers were out of all proportion to the profit, and England was already so deeply involved in India that she had no intention of taking on unlimited military commitments on the continent of Europe. The Treaty of Paris was a victory for trade: navigation on the Danube was freed, and the Black Sea was closed to all warships; and England was well pleased. But Napoleon III was carried away by the weight of his military prestige, and although in the beginning he had no doubt been sincere in his desire for peace, he could not stop halfway. He went on to take an interest in the Danubian provinces, in Serbia, and in Italy, and at that point England no longer supported him.

England had no doubt of its ability to conquer the world by trade, using armed forces as little as possible, and such a conquest, far from being costly, brought in handsome profits. France, on the contrary, fell back into her old military vocation: it was easy to levy troops from among the humbler French peasantry barely integrated into the economic life of the country, much easier than in England where young men tended to follow in their fathers' footsteps. So the French abandoned the maritime policy they had shared with England, and turned to continental expansion, as Germany had done. France tried, in fact, to make the best of both worlds. It imitated England in China; French diplomats and admirals settled *à l'anglaise* in Cochin-China and Cambodia; again, like the English, France tried to use Algeria as a Bengal from which French settlement would spread throughout the whole of the Arab world. But France was also looking towards her frontiers, and putting into practice a continental policy favouring Prussia against Austria, and especially favourable to Italy, provided this favour was returned in the form of a regrouping of territories.

In short, Napoleon III, weary of the court and castle round, turned to continental politics for a new diversion. At last he saw a career worthy of his genius opening out before him. He had rendered too many services to the capitalists (not always willingly) not to profit from their neutrality for a time. In the five years from 1859 to 1864, Napoleon III intervened everywhere. In Italy, he helped on a unification which the development of the railways was organizing from within. Having succeeded in this, he tackled Germany and Mexico (he had even thought of Scandinavia). But the industrial power of the United States was much stronger in America than that of France. The Mexican *débâcle* was followed by the tragic death of Maximilian. Similarly, the economic power of Prussia was stronger in Germany than that of France.

The disaster of Sedan was foreshadowed by the blunders of Napoleon III's internal policy: from the moment when he broke with the English alliance and departed from the policy of a capitalist peace which he had promised at Bordeaux, the Emperor found that in France itself he was mistrusted by the majority of businessmen. He held the peasant mass of electors and the majority of the urban lower-middle class by the prestige of his victories. Thiers, who had again become the mouthpiece of public opinion, realized this very well and did his utmost to widen the rifts separating the Emperor from the upper-middle classes whose diplomatic difficulties were now beginning.

In the early years of his reign Napoleon III had renounced his own social policy, and had been forced to allow the free development of bourgeois capitalism. Nevertheless, using the prestige his victories gave him, he had tried to make French capitalism benefit from technical progress. This aim he sought to achieve by forcing the industrial feudalisms, created in the first half of the century, out of the hothouses in which they had been enclosed by the protectionist laws. In 1860 he signed the famous commercial treaty with England which put French industries on the defensive and compelled them to make reforms. The result was a storm of angry protest against this abuse of this executive, which was taking advantage of its right to ratify treaties, in order to interfere in internal economic policy.

However, certain industrial changes were made, especially in the textile industry, although these were mainly the result of an acute crisis which hit Europe from 1863 to 1866, known as the cotton famine. The American Civil War ruined the Southern plantations which supplied the bulk of the raw material for Europe's cotton industries. In spite of England's attempts to support the South, European spinning-mills closed down, and an appalling poverty settled over Lancashire and northern and eastern France. Manufacturers adapted themselves to the situation as best they could. A change over from cotton to wool involved modification of plant; buying cotton outside America meant forging commercial links with India and Egypt and many merchants did attempt this, especially the enterprising Mulhouse industrialists who made the Le Havre *bourse* so prosperous. From this crisis the French textile industry emerged transformed. Although there were still 200,000 hand-looms in use for cotton-spinning in France in 1867, there were already 80,000 driven by power, 47,000 of which were in Alsace. As a result of a magnificent effort which had been particularly intense during the past two generations, and of which Heilmann had been one of the most distinguished initiators, Alsace became one of the world's great cotton centres. Normandy also was acquiring new spinning-frames, and in Flanders many small firms were being squeezed out of business and replaced by stronger ones. In consequence, a parallel change was taking place in the woollen industry. In 1860, imports of raw wool amounted to very little more than home production; twenty years later they were to be four times in excess of it. There again, Napoleon III was a witness of the phenomenon rather than its director.

The only point of his programme which he was able to carry through nearly as he wished in the 1860s was the transformation of the towns. The Emperor was unable to direct the economy himself, since the legislative body (the mouthpiece of the industrial middle classes) wished to maintain it on a private footing, especially by reducing the budget to extremely moderate figures; but he secretly helped certain of his own friends, bringing the whole weight of the state to the aid of his protégés. Amongst them must be specially mentioned the Pereires, whose banking activities we have already noted. Any *entrepreneur* who took part in the great plan for transforming the cities, particularly Marseilles and Paris, could count on the secret support of the executive, especially its Parisian representative, Haussmann. Advances were readily agreed to by the *Crédit Foncier*, they were given the backing of municipal finances and enjoyed a certain amount of governmental complicity in the delicate matter of accounting. All the financing of this urban reconstruction was done behind the scenes. The Emperor, who practised international politics in alcoves and in the discreet privacy of watering-places, carried on economic reforms in estate offices, publishing offices of business journals *à la Mirès*, and behind the fences of demolition yards.

The real advance achieved by the French economy in iron, textiles, commerce, banking, and even agriculture made new building projects fashionable. Louis-Philippe had already had the idea of finishing the Louvre of the Bourbons. Bonaparte took the scheme in hand. Meanwhile all the new rich were building themselves mansions and *châteaux* in the provinces, hesitating between the style of the *grand siècle* or that of feudalism, the Gothic which Viollet-Le-Duc's endless reproductions had made so fashionable.

The whole of France was hard at work building itself houses; there was speculation in the price of town sites, and by dint of borrowing impressive fortunes were built up. To speculate was to head straight for a title and those who succeeded were soon installed in lordly homes. The lower-middle class was lost in admiration of these amazing achievements. It could no longer recognize its broken-up streets, its demolished suburbs. A wind of pride was blowing, inflating the vanity of the townspeople, filling them with self-importance at being caught up in all this bold and feverish activity. After buying railway stock on the recommendation of Mirès and the securities offered by the *Crédit Mobilier*, the petty bourgeois dipped into his purse again for the debentures of the *Crédit Foncier* when Mirès suggested that he, too, might like to invest in real estate. Far more cautious, however, were the great financiers and all those who had learned wisdom from the accumulated experience of several generations, and the conservative and orthodox Rothschilds figured as defenders of tradition.

At first Napoleon III was delighted at seeing the country thus transformed in accordance with Saint-Simonist ethics and aesthetics.

All the kings of the earth paraded around him at the solemn opening of the exhibition of 1866. He may really have believed that he had only to follow the dictates of his ambition, and that the future would condone all his rash financial ventures, whose irregularities he tried to conceal. At all events, after 1866, the fear of bills being called in began to haunt his nights. Haussmann's fantastic accounts made credit uneasy. The Pereires, abandoned by the Bank, led to the downfall of the *Crédit Mobilier*. The railways, indeed, were doing well out of lines which were profitable to run, but the system of secondary lines was not yet completed. The leaders of industry, shaken by the cotton crisis and preoccupied by the enormous calls being made on them by the modernization of their businesses, grew anxious at the foolish waste of money on wars and imperial cities.

The political and financial world, remembering the closing years of Louis-Philippe, believed that the resources of credit could be reinvigorated only at the cost of political reform. It was in these conditions that the legislative power was granted a control over the budget all the tighter for being accompanied by a reform in the rules governing public accounting. By that time, however, the accounts had already become hopelessly entangled and suspect. Napoleon III had to abandon his recently adopted protégés. Although he was able to get Mirès out of prison, he could not prevent Jacob Pereire from selling his priceless collection of pictures and his brother Isaac from being twice disqualified for electoral corruption, or Haussmann, his favourite administrator, from being sacrificed to the liberals.

In the last months of the régime it seemed likely that the liberals were at last to assume control, and rescue the country from the crisis to which imperial adventures had led it. The legislative body attempted to canalize all the credit still available for those industrial concerns which were badly in need of it. Economies were ordered in every department of public expenditure including, of course, that of war. Unfortunately, however, the revolutionary changes brought about in Europe by the railway gave rise on every hand to rivalries which strained the 1815 frontiers to breaking point. The consequences of the imperial ventures in Mexico, beyond the Alps, and especially across the Rhine, began to appear at the very moment when the Emperor had exhausted his credit in unspectacular adventures in landed estate. There was no longer, Thiers said, a single mistake left for him to make.

Napoleon III had completely lost control over the machinery of politics, and was powerless to check the economic forces welding Hamburg to Munich, Venice to Rome. Ministers who had believed that their finest achievement would be the dismissal of Haussmann suddenly found themselves confronted by an insolent and cunning Bismarck. They declared war, in spite of the hesitations expressed by Napoleon who was bolstering up his courage with Eugénie's compliments.

It was a terrible year. The German railways did excellent work in concentrating troops; after all, they had the Rhine as their axis. The strategic moves were written on the railway map: France dispersed her troops, which were captured at Metz and Sedan before they had struck a single blow. The Tuileries and the lovely, new Paris were burning under Bismarck's eyes.

Socially the France of 1871 was in the same situation as in 1848. In May the Commune resumed, and lost, the struggle of June 1848. The middle-class business world again tried out a line of action which previously had always succeeded: as in 1815, 1830, and 1850 it allowed itself to be edged out of power, and underwent the revolution and the following reaction, only to emerge with a firmer grip on the reins of economic life. That was the real meaning of France's famous upheavals. Once the storm had died down, the same Thiers, the Montalivets, the Dufaures, Fraissinet the Marseilles shipowner and Freycinet the Ariègle engineer, all came to the fore again, until such time as the thriving industry of eastern France brought Jules Ferry to a position of authority. Their object was still a parliamentary régime, supported by sound business ventures. So the Republic resumed the building of railways, the best of which would be sold to private companies and the rest run at the expense of the taxpayer. It put forward a gigantic plan for canals and ports. French gold which had been in hiding now flowed in from all sides. Within a few months Bismarck was amazed to find that the Republic had freed France from German troops. It animated urban activity where streets, squares, houses, theatres (above all the Paris Opera) were completed according to the prescribed plans. Credit recovered and French firms were soon building railways in Greece, Spain, Algeria and Tunis, and making plans for Indo-China. Again, as before, the army, reduced to inaction in Europe, set sail for conquests overseas.

The break between Napoleon and the bourgeoisie occurred, as we have seen, towards 1865. By 1880 this same bourgeoisie had rallied to the Republic. More tenacious than the successive political régimes through which it had passed, modern French industrial capitalism, born in the *salons* of the Directoire and matured under Louis-Philippe, now entered upon its most successful phase.

10

The Town-Dweller

EVEN in the loneliness of exile, Victor Hugo never lost his faith in progress; it was his religion and he wanted to make it that of his people too. Baudelaire was more sensitive to the gloomy life of the streets in the new industrial towns, where a mass of human beings crowded together still secretly longing for the country life they had once known. The towns were tyrannical in their demands. They kept scientists and able men hard at work, forcing upon them tasks far removed from the cultured dilettantism which had been so delightful and valuable a feature of the old philosophical studies; these tasks were dictated by the needs of French industry and had to be carried out within a fairly rigid research organization, subdivided into specialized branches. The tasks drove millions of navvies and labourers to work. As for beauty, the townspeople were indifferent to it; insensitive to Daumier's criticisms, they revelled in reproductions of Meissonier, in the affected landscape painters, and in Millet's peasants praying in the fields. The important thing was to build quickly; style did not matter—Gothic, Greek, Louis XIV or Louis XV. Everything was grist to the architects' mill, nothing was too good for this greedy, uncouth bourgeoisie. Against this decadent taste, there were few rare reactions from a group of artists who detested the Philistine, bourgeois order. There was Courbet, painting crude, earthy men of the soil, and Wagner, celebrating the legendary heroes of olden days, the pure-hearted hero uncorrupted by gold.

THE SERVANT SCIENCES

In our discussion of the first half of the nineteenth century we ranked science before law as one of the motive forces of European life. In the second half, railways and banks were put in the foremost place, and science was relegated to a subordinate position. We must now examine the reason for this.

Science had lost its amazing coherence. Gone were the days when one single mathematical concept could give rise to a thousand experimental applications. Mathematics was divided into specialized branches separated if not by actual contradictions, at least by lively quarrels between the supporters of irreconcilable methods. As for the applied sciences, physics and chemistry, they were now almost independent, and depended as much on industry as on intellectual circles for the fitting out and successful working of their laboratories.

Confronted with this vast and strange phenomenon, the philosophers were unable to synthesize. Up to the time of Kant, philosophy had kept closely in step with scientific discovery and had even sometimes succeeded in disentangling the fruitful elements in it from the sterile. The Kantian philosophy, including its cosmogony, was a fairly good description of the Newtonian spirit. Once Kant had gone, it endeavoured to continue along the line of its own deductions. It tried, especially with Hegel, to deduce from these premises all the movements and the whole future of the world. But the *a priori* nature of this philosophy of identity, which blindly followed its own path, forced it to part company with the natural sciences. As each fresh discovery was made in these, leading to a correction of earlier ideas, it finally became obvious that the mental equipment of 1800 was no more than a shell which had to be broken out of. Hegel and the pure idealists continued to reason about this henceforth empty shell until Hamelin so sadly and humbly confessed their failure. The renewal was not to take place until the twentieth century when a new Newton was to mark an epoch calling for a new Kant.

In 1862 Helmholtz could write: 'The crucial proof [of the Hegelian identity principle] would have been in the natural sciences . . . at that moment [the Hegelian philosophy] failed utterly and completely. Of all the scientists not a single one could be found to follow these ideas. The philosophers accuse the scientists of being narrow-minded. The scientists retaliate by telling the philosophers they are crazy!' This admirable, mutual contempt reveals something besides mere pique; from now on it was no longer possible for one single man to embrace within his own mind all knowledge, to grasp the common nature of all methods.

The middle of the century was marked by one outstanding phenomenon, the division of scientific work. The encyclopaedic outlook was dying out. Each scientist entrenched himself in a domain which was exclusively his own, and so numerous were the discoveries being made that from one speciality to another, from one type of laboratory to another, no one had either the time or the inclination any longer to venture rashly into fields other than his own. Mathematics itself was split up in order to meet the requirements of such varied sciences. The old, sacrosanct unity of science was replaced by the doctrine of compulsory specialization. These specializations, however, and the techniques of laboratories which were beginning to fit themselves out with new equipment, did not in the least mean that each scientist was isolated within his own restricted sphere. On the contrary, the publication of scientific journals, the quicker postal service resulting from steam, the telegraph and soon the telephone, and travel, were to enable scientists specializing in the same subject to keep in close touch with each other and to cross all frontiers. There was a scientific internationalism which forced specializations to develop on what amounted to a world scale yet at the same time bound them ever more firmly to themselves.

The division, through discipline, was also reinforced by work in the universities. The mid-nineteenth century was the great age of university organization, or reorganization, of systematizations such as that suggested by Auguste Comte. The practical result was the formation of research groups in which students and assistants gathered around a professor for some special piece of work, applying a group of methods centring on one particular subject. This change in the universities took place extremely rapidly in Germany. In England, Oxford and Cambridge renounced their medieval universalism, of which Newton had been the finest flower, to open large numbers of specialized laboratories such as those directed by Maxwell, Cavendish or Forster. France, which had led the world between 1800 and 1830 because of the strong centralization of her Institute, found it more difficult to abandon this universalism, and resisted specialization. The wretched conditions in which Pasteur and Branly had to work, the hard lot of so many contemporary scientists, emphasized the slowness with which France was adapting itself to the new conditions.

Before embarking on a concise study of the scientific disciplines, we must explain some simplifications imposed by the need for brevity. We have abruptly cut the century in half and stressed the turning-point between 1840 and 1850. It is hardly necessary to point out that the break was not so clear-cut. If the record phase of the nineteenth century began much later than 1850, it started, as far as mathematics were concerned, at the very moment when Lagrange's rational mechanics was at the height of its popularity, for mathematicians were already assessing its results and preparing the next step. We must now return to Gauss, with whom we ended the last chapter.

If Lagrange and Laplace were men of their time, Gauss was well in advance of his. In his calculation of the trajectory of Ceres, he still showed his adherence to the Newtonian school, and it was by this calculation that the brilliant German established his reputation, entered the ranks of the great calculators, and ensured his own livelihood and his academic future. Similarly his work with Weber on electric physics was in the context of his time. But behind this imposing façade, which in itself would have been enough to make a man famous, another Gauss was concealed, a silent, secret worker, who accumulated the most extraordinary discoveries in his *Notizen Journal*. They were in a style so elliptical that some still remain an enigma today. This journal, written between 1796 and 1816, made quite a sensation when it was published in 1898. It is not therefore surprising that even *Disquisitiones arithmeticae* published in 1801 (and still published in Latin) opened up pathways so new that contemporaries failed to recognize their significance, and their extraordinarily rich potentialities became apparent only when they were taken up again by the generations of Dirichlet and Eisenstein. He was working on the monogenous analytical functions of complex variable from 1811, but his conclusions remained secret until Weierstrass rediscovered them forty years later. In spite of his undoubted genius, Karl Friedrich Gauss lived with difficulty on his meagre income, sometimes bitterly disappointed at having only three pupils —'one of them was mediocre and the other two ignorant'. He was less known than the learned Pascal, since he had no understanding sister to help him on the road to fame. He used to say jokingly that he had been able to count before he could read. At seven he had fathomed, quite unaided, the mystery of arithmetical progressions and could do instantly in his head the interminable sums with which his country schoolmaster burdened his young pupils. It was in this country school that he discovered the binomial theorems.*

Gauss's work on differential geometry was more spectacular still. The problem arose out of cartography—how

---

* Every student of higher mathematics is indebted to Gauss for a clear geometrical explanation of the meaning of complex numbers, and of the *i* (the square root of-1) so mysterious to the uninitiated. The *Disquisitiones arithmeticae* already foreshadowed the important new definition of congruence, which had led the study of uneven numbers out of the impasse in which it had remained since Fermat. Gauss returned to this subject in 1825 and threw new light on the problem of the congruences of quadratic binomials. He wrote a paper on cubic congruences which was found after his death. This work opened the way fifty years later for Dedekind, to whom modern students of higher mathematics owe the idea of the 'Dedekind cut', so useful in the new presentation of differential calculus and imaginary numbers.

to represent a curved surface on a plane. About 1820, as we have seen, a great deal of work was being done on representations of the globe. Studying in a new way how to determine the position of a point on a surface, Gauss analysed multiplicities in two dimensions: he then generalized his method, and ended with multiplicities to the nth dimension. This method of work enabled him to solve the problem of the map by distinguishing the conform representation which preserves angles from that which preserves distances; but it also showed the possibilities of mathematics in cataloguing any type of space whatever, even of more than three dimensions. The analytical functions of complex variables played an important part in this. And it was the conditions of calculus which, for those who were eventually to use it, gave the definition of space which most conformed to the phenomenon studied, much more than the conditions of sensitivity which played so great a role in the Kantian critique. A new age was opening in the history of man's mental equipment.

And now we move to the remote borders of Europe, to an obscure Russian university, which Alexander II had tried to stimulate by giving it new foreign professors, especially German or Viennese. At the whim of the imperial government Lobachevsky was in turn museum director, professor, rector, or merely a private individual, a suspect, whose movements were watched by the police, but through all these vicissitudes his unfailing passion for research resulted in a striking achievement: the definition of a surface (pseudosphere) which would enable several parallels to a straight line to be drawn through a single point. In 1855, at the age of 65, on his university's diamond jubilee, Lobachevsky presented his *Pangéométrie*, which he had just finished dictating, as he had become blind. It went right back to Euclid in order to escape from his postulates and start off again along paths which the old geometry had neglected in an attempt at rectilinear simplification. Its mathematics became exceedingly complicated* but the

* It is important at this juncture to stress the importance of Riemann. He was born in 1826. As a young man he had mastered the

main thing was that the tools needed to deal with the scientific problems of 1850 were now ready to hand. This new mathematics did far more than revolutionize philosophy, which for the next fifty years abandoned all attempts to understand it: it provided practical methods which simplified and activated the thinking of the experimenters in the physical and chemical sciences.

While this revolutionary new theoretical work was being carried out in eastern Europe, France still had Hermitte to carry on the great tradition of 1800. It seemed at times as if the Polytechnic and the University were intent on preserving the tradition of Laplace by clinging to the system and putting every possible obstacle in the way of Hermitte's 'pernicious originality'. Fortunately the aged Cauchy and the whole German school supported the young 'dreamer' in his application of elliptical functions to equations of the fifth degree; and the way was opened for his pupil, Henri Poincaré.

---

nine hundred pages of Legendre's *Théorie des Mondes* in six days. At thirty-three he defined the terms of an arithmetical problem with which Fermat had been given mathematicians sleepless nights for the past hundred and fifty years. At twenty-four he discovered that it was possible to establish a mathematics which would do away with all distinctions between the gravitation of electricity, magnetism and thermostatics—thereby fulfilling the dream of the early nineteenth century, but more important still, enriching geometry so immeasurably that a thousand new avenues were opened up. Gauss had suspected the importance of the analysis of position, the forerunner of our modern topology. From Gauss's uniformity of complex functions, Riemann, using the work of Abel, deduced the reasoning for a critique of multiform functions, the complexity of which he reduced by presenting a new interpretation of the plane and of space. We shall merely state here that in inventing a new geometry of surfaces Riemann made as much use of the obverse as of the reverse of the plane, and eventually evolved a general theory of the functions of the complex variable. The aged Gauss encouraged the young Riemann at Göttingen. At that period it seemed as if the whole story of mathematics was concentrated in Germany in the persons of Dirichlet, Kammer, Kronecker and Weierstrass, all of whom took a great interest in the young mathematician. In 1860, in a memoir on a problem of heat conduction Riemann, drawing inspiration from his geometry, perfected the reasoning from which, in the twentieth century, the theory of relativity was to emerge.

The theoretical work of the east Europeans brought a new diversity into mathematics and it is easy to understand why philosophers looked back wistfully to the age of enlightenment, when it seemed as if the whole life of the mind could be illuminated from one single source. Their attitude is accounted for by the diversity and the enormous complexity of the mathematical concepts which emerged from Gauss's revolutionary theories. To take just one example, there were interminable (and often friendly) arguments between the two protagonists of the rival German schools, Kronecker and Weierstrass: for the former, everything was number, for the latter, analysis. The field of thought covered by mathematics had become so vast that its extreme frontiers were in violent contradiction with each other. But it was so productive of ideas that, no matter what the demands of the natural sciences might be, they could almost always be profitably met; mathematical diversity encouraged the dispersion of scientific work.

We saw that at the close of the great creative period from 1800 to 1845, the problem which proved most resistant to the magnificent synthesis of the time was that of thermo-dynamics. The first person to tackle the problem was Sadi Carnot, the son of the 'organizer of victory'. Sadi Carnot made a theoretical study of the working of the steam-engine. It had been thought that just as the old mills were turned by the action of falling water, so the steam-engine worked under the effect of the fall of heat. Actually, Carnot had gone into the subject far more thoroughly, as the discovery of his papers was to show. The same careful observation is apparent also in the work of Lord Kelvin: not all heat is transformed into work. Joule had calculated the relations between the electricity expended and the heat produced in a conductor. Now, in theory, if the gravity machine is reversible, the heat produced by work is incapable, even in theory, and without friction, of reproducing the work which has engendered it. This is all the more important since in machines a vast amount of energy is irrevocably dissipated in heat, for theoretical as well as practical reasons. Furthermore, the new theory led to the liquefaction of gases: all that was necessary was to make them work. Faraday liquefied chlorine, and by the end of the century hydrogen had also been mastered. Most important of all, however, were the first industrial consequences of thermo-dynamics: the improvement of steam-engines and proof of the superiority of internal combustion engines.

In 1860, using Lebon's gas, the Belgian Lenoir produced his combustion engine. It was costly to run, using 3,000 litres of gas per horse power; a Nottingham engineer improved it by preliminary compression, then a German from Cologne claimed to have solved the problem —consumption fell to 300 litres in 1870, and eventually to 100 litres in 1890. The engine was ready and waiting only for petroleum.

Meanwhile advances in chemistry had been no less revolutionary. If Berthelot occupies a special place in the history of chemistry it is mainly because of the lucidity of his expositions, the convincing simplicity of his experiments. He was proud to be known as the creator of organic synthesis, of which he was the chief popular exponent. At times in his work he failed to give due recognition to some of his predecessors, to Berzelius, for instance. It is true that this brilliant Swede never abandoned his scepticism on the subject of organic synthesis in spite of convincing discoveries. However, Liebig in Germany had succeeded in achieving the synthesis of formic acid and urea; lactic acid was to follow. The Alsatian went one better, with the synthesis of ethyl alcohol thereby opening up innumerable avenues to industry.

The most important outcome of the new organic synthesis was artificial dyes. There were, of course, many mineral dyes already in existence. Pliny had described the Roman processes for making ceruse (white lead). Nevertheless, most high-grade dyes were obtained from vegetable products, indigo, campeachy wood (log-wood) brazil wood, and until 1880 competition from traditional dye-stuffs limited the industrial application of chemistry to the dye industry. Eventually, however, the new methods were adopted in all the great industrial dyeworks, a much for the novel brilliance of the colours they produced as for their cheapness. A number of German researchers were successful in this field. One of them, in 1826, distilled indigo and isolated aniline. Then a series of related substances of the same family were discovered, in isolation, in Germany towards 1850, when Hofmann perceived the basic unity of these substances and started large-scale industry. The explosives industry, too, dated from the 1850s. Up to that time, gunpowder was merely the mechanical mixing of a substance causing burning with a combustible substance. But the discovery was then made that organic compounds could be combined with nitric acid. The explosive power of gun-cotton, of picrate of potassium and of nitroglycerine made a terrifying impression on contemporaries, heightened by the results of the first practical tests, the effects of which in every case greatly exceeded expectations: scrap-iron and rocks seemed to have been volatilized.

There was so much rapid development during this period, that a number of important new products went unnoticed at first. The development of the rubber industry is an example. In the eighteenth century rubber was merely an object of curiosity. About 1825, in Glasgow, Mackintosh invented the raincoat, but if this peculiar garment was exposed to a too-hot sun it softened and ceased to be waterproof, and if it was exposed to cold, it cracked; all that Mackintosh got out of it was the honour of having given his name to a garment. About 1850, the American Goodyear discovered vulcanization; he had just gone bankrupt in an agricultural implement business when by a lucky chance he happened to heat a mixture of rubber and sulphur. 'Vulcanized' rubber resisted solvents, cold and heat. Goodyear's fortune was made: his firm soon grew to a huge concern, which dominated the American market by the close of the century. The new raw material was used not only for office erasers; it was drawn out into sheets, cut up into elastic, moulded into half-spheres out of which Lejeune in Paris made his celebrated balloons. It was hardened into ebonite, a valuable insulator for the new telegraph and telephone apparatus, and the development of pneumatics soon followed. This rubber was at first collected in the Brazilian Amazon; it was so profitable that a permanent shipping company was started on this dangerous river. Then trees were bled in Java, and there was a widespread search for these precious forests in Gaboon, as well as in China.

But it was electricity which effected the biggest change in industry. Ampère, one of the last great admirers and pupils of the *Encyclopédie*, carried on from the experiments of Oerstedt, and in 1820 demonstrated the relationship between electricity and magnetism, and propounded the law of induced currents. But he did not realize the full significance of his discoveries.

The implications were far-reaching. The foremost scientists, about 1850, doubted the possibility of inducing a current by mechanical means. In order to obtain high tensions, they continued to pile up voltaic elements on the model of the giant pile which had been in use for the past fifty years at the Polytechnic. This was not appreciably improved upon by the discovery of thermoelectricity. These piles supplied the current for experiments which soon moved out of the laboratory into the field of industry, one of the most important being electrolysis. Then the electric arc gave light and heat at temperatures never reached before, which enabled Berthelot to achieve his spectacular syntheses. Measuring instruments of ever-increasing sensitivity and resistance were devised. In 1880 an international congress determined the units of electricity which were to apply all over the world. Meantime, electricity had begun to have its effect on industry.

In 1831, Henry in the United States and Faraday in England carried out the decisive experiment which Faraday was the first to publish in a famous report to the Royal Society in London. 'Twenty-six feet of copper wire one-twentieth of an inch in diameter, were wound round a cylinder' reported the *Annals of Physics and Chemistry* thirty years later. Into this apparatus was thrust a magnet 'There was an immediate deviation of the needle.' It was the first electro-magnetic generator. In the following year

Hachette, the son of an Ardennes bookseller whom Monge had put in charge of the physics collections at the *École Polytechnique*, and who had just become a member of the *Institut*, read a paper by the son of a laboratory instrument maker: it dealt with a spark machine, which was probably the very first alternator. It was still of very low power. All over Europe men were at work inventing apparatus. In 1869 Gramme invented the machine which, according to the *Institut*, was capable of everything the pile had previously achieved. Gramme was a strange man. He appeared in Paris at the age of twenty-five in 1856, after attending free classes in Liège, and found a job as moulder in a lamp-glass factory. He taught himself by reading small treatises and dictionaries, and turned the kitchen of his small flat into a laboratory. Later he worked under Ruhmkorff with intense dedication. Finally he succeeded in building his continuous current dynamo which at first was greeted with scepticism. He perfected it and founded the *Société des Machines Électromagnétiques*. In 1880, at long last, he received his first reward—20,000 francs. Meanwhile he worked with Fontaine and studied the problem of the flow of an electric current. In 1890, the Society was turning out something like one thousand dynamos a year, the largest of which could keep 3,600 lamps alight on a consumption of 350 horse-power.

All these new industries which emerged from the laboratories were to change society. Before discussing this important aspect, it is worthwhile considering the mental and moral effects of these discoveries, particularly of the new strides which were being made in biological research.

Buffon had already put forward the tentative idea of linkage of creatures, but the pettiness of the criticisms that followed, particularly those of Diderot, whose chief aim was to annoy the Sorbonne, detracted greatly from the significance of his ideas. More important theories were proposed by Erasmus Darwin, a strange poet, a doctor by profession, who obtained some success with his *Botanic Garden*. The English are proverbially fond of their trees, their island flowers, the wild life of their countryside (Erasmus Darwin also produced a zoonomy), and

English rural society, unlike that of France, was as we have seen largely middle-class. It had leisure, and yet retained close connections with the towns. All the English took a close interest in agricultural experiments, cross-breeding, and seed selection; the successes of breeders and planters were discussed, appreciated, imitated, and the country was like one vast biological laboratory. Erasmus Darwin, then, was a doctor, so was his son Charles, and his grandson Charles was to have followed in their footsteps, but at Cambridge it became clear that he preferred hunting, dogs, gaming, and insect-collecting to medical studies. His career was typically English. He met in a club a member of the *Beagle* expedition who suggested that Darwin should go with him. His father was doubtful; his uncle Wedgwood, of Etruria, decided that he should go. Charles Darwin had paid no particular attention to the ideas of Lamarck, or Geoffroy Saint-Hilaire, or Chambers. He observed, noted, collected, and brought back from his cruise a huge mass of documents, which he endeavoured to put into some sort of order. He read hardly any theoretical works beyond the one which all England had been discussing for the past forty years, Malthus's *Essay on Population*. He read it in 1838 for entertainment, he said, and suddenly discovered the idea that favourable variations tend to be preserved, and unfavourable ones to be destroyed. This gave him a theory on which to work. Darwin said nothing about the causes which, in one and the same species, differentiated the innate qualities of individuals. But he explained with the utmost clarity how, of these innate qualities, those which have a survival value give to the individuals possessing them an advantage which enables them to live longer and to secure a mate which will propagate a durable race. Darwin formed his theory in 1844, but he worked at it for another twenty years, so that a year before publishing his own work, he learned that Alfred Russell Wallace had just arrived at the same theory, also from a study of Malthus. Darwin engaged in no recriminations, finished his book, published it, and won immediate fame.

In the bitter controversy which followed, he received valuable help from T. H. Huxley, who was known as Darwin's bulldog. A vast campaign of criticism and a violent quarrel of principle was unleashed. The Anglican clergy and all the Christian churches fulminated against the theory which made man 'a descendant of the apes', and relegated him to a position as the first of the primates. The Bishop of Oxford defied Huxley at the British Association, and sneeringly asked him whether it was through his grandfather or his grandmother that he was related to the monkey. It was Huxley who put into words the reason for Darwin's success (the first edition of the book had been sold out immediately). The *Origin of Species*, he said, supplied the working hypothesis they had been looking for. But he realized also the limits of this hypothesis: all good agriculturists, for whom Darwin soon wrote *The Variation of Plants and Animals under Domestication* (1868), know that the offspring of different, though related species, is sterile. The chief difficulty of the theory was therefore apparent at the outset, but did not hinder the popularity of the work. It was fairly popular in France, thanks to the materialists (as the socialists were called), who thus at one fell swoop, as they thought, got rid of the Revelation and final causes. In Germany, Haeckel declared that the new revelation was even more certain than universal gravity and that it should be taught instead of the catechism in all primary schools. And England buried Darwin (who died soon after the publication of his book) in Westminster Abbey near Isaac Newton.

The way to a solution of the difficulties inherent in Darwin's theory was opened up in 1865, though it was more than thirty years before this was realized. Mendel, abbot of a monastery in Brno, embarked on a series of experiments on the cross-fertilization of peas. He found that certain hereditary characteristics were indivisible and unchangeable units, and that particular hybrids, though similar in appearance, possessed in their germinal cells a pair of characteristics proper to each of the species which had participated in the cross. In this way he originated an atomist conception of biology, though its full significance was not recognized and exploited immediately. Before this could happen, Bateson and Devries had to study mutations.

In 1872 Darwin published *The Expression of the Emotions in Man and Animals*. He attempted to show that man can really be considered as ending the biological evolutionary series. This new publication of Darwin's gave great stimulus to the development of anthropology. Already Quetelet had been at work measuring conscripts. The shape of skulls was studied, racial demarcation fixed. Each race was defined by a group of interrelated characteristics. The geography of the European races was studied, their geological antecedents were traced. In 1856 human remains were discovered at Neanderthal; in 1886 more were found at Spy. A cousin of Darwin, Francis Galton, studied the transmission of the mental qualities of the individual, and stressed the importance of heredity. He drew graphs based on the work of Gauss similar to those which Quetelet had used. The final conclusion of all this research was, however, that the influence of environment had been overestimated. Education can and must foster only the best strains—an idea which became the ethics of eugenics, soon to become so popular in Germany.

Whilst English biologists were publicizing these extraordinary new theories, France seemed to be proving the evolutionists wrong. We shall deal at a more appropriate time with the work of Pasteur; he, too, was the butt of persecution. On the other hand, Berthelot, the friend of Renan, was a fairly typical example of the modern French approach. He embodied the militant secularism of the late nineteenth century which was in revolt against all the old religious ethics. In 1870, from one end of Europe to the other, to have a scientific mind, to be practical, meant to support the doctrine of evolution.

Thus, at a time when man was covering Europe with a network of railways which were to give him the greatest industrial power the world had yet known, Darwin showed him the immense historical perspective of his destiny. A new pride can be seen in the works of some Western intellectuals. The gradual development of this philosophy can best be illustrated by comparing John Stuart Mill and Spencer.

At thirteen Stuart Mill had read most of the Greek and Latin authors and a wide range of other books. Born in 1806, he was consequently steeped in eighteenth-century thought, and inevitably became a disciple of Hume, imbued with the learning of a previous generation. As a result he resisted the main research work of the nineteenth century, the exploration of the problems of evolution. But he did believe that the value of mental activity lay, not in the formal discipline it imposed, but in its capacity to enrich by experience and to co-ordinate a world of associations which created characteristics. It was this belief which enabled him to avoid Bentham's uncompromising hedonism, and to arrive eventually at a philosophy of general happiness, the greatest happiness of the greatest number. He followed this doctrine so far that he had no fear of communism, and condemned individual ownership of landed property since the land belonged to all alike. From this religion of humanity, he believed that we were justified in postulating the idea of God.

Stuart Mill had been employed by the East India Company, the suppression of which in 1856 left him without employment. Spencer, who worked for the London–Birmingham railway company, was a victim of the 1848 crisis. Born fifteen years after Stuart Mill, he was brought up in complete freedom by his father, a teacher who let him read every biological work on which he could lay his hands. At first Spencer was attracted by the doctrines of calculated ethics, but like Stuart Mill believed in a kind of communism of the land. Later he met the full force of German Romanticism through the works of Carlyle and Coleridge, and he discovered behind the evolution of societies a kind of permanent imperative, a mysterious force which might well be life itself. Society was no longer a mechanism, but an organism.

Everything was evolution, but the actual direction this

evolution was taking still remained to be discovered. On physical theories, he concluded that evolution is an integration of matter passing from indefinite homogeneity to definite heterogeneity. We shall mention later how much of this he owed to Clausius. The most important point was that Darwin's conclusions had been adopted: the mind adapts itself to external conditions; natural selection ensures the success of the best adaptations—which explains the intellectual studies made by psychology, and the effective combination by association of elements supplied by experience. Finally, though there is some evidence that he agreed with his German models in their theory of race, Spencer believed that evolution in general tended towards individualization. Society, militarist and monarchical in its early stages, tends to become industrial and liberal. He based his theory very largely on evidence provided by the entirely new and original study of savages. Thus he ended by rejecting the ideal he had at first adopted—agrarian communism. Biological evolution leads man to a perpetual improvement of his lot, the supreme triumph of which is political liberalism. Moral progress, imposed by force of circumstances, ends in individualism.

This was a cycle of mental evolution which ended in a curious way. First the mathematical liberalism of Bentham was rudely shaken by the crisis caused by the development of railways: people began to envisage a socialism à la Saint-Simon, even à la Proudhon, and for a short time middle-class society felt uncertain of its moral foundations. Then the drive for progress and modernization began again, in spite of Schopenhauer's scepticism, and biological science was taken to give a new basis for the middle-class liberalism in which England so implicitly believed.

THE INDUSTRIAL SOCIETIES

Both the natural sciences and the exact sciences seemed now to be furthering the ambitions of industrial enterprise. It was the knell of the old ethics, the triumph of uninhibited individualism.

We know how Flaubert's hero laconically summed up his sentimental education during the revolutionary days of 1848—'Je me réforme'. This kind of reform was apparently highly successful during the twenty years which saw the reappearance in France of manners as dissolute, though not as elegant, as those associated with the *roués* of Louis xv's reign. In Haussmann's new Paris, there were certain streets where gentlemen of fashion installed their mistresses in sumptuous apartments. Morny was outstanding in that strange society where literary *salons* were opened in the houses of the *petites amies* of princes of wit or wealth: the poets paid discreet (or even open) court to them. Moreover, many of these Egerias, having got themselves accepted, succeeded not only in living a decent life, but sometimes even affected a certain austerity; and at all events they remained faithful to their man. Those of the bourgeois who were less fashionable, or less wealthy, made love to the Cardinal demoiselles.

Men had no aim but pleasure; Napoleon III held a series of imperial fêtes in which the new wealth showed off its ostentatious luxury, in which Offenbach made fun in music of the old heroes and the ancient gods, where the waltz reigned supreme and crinolines were even more costly than the hoops so fashionable under the monarchy. But if the Emperor set an example of infidelity in the Tuileries, Eugénie was the very incarnation of the dignified outraged mother, for while the demi-monde was busy enjoying itself, virtuous boredom was the fashion in well-conducted families. The dreary evening parties at Compiègne showed what were the chief preoccupations of this virtue: to ensure the future of one's children, to arrange advantageous marriages and uphold religion and self-control. One town council went so far as to reward the latter by offering a prize to a citizen conspicuous for the moderate size of his family. The *Académie* set personal goodness amongst the virtues. Immorality and virtue had, at all events, one effect in common—a lowering of the birth rate. Fortunately, longevity was still on the increase owing to a number of factors. There was a better distribution of food supplies thanks to the railway, and a slight improvement in the lot of the workers; industries followed in the wake of the modernization programme which accompanied the completion of the railway system; standards of hygiene improved in the cities whose slums had been swept away by Haussmann's demolishers. This improvement in living conditions almost made up for the infant mortality rate; if the number of marriages increased slightly, families with few children kept the total population of France almost stable: from approximately thirty-six million in 1850, it rose to thirty-eight million in 1870, but the annexation of Savoy accounted for almost one million of this increase. It fell again to thirty-six million after the Treaty of Frankfurt, and from then on, after the usual post-war bulge, there was a marked drop in the fertility rate, and in the total number of births: in 1888, the number of deaths was exactly equal to that of births. From 1880 the total figure of the male population was stationary.

This was true of Europe in general after 1880, but not in the preceding thirty years. It is true that in England the 1848 crisis caused an abrupt drop in the number of births, but a rise in the birth rate had immediately accompanied prosperity. In the 1870s the gross reproduction rate was higher than that of the 1840s and expectation of life was increasing as satisfactorily as in France; but the death rate, unlike that of France, fell from 234 to 191 per thousand between 1840 and 1880. From 1860 to 1880, therefore, England's population increased at almost the same rhythm as in the previous forty years. Thus from approximately twenty million in 1840 it reached almost forty million in 1880. England's population doubled during the period when that of France remained nearly static.

The growth rate in Germany was similar, perhaps even more marked. There again the drop in the birth rate during the years of crisis was soon made good. The gross reproduction rate in 1880 almost equalled that of 1820. Although the increase in longevity had not quite kept pace with that of the West, the net reproduction rate nevertheless rose from one hundred per thousand in 1840 to more than one hundred fifty per thousand in 1880. From

1880, in Germany, as in England, the gross reproduction rate suffered a setback, though it was more than compensated by the fall in the death rate. But already the numerical superiority of the populations of Germany and England was assured. If France possessed more inhabitants than England and Germany put together in the eighteenth century, in 1880 the population of England alone equalled and surpassed that of France. By 1860, the population of Germany had equalled it; it surpassed it by fifty per cent in 1880. Demographically France had fallen far behind by the time of the railway revolution, a critical stage in the human evolution of Europe.

The consequences of these statistics must be obvious. It is true that the relative numbers of the populations of the three countries were not very different even up to 1860. But there is no doubt that the psychology of a people in rapid expansion is not like that of a stable people. Whilst England was flooding the world with emigrants, and Germany was responsible for a great movement of peoples, particularly towards America, France could barely populate the regions which its political and military power was still strong enough to hold. Neither Indo-China nor Mexico ever looked like being lands in which Frenchmen would settle. Emigration was limited to North Africa and was numerically smaller than that from Spain and Italy. Jean-Baptiste Say asserted, as it had been fashionable to do in eighteenth-century France, that the departure of families (and of capital) weakened nations. Between two dynamic powers, France drew false wisdom from the past.

Over and above these differences, there was one element common to the population throughout Europe. A new civilization was developing between 1850 and 1880 which led to an increase in numbers and also to increased expectation of life. The essential instrument of these new developments was the town. The growth of towns was concurrent with that of the railways, since it was the existence of urban centres, already firmly established, which attracted the railway and only the stations in big towns paid handsome dividends. Traffic paid its way between industrial cities, whereas country lines were costly to run. But if the towns helped the development on the first railways, the latter in turn brought enormous benefits to the towns. They mobilized labour and facilitated the transport of the many gangs of workmen from the country needed by the government contractors laying the lines. In 1848 the *Nord* alone employed 40,000 workmen. There must have been hundreds of thousands of workers whom the railway attracted from their fields and pitched into the towns. As a result the towns grew at an appalling rate. The crowds of workers lived where they could, in towns where the demolition of the old quarters, the creation of squares and streets had upset old ways of life. The lodging crisis passed through critical phases, and speculation in lands and houses was rife, in spite of the risks. New houses were so dear that they stood for months without tenants, and building societies went bankrupt because they could not meet their bills over such a long period. Then the new quarters filled up, but not as before with rich and poor intermingled from one storey to another in the same areas. Only the rich could afford to live in the city centres; the poor were pushed out to the periphery. The rag-pickers no longer swarmed in squalor around Notre Dame but took refuge in the area of the fortifications. Dingy suburbs encircled the rejuvenated towns.

It was of course the railways which brought food supplies to these masses of human beings who descended on the old towns. Almost from the moment of their inception they were making special arrangements for transporting provisions to the towns. In Paris the building of the central markets began in 1851. Companies lent capital to agriculture; contractors engaged in public works diverted the gangs of men no longer needed by the railways on to irrigation projects. In 1859 the old Moulin-de-Pertuis canal was re-opened and lengthened, and became the Cadenet canal, irrigating something like five thousand acres in Vaucluse. Two years earlier the Carpentras canal had been begun, planned to irrigate more than fifteen thousand acres. The railway was soon carrying an entirely new kind of freight intended to feed the towns it had populated. Modern methods of stock-breeding and cultivation, the development of slaughter-houses, the perfecting of mills, a whole body of changes benefiting the railway and increasing its profits, supported the increasing population of the new towns. Changes in the countryside also had similar effects on population. Better harvests were being produced with less labour, and the result was a surplus population which took the train to town. Whenever the population of a town increased new industries were attracted into the suburbs. The progress of the great textile mill made competition so fierce for the old country hand-loom weavers that they were gradually disappearing, worn out by the work of a day of more than twelve hours which scarcely brought them the price of a kilogramme of bread. In 1840 one third of the inhabitants of the Auge area were engaged in weaving; two generations later there was barely a loom to be found in the district. It was almost the same in Flanders and the Lyonnais: the town drew in the rural craftsmen, after the harshness of the struggle for survival had forced them to reduce their expenses to the barest minimum. In the old days in the countryside people looked to providence to feed their children; in the town everything had to be bought. If the bourgeois, eager to rise in the social scale, reduced the size of his family, the worker soon followed suit. And soon this new economic fashion spread even into country districts, first amongst the well-to-do, then wherever the railways took modern ideas—a little more hygiene and far fewer children. Since the population continued to increase because people were living longer, there was no resistance to this new outlook.

The reign of the towns meant the reign of capitals: the population of London doubled in thirty years; from approximately two million it rose to almost four million in 1880. The area of the city grew rapidly, absorbing great new suburbs, while at its centre the old city was almost completely uninhabited, so that all its unfurnished buildings could be set aside for trade: in 1880 it had only about 50,000 instead of the 200,000 there had been in

1840. It was because it was given over to offices that it could fill up during working hours with a crowd of more than 700,000. Night and morning an enormous migration set in between the periphery and the centre—a phenomenon which amazed the foreign visitor. But the vast cost of this daily migration made it logical to extend the Sunday day of rest to include Saturday, and later resulted in the institution known in France as '*la semaine anglaise*'.

The surface area of Paris developed less, since its centre remained overpopulated, and it was rather in the new quarters, the most expensive of which was the Elysée, that the new offices appeared. But the population piled up in the capital at almost the same rate as in London; from something like one million in 1840 it went up to more than two million in 1880. Within the same period, Vienna grew from 400,000 to 700,000 inhabitants.

But the most spectacular growth increase took place in Berlin. At the opening of the century it had barely 150,-000 inhabitants, but by 1896 it had more than 1,300,000. Berlin, which only a short time before had not been one of Germany's biggest cities, became one of the largest in the world. It took over from Danzig the role of corn exchange, from Breslau the role of textile capital, and from Essen that of iron capital (around the Borsig works there now stretched a huge black suburb). The University of Berlin was the first in Germany. The native population of Berlin included less than thirty per cent of Germans because there were so many descendants of French and Slav immigrants, so it was not by the power of race, as the Germans claimed, but by the power of industry (in which they were dominant) that Berlin became the key-city to Germany's future. In London, which had developed from trade, and in Berlin which had developed from industry, the destinies of the middle classes were comparable. But in Paris, a city still bound up in its long history —they were different.

Into this radically urbanized society the industrial results of scientific research were introduced. They created new middle-class dynasties. We have described how electricity had emerged from the domain of pure research.

The Siemens family demonstrated how it invaded industry. There were ten of them, brothers, from the same farm in Hanover and born between 1816 and 1836. By the end of the century they were the masters of the most extensive and successful group of factories in Germany, the new industrial Germany. At eighteen, Ernst had enlisted in the artillery. He became passionately interested in electricity, took out patents in galvanoplasty, and, once he was appointed director of the Berlin Arsenal, he invented the electric mechanism of underwater mines. At the same period he directed the installation of Prussia's electric telegraph. He resigned from the army in 1850 and founded a company for making telegraphic apparatus. He installed equipment in Berlin, northern Germany and Russia. He helped to install telegraphs in South America and South Africa. He competed with the English even in London itself. His firm became that of *Gebrüder Siemens*, for he had summoned his nine brothers to assist him. He was courageous enough to take on dangerous operations (like the Transcaucasian telegraph) and he also kept up to date with new electrical inventions. In England he learnt how to make submarine cables and was soon teaching his teachers. He adopted Gramme's machine and perfected it. In 1880 he astounded casual visitors to the quinquennial exhibition in Paris by running a small electric railway, and it was he who installed Berlin's trams. The nine brothers spread all over the world. Two went to England and stayed there; Karl was to become a baron and in 1883, as we have seen, he invented a new process for making steel. Friedrich was the inventor of a famous gasogene furnace which, through its ingenious system of heat recovery, appreciably lowered cost prices in metallurgy. Hans founded glassworks in Dresden and Bohemia. Gas, distillation, iron and steel industries as well as electricity, telephone and telegraph, all came from the *Gebrüder Siemens*.

Electricity was not alone in creating an influential middle class, for another branch of research invaded industry —chemistry. The whole world, in 1880, acknowledged that the Germans had a genius for chemistry, and one of those who best justified this opinion was Justus Liebig. About 1820 this talented pupil of the Gymnasium at Darmstadt, the son of a druggist, was working for an apothecary. He spent most of his time reading his way through the municipal library which had just been opened, concentrating especially on periodicals dealing with the new science. He was drawn to Paris, since all the great and learned theories were being formulated there, and worked there with Gay-Lussac and his collaborators, notably Dumas. Now a brilliant scientist, he returned to Germany and founded a small university in Giessen which he was to make famous, and where he established the world's finest laboratory. It soon acquired an international reputation. He found credits easy to obtain in the 1840s when industrialization was just starting in Germany, and eventually he was made a baron. His subsequent career was typical of every official of that time—he became a member of the German Academy, and a corresponding member of those of France and England. His great speciality was the analysis of plants and living organisms, the analysis of what is known as organic chemistry. It consisted in measuring carbon and hydrogen by oxidizing them, and he discovered constants in them which he expressed in radicals (C_2H_5). He never lost sight of the practical application of his work. Studying fats, he discovered the basic products of meat extract, and when studying changes in alcohols did not neglect to analyse the bouquets of the most famous wines. In continual contact with industrial firms, he was also one of the first to take a systematic interest in agricultural problems. He was responsible for important discoveries in the nitrogen cycle, and in the course of his work in this field he paid as much attention to the detailed procedure of Chinese agriculture as to the recklessly wasteful methods of Western farming. As a jam manufacturer, he made an enormous fortune.

The evolution of the industrial society presents curious paradoxes: whereas in Germany, the home of authoritarian régimes, scientists often adopted business careers, in France, thanks to the close connections between French power and the middle classes, French scientists often ended up in the seats of power.

The work of the Frenchman Jean-Baptiste Dumas was parallel to that of Liebig. He made a special study of alcohols and ethers and contributed to the discovery of the amides. Like Liebig, Dumas founded an institution, the *École Centrale des Arts et Manufactures*; but unlike his German colleague, he did not make a fortune in industry. He began, like Liebig, by being an apprentice-pharmacist from 1848 to 1870, but he became a Deputy, Minister of Agriculture and Commerce, then Senator. As President of the Paris Municipal Council he initiated major improvements in hygiene and in the supply of drinking water, and demonstrated the impurity of water from the Seine. The pursuit of science in France during these years led to power just as surely as American or German industry led to wealth. 'What a miracle of chemistry', wrote an Empire caricaturist. 'Retorts distil politicians!' Like Dumas, Berthelot ended up as a Minister, after being a Deputy, then a life Senator. The career of the Alsatian Kuhlmann serves admirably to illustrate the two roads to success; via industry in Germany and government in France. He was both an industrialist in Germany (he founded the complex industries in Loos which was to become so well known) and a politician in France (General Adviser and Governor of the Lille Mint). The two different attitudes certainly existed in the powder industry. The greatest precautions were necessary in the industrial preparation of these products, since they were so dangerous to handle. Between 1865 and 1870 terrible accidents had horrified public opinion. In San Francisco, Hamburg and Stockholm nitro-glycerine wrought such havoc that there was talk of banning it by international agreement. It was then that Nobel discovered that mixed with ethyl alcohol and especially with silica, nitro-glycerine was no longer explosive on percussion, but had to be detonated. This 'dynamite' exploded when ignited. In 1878, eighty victims died through the carelessness of a cavalry lieutenant who had brought a packet of dynamite too near an inadequately extinguished brazier.

Work went on ceaselessly to obviate these dangers, and above all to explore the possible applications of this new power. The vital question was, who should control it, businessmen or the state? In France the state took over and opened the gunpowder factory at Donges, whilst it authorized a very few private factories under its own control, and entrusted the direction of them to Berthelot. Elsewhere it was private capital which assumed control. Nobel was at the head of a consortium covering Germany, Austro-Hungary, Italy, Spain and the United States.

In conclusion it is worth mentioning the amazingly successful industrial career of a German chemist, Hofmann. He had been Liebig's pupil in Giessen and London, then in Berlin, where he earned a good enough reputation for himself as a scientist to found the *Deutsche Chemische Gesellschaft* in 1868. He then became 'official scientist' and a corresponding member of the great academies. In 1845 in Giessen, he had already analysed the ethyls and alcohols and discovered aniline in pit-coal. The whole new dye industry drew its roots from coal, which made it economical. It could be independent of costly vegetable imports since aniline, though difficult to purify, produced first a good black, then, properly treated, could give a red and a yellow. Another of Liebig's pupils working on indigo at Giessen enriched the range of synthetic colours and also worked in the *Deutsche Chemische Gesellschaft*. Aniline proved dangerous to handle because it was so toxic, yet in 1870 its industrial production increased greatly, and by 1890 had reached more than one thousand tons a year.

We shall not pursue further the history of all the chemical industries, ammoniac, soda, and later petroleum and celluloid. All had their part to play in the rebuilding of society; everywhere they contributed to the development of the towns; everywhere they contributed also to a reform of fashion.

THE DECLINE OF AESTHETICS

Industrial fashions had triumphed under Napoleon III. Parisian iron-founders could barely keep pace with orders for reproduction of old weapons, not, of course, in wrought iron, but in cast iron, since they were only meant to decorate halls and vestibules. After improving on the Louis Quinze style, the Faubourg Saint-Antoine then did the same for that of Nuremberg. The taste of the imperial court had not always been exquisite, but the taste of the new public opened the way to all manner of reproductions. Haussmann's new buildings gave a fairly good idea of this second-hand style in their interior decoration, which tended to luxuriate in innumerable fussy and elaborate imitations in every conceivable royal style; it was quite the thing to have a Henri II dining-room, a Gothic hall, a Louis XIV drawing-room, a Louis XV boudoir, and Louis XVI chairs. All these apartments were indiscriminately decorated with plaster or staff work. Even the cabinet makers tried to copy all these flourishes and their admirable craftsmanship did not compensate for the general lack of taste.

In all their reproductions, craftsmen were not content merely to excel; they wished to improve. Compare the imperial eagles of the First and Second Empire: the first made no claim to zoological accuracy, and was rather heraldic in inspiration, the second was a carefully observed copy of the eagle in the Jardin des Plantes. A scientific pretentiousness was substituted for an aesthetic sense: we have only to read the five volumes of the *Dictionnaire raisonné du mobilier français* or the ten volumes of the *Dictionnaire raisonné de l'architecture française* (1854–72), written by the famous Viollet-Le-Duc. This librarian's son was one of the first officials in the new Department of Historic Monuments; he first repaired then restored the Sainte-Chapelle and Notre Dame, Saint-Sernin de Toulouse, the Château de Pierrefonds, and the ramparts at Carcassonne and Avignon. His art aimed at scientific accuracy, inspired by learning and erudition. His popularity was as immense and as lucrative as that of Meissonier, the son of a chemist, and a prolific painter of the type of picture for which fashionable society paid fantastic sums, and which claimed to surpass in accuracy of historical detail the old Dutch masters themselves whom he was copying. When he wished to paint 1814, he made innumerable sketches of ploughland under snow to reproduce its exact appearance. His grenadiers were correct down to the last gaiter button, and he kept them on his easel until his imagination had encompassed every detail. It was the technique Flaubert used later to amass a wealth of detail for *Salammbô*.

Erudition in art! This was not exactly the kind of truth to which Vigny has aspired. Barely one generation had gone by and art was claiming to be 'scientific'. Was the old conflict between the artist and the bourgeois, between the poet beloved of Murger (who died in 1861) and the Philistine, at last dying down? In actual fact, although the so-called regard for truth which inspired artistic production satisfied the taste of the wealthy middle class in the case of a Meissonier or a Viollet-Le-Duc, and incidentally made their fortune, it was far from pleasing everyone. First of all Viollet-Le-Duc could not overcome the opposition of the young pupils in the *École des Beaux Arts*, who would not let him teach. Above all there was a certain form of truth which continued to arouse the violent dislike of the new society for, as Paul Mantz wrote, it 'touched the extreme frontiers of realist art'.

But before discussing this new aesthetic which originated in France, we should stress an important European aspect of the aesthetic revolution. The official taste of French imperial society left much to be desired, but it was no more dubious than the taste which prevailed in Germany or England. Munich was intended to be a new Athens and its creators were busy improving on 'Greek art'. In Berlin, too, Greek architecture on the grand scale was going up in stucco and brick. The Old Museum and the National Gallery, in a pompous Corinthian style, were no better than the Grand Theatre. Churches were constructed by the gross in every conceivable style in a vain attempt to capture for this city, which had sprung up so rapidly, the old historical traditions of the older capitals. At least one thing could be said for Germany's stations—they were enormous. Popular painters also went in for the large historical canvas: in painting the *Death of Wallenstein*, one artist reproduced the condottiere's ring so perfectly that the public mistook it for a real diamond. Menzel wasted a good deal of time in this sort of work. As for the English, they built in two styles, the Greek and the Gothic; their railway-stations looked like classical temples or cathedrals. In England, as in Germany, the statue in iron or cast-iron with an incredible wealth of dancing figures enjoyed a vogue which achieved its peak in the Albert Memorial. Germany was to be more sensitive than England to the lessons of French realist art, and in both countries alike the real reaction against this distressing modernism took an entirely different direction from that in France. We have seen that France's population figures in the 1860s revealed a trend which was not to be evident in the west and east until the 1880s. In 1860, just when the French were introducing realism in art, Germany and England were expressing their originality only by a return to Christian inspiration. At that time their demographic conditions were still those of a previous age.

This Christian aesthetic was expressed in England by the Pre-Raphaelite Brotherhood, founded in 1848. They drew a whole range of imagery from medieval legends and the books of the Bible which was essentially poetic in inspiration, although they endeavoured to depict it with extreme accuracy. Though they claimed to have revived the art of Botticelli, they achieved only Rossetti. The corresponding movement in Germany was that of the Nazarenes, founded well before its English counterpart, but more enduring. It drew its inspiration from Christian Rome, and its members carried sincerity to the point of conversion to Catholicism. They admired Perugino, but also went in for vast compositions like those of Michelangelo. In short the plastic arts in the two great industrial countries hardly ever surpassed the level of the most mediocre Parisian artists. Occasionally, especially when faced with the sarcasm of the new generation from 1860 onwards, they did introduce several new and original features.

We can now return to discussing the French realist movement which was far more than just a novelty. It began before Courbet, and its earliest expression was in *genres* which owed much to England; the caricatures of Daumier and the drawings of Constantin Guys. Baudelaire, as we know, was a great admirer of Guys. This Dutchman by birth had learnt from the English how to sketch in with deft strokes the characteristic attitudes of people and scenes from everyday life. Baudelaire again was one of the first to appreciate the quality of Daumier. Daumier's work was so much greater than that of Descamps that it is doubtful if he owed anything to Rowlandson, who had amused the English public at the expense of Napoleon I. From the indifferent material supplied him by real life and his third-rate journalists, Daumier built up a world, the restless, bewildered world of the railway age. He drew countrymen crammed together in a railway coach, lawyers defending the speculator, the people crushed by counter-revolutions, a whole collection of simpletons hastening to offer their money to rogues, scoundrels running the whole gamut of corruption, and lastly, lording it over all these humble folk, the newly rich bourgeois, pot-bellied, pompous and moralizing.

Two artists and a poet—Baudelaire, who is sometimes accused of having too limited a range, although it was he who captured to perfection the astounding originality of those bewildered human beings, of the cities which were growing around them like prisons and shedding their wan gaslight over all.

It was not easy to express this new way of life sincerely. Flaubert, who described provincial manners which aped those of Paris, and Baudelaire who allowed his friends to publish his poems, were both pilloried for outraging good manners. Daumier had plenty of time in prison to reflect on the unprepossessing features of Louis-Philippe, and Courbet was almost as unfortunate.

In the city Courbet saw little beyond his *Parisiennes*, who lived beside the Seine and looked as if they had stepped out of the *Fleurs du Mal*. But his country scenes were very different. On the fringe of the romantic movement a new landscape school had sprung up which shunned contact with towns. Corot, the son of a shopkeeper at the Pont-Royal, was swept off his feet by a love of nature as intense as that of Goethe. He had brought back from his travels in Italy, along with the inevitable historical pictures, paintings of classical ruins and landscapes. Then, snapping the last links which bound him to the Italian style and to history, he went to live at Ville-d'Avray and gave himself up to the beauty of a sea of indeterminate treetops, to the charm of everything that was vibrant with life 'from the plants and the flowers of the Île-de-France to the quivering of birches and willows'. At first mocked and scorned, and caring not at all, since he received an allowance from his father, he finally became most successful, but not before he had reintroduced into his misty landscapes the silhouettes of nymphs, fauns and dryads. There was nothing in Corot's landscapes to shock art lovers.

The paintings of the Barbizon school were somewhat cruder in style. In the last months of the reign of Louis-Philippe this school turned the forest of Fontainebleau into its open-air studio, painted trees *à la Théodore Rousseau* and ponds *à la Daubigny*. But there again, the artists who settled on the fringe of cities caused no one uneasiness. Their most typical representative was after all Millet, a painter in clogs it is true, but a painter of clean and decent human beings, whose peasants only harvested in broad daylight and prayed without despair. Millet's peasants easily made the artist's fortune, because they disconcerted no one.

It was a very different nature with which Courbet brutally confronted this public living in a whirl of business and not daring to look poverty in the face. Here were no *Parisiennes* strolling in the country, but human beings whose lives had been bound up with the land, but who were now being uprooted by the cities. Official criticism

voiced the indignation of the bourgeois: the faces of the
Ornans peasants accompanying the famous *Enterrement*
were not sad or moved, they were grotesque and unbearable. There was all the difference in the world between
Courbet's *baigneuses* and Corot's nymphs. The former
so completely disregarded all conventional and academic
standards of beauty that at the Salon, Eugénie de Mon-
tijo pretended not to see them. Proudhon accused those
who scorned his favourite painter of hypocrisy: he called
it hypocrisy to reject those slightly reeling *curés* in the
Retour de la Conférence; and hypocrisy to refuse to see
the world as it really is—a world in which the harsh law
of work deforms bodies and shatters dreams. Proudhon,
whom Courbet painted with his family, put into words
what the new socialist art was to be; Courbet was regarded as a dangerous revolutionary. After the Commune
he was obliged to flee to Switzerland: he was held responsible for the demolition of the Colonne Vendôme
and was expected to pay for its reinstallation.

With Courbet, painting had embarked on a new mission; it was no longer concerned with historical and anecdotal erudition, but with helping men to see, and to see
themselves as they were.

In 1867 Courbet, with that rebellious spirit and bois-
terous assertiveness which were always his characteristics, had a wooden shed put up on the Cours de l'Alma
in order to show his principal canvases which the official
salons had rejected. It was not long before a second shed
appeared beside it, to house the paintings of Manet.

In France, then, painting was revolutionary in trying
to teach men and to remind them of what they are. In
Germany there was no painting. The complex problems
and conflicts aroused by the nation's rapid growth could
only be adequately expressed in a torrent of music.
Wagner was born in Leipzig in the year of the Battle of
the Nations, which left him an orphan. He came of a
musical family and he was a pupil at the famous St
Thomas's school in Leipzig. Bach, Goethe, Beethoven
and Weber dominated the traditions of this small corner
of Europe. When he was twenty, Wagner, who had al-

ready composed several important works, found a job in a theatre and quickly made a name as a conductor in the cities of eastern Europe which had some pretensions to musical ambition. In the course of his travels he got to know Western and particularly Italian music, and came to Paris hoping to succeed there. He travelled by sea from Riga: a stormy voyage which inspired him to write *The Flying Dutchman,* the libretto of which, but not the music which Wagner had just composed at Meudon, was accepted by the Opera. French taste remained loyal to the Italians. In order to make a living Wagner had to turn journalist, music critic, copyist, and it was with no regrets that he made his way back to his small German towns. He crossed the Rhine in the year in which Victor Hugo published his *Rhin,* which he intended as a pledge of Franco-German reconciliation. When the musician came to the river which he was crossing for the first time, he saw in it the bitterness of his Paris failures and, overcome with emotion, swore loyalty to his German fatherland. The small German theatres were delighted to accept his *The Flying Dutchman.* Schumann realized that the new German music had at last found its fulfilment, liberated from all foreign influences. Wagner became director of the Dresden Opera to which Weber had brought such distinction; it was the era of *Tannhäuser* and *Lohengrin.*

Then Wagner discovered the true significance of his musical drama: music was not an end in itself, it was only a means of evoking the deep significance of man and his destiny. Arias and recitatives were dropped, since their significance was one of form alone: musical architecture was built up of motifs conveying an idea or a sentiment, a fate or a character. This music perfected the theory Gluck had advanced against Piccini. It also exploited to the full the revolutionary freedom which Beethoven had introduced into his later symphonies, and rediscovered and enriched the lessons of John Sebastian Bach with new orchestrations. Wagner was a revolutionary in every way. In Paris he protested against the materialism of bourgeois society which cared only for entertainment and nothing for art. In Dresden in 1848, he threw himself

passionately into the liberal national movement, going
as far as Proudhon in his demand that money should be
divested of its power to work evil. It was to be the regeneration of humanity by love. But all this fine enthusiasm suffered a serious setback when the reaction set in
against the liberals and Wagner had to take refuge in
Switzerland, where he did some serious thinking and discovered Schopenhauer.

Schopenhauer was a strange thinker, and very typical of
the Germany of the 1840s. He knew Kant, and unlike
the great philosopher's disciples applied himself in particular to the critique of practical reason and discovered
that idealist logic was an illusion, because it shut man up
within himself and because the world is will. Biology, so
popular in Germany, supplied him with numerous examples of this pressure exerted by nature on living beings
in order to force them into the paths it wishes them to
take. Without enormous self-control, man can be nothing
more than the puppet of the will, which bears him along
in the direction of the general current. The popularity of
Die Welt als Wille und Vorstellung did not become apparent until long after the first edition of the work, but
it had then been considerable, since it gave the vanquished of 1849 an explanation of their defeat—the defeat
of an over-abstract philosophy which had failed to recognize the imperatives of the inner life.

Wagner's time in Switzerland was spent pondering on
life and composing. He wrote a whole series of theoretical
works in which necessity and its counterpart, love, were
depicted, as in Schiller, as the foundations of destiny. It
was essential to destroy selfishness, and to burst asunder
the hard shell of hypocritical habits which shut the heart
off from the great creative surge of human history.
Schopenhauer believed that music was the only art capable of expressing the will, all other forms being merely
presentation. Wagner was eager to prove him right. He
started on his *Tetralogy*, the *Nibelungen Ring*, the history
of the pure-hearted hero who destroys the power of gold.
He said in music what German painters had been trying
in vain to express in their great legendary and historical

canvases, the story of Siegfried, soon a symbol of the chosen being, the chosen race which was to rid the world of the rule of those who lived for gold. (Wagner had already written *Das Judentum in der Musik* in 1850.) The vast *Tetralogy* led from the *Rheingold* to the *Götterdämmerung*, and its completion was delayed only by the love idyll *Tristan und Isolde*.

Wagner hoped that Tristan would be successful in Paris, since it was based on a French legend. It was his second attempt to please Parisian audiences, but it too ended in failure in 1860. Parisians did not take kindly to music which educated, preferring that which entertained. Wagner then drifted from place to place in Germany; the frontiers were reopened to the exile of 1848. Then from the depths of distress he was suddenly transported to the height of good fortune. When Ludwig II of Bavaria succeeded to the throne in 1854, he responded to Wagner's appeal of the previous year: 'The Prince who supports me in my work will ensure for his name undying fame.' Then Wagner's music poured in a vast flood over the whole of Germany, arousing a great wave of enthusiasm which so dazzled Wagner that he was moved to write a doubtful parody of the fall of Paris. But it also enabled him to realize his dream of Bayreuth, though not without difficulty.

This again reflects a contrast between France and Germany. In the work of Courbet, France grasped the whole human significance of a moment of time with great lucidity. In the work of Wagner Germany exalted feeling and traced its evolution from the biological origins of man through to the deliverance of the *Graal* in Paradise at the end of the road. The French remained true to painting, the possibilities of which they had been exploring for one hundred fifty years—and the Germans to music with which they had enriched Europe during the same period. The reason was that the French, swept up in spite of themselves into the industrial whirlwind, had never really become reconciled to it, and retained a wistful longing for their rural past. Germans, on the other hand, felt that they had been given a new chance when the exploitation of coal restored their country to the political supremacy it had lost four centuries ago. They could now draw a new certainty from Darwin's theories, and the 'historical appeal' to race was revived which German philosophers had been propounding at the beginning of the century.

Apart from the few creative geniuses of the age, the ordinary life of the people seemed to be overlaid with a cheap veneer of artificial and official aesthetics. This may well have been because man was still resisting the adaptation of himself as a human being to the great new industrial style of the cities. Hugo, exiled from Paris, far from the great cities, could continue to be the bard of progress. But Baudelaire, who was actually living in the garden of the new Paris, could only pluck from it the Flowers of Evil.

As a result, some poets and painters at the close of the century attempted to leave Europe, since they believed it was sullied by industry. But time was pressing, for the rest of the world was following hard on Europe's heels.

BOOK FOUR

THE CONQUEST OF
THE WORLD
1840–95

11

The Maritime Successes of
Western Capitalism

WHILST the continent of Europe was changing as a result
of the greatest technical innovation mankind had ever
known, sea traffic also was being transformed so as to
carry the news to every coast in the world, and with it
the produce of the industrial miracles of Europe. The
instrument of this expansion was first and foremost the
ship. In 1885 it was more or less in the middle of the
transition which was to lead in less than a century from
the sailing-ship, directly descended from the *Santa Maria*
of Christopher Columbus, to the steel liner driven by
turbines. In 1885, every harbour in the world was still a
swaying forest of masts and shrouds, but there was already one steamship to approximately half these sailing-
ships.

Naturally Great Britain played a decisive role in this
transformation. In 1850 steamships accounted for barely
six per cent of its total tonnage, but it was still the only
percentage of any consequence in the world. In 1870,
when England's rivals were tentatively going over to
steam, the proportion of steamships in England rose to
nearly twenty per cent, and had reached seventy-five per
cent by 1900—a proportion almost equalled by all the
western powers from Italy to Holland, Germany and the
United States. Only France still remained loyal to sail
with half her shipping, partly because there was not
enough export freight and the holds had to be filled with
sand; and also because the forests still provided wood
which was relatively cheap.

The engineer Fulton, encouraged perhaps by Napoleon,

but certainly discouraged by the *Institut de France*, returned to the United States with his proposed steamboat. Its first trials on the Seine had not in fact been too conclusive. England made the first voyage under steam to India in 1825. It was a long voyage, of course, but relatively simple, since the entire route lay along coasts where the ship could put in to refuel, in easy stages. This was an important advantage, for if these ships of traditional tonnage carried enough coal for the whole voyage they had no space left for cargo. The progress of the steamship was therefore bound up with an increase in tonnage, and that in turn with the progress of ship-building. In that sphere England achieved miracles. The substitution of iron for wood in the construction of hulls was enormously to her advantage, since her metal industry was powerful and her forest reserves exhausted. But an iron hull attracted marine deposits—colonies of barnacles which broke up its line and reduced speed. At first the builders merely edged wooden keels with iron. Then came the triumph of Bessemer steel, which kept the hulls completely clear.

In 1838, however, two cargo ships hastily fitted with steam-engines had crossed the Atlantic, and soon influential companies were founded. They were prepared to risk the financing of these costly ships, in view of the substantial returns which would accrue from regular swift transport, free from dependence on fickle winds. At that time the ships were called mail packets. There was the Peninsular and Oriental to Spain, the Mediterranean and India; the Cunard to the United States; the Royal Mail in England; the Collins Line to the United States, the *Messageries Maritimes* in France, and the *Compagnie Générale Transatlantique*; and before long the Hamburg-America Line in Germany, as well as the *Nord Deutscher Lloyd*. These companies could be certain of success, thanks to the vast strides in technical progress which transformed naval architecture between 1830 and 1860. Research was being carried out on the shape and resistance of hulls, engine power was increased and its weight per horse-power decreased by more than half; the condenser was adopted, the double-expansion engine was invented, and swifter engines did away with gearing; the propeller was substituted for paddles, subsidiary engines were fitted to move the vast rudder and, most important of all, accurate sea charts were compiled which did away with the slow, dangerous empirical method of taking soundings near coasts in order to find the deep-water channel.

By 1880 the triumph of the new lines was assured with the Cunarder *Gallia* and the *Compagnie Générale Transatlantique*'s *Normandie*. This had a capacity of 10,000 tons, and was equipped to take more than a thousand passengers; it was driven by steam, but in a good wind by sail as well. In this battle the rival companies met with varying success. The United States were powerful in 1860, but abandoned competition at sea during the tragic years of the Civil War. Though they resumed it in 1880, with a new fleet from which sailing ships had almost completely vanished, they could no longer catch up with England's lead. England faced stiff competition from 1850 to 1870, but was then unchallenged until the close of the century; this explains the English debates on shipping about 1860, and the unconditional return to liberalism towards 1880. Above all, England had one tremendous advantage: since it had at its disposal ports of call along every single route and excellent engine-coal (the early steamships were afraid of spontaneous combustion), it kept all the world's great ports supplied with its steam coal. It was the great purveyor of coal to the new ships, whose ports of call were dictated by the need to refuel. It sold coal all the more easily since English ships could offer it cheap and take it as freight on the outward voyage. They returned to port with a variety of the raw materials which England imported from all over the world, through markets increasingly controlled from London. English coal exports rose from three million tons a year in 1850 to nearly twenty-five million in 1884. One last detail explains England's predominance: the sailing ships carried their own repair outfits, but this was not the case with steamships. Damage could not easily be repaired except in ports specially equipped for the purpose. Moreover, these ports had to be fitted out in a special way and stocked with spare parts. The modern ship, like the railway, set the problem of standardization on a world scale, a requirement which naturally put the most advanced countries even farther ahead. Since England provided the coal and repair-yards it could impose its norms on ship-building all over the world.

This rapid rise of the steamship changed the rhythm of the world. The voyage from New York round Cape Horn towards the Golden Gate of San Francisco was shortened sufficiently to compete with the overland routes until the intercontinental railways were completed. The southern hemisphere, India and China, were brought nearer to the ports of Europe. Competition in the speed of transport reached such a pitch that a saving of a few days could be vital. The triumph of naval techniques opened up a commercial future for an old, and oft-deferred project, the Suez Canal.

The connection of the Mediterranean with India interested England all the more since its original settlement in Bengal was now spreading over the whole peninsula. By using the Afghan camel, English enterprise solved the Suez problem, and an army of camel-drivers ensured transport from the Mediterranean to the Red Sea. The French had long been planning a canal: Leibniz had already submitted a project to Louis XIV. Bonaparte rediscovered traces of the ruins of the canal attributed by Pliny to Rameses, and commissioned Lepère to see if it could be reconstructed. Unfortunately, Lepère subscribed to the theory that the two seas were not on the same level in spite of the observations of Laplace and Fourier. It was not until Enfantin invented an instrument capable of obtaining more accurate triangulations that this so-called difference in level was finally disproved in about 1846. A French vice-consul in Egypt, Ferdinand de Lesseps, presented with unexpected leisure by the 1848 revolution, sketched out the great financial plan which from 1854 appealed both to Mohammed Sahib and to Napoleon III. Even then it took five more years to collect the capital, since English financial circles were unco-operative; then ten years work. It was a mammoth task which required a special type of dredger and machinery which, in spite of the cheapness of labour, had to be of twenty thousand horse-power. At long last, the Empress Eugénie opened the canal in 1869 to the strains of the music of Verdi, who had composed Aïda in the Egyptian style for the occasion.

In 1867 Charles Dilke prophesied that France would soon realize that it had spent millions for the benefit of England, and he doubted whether this vast capital investment would pay. He was right on the first point, wrong on the second. Ten years later shares had risen by twenty per cent and dividends were higher than those in average English business. But in addition Disraeli had had the Khedive's share bought by the British Government. England's profits from Suez in 1879 were enormous: nearly two million tons of English freight were using the new canal, ten times more than the French. Subsequent progress continued to affirm this superiority of England, as Suez turned out to be a measuring-rod of sea-power.

Now that merchandise could be transported so rapidly by sea, orders, commissions and returns had to be speeded up still more. This led to another invention. In 1870 the telegraph cable connecting India with England was inaugurated; a message addressed to President Grant could soon be sent from Delhi to Washington using the two cables from India to England, then from England to the United States of America. The age of cables had been initiated in the 1860s from Norway to Africa and from Nova Scotia to the Gulf of Mexico. This second link was made possible by a more efficient use of rubber, and in spite of many failures. Until about 1862, three-quarters of the cables already laid at vast expense were of very little use. Then the money invested began to show returns in 1870, by which time the world network was more advanced. In 1872 Vladivostok was linked with China and Japan, and with England and Norway on the western side. In 1874 the Brazilian Company founded by Mauá, with English help, linked Rio with Recife and Lisbon via the

Cape Verde Islands. The great financial centres of Europe at the heart of this gigantic spider's web grew accustomed to commanding and following the economic activity of the entire world in detail and day by day. They soon penetrated into the heart of the continents, taking advantage of the progress made by railways and telegraphs, which were always guided by European and English capitalists and technicians.

We have seen how the coming to power of liberal capitalism had coincided with the onset of periodic crises, which shook the economy of the new industrial countries: England, the United States, France, then Germany. The vast extension of sea-borne trade brought this régime of cyclic crises into every country in the world, and the swifter a country was developing, the more violent were the crises it experienced. The great new economic powers began to share the chronology of Europe's crises.

A TRIUMPH: THE UNITED STATES

In the middle of the century, when railways and steel ships were starting up in Europe and were available to transport emigrants escaping from its countryside, the United States was also making ready to receive them. There were brand new trains waiting to welcome the immigrants and to carry them into the interior, and the railway companies often engaged the newcomers, especially the Irish, as workmen in their own yards, on tracks, embankments and building-work in the new towns created by the railway companies.

The first American railway linked New York and Philadelphia and proved to be so profitable that several companies competed for possession of it. Rivalry between companies was sometimes absorbed by amalgamation. New routes were sought: a line went out from Baltimore towards Ohio and the Mississippi valleys, comprising twenty thousand miles of track. Rivalries were sometimes taken up by the states, each subsidizing its own line: then competition went beyond all limits and the new lines were sometimes laid parallel to the old ones, especially in the east, where economic and urban development already provided plenty of passengers. Towards the south the railway continued to be less in evidence and less dependable. At the same time steamships were appearing on the great lakes and rivers, and in the north-east the development of canals was as rapid as that of the railways.

Above all the west was being populated, even along the Pacific seaboard where gold had just been discovered near the old Spanish settlements of San Francisco. Towards 1848, ironically enough, the adventurous crowds set out for Eldorado. To go from east to west was hardly feasible, nor was it wise. It was still necessary to cross wide areas occupied by hostile Indians. These pioneers first travelled southwards, either by sailing along the coast or by an overland journey, to the point where the continent narrowed and where there were fewer wide-open spaces to cross. They then took ship again on the Pacific coast, sailing northward towards the area of the placers. The journey was a tremendous adventure and through it the Americans learned to know the deserts which entered into their natural psychology and became part of their folklore—particularly Arizona, which had just been seized from Mexico. The richness of the seams transformed the settlement pattern of the Pacific coast. Perhaps the placer did not always bring wealth, but exploitation of the gold-seeker certainly did. The traders' stores and stalls attracted merchants and industrialists. Around the mining centres, the rich soil of the Californian valleys was soon used for agriculture, and population spread along them as far down as the Bay of Angels, Los Angeles. The rumour of all this new activity spread across the Pacific, and San Francisco began to expand and turn into a strange Chinese city where the sons of heaven achieved miracles in the commercial exploitation of the white man, a scornful but easy customer. If he was too poor to become a shopkeeper, the Chinese coolie accepted work under contract in the mines and the new concerns which were springing up on all sides—largely thanks to this source of cheap labour. Railways were built running parallel to the Pacific coast.

The Californian gold-rush had already halted and the economy evened out in a steady populating of the country, when gold was discovered in Colorado. Taken in hand more promptly by large-scale American capitalism, it was more quickly controlled. By the time Colorado had created in its turn a settlement around its gold-bearing valleys big enough to claim the title of state, the great battle of South and North had begun on the shores of the Atlantic.

It was a battle for or against slavery, but its significance went much deeper. Abraham Lincoln, the son of a Quaker, supported the cause of the poor peasants against the rich financiers of the eastern seaboard. He had worked on his father's farm and built his own house. On one of his trips down the Mississippi he had been incensed by the arrogance of the Southern planter and the poverty of the Negro. He embarked on various trade ventures, most of which were unsuccessful. He worked desperately hard to pay his debts. In this way he learnt how to speak to the section of the American people which lived by hard work and suffered so intensely from the repercussions of the general economic crises brought on them by the capitalism of the coast. His electoral victories were as much those of the western pioneers against the middle-class easterner as of the anti-slavery supporters. This made him an even more formidable opponent for the Democratic Party which was controlled by Southerners and the rich men of the east and had dominated the elections for twenty years. Abraham Lincoln had married into an old Virginia family. Now the least break in the solidarity of South and North meant that the new world from the west could irrupt into the cosy deliberations of the federal capital of the Atlantic coast. Lincoln had already inveighed against the injustice of the Mexican war, and had exposed the frontier incidents which served as pretexts for the Southern cavalry. He denounced the machinations of the South against the independence of Cuba. His election to the presidency, though far from resting on a large electoral majority, nevertheless signified the end of the old democratic compromise: the alliance between the rich of North and South in the name of the Union.

War broke out: when Southern and Northern troops came directly face to face on the banks of the Potomac, either the victory was indecisive or the ground remained in Southern hands. On several occasions the Southerners directly threatened Washington. The last Northern victory, the famous Battle of Gettysburg, was no more than a successful stand by federal troops solidly entrenched along the hill-tops against the assaults of the Confederates. The defeat of the South was due to the fact that its positions could be turned by the west; Grant marched along the Mississippi, leading troops recruited from western volunteers and conscripts equipped by Northern industry, transported by Northern railways, out-classing the South's river flotillas. The troops attacked the fortified towns along the river, and broke through at last on to the territory of the Confederate states: the capture of Vicksburg opened a wide breach to the eager North. The Southern cavalry and their loyal Negro troops fought heroically to defend the South's one railway junction, the city of Atlanta, but it fell, and the entire transport equipment of the Confederates was in the hands of the Union.

Authority Passes to the North

Lincoln's victory meant not only the abolition of slavery, but the end of an aristocracy and almost of a civilization. This most tragic and bloody of civil wars had the same significance as the 1848 revolts in Europe—the disappearance of a world in which the social hierarchy was based on the possession of lands and men, the disappearance of the world of the horse and the sailing-ship, of sophisticated luxury and vague law, of great orators and illusory pretence. The defeat of the South had really been implicit in the 1840s when traffic in the port of New Orleans caught up with that of New York, when the decadence of Charleston had become obvious, when the track of the Southern railway carried into the mining area of Birmingham the proletarian and capitalist civilization of the North. But the South went down fighting. When a fanatic, an actor by profession, assassinated Lincoln the tyrant, he firmly believed he was defending a democracy on the Greek model. Defeat did not just mean the emancipation of the slaves. The new Southern poor saw in the victory of the North the merciless invasion of a civilization of machines, shopkeepers, technicians, methodist preachers —all the advance rabble of the expanding urban way of life which made them grieve all the more bitterly for their old rural civilization.

During the presidency of Abraham Lincoln, insidious rumours were current in Washington. His wife loved luxury and extravagance; she adored her husband, but did not hesitate to ask the Minister of Finance to pay her thoughtlessly incurred bills. The victory of the people's infantry, though commanded by Quaker generals, was soon converted into a victory for the businessmen who cashed in on the success of the new Republicans. In order to win over the western farmers, the new Federal Government had made large distributions of land during the war (the Homestead Act followed in 1870). Each head of a family had the right to a plot of one hundred and sixty acres if he farmed it. This meant good business also for the dealers in agricultural material: the mobilization of young countrymen made it essential to mechanize agriculture.

The period of reconstruction saw the heyday of big business, especially during the two terms of office of the war hero General Grant. He was powerless to check the whirlwind of speculation which swept like a tornado across the length and breadth of the United States during the first years of peace. Up to that time it had always been the policy of the American Treasury to liquidate its internal debt at the earliest possible moment. During the war, however, there had been a considerable issue of Treasury Bonds (*Greenbacks*), but their withdrawal from circulation would have provoked a drop in prices, and caused serious embarrassment to all the new land-holders in the centre and west who had incurred debts in order to increase and stock their lands, as well as to farmers who would have to sell their produce more cheaply while still paying the same price to the landowner. Already Jackson, we have seen, had dismantled the cautious banking system favoured by the easterners. Grant gave a new lease of life to this policy of easy credit and generous guarantees by the state. Agriculture undoubtedly benefited as a result: the Timber Act of 1873 helped settlers engaged in afforestation, and four years later the Desert Land Act was to help those practising irrigation. However, the chief beneficiaries of this governmental generosity were undoubtedly the large-scale speculators.

There had been an enthusiastic programme of railway building during the war when their strategic advantages were obvious. The development slowed down when the thickly populated, economically equipped areas of east and west were more or less covered. The centre remained empty; it was still unpopulated, and no immediate profit was expected from it. Technically, however, the problem of linking the thickly populated east and the rapidly expanding west had to be solved. This was carried out in 1869; through the high passes of the Rockies, which had to be crossed through the high Californian valleys at heights of nearly 10,000 feet, over daring wooden bridges thrown across rivers and vast lakes, the junction of east and west was achieved at Promontory Point. It was celebrated by a huge fête, where most of the people were Chinese, since it was Chinese labourers who had built the substructure.

As for capital, though some was American, it was chiefly English. But shares were dropping on the London Stock Exchange, and dividends became insignificant. True, the ease with which the great American companies manipulated their assets and liabilities played some part in this, but the crisis of 1873 was also partly responsible since it was a poor year for agriculture and railway freight receipts fell accordingly. Railway law needed revising and, above all, an end had to be put to the disastrous competition which allowed two or three companies to operate the same route. Before any attempt was made to remedy this competition the government granted enormous advantages to the companies, including possession of a twenty-mile strip of land alongside the tracks they were laying down. Thus the railway companies were no longer just transport companies but actually huge land-owning companies, which attracted more English capital to the United States, and mobilized all the financial possibilities of America.

Unfortunately the 1880s were again critical years. More than three thousand companies went bankrupt, and some of them in circumstances of the utmost publicity. One of these was the company of Jay Cook, who had more irons in the fire than any other speculator during those years of reconstruction, who had built the Pacific Coast railway and founded the North Pacific Railway Company. There began to be a regrouping of interests. A pool was set up between several of the central companies, Chicago-Burlington-Omaha; each set aside for the pool half of its profits, divided again according to the number of shares. These agreements were arrived at partly for technical reasons; it was essential to co-ordinate time-tables over this immense continent, divided into five time-zones; the gauge had to be standardized, a problem to which the first eager pioneers had given no thought whatever; their hasty and often precarious tracks, with their over-sharp curves, their too steep gradients, their flimsy, temporary bridges needed reconstructing. Steps had to be taken to cut down the excessive number of accidents, to organize signalling, to adopt better brakes, as for instance the Westinghouse in 1873, to make automatic coupling safer, to replace iron by steel wherever possible, and to make passenger coaches more comfortable. It was the age of epic ventures: Vanderbilt, head of the Grand Central of New York, declared war on the Pennsylvania Company, though himself threatened by ambitious opponents in the region of the Great Lakes. The procedure of the struggle was always the same: first lines were built parallel to those of the rival one sought to ruin, then a fares war began. The travelling public benefited by each battle, but suffered as a result of each victory, and the English share-holder always footed the bill, both of the battle and the victory. Vanderbilt's successful rival on the Great Lakes was for a time the first great king of the American econ-omy—there was reason to fear that he might gain control of more than sixty thousand miles of railroad. In the centre and west, another kingdom was taking shape: that of Jay Gould. So much rivalry was, however, ruinous. In order to bring it to an end, the bank took away all the profit from the struggle. In 1885 the banker John Pier-pont Morgan formed a syndicate powerful enough to persuade the serious competitors to make peace and to eliminate the adventurers who had come on the scene too late. The result was an equitable sharing out between the Pennsylvanian and the New York companies, and a re-purchase of the Baltimore and Ohio; a unification move-ment went on from east to west, the development of the south was completed, and the American railway network became the admiration of the world because of its den-sity, its technical qualities and the efficiency of its per-sonnel and equipment.

The development of railways gave birth to new finan-cial structures—pools, syndicates, trusts and holdings—and also brought changes in landed property. At first the central areas benefited from an enormous increase in value once the railways were opened and this added to the importance of the gift given to the railways by the Government. Above all the agricultural movement bene-fited from the vast transport facilities offered to men and foodstuffs. This period, during which the great trans-continental lines were being built, also meant the end of the frontier.

The frontier was the vast area where the settler reached the limit of 'civilized' lands, in other words lands pro-tected against the Indian and under some measure of legal jurisdiction, and which were being opened up and developed in the normal way. This frontier was guarded by the Federal Army, but it was continually advancing, pushing before it Indian tribes and their herds of buffalo, enclosing them into their last reserves. The railroad now cut up into sections the belt of unexplored territory which framed the Rockies, an area of high grassy plateaux where agriculture was often difficult. But stock-breeding, not only of buffaloes, but of cows from the east and from Europe, flourished around the ranches, great farmhouses built of wood, solid as fortresses, and well able to defend themselves against the new immigrants. There was no need to worry about the cattle, except to protect them against theft: the cowboys kept guard over the prairie where the cattle grew and multiplied as on the pampas of the Argentine. The meat trade made considerable headway, especially as the cowboys' equipment was cheap and rudimentary—some good strands of barbed wire, a lasso, stout ropes and of course the indispensable Colt. In 1880, Buffalo Bill, the last of the frontier heroes, was twenty years old. Agricultural resources were beginning to be exploited. In Wyoming, Cheyenne already had more than ten thousand inhabitants, and the grave of La Ramée, a French trapper who died in the seventeenth century, had become Laramie, a small industrial centre, with five thousand inhabitants grouped around its station. From north to south of the high plateaux, colonization prospered and spread till it engulfed the islands of population which the search for and the exploitation of gold had brought there. Denver was no longer merely the site of a famous mint; it was a great capital of one hundred thousand inhabitants, the intellectual centre of this new country, with a slaughter-house nearly as famous as the one in Chicago. The technique of slaughter and preservation of meat was soon better than the methods used in the countries of the plain, and at La Plata. The canning and refrigerating industries were already making it possible to expand into European and world markets. A transformation was taking place in the Americans' diet, up to then based on cereals, which had given them the 'pasty face' at which the English poked fun; now they were eating more milk and meat and less bread and maize.

To the west of the prairies the small farm came off worst in comparison with the large estates, but in the middle west it was still firmly established, though in very varying forms. Between Omaha, the third abattoir in the country, and a city which won the admiration of Europe for the speed of its development, and Burlington, the terminus of the famous railroad, stretched Iowa, which took its name from the Indian 'blockheads'. Its territory with its perfectly geodesic frontiers was cut up into districts each of thirty-six square miles, then divided again into square miles each of which was split into four lots of one hundred and sixty acres in conformity with the Homestead Act. It was the best example of agricultural colonization in the 1880s; the streets of the little towns and even the field-paths were fixed in accordance with parallels and meridians. Sometimes traces were found of the first inhabitants, those who had cleared the forests, in the shape of caves hollowed out of the chalk hillsides or primitive houses built of clods.

The farther east one went, the more the agricultural scene became like that of Europe, particularly in the region of the Great Lakes where the Irish and the Scandinavians found soils and climates which were familiar to them. They built farmhouses which were exact replicas of the lovely country houses in their own country. On the east coast, even in the highly developed Massachusetts, a thorough enough search could reveal traces of a European land régime introduced two hundred years earlier by the Dutch. Towards the east also, crops were more varied. In New England there was an intensive polyculture. On the eastern grasslands there were no longer great herds wandering about over the arid grass, but small groups of animals confined to the stable in winter and providing milk, butter and cheese made on small farms and sold in village markets. In the south the cultivation of cotton, after a slight setback, continued to develop.

But everywhere in 1880 the small farm was on the decline. The farmer, even when presented with free land on virgin soil, could not make a fortune. The unfamiliar soil did not take easily to European crops, and in the west even crops which had been grown successfully in the east were a failure. Each small farmer had to find out on his own what resources the land had to offer, and this condemned him to a low standard of living. As a result the years of crisis quickly swallowed up the resources accumulated in good times. Furthermore, the increase in the number of farms meant that prices fell. These small farms were weighed down with an ever increasing burden of mortgages, and were sometimes sold to speculators or to large agricultural companies. Every year thousands of them were deposited as securities or sold. So the number of farmers began to exceed that of small landowners. At the same time the laws affecting afforestation or irrigation favoured the big combines. Rich and influential landed companies, often of English origin, carved out vast estates for themselves where they built towns, provided communications, and sold lots to small farmers whom they attracted by their offers of help and advice. Above all, they gave employment to many rural workers and ran agricultural concerns on industrial lines.

Thus, in California, there was one farmer irrigating as much as 1,200 square miles. A model farm in Minnesota covered 75,000 acres and owned 200 threshing machines, filling 75 wagons a day with corn at harvest time.

In a country where a small farm was approximately 125 acres, and a large one might be the size of one of Europe's smaller states, mechanization made tremendous strides. In 1880 the new threshing-machines drawn by large teams of forty horses were very popular. On the other hand, agriculture continued to be extensive rather than intensive. There was practically no use of manure, little study of the land, little research into genetics, yet the virgin soil gave good yields—almost too good, for soon there was difficulty in selling the harvest. Maize rotted in the fields, or was burnt, or used as fuel (1889). Nevertheless new products were added to the great harvests of corn, maize, cotton, and sugar-cane, especially in California, where the orchards had shown how profitable fruit-growing could be. Between the years 1880 and 1890 trees were planted in thousands, in millions, then in thousands of millions. This new development opened up a type of work that favoured concentration and only required seasonal labour at harvest time. Vegetables were little grown except on the outskirts of eastern towns. In 1887 the Hatch Act was passed providing for some of the money derived from the sale of state land to be used for the setting up of a fund for research into problems of land and soils. The best way of helping the farmer was to teach him about this new soil, instead of letting him find out for himself often at the cost of his own ruin.

Naturally the small farmer had long protested against the heavy burden of taxation, the dearness of credit, and the arbitrary and apparently haphazard way in which the railway companies fixed their rates, which were proportionately higher the less competition there was, hopelessly ruining the settler who had pushed far into the virgin lands. Of the farmers' associations, the oldest and biggest was that of the Grangers, which had grown to such an extent within seven years that, by 1874 when the crisis first became apparent, it already had something like one and a half million members. It tried to secure cheaper credit, less brutal evictions, lower transport rates. It intervened in political life against the trusts, the over-powerful financiers and the vast English concerns known as the Bonanza farms.

The farmers who had been given an unsatisfactory deal made common cause with the growing proletariat in the towns. In fact after 1874 immigrants no longer rushed to obtain free land immediately on disembarking, preferring to crowd together on the outskirts of ports. Wave after wave of them piled up in New York, and no longer moved off into the interior. If some did leave, it was because they were attracted by the growth of an industrial or commercial town. In the one year 1882, the United States took in from overseas almost eight hundred thousand immigrants, fewer English and Irish than before but more Scandinavians and particularly Germans, who went to swell the towns in the east or the middle west. The big capitalist companies were pleased to see them and made the most of the newcomers, since they accepted any terms and so sent down the price of labour in the factories. The large factory owners even went as far afield as Europe, especially to the Austro-Hungarian Empire and southern Italy, to recruit Slavs, Hungarians, Slovaks and Italians. These people were poor enough to accept any contract and only realized the severity of the terms they had agreed to after they had settled in America.

The Chinese recruited in China were so numerous that Congress had to put a complete stop to the immigration of orientals, and even to forbid the return of the many who had gone back home from the lands and cities of the west to pay a temporary visit to their relatives in China. In spite of this ban, a clandestine trade continued for some years in landing these sober and industrious Chinese on the Pacific coasts, making the old Chinese city of San Francisco bigger than ever and providing the fruit-growers with cheap and docile labour.

In any case, half the inhabitants of New York in 1880 had been born elsewhere, and three-quarters had at least one immigrant parent. The city had nearly two million inhabitants but, vast though it was, it was getting ready for a fresh expansion. It drained the surrounding districts, particularly New Jersey. This was a fairly widespread phenomenon in the United States and its significance was even greater than in Europe, where at about the same time honest folk were beginning to lament the flight from the countryside. Mushroom towns like Denver and Omaha sprang up within a few days. About 1890 this term 'mushroom town' was a fashionable way of describing cities like Kensington in Pennsylvania, which built five mills in two months and covered five square miles of a clearing which was soon being served by twenty-five trains a day. Speculation in urban land in the 1880s was one of the best possible investments. A town plan was traced out on the ground, the site of the public buildings was fixed, and the lots set aside for private houses were sold at a high figure. Sometimes speculation was unsuccessful; the wooden huts rotted on the spot. At other times, towns sprang up in a few months and profits were fabulous. Sometimes, after an existence of a few years, the town would disappear, sucked in by more fortunate neighbours, or moved *en bloc* from one state to another, from one resource to another. In 1885 Pithole City had houses, hotels, a station, a theatre, and public buildings; by 1890 nothing and no-one remained except ten or so obstinate creatures who had deliberately invited ruin by staying behind.

The queen of the cities which changed the map of America in the general surge and upheaval was Chicago. In the seventeenth century Joliet had made a cautious study of the ramifications of these marshy lake flats. In 1830 about a hundred people built huts on the site. Suddenly a town sprang up: land was drained, a port built on the lake, a railway constructed, and steam navigation turned Chicago into the great economic centre, the communication nucleus of the whole Federation. It was the meeting place of the committees co-ordinating the whole body of railway traffic and the transport rates between states. There was even some thought of making it the capital of the United States. St Louis, the great centre of the Mississippi, was outclassed. Then came catastrophe; the whole city, hastily built of wood, was burnt to the ground in 1871 and for six square miles nothing remained of it but a mass of charred debris. The vast column of smoke drifted southeast across the whole of America and almost half-way across the Atlantic. But the new city developed even more rapidly. In 1880 only one-quarter of the inhabitants were American born; Czechs, Slavs, Irish, above all Germans, vied with each other to reconstruct the city behind its frontage of parks stretching for twenty-five miles along the lake. Though the ground had to be drained, stakes fixed and deeper and deeper foundation piles driven, and though the houses were constantly threatened with ruin, the buildings being erected were more and more audacious. A vast hotel catering for thousands of travellers included among its public rooms a theatre to accommodate eight thousand spectators. In 1890 buildings of ten, fifteen and twenty storeys began to go up. The height of the New York blocks was equalled, then exceeded. Chicago was well fed. Its slaughter-houses were the best in the world, surrounded by vast paddocks where several thousand cattle grazed, providing half a million tons of fresh meat and almost a thousand million tins of meat. The trains were already being driven by electricity and carried millions of passengers a year.

Detroit was as yet only a small township near Chicago, but a new and rapidly prospering city came into being around the Pullman coach-works. The entire population of the mushroom towns could be fed without difficulty, because of the cheapness of agricultural produce, and new inhabitants were easy to recruit thanks to the great waves of immigration and migrations within the country. The people all depended on industry, which was vigorous enough to ensure handsome profits.

The gold fever had died down. The centre of gravity of the gold mines had moved from California to the interior (the eastern fringe of the Rockies from Arizona to Montana) where, moreover, it was silver rather than gold which brought wealth to the great concessionary capitalist companies which had gradually eliminated the lone prospector. Iron ore was being exploited on the shores of Lake Superior, and coal in Pennsylvania. Research was carried out, and iron and coal were mined to the south and east of the Mississippi. Better still, just before the Civil War reserves of mineral oil had been found in Pennsylvania.

Oil was not entirely a novelty since Genoa had been lighted by oil as early as 1802. The small Italian deposits were probably used as a result of lessons learnt from India and central Asia in the seventeenth century, but this was, however, a rare local phenomenon and had no economic significance. Up to about 1880, oil was merely a pharmaceutical product used particularly in the treatment of ulcers. In 1859 a retired American officer was digging a well in Oil Creek, Titusville, when oil suddenly spurted out: up to that time the Indians had collected it only by dipping rags into pools, but now it flowed out in such abundance that they did not know what to do with it, and it even fouled the rivers. Whilst Berthelot, Mendeleyev and other scientists were constructing strange theories about the origins of the new liquid, Rockefeller built a first refinery at Cleveland. There the various products were sorted out, benzines, lighting oils, greasing oils, tars, each of which sold well as the invention of suitable apparatus enabled it to be more widely used. From 1851 lighting by hydrocarbide attracted the admiration of visitors to the great international exhibitions, although their admiration was tempered with awe because of the risk of explosion. Oil ignites at thirty degrees. It was therefore essential both to improve lamps, which were merely modified versions of the old carcels, and to regulate the refining of lamp oil so as to produce a more stable product. But in any case the smell of the first lamps meant that they could be used only in kitchens and domestic offices. In 1890 the oil-lamp first appeared in the drawing-room. Between 1880 and 1890 Europe increased its imports of schist oil tenfold; in Germany and in Russia, where vegetable oils were costly, oil was soon being used to light the large city streets. Paris did not commit itself until 1880.

The small producer could not long compete in this swiftly expanding market. Though it had been considered a simple pharmaceutical product at first, oil was soon found to be good for lighting, though it still had to be purified. It was a useful fuel, but its sale had to be organized and a vast refining plant had to be built. For twenty-five miles around Titusville, wells were dug and crowned with pointed covers and wooden derricks. Over the country as a whole the yield of the wells decreased, but production increased, because the field of discovery was extended as far as California. Production could barely keep pace with demand, particularly as oil cooking stoves had been invented and large English shipping companies were thinking of burning oil in their ships' boilers, and were even busy exploiting Indian or Indonesian oils. Refining soon became a flourishing industry, and was much improved by the distillation of its costly by-products. Even before 1800 cracking had been introduced. The movement of oil from the oil fields of Pennsylvania and Cleveland or Pittsburgh became so great that the first pipe line had to be constructed. New York, Baltimore and Buffalo, with their very powerful pumping-stations, became the world's great refinery centres. On the edge of the Alleghany Mountains, carefully guarded stocks were stored in great tanks, lit exclusively by electricity ever since the terrible disaster of 1880 when a river of fire threatened to burn Titusville.

Michael Pupin may have deplored the fact that Americans had no taste for pure science, but they had a genius for its practical application. In 1876, the Philadelphia Exhibition displayed the telephone; its vibrating element was still primitive, but was improved in the following years until eventually it became the microphone. This transition from Graham Bell's telephone, strictly acoustic, to the electric telephone gave the world a new network of telecommunications. It was the achievement of a man who, more than any other, was typical of the age—Thomas Alva Edison. In 1880, Edison was thirty-three. He was the son of a Dutch gardener, originally a second-hand dealer who had emigrated to Michigan. At the age of twelve he was earning a living, and was one of the many youngsters whom the railway companies exploited as cheap labour, especially in America. He edited a newspaper in his goods truck for the use of travellers. He had a genius for doing the unexpected. As a telegraph employee he forgot to be there to transmit or receive messages, but invented a device which made his presence unnecessary. He caused a stoppage on the line, but invented the duplex telegraph (two telegrams being transmitted simultaneously along the same wire), and soon a quadruplex system. The Western Union Telephone Company made his fortune. In 1877, he invented the microtelephone which led to the telephone and the telegraph and ultimately to the telephonograph, and which was fantastically successful in the United States. Edison was a strange man, a jack of all trades, and a great reader, who had a genius for picking out of learned European reviews the tiny detail overlooked by other technicians, and from which he at once succeeded in deriving a wealth of riches. In turn millionaire and near-bankrupt, he invested everything he possessed in research work at his huge laboratory at Menlo Park, and drew lucky every time he played the dangerous game of double or quits.

One of the most outstanding inventions of the Menlo Park genius was undoubtedly the incandescent lamp. It deserves a few lines to itself. In 1878 Edison was bored. He visited the laboratories of a great American arc-lamp manufacturer, and realised the inconveniences of this lighting system which consumed enormous electrical energy and gave a dazzling light, but an extremely localized one. The problem of electric lighting could only be solved if the light could be subdivided. Then only could it compete with gas. Back in his laboratory Edison put aside all his photographic apparatus and applied his mind to gas lighting. He studied costs and concluded that electrical lighting could be profitable, on one condition: the solving of this problem of subdivision, which the world's scientists believed to be insoluble. Up to that time the electric lamp had been studied in isolation, whereas it should be regarded as one part of a much larger problem. The carbon had to be reduced to a very fine filament and brought to incandescence not in free air but in an evacuated glass ball. At first the filament consisted of a trace of carbon on paper; it lasted only a few minutes. Edison considered replacing the carbon by iridium or platinum, but they were too fragile. He passed from carbon to everything he could lay hands on in the way of raw material. He sent an assistant to China and Japan to bring back bamboo, which he drew out into the fintest of filaments, and then found a Japanese farmer who made a fortune out of supplying it to him, since other researches undertaken by Edison in Florida, Cuba and the South American forests were unsuccessful. The cost price of the lamp was almost two dollars. Edison founded the Edison Electric Illumination Company with branches in Chicago and New York, whilst waiting for his patent to be bought in Europe by Emile Rathenau. The reason for this prodigious commercial success was that Edison offered his two dollar lamp to his customers for one-fifth of its price—forty cents—reckoning that the flood of orders would soon justify mass production and the construction of powerful Gramme dynamos. His gamble proved justified and enabled him to win a substantial victory after years of hard credit, suspicion and near bankruptcy by equipping with electricity all the great cities of America, then of the world.

Electricity, like oil, showed that in future industry would have to be conducted on a large scale.

Large-scale Capitalism, Imperialism

The law of Pennsylvania, then the Sherman law, in 1880, prevented Rockefeller from controlling affairs outside the state. The oil-men decided to hand over shares to trustees, reliable people who, without any legal façade which could give the law a hold, were actually in complete control of production and distribution all over the United States. Millions of miles of pipelines enabled the distribution to be independent of the railways. Thus alongside the railway pools the great oil trusts were founded.

In metallurgy, too, holdings were created. The cotton textile industry still retained a character reminiscent of its distant origins (almost a century old), wheat moved from the north-east, where its produce was sold and traded, towards the south where it was produced, but the metal industry developed by a process of concentration analogous to that of the railways and which the Sherman Anti-Trust Act hardly affected at all. The Bank, which had acted as referee between the railway rivals, played the same rôle with Pierpont Morgan and soon with Carnegie. In this industry the enormous and costly plant had to be renewed every five years because of technical improvement and mass production resulted in such low prices that small businesses which could not raise the capital needed to keep up with frequent changes of plant had either to give in or to get out. In fact from 1864 the Bessemer processes were familiar in the United States and all the Pennsylvanian valleys were equipped with converters. Cheap steel contributed substantially to the progress of the railroad. Barely fifty years later the furnaces invented by Siemens and Martin were rivalling the converters and turning out steel of even higher quality. Then came improvements in blast-furnaces and cokeries, requiring new types of coal and recovery plant. Chemical industries combined with the coal industries and enabled prices to be lowered throughout the entire metal industry. In short, there was a whole chain of technical revolutions which pushed along the canals towards the lakes, and towards the new coal-beds (Birmingham was developed in Alabama). This all-conquering and powerful capitalist industry was well on the way to becoming the first and finest in the world; in 1890 it was producing more cast-iron than England. At the same time the total power of American steam-engines produced was greater than that of France and Germany together.

Finally, America's vast resources of cheap timber proved most advantageous to the paper and cellulose industries. Reserves of sulphur were discovered in Louisiana and Texas, which freed the United States from dependence on imports. The Michigan copper mines and later the Montana mines were the finest in the world. Between 1880 and 1890 the United States moved rapidly into the lead of capitalist industrial civilization.

The Civil War had interrupted the development of the United States navy at the precise moment when steam was replacing sail. On the Atlantic this vacuum gave England the advantage; on the Pacific no rival had a base sufficiently near to prevent the Americans from making astonishing progress: their penetration of the Pacific had been going steadily forward from the middle of the century, a continuation of their westward drive which had taken them from one ocean to another. They had got used to regarding the great ocean as theirs, as much theirs as the great desert. In 1867 they had bought the vast region of Alaska from Russia. The Russian shipowners, who had done so much to explore the Bering Strait and had established their posts as far as the Russian river to the north of San Francisco, were obliged to retreat. Similarly the United States installed itself in the Hawaiian Islands while claiming, this time, to respect the rights of the independent state of Kanake. This was a strange state, in which the natives had learned from all the sailors of Europe both to despise their gods and to fabricate a kind of constitution on Western lines. Now it was full of sailors from San Francisco who ousted all the others, protected ports and soon the whole state. Before long all the whites on the islands regarded themselves as Americans. The place was also an excellent stepping-stone to the Philippines.

After 1885 the land conquest of the American continent was completed. The great capitalists were dreaming of profits at sea. It was thought rather risky to venture outside the protection of the star-spangled banner and of the laws passed by Congress, but they were being pushed into the venture by the very success of their industrial expansion. From 1880 to 1890 coal-production rose from sixty million tons to more than two hundred fifty millions. The iron of Lake Superior was inexhaustible: iron output quadrupled. The first task, in any case, was to rebuild a fleet.

Unfortunately, however, America's very success led to a crisis of overproduction: prices dropped in three great waves from 1873 to 1897. It was a period which American historians acknowledge as being difficult to describe: there were agitations and violent disturbances, contradictory measures were passed by the authorities and the reactions of public opinion were unpredictable. Inevitably the ebb and flow of crises profoundly affected a nation where economic factors were so decisive. When prices were rising, farmers bought equipment, small farms pushed out westward, the mills paid good wages. When prices fell, the agricultural population flowed back to the east, increasing industrial unemployment, accusing speculators of robbing the little man. Huge combines were, in fact, buying up cheap the lands of ruined farmers, and enormous trusts were regrouping mills which had not a sufficiently sound financial basis. There were bailiffs running to call in mortgages but also strikes touching off more strikes and involving vast numbers of people: 750,000 railway workers supported the claims of the Pullman employees.

Naturally, here and there, appeals were made to the Government. When it decided to mint silver money, it brought new hope to the owners of those mines which had an excessive production, breathed a little oxygen into rarefied credit, and sent up prices, but it also compromised the currency. Similarly, if the Government fixed high customs tariffs it consolidated the market for American produce but also sent up the cost of living. The Republicans, who had been in power since the Civil War, were rent by endless quarrels. These divisions were turned to good advantage by the Democrat Cleveland who was twice elected to the White House, swept in for a second term by a tidal wave: an increase of 400,000 votes and an absolute majority in Congress. But Cleveland's two terms of office disappointed even his own supporters, for his solutions were self-contradictory, and his rigorous honesty was no more successful than the expediency of his opponents.

Nevertheless from all this confusion there emerged several important innovations. One was the creation of the Civil Service. Ever since the days of Jackson, more than ten thousand high administrative posts had been regarded as the perquisites of the party in power, and a change of government had involved even crossing-sweepers in a nation-wide upheaval for the benefit of supporters of the new majority. This system was now done away with, and the new-style officials were recruited by competition. The universities, too, were organized. The colleges were grouped into faculties. Wealthy patrons competed with each other to provide handsome endowments. Following their example the big business concerns abandoned their rule-of-thumb methods and set up research departments, created a permanent body of technicians, and embarked on a more systematic study of markets. Estimates were made of productivity and returns, on lines suggested by Taylor, the economist and statistician. The United States began to realize that it had reached its natural, geographical limits, and must now organize itself in depth. Immigration was restricted and customs barriers were erected.

But the United States had also to face the same intrinsic problems as Europe; the chief one was to find external outlets. The most venturesome spirits talked of colonies. Cleveland opposed this suggestion as forcefully as he could. He refused to annex the Hawaiian Islands as the American Minister in Honolulu, who had made all necessary preparations, urged him to do.

In 1897 there was a rise in prices, at first tentative, then more marked. Then the Republicans came back to power, supported by a reorganized capitalism. The National City Bank had important interests in the Pacific and also in Cuba, where it financed a major part of the sugar crop. Most of the newspapers had fallen into the hands of one important trust: the Associated Press. Public opinion was being schooled to a condition new in American history: imperialism at the expense of European possessions. A new era was opening for the United States and for the world.

A PROMISE: THE SOUTHERN HEMISPHERE

Within the space of a few years not only did the activity of Latin America make such strides that it was in a position to compete with Europe, but the new lands in the southern hemisphere began to acquire economic importance.

The Development of Australia

Up to the middle of the century, Australia had been regarded merely as a place of deportation, to the indignation of the few settlers already there. These settlers were thrusting back a strange indigenous population which had retained little of its matriarchal traditions beyond customs so hard on women that the tribes were already decreasing in numbers even before the fatal invasion of the white man. In thirty years, however, the population of Australia rose from 300,000 to almost 3,000,000 inhabitants. This advance was helped on by an influx of Chinese strong enough to disquiet the English majority. The increase was largely due to the rush for gold, which was discovered there in 1851. It was this gold which led to the development of the ports which had regular services to England, and of the railways already spreading over the south-east and tentatively pushing out across the desert towards Palmerston. The telegraph had also recently been introduced and it was proposed to continue it across the sea to

Ceylon and Vancouver. But the English contingent was not yet in a position to threaten the power of the squatters who had appropriated immense lands in spite of the laws; they owned thousands of acres each, on which only the rabbit, unwisely introduced, vied with them for the grass on which they grazed their vast flocks of sheep. These flocks were reckoned in hundreds of thousands, and their wool, sold to Europe, kept these lords of the land in princely luxury. Nevertheless, the towns had to be fed too, and around them the landscape was being marked out into fields of a European type. The ground was then divided into enclosed farms of average size, on the English pattern.

In 1885 there were three distinct zones and three types of society: on the coast, a landscape like that of England; farther inland, feudal land-ownership; and, tapering off towards the desert, an area peopled only by explorers and adventurers, bent on discovering a country still fraught with danger. There was one all-important city, Sydney, near Botany Bay, where the convicts had landed in former days. In fifty years Sydney had become one of the world's great cities, with almost four hundred thousand inhabitants. It was the queen of the south, a city of gardens and parks, a centre of learning, and above all a great capitalist city; it acted as the gateway through which English goods could reach a whole continent.

South Africa Becomes Industrialized

In South Africa, liberal England did nothing to hinder the expansion of the Boer state. She handed Orange over to them in 1854, then, after various vicissitudes connected with those of Gladstone's party, the Transvaal in 1874. Meanwhile the English in South Africa were grouped along a line of advance which pushed deep into the northern lands; they drew their supplies from the southern ports and particularly from the Cape.

The efforts made to reproduce the atmosphere of England did not prevent the Cape from developing a composite style of its own. Whites, blacks, Malays and Muslims from the Sunda Islands made up a population of fifty thousand inhabitants in which the half-caste was predominant, at least numerically. The lovely gardens of former days were now occupied by villas where the Europeans were installed as masters, directing the work of their employees and tenants, running business in the towns, and directing agriculture over large tracts of the surrounding countryside. They grew corn, and tried out viticulture, which made a promising start. Nevertheless, some foodstuffs had to be imported, especially since the ports, and particularly Port Elizabeth, had to provision passing liners. These ports were linked by railway and handled the bulk of the shipping. The South Africans relied on stockbreeding to pay for the imports, once the Dutch had acclimatized the cattle so profitably. In 1880, the bulk of the profit came from a most curious source—ostrich breeding. In twenty years the number of ostriches had risen from eighty thousand to almost one hundred and fifty thousand. The whim of Europe's best-dressed women had made its feathers as valuable as gold. In order to keep a monopoly of this magnificent trade, bringing in millions, the authorities strictly forbade the export of the eggs which all the breeders in the northern hemisphere coveted. The ostrich egg was then watched just as carefully as the tulip bulb had been two hundred years earlier. The vogue, unfortunately, proved just as ephemeral. In 1885 a caprice of fashion changed Europe's habits, and the Cape abandoned its ostriches and turned to more stable resources —the mines. Already the coal-seams had attracted Cornish miners, then copper was discovered, then when deep holes were being dug, diamonds came to light, not far from Kimberley. In 1887 alone seven tons were extracted. Police, guards, capital and covetousness abandoned the ostrich farms for the sites which yielded these precious stones, and the diamond-cutters of Amsterdam made them into the loveliest jewels in the world. Thus in spite of the rudimentary equipment of the first mines, and the cheapness of Negro labour, Kimberley experienced all the bustle of an up-and-coming industrial city, and speculation was rampant, just as in America.

Farther north, in the Boer republics, there still prevailed

the grand old tradition of stock-breeding, carried on by the isolated Calvinist patriarchs who lived cut off with their families in the middle of several thousands of acres, which they left only once or twice a year to take communion in a chapel isolated in the great expanse of the veldt. These huge estates were split up by inheritance, under the control of the Government of Pretoria. Pretoria, a large town full of huge country houses, watched like a father over the social evolution of the surrounding plains. Families were prolific and medium-sized farms rapidly increased at the expense of the ancestral lands, a process not so very different from that which changed the face of the pampas and created new nationalisms there.

Deposits of gold had also been found there, but of too poor a yield to warrant exploitation in 1880. Then came a sharp rise in the price of gold; with the invention of new mining plant and the discovery of dynamite, the number of prospectors increased, and bankers began to take an interest. By 1884 speculators were taking an interest in the little railway from Pretoria to Lourenço Marques; Germany supplied the material and the English capitalists at the Cape, Natal and Kimberley had shares in it too.

The great diamond king was Cecil Rhodes, who grouped all the mines into the De Beers Mining Company. He became the head of the Chartered Company, of which the Prince of Wales was one of the chief shareholders. Then he was Minister at the Cape in 1890, undertaking the colonization of Rhodesia. The railway pushed on and the old Boer stock-breeding was threatened on every hand by the new urban development. This was stimulated by gold in spite of the heavy taxes imposed by the Boer administration. Johannesburg rose from three thousand to one hundred thousand inhabitants in ten years (1896). The increase was bound up with the influx of innumerable Britons who claimed civic rights from the elderly Krüger, which the local government was afraid to grant. Already India was beginning to pour in a labour force which rivalled that of the Negro. A whirlwind of conflicting interests raged around the old patriarchal farms: the Dynamite Ring, the dynamite trust, hesitated between giving substantial support to the Boers and rallying to English interests. The German firm of Krupps undertook to provide, with the help of Le Creusot and the approval of William II, the vast material needed for building a railway between Pretoria and Lourenço Marques capable of stealing the thunder of the north–south railway envisaged by Cecil Rhodes. The *Berliner Handelsgesellschaft* poured in capital and technicians, and the *Deutsche Wagon Fabriken* material. Everything was building up to the war; the preliminary signs were apparent in 1895, and it broke out in 1898. The English, who had been accustomed to win without fighting, were brutally reminded that they had forgotten to keep their army young and their weapons sound.

Ephemeral Industry in Peru

The prosperity of the old Peru had come from her mining resources and her precious metals. The dreary city of Cuzco seemed as if it would never rise from its ruins. It had ruins of Inca settlements abandoned since the conquest, and more recent ruins of the palaces of Spanish noblemen, abandoned since the proclamation of independence and taken over, timidly at first then more confidently as the decadence of the town became more pronounced, by swarming families of half-castes and even by Quichuas. These Quichua Indians, with stern, forbidding faces, did little to enliven the small city of barely thirty thousand inhabitants. They only showed signs of animation and fell to prayer during the processions in honour of *Nuestro Señor de los Temblores,* behind whom they may perhaps have thought to see the tutelary power of their own gods. For as upper Peru was progressively deserted by its conquerors the old religion and the old customs revived, and supplications to the moon and the sun and the expectation of some fresh natural catastrophe brought a measure of relief to the melancholy lot of the great Indians.

On the other hand, Lima was becoming a brisk and flourishing city, animated by its port of Callao six miles away, with which it was connected by a tree-shaded road and a busy little railway. Callao was sufficiently prosperous and well-armed to have held out against a last Spanish attempt to retake it in 1866. Callao was the major gateway to Chile, the sister-nation on the edge of the Andes, and to Europe; and it was also an attractive holiday resort, gay with swallows. In Lima the two-storey houses built around a patio in Moorish style lined the approach to the old cathedral with its silver pillars. But Pizarro's cathedral was no longer without a rival: a Chinese pagoda was there as a reminder that the Pacific was no longer the limit of the white man's world, but a zone of communication with the Chinese world. The Chinese had been landing in great numbers for several years; they survived the coastal climate better than the Creoles, who succumbed helplessly to fever and childish diseases. Whenever there were Chinese and Negroes to do the work, the white man managed to get rich, in spite of the indolence of the dispirited Indian. Thus gradually a community of more than three million souls grew up in search of a national ethnical identity. The basis of its agriculture was still the tasty Indian maize, now improved in quality, and the various kinds of potato; but to these were being added wheat and barley, banana trees and sugar, and attempts were being made to grow coffee and cocoa, and even cotton (though the latter was only a passing phase). There were fewer agricultural innovations on the vast territories of the old landowners than on medium-sized farms where the state tried to install new settlers, and where England, as usual, tried to establish agricultural companies. The English also tried to scrape the last ounce of precious metal out of the mines, but very little gold, silver or mercury remained. Industry was almost non-existent.

In this context it is surprising that the magnificent railways were built. They were of no great length, but had immense difficulties to overcome, especially the rocky shelves more than twelve thousand feet high, which blocked the approaches to Lake Titicaca and the rich and coveted metal deposits on the high Bolivian plateaux. No financial help was available from Bolivia, for the suspicious Indians

were anxious to defend their national heritage. The capital
came from the guano trade. These deposits of seabird lime
on the islands were first exploited in 1840. They were
estimated at some tens of millions of tons, and the
Quichuas had already used them in farming. European
agriculture offered a good price for guano, more than
twenty times its exploitation price in the 1860s, and ships
by the hundred awaited their loads. In vast quarries,
the armies of Negroes and Chinese hacked down the
yellowish-grey manure, the new Peruvian gold. By 1880
Peru had exhausted all its reserves, and had built its railroads and a telegraph; but had still twenty years to wait
before any industries were started. It was an insecure society, and no parliamentary régime could last in it. Order
was preserved only by a military dictatorship.

The Adolescence of Three Nations

Chile, the sister-nation, continued to side with Peru
against Spain every time that country made an unwise
move. But Peru itself was Chile's major enemy on account of a stretch of coast which Chile won in battle in
1851 and 1881. This conflict must have had very deep
roots, for even before the European conquest the rebellious Araucanians had waged war with the Quichuas. It
was from this struggle that they had learned to stand up
to the white invader. These proud Indians were not defeated until the twentieth century, and then they were
only quelled with alcohol or absorbed by cross-breeding.
In the eighteenth century the Araucanians had seized
Spanish wives. In the nineteenth century the Creole Chil-
ians married Araucanian wives. In 1880 the pure Araucanian was in process of disappearing. Yet this interbreed-
ing did not prevent the white population from retaining
its predominance: it doubled its numbers between 1780
and 1810 to reach the figure of seven hundred thousand.
By 1880 it was already more than three million strong.
An aristocratic republic emerged, governed by the big
farmers and industrialists without too much difficulty after
the revolutions of the thirties.

On the arable lands, which were fairly rich though not very extensive agriculture developed on the American pattern. It was already largely mechanized, and its prices could compete with those of North America. At all events Chile fed the Pacific Coast on European standards, even producing the best wine in the New World. The success of this agriculture encouraged immigration, and Chile was one of the few countries to which Frenchmen were willing to go. The average-sized farms in the vicinity of the towns developed around the latifundia of former days. The industrialization of Chile, encouraged by European capital, grew rapidly from 1840 onwards. Since the country remained unexploited till comparatively late, it still possessed gold, silver and copper: and the foundries were prosperous at a time when the telegraph and ships used copper wire and sheet copper. The Peruvian guano was almost worked out but Chilean nitrate appeared inexhaustible. It was the industrialization of Chile which led Germany to supplant England and France in Chile's activity and external trade. It accounts for the fact that Chile could even create great financial companies in which the local governor fought against European influence. Above all, it explained the success of the Chilean capitals. There was Santiago with its luxurious shops sheltered by portals, Valparaiso where the *Sud-Americana* Company acquired a large share of the Pacific trade in the face of international competition; and Punta Arenas, the most southerly city in the world, a centre of sheep-rearing on the fringe of the sub-Polar latitudes. So although Chile was on the southernmost tip of the world, it formed a small but prosperous nation on European lines.

In 1880, the whole of Argentina was hardly more populated than Chile. As we have seen, the landscape of the eastern Cordilleras and the Upper Parana showed certain affinities with that of Europe and was suitable for wine-growing and corn, but the plains of La Plata were, by their very immensity, far more unusual. The northern plains were soon colonized for their sugar-cane, and the central plains developed a modest agriculture on European lines, especially on the outskirts of the towns and in particular Santa Fé; but the greater part created an economy and a society of an entirely original type. The problem here was not to wrest the land from the Indian (Pampians and Patagonians had retreated before the white man without too much of a struggle) but to organize it. Millions of horned cattle had bred from seven or eight animals landed by a Spaniard and a Portuguese about the middle of the seventeenth century. The abundant grass made this herd the biggest in the world; by 1860 the counting of heads would have been an utter impossibility, for no-one knew the boundaries of properties, or to whom the cattle belonged; no-one even thought in terms of land-ownership. A methodical German traveller, Brackebusch, was amazed that an Argentinian could have acquired almost a million acres for a trifling sum. But in this ocean of grass, what really mattered were the homesteads, the places where herds could rest, the *querencias*, near a spring, a drinking pool, if possible near a grove of trees. For the rest, the guardians of the flock, the bow-legged gauchos, lived with their herds. When they were hungry, they slaughtered an animal, carved out what they required for a meal, sometimes retrieved the hide if they were not too far from the drying rooms, and burnt the remains of the body if they could spare the time. Horses, bulls, and cows were caught by lasso, and stopped by having their pasterns broken. There was little or no sharing of land between the sons of landowners, and very little sharing of transit zones and heads of cattle. Their fratricidal quarrels sometimes turned into revolutions, and Buenos Aires was shaken by revolutions caused by disputes between great landowners. These quarrels were the more violent the nearer they were to the cities. Around Montevideo, Santa Fé and Buenos Aires ownership and property—the words and the reality—assumed increasing importance, a more definite meaning, in proportion as the urban civilization inspired by Europe developed. The problem of boundaries became more bitter, battles more violent. The alliances of great landowners became armies of horsemen disputing the great river valleys and fighting for control of the capital cities, and the towns tended to be organized like fortresses. It was for this reason that the Argentine, or rather Buenos Aires, could be held successfully by the Rosas dictatorship. For Rosas the vital point was to keep under the authority of the city all the plains of La Plata. Against Rosas there stood out the gauchos of the northern La Plata, of Montevideo, which the vast estuary effectively separated from its Argentinian rival. From this conflict a new nation emerged—Uruguay, supported by Brazil, the southern part of which also consisted of a large tract of pampas, where the Rio Grande do Sul felt itself as gravely threatened as Uruguay by the centralization policy of Rosas.

This quarrel of the gauchos gave rise to the most extraordinary adventure in South America in the nineteenth century: the tragedy of the ambition of Paraguay. Here and there the Indians had succeeded in defending a section of the land, but on the Upper Paraguay where the Jesuit missions had flourished more than a million Indians had founded a proud nation, quick to take offence, swift to violence, handing down the office of dictator-president from father to son in the Lopez family. In 1857 Solano Lopez proudly reckoned his subjects at more than a million and a half. In 1870 he launched them into the most pitiless of wars against a coalition of Brazil, Argentina and Uruguay. The struggle lasted five years. Its violence may be estimated from the census of 1877 which revealed that Paraguay now had no more than three hundred thousand inhabitants, chiefly women. It is true that the difference in numbers had perhaps psychological as well as material causes: it revealed the indifference of many families in the interior towards the 'census of defeat'. Yet it was not impossible that the victims numbered something like a million. Around its capital, the little Spanish-American city of Asuncion, Paraguay withdrew into solitude, the women inheriting the bitterness of their dead kinsmen. Yet this war served to make the frontiers clear and definite, and also crystallized the mentalities of three nations, the three republics of Argentina, Uruguay and Brazil.

Argentina and Uruguay evolved on parallel lines. Gradually the limits of property were fixed just as the nation had fixed its frontiers. The vast estate was still subdivided into huge *estancias*, but there were already some smaller agricultural units. The great ports open to emigration offered the newcomers a civilization similar to that of Europe. In 1876, Argentina, on the American pattern, divided the state lands into lots of 250 acres, distributed free to farmers on condition that they farmed them efficiently. This small farm changed the character of the towns, since it attracted shops, small trade, and craftsmen. Articles made on the spot by the European emigrants were substituted for manufactured goods imported from Europe. Cloth was still being imported, but fewer ready-made garments were brought into the country and weaving had already been started.

Suddenly and swiftly Buenos Aires began to expand. The houses, which up to then had been single-storey, rose higher. Hard stone was brought and mansions in Victorian style were built along the old streets. These were only twenty-two yards wide in conformity with a decision of the Indies Council, and they now stretched out into long boulevards. This over-rapid growth led to widespread epidemics, cholera and yellow fever, which claimed tens of thousands of victims. A sewage system had to be constructed, artesian wells sunk, and the distribution of water organized. Gas lighting was installed in the city. All this development entailed an enormous movement of money. In new marble palaces, the banks vied with each other in vulgar ostentatious luxury to attract the confidence and flatter the vanity of the rich. On the verge of bankruptcy, they telegraphed London, and London replied by sending credit. With it came English styles, furniture, and plant for handling goods or building railways. Within a few years the Spanish township became an Anglo-Saxon capital, the residence of the gaucho leader a great capitalist city. But though the style was English, the basis of the population, the proletariat of the city, was more and more Italian. About 1890, out of the four hundred thousand inhabitants of Buenos Aires, there were three times more Italians than Argentinians. It was the same in Montevideo.

The countries of the La Plata had to pay interest on all this new wealth and all this capital of European origin. Nothing could be easier; the casual, unorganized stock-breeding of 1860 was replaced by organized stock-breeding, in which Uraguay led the way.

The cattle were now branded by irons, watched over by the owner who chose the animals in good condition for the abattoirs, the *saladeros*. These factories were built on the American model: slaughtering and cutting-up were done on the conveyer belt system as in Chicago. The carcasses were carefully cut up, the skins were properly treated, and the meat was salted or dried, then loaded into the new ships for which steam ensured a swift and regular service. Argentina and Uraguay fed Brazil and Europe. England was one of the best customers for this cheap meat, and became quite accustomed to this tough diet until the invention of ships fitted with refrigerating plant provided a more palatable fare.

Positivist Brazil

Brazil was the largest country in the Americas after the United States, and almost equal to it in area; nevertheless it was one of the most backward in the world towards 1880 in that its social structure was based on slavery. This was the chief concern of the small *élite* of intellectuals which brought something of Europe's social and intellectual outlook to the tiny capitals from the Rio Grande do Sul to Ceara. These cities gave an outlet to the sea for the vast, almost unpopulated states which stretched away into the interior towards the impenetrable forests. The intellectuals called for the abolition of slavery, particularly those attached to the law faculties of Recife and São Paulo where the law taught was strongly impregnated with French liberalism. In São Paulo they went so far as to found a Republican Revolutionary

Party, which was prepared to break away from the rest of Brazil. They aroused some sympathy in the urban middle classes and even in certain rural areas where the farms were small, but the rulers of Brazil clung to a slave régime and expected the Emperor to maintain it.

Pedro II, though he was liberal in temperament, was also well aware how profitable slavery was to the Brazilian economy: it was slave labour which, in the eighteenth century, had worked the gold and diamond mines of Minas Geraes, and which had given Brazilian agriculture its present prosperity when the mines were exhausted. The staple crops were sugar and cotton in the north, and above all, from the beginning of the century, coffee in the centre, in the beautiful valley of Rio Paraya which linked Rio de Janeiro to São Paulo. Here the old court families had carved out large estates for themselves, where coffee grew of its own accord and supplied half the world's needs, in spite of rudimentary equipment. It was transported on mule-back to the markets and ports. These coffee barons constituted on the whole a fairly amiable aristocracy, professing a certain superficial liberalism and a somewhat *risqué* modernism provided it did not involve any threat to the ancient foundations of their wealth. However in the 1880s Brazil, like the rest of South America, was swept by a great wave of rejuvenation.

Just after the war with Paraguay, the southern frontiers were more clearly laid down and the huge prairies of the Rio Grande do Sul were organized around Porto Alegre, and those of Uruguay around Montevideo. There too, republican and anti-slavery ideas took root all the more easily since gaucho stock-breeding did not use slave labour. Farther north, European emigration populated small cities with Germans who introduced the customs and architecture of traditional Germany and supported the reformers. In the centre, commerce was beginning to transform the urban centres of São Paulo, Rio de Janeiro and certain privileged towns of old Minas. Average-sized farms came into being which could no longer afford to buy slaves (the trade was practically abolished from 1850) but which made a strong appeal to the immigrant and the settler, particularly the Italian. At the port of Santos tens of thousands of these immigrants landed to grow the new coffee. Since currency was limited, the settlers were often paid with gifts of land or small farms, which were not large enough to provide them with a livelihood, so that they remained dependent on the landowner, but were sufficient to keep their allegiance so that they were anti-slavery. All these immigrants, these *agregados*, increased the number of electors supporting reform. The prosperity of the central regions provoked an appeal from the poorer sugar-growing areas of the north, the bastion of loyalty to the Portuguese dynasty, which were fast losing their population to the more modern areas. Lastly, the very prosperity of coffee and its trade led to accumulated capital and closer ties with the countries of Europe, especially England; and all the capitalist organizations on the European model began to erect buildings in Rio and São Paulo in their usual palatial style.

The English had been watching developments in Brazil for some time. In 1807, they had asked John VI to put an end to slavery, and he had promised to comply. More effective than preaching was the display of new power with which financial capitalism dazzled the coffee barons —the power for instance, of Mauà, who built the railway from São Paulo to Santos for the transport of coffee. He was the moving spirit behind the great enterprises which carried the railway over the maritime sierras towards the vast plateaux of the interior; he founded banks, of which one in particular played a great part in the development of Buenos Aires and Montevideo; and he installed the transoceanic telegraph cable. It is true that after he was abandoned by Pedro II, he fell into bankruptcy in his old age, but the impetus towards a new capitalism had been given. The settlers, the small and medium landowners, the urban middle classes, strengthened by the success of the great maritime liberal capitalism on the European model, soon developed such self-assurance that the coffee barons were swept away. The Emperor gave way, and was glad to do so. In 1874 the law of free birth was passed (the children of slaves were to be born free); in 1888 the Empire abolished slavery and foundered along with it, to be replaced by a republic of Paulist inspiration in 1889.

Economic changes had paved the way for this dual, peaceful revolution of society and of the state by 1880; and the intellectuals were already preparing the way for the legal framework. The Brazilian middle class *élite* was only too well aware of England's century-old economic ambition and its pressure on Portugal, and at the same time they strongly admired French culture, which had already had a great influence in the eighteenth century in Lisbon itself; consequently they preferred capitalism on French lines to English capitalism, although the latter had built their harbours, their railways, and their telegraph. The young Brazilians of 1880 were positivist, and preferred to entrust the leadership of the country to scientists, technicians and theorists rather than to bankers. The part of Auguste Comte's teaching which particularly appealed to them was his polytechnician's belief in well-co-ordinated legal systems, in scientifically planned projects. Paraguay's young, victorious army studied Auguste Comte in its military academies just as many middle-class citizens in Rio read him in their libraries. The fanatics fostered in Rio itself a positivist cult which was far more successful than its counterpart in Paris. The most ardent of the Brazilian positivists accused the Parisians of hypocrisy. The new flag of the Brazilian Republic bore Auguste Comte's motto: Order and Progress.

This admiration for positivist technique led Brazil towards industrialization. From the eighteenth century mineral resources had facilitated the process, then coffee, cotton and sugar gave rise to the subsidiary industries of bark-stripping and drying, and the manufacture of alcohol. Now a search was being made for coal; the immense deposits of iron were being mined, and work had begun on currency reforms. The hopes of the new generation of Brazilians were not to be realized all at once, naturally. Buenos Aires reached the industrial stage more quickly than Rio, at the beginning of the twentieth century, simply because the mountainous forests of Brazil offered greater resistance than the Argentinian pampas. The economic policies of Brazil were ruthless but, together with the battle against the trees, achieved a good deal of land clearance. Brazil represented one of the most characteristic areas where European capitalism supported pioneer developments in the Americas. Ironically, the methods increased in efficiency just as the pioneer zones themselves were disappearing, swept out of existence by the success of capitalism in the United States. This efficiency enabled great numbers of people to be displaced to the interior of Brazil, and towns were created there which immigrants from Europe soon came to fill, so that the foundations were laid for an urban proletariat. As a result the rise in population was enormous. From three million inhabitants in 1880 it rose to fifteen millions in 1890, so that Brazil became in this respect the leading nation in South America.

A REVELATION—JAPAN

Towards the close of the century an entirely new topic was beginning to enliven conversation in political circles and to provide subjects for caricature in the illustrated papers—the great power of the little 'Jap'. The Americans had been following the evolution of the Pacific peoples fairly closely, whereas Europeans were less well-informed and therefore astounded by this revelation. A revolution was in fact taking place in east Asia and its results were noticeable throughout the following fifty years. The change in Japan was all the more surprising because of its isolation. In earlier chapters it was possible to devote long pages to the Asiatic problem without a single mention of Japan. The Japanese remained enclosed within their islands, and exerted hardly any direct influence on the rest of the world; and if their art, their historical remains, their language and their admirable paper were known and appreciated beyond the frontiers, this was due, paradoxical though it may seem, to Chinese merchants. Maritime China was in fact much more internationalized than insular Japan. Classical Japan had been built around entrenched camps at Yedo, the seat of military power which had defended Japan in the Middle Ages against the Tartar invasions and had withstood the great Kublai Khan. The feudalism arising from this military power had become so deeply rooted that the Shogun, the leader of the Daimoys, had become more powerful than the legitimate sovereign, who was reduced to the rôle of pontiff in his ancient palace of Kyoto. These Shoguns had at first welcomed the navigators from the West, and this people which had formerly proved so widely receptive of Buddhist teaching from China seemed prepared to offer the early Christian missionaries excellent prospects of evangelization. Yet barely had the conqueror's weapons been discerned behind the preacher than a violent reaction wiped out both Christianity and Christians in a sudden, sharp upheaval. In the eighteenth century Japan was closed to newcomers from the sea, as it was to those from the continent. The whole *raison d'être* of the Shogunate lay in the strong moral obligation felt by the Japanese to defend themselves against the foreigner.

Japan was less attractive to Western capitalism than China, and at first seemed to resist its infiltrations more firmly. The ports and deltas of China, which were after all very near the Japanese coast, were becoming Europeanized, and the whole of the Pacific was being commercialized by Western influence, as much through the activities of emigrant Chinese as by white men from Europe or America. But the Japanese proudly maintained their independence. Towards the middle of the century, however, pressure was becoming so strong that in a few years their resistance broke down. At first the Russians had tried to obtain in Yedo what they had obtained in Peking: they failed. Then the Americans appeared in force and in 1852 Commodore Perry made his entry at the head of a squadron. The Shogun authorized foreigners to trade in Japanese ports, but his capitulation did not mean that Japan as a whole had capitulated. At first foreign ships, especially steamships, were objects of curiosity and interest. Small local potentates had bought a number of these vessels and so acquired overwhelming prestige, but they left them to rust uncared for in the estuaries. Then the people themselves began to revolt; after all they had been taught to mistrust the foreigner for a thousand years. The Western fleets replied to the rioting by a cannonade. Then popular fury turned against the Shogun, understandably enough, for the régime had lost its *raison d'être* once it had become powerless to protect the country against the foreigner. One after the other the Daimyos acknowledged defeat. One set the example by knocking down his castle and ploughing up the land on which it had stood. Popular hopes now centred in the ancient Kyoto dynasty; it issued orders to the Shogun which he was powerless to carry out. Then the Mikado left his old palace, and installed himself as ruler in Yedo, out of which he created Tokyo as his capital in 1869. Tokyo, the capital of the east, was already 400 years old, and had been built around the palace of the Tokugawa Shoguns. All the Daimyos had built their own dwellings around it and had soon filled them with servants and dependants. In the eighteenth century it was a vast city, perhaps the biggest in the world. Strangely enough, although Japan had placed excessive restrictions on external trade it had always had an extremely active internal economy. Tokyo was, in fact, less like a city than a gigantic conglomeration of villages with innumerable temples, connected by lovely avenues along which sped thirty thousand rickshaws. It was not, however, organized like our Western cities: its population had almost vanished on the fall of the Shogun, then it reappeared when the new government was organized. Tokyo was a *parvenu* in comparison with Kyoto, the capital, which was a religious centre and the very shrine of the celestial dynasty. It was built on the lines of a beautiful garden and divided into two regions: that of the imperial palace and that of the day palace, the seat of the Shogun's representatives. Kyoto was a city of refinement, elegance, tradition and perfect craftsmanship, but after 1869 it became a museum city, with a thousand temples. Tokyo expanded with new activity and was largely run by businessmen, the over-whelming majority of whom went over lock, stock and barrel from the Shogunate to the Mikado.

One of these businessmen became famous. The name of Mitsui conjures up one of the most formidable eco-nomic forces of the nineteenth century. It had been borne by a Kyoto merchant in the twelfth century, and in the sixteenth century it was still the name of a merchant, but one living in Yedo in the service of the Shogun. In the seventeenth century Hashirobi Mitsui was perhaps one of the most original pioneers of modern business: he went in for publicity on the grand scale. On rainy days (it rains a great deal in Japan) he gave away to his fellow-citizens magnificent free umbrellas bearing his name in large let-ters. Mitsui was the government's banker, the biggest capitalist in Japan. In fact Japan had been a capitalist country since the eighteenth century. Its Shogunate struc-ture cut it off from the rest of the capitalist world, but inside its forbidding walls the most obvious of Western economic methods were practised. At the beginning of the nineteenth century large numbers of Japanese business apprentices travelled to the West to study the techniques of banking and commerce, property and law. Several members of the Mitsui family travelled in the United States.

The events of 1869 were not therefore a miraculous transformation, but rather the inevitable resolving of a paradox; for hundreds of years Japan had existed as a capitalist country in isolation, though all its neighbours had been won over to capitalism. There was no tidal wave when the trade dikes eventually collapsed: Japan took its natural place in the modern world, for which centuries of development had prepared it.

The Mitsuis gave their full collaboration to the Mikado of the Meiji era. The first essential was to give the country a flexible monetary structure. The Mitsui Bank was to serve as a model for the national banks which quickly increased in number, and for the Bank of Japan which co-ordinated their efforts. Paper money was no novelty. However, its circulation increased considerably. An increasing number of officials had to be created and paid, to import plant and offer capital to go-ahead businessmen. The state itself turned *entrepreneur* on a large scale. It prospected for deposits of coal and iron, and exploited them directly; it undertook cotton manufacture and bore the cost itself if any of these enterprises failed. If, however, they succeeded, private capitalists benefited, since in that case the Minister of Industry and Commerce, an associate of the Mitsui, proclaimed that in the name of liberalism these factories which had proved their worth were to be resold to private owners. Mitsui, Western fashion, knew how to play public interest and nonintervention against each other. Just as the government of Louis-Philippe defrayed the costs of the railway companies in order to sell them at a higher price, so the Japanese state created industry in order to sell it back to private enterprise.

If the Mitsuis were obviously the chief beneficiaries of this operation, they were not the only ones. Another famous success story was that of the Mitsubishis, but it was more sudden and spectacular: the founder of this family was only an unknown peasant in 1853. He was the trusted agent of the Daimyo of Nagasaki, and in 1868 became the owner of all his commercial concerns. He owned warehouses and ships, and increased their number. It was he who supplied the Japanese troops with transport for an attempt on Formosa in 1874. His power grew so quickly that it soon offended Mitsui. The latter, head of the 'liberal' party, blandly argued in favour of giving a justifiable twist to liberalism in the name of the general welfare of the nation (1870); the government was to have its own merchant fleet. But this government fleet bungled its affairs. Mitsubishi, who had succeeded in winning over to his side the best naval personnel, was able to buy back the state equipment at cheap rates. In 1882 Mitsui made a fresh effort. In 1885 Mitsubishi won another and similar success: this *parvenu* had become the master of Japan's sea-going trade. He had learned how to defend his interests in the new ministerial offices, he also had his own party which he called 'progressive' and his own political orators. He soon extended his activity into innumerable new branches, banks, business concerns, iron mines and so on.

Thus in Japan as in Europe political and economic activities were closely linked. And after the changes of 1869 the political framework was apparently the same as in Europe: the Supreme Committee corresponded to our Cabinet, and was, like it, anxious to have a supporting majority in the legislative Council, which corresponded to our Parliament. But under the superficial labels deep-seated differences did exist, precisely because Japanese capitalism was not a creation of 1869. It was Hashirobi who drew up the Charter of Ancestors which laid down the age-old traditions which were to remain valid to the present day. Two principles of this code deserve special note: first, 'the fortune of the dynasty depends on the harmony between the various families of which it consists. They should remain united in one group, remembering that an isolated branch is quickly broken. Next, each family must choose a head who will lead it intelligently, ready to seek advice but taking the decision on himself.' Thus family organization helped capitalist concentration. Mitsui had merely repeated the essential points of ancient tradition, so capitalism inevitably acquired such a directly feudal flavour throughout the whole of Japan. The influences that affected capitalism affected the state too. The Emperor was not only referee between the parties, but continued to be the incarnation of god, and therefore high above any constitutional suggestion. This attribute of his gave a very special significance to the privilege of direct access still enjoyed by naval and military commanders. It meant that the armed forces, as in the days of Shogun feudalism, retained an important place in the nation and represented it more fully than the representative assemblies. Capitalism had long known how to play on this military omnipotence; it should be remembered that Mitsui had been the banker of the Shogun, the military leader. The new business families formulated their policy as much in the war councils as in the councils of the parties. It was as easy to secure national unanimity for programmes of capitalist expansion as it had been to secure it during the past thousand years for rejection of the foreigner.

Therein lay the real meaning of the events of 1869 in Japan, which adopted Western-style capitalism and promptly conquered it instead of resisting it as before. The obvious course for Japan was to take full advantage of its place at the centre of the enormous bustle of activity which had erupted from the white man's world and which was in full swing all around. Japan joined in this activity, increased its vigour, and directed it to Japan's own advantage. Japanese capitalism only needed to copy Western methods to reach quick success, which explained why Japanese patriotism, forged by a thousand years of the Shogunate, was so quickly shaken. The Japanese peasantry soon became landowners on the French pattern, but here it was not, as in the West, new land legislation which drove the rural population to the towns, since agrarian 'reform' was a logical continuance of the past. Instead of paying the state a rent, they paid it a tax: the structure of land tenure was not upset.

In Japan, the increase in the urban population was not due to agrarian changes, but to the new conception of national honour which had been Malthusian but now tended to favour larger families. This rise in population filled the ports, the barracks, and the suburbs. After 1870 the population increased by more than three hundred thousand a year, and in 1890 Japan had the highest proportion of children and young people in the world.

All this surplus needed feeding. This was achieved first by more intensive agriculture, or rather horticulture, since the Japanese peasant worked only with spade and pick on tiny plots. One single crop, rice, could give a yield sufficient to feed the forty million Japanese. It was carefully sown by hand, grain by grain. Fish was more often used as manure than as food, since in that way it was more profitable. So Roman law, the return of which had encouraged stock-breeding in England, brought no modification of agricultural techniques in Japan. Fresh activity in the ports, combined with the introduction of new techniques, may possibly have led to improvements in fishing, and to a more efficient exploitation of the fabulous riches of the sea. But the huge old nets, almost a mile in length, drawn by a hundred men, already brought in thousands of salmon. On the whole, there was little change in the country's food supply, and industrialization never experienced the relatively slow phases which resulted in the West from the requirements of agriculture.

It is probable that in these conditions the reform of the Japanese economy was accompanied by a greater incidence of poverty. The disappearance of the Shogunate caused the people much hardship and suffering. Patriotism led to an increase in population, but it also had to teach endurance and patience to the starving. Theoretically the new political statute ensured for the workers crowded into the new factories the right to complain, to organize themselves and to resort to strikes, but in fact the terrible law of 1890 severely punished those who resorted to 'defamation' in order to ensure the success of a concerted action. The police force, in which most of the previous feudal guards of honour had taken refuge, could easily use this law as a pretext for putting any leader in a position where he could do no harm. At the turn of the century the strike of four hundred railwaymen was considered unique. With workers' unions paralysed, the bosses could play the father to their employees, and readily granted them advances on scandalously low pittances, so putting them at their mercy, sometimes for generations. Given these starvation wages, and the traditionally meagre diet, Japanese goods could astound the international market with their cheapness. Already the Japanese merchant was insinuating himself into every European capital; polite, gentle and modest, he excited more curiosity than fear, and won on every count. From 1870 on, Japan was integrated into large-scale Western capitalism, and was subject to the rhythm of its crises even as early as 1873. The same expansion and development took place in Japan that accompanied the railway age everywhere. Railways and post offices were built, large-scale trade was initiated, and an enormous inflation of notes and credit followed. The 1873 crisis in Europe meant a crisis in Japan too: the monetary system was readjusted and industry reorganized. Japan was then in a position to take ample advantage of the few years of prosperity around 1880.

The volume of business rose in three years from two to forty-eight million yen; then came the European crisis of 1883, as a result of which the building of Japan's railways was suspended for many years and the currency was in danger in spite of the continued daring of bank credit. Then, when the Japanese were thrown back on themselves, they supplied their own needs and rearmed, with the result that the iron and textile industries were booming. When prosperity returned, there was an extraordinary increase in the number and activities of business companies, unused capital was pooled and a feverish activity began on the railways, whose network was still further extended. It was the beginning of Japan's greatness, followed by the victory over China and the occupation of Korea.

Thus this famous series of crises which marked the years 1875–95, and brought about profound changes in Europe, as we shall see, produced a new phenomenon in Asia, the power of Japan. Korea more or less vanished before it. Japanese capitalism, together with Japanese diplomacy and armed forces, seized hold of the country in one fell swoop and directed its exploitation everywhere at once within a few weeks. This was, of course, the work of the Mitsui trust which founded a company in 1890 for the development of civilization in the Far East. But Mitsubishi was not idle, either. In 1893 he provided not only the ships needed for the transport of troops and horses but also auxiliary cruisers; he was in control of Korean shipping and also of its rice trade: both penetrated into China, set up factories in Manchuria, and established a skilful commercial apparatus intended to oust Russian competition from all their trading posts.

It is impossible here to go into the full details of this activity, decisive though it was in the evolution of the Eastern world, yet its significance must be stressed. Tokyo competed successfully with Peking, the city of the Manchu dynasty. The situation had taken a strange turn since the days when the Kublai threatened the coasts of Japan, compelling the Japanese to shut themselves up in their island. The effectiveness of Western methods was proved to the whole of the East. In Japan every village of six hundred inhabitants was legally required to open a school. Colleges were founded, universities had thousands of students, generous endowments were given to encourage education throughout the whole country. To the School of Medicine in Nagasaki, which was already half a century old, engineering schools were added, then a whole series of faculties, of universities which often recruited their first staffs from Europe or the United States. Foreign engineers and professors were, however, used only to educate the Japanese as quickly as possible, since their whole aim was concentrated on learning enough from the foreigner to be able to take his place. This activity and its success drove the Chinese to a strict searching of conscience, with what effect we shall observe later.

12

The Continents Resist

THE great world conquests of Western Europe had been achieved by sea. It remained to be seen how far they could penetrate inland. England and France would have to impose their own legal and intellectual structures on these new countries if they wished to ensure the success of capitalist industry, and industry itself would have to adapt to worlds whose heritage and entire outlook were so unusual and different; and if industry did become established in any new country, it remained to be seen if it in turn would lead to the adoption of Western institutions, Western ways of feeling and thought. In fact the outcome was different in each of the three major countries: technical success and spiritual failure in India; in China, success on the coasts and along the great navigable rivers, but failure in the interior; and finally, a unique result in Russia. Russia had been orientated westward since the sixteenth century, and Peter the Great had built his capital on the sea, but in the nineteenth century Russian interests turned to the vast expanse of Asia. In Western Europe the railways had secured the future of an industry that was geared towards export, but in Russia the railways served to consolidate an enormous continental bloc. In spite of external resemblances, no Russian achievement had quite the same meaning as any similar achievement in the West. In short, from the late nineteenth century, it became clear that there were limits to the assimilation of Eurasia by Europe. Because central Asia was less affected by Europe's revolutions it was the more affected by the slow Russian migrations, which consolidated a vast Empire.

INDIA EXPLOITED, BUT NOT CONVERTED

The Indian Mutiny is generally regarded as a turning-point in Indian history. Up to that time the peninsula had been run in the name of the Moghul Emperor by the East India Company. After the Mutiny, when the Company was abolished in 1858, a chain of events began which terminated in the celebration in Delhi in 1877 when Queen Victoria was proclaimed Empress of India. This may have represented a western triumph in the technical sphere, but was certainly not where customs, way of life, and religion were concerned.

It is impossible to deal adequately here with an event as important as the Indian Mutiny, and a brief outline must suffice. Lord Dalhousie was the most ardently modernist of governors. He worked to increase the Company's possessions substantially, extended them beyond the continental frontiers, and pressed for the modernization of the whole country. Progress was his religion, and he hoped that a vast technical expansion would bring back prosperity to India and reconcile its divergent races. He rushed changes through too quickly (hampered perhaps by the Crimean and Chinese wars), and precipitated the catastrophe, exactly as the over-hasty modernization of Europe in 1846 had brought on the revolutions. Almost as soon as it was annexed by the Company, Lucknow was the scene of a terrible revolt (1847) which soon spread to the neighbouring city of Cawnpore. The corpses of Europeans were piled up by the notorious Nana Sahib, who was never captured by the police, and there were sieges and counter-sieges. Eventually the Sepoy revolt was crushed by the electric telegraph and the mobilization of troops transported along the first railways and roads, and by the new swift steamers. Lucknow became one of the most Europeanized cities in India. The town was started in the eighteenth century, then fortified by the Frenchman Claude Martin in the early nineteenth century, until the old Rajput shrine became a formidable English arsenal as well as the English garden city of modern India. Dalhousie saw himself as the most progressive of governors, but he was, in fact, the cause of a terrible war. Nevertheless, modernism had gained a footing.

In the economic sphere new crops were more readily introduced in lands subjected to the new régime of ownership. The output of corn grew in proportion to the English and European demand, and even exceeded it in the 1880s, when the quantities exported increased fiftyfold. Vegetables from Europe, too, were being grown in market gardens on the outskirts of the great new cities. The demand from England in particular increased the production of coffee and tea. Coffee had been introduced before the English conquest by Muslims who imported it from Arabia. Tea was hardly known at the beginning of the nineteenth century except as a wild plant. The Company sent for workmen and young plants from China. In the middle of the century joint stock companies boldly launched out into tea-growing and the tea trade, and speculated so heavily that they went bankrupt. In the 1880s work was resumed and pursued more methodically; in ten years, exports to England increased fivefold. In London, tea from Bengal and Ceylon threatened the popularity of China tea. Then there was the strange story of opium: its sale was so profitable that the Company and the Government organized its cultivation under supervision, and the best land was set aside for it in Behar, Bengal, the Punjab and the Central Provinces. Elsewhere it was forbidden. The Government also organized its sale in China and Indo-China and the profits were so considerable that in 1880 they represented more than one-tenth of the revenue.

Although Indian rural life was transformed, the old spells of famine persisted. The violence of these cataclysms had not diminished during the past century: in 1868 in the Punjab there were more than a million dead. Over a million more died two years later in the plains of the Ganges, a region which contained the poorest peasants, though it also had the biggest estates and the richest lands in India. In 1877 all the previous appalling records of disaster were broken, and several million people died;

whole districts were depopulated and corpses strewed the towns and villages of Hyderabad, yet at the same time Bombay, Madras, and Calcutta were loading on to English ships their usual cargoes of rice and corn destined for export. Profit took precedence over all other considerations. With a monetary system replacing the old régime of collective mutual help, it was probably the poverty of the Indian peasants rather than insufficient production which was at the root of these great catastrophes. It is true that the government authorized distributions of corn and provisions, but the quantities were hopelessly inadequate. India had, in fact, reached the critical point at which the European régime was beginning to drain off the most substantial of her exportable resources, but had not yet built up technical equipment sufficiently to meet local requirements.

In the south the old dikes had been rebuilt, in the north canals had been redug and strengthened, and the admirable river network of the Ganges had been developed. But European scientists still knew too little about Indian land conditions and peasant psychology to be able to effect any appreciable improvement in the old traditional methods of farming. Great efforts were made in about 1880 to combat excessive money-lending, a habitual sore in countries with an old structure invaded by Western capitalism; but apparently they had little success. The effect of capitalism was all the worse because, though the draining away of local resources by the railways ensured a better redistribution of products, in certain areas its chief effect was to deprive the country of the products it needed in order to send them to the great export ports.

The Company's first great achievement at the beginning of the century was the construction of the highway from Calcutta to the Peshawar passes. That great trunk road with its network of subsidiary roads penetrating the countryside, covered in all some one thousand, two hundred and fifty miles. On the roads the cart replaced the ox with pack-saddles, and a good police patrol carried on the old tradition of guaranteeing the inviolability of the leader of the caravan. In 1834 the Company authorized merchants to penetrate into the interior of the country. At about the same time the optical telegraph system was completed. With the 1850s the new steamers appeared on the rivers, laden with merchandise. In 1853 Lord Dalhousie, who had been a pioneer of railways in England, succeeded in putting through one part of a great programme of construction when he opened the first line from Bombay to Thana. Within twenty years the backbone of the railway system linking Bombay, Calcutta and Madras had been completed. The contracting companies were all the bolder since in India, contrary to English custom, the Government guaranteed their profits: this was partly because the railway played an important strategic role in the country. Soon, it ran alongside the road from Calcutta to Peshawar and penetrated southward to the ports which looked towards Ceylon.

All this railway building attracted capital from London. The example was infectious: local princes undertook the construction of local railways at their own expense (often with an amazing disregard for such problems of coordination as the gauge of the lines). Gradually the wealth amassed by the princes joined forces with European capitalism. The electric telegraph was at first reserved for the state, but it became a public service after 1854, and from 1855 the postal service included almost three thousand post offices.

The areas to benefit most from these changes which were transforming the old India were chiefly the coast and the powerful chain of cities erected by the English a century earlier. For if the interior of India changed little, the seaboard was transformed. Agra and Delhi, which had been the capitals of the old Moghuls because of their strategic importance, had again it was true become important junctions, thanks to the railways. But though travellers still visited them to admire the remains of mosques and palaces and to search for treasures in the shops of the stone and marble carvers, most of the magnificent palaces were being used as barracks for English soldiers. Agra lost two-thirds of its population. Delhi, the capital of all the empires of India, and scene of

Queen Victoria's Durbar, was in turn eclipsed by a modern administrative Delhi which carried on the imperial tradition; yet this small modern city of one hundred and fifty thousand inhabitants seemed almost insignificant in comparison with the splendid ruins of old Delhi. These magnificent remnants of vanished continental empires which had lasted nineteen hundred years, covered an area of some sixty square miles, though they were now overgrown with scrub and brushwood.

In striking contrast, Calcutta, a city of almost a million inhabitants, the second city in southern Asia after Bombay, had risen over the mud of the Ganges delta on the site of a sparsely inhabited village. In former days European sailors had died so quickly of disease here that they had nicknamed it Golgotha. The huge citadel of Fort William was still standing, though after Plassey it had been very little used. Systematic drainage had made the site more healthy, and the colonnaded Greek architecture so fashionable in nineteenth-century Europe was much in evidence, particularly in the massive banks, commercial houses, and administrative offices erected by the capitalists. This city of foreign merchants had soon attracted crowds of Indians, accustomed to moving wherever the possibility of trade or work held out the alluring prospect of making money. Up to the middle of the century, all the Indians lived in the filthy and unhealthy mud to the north and east of the new city. It had been necessary to clean up the native quarters, since they formed centres of disease which mowed down the conquerors. Through the tangle of noisome hovels and small dark streets, great avenues were cut which let in air and light. All these improvements sent up the price of land, and so forced the poor out towards more distant outskirts, a dangerous neighbourhood in which to have them.

Calcutta was a success, and Bombay was an even greater one. The uninhabited island had undergone an even more spectacular transformation. At high tide the sea flooded the low-lying areas, so that the Europeans had to overcome it to build the city. Towards 1840 the caravans from Suez unloaded their English cargoes for

India into Red Sea ships, and Bombay was the economic centre of the west coast of the peninsula. In 1860 the American Civil War deprived Europe of cotton. India's entire cotton harvest was collected in Bombay and sent through Suez or round the Cape to London, Le Havre and Hamburg. In 1869 the Suez Canal ensured for Bombay the place of the first city in southern Asia. Asia was changing from year to year almost visibly. In the prosperous 1860s the English in Bombay declared that they would make the city bigger and more flourishing even than London. The restoration of peace in America led to some bankruptcies and disillusionments, but nevertheless the city continued to grow. There again it was necessary to battle against epidemics, transform swamps into boulevards, eradicate cholera and the plague, and find a pure water supply. There the prevailing style was not so much Greek as Italian in the Lombardy Gothic, and around this European enclave of *nouveaux riches* the huge suburbs spread out into the nearby forest.

Calcutta and Bombay became industrial centres. We have already seen how in the eighteenth century the urban depôts attracted country cotton weavers. A century later factories were being built in the suburbs, and the weavers left their old looms to swell the urban proletariat. The concentration of Indian cotton manufacturing in the 1860s marked the end of the old rural weaving and mobilized raw material to the advantage of the coastal merchants, whose trading activities were even beginning to alarm Europe. The cotton industry attracted others, silk, jute, and also lace, and before long the need to keep all these factories supplied with machines led to the creation of a metallurgical industry.

Yet the development of European industries and the introduction of European plant and equipment did not necessarily imply any radical change in the Indian way of life. The English offered increasing rewards for the killing of snakes or wolves, but the people continued to worship them. A ruler still passed solemnly through a hollow cow of specially melted gold in order to become a Brahmin, which meant that any organized system of cattle-breeding was, as yet, out of the question. A few Christian missionaries acquired some little authority, but only in so far as they respected the caste system; the clergyman being carried from place to place in a litter did not dare to greet his brother evangelist on foot if he was an outcast. The poor people were ready enough to be converted to Christianity, but since they made it unclean by their contact they limited its influence.

After 1870, widows no longer threw themselves on the funeral pyres of their dead husbands, but the priests of Kali continued their human holocausts and did not lack suppliers. Siva, the favourite god of the trinity, underwent several surprising metamorphoses, and even acquired a blonde moustache; people worshipped the statues of the most ruthless English generals, and even the Prince of Wales. After all, for the English themselves, the traditional religion was a good instrument of government: it was understandable that the administration preferred it to Mohammedanism, especially to the intractable Wahabites who went regularly to Mecca to renew their faith and declared India to be the land of the Holy War. This sect aimed to reinstate the former rulers of India and tried to win Persia over to its cause; this alarmed the English sufficiently for them to increase the number of guards on the great routes to Islam. The English had the telegraph on their side, and were backed up by realistic Muslims, but they gave up the attempt to convert the mass of the people to the capitalist and liberal way of life.

The last resort of the moneylender or usurer was to present himself at his debtor's house, dagger in hand, and threaten to kill himself on the spot and to bring down an everlasting curse on the family; this course of action succeeded where the regular courts had failed. Before 1858 the Company had made little attempt to develop education on a scale comparable to the tremendous needs of the population, and was less enterprising than the local potentates. In 1877 the entire activity of the great city of Bombay was brought to a standstill by a curious strike: the English municipal police had insulted a number of coolies. Passivity was India's reaction to the invasion of technical progress. This passivity was surely not so much a sign of weakness as the ultimate and decisive strength of India.

INLAND CHINA REJECTS CAPITALISM

The story of China at the close of the century was indeed a strange one. The Westerners were under the impression that they had conquered the dynasty: in actual fact they had strengthened it in its reactionary and conservative power, and had restored the old Manchus, who were being threatened by a wave of revolts and reforms which was affecting the whole country.

The End of the Celestial Mandate

The opening of the southern ports had not completely satisfied the commercial ambitions of the West. The cunning of the Chinese merchants of Canton was legendary, and the Europeans had the impression that China was selling them only what she wanted to sell. They therefore aimed to approach nearer to Peking, and open the ports of northern China. In 1856 the execution of a French missionary and the confiscation of a British ship provided an excuse for a fresh campaign: the time was admirably chosen, since China was being overwhelmed by the greatest disasters yet suffered by the Manchu dynasty.

The Taipings had been growing in strength since 1830. Starting from Kwangsi, the band was continually increased by conspirators who had been trained by secret committees for two generations. It seized Hankow, Kiukiang and Nanking in succession between 1852 and 1854, and constituted a serious threat to the north. They reached Tientsin and the Peking government became alarmed, since all the prosperous regions were affected.

Then catastrophe came. The Yellow River, the Hwang-Ho, left its bed, and people told how in 1780 the Emperor Kien-Lung had got together an army of workmen to dig a canal sixty-two miles long, capable of diverting the flood-waters of the 'Incorrigible River' towards a lake.

The upkeep of these secondary canals and of the dikes which protected the surrounding countryside called for continuous effort, especially as the dikes were at a lower level than the river-bed. The civil wars disheartened the peasants and depopulated the regions where work was most urgent. In 1851 a breach almost a mile long opened up along the middle course of the river. For two years it gradually grew wider, and the river spread over the northern plains, until it found an adequate outlet some five hundred and sixty miles to the north. This left on the one hand the vast marshes of the old flood area, in places fifteen miles wide, and on the other deserts of sand between the walls of the old dikes. These useless ramparts no longer protected anything but an eternally drought-stricken tract of land. Villages were destroyed and cities abandoned, the countryside was choked with mud, flooded or dried up, and millions perished. Many complaints were directed towards Peking but with no result. If the Emperor was so powerless, people argued, did it not mean that he had lost the favour of Heaven? Was not this a sign from Heaven that the dynasty's rule was at an end? In 1870 there occurred a fresh breach, fortunately a less serious one, on the south bank. A period of insecurity followed; the great canal had been cut into sections by the immense cataclysm, and liaison between north and south could no longer be effected except by the sea, which was controlled by foreigners. It seemed the end of the old China.

These great upheavals, which turned the discontent of the masses against the Emperor himself, were no new feature of Chinese history. They usually heralded the downfall of the dynasty. The legality of such a procedure was sanctioned by tradition: it was the method by which the Mings had ousted the Mongols. The situation was aggravated this time by the Muslim movement. This had reached China along the southern routes from India and along the northern routes from central Asia, and was provoking the usual unrest wherever it went. In 1855 a quarrel developed between Chinese and Muslims who were joint exploiters of a silver-bearing lead mine. The Chinese officials lost their heads, appealed to Peking and the Muslims were massacred. A wave of fanaticism (the real cause of the Anglo-French incidents of 1856) led to fears of a St Bartholomew of Muslims and Christians. An aged Muslim priest, Mateh-Sing, organized the resistance. He had travelled with the merchant caravans, visited the Arab worlds, made the pilgrimage to Mecca and Constantinople, and had witnessed the superiority of the seafaring nations. Soon, under his orders, thousands of men embarked on a campaign. They, too, marched northward and swelled the number of their troops from stage to stage of the march to Peking. Meanwhile disturbances were continuing in Kashgaria.

It was therefore in favourable conditions that the French and British attempted once more to force the Chinese stronghold. In spite of the Indian revolt which weakened the English expeditionary corps, the combined forces seized Canton and settled there (1858–61). The Chinese hedged. They accepted the preliminaries of a treaty, then shot the plenipotentiaries who came to negotiate. In 1858 France and England had to stage a full-scale war: in all, something like thirty thousand men were armed and dispatched towards Canton and Shanghai. In 1860 they captured the mouths of the Pei-Ho, and marched on Peking. The Chinese attempted to delay this advance by alternating cunning negotiation and sudden ambushes. Their action was not so much the result of concerted will-power as the effect of the confusion prevailing at court, where counsellors were at each other's throats, and half a dozen conspiracies were on foot at one and the same time: the central authority hardly existed any longer, and the local chiefs did not agree among themselves, uncertain whether to give way or to fight to the death. The combined European forces failed to understand these inconsistencies and attributed them to what they called Chinese duplicity. After the hard-won victory of Palikao, they made a furious onslaught on the gardens of the Summer Palace and embarked on the notorious looting and burning sanctioned by Lord Elgin. Peking capitulated. This time the Europeans installed themselves in the heart of China: they insisted on having their ambassadors at the court, and exacted handsome compensation for all the damage suffered by their protégés. Above all, their greatest victory was to ensure that Tientsin was opened up to international trade. It may have seemed that China would at last take its place on the list of great powers enrolled in the economic system of Europe; but this was by no means the case. Once again China's infinite complexity got the better of its conquerors. These were proud at having secured a treaty which brought the Manchu ruler from his sacred altar and gave their ambassadors the right to come before him without the kow-towing due to a descendant of the gods and master of the world, so they had now but one idea: to support the dynasty against its internal enemies. In 1861, then, the French and British turned their arms against the Taiping, who retreated, making a stand here and there, then disbanded, but not before large sections of their troops had descended into Indo-China, creating endless difficulties for the French troops. By 1864 the Taiping menace was averted. There remained that of the Muslims. In 1860 Mateh-Sing agreed to sign a treaty with Peking, but the holy man exacted merely trifling conditions, then failed to persuade his followers to continued obedience. The unrest continued until 1873. At Tali an independent sultan reigned for several years, attempting to recreate a southern Muslim empire; and until 1877 Kashgaria too was organized into an independent Muslim state under Yakub, who was proclaimed Emir by Constantinople and Commander of the Faithful by Bukhara.

If the Muslim resistance was broken, it was thanks to the help Peking received this time from Russia. Yakub, before defending his Kashgaria against China, had defended it in the name of China against the Russian claims. In 1871 it was the Russian technical missions which suggested to Peking the raid against Yakub; it was not therefore surprising that he was defeated. For a time in 1881 the Russians thought they could settle in the western part of the Kulja territory, but even Kulja returned to China. In short, after twenty years of crisis the Manchu dynasty won a comparatively unexpected victory with the help of the Europeans, who did not fully understand its significance for several years to come.

Inland China Remains Conservative

Towards 1868, a Chinese embassy, led by Westerners and presided over by a former American minister-plenipotentiary, travelled everywhere abroad to prove that this time China was well and truly converted to international collaboration, that 'crosses gleamed on the hilltops', that there were profitable openings for trade, and that progressive ideas were gaining favour there. It was all an illusion. The reality was very different. In 1870 some thirty Frenchmen (including the Consul) and French protégés were massacred at Tientsin. In 1873 there was an extensive massacre of Muslims of the Szechwan in south China in the kingdom of Tali, whose 'celestial king' had committed suicide a few years previously by swallowing gold. It wiped out his former followers. Eighty per cent of the population of Mongtze were assassinated. Tali was reduced to six thousand inhabitants. It was said that the number of victims ran into millions; certainly any subsequent Muslim coup in China was impossible. Though China allowed a few Englishmen to visit Tibet, which she wrote off as useless, she opposed English penetration of Burma, towards Yunnan. In Peking, the real authority fell into the hands of the Dowager Empress Tzu-hi who clung stubbornly to power. The Europeans had to wait for help from Japan before they could really penetrate the Middle Empire.

Nevertheless the Western world did reap something more than mere rebuffs from all these expeditions, embassies, and investments of capital: though the Chinese continent remained closed to them, they had a fairly firm hold on the ports and the seaboard. It was also in the Chinese imperial tradition that rebellious intruders should be in permanent possession of the outlets to the sea, to which the continental victors had driven them back. It was the logical consequence of the growth of coastal China, whose surplus population of industrious workers and skilled traders poured out across the Pacific. They were absorbed into the meshes of Western capitalism and in turn strengthened capitalism along the very borders of the inviolable Asiatic continent.

In 1880 then, there were two Chinas: one vast, impenetrable, remaining proudly loyal to the traditions of the Middle Empire; the other, intangible, mobile, efficient and growing in wealth, spilled out from Tientsin and Shanghai towards Saigon, Batavia and Singapore and even to Callao, Lima and San Francisco, which developed into the largest Chinese city outside China. Each needs understanding in its own right.

There was no difference between Chinese agriculture in 1880 and in the previous century, except that the Europeans knew it better and evaluated it more accurately. Consequently they praised it a little less fulsomely and it was noticed that the Chinese left considerable stretches of good land lying fallow. Moreover, much of the land was sacred, that of the pagodas, the cemeteries (which could apparently only be brought under the plough with each change of dynasty), and some territory belonging to the Emperor. In short, it appears to have been only in Shantung that more than half the land was cultivated. Another surprise was the scarcity of trees. Outside eastern China, with its forests and spinneys, there was hardly anything but bamboos growing around the sacred places and around a few privileged dwellings. The Chinese peasant had no fire in winter; he dressed in furs if he could, or put on several garments. For cooking, a tiny fire of twigs or roots served to cook food cut into very small pieces.

But the genuine merits of this agriculture were also studied scientifically. The harvest was rich in lands where the loess was deposited in layers several yards thick, where the streams cut steep cliffs, and where embanked tracks wound along the marshy hollows through the capricious waters. There, the soil was continually being renewed. The German chemist Liebig praised Chinese thrift and wisdom. Nothing which could benefit the land was neglected: refuse, human manure, crushed and powdered bones, ashes, everything, in short, was put back into it which could be recovered from organic waste. With his ancient rudimentary tools the Chinese peasant continually lightened his soil by breaking up the clods, levelling out the irregularities in the ground, finishing off this careful work with feet and hands, getting rid of every single weed, calculating irrigation to a nicety, analysing by long practice the least variations in soil so as to sow at the most suitable time of year the seed which experience had shown to be most likely to do well. It was gardening, rather than agriculture, a technique of perfection which continued to be held in high esteem; the Emperor himself opened the working season by planting a field near his palace. There was little livestock. Land was too scarce to be left for pasture. The larger-scale stock-breeding which the northern conquerors had wanted to reintroduce had always been quickly rejected. The ox and horse were pack and draught animals, old friends whom it would have been unthinkable to eat. It was permissible, on the other hand, to eat the pig and that very special delicacy, the duck, which the children guarded in enormous flocks beside pools or calm rivers. The farmyard was well stocked, and methods of artificial incubation had long been practised, as well as the correct feeding needed to produce good laying hens. Thus the Chinese succeeded in getting a living from their land.

Nothing, as we know, is more difficult to study than the system of Chinese land-ownership. Its history includes phases of collective village ownership, and of great feudal estates. In about 1880, at all events, there was no such thing as a single system of ownership. Observers noted that there were undivided lands, where families shared the work and the harvest. There were also small farms crowded close together, each of only a few hectares, which managed to keep a large peasant family alive. Ownership, moreover, implied responsibility in a country where famine was always just around the corner. The village headman could be beaten for having permitted lands to lie fallow, and after three years he had the right to take them away from their owner and to hand them over to someone more industrious. Then, too, since the tax on land was very light, there were great estates, so big that a part could sometimes be set aside for stock-breeding.

The peasant had to get all his food and indeed all his livelihood from his land, and in the same way the craftsman was responsible for every process involved in making the objects of his trade. Vases, materials, furniture, tools, wicker baskets, were fashioned by him right through from the raw material to the perfect finished article demanded by rigorous Chinese standards. Moreover, many peasants were also craftsmen: they grew, spun and wove their cotton themselves. Thus manufacturing secrets were handed down from father to son, from one family to another; the quality of enamel, of dye, of fabrics, could vary, yet be perpetuated from generation to generation in a well-guarded secret. A family without children (and in Chinese eyes that was a calamity, a punishment sent by Heaven which broke the continuity of ancestor worship) also meant the end of a manufacturing secret, an irreparable loss to art or industry. There were some larger enterprises to obtain salt by drying sea-water, and to extract coal from the seams. Bamboo was still the chief raw material for tools. These old traditional methods did give a limited opening to Western techniques; miners from Europe and a few machines were actually landed, and local groups were formed to work them, but only on the edges of the country, in Manchuria, near the sea coasts in Formosa or Pe-chih-li.

Everywhere the workmen tried to protect themselves. They had their own associations, which were more like groups of comrades than unions, drawing their strength from discipline. Strikes were always hunger-strikes and the workmen held out until they died if necessary in order to make an obstinate employer yield. Moreover, the claims advanced were always for such a small rise in wages that harmony, except in an agricultural crisis, was not broken for long.

Transport in the interior of the country remained the same as it had been for centuries. Heavy junks were towed along the rivers, and were dragged from one river to another, often by sliding along short stretches of clay. Most transport was still carried on the backs of men or animals, not along roads in the ordinary sense, but along tracks which crossed rice fields and pools on flat stepping-stones. The towns were very varied in appearance; many were both town and fortress, surrounded by walls as thick as they were high, pierced with gates which were shut at night. Outside were great encampments like a fair in which all the commercial activity was carried on. There was always the juxtaposition of the Tartar and Chinese city. During troubled times, the outer town vanished, and the inner town shut itself up in its redoubt. Once peace was re-established, the bustle returned. The insides of the houses, at least of the well-to-do houses with their court-yards gay with flowers, were as clean as the squares and streets were dirty and stinking, at least in the late nineteenth century. Peking had greatly declined. Acres of un-occupied land and cemeteries stretched away even inside the ramparts. Some temples were better cared for than others, buildings were falling into ruins, and some of the palaces were deserted. The city may have lost a fair pro-portion of its population, and Bertschneider was probably right in putting its inhabitants at no more than half a million.

Inland China, in 1880, was full of gigantic ruins, but life was slowly returning to them. On the Upper Hwang-Ho in the heart of the rich loess country and amongst the coalmines already reckoned the richest in the world, the great city of Hangchow, the starting-point of the Muslim rebellion, had completely disappeared, razed to the ground in the repression which followed. In the district around Sining, merchants still went about armed, and business deals often ended in a pitched battle. A few large cities had been comparatively well preserved by their walls, as for instance Lanchow (which was re-built in European style and had kept its cannon-foundries and cloth fac-tories). The Fuen-Ho basin, which derived so much wealth from its thick salt deposits, had been devastated by the Taipings. In the region of the Upper Hwang-Ho the population, which numbered approximately eighty mil-lion in 1840, had fallen by half in 1860, then picked up again about 1880.

On the Yangtze basin the devastation was equally great.

The twelve thousand salt-pits at Tsuliu-Cheng were resuming work. They still used bamboo for their drilling, and after patient efforts over many years they had reached depths of several hundred yards. The workers forcibly opposed the introduction of European methods which many wealthy mandarins wished to adopt; they claimed the credit for extinguishing the devilish fires which had lit up the nights of the civil war. At Chungking an English consul had reorganized the great trade of this urban centre in 1878, and its prosperity was now reviving. The people were no longer reduced to baking rolls out of the greasy local earth. At Hankow, or rather in the group of three 'tributary' towns which had had nearly eight million inhabitants in the eighteenth century, the population began to come back and rose within twenty years from one to two or three million. Business was exceedingly brisk, but no longer based on the fabulous wealth of the subsoil as in former days (though the coal trade was starting again and doing well, owing to steam navigation which was developing on the Yangtze). The bulk of the trade was in tea, which accounted for the prosperity of the rich European quarter where English and Russians lived side by side. Downstream the famous ceramic centre of Kingte had not regained its past glory and seemed to have lost its trade secrets. But Nanking paid a heavier price than any other for its transitory fame as capital of the heavenly king of the Taipings (1853–63): the city was razed to the ground, its inhabitants were massacred or dispersed. Nevertheless it came back to life and retained its character as an intellectual capital.

As for the interior of China, it presented a picture of human desolation on land which was the most fertile in the world and which had been the longest inhabited by human beings. The Westerners took advantage of the disorganization to line their own pockets along the navigable rivers.

Nearer the coasts, the spectacle changed. In the ports business grew from year to year and was becoming increasingly international in character. China was importing the notorious opium. The Imperial Government had resigned itself to the fact; it had gone further and entrusted to an English official the organization of customs and duties, in order to extract as much revenue as possible from the accursed herb. China—and this was something new—was also importing part of her foodstuffs. This was, indeed, an innovation, since the Middle Empire had prided itself on being independent of foreign countries for its food supply. As for China's exports, silk was still, as in former days, a great source of wealth, and so increasingly was tea, which had become the habitual drink of the Anglo-Saxon world, whilst the poverty-stricken Chinese had to make do with elder leaves. It is interesting that the silk and tea trades had also kept to their two old continental routes: not this time, however, towards the Mediterranean, but towards Moscow across Russian Asia. All this expanding trade was not the exclusive monopoly of Europeans. The Chinese themselves took an active part in it, and with growing success, so skilful were they at manipulating money. Sometimes, too, they showed themselves to be intrepid sailors. China was familiar with paper money long before it became current in Europe and she even perfected Western improvements. Eventually the Chinese gained a monopoly of commercial coastal shipping, ousting the Europeans and restricting them solely to large-scale international trade.

There were few railways. Technicians and financiers from England and America drew up imposing plans, but the Chinese Government rejected them all. Short lines ran along the quays in the ports, and in a few mining districts. One line had experienced a real popular success in the suburbs of Shanghai, but the Chinese Government bought it and dismantled it in order to transport the material to Formosa. Similarly, very few steamers plied the rivers; porters and boatmen monopolized the river traffic. Everywhere China tried to prevent the commercial influence of the barbarians from penetrating inland with its hated equipment. Thus the contrast increased between inland China which clung to old traditions and maritime China which had been seduced by Western trade. The great city of coastal China was Shanghai, which was fast becoming the largest mart in Asia. The Peninsula Company, the *Messageries Maritimes*, and a growing number of companies of all nations had their offices there and their place on the quay. Western banks and trading firms tended to make it their administrative centre for business in all the free ports. From Shanghai they tried to control the river trade, concentrating more on that of the Yangtze towards Hankow than on the famous but obsolete Imperial Canal leading to Peking. Shanghai, an old city, already recorded in the fourteenth century amongst towns of the third class, was very decadent in 1870 when it numbered barely 50,-000 inhabitants. In 1885, an abrupt expansion raised their number to more than 350,000, and the foreign quarters comprised more than 3,000 English and French (5,000 when troops were stationed there).

This prosperity of the new Shanghai contrasted with the ruins of its neighbouring rival Hangchow, the ancient city of Quinsay, celebrated by Marco Polo as the city with 1,600,000 houses and 12,000 bridges. In the seventeenth century it had an estimated circumference of one hundred miles, and there were still two million inhabitants in 1850. It had no more than half that number in 1880; the war against the Taipings had reduced it to a most appalling scene of desolation, but it was still charming nevertheless, with its picturesque ruined pagodas and its overgrown gardens. Shanghai and Hangchow were opposites: two Chinas in confrontation.

This swift progress of maritime China revealed also the amazing adaptability of the Chinese, under the aegis of Tsai-Chin, the God of Trade. Their sobriety, their moderate tastes, enabled them to make rapid progress in competitive Western ways. They observed the Europeans carefully, but at the same time, partly from national pride but also out of an innate critical ability, preserved their own way of life and dress. They realized the superiority of certain foreign techniques, and tried to assimilate them. They had always been brilliant scholars, and were equally quick to assimilate new ideas from the barbarian foreign devils when they were travelling in Europe. Schools and newspapers were started. The Shanghai *Journal* had eight thousand subscribers in 1877. Maritime China was rapidly becoming modernized and the Japanese were working towards it even more than the Europeans. At first no one took these little Japs seriously, they looked so quaint in European dress. Loti in 1890 informed his French readers that 'the Japanese look like little old men, shrivelled and bloodless'. They were 'aware of their mummification'. Loti poked good-natured fun at this 'tiny, obsequious race, tainted with congenital affectation and an ineradicable apishness'. Writing at the same time, this same Loti praised the great and powerful Chinese, so majestic in his noble silken robe. Unfortunately he proved a false prophet. In 1895 the affected monkey crushed the incarnation of noble majesty. England, which had assured China of its goodwill, advised it to come to terms with the victor with all speed. The United States and Russia, more far-sighted, were becoming alarmed at the progress of Japan, which they were anxious to contain. After its victory Japan retained only Formosa and control over Korea. Russia had taken the measure of China's weakness, and now built a railway across Manchuria towards Port Arthur. Europe followed suit; it was the break-up of China. But although Europe was busy carving off pieces of the China seaboard, the aged Dowager Empress Tzu-Hi kept the centre of the Empire intact for another fifteen years. The story is a fascinating one.

In 1885 a book entitled *A History of the Japanese Revival* appeared in Canton. Its author, an educated young Chinese who had studied for a long time in Japan, insisted, and quite rightly, on the role played by Japanese patriotism in the changes which had been inspired by the West and which were intended soon to supplant it. The book met with violent opposition from the conservatives, who ridiculed this pretentious author and his ambition to be a modern Confucius. Nevertheless his appeal awoke some echo. The young Sun Yat Sen explained that the Young China Party was created in order to associate the throne with the much-needed reform movement 'in the hope that the aristocrats of Peking might come to understand the principle of constitutional government' and to beseech them 'in all humility to move towards a form of liberal government'. In 1898 the young Emperor was persuaded by his entourage to read the modern Confucius. He accepted the principle of reforms; the subject of the traditional mandarin examination in 1895 had been 'Confucius has said: *They were three*'. The problem was to transform the mandarin circles into schools where European and Chinese learning would be imparted at the same time. It was necessary to create cadres and to refashion the law, and something in the nature of a code was drawn up. If there was as yet no question of a ministry on European lines, or of a responsible cabinet, at least there was envisaged the creation of government departments one of which would deal specially with agriculture, the printing of technical journals, and the purchase of machinery. Furthermore, there was to be an attempt to reform the army on European lines.

This Chinese army was an interesting body. It consisted of a few corps organized on European lines; some bands hastily levied by the provincial war lords for a definite action; and the two most famous and important elements, the Eighteen Corps of the Green Flag and the Eight Banners. The Eighteen Corps were composed of Chinese but dispersed over the eighteen provinces and employed chiefly in the preservation of law and order and on certain public works; the Eight Banners was an army of Manchus and Mongols. It was they who ensured the security of the dynasty and who, in other words, were in complete control of the Tartar cities. These fortresses set in the middle of the great Chinese cities were a perpetual reminder of their defeat and subjection. These corps were the great beneficiaries of the Manchu régime. They were loyal to the old dynasty and the old principles, especially since soldiers and captains had received substantial grants of land on which, once they had settled, they brought up prolific families. Although they were of little use in a modern war like that with which Japan was threatening China, they formed a strong conservative element against which the reform party was broken. There were approximately three hundred thousand men in the Eight Banners, and the most dangerous were the sixty thousand who occupied Peking and guarded the palace; those occupying nearby Tientsin were also dangerous. The young, reforming Emperor forfeited all hope of success by threatening the privileges of these old seasoned troops, particularly as the old Dowager Empress Tzu-Hi was quite ready to oppose her grandson and assume the old, venerated, traditional authority. The small reform group was well aware of the threat: it appealed to the modern contingents commanded by Yuan Che-Kai, a young and brilliant general, the only one who had shown a clear grasp of Korean affairs, a friend of the reformers who in every possible way supported and accelerated his success and his career. Yuan Che-Kai arrived in Peking and the crisis was precipitated. The young Emperor put himself in his hands. The general weighed up the difficulties that reform would entail. He temporized, and warned Tzu-Hi. In a violent rage the Dowager Empress boxed the ears of the young Emperor and had him shut up on an island in the imperial park. Counsellors were executed or exiled, and Yuan Che-Kai was master of the situation. The privileges of the old China were restored for the benefit of Tzu-Hi. The age of reform had lasted only a few months and came to an end in September 1898.

Outer China Lets in the West

The failure of the reform movement in China which ended by closing the country to direct Western influence, at least during the few years preceding the proclamation of the Republic, should not lead us to underestimate the increasing importance being exercised by 'overseas China'. Three to five million emigrants kept up the traditions of Chinese trade throughout the whole of maritime Asia in innumerable ports on the Pacific archipelagoes. These shopkeepers, merchants, and bankers were the indispensable middlemen between the native populations and the great European business firms. They were rarely liked; the superiority of their culture shut them up within themselves behind a barrier of politeness which often rebuffed the casual, easy-going European, who nevertheless could not do without these valuable collaborators. At heart the Chinese always remained loyal to their Empire; it was this loyalty which made them abandon their indigenous wives and daughters, though they regarded it a point of honour to keep their sons and bring them up in the Chinese way, and if possible in China itself. Their greatest ambition was to acquire as soon as possible the sumptuous coffin which would bear their bodies back to the land of their ancestors. These Chinese controlled the middle branches of the trade of the archipelagoes, and in the Indo-Chinese peninsula they possessed entire cities, like Cholon, forming colonies totalling more than a million men.

Obviously the waves of emigrants in the last decades of the nineteenth century could not preserve this aristocratic character. On the contrary, the movement was almost a repetition of the slave trade, bringing a million workers to the lands occupied by the whites: one hundred thousand to the United States of America, nearly one hundred thousand to Australia or Peru. As on the old Atlantic slave ships there was a frightful toll of human life, partly because of the exceedingly primitive conditions on board, and partly because of fearful revolts which sometimes ended in the total disappearance of ships, passengers and cargo. But at this high price, and thanks to several agreements between the Chinese and the reception countries, new Chinese colonies were founded in most of the new worlds in the Pacific.

In Indo-China, direct Chinese influence even exceeded that of the immigrants. The proximity of the great Empire and the long tradition of subjection had preserved habits of work, of reasoning, and of feeling which even threatened the Annamites' own way of life. The human population of Indo-China was in fact the result of a series of waves; the Chinese wave pushed back the Annamites, who had themselves ousted the Moi. The latest wave was French, borne on the flood tide of Western capitalism. The causes and significance of this would take too long to describe here. One important factor was Gialong's eagerness, nearly a century ago, to be surrounded with French missionaries and officers, so that for the following hundred years any Frenchmen looking for conquest had found this a favourable ground for their ambitions. France helped Indo-China to detach itself from China, then, swept on by its own impetus and reinforced by the power of its new industrial and maritime equipment, took the place of its former master. This Annam was a strange political state in which prefectoral institutions were intermingled with mandarin customs. There was a strange civilization in the cities, where a dialect was being forged from three or four major languages, borrowing words and expressions best fitted to describe the changing facets of economic activity. There was a continuous influx of new merchandise under the impact of which harbours were widened and deepened, and estuaries and great rivers were penetrated. Yet another new quarter was added to these already extensive peninsular cities. It introduced the architectural decorations of the style of Napoleon III into the monsoon climate. The old roots of Catholicism planted in the seventeenth century, then forbidden, began to show signs of renewed life, attracting communities of as many as one hundred thousand worshippers. Strange sects were founded which tried to assimilate the mysteries of the West into the traditions and customs of the East. And here again the influence of moral and economic forces proved stronger than the direct action of the immigrants from France: there were less than a thousand officials, whether officers or businessmen, in Cochin-China in 1881; but Victor Hugo was revered by everyone.

The Europeans were paying a good deal of attention to south-east Asia; the French especially profited from it. At almost the same time that the Anglo-French war was developing in China (1858), a French fleet bombarded Tourane in order to avenge the execution of Christians in Annam. But a landing attempt failed and the admiral decided to divert his attempt to Cochin-China. He took Saigon, and entrenched his position so thoroughly that the Emperor of Annam was compelled to confirm him in possession of it. In 1862 a naval officer succeeded in making a protectorate treaty with the King of Cambodia. The main preoccupation of the naval officers, not disavowed by Paris, though not exactly encouraged, was to find a way through into China. They had soon to recognize that the River Mekong was no use to them in their project. The activity of the French Far-Eastern fleet then turned northward to Tongking. In 1873 Francis Garnier succeeded in seizing Hanoi, but could not hold on to it for long. Ten years later, more strongly supported by a French ministry (which was soon, however, disavowed by Parliament), the French fleet succeeded in occupying the whole of Tongking and forced recognition of its protectorate over Annam itself. China, which was claiming a right of suzerainty over these countries, acknowledged the *fait accompli* in 1884. Siam recognized the French settlement in the Indo-Chinese peninsula: the interplay of Anglo-French rivalries enabled Siam to remain an independent state and safeguard its freedom.

In 1885, England, uneasy at the progress France was making, established a footing in Burma, not without a tough war which dragged on until 1898. The English also retained the Malay peninsula, a former Dutch possession on which Singapore had been created in 1819. In 1824 they bought back Malacca from Holland and developed and systematically legalized their authority there by a series of protectorate treaties from 1874 to 1889.

The outcome for Malacca was rather different. This insignificant remnant of a once flourishing maritime kingdom had been taken over by the English in 1824 from the Dutch, who had themselves taken it over from the Portuguese. England's chief preoccupation was apparently to compete effectively with the splendid port of Batavia, which she had been forced to return to Holland when the Dutch legitimate monarchy was restored. The principal weapon of the English was economic freedom which, as we noted earlier, acted as a powerful attraction. The more Batavia surrounded itself by barriers, the more Singapore congratulated itself on its liberalism. Dutch ships had a monopoly of the one: the other had the privilege of sheltering all the rest of the world's shipping. The harbour of Singapore had to be continually widened and deepened.

Along its shores a mushroom city was growing in the mud of the foreshore, bustling with a hundred thousand inhabitants drawn from every race in the Eastern world, and governed by a handful of Englishmen. They were responsible for directing raw materials, especially the new rubber, to English markets; the local trade and its profits they left to the Chinese, who, as elsewhere, assumed control.

These same Chinese numbered more than two hundred thousand in Java, where again their trade 'flowered like the lotus' and was even more influential than that of the Malays. As for the Dutch, they had little interest in shops. The Netherlands Government was more preoccupied with discouraging any European venture not strictly necessary for the exploitation of the island. Their own particular form of exploitation was a curious system initiated in 1832 by the Governor Van den Bosch. Since the English style land tax was far from covering the expenses of the colony, he replaced it by the 'system' partly inspired by old local customs which became famous. One-fifth of the natives' land was brought into cultivation by the government or by concessionaries, and farmed in modern plantations, coffee, sugar, spices (and soon rubber), the largest of the profits going to the Dutch exchequer. At first it was amazingly successful, and aroused the admiration of numerous economists, then it declined when the regulations had to be relaxed and slavery was abolished in 1861. The growth of transport and the development of the railways after 1870 possibly account for the increase in population which trebled during the century. It reduced the peasants' holdings to minute plots, often collectively farmed; rice was the only crop they could grow which would support so many people. This did, in fact, explain the rapid rise of Batavia. The harbour had silted up; the city, several miles away from the coast, had had to select a new port in deep water, and the residential areas had abandoned the marshes and moved up to the inland plateaux. Two Chinese cities were included in the settlement. It was curious to see the luxuriant vegetation of the wealthy quarter trained into formal gardens in the Dutch manner, restoring to the name Batavia something of the authenticity it had lost when the canals in the first city, dug like those of Amsterdam, had silted up. The Dutch were well aware of the necessity for keeping their prestige intact. They had been accepted by these kindly Javanese who had successively welcomed so many different peoples of such varying customs and religions; the Javanese still had a great respect for the numerous Arabs and the Muslim faith; the Dutch could probably have got both their language and their religion easily accepted, but they chose to forbid both to the natives, at least until 1870. By so doing they left the door wide open to Chinese civilization.

RUSSIA DEFENDS ITS TRADITION

Russia was entering an era of far-reaching reforms which might have made its enormous empire into one of the great middle-class capitalist nations.

Ancient Russia in Search of Itself

The originality of the Russian intelligentsia should not be underestimated. They were recruited partly from the aristocracy, and even from the ranks of the clergy, but chiefly from a middle class still indeterminate but everywhere respected, even at court. These intellectuals had a shrewd knowledge of European methods, and knew and loved their own country too well to rush into blind imitation of them. The great reforms of the 1860s were by no means a hurried copy of Western laws, as is evident from the temperament of those mainly responsible for them. Milyutin was State Secretary in Poland, which had rebelled again and been defeated again; he was the brother of a Minister of War who held his post for twenty years and was one of the conquerors of the Caucasus. Milyutin was convinced of Russia's greatness, and had no intention of aligning Russia with the West; and if he hated the nobility, it was not for the same reason as the French liberals, but because he wanted to liberate Russia's ancient traditions from their state of aristocratic hypertrophy. Samarine, after ten days' imprisonment, had been paying the penalty in Siberia for a biting satire on social life in Riga, in which he showed no love for the German aristocracy, a Western aristocracy settled on Russian soil. He was an ardent supporter of reform, but chiefly from his desire to revive the Russian rural peasant community. In Russia, the abolition of serfdom was part of a historical process and was nothing to do with the principles of 1789. It was the rejection of a feudal institution, Western in character, more or less artificially grafted on to the country in the fifteenth century in imitation of Europe.

At any rate that was the theory of the mystical reformers who ardently championed the Russian spirit. In practice the reforms of Alexander II, which liberated the serfs on the great imperial estates and then those of the nobility, posed problems which the legal expert of the reform movement, Prince Cherkasky, could not solve without resorting to Western legal and financial procedure. The peasant's real independence could only be secured by giving him complete ownership of a plot of land. The fundamental problem was therefore one of ownership, as much for the newly freed serf as for the former dispossessed seigneur, who demanded compensation.

Of course, wherever possible (as in the Ukraine) it was the peasant community, rather than the individual peasant, which was given the benefit of the reforms, but this did not simplify the financial problems. A credit organization had to be set up which would enable the new landowner to pay yearly instalments on the total amount which the seigneurs wanted to receive in a lump sum. When it came to starting this credit technique, it was once again Western institutions which offered the most appropriate experience on which to draw.

A similar situation arose with the reform of the Zemstvos. In principle there was no question of liberalism on the Western pattern, but of bringing the Russian land once again under its old traditions of government and local administration. All the same, the creation of departments and officials, and the clarification of judicial powers, involved recourse to reforms on the Western model. All this surge of new ideas demanded an educational programme, an expansion of the teaching service, and encouragement of the press. Inevitably this meant opening the door to Western ideas, which flooded in whilst the old local culture and the Russian tradition proved more difficult to diffuse, since they were vague and unformulated.

The new Russians were therefore in a paradoxical situation: they disliked Western capitalism yet were compelled to watch it irrupting over their frontiers in increasing measure as they tried to rid the country of Western feudalism and get back to the old Russian institutions and their own modes of thought. The reformers were eager to shake off the Europe of yesterday and get back to a more distant past, but it brought them up against the Europe of today.

It was not therefore surprising that the 1880s were years of confusion. Probably never before had the entire cultured *élite* engaged in such profound heart-searching, nor had the diseases of collective psychology ever broken out in stranger forms. The most spectacular was that of nihilism, of which one of the first victims was the reforming Tsar himself in 1881. Paradoxically his successor, in order to ward of nihilism, tightened the framework of autocracy and gave back to the nobility some measure of privilege. He entered into the famous agreements with capitalist France which resulted in reconciliation with the hated England; and Russia's financial future was put at the mercy of speculators on the Paris *Bourse*. But it was a paradox only in appearance, since it was profoundly characteristic of the economy of the Russian people to stand at the crossroads between the maritime civilizations and those of vast Eurasia.

The future of Russia still lay in the balance at this time. The people were zealous and hard-working in the 1880s. The prospects of agriculture were certainly far better than those of industry. Russia was still one vast village, but a village whose system of land-ownership was exceedingly difficult to define. There were small landowners on the French pattern in the West, Poland or the Baltic countries, and apparently a few also in the south of the Dnieper and Don region. The majority were settlers of foreign extraction: notably the Cossacks, and those in the Urals, who became farmers but remained organized in hierarchies. In those regions, therefore, there were estates with a social class structure similar to that found in the West.

However, on the majority of lands, the Russian usage prevailed. It was not the individual who was the owner, but the village. The law of emancipation authorized the formation of individual farms but some Ukrainians rejected individualism to group themselves into *Mirs*. Even Germans from the Volga pooled their lands. Land was not united under the collective authority of the village in order to improve agricultural techniques: for as a rule the work was still done, if not by individuals, at least by families. The predominant motive was the desire for a brotherly sharing of liabilities. Taxation, conscription, and financial arrears were borne not by each family, but by the whole village, and it was now the village which fixed each man's share in proportion to his potentialities. The village fed the children, widows and old people, and asked only small tasks from them in return. When the demand for education began to spread, the village sometimes set up a fund in order to start its own school, or more often to send selected children to the school in a small neighbouring city. At periodic intervals the village redivided its lands into plots, so that each portion constituted a balanced farm which bore some relation to the capabilities of the person who was to run it. In case of uncertainty the plots were allocated by lot.

These redistributions of land were made on a basis of 'souls', that is to say of able-bodied men capable of giving the land all the attention it required. The method by which the reallocation was carried out varied greatly. In most cases the sharing out took place every year, but it might also be only every two years. There were fairly rare instances where the custom of sharing had been abolished, but even in these cases solidarity persisted and the harvests had to suffice for all. The *Mir* takes pity on everyone, said the proverb. There were various methods of sharing which deliberately created inequalities in favour of the most deserving, or of the families who had most men, equipment or cattle; two horses equalled one soul. Receipts and expenditure did not always balance at the end of the year. The village sent labourers and craftsmen to the town, especially in winter; all who could earn a little money by some sort of work brought it back to the community, and if there was still a deficit it was the village which was in debt and the mortgages were collective.

Of course land belonging to the nobility was governed by laws which were much closer to Western practice. Men of the middle class and merchants also bought land in quantities large enough to displace the peasant and bring ruin on villages the population of which then moved off to the growing town. As in Europe a century earlier, the advance of progress created the agricultural then the urban proletariat. 'Where I settle, the mujik no longer sings', was the saying traditionally imputed to the moneylender, who acquired possession of whole villages and appeared on the scene whenever hunger and disease were rife. The moneylender paid the taxes and the debt, but was then the owner of souls, or, taking advantage of the new law, the owner of lands which the peasants were forced to leave.

The traditional social structure varied in this way from one part of Russia to the other, and the people's existence and their way of life also varied a great deal according to local resources. In the north they existed chiefly on fishing, hunting, and trade in power, game and furs; and they were more dependent than elsewhere on corn. On the shores of the Caspian the fishermen who were also organized in communities caught more fish, it was said, than all the fishermen between Europe and Newfoundland. In the sparsely populated areas, villages selected their fields from the vast stretches of land which belonged to them, since they could not farm them all. There were said to be enormous *Volosks*, consisting of groups of hundreds of villages. Sometimes the lands had to be wrested from the forests, which were devastated so rapidly at this time that the price of wood dropped to a tenth of what it was in Europe. As a rule, empty lands were sought, the population increased more quickly there than elsewhere, and then the *Volosks* split up into *Mirs*. Sometimes also villages rented tracts of land by the year on the fertile lands of the south belonging to great land-owners or to the crown. On these new lands agriculture was somewhat haphazard. After three crops of corn and two of flax in five years, the land was left fallow. Many rich private individuals also rented land belonging to the crown or to great landowners, in order to practice a similar itinerant agriculture.

In general, Russian agriculture remained extensive: there was little use of manure and not much attempt at seed selection; the techniques employed depended solely on the chances of the great migrations. The fairs tended to encourage the production of cereals which were much favoured for export; the poor cereals were good enough for the mujik, and wheat was usually sold. Thus the export movement continually increased. Formerly it had brought handsome profits to the large landowner, ena-bling him to live in Parisian luxury and follow court fash-ions. Now commerce had an influence on the whole of rural life, from the moment when the smallest village had to muster enough money to pay the state the arrears of a heavy land debt together with the taxes. Commerce was relatively easy when the farms were those of the rich black lands of the south. The sacks of grain piled up at Odessa, putting Russia at the head of all the world's leading grain exporters during the first half of the nine-teenth century. In 1880 Russia was still second on the list. In default of corn, flax was sold. The demands of Western industry had become all the heavier since Rus-sian prices were extremely low, and Russia became the leading supplier in the world. On the other hand although the immense pasture lands of Russia were ideally suited to stock-breeding this had barely been begun. This may have been due to carelessness, or to the influence of religious fasting. Whatever the reason, the cattle were of poor quality and nothing was done to turn them into a paying proposition; but the country was rich in horses, the mujik's faithful friends.

Rural trade brought the introduction of new crops.

The innumerable orthodox Jews faithful to their race and religion in south-west Russia had not made a great success of cultivating the lands on which Catherine had wanted to settle them as farmers; but they had succeeded admirably in stimulating trade in the frontier region of the Ukraine. In the region of Kiev initiative and capital were soon available to develop a vast beet-growing industry, and this in turn was followed by a sugar industry. The potato, too, did very well in Russia. Beet and potato were used instead of barley in the manufacture of alcohols from which the state derived very substantial revenues.

Prosperous villages ran small industries on their own: craftsmen provided the basic requirements of the collective, including, of course, icons. In these crafts some villages were fortunate enough to find an additional source of income, as there was considerable demand in western Europe for the many wooden articles, for the famous Russian leather and for lace. This small village or 'cottage' industry was, however, steadily declining, threatened by competition from the new urban concentration. The new mills could deal with millions of hides at a time; distilleries and refineries were grouped together, and a few major flour mills were replacing the number of small ones distributed throughout the country. Eventually some of the major industries became as concentrated as their counterparts in Europe; this was especially true of textiles, fats, and even at this early stage metallurgical and chemical products.

The first locomotive was apparently assembled in 1825 by technicians from the New World. At first there was merely an assembly shop, then a state depot, and by 1880 Russia was making one-fifth of its own locomotives. The Government also increased facilities to foreign contractors and there were already more than two hundred works, each employing more than three hundred men. An intensive search was being made for coal; the Polish mines were being exploited, and also the Donets mines which had been discovered early in the century and fitted out with rudimentary equipment during the Crimean War. In about 1880 the Gruchovka mines began to turn out enough coal for the Black Sea and Don shipping. In this basin alone, production was stepped up in fifty years from a few thousand tons to more than a million. Seams of coal were near at hand, and the Crimean War revealed how superior the strategic value of this mining area was to that of the distant Urals. So an industrial Russia was gradually being built up and the network of railways was providing its framework.

Noblemen were eager to increase their incomes, villages were being driven to commercialization, yet Russia's roads were primitive in the extreme. They were earth tracks not kept in repair, so that in spring and summer they were nothing more than quagmires or dust-bowls. Serious transport was conducted on sledges during the winter when there was always a firm, solid track for five or six months and ice bridges across the rivers. Groups of countrymen were past-masters at exploiting natural communications and at the opening of the railway era achieved greater speeds than the first steam trains.

The huge rivers naturally made splendid trade routes. The old shipping had used heavy wooden boats sometimes built for a single trip and demolished at the end of it. Then, with the arrival of the steamship, these wonderful natural arteries came into their own and carried vast quantities of grain in the middle of the century. The system of interjoining canals dreamed of by Peter the Great had never been realized, but in spite of a late start the railways were built in record time and completed the river network by about 1870.

At first trains drawn by horses linked the Don and the Volga. Then Alexander II, it is said, marked out the line from St Petersburg to Moscow with a ruler. However that may be, the railway completely by-passed a number of important towns, and the roads were so bad that it took more time to get from a town to its station than to cover the whole distance by rail. In 1880 however, almost twenty thousand miles of track were opened. Their special gauge separated them from those of Europe. Above all they emphasized the natural centre of Russia, Moscow.

Moscow was in process of becoming the first city in the Empire. Its population was almost equal to that of the capital chosen by Peter the Great. It retained in its plan something of its curious eighteenth-century appearance. However, the seigniorial parks had been divided into lots on which had been built small houses clustered around parish churches, and which were intersected by wide avenues of trees. All these suburbs were themselves grouped around the city, the fortress and the Kremlin. Economically, the new centre was constituted by the railway stations of the five big Russian lines, the combined traffic of which was twice that of St Petersburg. Thus in the suburbs of Moscow the aristocratic mansions and the monasteries were being shouldered out by the new factories; the spinning mills, weaving mills, dye works and distilleries employed more than fifty thousand workmen.

Nevertheless in 1880 St Petersburg was still undeniably the capital, although it had less industry than Moscow and it would have had even less but for the luxury trades—tapestries, mirrors, porcelains—all the accessories of court life. The presence of the Government attracted the wealth of the country as well as the great banks. In an economy still largely dependent on Europe and the sea, English, Jewish and German finance contributed to this convergence of wealth and income.

Moscow was the city of popular and religious publications, and St Petersburg was the centre of scientific and literary works and of luxury publications. The two cities were a contrast: one with its classical palaces and French gardens, and the other with its elaborately Eastern churches and monasteries standing in remnants of forests. The two economies were a contrast; one agrarian, though this did not prevent the peasant from experiencing disastrous famines and the ever-present evil of usury; the other was commercial and piled up cargoes of foodstuffs on the quays of the Baltic and the Black Sea for England to buy cheaply. It was almost as if there were two Russias.

We shall stress later the efforts, first of Count Witte, then of Stolypin, to make the capitalist system prevail, but here at the outset we should do well to recall the essays written by the young Lenin. They constitute an admirable study of capitalism in Russia, and emphasize its ill-adapted, artificial and dangerous nature. It is important also to stress another important fact: the Western powers dominated the maritime worlds because their economic liberalism was so attractive and their financial resources so powerful, but the Russian influence grew strong in continental Asia for quite other reasons and by very different techniques.

The Russian People Conquer Asia

The Russians who were acquainted with Siberia realized that it was not empty. Ethnographers in 1880 had already described several successive layers of civilization to be found there. The peasant admired its curious cattle and particularly the pig known as the *chude*, which was also the name of a very ancient people who had probably come down from the Altay. The empire of these Chudes extended as far as the Dnieper, and it was almost certainly they who came into contact with the Mongol conquerors from whom the Siberian peoples inherited their high cheek bones and slit eyes. Centuries of common life, in which there was increasing intermarriage, and the endless movements of tribes from one end of the country to the other, resulted also in the creation of a composite religious life. This predisposition to amalgamate worked out to the advantage of the Russians who were always in a majority; there were several millions of them in comparison with barely one million natives. The Russian was good-natured and sentimental. Even if he were a merchant, he adopted the orphan and welcomed the Yakut or the Tungus. In the vast spaces of Asia races probably co-existed more than anywhere else in the world, yet there was no racial problem, barely even a national one. There were only human beings who suffered together, toiled together, and certainly tried to get rich, but without forgetting the consolations of the heart and the blessings of solidarity. In the crucible of a nature so vast and overpowering, man became more human.

The backbone of this Asiatic world was the Altay, the Gold Mountain, a solid mountain range which separated Russia from Mongolia and China. Even greater efforts were being made than in the previous century to extract its wealth of gold and silver, which in the past had contributed to the greatness of the Chudes. The mines belonged to the Tsar and if yields had been fairly good up to about 1870, it was due to the forced labour of political prisoners or to the cheapness of serf labour. Then interest in gold began to wane, partly because fantastically rich seams of coal were discovered in the Kuznetsk basin. The attraction exerted by these distant countries was far from diminishing. Barnaul had been growing for the past century and already had twenty thousand inhabitants. It was almost like a capital on which the slow-moving convoys converged. Tradition, allied of course with self-interest, ensured the caravan leader the respect of the peoples. Traffic was not much improved by the convoys of steamers sailing up the Ob, where the imperial foundries were situated. It was around such small centres as these that the Russian peasant showed a desire to settle, though they were forbidden imperial lands. At first the police generally ignored them or pretended to do so; then the peasants began to grow crops, to harvest them, to build villages. When attempts were made to drive them away before an over-lengthy occupation gave them indisputable rights, they wept and pleaded and wrote to the Tsar, asking to be allowed at least the delay necessary for a reply to be received—a reply which never came. By thus letting the situation drift from delay to delay, Russian obstinacy conquered Siberia and the peasant was firmly settled on the land.

This slow infiltration of the peasants began to oust the old hunters, although they carried on their activity as before. Yakuts and Tunguses continued to pay their taxes in furs. These furs were world-famous and came from more than fifty different animals, amongst them marten, sable and black fox. Hunting provided food too, but less than fishing in the lakes or inland rivers, which were as big as our Western seas.

The deportees provided an *élite*; those who survived the lengthy convoy built the rudiments of villages around small army or police forts, and created small towns where each man did his utmost to acclimatize himself to exile, to live in mutual love and friendship an existence whose torturing fatigue ended only with death: they discussed and read, and small cultural centres sprang up in the heart of Siberia. The deportees were fairly well received by the population. They were regarded less as criminals than as unfortunates. The arrival of a new contingent brought a little novelty: the newcomers were bombarded with questions and asked for news of events in the faraway country in the west. Life's true values were prized. Dynamism could certainly not be expected from these peoples, but the new land easily guaranteed a minimum of subsistence. Escapees were taken in, hidden, assimilated, and the police soon got tired of looking for them.

All the time peasants were continually arriving to swell the population. They came in bands, bringing their *Mir* with them. Their agricultural methods were undoubtedly haphazard; they did not use manure, or select seeds, but the best possible use was made of local resources. A period of fallow refreshed the land, new plots of which could easily be found when the old ones were exhausted. The lands were carelessly farmed, and weeds competed with corn. Whole herds sometimes reverted to the wild state. Nevertheless something had to be sold to pay the tax, to buy rudimentary tools, and to acquire the necessary luxury of a bowl from Europe or leather boots. A primitive local industry attempted to make articles cheaply if they were expensive in the shops because they had to be bought from the caravans. Thus a few hamlets began to look like villages, and then like miniature towns. The centre of these was often the tavern in which the miner, the peasant, and the merchant came to drown their sorrows in potato whisky which the Government readily allowed to flow since it brought in a handsome revenue from taxation. The Russian had as yet done no more than scratch the surface of the vast region stretching from the Urals to the Pacific, but at least he had taken possession of it. Though the population was very scattered it had quickly struck deep roots. From village to village, from post to post, settlement continued to the very borders of Manchuria; hence the attraction of a more organized way of life, which began to appeal, if not to the peasant, at least to the military or merchant adventurer. The essential features of the Russian colonization of Asia were beginning to emerge.

This progressive occupation of Siberian land by the Russians was not altogether unconnected with the consolidation and progress of the Russian positions in central Asia where Russia had also been expanding for more than half a century.

At Baku the watchtower had been converted into a lighthouse, but in 1880 the future oil capital was still lit at night only by Cossack torches. The town was wholly Eastern in appearance, that dusty East characteristic of central Asia in the nineteenth century. The ships in the ports took on Tartar crews. The railway from Batum to Tiflis had not yet been extended as far as this, but agriculture was progressive at the expense of hunting and fishing. Cotton was flourishing. French missions, in 1848, had arrived to observe the progress of silk manufacture and to attempt to direct its trade towards Lyons. These textile crops in Caucasia were very successful at the time of the American Civil War. The vine did extremely well there, and was soon producing the best wines in Russia. Tobacco soon followed. Meanwhile the primitive industry was being expanded. Almost modern equipment began to replace the old tools of wood and stone. With the exploitation of copper and naphtha, Georgia came to life under the protection of Russia. In Transcaucasia Russia's advance found its point of equilibrium in 1880 when it came into contact with Turks and Persians, but the same could not be said east of the Caspian. There everything was still in a state of flux, and in 1880 Merv was still independent, a relic perhaps of past splendour, yet at the end of the eighteenth century this famous city had been almost destroyed in the course of its struggles against the Emir of Bukhara. Its population had been deported almost in its entirety to the rival city. In the nineteenth century it numbered only a few thousand inhabitants, sheltered within the imposing-looking walls. It kept alive the tradition of the old caravan capitals of central Asia, for the nomad Turkmen still pitched their tents under the city walls during fairs. All around it stretched the oasis, the irrigated area where corn and sorghum gave yields of one hundred per cent, but not far beyond was sand and swamp, both equally treacherous: these men of Merv were chiefly robbers and still had a bad reputation in 1880. Nevertheless, habits were changing: the area was pacified by the Russian conquerors and already the nomad encampments were turning into fixed villages and gradually growing into large townships.

Bukhara had lost its warlike impetuosity, though not because it had resumed its fine past as the intellectual capital of Asia. The ruins of this Rome of Islam were as strong and solid as its faith had once been, and the most sordid poverty went hand in hand with the skilled craftsmanship of some of the last of its leather workers and cotton or silk weavers. But Bukhara was a Russian protectorate. It was from Russia that it obtained the manufactured goods in common use, and it was through Bukhara that tea made its way towards Russia from Afghanistan. But whether Russian trade and a Russian protectorate had the power to save Bukhara from destruction was not yet clear. The century was marked by a series of disasters: each year the inhabitants emigrated by hundreds, sometimes by thousands, northward or in the direction of Samarkand. Bukhara seemed to be giving up the struggle against the encroaching sand dunes from the desert. Its canals were silting up, its suburbs were buried. Central Asia, the land of marvels, had become the land of ruins and it was precisely this threat from the desert, combined with the decay of its important trade, which gave a powerful impetus to the Russian advance.

The Tsar was the protector not only of Bukhara but also of Kiva. Here, however, up to 1863, the Khans were not only independent but actually prided themselves on the Russian Christians they had captured and enslaved. The Russian slaves had revolted; they were tortured, massacred, hacked in pieces. Russian troops came to save those who survived, though many more died on the long return journey. The Russian troops found admirable ruins, but few inhabitants. They had fled. Those who remained were besotted with opium and hashish.

Moving eastward again to Samarkand we find ourselves once more in Russia. Tamburlaine's city had become the capital of a province and around the ancient streets with their famous ruins, new suburbs had sprung up, inhabited by Russian merchants. Old and new blended harmoniously in the centre of a cultivated zone in which the ruins of the old walls of the head of Islam were still standing here and there. The tomb of Tamburlaine was overgrown with bushes. With the arrival of the Russians, the Zerafchan had returned to life, and soon all the surrounding regions with it. The Ferghana was the richest of these Asian valleys, once its irrigation canals were restored, the trees in the orchards renewed and the cotton and mulberry plantations which fed the silk worm recultivated. The produce was exported to Russia in loaded caravans which brought back consignments of tools, utensils and cloth from Nijni-Novgorod. Some of these goods also went to enrich the bazaars of Tashkent, the leading city in central Asia, which vied with Tiflis for recognition as the chief Russian city in Asia. More than one hundred thousand inhabitants of every race crowded its still illdefined streets, surrounded by houses of dried mud. But the Russian quarter was already easily distinguished, with its solidly built houses surrounded by gardens. Remnants of disease still dominated the old Tashkent, and whole districts had had to be evacuated, since half the Russian soldiers were afflicted with goitre. There had even been an attempt to move the site of the bazaar. Nevertheless Tashkent was developing rapidly and producing enough money to endow the nearby leper asylum with alms and to order the newest literary works and the very latest products of fashion and good taste from Europe.

For centuries central Asia had controlled the East-

West relations of Eurasia until the English conquest seemed to have robbed it of its last chances of survival. But now it gradually came back to life as Russia's economic influence was extended. The Russian economy was still very rudimentary by European standards, but this in itself meant that it could graft itself effectively on to these primitive countries. The railway was not to come for many years, but the long files of horses, heavy wagons, and flat-bottomed boats were a continual source of wonder.

Even the slowness of postal communications helped on the Russian conquest. In St Petersburg, in other words more than 1,250 miles from the area of operations, ministers and diplomatic officials would reassure the chancelleries of Europe as to the peaceful intentions of the Tsar, and assure them that the advance of Russian troops had finally reached its ultimate limit; and influential military circles would endorse these assurances, which they believed to be sincere. But on the actual spot the small armed groups in the most forward positions, the light infantrymen, continued to live the life of Cossacks, Tolstoy's stirring picture of whom has already been mentioned: the soldiers would perhaps have liked in their heart of hearts to settle down and stop moving forward, if only they could obtain a piece of land. But the endless skirmishes with the opposing Kirghiz cavalry continually drew them on. There was always the spur of a hill to be captured, a dune to be outflanked, an old fort to be occupied, a village or a town to be cleaned up, a group of Russian slaves to be set free. The decay of the central Asian trade routes had created this vacuum, which kept drawing the Russian peoples onwards. This forward movement awoke a lively response in the Russian trading population, and particularly among the Jews. In a city which had barely been completely conquered the first operations were not without danger, and the merchant risked his life, but for what handsome profits! Soon, newly rich, he returned to his little native town flushed with success, which proved a strong incentive to new departures. The peasant soon followed, for the rights of property were not yet rooted deep enough in the Russian soul to tie the peasant to the land.

One important result of the abolition of serfdom had been to encourage that love of travel which, from time to time, obsesses the Russian soul. Change, sometimes for the worse but change at all costs, is an old saying in the Ukraine. It was an atavistic cast of mind going back to the remote struggles of Russian Christianity against the pillaging Muslims, and it relieved a host of pent-up bitterness which had been accumulating ever since the days of Genghis Khan and Tamburlaine, and which no agricultural technique could efface as long as Russia remained so close to a nomad culture. It played a bigger role in the Russianization of the regions bordering on Muscovy than all the ukases issued from St Petersburg by the Tsars.

This irresistible movement, which carried the full weight of Russia's power so decisively into the frontier areas, was halted in central Asia only when it came up against Persia and Afghanistan. They had the support of the English, who were beginning to reach these areas at about that time after the long voyage around Africa or through Suez. With Russia checked in central Asia, this racing tide fell back like breaking surf along the Tianshan and reached the Amur River and the borders of China. The Russians hesitated to enter China but continued to send in their luxury-laden caravans and tried to win the goodwill of Peking, which was alarmed by the barbarians from the sea. The Russian drive reached Mongolia and Manchuria through the activities of businessmen. A *camarilla*, eager to carve out great estates in the frontier areas, went as far afield as the Pacific and even appeared in Korea. For the first time no buffer state separated the power of Russia from the maritime capitalist powers. The first check to Russian expansion came from Japan.

13

Changes in Europe and Africa

BOTH the success of European institutions in America and their failure in Asia had adverse effects on Europe itself. The one brought competition, the other, resistance. These were the underlying causes for the long-lasting crisis which set in at the end of the nineteenth century and forced Europe to push to the extreme its programmes of industrialization and social reform. The demands of capitalism had never been so exigent or its imperialism so blatant. One continent, Africa, still remained free. It had been ignored during the years when America and Asia were easy to conquer and had also been impenetrable until adequate methods and techniques were available; but now it was seen as the last world left for Europe to conquer. It represented Europe's last great victory in a series which stretched around the world, and carried European influence to every continent. Europe had reached the height of its power. Yet at the very heart of Europe, numerous regions had more or less escaped the influence of industrial civilization, particularly the regions contiguous to Russia.

In effect there seemed to be two Europes, one linked to Asia, the other washed by the Atlantic. This second Europe, however, was not wholly maritime, for the great continent of Africa was within easy reach. The interior of Africa was until then both feared and unknown, but now Europeans attempted to penetrate it.

THE BURGEONING OF INDUSTRY
FROM 1880 TO 1895

By 1873 the last echoes of the Parisian revolution had died away and the hopes it had aroused among small groups of advanced thinkers from Budapest to Warsaw had vanished. Bismarck had brought his war to a successful conclusion. Calm reigned in Europe for almost half a century.

Yet in the next twenty years, a succession of crises transformed the structure of societies and the destiny of nations. A major factor in these crises was the fantastic rise in world production which meant that the European markets were facing stiff competition for the first time. These crises were reflected in the periodic financial fluctuations which had occurred from the beginning of industrial capitalism.

Outward Appearances: Financial Crises

This new crisis was first apparent in Vienna, where it touched off a series of bankruptcies which wrecked the precarious financial institutions of Germany. Financiers in Switzerland had been cautious, and were therefore very little affected, but the new Italy was badly shaken. France survived the crisis fairly well. The war of 1871 and the great financial effort required during the years 1871–3 to pay the indemnities laid down at Frankfurt had clipped the wings of speculation. On the other hand, London was the scene of activity. From March to June 1873 the discount rate of the Bank of England rose steadily from three and a half per cent to seven per cent. Yet in spite of this rise, gold drained away from the City and crossed to the continent notwithstanding England's gold credits on France. On 7 November 1873 the English bank rate rose to nine per cent. One reason was that the wave of bankruptcies had no sooner begun to spread over the continent, in the summer of 1873, than the Atlantic economy was called on to face a wave of American bankruptcies. Liabilities amounting to over two hundred million dollars could not be met and more than half of them were placed in New York alone. Prices on the stock exchanges collapsed. At the Bank of England there was thought of suspending Peel's Act. Then English credit strengthened rapidly. The Governors of the Old Lady of

Threadneedle Street returned a rather curt refusal to the presumptuous offer made her by that Berlin *parvenu*, the Bank of Prussia. It had now become the Bank of Germany and was rich with French gold. The general uneasiness showed itself in a permanent demand for gold, the price of which rose everywhere, gradually creating a climate of anxiety. In addition so much silver was being produced from the mines of Nevada and Mexico that its relationship with gold collapsed. In twenty years silver was devalued by half. Silver coins were still common currency, even in England, and they were now regarded almost as paper money. The Imperial Bank of Austria was in serious difficulty, since its important metal reserves were in silver. In the United States of America the owners of silver mines started an energetic campaign for the defence of the silver standard. In fact, though the minting of silver continued, from then on bank reserves were only in gold; many business firms lost their independence in this tightening up of financial discipline and closed down. In 1878 the City of Glasgow Bank had to suspend payments; the result was a chain of disasters which lasted through the next two years. Its effects were all the worse since the Bank of Glasgow was not a limited company, so that the shareholders had to bear losses much greater than the capital subscribed and had to liquidate their personal property.

The year 1883 saw a great French bankruptcy case, that of the *Union Générale*, which was deeply involved in the affairs of the railways and in industrial expansion as well as insurance, then in full swing. In 1890 there was another serious scare, but this time in England, where Baring's Bank, one of the oldest-established and safest in the country, went bankrupt through having been over-venturesome in Argentina, where the Government had recklessly abandoned all scruples about foreign currency. Although 8 November 1890 was a Saturday, the most influential financiers in the City went to their offices to decide the fate of one of the most powerful families in England which was liquidating its own bankruptcy. For months it took all the vigilance of the British Government and of a committee of famous bankers who had decided to cover the Bank of England, for the affair not to assume the proportions of a national disaster.

Finally, about 1896, not before a new wave of bankruptcies had again swept over America and Europe, the situation appeared to be in hand. At last the bank rate was stabilized. Credit became cheap; the movement of gold from one country to another was organized on the basis of the deficits or surpluses of each country's balance of payments. This was the beginning of the epoch of financial orthodoxy, which lasted until 1914.

This series of financial disasters had some important consequences. Gold was substituted for silver as the monetary standard, and a new demand for gold arose just as it had done in Europe in 1845, when it touched off the great revolutions of 1848. The clamour for gold, at all events, was soon satisfied by the systematic exploitation of the African and Australian reserves, an operation which could now be carried out more economically than ever before, thanks to the new dynamite which allowed the ground to be excavated cheaply. The economies certainly needed some such reinforcement of precious metal, since the new gold standard now applied not only to the millions of inhabitants in the Old World but also to the millions of America and Africa, and was also beginning to penetrate into Asia through Russia, India and Japan. China alone retained her old silver currency. Naturally the development of paper money and cheques made up for the deficiency of metal coinage. In Austria and Germany, where banking was still too recent to meet all the demands, the technique of the postal cheque was devised.

Competition took a new turn. The basis of Europe's economic activity in 1885 was still agricultural. In Great Britain the population of the towns was, it is true, already much greater than that of the country areas, but British agriculture employed more labour. Germany and France had more peasants than town-dwellers. Now this age-old foundation on which Europe's economy rested was shattered by a phenomenon quite new in history: massive quantities of agricultural produce began to arrive in Europe from overseas. The path for this invasion had been opened up by England, which had been choosing to buy foreign foodstuffs for a long time even if they were expensive, in order to be able to sell more industrial products and to be sure of making money on trade and transport. We noted the growing activity of the rural areas of America, Africa and Australia in the 1880s. Everywhere enormous harvests were choking up the farms, so that great sheds had to be built and the first silos were introduced. Prices fell in the great new markets of Chicago and Buenos Aires, and Europe could no longer control world prices. Ships crammed with corn sailed into French and German harbours to dump the surplus not required in London; the result was a general drop in world prices. The statistical graphs showed a halt in the continuous rise in prices which had buoyed up Europe's activity since 1850.

This drop affected different countries in different ways, but by and large in twenty-five years it represented a nominal loss of fifty per cent on commercial stocks and realizable assets. Agriculture was the first to be affected; but later industry was the victim of its own expansion. Europe was not only worried by American competition; competition within Europe itself and within each nation had become as keen as it had been in 1830, when the middle classes had suffered a severe shock. As in the 1840s, the clamour for gold brought a fall in prices.

This poses a problem: a drop in prices lasting only a few years had led to the revolutions of 1848, yet this new drop lasting twenty-five years had produced practically no visible change in European events. The solution is that the very structure of Europe was changing in depth. Its industry was stronger, it had a more flexible financial system, and a commercial system which could reabsorb stocks more easily. It had at its disposal an amazing accumulation of inventions which were waiting in the laboratories until they could be used. The fall in prices forced producers to do their utmost to make better use of the new methods and techniques.

We have already noted that in England, which was already highly developed, the events of 1848 had led to major demographic and social changes rather than to political revolution. Half a century later the same phenomenon was occurring on the continent of Europe, from the North Sea to the Vistula. Using its technological banking potential, western and central continental Europe transformed its methods and its whole organization.

Events in France: Industrialization

It is unnecessary to labour the point already made that French agriculture strongly resisted any innovation affecting its structure and its equipment. In 1882 it was France which had the highest proportion of smallholders and they were still predominant in 1892; there had in fact been a slight increase, from 2,150,000 to 2,200,-000. Similarly, the number of farmers had risen slightly from 970,000 to 1,000,000 and the number of *métayers* (farmers paying rent in kind) from 342,000 to 344,000. Taken all together these figures revealed a marked number of new land proprietors, bringing the total to the record figure of 3,100,000. During the same period the number of agricultural workers dropped from 3,400,000 to 3,000,000. The French, then, remained unchangingly devoted to their small farms, and their smallholdings, and still resisted any industrialization of the countryside. Nevertheless, a careful analysis would show that this small farm was no longer quite the same in 1900 as it had been in 1880. First its area had increased a little. Several large farms had been so hard hit by the fall in agricultural prices that they were put up for sale. The number of farms of more than 250 acres fell appreciably, and thrifty peasants bought small plots for a reasonable figure. So the small farm was increasing in size at the expense of the large one; but it also increased at the expense of the very small one. Day-labourers who had a small plot of land of less than a hectare left the countryside, attracted by the rise of industry in the towns. In the country, wages were becoming more difficult to earn, and remained at the same low level. The small owner, therefore, seized the opportunity to buy up portions of field and additional garden plots. On an average the gain was fairly meagre, hardly more than a hectare, but for farmers working ten or so hectares (25 acres), it was a source of new confidence; it filled them with optimism, and gave them a new incentive to remain attached to the land and to farming.

Moreover, the peasants did even better; they also bought new equipment. They ventured to agricultural shows and to exhibitions of farm equipment in the neighbouring town, and acquired new plant. True, there was as yet no question of using the powerful American and English combined harvesters: they bought chiefly hay-making and mowing machines. To possess one's own threshing machine became the hallmark of success, and within fifteen years their number doubled. Weeders were the cheapest implement, and ten times as many of these were bought in the same period. Certain regions seemed particularly progressive, for instance Haute-Garonne, where the number of mowing machines and binders increased tenfold within ten years. Within the same period, the use of fertilizers became more systematic; after the popularity of guano, farmers cautiously began trying out the synthetic nitrogenized manures and especially basic slag, which could be obtained cheaply near the government foundries. Production was also reorganized to meet requirements, less corn was grown, more potatoes and much more beet. In 1900 sugar production reached ten times its level of 1870. Sheep were given up, since their wool could certainly not compete with that of Australia and the Argentine, and the byres were filled with two or three additional horned animals which the town butcher would buy at a fairly good price. Their pigs were protected against the cheap pork from Germany or America with the help of the Government, which fixed high import duties. These changes did not amount to an agrarian revolution, but they indicated a slightly more progressive approach to the old traditional farming methods.

In the French countryside of 1890, some men were

lucky, others unlucky, and fate selected both impartially from amongst very small landowners and very large ones, from farmers with an average holding of a hundred acres and those with large farms of 125 acres. France continued to be the country of the small and medium farm. This fairly homogeneous peasant class began to organize itself into embryo societies; though the *Société des Agriculteurs de France* was more anxious to make complaints to the Government than to teach the countryside. In Loir-et-Cher a famous syndicate, founded in 1883, made arrangements to buy manure cheaply. Certain agricultural syndicates took timely advantage of the law of 1884.

All these associations laid their grievances before the Government, and their complaints were all the stronger since the vines were threatened not only by foreign competition but by the dreaded phylloxera which cut down production by two-thirds in 1890, and made it necessary to import wine from Italy and Spain. The Government dealt with these complaints by protectionism. Méline, the protector of agriculture, was supported by the members of the rural syndicates who soon numbered half a million; he made France adopt a strongly protectionist customs policy and tried to convert all the states in Europe to the same policy of protection against the American agricultural invasion. It was also at this period that Parliament enacted a series of specialized laws connected with vines and wine which hindered France's entire agricultural policy in the twentieth century.

The way in which the marketing of new products, such as fruit and vegetables, was organized was also indicative of the slight but unmistakable advance in French agriculture.

The PLM Railway Company was interested in the construction of an irrigation canal and the producers formed themselves into local and regional unions to ensure the quality of their produce and the exploitation of markets. This tendency towards organization also affected dairy produce. A new feature was the granting of loans by the *Banque de France* to the groups of producers, though it was, of course, covered by the state against attendant risks. The peasants were still making complaints in 1900 against the farmers-general, intendants and *métayers* as they were still occasionally called; but the grievances of the proletariat were finding expression in strikes, in the Nièvre for instance, which were a prelude to the great vineyard strikes of 1907.

A major revival was taking place in France towards 1890, just as it was in the world as a whole, but it affected agriculture less than industry. French industry had previously been the most backward of all, but it became the quickest to develop. The year 1890 saw the greatest migration from the countryside to the towns. The great landed proprietors left their country homes and settled in Paris. Whatever capital they had been able to amass by selling lands, town houses and *châteaux* they invested in industry. The farm labourers went to form the urban proletariat. Thus from 1875 to 1900 coal production doubled while imports of coal trebled. The output of cast-iron doubled and that of steel was almost tenfold. Phosphorous ores were exploited by the Thomas-Gilchrist process and France became the second country in the world for ore; Bessemer and Thomas steel, thanks to coke, was either made in France or imported from Germany and England and supplied most of France's needs. It was a great time for builders of blast furnaces and coking ovens. Le Creusot acquired steam-hammers and rolling-mills, and the north began to develop into a great metal and chemical region. Steel plates and girders were made in the urban centres, now surrounded by entirely new factories; Belleville made boilers and Saint-Denis built rolling-mills; the workshops of Eiffel were constructed at Levallois-Perret. The future automobile industry was already building the Darracq works. Paris ceased to be a city of craftsmanship and became industrial. This great industrial advance of the 1880s can best be measured by the increase in the use of the steam-engine: their number rose rapidly between 1885 and 1892. This did not mean that France had suddenly become industrialized at one fell swoop. But there had never before been such an effort at modernization; in

Normandy the textile industry was strongly concentrated at Elbeuf, where the number of mills dropped abruptly from two hundred and fifty to twenty-five. This effort was all the more astonishing and admirable since France had lost the industries in the east, the fine spinning-mills, the machine-tool works at Mulhouse, part of the iron-works and all the coalfields in Lorraine.

A new period was opening in French history: silk-worms were no longer being raised in the Rhône Valley, but Lyons became the world silk market. The markets at Le Havre, Roubaix and Tourcoing put French industries in a favourable position to compete in world trade. Better still, France led the world in the hydro-electric industry, thanks to Bergès. The French launched the processes of electrolysis for the making of aluminium and the techniques of reinforced concrete.

There was marked progress in the fleet too, in spite of the curious attachment to tradition (France was one of the few countries where the number of sailing-ships went on increasing after 1870, and wooden ships were still being built). The French liners were the finest in the world on the Le Havre–New York run, and withstood the competition with English and German rivals. French ship-building techniques in iron and steel gained the same high reputation as the designs of the last sailing ships had had sixty years earlier.

Events in Germany: Phenomenal Development of Industry

France was the country in which the 1890s marked the most abrupt turning-point of industrialization, but Germany's industrial drive had not lost its impetus—quite the reverse. In the early stages, German agriculture had remained solidly organized around large farms, in spite of a trend, analogous to that in France, towards the development of the medium-sized farm at the expense of the very small one and of the large one. Half Bavaria was still no doubt predominantly a land of small farms where land tenure was on the French pattern, though the farms were noticeably larger than in France; but there were still only large farms in Mecklenburg. This persistence of the large estate was apparently connected with the division of common lands and the redistribution of fields, which finally came to an end in the 1890s. It was a difficult task. In Brunswick, the first country affected, the change was completed only in 1905. This agrarian reform was, however, a remarkable achievement. Some areas in the west resisted it at first, and Alsace never abandoned its opposition to the movement. But there was a marked development in sugar beet and even more extensive cultivation of the potato than in France; as in France, too, there were changes in livestock; sheep were no longer kept and the number of pigs was greatly increased. But, in contrast to France, Germany sowed more wheat and increased her yields. She was still not producing enough corn for her needs, but harvests were steadily increasing. Several sandy wastes and marshlands in the north-east were reclaimed. This transformation of German agriculture was supported throughout by the development of banking, which had made great strides by 1860. All the establishments created on the Prussian model, central co-operative banks and co-operative agricultural societies were merged into an Imperial Union, working in association with the *Raiffeisen* Union. At the beginning of the twentieth century, the co-operatives had in all four million members, and one-third of these co-operatives were affiliated to credit societies.

Thus the German peasantry remained economically more effective than the French, worked in better conditions, and were better integrated into the financial movement.

As in France, the development of the medium-sized German farm drove the very small farmer to the towns. Between 1885 and 1900, the number of working miners doubled, while during the same period the concentration of mining concerns substantially increased the number of workers per pit. With an average of more than a thousand workers per mine, German business was among the most concentrated in the world. German iron production had almost equalled that of Great Britain in 1900; the same year the German steel output already exceeded the British amount and was three times as great as that of France. There was a marked move towards concentration in industries which had previously been dispersed, such as cutlery at Solingen or silk at Crefeld, although the introduction of electricity was bringing a new lease of life to various country factories. The concentration of the German silk industry at Crefeld between 1890 and 1905 was so successful that it became a threat to the Lyons market. A parallel process of industrialization was affecting the spinning and weaving districts. Whereas in 1880 two-thirds of the weavers were still small craftsmen working in their homes, twenty years later all the workers were employed in huge mills. In spinning, the hand-worker was nothing but a memory. There was now hardly any hand-work except in the flax and hemp industries. The number of German cotton spindles and looms had been increased by the contribution from Alsace, so that there were slightly more than in France, and though the industry was late in developing it became well-established in the European market. By dint of technical improvements and a systematic study of cheap production, German yarn and cloths became famous for both their mediocrity and their cheapness. They sold admirably in South America or in Turkey, and even in England. On the whole it was the cheapness of its goods which gained Germany a place in the international markets, in spite of her rivals' attempts to denounce German 'shoddiness'. In fact, in self-protection the English imposed on all goods a label of origin. At first the mark 'Made in Germany' was associated with goods of very poor quality, but about 1900 the famous label became a piece of propaganda for German trade; the middlemen in the City soon noticed that even some of their Dominions' customers were deserting them to deal direct with Germany.

Naturally, it was in the chemical and electrical industries that German progress was most spectacular. Within twenty years, the production of sulphuric acid increased tenfold, and superphosphates were already in general use. Ammonia made even more progress, and artificial dyes were being exported in large quantities. In 1882 German statistics did not include workers in electricity, but twenty years later they numbered more than one hundred thousand. They made the electrical dredgers which caused a sensation at the Frankfurt and Paris exhibitions, and even electric ploughs.

From 1887 the telephone became exceedingly popular. As early as 1890 Germany was a large exporter of electric cables, and in 1900 she cornered the market. All this production was dominated by two great firms, Siemens and the *Allgemeine Elektrizitaets Gesellschaft* which was launched in 1883, and soon became transformed under the skilful management of Rathenau, one of the most powerful figures of European capitalism. All this industry greatly stimulated Germany's large-scale trade. The German fleet, after 1890, was built at record speed. Fine steel ships were launched on the North Atlantic routes, and although they were newcomers they were soon in the first rank of competition. Bismarck had abandoned the policy of free trade which had served him so well in the sixties, in favour of *Realpolitik,* a protectionist policy. He imposed moderate duties on corn and manufactured goods in 1890, and made them heavier after 1890 at the moment when American and French protectionism was becoming more clearly defined. In 1902, Germany had the best planned system of customs duties, devised by Caprivi's government, and income from it provided subsidies for the export industries. This business acumen irritated the old-established trading nations, and England denounced its treaty with Germany to protect Canada against an invasion of products 'made in Germany'. Almost everywhere Germany gained the reputation of dumping in order to conquer the markets.

Events in England: Trade Predominates

So in 1880 French industry expanded rapidly and Germany continued its phenomenal advance. England meanwhile was living on its great past. In 1884 Randolph

Churchill declared that England's iron industry was dead, 'as dead as mutton', its coal industry was languishing, its silk industry was dead, killed by the foreigner, its woollen industry was *in articulo mortis*, and its cotton industry was seriously ill. This was, of course, a rather gloomy picture. He was making a speech at Blackpool to try to convince the public that it must support the Fair Trade League, which demanded the imposition of a customs duty of ten to fifteen per cent. Only the goods of nations freely admitting English goods would be exempt. The years of the Jubilee celebrations were difficult ones for England, and there were many Englishmen who put their complaints into words. Travellers returning from Sweden, Norway, Switzerland or even Germany and France were disappointed to see their country so slow to adopt electricity. Hydraulic dams, new processes in metallurgy, electric furnaces, and improvements in coke distillation were all frowned upon in England, and meanwhile people on the continent were beginning to poke fun at Britain's traditionalism and smug self-satisfaction.

Many of these British anxieties were justified. Of course English blast-furnaces were being rebuilt, but they were no longer the kings of steel. American or German plant was producing more than that of England in 1900. Electro-metallurgy had made scarcely any headway in Great Britain and its metallurgists ridiculed the progress made on the continent and in America in special steels; yet these steels could be turned at immense speed and by 1900 they had transformed the market for machine tools to the great advantage of America. America also led the way in pneumatic machines, steam-hammers, and riveters, which were increasingly being used, and even in shipbuilding. English industrialists were very slow to adopt the new coke ovens for the recovery of the new ammonia gas. The English Aluminium Company was not formed until 1895 to exploit the processes which America and France had already introduced some years previously. The electrification of English coal-mines had barely begun in the 1890s. Many worthy French and German mine-owners were indignant at the antiquated gear of England's coal-mines; the equipment was installed with little apparent regard for the miner's life, and it was so cheap simply because it was so primitive. It was not only in the art of building that England had remained backward. The country had made amazing progress in the years 1830–70, but seemed now to have lost all its economic supremacy.

This may have been true of industry perhaps, but not of finance. The new developments lowered prices and changed the direction of the flow of goods, but at the same time the circulation of foodstuffs around the world increased appreciably; and this benefited freight, insurance, the activity of ports, of pools and banks. England adapted itself well to the new financial conditions between 1880 and 1900, and if it could afford to neglect its industry it was because its commercial power was at its height. If business was slack in Europe at any time, it was sure to be flourishing in China or Japan. If the price of agricultural produce dropped, all the better for the pockets of consumers in London or Glasgow. And the development of new industries benefited England indirectly. The new rubber industry was slow to catch on in England, but it was the English who shipped it and bonded half the world's rubber production, until in 1905 English financiers encouraged planters to settle in Malaya. With a rare flexibility England weathered the years of crisis and competition, not so much modernizing itself as skilfully manœuvring both its fleet and its capital, steering them always into the main stream of trade and keeping them away from reefs. When the fresh rise in prices led amongst other phenomena to an increase in gold production, it was soon apparent that the sources of these new treasures were all in the hands of England, exploited by English machines and English dynamite, and soon guarded by English soldiers.

England's strength lay in its genius for making good investments rather than pushing on with the modernization of the country, but there were risks inherent in this policy, and particularly the risk of unemployment. The trade union statistics show high levels of unemployment at various times between 1885 and 1895. It may have been good business to choose German steel if it cost less, rather than home-produced steel, but it threw many men out of a job. Actually the threat was not particularly heavy, and there was a great boom in building. Houses, offices and modern blocks typical of the later years of Queen Victoria's long reign were built at a great rate. As this century, which had been such a great one for England, drew to its close, peace and quiet, calm and comfort prevailed. The privileged regarded the earth, as Lord Asquith said in later years, as the playground of the rich. England was a country good to live in in those days, making progress in hygiene and with fairly good wages. Many English emigrants returned home about 1900.

Moreover, at this same period England was making a slow but determined effort at modernization. A law was passed allowing municipalities to build electric factories. The chemical industry, long regarded by the majority of English businessmen as a German monopoly, began to take advantage of the wealth of England's coal. The springs of industry were wound up once again.

RURAL LOYALTIES

The North and North-East: Modernization of Agriculture

To the north of Europe's vast industrial backbone lay a broad agricultural belt stretching from Ireland to Finland and covering Scandinavia.

This zone, so different in character, opened up at the very gates of the great cities of steel and steam, to which it offered so violent a contrast. Ireland in the nineteenth century presented a strange and tragic spectacle. Poverty there had been extreme in the eighteenth century, but it seemed at the opening of the industrial century as if things were about to change, because of the recent discovery of the potato. It was cultivated everywhere and the yields were good in spite of primitive methods because of the suitable soil and climate, so that it ensured an almost completely adequate food supply. A great wave of hope swept the country. Even the English were beginning to display comparative tolerance, and they allowed the tithe on their Catholic subjects for the benefit of the Church of England to be collected with the farm rent. The Irish Bill brought Catholics into the English Parliament. The position of the Irish peasants had improved. The population increased in a few years; between 1800 and 1845 it rose from six to eight millions. The towns expanded, life became more civilized.

The Irishman has always had in his speech a strain of poetry, a lively wit often envied by his English neighbour. Great orators popularized the English language, the old Erse was lost. Matthews, an earnest preacher, succeeded in converting the Irish to sobriety. A country-wide movement closed the drink shops and converted almost the whole country, village after village. The peasants began to save a little. Some grew accustomed to working in England's industrial cities where they were given the hardest jobs ('what on earth should we do without the Irish?') and, by depriving themselves, sent their savings to their families which had remained in Ireland.

Since they had been forcibly compelled to abandon the old system of collective ownership, the Irish had begun to realize the advantages of individual ownership, though these peasant holdings, often tiny, were redivided into even smaller plots each time they were handed down. The old pagan traditions preserved by poverty and loneliness began to disappear, and lingered on only in a few of the islands. Railway lines were built from Belfast and Dublin. A little trade brought life to the countryside. English landowners began to go and look after their vast estates on the spot.

All this surge of hope came to a tragic end with the famine of the black years of 1846–7. The potatoes developed a disease; the harvest was practically non-existent; famine threatened, the small herds of pigs were soon eaten, cattle could barely crawl about in the inadequate fields and died there. The peasants carried these starving animals to the stables but this made no difference, for exclusive concentration on potatoes had led to the neglect of hay and fodder. On the roads, in the hamlets, death struck mercilessly. It was a famine as disastrous as any in the darkest eras of the Middle Ages and people soon stopped burying the dead. Huts, cabins, whole villages were burned down to get rid of the corpses. In the towns, the healthy no longer even cast a glance at the weakling who dropped in the streets. It was difficult to count the number of victims, but there must have been between one and two millions. In a few years the population fell to a figure below that of the eighteenth century. Naturally, emigration had completed the work of the famine; all who could get to a port set sail for America and left their country which they sadly called 'the poor old lady'. The emigration itself was tragic enough. More than a third of the emigrants died on the voyage or on disembarking. By 1880, paradoxically, there were more Irish in America, particularly in the United States, than in Ireland itself.

But the disaster was followed by a period of new growth. The peasant farm was somewhat enlarged by so many departures. English landowners took advantage of the cheapness of land to round off their estates, but at the same time some large estates were divided to the profit of the small ones. The English Parliament had some pity at last and granted the Irish tenant the right to receive compensation if evicted by an English landlord. During the famine a few subsidies had been paid out. Above all the Irish exiles in America had found it easy enough to get work since they were not afraid of heavy labouring, and they saved enough to send millions back to the old abandoned country. Sometimes of course the Irishmen in the homeland gave way to fits of black depression and forgot the good resolutions made before 'the troubles', so that some of the money went on liquor; but agriculture did benefit from it as well. A current of trade began to flow from Ireland to England, bringing corn and especially dairy produce and meat. Flax-growing provided the raw material for the textile industries of

Scotland and even of Ireland, where an industrial area developed around Dublin and particularly Belfast. Dublin never regained the prosperity it had known before Cromwell but it began to look like a capital once more. American Ireland had saved European Ireland. Soon the countryside regained the mellow prosperity it had lost for centuries. In 1880 Ireland was on the way to becoming one of the finest agricultural countries in Europe.

Holland had experienced no such tragedies or hardships. It was, in fact, because she was so wealthy that she had been able to remain placid and untroubled on the agricultural fringe of Europe. This amazing country, which in the seventeenth century had set the world an example of modern organization, seemed to have forgotten its urban vocation in the nineteenth century and devoted all its effort to the countryside. Railways were introduced late, for there was already a fine system of canals; and the construction of railways across the unpredictable flats and dikes involved enormous work on bridges and viaducts, which needed continually to be strengthened in the light of experience.

Industrial technique penetrated Holland only gradually, but it was a tremendous help in conquering these lands: the old windmills were still turning, but steam pumps were more efficient and made it possible to plan such ambitious projects as the draining of the bed of the Zuyder-Zee. The country already had splendid achievements to its credit: the sea of Haarlem had been drained and islands lost for a hundred years had been recovered. From the end of the imperial wars in Holland up to 1880, the country had reclaimed 150,000 acres. It was rich land which responded excellently to the new agricultural techniques, the use of manures, the selection of seed and of stock. There again, the proximity of the consumer markets of England and Germany ensured a profitable flow of trade. The growing volume of shipping made it essential to dig the fine canal from Amsterdam to the sea, and Rotterdam in turn had to improve its stretch of estuary. These investments of capital were soon made to pay, thanks to the amount of traffic which increased with each fresh advance of German metallurgy.

The Dutch also had their Indian colonies which brought in revenue. Holland was prosperous enough to concentrate her ambitions on maintaining the neat and well-tended countryside, which had been typical of the Dutch since the finest periods of their history. They did not abandon their industrial activities, but concentrated on those which were in keeping with their traditions; luxury fabrics and lace, which was not yet being replaced by cotton; glassware and particularly food industries.

Denmark was also mainly agricultural and reaped the benefit of English free trade. There, the farmers were still content with poor-quality cereals for themselves but they grew more and more wheat which sold at a good price in England. A flourishing stock-breeding was soon started too, and came to be considered the finest in Europe. Denmark offered England its bacon, lard, dairy produce and beef. The Danish population doubled in sixty years. Although there were still important aristocratic estates in Denmark and enormous inequalities in wealth remained yet the development of the agricultural revolution worked out to the advantage of the small farmer who acquired more land, cleared moorland, took possession of the common lands, drained marshes and by care and thrift succeeded in swelling his bank balance. The Danish countryside was more prosperous even than the towns; education developed more quickly, there was scope for ambition, and the countryman was more active in politics than the townsman. Naturally Copenhagen remained an important centre, favoured by its admirable site: nevertheless there were few industries and little fishing, and agricultural trade and shipping were its mainstay.

The Scandinavian countries were all agricultural. In the three Nordic countries there was certainly a marked trend towards urbanization, but except perhaps in Norway it never reached the same proportions as in industrial Europe. The population was not immobile; here as elsewhere a progressive countryside meant a deserted countryside. But from 1875 the towns which attracted the northern migrants were those of America. The progress of Scandinavian agriculture assisted England's towns by feeding them and the towns of the United States by populating them. This agricultural advance took two forms. First of all numerous clearings were made in the peat bogs, the moorland and the forest areas: within ten years (1865–75) two and a quarter million acres were brought into cultivation. In Sweden the government gave considerable help with the draining of lands flooded by lakes. Norway was reclaiming her fiords. The victors of this battle were small farmers, who soon became small landed proprietors and settled firmly on their new lands to bring up large families in a Lutheran and Republican atmosphere. Even the Laps took part in this expansion.

A more sensible method of farming was adopted. More care was taken over stock-breeding. Scandinavian breeds were formed by a continuous and increasing adaptation of genuine Nordic elements. Scandinavia exported foodstuffs, whilst the newsprint and cellulose industries gave the forests a new value, and the woodcutters moved ever farther north, covering the rivers with innumerable log rafts. The Norwegian or Swedish peasant owned his own land. If he were a farmer, he was protected against serfdom by the tradition of a country into which it had never been introduced, since it was restricted to the south of the Skagerrak. Then, too, collective ownership persisted stubbornly in the north. In the south the vagaries of the civil code on the French model were experienced only after 1850.

Railways had not been started until the second half of the nineteenth century and were slow to develop. Denmark was intersected by the sea, Sweden by lakes and Norway by mountains, so that each called for great feats of engineering. The railway network was not yet sufficiently developed for the great mineral deposits of the northern regions to be exploited, and Swedish industry in the central areas still retained its traditional character based on good craftsmanship and excellent ores. There was a sudden movement towards urban expansion especially in Norway, round about 1880, caused by the coastal shipping and the fishing. The cod and herring fishing kept to its medieval techniques until the end of the century, though it widened in scope and it was able to send copious supplies to the German and English markets.

The movement of change had not yet penetrated to Finland where a Swedish aristocracy (self-styled) passed under Russian rule as a 'Western' people. The peasants living in their smoky dug-outs, hollowed out of the ground, took their first steps forward only where they adopted the Russian *isba* built of round logs. Finland had been equally free from serfdom, but the rule of the seigneurs was restrictive and the government clashed violently with it in the attempt to give the peasants a little more land. The railway was still so recent an innovation that it was not yet possible to speak of modernization.

On the opposite side of the Gulf of Finland, the Finnish peoples fared little better in the matter of land, with this small difference, that the Germans disputed the ownership of the land with the Swedes and introduced serfdom. When Russia became the new master the peasants were offered freedom on condition that they were converted to the Orthodox Church, but they often had to go to faraway Siberia to enjoy it, for on the spot the Germans ruled and even succeeded in imposing Protestantism in the country districts near the cities whose trade they controlled. The landless peasant remained closely dependent on the seigneur. In 1880 a small movement began to take shape in favour of individual ownership but it benefited only a very restricted number of native inhabitants.

The peoples of northern Europe reveal certain common characteristics in their economic systems, above all an attachment to agriculture; but the Slav population which formed the eastern fringe, the intermediate zone between Europe proper and Russia, is more difficult to define briefly. We have seen that part of Bohemia became re-attached to the great industrial backbone just as southern Poland did, but beyond the Carpathians, Slovakia, northern Poland and Lithuania retained all their ancient characteristics. In fact the whole of the region between Warsaw and the North Sea up to 1878 was fairly similar in structure to that of the Baltic and Finnish countries. It formed an enormous group of servile peasants dominated by a few great lords, Polish or German in Posnania, Austrian in Galicia, Russian in the east. Trade was entirely in the hands of Germans, Rhenish Jews who were all-powerful in the cities.

Poland's revolutionary struggles were the product of an old-fashioned Polish patriotism and were rapidly suppressed by Russia. But they had the paradoxical effect, in the Russian zone at least, of hastening the liberation of the serfs and developing a small peasant farm on something approaching Western lines. The Russians were more skilful than the Austrians in Galicia; they wished to destroy the influence of the arrogant Polish landowners, and they steered the conflict between them and the peasant classes into economic spheres. The estates of the nobility were dismembered, villages and farms given back to the peasants, lands redistributed. At the same time the peasant was allowed to keep his old communal institutions analogous to those of the Russian *mir*. He used them as a kind of trade union to enable him to fight against the Jewish or German moneylender. When a straightforward system of landownership in German Poland had been established, it ended after a brief opposition in the peasant's subjection to the landowner. But the composite Russian régime gave this Polish peasant a chance to develop his vocation: agriculture improved in quality and quantity at the expense of the dismembered seigniorial estate, and the rural population increased noticeably. Within twenty years it rose from four to seven millions. The peasants moved out of the hamlets to the villages and from the villages to the towns, and provided the labour pool of an industrial Poland, which made marked progress. The same phenomena were occurring in Lithuania, at the expense of the German and Polish rulers. Here the reform of serfdom had the effect of westernizing Poland. The success of this policy of landownership not only enabled the Russians to wean the mass of the Polish people away from the heroic, but short-sighted patriotism of the seigneurs, but made Russianization bearable. It also made tolerable the attempts of the Orthodox Church to supplant Catholicism, and the compulsory use of the Russian language in schools. This obligation did not prevent a surprising growth in the number of Russian schools paid for by peasant contributions; they increased fourfold within ten years. It is true that in the privacy of their homes the Polish people remained faithful to their religion, their language and their country. But their attitude towards their Russian masters was different from that towards their old aristocratic rulers. Economically and socially the Russians were seen as liberators all the more readily since the oppressive power of the landowners had been strengthened in the German and Austrian zones, and since urban capitalism, urban trade and money-lending remained in the hands of foreigners. The Polish noble looked to the West, the people to the East.

The East and South-East: Prisoners of Their History

Wretched though the *Wasser Polaken* might be, the Ruthenians were even more so. This hinterland of Europe was a curious crossroads of the East. Races, languages and religions cut across each other in an incredible confusion, and economic life was completely controlled by the Jews. The Ruthenian sometimes felt himself a Russian at heart though he had his own language and practised the Orthodox religion. The racial, linguistic and religious influence of the Poles extended to the Upper Dnieper, but Hungarians and Rumanians also penetrated as far as the Dnieper, whilst the Czechs crossed the Carpathians.

Bukovina was famous in 1880 for the scene of political confusion it presented. There were for example eight or ten religions currently being practised there. This mixture and confusion were increased at the end of the nineteenth century when a start was made on exploiting the resources of the subsoil and the hitherto neglected naphtha. This drew fresh waves of immigrants of every nationality from all the surrounding areas. The people benefited hardly at all. A primitive agriculture barely enabled them to keep alive in the good years, and to renew their debts with the obliging Jews when times were bad. Here the reform of serfdom or the rights of property had very little meaning—every town was a law unto itself. It was a relic of the old Europe of feudal days, before the social movements brought reforms and led eventually to capitalism.

Moving southward, we come to Transleithania, the Hungarian half of the double eagle. The traveller arriving from the north was immediately struck by one most unusual feature—there were very few trees, sometimes none at all. The Alföld stretched for almost twenty-five thousand square miles with no growth but plants and the few shrubs bordering the roads near the villages. As in China, the peasant's fuel in these parts was cowdung. The lands of the *puszta* were rich enough not to need manuring. As on the Asian steppes, flocks and herds roamed about in the care of shepherds; this way of life was a fashionable source of inspiration to the Romantics and was illustrated by Petöfi. The uniformity of the countryside created an illusion of racial unity in this pocket where the Eastern steppes came up against the mountains of Europe. There was certainly a unity of landscape, but far more important was the unity of language. Though the Magyar tongue prevailed, the Magyars themselves were not really in control of the country. They had long been aware of the delicacy of their position, surrounded as they were by such a variety of Slavs who were beginning to realize their common claims against the Hungarian overlord. Like Turkey, Hungary was beginning to look like an Asian enclave planted in the middle of Europe. Though the formidable courage of this race of horsemen had compelled the Habsburgs to concede their rule over the plains of the Empire, it seemed that the dual monarchy might become a triple one: there were in fact too many Slavs.

As for the German masters, they were firmly installed in the Alpine mountain regions, in control of the passes and the great valleys, of the fortress from which they had started the conquest of the lowlands. But today it was the very diversity of Austria which paralysed it. The Austrians had certainly made great efforts to finish the dense network of railways in the 1860s, but the difficulties were immense. Then came 1873: we have seen how the crisis which shook Europe broke first in Vienna. The disaster of 1883 followed, when the Austrian railways played a decisive part in the failure of the *Union Générale*. The die was cast. Austria had missed the opportunity for industrialization in Hungary and could no longer follow the rhythm of development in rival countries.

Nevertheless Vienna still retained its aristocratic air, chiefly because the Viennese plain was effectively industrialized on Western lines and the Alpine country region had almost caught up with the movement of modernization. The radius affected by this revitalization was limited, but it accounts in part for the extraordinary vitality of Vienna. The Austrian monarchy had been doing everything possible to consolidate its position for the past hundred years and had at least succeeded in making Vienna the gala capital of Europe. The land of Mozart and Haydn had become that of Strauss. His waltzes were still full of the imperial splendour which set all Europe dancing, delighting each generation afresh with their unusual rhythms, drawing wild applause alike from the Sunday crowds in the parks and from the aristocratic circles which were the last remnants of the feudalism of the *ancien régime*. The palaces of these nobles had now shed yesterday's gilt baroque only to adopt the ornate modern style based on the latest botanical fashions, and which became all the rage in London, Milan and Barcelona. It was the prestige enjoyed by this ancient aristocracy and its old-world standards of honour which held the Empire together. Its officials were intensely proud of their calling, its soldiers gloried in their high vocation, and its priests were tolerant because they were troubled by no doubts. Vienna lived on its past, it set Europe an example of wonderful solidarity, and resisted the assaults of nationalism by diplomacy and a kind of resigned wisdom which made the Austro-Hungarian yoke bearable. All its subjects were eager to be educated in German-speaking schools while waiting for the day when, like Italy, they would break free from the antiquated imperial city.

To the east the German people were pushing forward everywhere and colonizing the Slav lands.

Italy: Capitalism Builds Unity

Italy had succeeded in winning independence and had forged a national unity. What a railway had failed to do in Austria it had achieved in Italy. As in Germany the construction of the peninsular railway had prepared the ground for political unification. Brindisi could claim to be playing a pivotal role in the new Mediterranean economy, although it had still to be connected up with the great continental axes. In Italy every form of transport was slowed down by the presence of the Papal States cutting across the country like a scarf from one sea to the other; the administrative indifference of the Papacy enraged engineers and businessmen who were battling against the keenest international competition. Above all, the richest part of the country was in the hands of the Austrians, whose financial administration was cumbersome and inefficient. On the other hand Genoa which had lost its independence in 1815, when it joined up with Piedmont, was enjoying a genuine prosperity and was sufficiently vigorous to threaten the Austrians in Trieste.

Italy's economic progress could not be compared with that of the northern nations, especially contemporary Germany. It was not an irresistible drive towards industrialization which carried Italy to unity. Its wealth was still agricultural, and in spite of spinning mills, textiles and luxury industries of all kinds, it was trade in agricultural products which kept the lovely museum cities going. In that respect Italy was more akin to France than to any other European country. Like France, Italy was fortunate enough to have a brilliant political ideology, at once speculative and romantic, which imbued the unification movement with the idea that love of one's country was more important than material interests. The most ardent patriots had full belief in the power of French revolutionary ideals and were never discouraged by military setbacks.

Cavour is a typical example of the evolution of these sentiments and these needs. He was the godson of Pauline Bonaparte (Camillo's father—the Marquis Benso di Cavour had been Great Chamberlain to Camillo Borghese) and as a young man began by deliberately expounding such radical ideas that Charles Albert kept him away from his Court, and even withdrew him from Genoa to which he was attached. Cavour himself tells how he learned to moderate his passions and to appreciate the delicate situation in which his country was placed, between the threat of Papal excommunication and Austrian bayonets. He travelled, got to know England, and wrote a penetrating book on the English public assistance scheme. He realized the progress being made by Germany. Most important of all, he made many close friendships with Frenchmen, and this aristocrat, like so many Italian patriots, learned in Paris that it was the progress of the people which would forge the future. Debarred from holding any public office but a modest post on his country's statistical commission, he devoted himself to running and improving the family estates. He drained and ploughed and introduced new breeds, did an extensive trade in food produce, made money, studied economics, founded schools and hospitals and even tried his hand at industry. He founded an agrarian association and published a great many practical articles in his newspaper. He believed the rôle of the railways to be ethical rather than economic. In spite of this activity, Cavour was suspect to the monarchists in power and to the democrats in opposition, for he had to pursue a delicately-balanced policy which would enable agricultural Italy to profit from the industrial revolutions of northern Europe. He started a new newspaper, *Il Risorgimento*, in 1848. His political beginnings were marked by setbacks which gave him time to forge more solid links with London and Paris. He made the acquaintance of Louis Napoleon. Following England's example, on his return to Piedmont he freed the corn trade and was instrumental in promoting the railway from Genoa to Turin. The rest is history: his activities during the Crimean War and at the Congress of Paris, and the way in which he served Italy 'in the only way permissible in the existing state of Europe'. He succeeded at last in winning popularity through his friendship with France, and with good reason, since the Emperor's intervention drove the Austrians from Milan and enabled Piedmont to annex Tuscany, Parma, Modena and Romagna, and to transform itself into the Kingdom of Upper Italy. Cavour finally wrested from Napoleon III the authority to install himself in Naples in place of the Republicans and Garibaldi when the latter drove the Bourbons out of it.

After Cavour's death, his policy was carried on, but by then it was not France which was the leading industrial power on the continent, but Prussia. Each Prussian victory brought the young kingdom of Italy its share in the expansion; Venice after Sadowa, and Rome after Sedan.

The achievement of Italian unity was followed by an outburst of activity. Italian engineers won general admiration, and their bridges and canals were examples to the rest of Europe. In industry, Italy tried to develop away from the old crafts for which the country had been famous; but there was little coal, and the iron on Elba was not sufficient for the whole country. There were fortunately rather more resources for the chemical industry. In order to succeed in heavy industry, Italy had to rely more on ingenuity than on natural resources. Italy had been the first to introduce commerce into Europe and now the country's efforts were concentrated on it again. The elements of a transoceanic fleet were evolved from the extensive coastal shipping, and the first Italian vessels began to cross the Atlantic.

Nevertheless the excessive population presented a serious problem. Its density was too high, and was caused by a high birth rate rather than by longevity. Italy was therefore still at the stage which Europe had first reached on the eve of the industrial changes. There were few country districts in Italy except in the north which did not show the two infallible signs of poverty: famine and rickets. Italy, like England, exported as many able-bodied men as she could to America, but she also developed her own brand of emigration; large numbers of Italians slipped secretly across frontiers to France, Switzerland and North Africa. These emigrants remained loyal to the families they had left behind in Italy, and thus made substantial contributions to the state, whose finances showed a continual deficit.

But this emigration was not enough to compensate for deficiencies of industrialization. Ignorance and poverty kept alive certain picturesque features with which the Italians could well have dispensed, and maintained a body of peasants who were little more than relics left over from bygone centuries. One of the picturesque elements was banditry. In 1865, brigands were still the real rulers of the country districts of Palermo, for example, where they had their own law, the *omerta*, which they claimed went back to the days of the Normans. When the farmer harvested his corn, his oil or his wine, he had to pay tribute. At the end of the century according to official statistics the Mafia still numbered thousands of members who exploited the general fear of risks and the hatred felt for the gendarme who received his orders from Rome. The situation was serious not only in Sicily, but also in Calabria, and in many regions in southern and central Italy.

All this was the legacy of the wretched past. Venice had reached the lowest point of its decadence round about the 1840s when its palaces were in ruins, its squares were overgrown with grass, and its population dwindled to less than one hundred thousand inhabitants. At the close of the century the city was reviving and there were almost one hundred and fifty thousand inhabitants. New houses were built, the glass and textile industries were in full production, and maritime trade was making a fresh start. The same was true of Milan; of Naples, which was beginning to develop; and of Rome, the new secular capital, where the historical ruins were being classified and protected, and new and modern administrative buildings were being built.

Spain: Capitalism Encourages Disorder

Italy was being reorganized on modern lines, but Spain had not the same opportunity for doing so. The natural resources of Spain were exploited by foreign capital, and by English, French and Belgian engineers. For example, from 1861 the Carthagena zinc mines brought as many as twenty-five thousand people to live in the vicinity of Las Herrerias mines. The majority of Spain's railways too were built by foreign capital and engineers, and sometimes at a heavy loss, for the geography of the peninsula put so many obstacles in the way of the constructors. All these thousands of millions of pounds invested by foreigners shored up the economy of a country whose own inhabitants seemed to reject the demands of the modern world in order to cling to what remained of their past. The budget showed a continual deficit and the bulk of Spain's expenditure went on the upkeep of its army. This numbered two hundred thousand and was recruited with much difficulty by a system of conscription which gave exemption to cripples, invalids, defaulters, and those who were bought out; the latter class grew as the national finances became more and more shaky. A considerable part of this army was permanently immobilized in Cuba and the Philippines. Since the revolutions of 1855 the monasteries had emptied, but as Catholicism remained the state religion ecclesiastics formed a caste far more numerous than the businessmen. No one took the trouble to verify a nobleman's claim to his title: the number of hidalgos apparently amounted to something like a million. It was through this hard crust of age-old traditions that modernist ideas had to penetrate. In Spain as everywhere the reformers attempted to win adherents in the poverty-stricken country areas and towns, and among the discontented lower middle classes. Since there was no satisfactory outlet available in industrial life, the urge to change led to continual revolts; it was the root cause of an insecurity which never really succeeded in changing the country but unleashed an unending chain of disorders. There were movements against the clergy, against the monks, against the aristocracy, against the royal family. From 1835 to 1868 the crisis was latent. From 1868 to 1880, after driving out Isabella II, Spain tried every possible expedient: a military dictatorship, monarchy (with an Italian prince), a republic . . . Though Isabella's son reigned from 1876, he was unable to win over the legitimists of the north; from the Basque provinces to Catalonia, these recognized none but Don Carlos. That explained why Spain's military expenditure was so excessively high.

This perpetual civil war had an economic motive. The railways had helped to keep Madrid the most important city in Spain. It had nearly half a million inhabitants who made their living by genuine industrial activity. But the plateaux around it had emptied. Spain's entire population, outside the capital, appeared to be ebbing away to the coasts, attracted by the new maritime ventures, and by vine-growing. The region of Cadiz, for instance, supported two hundred thousand hard-working citizens. Some went to Santander, Santiago, Bilbao, or Carthagena, and many to the incomparable Barcelona, which clung tenaciously to its activity and showed every sign of becoming one of the most prosperous Mediterranean cities in the French style. Between Madrid, which was isolated at the centre and needed to set up a strong union at all costs, and these provinces which clung to their regional independence there was a continual struggle. Foreign capital gave as much support to local capitalism as it did to the construction of the railway which favoured Madrid, and so gave ammunition to both sides: the very modernization of Spain kept alive the conflict it sought to bring to a close.

INDUSTRIAL EUROPE SPREADS INTO AFRICA

European settlement in Africa was one of the outstanding phenomena of the late nineteenth century. In order to get there, the Europeans had had to cross the barrier which Islam had erected across the world from India to the Atlantic. This had already been extensively breached by France, as we have seen, through the newly-emerging nationalisms. Once this gap had been widened, Africa was open to every influence of the Western world.

The Defeat of Islam

For a full understanding of the situation, we must go first to Teheran, a capital reft by Russian and English ambitions. From 1857 the Shah had been travelling abroad and forming economic alliances. In 1864 the telegraph was working and astounding the crowds, whilst the learned men of Islam looked inside the wire for the hole through which the messages were transmitted. About 1870 a modern city was growing up around the huge English bank, known as the Imperial Bank, and endowed with the magical telegraphic address of 'Pehlevi' (a name which was to become that of a ruling house). This city soon boasted gas and trams. Good roads were constructed to link it up with the Caspian and the Persian Gulf. Here, between the equally balanced power of Russia and England, a new nation emerged which no longer owed anything to the 'unity' of Islam. It adopted Western numerals (known as Arabic though the Arabs count by letters) and the decimal coinages. French (and Western) thought brought a new stimulus to education. In 1896 when the ruler did not appear enough of a reformer, he fell victim to a plot. Progress swept him away.

As for Turkey, it was cut off on the eastern flank by England's advance to India, by Russia's advance across the steppes and by progress in Persia itself. It is true that the Sultan Mejid had achieved a master-stroke and was posing as victor in the Crimean War, which ended the quarrel over the Holy Places between Russia and the West with the fall of Sebastopol. Constantinople was growing. The sultans abandoned the old Seraglio and built new palaces on the Bosphorus, to the north of the Golden Horn. The suburbs of Galata with their many foreign inhabitants thus became the centre of the city. The Sultan Abdul Hamid, who was detested by the West, hoped to take advantage of this revival to re-establish the unity of Islam. He intrigued with Bismarck, strengthened his army, surrounded himself with Arabs and assumed the title of Caliph, which none of his predecessors had ventured to do. But his attempt to restore Islam did not succeed. Hated and lonely, he went in fear of his life, hiding first in one room then in another, terrified by the Young Turk movement which had succeeded in assassinating his predecessor. These Young Turks, carried away by the success of the Young Persians in Teheran (1896), abandoned the turban for the fez and took an interest in the economic advance which enabled Trebizond to benefit from the Persian renaissance. The Sultan-Caliph's great problem was to win them over with all speed by making himself the champion of modernism.

It was not the old masters of the Mediterranean, Italy and Spain, which reaped the benefit of its commercial revival; nor was it Turkey, although on the map the Sultan's nominal possessions were still considerable. But they were rarely put to any good use. If an attempt was made to bring fertile lands which had been lying fallow into cultivation, it turned out that they belonged to a mosque, or to the Sultan. The wretched farmer found himself in prison and his goods confiscated by the Seraglio, and not without a substantial rake-off for the local authorities.

For the Sultan's one over-riding and incessant preoccupation was to get money, a lot of money. One excellent reform was the reduction of the vast army to a well-equipped, well-disciplined corps of one hundred thousand men. At far less cost to itself, the sovereign power was now more secure against the revolts of subject peoples, but it was also more exposed to the danger of praetorian revolts. As further economy the Turk wrote off two-thirds of his fighting fleet, so as to be spared the trouble of equipping and maintaining it. Turkey's strategic position had until recently made it the focal point of the ambitions of neighbouring nations. Now these nations were conferring together to ensure that, under the close supervision of them all, no single one should reap the benefit of an easy windfall. Thanks to their efforts, the last of the sultans were left free to enjoy the pomp and luxury of power without any of its accompanying responsibilities.

So in the gardens of the Seraglio and the new palaces costly summerhouses and follies were built and valuable furniture and precious objects were installed. Six thousand servants were barely enough for this fabulous household, which also included a host of parasitic retainers. The food contracts show that one thousand two hundred sheep a day were taken into the palace kitchens. Although he had reduced his administrative expenses as much as possible, and encouraged the extortion of money out of his subjects, the Sultan did not scruple to borrow money to keep up this luxurious way of life. He was encouraged in this since he always found one or other of the Western nations eager to seek his favour.

The land was still rich and the people were stubborn, so the rural economy with its strong tradition of craftsmanship kept alive, in spite of the pretentious way of life of the court. Constantinople remained the city of mirages: six hundred thousand inhabitants were still herded together in wretched wooden shacks and the watchmen on the Galata Tower discovered five or six major fires a week in the quarter. The city was a medley of races, religions, nationalities. Yet the Franks, tolerated by the easygoing Sultan since it was in his interests to do so, seized the bulk of the business and built in stone; the suburb of Pera replaced the Phanariotes. When the railway linking Constantinople with Vienna was completed it became an advance-post of the European economy.

For a hundred years the collapse of the Turkish Empire had been confidently awaited; it was expected that Constantinople would become a market for Western goods. But there was no evidence of this in 1895. The masterpieces of craftsmanship still displayed in the bazaar seemed rather to prove the permanence of the economic and human structure of the Muslim worlds of continental Asia. And although it went underground the slave market was nevertheless very busy. Although the Christians were more numerous they were less active in local politics: the Greeks looked to Athens, the Armenians to Russia. The various Muslim peoples, in turn, were more preoccupied with their own countries of origin than with the fate of the old capi-

tal, and with every year that passed they drew a little farther away from the Turks, leaving it to them to criticize
the Seraglio and its antiquated politics. The Sultan, in spite
of his ambitions, was no longer regarded as master of a
world, the head of a religion covering the globe, but as a
local potentate whose insensate extravagance could no
longer be justified. The young generation of Turks in particular were ready to abandon dreams of world-wide
domination in order to work for the effective creation of a
limited country run on modern lines. Whether or not
Constantinople was to predominate in Turkey, it could no
longer claim to do so in Asia, Africa or the Mediterranean, which had been taken over by the economy of
the West.

In Egypt the Albanian Pharaohs were carrying on with
their programme: roads, canals, towns and palaces transformed the country. Ismail built Ismailia and improved
Alexandria, the population of which rose from two thousand inhabitants in 1800 to four hundred thousand in
1900, catching up with that of Cairo. The total population
of Egypt reached almost ten millions at the end of the
century. This was all accompanied by a great drive for
education, and an expansion of the universities and even
of popular education.

This progress was spectacular but short-lived. The
Egyptian people, the fellaheen, suddenly realized that they
belonged to a nation and called on Araby 'the Egyptian'
against their Albanian masters who represented the hated
Turkish rule. Turkey's influence had been incautiously revealed when Sultan Abdul Hamid deposed the Khedive
Ismail in 1879. Ismail's successor, the young Tewfik, was
in a most difficult position. His predecessors had spent
wildly and borrowed at heavy interest. It had been necessary to do so in order to modernize the country, but the
creditors were pressing; Tewfik, caught between Egyptian
nationalism, the claims of the Turkish Sultan, and the demands of French and English bankers, was compelled to
accept the 'protection' of England. The English acted
single-handed in 1881 when France delayed over her
reply.

The whole of North Africa was therefore cut off from Arabia, from which its conquerors had set out ten centuries earlier.

Europe's Future in Africa

We have described how the failure of the old-established Mediterranean countries to exploit their sea had enabled France to gain a footing in Algeria; and it is easy to see now how the French were able to extend their field of action to the whole of North Africa. First there was a sudden increase in the French and European populations in Algeria. This had three causes: the Crémieux decree granting naturalization to the Jews, the immigrations of Spaniards, Italians and Maltese who were also eligible for naturalization, and the considerable French immigration since 1871. Some Arabs objected, some considered naturalization themselves, although they hesitated for fear of betraying the Law and the Prophet. In any case the major language was either French or Sabir, and work was done more and more on European lines. Unfortunately much of the work consisted of cutting down the woods spared by the gigantic fires of 1865, 1881 and many others caused by imprudent new colonists. But farms also were being built, with earthen floors, on the lands granted to settlers by the state. It was hard work. The draining of the Mitija was also a miracle of rural heroism. More than fifty villages were founded for the refugees from Alsace and Lorraine. Work was started on a land register which even allotted some ground to the natives. In addition, improvements were made in the organization of workers, the miners were being exploited, roads were opened up, and caravan traffic across the Sahara had been resumed. The volume of shipping increased at the ports and new districts were built in Algiers around the old Kasbah and along the busy port.

The railway followed the coast and had reached the very heart of Tunisia, taking French power as far as Tunis. It had been laid down by the French, whose task was made easier by the imprudence of the Bey. He was nominally a

Turkish official, but in fact independent; he had borrowed money from all over Europe, especially from France, without thinking too much about how it was to be repaid. It was to put his finances on a sounder footing that the Treaty of Bardo in 1881 associated a French resident with the government of the country. The army of occupation numbered forty-three thousand men, and although it was quickly reduced to ten thousand, it brought in its train a crowd of Algerians, more Arab than French, who followed their new rulers hoping to improve their frugal way of life by accompanying the spearhead of the modernization drive. At all events, the French were now firmly entrenched in Algeria and the way was prepared for the supremacy of the French language and way of life, as well as for French institutions, in spite of the other Europeans, particularly the Italians, who up to that time were the most numerous and the most active.

The new French influence not only resulted in the efficient ordering of the budget, which doubled from 1883 to 1886, but also vastly improved the city of Tunis. New quarters were built in what had previously been the refuse dump, which the Jews had been obliged to empty from time to time. The drainage of land for building brought Tunis nearer the sea, where a great artificial harbour was planned in the creek with its picturesque fishermen. These were the first stages of a far-reaching programme. As the tribes fleeing from the Christians made their way towards southern Algeria, a growing number of immigrants was arriving from the Mediterranean countries, and these all helped to draw the country away from its Eastern traditions and to link it to the modern way of life, which was dominated by French speculation. At the other end of the Atlas range the supervision of the Algerian borders led to the exploration of Morocco. The most daring of these explorations was that of Charles de Foucauld who crossed the Atlas Mountains and travelled across areas of the south where hardly anyone had ventured before. The region of Rabat at Fez was, however, better known, and people from every nation could be found travelling there. The question then arose whether Morocco should be independent, under international supervision, or French. In any case Morocco was opening up to foreign influence. The Moroccans were no longer forbidden to offer hospitality to the Christians. European greed found effective ways of flattering the Sultan. His personal fortune was mixed up with that of the state, after the Turkish custom, but he had no need to borrow, for the income from his taxes and the gifts which accompanied them was substantial. French settlement in what was still called Barbary China was to be no easy task. The process was the result of a vast international movement which involved Europe in the seizure of the whole of Africa.

Europe's appropriation of Africa was the greatest outcome of its drive to expand, the last and strongest of the series which emanated from the old world. And no other power, even among those which competed with Europe for Asia, thought of disputing the European claim to Africa. Nevertheless, Africa only forms a single continent for the convenience of modern geographical classification; in reality this great and varied land mass is criss-crossed by innumerable trends and currents. Its Atlantic coast, as we have seen, had long been exploited by the slave-traders. Then the traders seeking gold, ivory, fruit, cocoa and wood established their trade settlements, but as yet did not venture into the interior. But the progress of steam navigation and the creation of ports of call stocked with the coal these ships required meant that the coastal ports were being developed. Then Faidherbe emerged from the island of Gorea, occupied Dakar and ventured a little way into the interior. All around these coastal bases patches of oil began to appear in the sea. The same phenomena occurred in the east as in the west. In the east, for instance, the Piedmontese Sabato explored a region which gradually began to take shape as Eritrea, around Massawa. England penetrated up the Zambesi and German merchants traded around Zanzibar. Along the whole of this coastal belt the traces of the great commercial empire of Zanzibar formed a powerful motive for penetration inland. The Arabs by the Red Sea, along the route from India, had as we have seen developed a kind of thalassocracy. The Sultan of Zanzibar claimed sovereign power over the territories in the interior of Africa into which Arab caravans penetrated in search of slaves, spices and ivory, which he re-sold to India. These warlike caravans relied for their defence on young Negroes, kidnapped and trained to serve as escorts. They no longer bothered greatly about concealing the routes they followed, and so opened up the way to adventurers from Europe. Something in the nature of a European condominium in fact controlled the Sultan of Zanzibar, who was soon consoled for the loss of his empire since the pressure of Christian competition quickly filled his coffers. Lastly, there was an extensive thrust into the interior from the Dutch territories in South Africa. The north seemed to fall into an easy division between the English in Egypt and the French in Tunisia and Algeria; the Italians tried to gain a foothold somewhere in between.

There remained central Africa itself. The problems it raised were complicated by a geographical error. From ancient times there had been argument about the course of the Nile, the miracle river of the desert. It was known from Negro folk-lore and from several explorations that there were enormous lakes in the centre of Africa; it was out of this lake Zaïre that the Nile was believed to flow, as well as the river which emptied itself into the kingdom of the Congo. At the end of the eighteenth century the Portuguese had made a last attempt to link up Angola with Mozambique. Little is known about what these Pombeïros achieved on their journey, which continued into the early years of the nineteenth century. Once again in 1843 Graça followed in their footsteps, apparently with no more success. The Portuguese were followed by the English. From 1887 they penetrated inland in their turn, in search of the central empire which might possibly have become the refuge of the mythical Prester John. In 1870 Livingstone set out, followed a few years later by Stanley.

The Partition of Africa

This time a new era was beginning. Western explorers were becoming increasingly confident in their methods, their tools, ships, weapons, and medicine chest. They drew up more accurate maps, and were quicker at understanding native dialects; among the Bantu tribes, for instance, forty, and ultimately fifty, variant dialects were recorded. Then Stanley undertook his fantastic expedition on the Livingstone (as he wished to re-name the old Zaïre which in the end retained the more politic name of Congo). The journey covered twelve thousand miles of jungle, forest, reeds, lakes, cataracts, waterfalls and mountains, including the Mountains of the Devil! It took three years and cost hundreds of lives, three or four of the casualties being white men. Stanley was, however, the first to give an informed description of the heart of Africa (1877). On landing at Marseilles he found waiting for him two emissaries from the King of the Belgians. For the past fifteen years Leopold had been looking for a colonial venture, not so much because he was an explorer at heart but because he was a far-sighted businessman and had shrewdly appraised the wealth which skilful exploitation of these new worlds had heaped up in England's coffers. Stanley would have preferred to work for England, but the latter rejected the explorer's offers. Consequently he agreed to become Leopold's man, or rather, officially the representative of an association which was called in succession the *Association de Géographes*, then the *Internationale Africaine*, then the *Études du Haut-Congo*, and finally emerged as the *Association Internationale du Haut-Congo*. Its aim was to root out the remnants of slavery from the Congo and to carry to the Negroes the Gospel and the benefits of civilization. It was to work through national committees in several countries. It would perhaps be more to the point to ask what was Leopold's aim: it was to gain a vast stretch of territory for himself, and the means which would enable him to do this were the credits which the Belgian banks were obliged to grant their king. Leopoldville was founded in 1882 by Stanley, who had gone back to the Congo in fulfilment of the Association's statute which sought to 'set up civilized establishments along the banks, to conquer the country by peaceful means, to cast it in a new mould more in keeping with modern ideas, to foster states in the bosom of which the European trader would fraternize with the Negro, the African trader, and from which murder and the slave trade would be banished for ever'. Meanwhile in order to resume the exploration of the country, this time from west to east and moving towards the Nile, Stanley made an agreement with the Arabs and used their squads of slave hunters. It is only fair to note that while Belgian money was enabling the European to replace the Arab, a movement was growing to transform numerous Negro states, previously warlike, into agricultural countries where manioc was grown, the forest cleared, and agricultural produce sold rather than prisoners of war. But during these early years the Congo was far from bringing Leopold the quick profits he had been expecting.

This did not, however, prevent the Belgian venture from arousing much keen jealousy. For more than ten years Savornan de Brazza, starting from the Gabon estuary, had been pushing into the interior on expeditions which took him too to the Congo. He recruited troops on the spot and exploited native rivalries to establish himself in an enormous tract of country. He laid claim to Stanley's river and established an impregnable post on the banks with a garrison consisting of four Negroes.

The Germans in Zanzibar, for their part, made many marches westward in order to annex as much as they could of the region of the Great Lakes. In such circumstances the *Association Internationale* did not appear a very formidable rival: there was open talk in Berlin of carving out a good empire at its expense. The Portuguese in Mozambique and Angola fought bitterly to assert their historic rights, and England suddenly gave them noble support after having considered sharing with Germany. In short, central Africa became a great centre of rivalry between the European powers. There was, however, no question of actual war: however eager the new nations were to paint the maps of the world in symbolical colours, the forests, swamps, and fevers of Africa did not inspire them with the requisite greed. Each power was concerned mainly with playing off its rivals. It used its traders and engaged in diplomatic disputes, the more readily since both Leopold and Portugal appeared an easy prey. Bismarck suggested that France should convene an international conference on Africa in Paris. France affected to prefer Berlin. The purpose was to ensure 'the most favourable conditions for the development of trade and civilization in Africa'. In practice the Act of 1885 established a kind of working rule: Stanley, Brazza and the Germans in south-west and east Africa, the English in the Sudan and the south, majestically presided over the distribution of flags. The 'conqueror' arriving in a village negotiated with the chief, offered him gifts, all with the greatest solemnity, and handed him the flag of his own nation: the conquest was completed. Brazza found flags a more valuable item of baggage than footwear. In future, treaties were to be notified to the European chanceries. Each power naturally had great bundles of treaties, except perhaps England, which more often than not merely marked her zones of influence on the map, often not even bothering to go there, accustomed as she was to being the only nation on the spot. Moreover, and this was the most important of all, the Act of Berlin granted to each owner of a stretch of coast first claim to its hinterland. This effectively barred England's route to the north. On the other hand, in return for heavy sacrifices on the banks of the Congo River, the Congo was recognized as an independent state, charged only with the obligation to leave trade free and equal for all. The Brussels Parliament resigned itself in turn, with reluctance, to allow its constitutional King to become an absolute monarch in the Congo. France was momentarily appeased by the promise of a right of preemption and allowed the measure to go through.

Leopold, though sovereign ruler, was short of money and deeply in debt and the Congo, far from bringing money in, swallowed up enormous amounts of capital.

The Belgian Bank was no longer adequate, and the Belgian Government was forced to lend millions to its sovereign. He had to negotiate the right to establish customs duties in order to bring in the resources needed for the abolition of slavery. No sooner had he obtained this concession than the world witnessed the strange spectacle of Leopold behaving as a landowner more brutally than the harshest slave-master in pre-abolitionist America. It was the rule of the Chicote, a whip made of hippopotamus hide. It was all the easier for the régime to go unchallenged since the last Arab rivals were crushed in 1893. Negroes were recruited compulsorily, populations were transplanted, and forced labour was instituted particularly in the rubber plantations; 'red rubber' as the opposition called it. Leopold became the most colossal landowner in the world, living sumptuously in Europe, building palaces and collecting mistresses on an equally lavish scale.

There were sporadic insurrections, some indignation, and a good deal of jealousy. Nevertheless, the change which had come over the management of affairs in the Congo had noticeable repercussions in several other parts of Africa. France took possession of Madagascar, and England of Zanzibar: each allowed the other a more or less free rein. But Madagascar was shaken by revolts; costly expeditions had to be sent and many lives sacrificed. It was found necessary to depose Queen Ranavalona and introduce direct rule. In the Niger, France and England had joined forces to oppose the claims of Samory, the champion of Islam. The French, in pursuit of slave hunters, reached the Chad: thus at last achieving the internal link between west and north Africa. It was chiefly in order to extend this internal domination as far as the region of the Upper Nile and of Bahr El-Ghazal that the Marchand expedition set out in 1896 from the Congo in the direction of the Sudan. Two years later, after innumerable adventures, it reached the post of Fashoda only a few days before the English expedition commanded by Kitchener arrived at the same point, having come up the Nile. Although France was traditionally a militant nation she ceded Fashoda to the English. In colonial territories French policy was peaceful, more concerned with human contacts and economic progress than with spectacular *coups*.

A whole generation of young colonial leaders was now growing up, following in the great tradition of the Faidherbes and the Brazzas, and adding new lustre to it by their magnificent achievements. There was Galliéni on the Niger and in Madagascar, Laperrine in the Sahara and Charles de Foucauld exploring unknown Morocco. Lyautey has described how this new spirit came into being. In 1889 he was received at Saigon by Galliéni, who asked him for the books and papers he had brought in his kitbag (the tactical manual, army service book and other aide-memoires). Galliéni firmly tied them up into a parcel. 'Forget the lot,' he said, 'nothing they contain has anything to do with our job out here. We have to begin by observing, listening, reflecting and re-reading Joseph Chaillez: colonial policy is not so much a matter of continual expansion as of carefully planned progress. A European capital cannot possibly administer or govern by *its* methods, its laws and its European officials . . . In order to pacify a country one has to use peaceful means.'

The brilliance of France's industrial development during these years enabled it to rely confidently on this policy that was so essentially English in conception; at this time England, whose economic superiority was now threatened, was embarking on the most terrible war in the whole of her colonial history in South Africa, although its record there had been one of great tolerance up to that point.

CONCLUSION

Danger Ahead

ONE CAPITALISM OUSTS ANOTHER

IN 1890 the stock exchanges of London, Paris, Berlin and New York controlled the economic progress of the whole world. The liberal middle class had reached the height of its power and influence. There was, however, a tremendous difference between the businessman of 1890 and the bourgeois of 1830. An entirely new society was coming into being which called for a new type of person, was organized in new ways and used new methods. Above all it was preoccupied with a new and unusual source of anxiety. Hitherto the European bourgeois had made money at the expense of the other classes and the other continents; it had left it to providence to take care of poverty and relied on progress to eradicate it. In 1890, those in control of Europe's economic life were obliged to organize and integrate the European working classes who were now powerful enough to make themselves felt as an essential factor in this evolution; they were also forced to reassess Europe's place in a world which had itself awakened to new life.

We have noted that the economic history of the 1880s posed this problem in the form of a paradox. These years saw the introduction of a range of technical processes invented in the new scientific laboratories which had the effect of stimulating the economy even further. During these years, too, great factories were set up on the continent with modernized plant, and the mechanical civilization they created was far more powerful than the one which excited the progressives in 1850. But at the same time this period was marked by the biggest drop in prices yet experienced in Europe's history, and that without the accompaniment of revolution or of war; a profound transformation of society was taking place.

The year 1850 had been, as we have seen, that of the

railway, and the vogue for railways persisted up to 1880, when Freycinet drew up his grandiose projects for it in France. The fact was that the business world was under the illusion that the mileage returns from lines built in 1880 would equal that of the lines built in 1850. Unfortunately, it is quite obvious that branch lines of small secondary centres, on which moreover traffic was slower, could never bring in as much as the great main lines. In 1882 thousands of miles of track built by the French Government could not find a bidder, and the exchequer had to bear the cost until almost the end of the century. Furthermore, the *Compagnie de l'Ouest*, for instance, managed its affairs so badly that it had to be nationalized in 1909. It was the same in Belgium; the state was obliged to buy back certain lines, and doubled its network in 1873; in 1880 it built three-quarters of the railways and almost completed the system in 1908. In Germany the completion of the railway system had largely been facilitated by the war indemnity paid by France. All the same the Prussian Government also had to buy back the networks of Hanover, Hesse and Nassau. The Imperial Government bought back the Alsace-Lorraine network and set up an organization that by and large turned the railways into a state concern though it was opposed by some countries, among them Bavaria. In Prussia the state lines increased from three thousand to nearly twenty-five thousand miles, while the private lines fell from something like eight thousand to less than two thousand. This concentration of railways in government hands is worth noting, since it could be considered the beginning of state capitalism. In the 1880s financiers were continually complaining of the small profits now to be made on the railways. The fact was that the concentration of lines, the simplified and reduced rates, no longer made profits possible except for very large concerns. By 1900, only the very big French companies had come near to repaying the credits borrowed from the government. Only the Prussian railways were bringing their owner, the government, substantial profits; moreover these remained outside parliamentary control and made possible a close connection between the railway and the military administrations. A similar situation was developing with the canals and roads; the age of individual enterprise on the English pattern of the 1830s was definitely over. Only vast organized systems could meet the costs and guarantee profits. These hard facts were obvious only to a very small group of thinkers who met with such a hostile reception when they forecast the end of small-scale middle-class enterprise that they did not dare express openly either their belief in 'state control' or their 'socialism'.

This trend towards concentration in transport was equally apparent in other spheres of economic life. Financiers were now familiar with the rhythm of crises. When the currency circulation of the bank of issue increased, the increased number of bills and acceptances indicated widespread activity by private enterprise. A large number of industrialists attempted to try their luck. The consumer's market, strongly influenced by advertisement and by a growing volume of publicity, made its choice from the mass of new products and those it rejected piled up in the factories which soon had to close down. Then the discount rate rose. Credit tightened. Reserves dwindled, the issue of paper currency slowed down and the crisis had arrived. The small manufacturer faced bankruptcy, total ruin, or at best the sale of his business at a low rate to a much larger concern whose floating capital was substantial enough to surmount the credit difficulties provoked by the rise in discount. Consequently there occurred vast ebbing and flowing movements of credit, which assumed an approximately five-yearly rhythm.

Each period of recession was characterized by concentration. This was so intense that private family capital, the bourgeois capital of the 1830s, could no longer cope with it. The joint stock company was essential, since that alone could make good in each phase of prosperity the retrenchments which had been imposed by the slump. In France, three hundred companies a year were being founded in 1880 and more than a thousand in 1900. In Germany there were more than two thousand new ones by 1885, and approximately four thousand by 1900; these latter figures included only the *Aktien Gesellschaft* or very large businesses, small limited liability companies being much more numerous.

A large number of these joint stock companies were banks, which were becoming more and more necessary to provide floating capital for businesses. The development of banks was widespread in England and in France, but in Germany it was phenomenal. In France the deposit banks already had two hundred and fifty branches in 1890 and the total passed the thousand mark at the beginning of the twentieth century. In Germany the banking organization was more complex. There were a great many regional and local banks, and it was by direct or indirect control of them that the great central organisms grew to vast proportions. At the opening of the twentieth century, the *Deutsche Bank* participated directly in the management of thirty banks and indirectly in that of fifty-seven. These growing organisms, sometimes monstrous in size, amassed a large quantity of deposits for the three great Western countries, France, England and Germany. These must have amounted to something like four hundred million pounds in 1880 and nearly two thousand million twenty years later. The bank completely dominated industrial credit. Any business concern however well equipped from which it withheld its support, especially in the rather risky economies such as that of Germany, would certainly go bankrupt or would be compelled to merge with a more important firm or one more favoured by the bank. Yet the bank was able to accumulate such vast deposits only by constant contact with a growing and increasingly trustful clientele. It was these who, in actual practice, controlled the placing of shares, thus playing in the distribution of long-term credit a rôle equivalent to the one they played in short-term credit. Hence the enormous power wielded by these enormous banking houses which erected their proud façades in the new capitals of 1900. In Germany, four great banks practically shared out between them the financial market of the whole Empire by a gentleman's agreement. The *Dresdner Bank*, for instance, controlled the steel and electrical industries, as well as business concerns in west Africa and Brazil; the *Deutsche Bank* was more concerned with communications, chemicals, and also the central European and Turkish markets.

Behind this concentration of banking and finance, an industrial concentration was also in progress. In France the owners of coalmines and foundries entered into joint agreements known as *comptoirs*. In 1876 in Germany the Westphalian coalmines had, as we have seen, agreed to fix prices, a move towards organization which was a reaction from the fever of the *Gründerjahre*. In 1890 came a further step: a cartel organized sales; three years later it controlled half the country's production by a merger with the briquette union and the coke syndicate. Similarly, cartels were set up for steel, iron and metallurgical plant (the *Stahlwerksverband*). We have seen that from the beginning the electricity industry was concentrated. Under the direction of Rathenau, the AEG joined forces with Siemens to exercise almost absolute control over the whole of German production. The *Kalisyndikat* was created in the same way. Powerful new men came to the fore, amongst them Kirdorf, Thyssen and Krupp in the Rhineland.

In reality, economic power, though organized empirically, was nevertheless as closely knit as political power at the end of the nineteenth century, and it is important not to regard it merely as an outward expression of the personality of some captain of industry or influential financier. Industrial concentration proceeded at such a pace, because of technical progress and under the impact of the long slump, that in effect it created an economic administration. This was no longer on the classic lines of middle-class liberalism, but it employed an army of officials who were as active and influential in the nation as the officials in the public services.

The innumerable employees of the banking houses and the industrial managements really were officials. The hierarchy, though it may have been less obvious, nevertheless exerted great power; the head of the system was not parliament but the boards of directors. In principle these bodies were responsible to the general body of shareholders. In fact the majority of shareholders empowered their banks to negotiate on their behalf and the zeal and vigilance of a few bankers were all that was needed to ensure the stability of the board. Administrative officials dealt with one transaction after another whether or not there was any connection between them. Plurality of seats thus reinforced economic solidarity and added a new 'princely' hierarchy of directors, in which each man's rank was determined by the number of 'seats' at his disposal. It was a far cry from the middle-class employer paternally managing a small factory of some tens or even hundreds of workers. This was a polysynody of great aristocrats which exercised absolute control over hundreds of thousands or even millions of workers.

The new social régime needed new men to fill posts at every level of its hierarchies. Up to 1880 the problem of education had been chiefly a political one: the elector had to be educated, and the major subjects had been philosophy and the teaching of liberty, law and politics. After 1880 the problem was increasingly a technical one. The controversy on the problem of 'special' education in France towards 1870 provides an illustration. Whilst secondary education in the *lycées* continued to teach Latin rhetoric, Victor Duruy had selected for special education some young men who had not studied Latin but wished to be initiated into the modern disciplines of science. Classical instruction held its ground for nearly fifteen years against this despised competition; it made concessions; in order to save Latin it did away with the old-fashioned exercises in Latin verse, and split up the *bachot* so that the second part could be either scientific or philosophical, to the great despair of cultured minds for whom philosophy remained the true end of education. But the special education continued and began to attack the privileges of the *lycées* cautiously at first, then in strength; finally it organized a system of 'modern' education without Latin, and with its own literary and scientific divisions. In 1892 it triumphantly achieved parity with the old *bachot*. In 1894 the two teaching bodies were merged. This merger was all the more important since a marked increase in the numbers attending *lycées* took place at the same time. Every year this new economic way of life called for more officials, more engineers, more business managers: the old middle-class grounding in Latin and philosophy was no longer adequate.

England, as we have seen, remained sentimentally attached to its Victorian economy even after 1890. Its universities turned out clergymen and theologians: the sons of great families went there to acquire a veneer of culture.

Technical education was equally limited. An official report in 1884 deplored the total lack of elementary institutions, and the scarcity of higher education. It was customary in England for the businessman and the technician to be trained within the firm itself, which naturally made it much easier for sons to make a career in the family business in which they served an apprenticeship under covenant. Yet the incessant demand for labour which characterized this vigorously expanding economy did not deprive the poor man's sons of all hope: he too made his way in the world. Starting as one of many, he proudly attained a directorship forty years later. Nevertheless a systematic modern education was vitally necessary. Many English scientists (or scientists who had migrated to England) heard the call of science in the great public lectures of the Royal Society. When a well-known expert was lecturing, he easily attracted several hundred attentive listeners, most of whom had just come from the office, the laboratory or the shop, in search of a little knowledge. As in the age of enlightenment, it was through personal contacts, chance meetings, the friendship formed between an expert and his faithful disciple, that the experts of the future were recruited.

After 1850 the secularization of Oxford was decided upon, but it was not until 1870 that the monopoly of examinations was taken from the old medieval universities and that examining bodies were set up in London with power to grant degrees to the pupils of the independent schools. These were springing up here and there in cities such as Birmingham and Manchester. However, the well-known Industrial Museum at South Kensington was beginning to disseminate elementary and secondary technical education. Although the universities were slow to widen their scope, they began to acquire laboratories in modest premises presided over by some great scientist such as Faraday or Maxwell. Modern higher education began to take shape in 1880.

In France, too, higher education still preserved its middle-class character at about this same period. The lecture-halls of famous professors were crowded with fashionable people, men of learning and wealthy young men, rather than with students. It was not until 1875 and the advent of Liard that higher education began to be more concerned with turning out technicians than with philosophizing for the benefit of the cultured people. It was only at the end of the century that the faculties gradually overcame their administrative autonomy and were grouped into universities. We know how wretchedly equipped were the laboratories of Berthelot and especially of Pasteur. The great scientific movement was almost as slow to get under way in France as in England. Nevertheless France had her schools, *Polytechnique*, *Normale Supérieure* and *Centrale*, already long-established. To these new schools were being added, built in the same spirit; particularly the *École des Sciences Politiques* founded by Taine and Boutmy and intended to train suitable men for the new public and private administrative posts. Then too there was the *École des Hautes Études*, which through Duruy's foresight answered in advance the complaints set out by Renan in *La Réforme Intellectuelle et Morale*—a treatise in which the historian and the philologist deplore the lack of technical training in French culture. The great reformers of 1890 urged on the development of the university in the hope that it would succeed in absorbing all the special schools born of the imperial tradition.

Renan attributed part of Germany's victory to the excellence of its universities. These had, in fact, been regarded as a model throughout all the latter half of the nineteenth century. They had forged the idea of German unity and they celebrated the victory of the Empire as their victory. Most of the old universities had doubled their numbers. Faculties of political economy had been inspired by the teachings of List, while the faculties of philosophy split into two sections, history and sciences. The system of seminars brought masters and students into more direct contact for practical work also, and the system of the *Privat-dozent* enabled men of talent to use their popularity with the students in order to become candidates for official chairs, thus undermining the position of the old-fashioned lecturers by competition. Seminars and *Privat-dozents* competed with each other for students who made a point of going the rounds of three or four universities before settling down in one of them. This competition encouraged the public authorities of a university city to keep excellent libraries and laboratories, and led to a close liaison between research and teaching within the framework of the states of the Empire. The staff of German universities had such exceptional privileges that in contrast with the situation in France legislation sought rather to reduce than to extend them. In 1880, the imprisonment of members of university councils was actually limited to a fortnight! The life of the student guilds which Germans sometimes liked to trace back to the Middle Ages, with their curious customs (particularly the duel, the *Mensur*), dated in fact from the time when rapid progress took the universities from their medieval structure of the 1830s to the large-scale capitalist structure of the 1880s; so that in only two generations the whole of the middle-class era was spanned.

Economists, lawyers, engineers, technicians of every kind, armed with testimonials in England and diplomas in Germany, filled the new posts created by the capitalist economy. Renan made the suggestion that a country's educational system was a clear indication of its worth. Germany was methodical, erudite, ambitious, confident; England cautious, self-assured, haughty; and France divided between the technical achievements of her schools and the too-generalized culture of her university.

The 1880s also witnessed a general encouragement of primary education. The school set out to attract the most gifted young men of the nation in order to carry them towards posts in private businesses or with the government by a process known as 'social capillarity'. Schools were opened in the countryside. It need hardly be said that though the nation's hierarchies were being radically changed and Republican statesmen in France (Ferry and Berthelot in particular) did all they could to make the new capitalist structure democratic, it still remained easier for the rich than for the poor to attain the key positions. A curious instance of this was provided in France between 1789 and 1880. Higher education for girls created at the instigation of Camille Sée was at first free. It was a failure. The municipal schools could get no pupils. The idea was then conceived of making it appeal to its 'natural' clientèle, so the education consequently had to be paid for; and it was soon a great success. It is hardly necessary to recall here that the cost of the actual tuition represented only a fraction of the total cost incurred in a young man's education. The son of a peasant or a workman was hardly in a position to embark on the long course of secondary and advanced study. The lower middle classes sometimes went as far as the fourth grade, or to a public school in England, and there were various generous schemes afoot to carry education to wider sections of society; the University of Cambridge launched the University Extension movement, offering a course of popular lectures designed to cover the normal school syllabus in three years and enabling students who had passed a qualifying examination to take the final years of the university course. The popular universities in France, and even more in Belgium, also made provision for this movement, which continued throughout the expansive phase of the modern technocratic society.

The nineteenth century offered many striking instances of tradesmen's sons attaining the highest honours by way of either science or industry, but it was comparatively rare for such eminence to be achieved by the sons of peasants or of artisans, or by anyone from the ranks of those who in the 1830s were known as 'the people'. However, a middle-class parent still deplored the fact that he had to send his children to universities and schools in which they might have to rub shoulders with the sons of the people. A large new lower middle class was also emerging from which the army of officials was recruited; this class was dominated by powerful industrial and financial circles.

And what of the people? Michelet no longer regarded them as synonymous with the working class which had come into being in the great urban centres, and which might more fittingly be called the proletariat from 1880 onwards.

A SETBACK FOR THE MIDDLE CLASS

The closing years of the nineteenth century also brought about a growth in population. This time, however, the rise was due not to an increase in fertility, since this was in fact steadily declining, but to improved expectation of life. Although man's life-span now extended into the middle years of the fertility period, this increased longevity was from 1880 onwards no longer accompanied by a rise in the birth rate. The two-fold movement from the country to the town, and from the agricultural fringes of Europe towards the industrial areas of Europe or the New World, meant that populations were being shifted by rail or by boat on a hitherto unprecedented scale. The people were moving along the channels opened up by the techniques of capitalism. The rise in the birth rate was not very marked, and a few years later the rise was to slow down, then stop altogether.

The urban working population took on a new lease of life in this time of flux. Amongst these uprooted people the first stirrings of a new spirit were beginning, a feeling of brotherhood uniting all the workers of the world. Not that socialism had suddenly won the day: its growth in the early years was hesitant and impeded by the continual fluctuations of the economy. It was nevertheless favoured by a slight but continuous rise in wages. The great mechanized industries paid best and gradually absorbed the ragged proletariat, the victims of the sweating system, but not without terrible sufferings: the last days of the rural hand-loom weavers were agonizing whether it was in Cambresis, Silesia or Lancashire. Parliamentary investigations in every country revealed the poverty of these families, toiling away fourteen hours a day at their old looms to earn barely enough to buy bread. The fact was that mechanized industry now worked at such cheap rates that the craftsman was being driven out from many sections of the economy, and particularly from textile manufacture. In the factories, there was as yet no question of a systematic organization of work, and the multiplication of machines necessitated a new team work and created a new feeling of solidarity. In the towns the building of new housing estates for the newcomers brought working-class families into the closest contact with each other and created for them an urban setting which, though still rudimentary, was already establishing a uniform pattern of living amongst workers all over the world. Shrewd minds were shaping this new army for the coming class struggle; Marx believed he had seen the first signs of it in England twenty-five years ahead of the times.

A new working-class solidarity was beginning to emerge. In 1880 most of the workers were craftsmen in the direct tradition of the old guilds, and the rapid or gradual disappearance of the old rules had unleashed rivalries which set tradesman against tradesman. The people of 1900 still bore the mark of the harsh treatment meted out to them by the early liberalism, but pressure of circumstances forced the working classes to recognize that solidarity was far more essential than competition. The poor began to realize that it was foolish to try to succeed in isolation. Shared migrations and the common difficulties involved in settling on new lands or in the vast collective tenements and new suburbs gave them a better opportunity to bring about communal improvements in material conditions. Common funds, capable of financing common action, came into being side by side with the old savings banks advocated by the philanthropists of 1830. Mutual aid societies and unions were modelled on the pattern of those in Germany, which claimed to be the inventor of social insurance.

The great problem was the recruitment of labour. Labour exchanges were a French idea of about 1848, which had gradually gained ground under the Second Empire without any backing from the public authorities, who preferred their own system of employment bureaux run by each mayoralty. Other countries took up this idea and it almost succeeded in Austria and Belgium. The power of the unions in England succeeded in establishing it there. Each union tried to control the labour market by employing a special secretariat; they also made use of publicity which was timid by modern standards but nevertheless well-planned. In 1876 at Philadelphia, in 1880 at Le Havre, workers' conferences put the question of labour exchanges on their agenda. In 1888 the Paris Municipal Council granted the Paris Labour Exchange a huge office block in the Rue Jean-Jacques Rousseau. It included an assembly hall seating one thousand five hundred. The early days were difficult. The Caterers' Bureau succeeded in finding employment for two-thirds of its members, but the labourers were not nearly so well served. It was also not clear whether the Exchange should support other needs of the workers. Numerous though the exchanges were, they were soon quite inadequate and it was necessary to plan the building of a Central Exchange near the Place de la République.

In any move towards working-class solidarity, the problem of labour recruitment involved that of wages. The laws of 1871 in England and of 1884 in France opened up a wide field of action to the unions: each new crisis led to fresh unrest and agitation among the workers. Sometimes the new proletariat would erupt with an isolated act of anarchy; sometimes a group plotted together; there was the attempt to dynamite Wilhelm II at the unveiling of the statue of *Germania* in 1889, and the French *Chambre des Députés* in 1896. President Carnot was assassinated in 1898, King Umberto in 1900. The working-class organizations openly condemned these anarchist moves, and the International excluded anarchist theorists from its membership. Anarchism, a label rather than a programme, was abandoned almost everywhere except in Spain. For though the anarchist movement had its theorists like Kropotkin, it was chiefly the symbol of a discontent which working-class organization alone could cure. This derived its strength from the struggle for better living conditions, higher wages and more stable employment. Once strikes were legalized in 1880 they were widely used in times of crisis. Strikes affected the exploitation of raw material in the Borinage and in the Ruhr; and were used with even greater effect against the means of communication (as in the Italian telegraph service in 1893). A strike could rally enormous crowds around its committees; there were as many as thirty-five thousand in St Petersburg in 1896. As the proletariat organized itself, it grew increasingly conscious of its strength. Jules Guesde reproached the Germans with not putting enough revolutionary fire into their action. Pelloutier urged the use of the general strike. The ground was prepared for the great waves of general revolutionary strikes which marked the opening years of the twentieth century.

This movement had a considerable revolutionary element in it and originated largely in Paris. In 1880 Paris was undoubtedly the city in which large-scale industry was the least developed of any in the world. Average-sized businesses with craftsmen operating in suburban workshops were still the rule. In this respect, French working-class agitators used similar methods to those of 1789, and the quarrels of the Commune were revived after twenty years. But it was in France, too, that the struggle for working-class education was strongest, precisely because the frontier between the proletariat and the lower-middle class was less clearly defined. It was this democratic opinion which supported Ferry's educational programme and gave colour and strength to the work of Pelloutier, a bourgeois in the service of the people. Outside France, the demands of the workers were more closely linked to their conditions of work. Americans were the first to stipulate an eight-hour day, and the celebration of the First of May as Labour Day. Differences began to emerge in temperament and outlook between the various countries. Their delegates clashed in speeches and motions at international conferences. At Zurich in 1893, a great Dutch trade unionist reminded his audience that chauvinism existed among socialists just as among the middle classes. In 1889, the year of the birth of the Second International, the Congress of Paris was divided between socialists and trade unionists. As for the Germans, they had turned socialism into an enormous political party of more than a million members in 1890; but it grew too quickly, lost its fighting strength, and collaborated in parliament with the middle-class parties.

Amidst all this upheaval and conflict of ideas, one fact was indisputable: the proletariat existed and its strength was growing. Intellectuals of every order recognized it, from Lyautey to Léon Bourgeois. Sorel discussed the problem of violence, the English discussed Henri George's book on progress and poverty; the readiest answers to the proletarian problems of the day were found in Karl Marx.

In 1887, the young Lenin was seventeen when he learned that his brother had been hanged for complicity in a plot to kill Alexander III. In his subsequent embittered search for a more effectual way of reviving and emancipating the people, it was in the works of Karl Marx that he discovered the guidance he was seeking.

A SETBACK FOR EUROPE

The 1890s marked the zenith of European power; Europe's conquests were still continuing in Africa and Asia, but it was the peak of the graph. And though the decline may not yet have been perceptible, the forces of opposition were already lining up and taking up positions of strength. The United States in their westward advance and Russia in its thrust eastward were becoming imperialist powers that were soon to surpass Europe in strength.

We left the United States on the verge of imperialism, poised on the shores of two oceans and eager to exert their young strength over both. The attempt was made in 1895 and the first victories were astounding. At first Madrid feared nothing and suspected nothing; revolts in Cuba were only too frequent. The usual way of dealing with them was to send a few troops and a ruthless general. But this time there was a new feature. Cuba's complaints were noisily and prominently ventilated in the press, first of New York, then of all the states. Though American mobilization was clumsy and its navy mediocre, its forces demoralized the Spanish troops who were a long way from their base, and were beaten before ever they fought. As a result, Cuba became an American protectorate, Porto-Rico was annexed and bought for twenty million dollars. This sum almost equalled the indemnity received by the United States after the Boxer risings; they had used the indemnity to attract large numbers of Chinese students to the States. The Filipinos were skilfully won over by an agrarian reform, which secularized monastic property and greatly increased the number of small farms. The north Pacific became a zone of American influence.

It is in the context of this great westward expansion of the United States that the history of Japan assumes its full significance. The furthest spearhead of the American thrust touched Japan in 1854; the Americans had then been forced to withdraw at the time of the Civil War and Japan was left to work out its own transformation. By the time the Americans returned they had only to set themselves up as protectors of the new nation. The Japanese proved themselves the best of all America's pupils. Victory over China had won Japan the Liaotung peninsula, but its possession was disputed by Europe. The Japanese were finally obliged to return it against an indemnity of thirty million taels, which China could get together only by appealing to Russia. This gave Russian capitalism the chance to make a bold move, and it took over at China's expense a territory almost equivalent to the Japanese conquests; it extended as far as Port Arthur and included control of Manchuria. In December 1895 a Russo-Chinese bank was opened in St Petersburg, and three months later it opened a branch in Shanghai. The great Parisian houses, particularly the *Crédit Lyonnais*, the *Banque de Paris* and Hottinger took part in the transaction; for some years past French savings had been deeply involved in the Russian economy. Russian capitalism had crossed the whole of Siberia and reached the China seas by the land route.

Parallel to the changes in America in the 1840s, so developments of equal importance were taking place in Russia during the same period. After the vacillations and uncertainties which followed the great reforms of the 1860s there had been a marked advance, at first demographic: in the later years of the century, Russia's population increased by thirty millions. The great fair of Nijni-Novgorod in 1896 astonished the world; it was a real international exhibition comprising ten thousand exhibitors, amongst whom were Chinese, Japanese, Persians and Europeans. This last great survival of Europe's medieval trade had now become an ultra-modern showpiece. Exhibits of the most famous craftsmanship in the world created a sensation, but so did the modern plant and equipment manufactured by ancient Russia. Already statistics showed Russia to have eighteen thousand factories and more than a million workers, using three hundred thousand horsepower of steam. Output of coal and cast-iron remained poor, but an immense effort was getting under way everywhere: there were, it was claimed, two hundred and thirty-five thousand men at work in the Urals. The progress in naphtha production was very considerable; a first pipeline was functioning in Transcaucasia. In the science of petroleum, the Russians were so brilliant that American technicians were soon turning to them for the solution of their problems.

Changes in rural life were less clearly defined. There were great variations in livestock because of the chronic insecurity of stock-breeding, but a determined effort was being made to find out more about the different strains and their diseases, about the land and its requirements. Russian laboratories also made the most outstanding contributions of the twentieth century to the study of soils and their treatment, which led to a true agronomic revolution whose effects were apparent in the twentieth century in every country and particularly in the United States. Most of the agricultural produce, moreover, was exported, and thus stimulated the development of a growing merchant fleet. The Russian Trading and Shipping Company owned eighty ships of one hundred and forty thousand tons. In 1877 a new company was founded, which was sufficiently unusual to deserve mention; it was not a capitalist creation on English lines, but was started by national subscription just after the Russo-Turkish war of 1877, accompanied by a campaign explaining the urgent need to develop transport. This 'volunteers' fleet soon numbered fifteen vessels. Once the capital had been assembled, this national enterprise became a private one (1883).

In the field of transport, however, Russia's truly great achievement was in the development of transcontinental railways. With the help of French industry the railways had already been extended as far as Merv and soon Tashkent. The pace of progress quickened after Count Witte came to power in 1892; his career had been in railways and he hastened the building of the Trans-Siberian, for which construction yards had been opened the previous year. Rivers, swamps and rocky spurs were crossed. In ten years the whole continent had been crossed, the last obstacles being the Baikalia tunnels. Already capitalists and engineers were busy in Manchuria, and plans were going ahead to reach Peking. There was also a tentative project to carry the southern line on towards Persia and even India. This meant in effect that overland lines would short-circuit the shipping routes which for three hundred years had been draining Asia's trade towards western Europe and the Atlantic. A self-important and unscrupulous group was busily intriguing on the fringes of the government—the Russian equivalent to American 'Grantism'. Companies were founded to exploit the distant territories which the railway had suddenly brought within reach of Europe. When there was talk of mineral wealth in Korea it was a question of forestalling Japanese claims: woodcutters, soldiers and workmen disguised as peasants infiltrated into the peninsula and paved the way for capitalist conquest. Statesmen like Bezzobradzov, service-chiefs like Admiral Alexeyev, and bankers like the Gunzburgs were already making a name for themselves with this sort of project. Count Witte himself became uneasy and gave warning against the dangers to which this uncontrolled spirit of adventure was exposing the Empire. But he admonished and implored in vain. The capitalist group succeeded in opening a free-water port in the Liaotung peninsula which enabled it to control both China and Oceania.

These great movements of expansion were accompanied by a real advance in education and culture. Although police kept a strict watch on academic establishments and bookshops, schools and books multiplied. Villages subscribed to get schoolmasters, advertised for them, went to the cities to look for them. It was a point of honour with the Zemstvos to open as many schools as possible. To celebrate the marriage of Nicholas II, the Moscow Zemstvo prided itself on opening twenty new schools. Russian literature was popular all over the West, particularly in France.

A good deal of capital was needed to finance so much activity. We have stressed the difference between American and Russian institutions. The expansion of America may have been greater but Russia's was amazing in view of her poor banking facilities. However, St Petersburg had found considerable resources in France. It was the age when the great Jewish families in the old Russian cities, the traditional representatives of big business, set up large banking concerns. Once they were protected by court privilege and had become very wealthy, they were granted the Russian nationality previously refused them. They opened sumptuous offices in Paris and set up small courts which fashionable artists and literary critics did not disdain to frequent. Close contacts were established with the French credit network. For twenty years the *Crédit Lyonnais* devoted much of its energies to placing Russian loans. Whilst finance was hard at work, the Grand Dukes were amusing themselves in Paris. In this way they gave the most spectacular publicity to Russian credit. At the 1900 exhibition the French people, who had risen up four times in rebellion against its own princes, gave an enthusiastic welcome to the Russian princes. As a result the Russian budget was the only one in the world which showed a substantial surplus every year. The gold debt rose by three thousand million francs in the last years of the century, yet the interest on this debt was not increased. Public infatuation, especially among the French public, was such that it permitted skilful reconversions, investments at par, and above par. Russia's finances were the soundest in the world thanks to the French treasury.

Thus, from London, New York and San Francisco, a wave of expanding capitalism reached the China Seas, while at the same time a bid for economic domination from London, Paris and St Petersburg was developing; though certainly smaller in scope, it was no less intense, and its influence extended as far afield as Mukden and Port Arthur.

A new world was indeed emerging at the close of the century, a world in which the two great new powers were attracting both intellectual curiosity and financial resources. It foreshadowed the world in which we are living today. Its general outlines were even more clearly discernible at the close of the nineteenth century than at the beginning of the twentieth, and two generations were to go by before the picture was complete. It is tempting to suggest that it was precisely the rapid progress of Japan which halted both America and Russia; but it was chiefly the instability of Russian capitalism and the national rivalries of the Western worlds which gave Japan the great chance of appearing to check the two new colossi during the next fifty years.

The essential features of Russian and American development had already been determined by the railway and the steamship. When Stephenson demonstrated his first engine the *Rocket* to a group of pioneers and incredulous transport contractors at the beginning of the century, he was setting in motion forces which changed the whole world. He was opening the way for economic exploitation of the great continents. Up till then the Westerners had only explored their coastlines; they were the sons of Mediterranean sailors and did not willingly venture over high mountains and across vast rivers. Grandiose though Saint-Simon's dream may have appeared, it was soon surpassed. In any case his Mediter-

ranean system stopped at Baghdad, whereas the fate of
the world was to be played out in the seas around Korea.
The railway age brought with it a wealth of invention
and a great eagerness for conquest; it gave the world a
new youth, so that within four generations the pattern
of the past thousand years was swept away.

In 1780 we described London as the capital of the
seafaring world, and Berlin as the city most typical of
the continental civilizations. A century later the capital
of the seas had shifted westwards towards America, and
the centre of the continents had been shifted far to the
east by the expansion of Russian Asia. We described
Paris of 1780 as being between two worlds. In 1900 it was
the whole of Europe which was threatened by these new
expansions, for Europe was the hinge and pivot on
which they turned. There was no guarantee that a re-
planning of the European railway system would ensure
unity; it seemed possible that Europe would break somewhere, perhaps on the Channel, the Rhine, or the Vistula
under the weight of these two new gigantic wings. It was
a question which the generations of the future had to
answer in blood and fire. The end of the eighteenth century held no intimation of the profound crises which were
to come in the 1880s, which compelled societies which
had remained stable for centuries to make fundamental
changes in their structure, their tools and their way of
thinking. But these crises themselves stemmed directly
from the development of new worlds.

The Europe of 1900 knew nothing of the world catastrophes which were to come. It was dazzled by its own
success and proud of the triumph of its unique civilization; 'like the Berecynthian in her chariot', it exulted in
having brought forth so many gods.

But the new science which had been the foundation
of Europe's success was undergoing profound modification; and its centre of growth would perhaps no longer
even be in Europe.

A SETBACK FOR NEWTON

There had always been some contradictions implicit in the accepted scientific principles of the nineteenth century. On the whole they were dismissed as insignificant until Einstein in 1905 gave an unforeseen direction to the controversy. He showed that the ideas of absolute time and space were fictions of the mind. Two vital concepts which had been the basis of all intellectual effort since Newton and Kant were therefore being challenged.

Einstein's conviction was, indeed, far from being unanimously shared. Here again a generation would have to go by before it was generally accepted. Nor did his discovery, which we regard as belonging to the twentieth century, spontaneously appear in 1905. It was prepared by half a century of critical and original thinking by men whose work must at this point be mentioned.

In England about the middle of the century the mathematicians had been lulled to sleep, as we have said, on the downy pillow of Newtonian fame. Pedagogues and philosophers spent their time criticizing the mental paralysis which mathematical disciplines inflicted on students, although it must be admitted that they themselves seemed quite incapable of doing anything to remedy the situation. But one of the most original minds of the age distinguished himself by his defence of mathematics. George Boole, the son of a small shopkeeper, had tried various ways of making a living—business, the Church and the University. He achieved fame by a work of unusual daring in which he suddenly brought new life to logic if not to metaphysics (which remained as entrenched in tradition as it had always been). His book was entitled *An Investigation of the Laws of Thought, on which are founded the Mathematical Theories of Logic and Probabilities*, a study of 'the operations of the mind by which reasoning is achieved', and which he expressed in terms of calculus. Boole's work did not revolutionize contemporary thinking, but it already marked the opening of a new era, that of the axiomatic.

At about the same time the German Clausius, making a special study of temperatures, and observing their tendency to equilibrium in a closed system, revealed a general tendency of the universe: work is changed into heat; the lower the temperatures, the more they tend to fall; energy is degraded. In order to measure this reduction, Clausius suggested the idea of entropy, which has assumed such importance in the twentieth century.

Proof of its importance is furnished by a study of the kinetic theory of gases. In 1848 Joule had succeeded in calculating an approximate figure for the speed of molecules by establishing the relationship between the speed, volume, pressure and temperature of gases. The total available energy of molecules in a closed system is measured by the total heat of the gas, and the energy of each molecule contributes to the temperature of the gas. These startling observations confirmed Mariotte's Law for approximate values but invalidated it for more accurate observations; the same applied to the theories of Boyle, Avogadro and the whole group of physicists of the 1800s. It was noted that molecules tended to achieve the arrangement which would most probably produce a levelling out of heat in a system; this introduced the notion of entropy into the theory of gases and thus into the composition of matter. It should be recalled that this notion of the most probable was related to the probability theory which had been the subject of study from the seventeenth to the nineteenth centuries, and had been clarified by the gifted Gauss. Thus thermodynamics and the constitution of matter introduced into science a revolutionary form of determinism: statistical determinism. The approximate number of molecules per cubic centimetre was established, and observation of this movement of molecules showed that it did not always proceed in a straight line: it took all the refinements of mathematics that we mentioned earlier to calculate the molecular energy of a few diatoms.

All this represented a transformation and expansion of the conclusions to be drawn from the surprising observations made by Brown. As early as 1827 he noted the small movement of particles in collision with the molecules of the liquid in which they were immersed. Soon Maxwell linked up all this body of reasoning and observation by showing that the sun's rays warmed the molecules and made them bounce off the surface of the ground, particularly if they were very absorbent, in short very dark. So a small mill with arms white on one side and black on the other could be made to revolve in sunlight.

This molecular study of gases had, one may well imagine, many repercussions in the sphere of chemistry. Newton had foreseen it and Berthelot almost formulated it in his work on the speed of chemical reaction. The whole question was, however, reopened in 1850 by Wilhelmy. From monomolecular to dimolecular phenomena, all this movement was related to the principles of thermodynamics, and resulted in the law of action of chemical mass in 1864. The speed of reaction could change under the action of a substance which was present in an active state but not yet itself transformed. This was the idea of catalysis, formulated by Berzelius and studied by Berthelot. It resulted in 1880 in the definition of enzymes, which have been the subject of a good deal of study since then.

In studying solutions it was noticed that the speed of diffusion varied according to the substance, and Graham distinguished colloids from crystalloids. Applied to solutions, electricity produced marvellous results. In 1840 Faraday had easily explained numerous phenomena by calculating the speed of displacement of ions to electrodes, and electricity adopted the ion as its atom. By 1860 the relative speed of ions was calculated with comparative accuracy. The discoveries of Clausius were of the greatest help, and the relationships between the composition of matter and electrical phenomena were clarified towards the end of the century. The relationships between the electrical properties of solutions and osmotic pressures were also worked out. Thus the ground was being prepared for the twentieth-century discovery that electricity lay at the very centre of the composition of matter—a body of knowledge which was still theoretical and was not to be applied until the twentieth century.

From 1850 to 1900 there was an astounding variety of discoveries in every sphere, the relationships of which were sensed by the most distinguished minds, though they could not always reduce them to the unity of a formula. From this extraordinarily widespread creative activity, the finest example that can be given is in the branch of science unrelated to all the preceding ones. About the middle of the century, Foucault and Bensen tried to apply the principles of thermodynamics to the composition of the universe, and in this way they gave a great impetus to the spectral study of the stars. Newton had indicated the importance of this without reaching any decisive conclusion on the subject. The movement of rays across the microscope revealed the speed of displacement of the source of light. This spectral analysis led on to the discovery of substances in the sun which were not found on the earth for another twenty years (as for instance helium, detected in the solar spectrum in 1878, and not on earth until the end of the century). Thus infra-red and ultra-violet rays too came to be studied. Most important of all, however, was the fact that all this research suggested a solution to the problem of the velocity of light.

In 1887, Michelson in Chicago reached an amazing truth: working on the effects of motion on the velocity of light, he obtained a series of results which had only one possible explanation: the velocity of light is invariable whatever the relative speeds of the sources of light and of the observer, a discovery which rendered classical mechanics and the principal hypotheses of Newton completely out of date.

Towards the end of the nineteenth century then, a whole age of scientific thought was drawing to its close. At the very time when the United States was supplanting the old Europe, when Asia was awakening, when the social structure of Europe was being transformed, Newton's star was waning in the scientific sky and the principles of general mechanics were superseded.

CONCLUSION

There could be no more fitting or thought-provoking theme with which to conclude. European expansion had originated with the conviction that the earth was round, and that man would therefore have to reconsider the position he had assigned himself in the universe. From the age of Tycho-Brahé and Kepler to that of Newton and Laplace, who finally completed the system, ships had steered by this new knowledge of the heavens and gained the mastery of the seas, conquered unclaimed territory all over the world and assumed control of the coastal areas which fringed the ancient civilizations.

The possession of great territories and the control of communications encircling the globe were new factors which rendered the old methods of political and economic government completely out of date. Businessmen and industrialists, using the new techniques which had also been developed by science, overthrew the old courtly society founded on privilege, initiated economic liberty, founded a system of credit and created belief in the future and in progress. The result was a victory for those who were proud to be called the middle classes. It was they who controlled the cities, industry and commerce, and the world.

Every advance in science contributed during those years to the wealth and authority of the middle classes and did much to renew and strengthen the power of Europe. Yet just as the privileged few of the *ancien régime* had been unable to gain control of scientific progress, so the middle classes of Victorian Europe were unable to retain the monopoly of its benefits for long. Society underwent a series of structural changes, as a result of which the middle classes were swamped by a rising tide of technicians drawn from the ranks of the people and educated in the new schools. From Monge to Gauss and Lobachevsky the new mathematics spread across the continent to Russia; from Fresnel to Michelson the most brilliant research crossed the Atlantic. Scientific thought found a solution to the problems propounded by Michelson in the geometries arising directly out of Lobachevsky's work. Just as the Vatican Library had been powerless to keep Galileo's thought enclosed within its walls, so the laboratories and libraries of Europe did not prevent science from re-entering the world; they had, in fact, thrust it out themselves.

The European middle classes were proud of their triumphs, but were they justified in claiming them as their own? They were surely the triumphs of science, and they themselves were merely its instruments, suitable enough because they believed in science implicitly. The laboratories and libraries of America and Asia undermined the foundations on which the power of the European middle classes had rested. It was not long before they began to feel uneasy at the growth of technocracies and socialisms and the rise of new continents. Soon they were being gradually deprived of their power and by exactly the same forces that they had themselves employed to despoil the privileged of a previous generation—by belief in progress and respect for its laws.

Even the deadliest of wars do not achieve their purpose, since their ultimate effect is to speed up evolution. Science and humanity are one, and the future of knowledge will decide the future of the world.

BIBLIOGRAPHY

ANSTEY, V. *The Economic Development of India*. 1929.
ARIES, PH. *L'enfant et la vie familiale sous l'ancien régime*. 1960.
ASHTON, T. S. *An Economic History of England in the Eighteenth Century*. 1955.
BAKER, J. N. L. *A History of Geographical Exploration and Discovery*. 1937.
BEAU DE LOMENIE, E. *Les responsabilités des dynasties bourgeoises* (3 vols).
BELLET and DARVILLE, W. *Les plus grandes entreprises du monde*.
BERNAL, J. D. *Science and Industry in the Nineteenth Century*. 1953.
BIGO, R. *Les bases historiques de la finance moderne*.
BIRNIE, A. *Histoire économique de l'Europe, 1760–1932*.
An Economic History of the British Isles. 1935.
BLOCH, M. *Esquisse d'une histoire monétaire de l'Europe*. 1954.
Les caractères originaux de l'histoire rurale française (2 vols).
BLUM, J. *Lord and Peasant in Russia from the Ninth to the Nineteenth Century*. 1961.
BOUTHOUL, G. *La population dans le monde*. 1935.
BOWDEN, KARPOVITCH and USHER. *Economic History of Europe since 1750*.
BOWMAN, L. *Pioneer Settlement*. 1931.
BRIGGS, A. *Age of Improvement, 1780–1867*. 1959.
Victorian People, 1851–1867. 1965.
Victorian Cities. 1963.
BROGLIE, L. DE *Savants et découvertes*.
BRUFORD, W. H. *Germany in the Eighteenth Century*. 1965.
BRUUN, G. *Europe and the French Imperium*. 1954.
CAMERON, R. E. *France and the Economic Development of Europe 1800–1914*. 1961.
CAULLERY, M. *Le problème de l'évolution*.
La société française depuis le XVIIe siècle.
CARR SAUNDERS, A. M. *World Population*. 1936.
CHASLES, M. *Rapport sur les progrès de la géometrie*. 1870.
CHAUNU, P. *L'Amérique et les Amériques*. 1964.
CHEVALIER, L. *Classes laborieuses, classes dangereuses à Paris dans la première moitié du dix-neuvième siècle*. 1958.
La formation de la population parisienne au dix-neuvième siècle. 1950.
CIPOLLA, C. *The Economic History of World Population*. 1962.
CLAPHAM, J. H. *An Economic History of Modern Britain. I: The Early Railway Age, 1820–50. II: Free Trade and Steel, 1850–86. III: Machines and National Rivalries, 1887–1914, with an epilogue, 1914–29*.
The Economic Development of France and Germany, 1815–1914.
The Bank of England.
CLARK, C. *The Conditions of Economic Progress*. 1940.
CLOUGH, S. B. and COLE, C. W. *Economic History of Europe*.

COLE, G. D. H. *Life of William Cobbett.*
COLLINS, I. *The Age of Progress: A Survey of European History from 1789–1870.* 1964.
COLQUHOUN, A. *China in Transformation.*
Congrès internationaux de la population.
COURT, W. M. B. *A Concise Economic History of Britain.*
CROCE, B. *A History of Europe in the Nineteenth Century.* 1965.
CROUZET, M. (ed.) *Le dix-neuvième siècle (Histoire Générale des civilisations).* 1955.
CURTIN, P. D. *The Image of Africa; British Ideas and Action, 1780–1850.* 1965.
DAUMARD, A. *La Bourgeoisie parisienne de 1815 a 1848.* 1963.
DAUMARD and FURET. *Structures et relations sociales à Paris au milieu du dix-huitième siècle.* 1961.
DECARY and CASTEL. *Migrations intérieures récentes des populations malgaches.* 1941.
DION, R. *Essai sur la formation du paysage rural français.* 1943.
DOUGLAS, R. K. *China.*
DUMONT, A. *Dépopulation et civilisation.* 1890.
DUNHAM, A. L. *La révolution industrielle en France, 1815–48.*
DURKHEIM, E. *De la division du travail social.* 1893.
DUVEAU, G. *La vie ouvrière en France sous le Second Empire.* 1946.
ENGELS, F. *The Origin of the Family, Private Property and the State.*
EPSTEIN *From Opium War to Liberation.*
FÈBVRE, L. *La terre et l'évolution humaine.* 1922.
FIRCKS *Bevölkerungslehre und Bevölkerungspolitik.* 1898.
FLORINSKY, M. *Russia, II.* 1953.
GALLAGHER and ROBINSON *Africa and the Victorians.* 1961.
GLASS, D. V. *Population Policies and Movements in Europe.* 1940.
GOODFELLOW, D. M. *Modern Economic History of South Africa.* 1930.
GUILLET, E. C. *Pioneer Days in Upper Canada.* 1965.
HACKER, L. and HENDRICK, B. *The United States since 1865.* 1946.
HALBWACHS, M., SAUVY, A. and ULMER. *Le point de vue du nombre. Encyclopédie française,* vol. VI. 1936.
HALEVY, E. *History of the English People in the Nineteenth Century.*
HARTWELL, M. *The Industrial Revolution.* (Historical Association Leaflet.) 1965.
HEATON, H. *Histoire économique de l'Europe* (2 vols.). 1950, 1952.
HENDERSON, W. O. *The Industrial Revolution on the Continent; Germany, France, Russia 1800–1914.*
HOBSBAWM, E. *The Age of Revolution.* 1962.
HOLBORN, H. *A History of Modern Germany.* 1959.
HUBER, M. *Cours de démographie.* 1938–41.
HUETZ DE LEMPS, A. *Australie et Nouvelle-Zélande.* 1954.
JANET, P. *La Famille.* 1919.
KEYSER, E. *Bevölkerungsgeschichte Deutschlands.* 1941.
LABROUSSE, C.-E. *La crise de l'économie française à la fin de l'Ancien Régime et au début de la Révolution.* 1943.
LANDRY, A. *La révolution démographique.* 1934.
LANG, O. *Chinese Family and Society.* 1946.
LATOURETTE *A History of Modern China.*
LATTIMORE, O. *The Making of Modern China.* 1954.

Lefèbvre, G. *La Grande Peur de 1789*.

Lemaitre, J. *Les contemporains*.

Le Play *Les ouvriers des Deux Mondes*. 1878.

Levasseur, E. *La population de la France*. 1889–92.

Linder, R. *Die Schwedische Landerbevölkerungs unter dem Einfluss der Industrialisierung*. 1938.

Lorimer and Osborn *Dynamics of Population*. 1934.

Lyaschenko, P. *History of the Russian National Economy*. 1947.

Mackenzie, K. *The Banking Systems of Great Britain, France, Germany and the USA*. 1945.

Mantoux, P. *La révolution industrielle en Angleterre*. 1906.

Mavor, J. *Economic History of Russia*. 1925.

Milioukov, L., Seignobos, C. and Eisenmann, L. *Histoire de la Russie*. 1932.

Mondaini *La colonisation anglaise*. 1925.

Morazé, C. *La France bourgeoise*. 1946.
   Introduction à l'histoire économique.
   Les trois âges du Brésil.

Morrison and Commager *The Growth of the American Republic* (vols. 1 & 2). 1962.

Orsi, P. *Histoire de l'Italie moderne*. 1911.

Pannikar, K. *The Future of South East Asia, An Indian View. Asia and Western Dominance, A Survey of the Vasco da Gama Epoch of Asian History, 1498–1954.* 1954.

Parnaby, O. W. *Britain and the Labor Trade in the South-West Pacific.* 1964.

Pearl, R. *The Natural History of Population*. 1939.

Philip, P.-D. and Wood, G. L. *The Peopling of Australia*. 1928.

Pilon, E. *La vie de famille en France au XVIIIe siècle*. 1928.

Poincaré, H. *Dernières pensées.*
   La valeur de la science.
   Les fondements de la géométrie.

Popper, K. *The Open Society and its Enemies.*

Portus, G.-V. *Australia. An Economic Interpretation*.

Redford, A. *Labour Migration in England, 1800–1850*.

Reeves, W.-P. *New Zealand*.

Reinhard, M. *Histoire de la population mondiale 1700–1949*.

Renouvin, P. *Transformation de la Chine et du Japon de 1850 à 1952*.

Rist, Ch. *Précis des mécanismes économiques élémentaires*. 1947.

Roessle, R. *Die pathologische Anatomie der Familie*. 1940.

Roupnel, G. *Histoire de la campagne française*.

Sagnac, P. *La formation de la société française moderne*.

Schnabel, F. *Deutsche Geschichte in XIX Jahrhundert*.

Sée, H. and Schnerb, R. *Histoire économique de la France* (2 vols).
   Les origines du capitalisme moderne.

Simiand, F. *Le salaire, l'évolution sociale et la monnaie*. 1932.

Soyeshima, Michimasa: *Oriental Interpretation of the Far-Eastern Problem.*

Sundbarg, C. *Bevölkerengsstatiskik Schwedens, 1750–1900.*

Taton, R. *Histoire du calcul.*

Tawney *Land and Labour in China*. 1932.

Thomas, D. S. *Social Aspects of the Business Cycles*. 1927.

THOMPSON and GARRATT *Rise and Fulfilment of British Rule in India*. 1934.

TOLEDANO, A. D. *La vie de famille en France sous la Restauration et la Monarchie de Juillet*. 1943.

TREVELYAN, G. M. *English Social History*. 1942.

USHER, A. P. *A History of Mechanical Inventions*.

VACCHINO, A. *La populazione italiana. Storia delle populazione e demografia italiana*. 1941.

VANDENBOSCH, A. *The Dutch East Indies*. 1941.

VAN SOMEREN BRAND *Les grandes cultures du monde*.

WEBER, M. *Gesammelte Aufsätze zur Social- und Wirtschaftsgeschichte*. 1924.

WILLCOX, W. F. *Studies in American Demography*. 1940.

SOME NINETEENTH-CENTURY TRAVELLERS

ALCOCK, SIR R. *Art and Art Industries in Japan*. 1871.

ARDENNE DE TIZAC, H. d' *La sculpture chinoise*. 1931.

AUBERT, L. *Les maîtres de l'estampe japonaise*. 2nd ed. 1922.

BALLOT, M. J. *La céramique chinoise* (Louvre Museum).

BRUCE, J. *Travels to Discover the Source of the Nile in the Years 1768–73*.

BURNES, M. A. *Voyages de l'embouchure de l'Indus à Lahore, Caboul, Balh et à Boukhara et retour par la Perse, pendant les années 1831, 1832, 1833*.

BUSHELL, S. W. *Chinese Art* (Victoria and Albert Museum, 1924).

CAILLÉ, R. *Le voyage de R. Caillé à Tombouctou et à travers l'Afrique, 1824–1828*.

CORNET, CAPT. *Au Tchad. Trois and chez les Sennoussites, les Ouaddaiens et les Kirdis*. 1910.

COSTE and FLANDIN *Voyage en Perse* (with an atlas).

DEMIDOFF, A. DE *Voyage dans la Russie méridionale et la Crimée par la Hongrie, la Valachie et la Moldavie*. 1840.

DJELAL ESSAD *Constantinople*. 1909.

DOOLITTLE *The Social Life of the Chinese*. 1866.

DU HALDE, FA J.-B. *Description de la Chine. 1736–1737*.

DUMONT D'URVILLE *Voyage pittoresque autour du monde*.

GANDAR (the elder) *Le canal impérial. Étude historique et descriptive*. 1894.

GUIMET, E. *Promenades japonaises* (2 vols). 1879–80.

HOMMAIRE DE HELL, X. *Voyages en Turquie et en Perse exécutés par ordre du gouvernement français, en 1846–48*.

HUC. FA. REGIS *Souvenirs d'un voyage dans la Tartarie, le Thibet et la Chine*. 1850.

L'Empire chinois. 1855.

KOULOMZINE, A. M. DE *Le Transsibérien*. 1904.

LA PÉROUSE *Voyage autour du monde*. 1797.

LE BON, DR G. *Les civilisations de l'Inde*. 1887.

La civilisation des Arabes. 1884.

LIVINGSTONE, D. *Exploration à l'intérieur de l'Afrique Australe*. 1881.

MAGE, E. *Voyage dans le Soudan occidental, 1863–1866*.

Nansen, F. *In Nacht und Eis. Die Norwegische Polar-Expedition, 1893–1896.*

Nordenskiold, A. E. *Voyage de la 'Vega' autour de l'Asie et de l'Europe.* 1883.

Nouvelle bibliothèque des voyages. Paris, Lecointe, 1823–30.

Palgrave, W. G. *Une année de voyage en Arabie centrale, 1862–63.*

Pallas *Russie et Asie septentrionale, 1788–1793.*

Parode, Miss *The Beauties of the Bosphorus.*

Playfair *Cities and Towns of China, a Dictionary.* 1880.

Soltykoff, Fa. *Voyage dans l'Inde.*

Voyage de Perse. Le Cou, 1854.

Stanley, H. M. *Divers voyages.*

Sven Hedin *Durch Asiens Wüsten. Drei Jahre auf neuen Wegen, in Pamir, Lopnor, Tibet und China.* 1899.

Sykes *The Taiping Rebellion in China.* 1863.

Vambery, Arm. *Voyage d'un faux derviche dans l'Asie centrale.* 1865.

INDEX

ANCHOR BOOKS

HISTORY

AFRICA AND THE VICTORIANS: The Climax of Imperialism—Ronald Robinson and John Gallagher, A614

THE ANCIENT CITY—Fustel de Coulanges, A76

THE ARAB WORLD TODAY—Morroe Berger, A406

BAGEHOT'S HISTORICAL ESSAYS—Norman St. John-Stevas, ed., A451

THE BIRTH OF CIVILIZATION IN THE NEAR EAST—Henri Frankfort, A89

THE BOOK OF THE COURTIER: Baldesar Castiglione—Charles S. Singleton, trans., A186

THE BRUTAL FRIENDSHIP: Mussolini, Hitler and the Fall of Italian Fascism—F. W. Deakin, A508a

CRISIS AND COMPROMISE: Politics in the Fourth Republic—Philip M. Williams, A518

CRISIS IN EUROPE, 1560–1660—Trevor Aston, ed., A575

DARWIN, MARX, WAGNER—Jacques Barzun, A127

DISCOVERIES AND OPINIONS OF GALILEO—Stillman Drake, trans., A94

THE DISCOVERY OF INDIA—Jawaharlal Nehru, Robert I. Crane, ed., A200

THE EARLY CHRISTIAN CHURCH—J. G. Davies, A566

ENGLAND: From Pre-History to the Present—Martin J. Havran and Arvel B. Erickson, AO2

1848: THE REVOLUTION OF THE INTELLECTUALS—Lewis Namier, A385

THE ELIZABETHAN JOURNALS, Vol. I: Being a Record of Those Things Most Talked of During the Years 1591–1597—G. B. Harrison, ed., A458a

THE ELIZABETHAN JOURNALS, Vol. II: Being a Record of Those Things Most Talked of During the Years 1598–1603—G. B. Harrison, ed., A458b

THE ERA OF TYRANNIES—Elie Halévy; Robert K. Webb, trans., A463

ESSAYS ON OLD TESTAMENT HISTORY AND RELIGION—Albrecht Alt, A544

THE FALL OF PARIS—Alistair Horne, A562

FOUR STAGES OF RENAISSANCE STYLE—Wylie Sypher, A44

FROM HEGEL TO NIETZSCHE—The Revolution in Nineteenth-Century Thought—Karl Lowith; David E. Green, trans., A553

THE PURITAN REVOLUTION: A Documentary History—Stuart E. Prall, ed., A602

QUEEN ELIZABETH I—J. E. Neale, A105

THE RUSSIAN REVOLUTION—Leon Trotsky, F. W. Dupee, ed., A170

SEVENTEENTH CENTURY BACKGROUND—Basil Willey, A19

SEVENTEENTH CENTURY FRANCE—Geoffrey Treasure, A592

THE SIX HUNDRED DAYS OF MUSSOLINI—F. W. Deakin, A508b

THE SPLENDID CENTURY—W. H. Lewis, A122

STATES AND NATIONS—Benjamin Akzin, A493

THIRTY YEARS WAR—C. V. Wedgwood, A249

TODAY'S LATIN AMERICA—Robert J. Alexander, A327

TO THE FINLAND STATION—Edmund Wilson, A6

THE WANING OF THE MIDDLE AGES—John Huizinga, A42

THE YORKIST AGE: Daily Life During the Wars of the Roses—Paul Murray Kendall, A466

ANCHOR BOOKS

Limits on Liberty

LIMITS ON LIBERTY

The Experience of Mennonite,
Hutterite, and Doukhobor
Communities in Canada

William Janzen

UNIVERSITY OF TORONTO PRESS
Toronto Buffalo London

© University of Toronto Press 1990
Toronto Buffalo London
Printed in Canada

ISBN 0-8020-2731-8

Canadian Cataloguing in Publication Data

Janzen, William, 1943–
  Limits on liberty

  Includes bibliographical references.
  ISBN 0-8020-2731-8

  1. Mennonites – Government policy – Canada.
  2. Hutterite Brethren – Government policy – Canada.
  3. Doukhobors – Government policy – Canada.
  4. Minorities – Government policy – Canada.
  I. Title.

  FC104.J36 1990   322'.1'088289   C90-093728-9
  F1035.A1J36 1990

This book has been published with the help of a grant from the Social Science Federation of Canada, using funds provided by the Social Sciences and Humanities Research Council of Canada

In memory of Andrew Janzen, 1983–1986

Acknowledgments

It is a privilege to publicly thank at least some of the people who assisted me in preparing this book. Professor Kenneth D. McRae and Professor Khayyam Z. Paltiel (since deceased) served as my supervisors when I worked on it as a PhD dissertation in political science at Carleton University. Others who helped with advice, resource materials, and encouragement, either at the dissertation stage or in the later revisions, include Professor Frank H. Epp (since deceased), Professor Adolf Ens, Koozma Tarasoff, Roy Baker, Michael Radcliffe, David Luthy, Professor Ian Hunter, Rev. Jacob Kleinsasser, and Lawrence Klippenstein. The encouragement of Virgil Duff of the University of Toronto Press, the assistance of copy editor Lydia Burton, and the publication grant from the Social Science Federation of Canada are also gratefully acknowledged. So too is the contribution of my employer, Mennonite Central Committee Canada, which gave me a sabbatical so that I could transform the dissertation into the manuscript for this book and which also authorized Grace Mann and Eleanor Dyck to do the necessary typing. Last but not least is my wife, Marlene, without whose personal support this book would not have become a reality. While I am deeply grateful to these and others, responsibility for any errors rests with me.

William Janzen
Ottawa, Ontario
January 1990

Contents

viii   Contents

Part Six: Conclusion   287

Introduction

The discussion of Canadian minorities in Thomas Berger's popular 1981 book *Fragile Freedoms* indicates that their problems are not all of one kind.[1] In some instances individuals from minority groups have wanted to participate more fully in Canada's economic and political life but have not been allowed to do so. In other instances, groups have wanted to live separately, with their own land-base or their own school systems, but have also encountered obstacles. Some groups have based their claims on aboriginal status. Others are identified by their ethnic background or by their religious commitments.

This book deals with only one type of group and only one kind of pursuit. The pursuit is that of living in a more communal manner somewhat separate from the larger society. And the groups consist of Mennonites, Hutterites, and Doukhobors. Admittedly, there are differences both within and among these groups, but a significant number of people in these groups have sought communal landholding systems, special arrangements for the education of their children, exemption from military service, and certain modifications in welfare-state matters. In each of these four areas they have needed accommodations, or liberties, from Canada's federal and provincial governments. The governmental response, though not entirely negative, has been ambivalent and limited. That response is the subject of this book.

The issue of accommodating groups who wish to live in a distinct manner is facing many governments in the contemporary world. It also has historical and philosophical dimensions. The 'millet' system, which existed in the Ottoman Empire from the fifteenth century until the First World War, gave a substantial autonomy to non-Muslim minorities, such as Greek-Orthodox, Armenian, and Jewish groups. People belonged to these groups and were subject to them even if they did not live in contiguous territory. In the period between the two world wars the problem of accommodating groups was a major issue in central and eastern Europe where there were many groups with ethnic, religious, and linguistic distinction. And in Switzerland, Belgium, and certain other European countries, group accommodations, some of which can be traced to the Protestant Reformation, continue as fundamental aspects of the political systems.[2]

The accommodation of minority groups also has a long history in Canada. The Quebec Act of 1774 included significant accommodations for the language, religion, landholding patterns, and internal autonomy of the French Catholic people of Quebec. These arrangements were continued in the British North America Act of 1867, now known as the Constitution Act, 1867, which also provided certain protections for Catholic minorities in other provinces and for the English Protestant minority in Quebec. Canada's Indian people also have a particular status, both on and off the reserves.

Even though these arrangements for accommodating groups are important in Canada's structures, some of them have been strongly challenged in post-Confederation history. This is evident in a number of developments, particularly in the restrictions imposed on French-Catholic education systems in New Brunswick, Ontario, Manitoba, Saskatchewan, and Alberta in the decades around the turn of the century, and in the historic treatment of the land claims and other concerns of native peoples. This antipathy toward accommodating distinct groups has often been attributed to the size of the English-speaking majorities in the affected provinces but it is also a result of their political culture and philosophy. Kenneth D. McRae wrote in 1974 that 'special accomodatory devices may be needed for resolving inter-group differences. English Canadians collectively have never grasped this fundamental point. This majoritarian attitude ... I suggest ... is the *damnosa hereditas* of Anglo-American democracy and Lockean political theory and liberal society, though in fairness one must note its all too frequent appearance in other political traditions also.'[3]

This suggests, then, that there are two contradictory influences in the Canadian political system on the issue of accommodating minority groups. On the one hand, there is a long history with some basic structures for the accommodation of certain groups. On the other hand, there is a 'liberal' political culture that has emphasized individualism, a certain egalitarianism, majority rule, integration, and participation, with only limited appreciation for the significance of distinct groups. Admittedly, this culture has been modified with the more recent emphasis on bilingualism and multiculturalism and the efforts to address some of the concerns of native people. Nevertheless, in some respects the historic dilemmas of accommodating groups persist.

The fact of these differing influences in the Canadian political system begins to explain the ambivalent experience of Mennonites, Hutterites, and Doukhobors. As succeeding chapters will show, these groups have found a degree of accommodation, a measure of liberty. The survival of the Hutterite way of life is one of several substantial indications of that. But many of the liberties given to these groups were quite limited in their breadth and vulnerable to public pressure. In the 1920s, approximately 6000 conservative Mennonites from Manitoba and Saskatchewan immigrated to Latin America because of the refusal of the provincial governments to let them continue with their private school system (see chapter 5). Earlier in this century, 250,000 acres of homesteads land allocated to the Doukhobors were withdrawn largely because of Doukhobor communal cultivation practices (see chapter 3). Later, in British Columbia, the Doukhobors also encountered serious difficulties in education matters (see chapter 6).

In order to deal with these various developments, it is necessary to describe the history of these groups, their religious motivation, and how they pursued their objectives. But my primary concern is to show how governments have responded on the four issues, to identify the underlying patterns in those responses, and to probe the political culture and institutions that help to explain those responses and thus account for the limited liberties that were given. For these purposes, it is useful to follow the experience of three groups rather than just one and to use an issue framework rather than one of simple chronology. One particular question that comes up at a number of points relates to the breadth of freedom for religion. Is it limited to matters of belief and worship or can it include a group's way of life? The answers that emerge are not always consistent but a pattern does appear. Also evident is the dilemma that giving liberties to groups can mean restricting certain liberties for individuals within those groups.

The three groups are not entirely alike. Doukhobors are less institutionalized than Mennonites and Hutterites. The Doukhobors also have a more anarchistic view of government, no doubt related to their theological emphasis on 'the God within' each person rather than on the God as taught by a sacred book or by a formal church structure. Also, while Hutterites are quite unified in their orientation, Mennonites and Doukhobors are diverse in their approach to the larger society. This diversity is such that many Mennonites and Doukhobors would not identify with the desire to live more communally and separately. Instead, they would hold that faithfulness to their religious teachings should lead to a constructive involvement in the larger society. Because of this orientation, these more integrated Mennonites and Doukhobors have different relations with the larger society and are not the concern of this book.

The groups also differ from one another in size. The 1981 census reported that there were 189,500 Mennonites, 15,500 Hutterites, and 6700 Doukbohors in Canada. (In 1941 figures were 106,000, 5000, and 17,000 respectively.)[4] However, according to a Doukhobor historian there were, in 1982, 30,000 Doukhobors in Canada.[5] Whatever the exact numbers, they can be misleading because, as noted, many Mennonites and Doukhobors are integrated with the larger society and would not identify with all four issues analysed in this book.

Still, a substantial number of people in each of the three groups have followed particular practices in regard to the four issues considered in this study. They have done so because they desired to live more communally and somewhat separately from the larger society. As a result they forced the Canadian political system to address the subject of the limits of liberty in ways that are important both for them and for what they reveal about that system.

1 The Background of Mennonites, Hutterites, and Doukhobors

The idea of living in separate communities is deeply rooted in the history of these groups. Each began with an effort to separate from the institutions and values of the societies in which they lived. For Mennonites and Hutterites, who have a common origin, the setting was Germanic Europe in the sixteenth century. For Doukhobors it was Slavic Russia in the following century. In each setting the institutions of religion and those of politics were closely integrated. The prevailing view was that uniformity in religion was necessary for maintaining the social order. Accordingly, political power was used to enforce religious practices.

The people who formed these groups took a different view. They believed that the institutions of religion should be separate from those of politics. They held that true religion was a voluntary matter and could not be forced upon individuals. They rejected the authority of the existing ecclesiastical hierarchies and discarded many of the elaborate religious forms that had developed. They did not give full allegiance to political rulers or serve in military forces. Not surprisingly, their views were perceived as dangerous. As a result they were persecuted, so they migrated from one region to another.

This general pattern is evident in the history of each of the three groups. For Mennonites and Hutterites it began in Zurich, Switzerland, in the mid 1520s when some people broke away from the established church led by Ulrich Zwingli under the auspices of the City Council. The people who broke away then formed their own community, where they studied the Bible by themselves, chose their own leaders, and refused to have their new-born children baptized even though doing so was required by law.[1] This refusal, together with the refusal to use force and to swear oaths of allegiance, did not, however, represent a complete rejection of the institution of government. They simply believed that government should serve a more limited role. Their 1527 Schleitheim Confession 'acknowledges and accepts the state as "an order of God," but places it outside the "perfection of Christ"; ... the Confession establishes a dualism of two distinct realities ... Both are equally valid within their respective realms, both have their principles and standards. The work and office of government are utterly necessary in the world, but they are not necessary for the Christian. On the other hand, the law of Christ is clear and absolute, but it has validity only in His church.'[2]

When persecution set in, these groups fled in directions that would eventually lead some of them to Canada. For Mennonites, there were two migratory streams. One stream originated in Switzerland. People from there first fled to the regions of Alsace, Lorraine, and the Palatinate. On one occasion, Count Karl Ludwig welcomed them to the Palatinate because he 'desired thrifty farmers to build up the deserted agricultural lands laid waste by the ravages of the Thirty Years' War.'[3] But conditions were not secure. There were wars, and rulers with less tolerance for minority groups came to power. Because of these developments the Mennonites were receptive to the news about settlement possibilities in William Penn's new colony in America. A few departed for Pennsylvania as early as 1683 and over 3000 migrated in the following decades.[4]

Conditions in Pennsylvania were more than satisfactory, for a time. The Mennonites were able to settle in communities. The soil was fertile. They set up schools for their children. Indeed, one of their schoolmasters, Christopher Dock, is credited with writing the first treatise on pedagogy in America. But by the middle of the eighteenth century, circumstances were changing. Pennsylvania's involvement in the Seven Years' War (1756–1763) caused uneasiness. A generation later when the American War of Independence broke out, Mennonites were in an awkward position. They did not fight for either side. But in some instances the rebelling Americans impressed their horses, took their grain supplies, and even threatened their lives. The Continental Congress in 1775 assured people 'who from religious principles cannot bear arms' that it intended no violence against their consciences. Nevertheless, some Mennonites became interested in what remained of British North America, seeking both a stable government and more land. The migration began in 1786. In a few decades there was a substantial flow to Upper Canada.

The second stream of Mennonites originated in the Netherlands and came to Canada via Prussia and Russia. When they were persecuted in the Netherlands they fled eastward to areas near the North and Baltic seas. The rulers here wanted their lands developed agriculturally. They were also more sympathetic to religious reforms and less concerned about the homogeneity of their populations than were rulers in western Europe. The rulers further east promised the Mennonites exemption from military service and considerable internal freedom, but in some instances they restricted the Mennonites to certain geographical areas and barred them from certain occupations and educational institutions. Despite these limitations, the Mennonites enjoyed relative peace and tranquillity until the second half of the eighteenth century, by which time many of these areas had been consolidated under Prussian rule.[5] Difficulties then arose in relation to Mennonite exemption from military service and their right to acquire land for their growing populations.

Fortuitously, the possibility of migrating to Russia then appeared. Russia had just expanded its southern frontier. It was eager to consolidate its political control over the new territories and to develop their agricultural potential. For these purposes it needed people. Czarina Catherine II (1762–96) was willing to accommodate various particularities in order to attract immigrants. Before long, Mennonite leaders had negotiated arrangements that included substantial autonomy over internal affairs, exemption from military service, and freedom of religion including the right to operate their own schools.[6] The Mennonite migration to Russia began late in the 1780s and for almost a century these insulated German-speaking colonies flourished.

By 1860, however, Russia was becoming less hospitable to many colonies of foreigners. The ideals of Western liberalism about equality before the law, individual rights, and public participation in the affairs of state were becoming stronger in Russia. In addition there was a romantic movement, determined 'to purge the Russian soul of all foreign influences.' Both these factors militated against the particular status of Mennonites and other foreign groups in Russia. According to E.K. Francis, 'both movements were nationalistic, aiming at the integration of all the subjects of the Tsar in one culturally, economically, and socially unified, cohesive, and powerful social system after the image of the modern nation.'[7] These new ideas were soon expressed in law. In 1861 a land-reform law liberated serfs. In 1870 the system for the colonies of foreigners was changed, reducing their insulation, their internal autonomy, and their privileged status. Their schools would now be administered by the Russian government. Russian would be the main language of instruction. And military service would be required of all young men.[8]

Naturally, the Mennonites were alarmed. They made strong appeals to the Russian authorities. Eventually, the government, prompted by fear that all the Mennonites might emigrate, agreed to permit their young men to render a non-military form of national service. To some Mennonites this was an adequate solution; others wanted to explore new settlement possibilities. The latter's interest coincided with the interest of the new Canadian Dominion to attract settlers to the western prairies. As a result, special arrangements were soon negotiated, and in the 1870s approximately 7000 Mennonites migrated to Manitoba. Another 11,000 migrated to the United States. Of those who remained in Russia, another 21,000 would come to Canada in the 1920s.[9]

The Hutterites grew out of the same movement as the Mennonites, but when the persecutions set in they migrated in a different direction, finding refuge in parts of Moravia. In one migration they committed themselves to the principle of communal property, which has remained their distinguishing characteristic. They base it on the example of the early Christian church in which 'all who believed were together and had all things in common.'[10] An early leader, Jacob Hutter, from whom they derived their name, emphasized this principle. His 'theology of Gelassenheit' called for a 'peaceful submission to God and to the believing group ... looking to the future for the ultimate vindication of their faith.'[11]

Despite the early persecutions, the second half of the sixteenth century was a 'golden age' for the Hutterites. Secure under the strength of the Moravian nobles, they grew to over 100 'Bruderhofs,' as their colonies were known, and their total membership rose to over 50,000.[12] They worked in agriculture, carpentry, saddle-making, and tailoring. Their education programs placed them well ahead of their time and their 'home-made' physicians were in high demand by leaders of the larger society. Unfortunately, late in the 1500s, circumstances changed. There were decades of war, followed by the Catholic counter-reformation in which 'children were permanently removed from their parents ... older people ... were placed in monastic institutions [and] ... all worship outside the prescribed state churches was forbidden.'[13]

These events had a devastating effect on the Hutterites. Those who survived migrated to Russia in the 1770s. There they were given freedoms similar to those of the Mennonites but their century in Russia was not singularly successful. Perhaps their energies were too dissipated. By 1819 they abandoned the practice of living communally on Bruderhofs and took up the Mennonite village pattern where each family had private property. However, a revival in 1859 led many to re-establish the Bruderhofs. In the 1870s, when Russia set out to partially integrate the foreign colonists into Russian society, the Hutterites migrated to the United States, along with many Mennonites.

In the United States, however, the Hutterites were not entirely secure in their freedoms. In 1898, when uncertainties arose because of the Spanish-American War, they explored the possibility of migrating to Canada. However, they did not make a permanent move until twenty years later, near the end of the First World War. At that time, much public anger was directed against them because they spoke German, the language of the enemy; they refused military service; and their colony life-style made them conspicuous. At one point, the colonies were charged with false incorporation on the grounds that 'the Hutterite corporation, instead of serving religious purposes as called for in the charter, was really used for economic gain.'[14] Also, they were described as 'a menace to society, depriving children of the right to attend county fairs and mingle with the outside world.' Even more serious was the fate of their young men who refused to render military service. They were harassed and tortured to the extent that two died in prison.[15] Because of this most difficult situation, the Hutterites made a hurried move to Canada in 1918, where the government welcomed them as agriculturalists with generous promises of religious freedom.[16]

The history of the Doukhobors is distinct from that of the Mennonites and Hutterites. They arose in Slavic Russia, probably in the social upheaval that followed the Great Schism in the Russian Orthodox church in the 1650s.[17] Like Mennonites and Hutterites, the Doukhobors rejected the established social and religious frameworks. Indeed, the Doukhobor rejection was even more far-reaching than that of the other two groups. Institutions like the priesthood, baptism, and the eucharist that, in a reformed way, had remained important for Mennonites and Hutterites were not used at all by the Doukhobors. The Bible, too, played only a minor part. Instead, the Doukhobors held that each person could be guided by 'the Christ within.' This principle, with its strong egalitarian implication, pointed towards a view that minimized the need for government. According to one early observer: 'Inasmuch as all men are equal, and the children of God do good willingly, without coercion, they do not require any government or authority over them. Government, if needed at all, is needed only for the wicked ... To go to war, to carry arms, to take oaths – is forbidden.'[18]

Doukhobor history in Russia is marked by periods of severe persecution. In the 1770s, one strong leader, Pobirokhin, championed the causes of the peasantry and spoke of the antagonists as 'those in authority, those who live at the expense of the toil of others, those who as thieves and robbers withhold from the people the divine truth that should be freely available.'[19] Pobirokhin emphasized that the struggle against these antagonists had to be carried on with love and not with anger, for 'war and the taking of human life and all forms of hate towards our fellow men are the most impermissible deeds for a servant of God.' Despite this non-violence, the government, encouraged by the Russian Orthodox church, set out to eradicate Doukhobor beliefs, leading to years of severe and brutal persecution.

Early in the nineteenth century, Czar Alexander I (1801–25) took a more tolerant view. He ordered that the Doukhobors be allowed to locate in a separate colony in a new frontier region in Taurida province not far from where the Mennonites were settling. The government gave them land, helped them with transportation to the site of the new colony, and exempted them from taxes in their pioneer years. The move satisfied the Russian Orthodox church, which wanted the Doukhobors isolated so that their teaching would not spread further among Orthodox adherents. It also helped the government to populate and develop some newly acquired territories and thus to broaden the empire's sphere of control.

For the Doukhobors, the early decades in Taurida province were a time of consolidation. A man named Kapoustin gave them good internal leadership. They adopted the principle of communal property. They tilled their fields together, divided the harvests among all the people, and built storehouses for the lean years. The Doukhobors also adopted some agricultural improvements from the nearby Mennonites. According to a governmental report of 1807, 'they were sober, well-to-do people; exceedingly punctual taxpayers. In intercourse with the Russian officials they were submissive. They were accustomed to help one another.'[20]

Unfortunately, after a few decades there were difficulties. A new czar, Nicholas I (1825–55), was less tolerant, and with the death of the Doukhobor leader Kapoustin, some serious internal problems arose.[21]

After an investigation, the authorities dissolved the colony in 1841 and sent the Doukhobors to the Transcaucasian regions. The government's official explanation stated that they had denied the historic dogmas of the church and that 'public peace demands that you be transferred to distant regions where you will no longer be injurious to your fellow men.'[22] But there may have been another motivation. The Transcaucasian regions were Russia's new frontier. Russia needed settlers there, just as it had in Taurida forty years earlier, and just as Canada would later.

The period in the Caucasus followed a pattern similar to that in Taurida province. After initial pioneering difficulties, the Doukhobors became prosperous in their agricultural communities, but again the situation did not last. There were internal disputes and a new czar, Alexander III (1881–94), was not tolerant. Influenced by the Russian Orthodox church and the army, this czar introduced conscription into the Caucasus in 1887.[23] This divided the Doukhobors. Some complied with the law and allowed their young men to 'enter the army, warning them, however ... not to become murderers, and to be sure, if they had to go to battle, to shoot high so as not to hit anybody.'[24] Others saw themselves as a pilgrim minority destined to be persecuted. The latter group was led by exiled Peter Verigin. Its young men suffered severely when they refused to obey the orders of commanding officers and carry arms.

The internal Doukhobor division became deep. The Verigin followers sought to purify themselves by reinstituting a more thoroughgoing communism, by sharing their excess wealth with poorer non-Doukhobor neighbours, and by abstaining from tobacco, alcohol, meat, and, for a time, from sexual relations as well. They also burned their guns. This action was critical. The burnings took place in several localities on 29 June 1895. The Verigin group saw these burnings as acts of religious devotion and accompanied them with all-night prayer vigils.[25] To political authorities, however, the burnings appeared as acts of defiance. They responded brutally. The persecution that followed was so severe that Count Leo Tolstoy and certain English Quakers, who had had contact with the Doukhobors for some time, undertook a major effort to help them. Before long they decided that the best way to help was to arrange for the Doukhobors to emigrate. As a result, the Verigin Doukhobors, numbering about 7400, were on their way to Canada before the end of the century.[26] A larger number remained in Russia.

THE TERMS OF THEIR IMMIGRATION TO CANADA

When these Mennonites, Hutterites, and Doukhobors immigrated to

Canada they did so on the basis of letters or orders-in-council assuring them that they would be allowed to live according to the teachings of their religions. Many issues would be negotiated later, but these initial arrangements represent the first efforts of these groups to enlarge the limits of liberty in Canada. The arrangements also indicate a positive governmental response.

The Mennonites who began to migrate from Pennsylvania to Canada in 1786 did not enter into elaborate negotiations with the authorities before their arrival. They assumed that the British would give them the same liberties that they had long enjoyed in Pennsylvania. There is, however, a noteworthy letter sent in 1792 by John Simcoe, lieutenant-governor of Upper Canada, to Henry Dundas, British colonial secretary. Simcoe stated: 'There is every prospect of very great migrations taking place out of the United States into His Majesty's Dominions and I have not hesitated to promise to the Quakers and other sects the similar exemption from militia duties which they have always met with under the British Government.'[27] The importance of Simcoe's promise became evident one year later. In 1793 the Assembly of Upper Canada passed an act exempting 'persons called Quakers, Mennonists, and Tunkers' from militia duties.[28] (The Tunker church adopted the name Brethren in Christ early in the twentieth century.)

The Mennonites who came from Russia to the Canadian prairies in the 1870s negotiated a broader range of concerns. They raised them already in January 1872, when they first approached a British Consulate in Russia about settlement possibilities in Canada. Their interest was then relayed to Ottawa, where the government, on 26 April, passed an order-in-council stating that 'free grants of land may be obtained or purchases made on easy terms and at merely nominal prices. The settlers may obtain contiguous lots of land, so as to enable them to form their own communities.'[29] A 25 September order-in-council promised them 'absolute immunity from military service.'[30]

In 1873, after various other communications, the groups in Russia sent a twelve-member delegation, including two Hutterites, to explore settlement possibilities in both Canada and the United States. Four of the twelve favoured Canada primarily because of the stronger assurance that they would be allowed to pursue their particular way of life.[31] This assurance was described most fully in a letter dated 25 July 1873 from John Lowe, the secretary of the Department of Agriculture, which was then responsible also for immigration matters.[32] The letter's fifteen points gave the Mennonites an exemption from military service, a reserve of eight townships, full freedom to exercise their religious principles and to educate their children in their own schools, and the privilege of affirming instead of swearing oaths. For the Mennonites, this letter outlined their basic relationship with government. On 13 August 1873, the government approved the letter as an order-in-council, with a slight modification in the reference to schools.[33] Satisfied with the arrangements as they understood them, about 7000 Mennonites moved from Russia to Manitoba in the 1870s.

The Doukhobors, who came from Russia to Canada in 1899, also entered into negotiations with Canadian authorities before their arrival. However, these negotiations were not entirely clear, perhaps because they went through several intermediaries. One intermediary, Prince Peter Kropotkin, well known for his writings on anarchism, had visited Canada in 1897 and now felt that the Mennonite settlement in Manitoba could serve as a model for the Doukhobors. Writing to James Mavor, professor of political economy at the University of Toronto, on 31 August 1898, Kropotkin stated that the Doukhobors would want exemption from military service, block settlement, and internal autonomy. Within two weeks, Mavor met with James A. Smart, deputy minister of the Interior, and presumably conveyed these concerns.[34] At the same time two Doukhobor families, together with other intermediaries, were in western Canada looking for a suitable location.

In October 1898 there were further meetings with government officials. Now it was confirmed that the Doukhobors would settle in two blocks instead of one. Early in 1899 a third block was added. Also, in these October meetings the English Quaker Aylmer Maude seemed to speak for the Doukhobors but there is speculation that he neglected some of the Doukhobor concerns. At least there are no written references to schooling, swearing allegiance, or registering births, deaths, and marriages, all of which would become contentious later. The order-in-council of 6 December 1898 promised only 'absolute immunity from military service,' after noting that the Doukhobors appeared to be a most desirable class of settlers for the vacant lands in the west and 'that it is expedient' to give them this promise. Early in 1899, approximately 7400 Doukhobors arrived in Canada.[35]

The Hutterites entered into negotiations with Canadian authorities on two occasions before they made permanent settlements. Their first contact was in 1873, when two representatives from their colonies in Russia accompanied ten Mennonites in an exploratory visit to North America. However, like a majority of the Mennonites, the Hutterites opted for the United States at that time. Their second contact with Canada was in 1898, when the Spanish-American War left them uncertain about their exemption from military service. This time the negotiations became more involved. They sent three delegates to Winnipeg, where the immigration office responded by sending an agent to visit the colonies in the United States. This agent then reported: 'Any inducement possible should be made to secure them.'[36] In the spring of 1899 one colony moved to Manitoba, even though the negotiations were not yet complete. On 12 August 1899, the federal government passed an order-in-council that promised the Hutterites 'absolute immunity from military service.'[37]

In September of that year the Hutterites raised additional concerns in a six-point petition to the Winnipeg immigration office. They asked, among other things, that they be allowed to have their own schools, to hold property in common and to pay taxes accordingly, and to be exempted from voting and from using the oath.[38] The Winnipeg immigration commissioner, W.F. McCreary, sent the petition to Ottawa where James A. Smart, deputy minister of the Interior responded favourably to each concern.[39] Despite these assurances the Hutterites did not move at the time. Their anxieties subsided when the Spanish-American War ended; and the one colony that had moved to Canada soon returned to the United States. However, in 1917, when they encountered severe difficulties because of the American involvement in the First World War, they asked Canadian officials whether the earlier arrangements would still hold. The deputy minister of the Interior, W.W. Cory, said that they would, so the Hutterites moved quickly, purchasing land for six colonies in Manitoba and nine in Alberta.[40]

Canadian hospitality did not last, however. The social atmosphere of the war had left many Canadians hostile to those who were unwilling to render military service. Before long, the press carried reports that 30,000 to 60,000 Mennonites and Hutterites from the United States were being admitted to Canada.[41] The minister of Immigration claimed that only about 1000 Hutterites and 500–600 Mennonites were crossing into Canada. Nevertheless, the opposition from citizens' groups and from the provincial governments in Alberta and Manitoba became so strong that federal orders-in-council were passed on 1 May and 9 June 1919, prohibiting Mennonites, Hutterites, and Doukhobors from immigrating to Canada.[42]

This action caused considerable difficulty for those Hutterites who were still disposing of their possessions in the United States. They appealed to the Canadian government to reconsider its action. The Mennonites made appeals, too. They were concerned about Mennonites in Russia who had remained there in the 1870s and were now suffering severely because of the Great War, a famine, and the Communist revolution. William Lyon Mackenzie King, leader of the Liberal party, proved to be sympathetic: on 2 June 1922, after he had become prime minister, a new order-in-council was quietly passed rescinding the order barring Mennonites and Hutterites from Canada.[43] Four years later, on 17 March 1926, the prohibition against Doukhobor immigration was also lifted.[44] (The government's sympathy was selective: in 1923 it imposed restrictions on Chinese immigration.)[45]

When the prohibition was removed, in 1922, the Mennonites acted quickly. In the next few years they were able to bring nearly 21,000 of their people from Russia to Canada. These came on the basis of an understanding that they would find shelter and support among other Mennonites, that they would be placed on land as farmers, and that they would not become public charges. On the matter of military service, the government no longer wished to issue special orders-in-council, but it assured these immigrants that they would be covered by the Militia Act, which exempted all who 'from the doctrines of their religion are averse to bearing arms or rendering personal military service.'[46]

These terms for the immigration to Canada of the Mennonites, Hutterites, and Doukhobors do not deal with all the issues that would arise later. Nevertheless, they indicate that these groups asked for particular liberties and that, to a considerable extent, the Canadian government accommodated them.

PART TWO

Landholding

For most of their history in Canada, Mennonites, Hutterites, and Doukhobors have been agrarian peoples. Land, therefore, has been important to them and, in accordance with their religious orientation, they have sought to hold it communally.

The groups have differed, however, in the form and extent of their communalism. The Hutterites have rejected the idea of private property. When they arrived in Canada, as the First World War came to an end, they bought land and set up colonies in Alberta and Manitoba. Each colony had about fifteen families and they held their property in common. The Hutterites have continued to live in this way even though each prairie province has, at least for certain periods, imposed significant restrictions on their landholding rights.

The Doukhobors were somewhat different, but a majority of them also opposed private property when they arrived in 1899. They had special governmental arrangements for settling in a communal manner. However, within a decade, they encountered serious difficulties; a large portion of the land initially allocated to them was reclaimed by the government. Following this traumatic development some Doukhobors accepted regular private homesteads on the prairies, while others purchased land in British Columbia and rebuilt a community life there. That community broke up in 1939 because of both internal and external problems, including certain government actions, but there was no specific prohibition on the right of the Doukhobors to hold land communally.

The Mennonites were less thorough in their communalism. They accepted private property. But many of them wanted to live in blocks of land by themselves. However, not all their efforts to do this were successful. Early in the nineteenth century some Mennonites who had recently come from Pennsylvania to Upper Canada petitioned the governor for 'any portion of one of the Townships now about to be surveyed ... to be located by the Mennonists only.'[1] They explained how such exclusiveness would help them to preserve a community way of life that they, for religious reasons, regarded as important. However, the authorities denied the request, stating that 'no lands [would] be granted to persons who will not enrol themselves in the Militia.'

A more successful effort began in the 1870s, when 7000 Mennonites migrated from Russia to the Canadian prairies. This time the government, responding to their requests, reserved certain areas of land and stipulated that only Mennonites could claim homesteads within them. It also allowed the Mennonites to live in villages. A few decades later, when these Mennonites asked for similar accommodations in the northwest, soon to be known as Saskatchewan, the government again responded favourably.

The willingness of the government to make such arrangements did not continue indefinitely. Late in the 1920s, Mennonites from Manitoba were looking for another 'suitable tract of land where to settle in a colony the younger generation.'[2] They asked the government to reserve 'from 10 to 20 townships' in the Peace River valley of Alberta for them. Government officials discussed their petition at some length but in the end rejected it. The government now wanted to preserve the principle 'that the lands are available to the first eligible applicant.'[3] There were concerns also about difficulties that had been experienced in administering such reservations earlier.

There are, then, three occasions on which Canadian governments, federal or provincial, granted these groups the right to hold land in communal ways: the Mennonite reserves created first in Manitoba in the 1870s and then in the northwest around the turn of the century; the Doukhobor community created in the northwest in 1899; and the Hutterite colonies that continue in each of the prairie provinces.

Each of these three occasions involved a complex governmental encounter. For the Mennonites and Doukhobors it was with the federal government because at the time of their arrival that government was engaged in a major effort to settle the prairies. For the Hutterites it was with the provincial governments because they obtained land, not by homesteading, but by purchase. This was within provincial jurisdiction. In spite of these jurisdictional differences, each government allowed a degree of communalism, though for the Doukhobors the federal government made a drastic change of direction.

2 The Mennonite Reserves

The Mennonites who came from Russia in the 1870s had a view of landholding that was more communal than that of Canada's new homesteading system. The Mennonite view had been formed not only by their religious teachings but also by the Russian laws for foreign colonists. In Russia the Mennonites had had several large blocks of land unto themselves. These were owned by the church community and each block, or colony, contained several dozen villages. Each village had at least a dozen individual farms but the land on these farms was owned privately. Each village also had some common land for pasturing cattle. If the common land had wooded areas, they could also be used by all villagers. The cultivated land around the village, though individually owned, was farmed in a way that required close co-operation among the villagers. The system, according to sociologist E.K. Francis, 'presupposes and fosters strong social coherence, intensive interaction on a face-to-face level, readiness to cooperate and offer mutual aid, and a common value system which leaves few alternatives in one's everyday conduct, and which is enforced by strict social controls based on both inner and external sanctions. In fact, it would appear that it cannot be made to work adequately unless these sanctions have a distinctly religious connotation.'[1]

In contrast, the new Canadian homesteading system had a more individualistic orientation. Adopted from the United States, where it had facilitated massive settlement in the midwest, it was now applied, in modified form by the Canadian government, to the western prairies. Officials surveyed the land and divided it into townships and sections. The sections were one mile square and the townships six miles square, thus consisting of 36 sections. A settler could obtain a quarter-section, with 160 acres, by registering a claim and paying the nominal fee of $10. This was known as a homestead 'entry.' The settler then had to meet both a residence and a cultivation requirement, meaning that he had to reside on his homestead and cultivate at least a portion of it. After three years he could obtain the legal title, officially known as the 'patent.'[2] If the settler was an immigrant then he first had to become a naturalized British subject, which involved taking the oath of allegiance, before he could obtain the patent.

Not all sections of land were open for homesteading, however. Some were withheld for the Hudson's Bay Company and a few were identified as school lands. More important, in many areas the odd-numbered sections were designated for the railway companies. The settlers, it was assumed, would purchase these from the railway companies as they became more established on their initial homesteads. In this way, these companies would receive a financial return for building the railway and have an interest in attracting settlers to the west. It was an elaborate scheme and, according to C.A. Dawson, it was 'a natural outgrowth of a competitive system whose outstanding characteristic was an experimental individualism.'[3]

Not everyone favoured this grand new scheme. The Métis tried, with only limited success, to have the government recognize their strips along the rivers. But immigrant groups tended to be more successful in their requests for concessions.[4] The Mennonites wanted, among other things, a block of land reserved for themselves, exclusive access to the odd-numbered sections within that block, permission to reside in villages rather than on individual homesteads, and reassurance that taking the oath of allegiance would not make them liable for military service. Significantly, the government agreed to these requests but there were innumerable practical difficulties, first in Manitoba and later in Saskatchewan.

THE RESERVES IN MANITOBA

The most basic accommodating step that the government could take was to reserve a block of land and allow only Mennonites to claim homesteads in it. The government indicated its willingness to do this in response to the first Mennonite inquiry. The order-in-council of 26 April 1872 stated that 'the settlers may obtain contiguous lots of lands, so as to enable them to form their own communities.' A government report published soon after stated that the settlers 'can obtain large grants of land *en bloc*, they can form a settlement or settlements of their own, where they can preserve their language and customs.'[5]

This clear intent was translated into reality with an order-in-council on 3 March 1873 that set aside eight Manitoba townships for the Mennonites.[6] But now the first complications arose. It was learned that a number of Canadians had already settled in one of those townships. These Canadian settlers 'entered a strong verbal protest,' so another order-in-council was passed, on 23 May 1873, changing the boundary of the land reserved for the Mennonites in order not to interfere with the settlement established by the Canadians.[7]

There were other problems in the spring of 1873. The Mennonite delegates from Russia who had come to see the land were not impressed. Parts of the eight townships were marshy. Others were subject to drought. The mosquitoes were 'terribly bad.' Grasshoppers were plentiful. And the transportation facilities necessary for starting farms seemed seriously inadequate. These disappointments led a number of delegates to favour the United States for settlement.[8] Even the four who preferred Canada, because of its clearer promises of religious freedom, sought and obtained assurances that the government would reserve land in a different area if, upon arrival, their settlers would desire a new location.

The willingness of the government to reserve additional land proved to be important. The townships reserved first were on the east side of the Red River and most of the 1300 Mennonites who arrived in 1874 settled there, but their fears that sizeable parts of the reserve were not suited for farming were soon confirmed. As a result, some of them began to settle on the west side of the river even before it was officially reserved for them. The movement to the west side became substantial in 1875 when over 3000 Mennonites arrived from Russia.[9]

Even though formal arrangements for settling on the west side had not yet been made, government officials did not object. According to one official, Canadians regarded the west side as unfit for settlement because of it 'being destitute of timbers.' The Mennonites, in contrast, were familiar with open plains. They knew how to build homes and set up farms with only a small amount of wood.[10] They believed that the land was of good quality and the government, eager to have them, passed an order-in-council on 25 April 1876 reserving seventeen townships for the Mennonites on the west side of the Red River.[11]

Once again, however, there were complications. Some settlers from

Ontario had already located in one wooded corner of the seventeen townships. They complained to government officials that they were hoping for more 'British Subjects from Canada' and that the creation of a Mennonite reserve deprived them of the possibility of a Canadian neighbourhood. They would now be too few to establish their own schools and churches.[12] A number of Canadian settlers came to the area even after it had been officially reserved for the Mennonites. These were squatters and according to William Hespeler, an energetic immigration agent who had worked with the Mennonites from the beginning, 'they entered upon the lands defying anyone to interfere with them.' He reported that they were 'going as far as to threaten the lives of the Mennonites, should they remove any wood from such lots that they [the settlers] had trespassed upon.'[13]

The problem of squatters became quite serious. In July 1877 one Dominion Lands agent, A. Belch, wrote that 'the Government must either abandon the system of special reserves for particular classes of immigrants or else protect them in the enjoyment of the privileges conferred.' He asked for authorization 'to compel these squatters to abandon the lots upon which they have located.'[14] In spite of his request, the evictions did not take place and the Mennonites became increasingly concerned about being 'prevented from cutting wood upon lands undoubtedly in their reserve.'

In November 1877 the Department of the Interior made an investigation. William Pearce reviewed the problems in detail and said many of the complaints of the English-speaking settlers were either unjustified or frivolous. He pointed out that if the Mennonites had not demonstrated that it was possible to settle on the 'treeless plain' on the west side of the river, then others would probably not be doing so either. He reported that some squatters had said that 'no Gov't would dare to eject them and there was not force enough in this Province.'[15] By way of a recommendation, he said: 'I think the best solution of the difficulty to be an ejectment of the squatters at once, and if the few legal settlers who really have a grievance would take a reasonable compensation in land or money for the disadvantages under which they have been placed it would perhaps be advisable to do so.' Another official reported that the feeling among the Mennonites was such that if the squatters were not removed, then the flow of Mennonite immigrants would decrease sharply. Officials also feared that land agents from the United States would use these problems to persuade the Mennonites to leave Manitoba and go to the United States.[16]

These reports may have exaggerated the problems. The Mennonites at this time had taken up less than one-half of the reserved lands. And the squatters, it appears, had taken up considerably less than one-half of the remaining portion. Still, the fears are understandable. To deal with the situation, the surveyor-general recommended that the squatters be ejected and that several government representatives, including William Hespeler, be sent to negotiate a change in one of the borders of the Mennonite reserve so as to accommodate the English Canadians who had settled there legitimately.[17] This was soon accomplished. The Mennonites gave up part of their reserve on one side and received additional land on another side. One local land agent christened the new border as the Meno-Canuck line.[18]

Despite these significant efforts, the problem of the squatters was not resolved, and, gradually, some government officials became sympathetic to their situation. By 1879 the flow of Mennonite immigrants from Russia was down to a trickle and sizeable portions of the reserve remained unsettled. Land agents began to fear that in light of the 'abundance of unoccupied land within the reserved townships,' the removal and exclusion of non-Mennonites 'will soon be made a public grievance.'[19] In the fall of 1879 one official wrote that 'the popular feeling is becoming so strong that it will be difficult or impossible to remove future squatters.'[20] He recommended that the unsettled portions of the reserve be 'thrown open for general settlement.' The surveyor-general also became sympathetic, stating that 'it would be a great injustice to go on retaining for the children of these foreigners land that we refuse to permit our own people to enter and cultivate and that is precisely what continuing the reservation means.'[21]

The sympathies of officials and the numerous appeals that came directly from squatters led to another effort to resolve the problem. In March 1881, the minister of the Interior made a submission to Cabinet and noted that 'great pressure is brought to bear ... by persons desirous of securing the unoccupied portion of those lands.'[22] He then proposed, 'in order to prevent complaint of favouritism and to realize at the same time their fair value in the public interest,' to sell, by public auction, those lands in the reserve that the Mennonites had not yet occupied. The Cabinet approved the plan and the sale was scheduled for June.[23]

Once again there were complications. Because of discrepancies among lists in local, regional, and national offices, there was uncertainty about precisely which quarter-sections could be sold. Accordingly, the sale was postponed until 19 September. However, when the list for the

September sale was made public, it was found to include the sites of several established Mennonite villages.[24] This information created such an alarm that four local members of the federal Parliament cabled the minister of the Interior urging that the sale be postponed again to allow for further investigations. A sale finally took place on 19 October 1881, using a greatly reduced list of lands; but even then some lands occupied by Mennonites were inadvertently sold.[25] Alongside the auction sale, officials made arrangements to permit the growing number of squatters to purchase the lands that they occupied, 'notwithstanding the manner in which these squatters have gone into occupation.'[26]

A second issue that had to be dealt with involved the odd-numbered sections within the areas reserved for the Mennonites. The odd-numbered sections were generally not open for homesteading. The government had agreed to grant most of them to the Canadian Pacific Railway Company (CPR), which would then sell them to the settlers. For the Mennonites, however, the government had made an exception. It permitted the Mennonites to make homestead entries on both the even- and the odd-numbered sections within their reserved areas. However, some officials seemed unaware of this arrangement. Consequently, on 9 July 1879, when the Department of the Interior announced that the odd-numbered sections in certain areas of Manitoba belonged to the CPR and would be purchasable as of 1 August, it was found that the lands thus described included parts of the large Mennonite west reserve.[27]

Understandably, this announcement raised questions. Why were the Mennonites now not to claim these odd-numbered sections as homesteads? And if Mennonites could now obtain the odd-numbered sections in the reserve by purchasing them, could non-Mennonites do so, too, and thus intrude on Mennonite exclusiveness? Land agents in the west quickly contacted Ottawa but were informed that the intent to sell these odd-numbered sections was government policy now. Nevertheless, one local land agent continued to register homestead entries for Mennonites on the odd-numbered sections. However, when this agent's activity was discovered he was forced to cancel these entries.[28]

The new policy, though disappointing, was not an overwhelming hardship for the Mennonites. They acted quickly and purchased 'a considerable amount of land between their villages.'[29] Indeed, a local land agent worked to prevent non-Mennonites from buying land within the reserve, thereby helping the Mennonites to maintain their exclusiveness. Also, some Mennonites who had first homesteaded in the east reserve, and were disappointed by the quality of land there, now bought land in the west reserve. A few Mennonites from the United States also took advantage of this opportunity and moved to Manitoba.[30]

The new policy was not to last, however. Officials in Ottawa, having considered the concerns expressed by the land agents in the west when the policy was first announced in summer 1879, issued orders in February 1880 that the sale of odd-numbered sections in the Mennonite reserve was not allowed. One agent, who had sold over 8000 acres in the intervening months, was then ordered to cancel all sales. This turn-around caused substantial confusion. Land agents in the west sent cables to Ottawa and Mennonites wondered why they were 'forbidden to either purchase or homestead odd numbered sections.'[31] Some weeks later, on 23 March 1880, the old policy was reinstated, meaning that the Mennonites could now homestead on the odd-numbered sections. Those who had purchased such sections were now given a refund of their money and allowed to make homestead entries instead.

Unfortunately, questions about the status of the odd-numbered sections reappeared. Early in 1883, when another order-in-council granted odd-numbered sections in another area to the CPR, which then set out to sell them, the list was again found to include lands in the Mennonite west reserve. When this inclusion came to the attention of the deputy minister of the Interior, he stopped the railway company's planned sale, claiming that the Mennonite reserve had been created before 'any right of the Company had accrued.' The issue developed into a decade-long controversy, involving the Justice Department and the Cabinet. Finally, in 1893, the government took the position that it had first given the lands to the Mennonites and therefore could not have given them to the railway company.[32] In this way the thrust of the initial promises made to the Mennonites was upheld but the extended uncertainty and several reversals created considerable difficulty for them.

A third issue involved the desire of the Mennonites to live in villages rather than on individual homesteads. Their methods of farming, the operation of their schools, and numerous social and religious practices presumed settlement in villages. However, the government's grand homesteading scheme required settlers to live on their individual homesteads, at least for the first three years. It appears that the Mennonites were not aware of this proviso when they arrived. They simply proceeded to settle in villages. Fortunately, in April 1876, Parliament moved to allow village settlement by inserting, into the Dominion Lands Act that, 'In the case of settlements being formed of immigrants in communities (such as those of Mennonites or Icelanders) the Minister of the Interior may vary or waive, in his discretion, the foregoing requirements as to residence and cultivation on each separate quarter-section entered as a homestead.'[33]

In keeping with this change in the law, the form with which a settler was to apply for the patent, that is the legal title for his homestead, was eventually changed, too. The first version required him to declare: 'I ... have been actually residing on my homestead.' Obviously, this wording was not suited to people living in villages. The problem was brought to the authorities on several occasions and in 1883 a more appropriately worded form was developed.[34]

A fourth government accommodation related to the oath of allegiance, which had to be taken by an immigrant in order to become a British subject, which in turn was necessary to obtain the patent, or legal title, for one's homestead. Mennonite settlers certainly wanted legal title for their lands but they had a historic antipathy against taking oaths. Also, the words in the oath suggested a willingness to render military service. One official reported to Ottawa that: 'They hesitate to become naturalized owing to a professed difficulty in taking the oath of allegiance and also because should they become subjects of Her Majesty they would be called upon to take up arms in her defence ... They claim that they were promised ... that they should be relieved from Military service and they object to naturalization until they have a reassurance of this promise.'[35]

The government then passed an order-in-council on 27 August 1877 giving the desired reassurance. The order referred to the earlier promise of exemption given to the Mennonites and then stated: 'Taking the Oath of Allegiance ... will not be construed as interfering with the immunity from Military service secured to them.'[36] Despite this reassurance, a few Mennonites remained hesitant. Several tried to purchase their land and thus become owners without taking the oath. For most, however, the arrangement was satisfactory. They affirmed the oath, became British subjects, and acquired legal title to their land.

The commitment to reserve a block of land for the exclusive use of Mennonites was not to continue indefinitely. It had served the basic purpose of helping the Mennonites to become established in an area by themselves. But some of the reserved areas had remained unsettled, providing one reason for the problems with the squatters and for the pressures from other settlers. One official argued that the Mennonites, having 'failed in completely settling the reserve, had lost their right to it.'[37] Other officials felt that 'good faith to the Mennonites requires that we shall continue these reservations indefinitely until the lands have all been taken up by Mennonites.'[38] Several Mennonite leaders expressed the hope that the government would follow this policy. It was clear, however, that the few areas within the reserves that had not been taken up were of poor quality and not desired by Mennonites. Moreover, a few Mennonites were selling their land to non-Mennonites. For these and other reasons, the government moved, in 1898, to terminate the special arrangements, so that the land in the reserves that had not yet been settled became available to the public at large.[39]

THE RESERVES IN SASKATCHEWAN

By the 1890s some Mennonites in Manitoba were looking for another place to settle. Virtually all the better land in their Manitoba reserves had been taken up. Another wave of Mennonite immigrants from Europe was coming. Most had large families. And children of the first settlers were now eager to set up their own farms. At the same time, railways with various branch lines were being completed in the North-West Territories, as the area was then known. Also, the government was eager to promote settlement there.

The movement of the Mennonites to the northwest began slowly. Several Mennonite families from Manitoba moved in 1891.[40] Soon after some Mennonites came from Europe directly. These, however, settled more on the individual basis suggested by the general homestead system. A more group-oriented effort began early in 1894, when leaders of the Mennonites in Manitoba asked their solicitor, J.B. McLaren, to write to the federal government 'with a view to securing another small reserve further west.' They suggested that the land be reserved 'for a period of say five years.'[41]

In the following months there were discussions with officials about the best-suited areas. When Manitoba Mennonite leaders visited the north-west in the summer of 1894, they selected four townships near the town of Hague.[42] They then met with the minister of the Interior and asked that the even-numbered sections in these townships be reserved. According to their account of the meeting, they dealt with the question of the odd-numbered sections by asking the minister to help them to make arrangements with the railway company so that it would 'reserve these lands for sale to the Mennonites for a term of say at least five years.'[43] This was not part of the minister's account of the meeting but he indicated a willingness to take their general request to the government and stated that the good record of the Mennonites would make things easy.

An order-in-council granting a reserve of the four townships was passed on 23 January 1895.[44] It noted that the principle of reserving land for Mennonites had begun in 1873, and that a new reserve was now needed 'in order to meet the growing needs of their families, and to encourage the settlement of their fellow-countrymen in Canada.' It also assured them that they would 'be enabled to carry out the principles of their Social System, and to settle together in hamlets (for which provision is made by section 37 of the Dominion Lands Act) by obtaining entries for contiguous lands.' Following this approval the Mennonite group settlement began. The movement grew beyond initial expectations so the Mennonites asked for and received a fifth township. It was added to their reserve with an order-in-council on 24 June 1898.[45]

With these orders-in-council the matter of reserving an area of land for the Mennonites was firm in an official sense. However, as in Manitoba, there were practical complications. Some of these were related to an effort in 1898 by the immigration commissioner in Winnipeg to settle a colony of Galicians in an area nearby. This effort had 'encountered very great difficulty.' As a result, many Galicians had returned to the more settled areas in Manitoba. A few had been prevailed upon to remain but these, according to a Dominion Lands agent, had consented to stay 'only on the condition that they would be allowed to make their own selections of lands, which they did on the Mennonite reserve, and as the Mennonites in the locality did not offer any objection it was deemed best to allow them to remain there.'[46]

Understandably, this deliberate settlement by government officials of non-Mennonites on land within the reserve became contentious. One official, C.W. Speers, recounted the trouble they had had with Galicians and expressed the hope that the Mennonites would now be asked to make an adjustment 'in the interest of the Galician settler.'[47] However, the deputy minister of the Interior was reluctant to withdraw land from the Mennonites after the government had formally reserved it for them. He advised Speers to 'adjust the matter as best you can.'[48] When more Mennonites found 'that lands selected by them were homesteaded by non-Mennonites,' they asked their solicitor in Manitoba, J.B. McLaren, to appeal to Ottawa. In a letter to the secretary of the Department of the Interior, McLaren wrote:

While the Mennonite Association appreciates the kindly recognition given to them as settlers in setting aside this reserve for them and while they do not wish to appear as carping at small matters they feel very keenly in regard to outsiders being allowed to settle on their reserve. As you are aware they live largely in the village system or at all events on the community system. They have their own Mutual Aid Societies, Mutual Fire Insurance Companies, Mennonite schools, commune system of herding cattle, together with other institutions peculiar to themselves and under the control of or in connection with their church. These institutions, as you will readily see, are based on the settlement being exclusively Mennonite, and a very few non-Mennonite settlers could prevent their successful operation.[49]

The authorities were in an awkward situation. The land in dispute involved primarily the fifth township, which had been added to the reserve with the order-in-council of 24 June 1898. Mr Speers, it seems, had not been aware that this township belonged to the Mennonites. Also, the Mennonites who were said not to have raised objections to the settlement of the Galicians may have been those who had settled on a more individual basis near this reserve. Whatever the situation, the understanding between officials and the Galicians appears to have been quite firm. A senior land agent in the region warned that 'any appearance of breach of faith with them might lead to undesireable results.'[50] It is understandable, then, that the reply that McLaren received from Ottawa on 24 April 1899 said little more than that 'Mr. Speers ... has been instructed to see the persons interested and do what he can to have the matter satisfactorily adjusted.'[51]

The problem was discussed at some length in the following weeks. On one occasion the Mennonite leader, Franz Froese, wrote to the minister, the Hon. Clifford Sifton. On another occasion some thirty-five Mennonites signed a petition requesting the government 'to make arrangements so as to keep the Galicians from settling among us in our Reserve.'[52] Meanwhile, officials wanted to protect at least those Galicians who might have settled on the land before it was declared a reserve. But this was not easily done because some Galicians had moved around, taking possession of land without bothering immediately to make official entries in land offices. When officials sought more definite instructions from Ottawa, the department refused, saying: 'It is impossible to give any definite instructions to Mr. Speers in this connection but he should go there, look into the matter on the spot, and make the best arrangement possible.'[53]

In August 1899, Speers undertook to work out a settlement. He visited many of the settlers concerned. In some instances he recommended that entries made by Mennonites be cancelled and that the claim of the Galicians be allowed. In other instances the Galicians were refused.[54] The Department of the Interior proceeded to ratify his recommendations but several Mennonites whose entries were cancelled protested strongly. Eventually it was found that Speers had favoured those Galicians who had made a claim to land in the summer of 1898 because he had understood that the land had been reserved for the Mennonites only in October 1898. In fact, the fifth township had been reserved on 24 June 1898.[55] The discovery of this fact, in January 1900, strengthened the claim of the Mennonites, but some Galicians, when so informed, protested strongly. There were threats of violence.[56] The conflict continued into the summer of 1901. Speers made another personal visit. Eventually, the few contending Mennonites were persuaded to surrender their claims and to take land in another part of the reserve.[57]

In addition to these difficulties with the Galicians, there was a problem regarding the desire of the Mennonites to live in villages. It surfaced in 1899, when some Mennonites who had held their homesteads for the required three years applied for patents and were refused. Changes in the hamlet clause, first inserted into the Dominion Lands Act in 1876, had created some confusion. The 1876 provision, which allowed the minister of the Interior to waive the requirements that a homesteader reside on and cultivate his particular homestead, had been replaced in 1883 with one allowing only the residence requirement to be waived, and even that was now subject to new conditions. The law, as of 1883, stated: 'If a number of homestead settlers, embracing at least twenty families, with the view to greater convenience in the establishment of schools and churches, and to the attainment of social advantages of like character, ask to be allowed to settle together in a hamlet or village, the Minister may, in his discretion, vary or dispense with the foregoing requirements as to residence, but not as to cultivation of each quarter section entered as a homestead.'[58]

In keeping with this change, officials informed the Hague Mennonite settlers that the law did not allow a homesteader to obtain a patent if he had not cultivated at least a portion of his particular homestead. This point was of concern to the Mennonites. In addition to an exemption from the residence requirement, the Mennonites also needed some flexibility regarding the cultivation requirement. In the negotiations for the Hague reserve they had stated their desire 'to perform their homestead duties according to the village system in the same way as they had been permitted to do ... in Manitoba.'[59] Moreover, the order-in-council of 23 January 1895, which established the reserve at Hague, and the one of 24 June 1898, which added one township, had stated that the Mennonites would be able 'to carry out the principles of their Social System, and to settle together in hamlets.'

Fortunately, the issue was soon resolved. The solicitor for the Mennonites, J.B. McLaren, approached the minister of the Interior who then agreed to accept a solemn declaration from the Mennonite leader Franz Froese about Froese's understanding as to what had been agreed to in the early negotiations. As a result, an order-in-council was passed on 6 March 1900 acknowledging that the Mennonites who had settled in the northwest had 'received assurance from the Department in the year 1894 that the privilege of residing in hamlets and cultivating land in common, which was at one time enjoyed by Mennonites in Manitoba,' would continue to apply to them, and that they had relied on such assurance and had proceeded to settle accordingly. The order then stated that they could obtain the patents for their homesteads without residing on them.[60]

The issue of the odd-numbered sections belonging to the railway company seems not to have caused problems. At one point the minister advised the Mennonites to go directly to the agents of the railway company with plans to purchase the odd-numbered sections. The surviving records do not indicate what happened but the rapid emergence of more than twenty villages in the Hague settlement suggests that there were few major difficulties.[61]

A second Saskatchewan reserve near Swift Current, 200 miles south of Hague, was opened almost a decade later, again at the initiative of Mennonites in Manitoba. After finding a suitable area, two of the Mennonite leaders, Franz Froese and John Wall, went to Ottawa in July 1904 to ask that it be reserved.[62] The Hon. Clifford Sifton, minister of the Interior, acted quickly. He instructed his officials to make the necessary inspections without delay, and on 13 August 1904 the government passed an order-in-council reserving six townships for the Mennonites. The order noted that the lands were not of particularly good quality: 'They are reported as not being of a class which would make them suitable for farming by ordinary settlers ... but ... guided ... by the results which have attended the efforts of the Mennonite community in other parts of Manitoba and the North West Territories in founding colonies ... they will be able to work the lands applied for with success.'[63]

The odd-numbered sections in the Swift Current reserve did not pose a problem. Some of these had already been made the property of the railway company but they remained under the administration of the government, which now gave the Mennonites an exclusive right to purchase them. For the other odd-numbered sections, the government agreed to let the Mennonites homestead on them just as on the even-numbered sections. The order also stated that no one, unless approved by the 'Mennonite Association' or otherwise authorized by the Department of the Interior, was to have homestead rights within the reserve and that 'such reserve shall be continued for three years.'

These official provisions seemed adequate but once again there were problems with non-Mennonite settlers. The Mennonites, eager to avoid such problems, had 'deliberately selected lands which had been in the market for nearly a generation' and for which there had been no demand. Indeed, the department had felt that the lands were not good enough to warrant efforts to encourage settlers to locate there.[64] Nevertheless, in the summer of 1904, while the Mennonites were negotiating for the reserve, some non-Mennonite settlers claimed homesteads in the area. Others were approved later when officials 'inadvertently overlooked' the order-in-council creating the reservation.[65]

To deal with the situation, the solicitors McLaren, McLeod, and Black, of Morden, Manitoba, who had long served the Mennonites, wrote a strong letter to the new minister, Frank Oliver, in spring 1906. They said that in their extensive experience with helping Mennonites to settle on reserves, they had 'always had interminable trouble maintaining the reserves for the Mennonites' and that 'the underlings in the Department seem to be opposed to allowing the Mennonites to have their reserves undisturbed.' They noted that Mr Turriff, the commissioner of Dominion Lands, had 'openly avowed his objection to these reserves.' They described the predicament of the Mennonites in the following way:

Mennonite settlers who are entitled to entry under the terms of the reservation, went up from here to Swift Current, taking their effects with them, and seven of them have found the lands which they selected taken up, and they are now stranded on the prairie awaiting your intervention in the matter. This Spring, 104 cars of stuff have left this district for the Swift Current Reserve, together with about 450 persons in all. So far 230 entries have been made, and there is a large number yet to be made. We do not know whether any further entries have been made by non-Mennonites or not, but we would ask you to take immediate steps to have the entries already made, cancelled.[66]

The solicitors also referred to their earlier suggestion, partly incorporated in the order-in-council, but not operationalized, whereby every Mennonite, when applying for a homestead, would 'have a certificate from Mr. Franz Froese, the agent of the (Mennonite) association, showing that he is entitled to a Homestead on the Reserve.' Land agents would grant entries only to applicants who had such a certificate.

In reality the problem was not widespread. Less than ten homesteads had been approved for non-Mennonites through the oversight. Still, the Department of the Interior now accepted the suggestion and instructed the lands office in Regina that 'applicants for entries should first obtain a certificate from an accredited representative of the Mennonite Association.'[67] It warned the particular official involved in the oversight that any repetition would lead to his immediate dismissal. But it ruled that the several homesteads that had been granted to non-Mennonites should be allowed to stand because they were 'granted to bona fide settlers.'

The issue of village settlement was complex, too. When the Mennonites arrived and began to settle in villages, some local officials objected. The Mennonites then petitioned the minister to 'allow them to perform their homestead duties on the hamlet system,' arguing that they had been allowed this privilege before and that it had contributed to the rapid development of the areas where they had settled. They stated further that it was particularly important in the Swift Current area because of the difficulty and expense of digging the very deep wells necessary to get water. If this burden were placed upon each individual homesteader, then the development of the area would be much slower than if they could have wells together in villages.[68] They also referred to the importance of village settlement for their social and religious life.

A reply from the department came in the spring of 1905. It was willing to let the people settle in villages subject to a strict interpretation of the legal provision which, according to the 1883 amendment, required a petition from 'a number of homestead settlers, embracing at least twenty families.' This strict interpretation created problems. The formation of hamlets or villages was naturally a gradual process; they did not suddenly have twenty settlers in them. When some officials expressed concern about this matter, the solicitor for the Mennonites, A. McLeod, wrote another strong letter to the minister in July 1906:

None of the hamlets yet have twenty settlers in them, and the inspectors of the Department are poking around and notifying the homesteaders in these hamlets to get on their land. I cannot understand what the inspectors are doing there at all, unless they are there for the express purpose of worrying these people. No one can homestead the lands except Mennonites who get certificates from the society, and they will not give two certificates for the one piece of land. The society has three years to settle the reserve, and before that time is up, every homestead that is worth taking in the reserve will be settled if the officials simply let them alone.[69]

The minister's officials did not respond immediately and McLeod wrote again, this time with a tangible proposal. He explained that eight hamlets were in the process of being formed but that none of them had twenty settlers yet. He then asked that the entries of these settlers be protected until the required number had been reached, at which time the formal application for hamlet status would be submitted.[70] The department accepted this proposal. The 'hamlet privilege' was abolished in 1907, but when four Mennonite villages applied soon after, each having the required twenty residents, their applications were approved because for the Mennonites 'the arrangements were made before the change in the regulations.'[71] The formation of several more villages was helped, it appears, by the fact that they were able to purchase certain odd-numbered sections.[72]

In reviewing this Mennonite settlement experience, it is clear that the federal government made significant changes in the homestead laws and thereby extended 'the limits of liberty' so that Mennonites could become established in their desired communal way. The government reserved areas of land so that only Mennonites could homestead within them. It helped the Mennonites to obtain the odd-numbered sections within those reserved areas. It waived the normal requirement that homesteaders reside on their individual homesteads and proved flexible also with regard to the cultivation requirements, thereby facilitating the village settlement that the Mennonites desired. These concessions, taken together, represent a fairly broad liberty.

Although the government's actions to accommodate the Mennonites were significant, they were accompanied by innumerable practical problems. That these kept reappearing may suggest that the issue involved more than inadequate administrative practises and that the basic institutional framework for landholding was not well suited to accommodating communities. The framework was not like the one for colonies in Russia before the 1870s. The framework in Canada was oriented more towards the individual: it could be modified but it was not to be changed in a basic way. Also, Canada's political culture was not in harmony with communalism. The lack of enthusiasm for the Mennonite reserves on the part of some officials appears to have come not from any general dislike of Mennonites but from a sense that the idea of a reserve for a particular group of people was somehow unfair. This view is understandable. The broad settlement plan, that homestead entries would be given to the first eligible applicants, suggested a process of egalitarianism and individualism. The Mennonites, in contrast, were given privileges on a communal basis. It is not surprising that officials, when pressured by other settlers, did not always support the idea of reserves for Mennonites.

If these institutional and cultural dimensions help to explain the difficulties, what factors help to explain the relative success of the effort? Clearly, the eagerness of the federal government to attract settlers was a major factor in its willingness to make concessions. Also, the fact that there were few settlers in the west at this time made it easier for the government to be flexible. Moreover, the 'political process' with the Mennonites seems to have been open, direct, and marked by good faith. The Mennonites, despite their separatism, were not anarchists. Their theology had a definite place for government. They did not hesitate to approach government with what they felt were legitimate concerns. They sent numerous communications to officials, both directly and indirectly through solicitors and other intermediaries. They made complaints and proposed ways of resolving difficulties. The Mennonites were also willing to make some compromises. This willingness to compromise and to communicate in a forthright manner is suggested in an 1880 letter from Isaak Mueller, a Mennonite leader in Manitoba, to Sir John A. Macdonald, who, in addition to being prime minister, was also the minister of the Interior. Before describing his specific complaint, Mueller said: 'The Government of which you are the Honourable head has always met our complaints with justice remedying mistake where it was possible to do so and we again have always endeavoured to yield any point your department has demanded.'[73]

This good faith on the part of both Mennonites and the government, the open and direct communications about the problems, the general flexibility on both sides, and the usefulness of the Mennonites in advancing the government's objective of settling the west may help to explain why, despite numerous difficulties, the arrangements for the Mennonite reserves were moderately successful.

3 The Doukhobor Community

The Doukhobors came from Russia to Canada in the first half of 1899; they numbered approximately 7400.[1] They wanted to follow a communal agrarian way of life. To do so their representatives had made special arrangements with the federal government. Within a decade, however, the government changed its mind.

The history of communalism among Doukhobors is uneven. To a degree it is implied in their religion but they did not practice it consistently. For some periods the traditional Russian village system, which included many forms of co-operation but allowed for private property, seems to have been sufficient. Late in the eighteenth century, however, the Doukhobor leader Pobirokhin 'sought to establish a form of religious communism.'[2] But he was not able to go far in implementing his ideas before the Doukhobors were banished to 'various regions on the periphery of the Russian Empire.' The ideas did not disappear, however. Early in the nineteenth century when a more liberal czar, Alexander I, stopped the persecution and arranged for the Doukhobors to settle by themselves in Taurida province, they followed a more thorough communalism for one generation. According to one account:

There were common herds of cattle and sheep. The land was tilled in common, and in the villages there were common granaries and mills and also communal baking ovens, which supplied to the various households all the bread they needed. The members of the Community were encouraged to make farming their principal occupation, though, apart from the crafts necessary to self-sufficiency, such as metal-working and weaving, there were also a few cottage industries, such as the manufacture of linen and of gaily coloured woollen sashes and caps for sale outside the Community. Individuals were discouraged from trading. This was done by the elders on behalf of the Community as a whole.[3]

After about two decades this communalism weakened. There were internal problems as well as external pressures. Gradually, families began to keep their own cattle and fields, but they still had some 'gardens and flocks which belonged to the whole community.'[4] After 1841, when the Doukhobors were again exiled, this time to the mountainous regions in the Transcaucasian provinces, they did not establish such a thorough-going communalism. They shared generously with those in need but they held their property privately.[5]

Late in the nineteenth century, when a division occurred among the Doukhobors, one group, led by Peter V. Verigin, made a new effort to live communally. Verigin was sent into internal exile in 1887 but this did not remove his influence. Indeed, it was in exile that he met followers of Leo Tolstoy and accepted many of their ideas, which he then sent back to his Doukhobor followers. By 1893 Verigin was calling his followers 'to return to the ancient Doukhobor traditions of Christian communism.'[6] Debts among the Doukhobors should be forgiven and those to outsiders should be paid. Property should be pooled so that 'all things would be held in common.' Military service, including non-combatant service, was to be refused. As for the oath of allegiance: 'Christ had forbidden oaths; therefore no Doukhobor should swear allegiance to the tsar.'[7]

The authorities had little tolerance for the refusal of the Doukhobors to take the oath and to serve in the military. As a result the Doukhobors suffered severely. The Doukhobor plight now came to the attention of prominent outsiders, including Count Leo Tolstoy and Prince D.A. Hilkoff. The latter had once served with a military regiment stationed near a Doukhobor village. These men now joined in the efforts to help the Doukhobors. Before long, plans were under way for an emigration. As they prepared, Verigin, who was still in exile, sent a further message about communalism: 'I want the Doukhobors to live in communities but they ought to be based on a free principle. Each family should have a separate house, a pair of horses, and a cow at their disposal. The increase of the cattle should join the common herd and be common. All the work in the fields should be done together. Each family should get its allowance in corn for itself and the forage for the cattle. The remaining revenue should be common and be kept in the cash office of the community.'[8]

The desire for a communal life was a factor in the negotiations with the government of Canada but it was not dealt with in a precise way. When Prince Kropotkin wrote to Professor James Mavor in Toronto in August 1898, he stated that in addition to an exemption from military service, the Doukhobors would want 'land in a block' and 'full independence in their inner organization.'[9] Mavor met with Department of Interior officials in September and probably conveyed these concerns, but details are not known. Soon after two blocks of land, consisting together of twenty-one townships were reserved for the Doukhobors.[10] These were located near the town of Yorkton, in what became the province of Saskatchewan in 1905. The deputy minister of the Interior, James A. Smart, made arrangements with the railway company so that the Doukhobors could have both the even- and odd-numbered sections within the reserved areas.[11] Later, more land was reserved several hundred miles north, near the town of Blaine Lake, along the North Saskatchewan River. This would be referred to as the Prince Albert or Saskatchewan reserve, but here only the even-numbered sections were held for the Doukhobors. The Doukhobors who settled here, being more individualistic, accepted this arrangement.

While sizeable amounts of land were thus reserved, certain important questions were not adequately addressed. It was not clear whether the Doukhobors were to make 'entries' for their homesteads individually and whether they had to reside on and cultivate each homestead. When problems arose several years later, the English Quaker merchant Aylmer Maude, who was also involved in the negotiations, reported that there had been an understanding that the Doukhobors would 'make entry for their homesteads individually' but that they would be allowed to cultivate their land in common.[12] If this was the understanding in the negotiations, it is doubtful that the Doukhobors were aware of it.

Although there were difficulties ahead, at the time of the negotiations the prospects were good. When the first Doukhobors arrived at Halifax, early in 1899, they were greeted warmly. Smart, the deputy minister, was there and newspapers carried glowing accounts.[13] The Doukhobors spent some time in immigration halls and proceeded to their land in the spring. They settled in villages. A number of the men took jobs on the railroad to earn money for the community. Others began to use their many domestic and farming skills. Quakers from Philadelphia sent 300 spinning-wheels and other forms of assistance as did a number of Canadian groups. The government also provided funds. It appeared that the Doukhobors would soon become a self-sufficient and well-established community.

THE 'ENTRY' PROBLEM AND OTHER DIFFICULTIES

In spite of the good prospects, difficulties soon appeared. Already in January 1899, after the land at Yorkton had been reserved but before the Doukhobors had settled on it, there were protests. A local newspaper headlined: 'No Canadians or Britishers Allowed.' It criticized 'the action of the Minister ... in thus arbitrarily appropriating it (the land) for the sole use of his Doukhobor pets.'[14] Officials reported that about thirty-five homesteaders in three townships 'are going to stoutly rebel [sic] against the government if they allow Doukhobors to settle among them. When the Doukhobors learned of this and other protests they agreed to release the three townships in question, which happened to be inside the Manitoba border.[15] In return they received two townships on the other side of the reserve, close to the Swan River.

In the discussions for this exchange of townships there was a misunderstanding of some consequence. The Doukhobors, so it was later reported, 'were told by the Interpreter employed by the Immigration Department ... that while they would not be permitted to settle in Manitoba, they might go west and settle anywhere in Swan River that they wished.'[16] They used this freedom but when it was found, a year later, that they had set up several villages outside the boundaries of the reserves, there was concern. Herbert Archer, and English Tolstoyan who lived among the Doukhobors, made strong pleas on behalf of these villages. He pointed out that the land within the two added townships was of poor quality and that these Doukhobors had 'built good villages, plowed a good bit of land, [built] bridges over the Swan, ... in general made a good start, ... [and] ardently desire to be in communities according to the understanding when they arrived in Canada.'[17] He was 'convinced that their settlement outside the Reserve ... was done in perfect good faith.'[18] In spite of Archer's efforts, the Department of the Interior refused to give reserve status to the areas in which these villages were located.[19]

Two more townships were added to the reserves in the spring of 1900. Here the Doukhobors settled in villages as they had elsewhere but in summer 1900 they learned that, in these townships, the status of the odd-numbered sections was not clear. Smart, the deputy minister, held that since these had been reserved at the same time as those at Prince Albert the same provisions applied, namely that only the even-numbered sections were reserved.[20] Once again, Herbert Archer pleaded on behalf of the Doukhobors. He explained that unlike the Doukhobors at Prince Albert, who had always known that they had access only to the even-numbered sections, the local group had assumed that the odd-numbered sections were for them, too. They had built their villages in good faith, he argued.[21] Once again, however, his efforts were not successful. By the fall of 1900, after various other discussions, Archer advised the Doukhobors to leave the area and to settle within the original reserve.[22]

The surrounding residents also expressed their displeasure. In summer 1900 a group of settlers in the area sent a petition to the House of Commons asking that the exclusive settlement rights given to Doukhobors be rescinded.[23] Some ranchers expressed their views in other ways. According to one Immigration official: 'The Doukhobors informed me, and I believe they were right – that some of the Ranchers there actually came at night, pulled the fences down and drove their cattle into their crops.'[24]

Alongside these difficulties there was a more basic problem. It involved the requirement that settlers register or 'enter' applications for individual homesteads. If the Doukhobors agreed to do this, they could be taking a step away from communalism. They had vigorous internal debates on this question. Some argued that 'the fullness of Doukhobor life' required a thoroughgoing communalism and that any individualism would lead to moral decline.[25] Others were prepared to accept a measure of individualism. Certainly, some of the Doukhobors in the Prince Albert colony were willing to register applications for individual homesteads. The debate was difficult because most of the Doukhobors were illiterate and there were strong outside influences. Peter Verigin, who at this time was still in exile in Russia, counselled communalism.[26] Leo Tolstoy, having heard of possible steps in the direction of private property, advised them against it. In a lengthy letter dated 27 February 1900, Tolstoy wrote: 'If you wish to continue to live a Christian life, and do not wish to disavow all for the sake of which you suffered and were exiled from your fatherland, then you must not live as the world lives, each accumulating property separately ... property means – that what I consider mine, I not only will not give to whoever wishes to take it, but will defend from him ... property is defended by the threat of violence ... to acknowledge property is to acknowledge violence.'[27]

In June of that year the Doukhobors made a lengthy appeal to the government. It was entitled 'Petition to the Canadian government from the delegates of the Society of Universal Brotherhood, near Yorkton.' The petition was signed by twenty-eight Doukhobors but drafted by the Russian anarchist Alexander Bodyansky who lived among them. In it they said:

We ask you not to enforce against us such of your laws as contradict our beliefs, and thus to give us the possibility of living in your country without breaking openly or tacitly, directly or indirectly, our conception of the Truth ... The laws of your country require that every male emigrant, 18 years of age, who wants to settle on vacant government land, has to record it in his name, and after a certain term, such land becomes his property. But we ... cannot record homesteads in our individual names, cannot make them our private property, for we believe in so doing we should directly break God's Truth ... there is no excuse for a man who, knowing the Law of God, still appropriates as his own something that is not the fruit of his labor, but was created by God for the use of everybody. Is not the division, the ownership and the recording of land the main cause of wars and strife among men, and is it not the cause of their being masters and serfs? ... We petition you to let us have the land for settlement and agricultural purposes, not upon your general conditions for emigrants, but upon the conditions given to your Indians – that is, the land to be held by the community and not by the individual members. It matters not to us whether that land be considered our community property, or the property of your country; but we would like it to be considered as given to us for an indefinite period of time, and if you wish us to pay rent we are willing to do so, provided we shall be able.[28]

The government did not respond to the petition immediately but 'quiet measures were taken to have known friends and benefactors of the Doukhobors attempt to dissuade them.'[29] The Doukhobors received lengthy appeals from Aylmer Maude, from the Quakers in Philadelphia, and from those in England. The letter from the Quakers in England, written in November 1900, stated:

You say it is breaking the truth of God to write down parcels of land in your personal names, to make them your property, because God made the land for all people. But ... with so large an area of land being occupied by new settlers, it would be impossible for the Government to know what parts are still left free if it was not all measured and written down. If this had not been done it could not, without a long delay, have given you the land you needed; and you might have gone on to lots already taken up by other people, without your knowing it, thus causing great confusion and disappointment ... We trust it will be your hearty desire to show your gratitude to the Government that has been so generous to you; and to help others who come, like yourselves, to settle in Canada; and we therefore counsel you by all means to comply with the reasonable laws which require that each quarter section shall be written down in the name of the man to whom it is granted ... There is no duty more clearly inculcated in the New Testament than obedience to rulers and governors, and to their laws, so long as these do not conflict with the higher law of God.[30]

While various intermediaries were attempting to persuade the Douk-hobors, their petition of June 1900 was also being discussed among government officials. Finally, on 7 January 1901, J.G. Turriff, the commissioner of Dominion Lands, replied: 'In reference to the question of taking up land it can only be done in the ordinary way. We have only one system of granting free homesteads to settlers, and the same rules apply to every settler ... irrespective of his nationality or religious belief ... The government is quite willing that your people should reside in villages, the cultivation of course to be done on the individual home-steads.'[31] Turriff explained further that 'after your individual settlers have completed their homestead duties a patent will issue to each homesteader, giving him the full and absolute ownership of the land,' and if they would decide then to hold the land in common the government would not interfere in any way.

This government position did not satisfy the Doukhobors. Consider-ing a compromise, one Doukhobor village proposed: 'We'll give you a list of those men who have according to your laws a right to obtain land ... by the law of the country you are obliged to fix the name of a man to his farm. You can do this ... But we want common land.'[32] Another proposal, made later in 1901, asked that the government sell the land to a loan company and then let the Doukhobors obtain it by purchase. This proposal had been approved at a meeting of representatives from the various Doukhobor villages but government officials rejected it, as they had the earlier proposal.[33]

The differences between the Doukhobors and the government were becoming sharper. Some officials began to suggest that the land be taken away from the Doukhobors. In January 1902, J.O. Smith (who had succeeded W. McCreary as commissioner for Immigration in Winnipeg) wrote: 'I am convinced that some of these people will not take up their homestead entries in the ordinary way until they realize that by their neglect the land which is freely offered to them has passed from their possession.'[34] Soon plans were made to implement this idea and to open some of the lands reserved for the Doukhobors to the general public.[35] Before these plans could be carried out, however, two Doukhobor delegates met with the minister of the Interior, the Hon. Clifford Sifton. As a result, the minister, in a 15 February 1902 letter, made an important accommodation:

It is ... necessary for your own protection against outsiders that you should make individual entry for the land, and at the expiration of the three years you can do as you like with the same, either conveying it to some person as trustee of the village or ... the Doukhobor Community ... I have decided that those who will take their homesteads and accept of free land from the Government may live together in one or more villages and instead of being compelled to cultivate each quarter section held by each Doukhobor, that the land around the village itself may be cultivated and the work which otherwise would be required on each individual homestead may be done altogether around the village ... If, for instance, a village wants 50 homesteads around the village, I will be satisfied if the amount of improvements required for each quarter-section is done around the village, only for the whole fifty. This would enable all those in the village to live together and to work together in and around the village without being compelled to go a long way out to their individual homesteads.[36]

In effect, Sifton's letter waived both the residence and the cultivation requirements but not the requirement that 'entries' be made for individual homesteads. The Doukhobors would be able to practise communalism once they had made the entries.

While the Doukhobors were trying to resolve the 'entry' problem, significant internal differences began to emerge. Approximately 1700 people from among the more communistic and poorer Doukhobors set out on a pilgrimage across the prairie, claiming to follow the call of God. Some rejected the use of work horses, the keeping of cattle, the use of money, the idea of cultivating the soil, and physical labour. After all, they said, the early apostles had also left their labours in order to follow Christ.[37] The pilgrimage became a four-month adventure and led to further public criticism. Government officials believed that it was caused in large part by the unresolved entry problem but other factors may also have been at work.[38] Officials now began to place their hopes in Peter V. Verigin, the Doukhobor leader who was still in exile in Russia. Indeed, the Canadian government may have asked the Russian government to release him.[39]

Verigin came to Canada in December 1902. When his train stopped in Winnipeg, the *Manitoba Free Press* carried a positive account of him: 'His eyes are dark and thoughtful, and his whole expression is that of a man who has suffered much and has triumphed over everything through the force of kingly courage and constancy.'[40] The acting immigration commissioner was quoted as telling Verigin: 'You will know all about the troubles the Government has had with the Doukhobors when you get among them. We hope your coming will have a very good effect. We will do anything possible to help you.'[41] When Verigin arrived among the

Doukhobors he received support from all of the different elements in the community. Even those who had participated in the pilgrimage agreed to moderate their behaviour.

Verigin acted quickly on the entry problem. Early in January 1903 he invited J.S. Crerar, the Dominion Lands agent in Yorkton, to meet with him and other Doukhobor leaders to find out 'the true particulars of the Land Act' and the duties that the Doukhobors needed to perform.[42] When he asked Crerar whether the government would consider making further changes, Crerar replied that 'there was no hope in making any change as the matter was decided that they must make their homestead entries the same as other people.' He noted that many people were 'waiting for the Government to throw open the Douk' [sic] Reserve.' After a lengthy discussion, Verigin stated that they would soon have 'a big meeting at a central village with a representative from all other villages when the whole land question would be settled.'

This 'big meeting' took place on 10 February 1903. It lasted nearly a whole day and both Crerar and Hugh Harley, the Dominion Lands agents at Yorkton and Swan River respectively, were there. In addition to matters relating to homestead entries, the officials explained 'that they would have to become British Subjects before they would be granted a patent for their lands.'[43] This 'was for some time a stickler with them' Crerar later reported. They asked for two weeks' time to think about it but Crerar and Harley refused, saying that the matter had to be settled that day. According to Harley, 'I told them that they had been humbugging and playing with the government ... that they must settle it now or never, as if not the land would be thrown open to other settlers at once.'[44]

At this, the Doukhobors decided to take up the land. They asked, however, 'that they not be compelled to apply individually.'[45] Accordingly, they set up a three-member committee and gave it power of attorney to make the entries for them. In this way the individual Doukhobor would not know which quarter-section had been 'entered' in his name. Thus, the idea of holding the land communally was preserved and legalized. The willingness of the Doukhobors to now make entries prompted the *Manitoba Free Press* to write, under the headline 'The Doukhobors Will Homestead,' that they 'will have no other aim but to settle in Canada and become Canadians ... They will have a stake and interest in the country.'[46] By spring 1903, the committee had made entries for over 2000 eligible Doukhobors.[47]

After the Doukhobors had made their entries, 31 per cent of the land in the reserves remained unclaimed. These lands became the next object of contention. Inquiries from other settlers were becoming stronger. There were squatters. And authorities began to make plans for opening these unclaimed areas within the reserves to the general public. When the Doukhobors first learned of this possibility they were shocked. They had thought that these lands would remain available for their children and for other Doukhobors still in Russia. The authorities then agreed to let them make some claims for males 17 years of age. However, on 15 December 1903 the unclaimed areas, including 100,640 acres of the 448,615 originally reserved in the Yorkton area, were opened to the public.[48]

TOWARDS A WITHDRAWAL OF ACCOMMODATIONS

The resolution of the 'entry' problem and the firm leadership of Peter V. Verigin brought on a brief period of prosperity. Verigin purchased thirteen additional sections of land right beside the railway and set up his headquarters there for directing the affairs of the community, now formally known as the Christian Community of Universal Brotherhood (CCUB). Verigin also began an intense modernization effort. He set up a Doukhobor trading company to handle all commercial transactions for those in the Yorkton reserves and purchased farm machinery and horses to bring more and more of the land under cultivation. By 1905 the Yorkton colonies had 16 steam plows, 11 threshing machines, 6 flour mills, and 5 sawmills as well as a large brick plant.[49] It was a sizeable industrial enterprise.

Despite these improvements, there were problems. Some Doukhobors moved out of the Community and claimed individual homesteads like other settlers. (Later, these Doukhobors organized themselves as the Society of Independent Doukhobors.) At this time, however, it was difficult for individually minded Doukhobors to move out of the community. A local justice of the peace stated: 'There is a good deal of persecution going on on those who have left the Community.'[50] Other Doukhobors criticized Verigin for becoming too materialistic, for getting too many machines, and for departing from the ideal simple life in other ways. Approximately fifty Doukhobors went on a nude pilgrimage in May 1903. When some of these, in an attack on materialism, burnt a canvas on a harvesting machine belonging to the Doukhobor community, Verigin pressed charges with the result that six Doukhobors were jailed for three years.[51]

Though irritating, these internal differences were not as serious as the external problems were to become. There was growing criticism from outsiders that much of the Doukhobor land was not being cultivated.[52] In reality, the Doukhobors were cultivating steadily increasing portions. However, they began with the land near their villages so their progress was not immediately evident in the outlying areas that others now wanted to occupy. Some squatters went to the land offices and applied to have the Doukhobor entries for certain homesteads cancelled and their own claims registered instead. A few land officials agreed to this practice.[53] They claimed that it was justified because the Doukhobors were not cultivating the particular homesteads in question.

Understandably, Peter Verigin protested. In a letter of 21 February 1905, he explained that the Doukhobors were cultivating as much land as they could but that, in keeping with their communal cultivation practices, for which he claimed governmental approval, they were working the land near their villages first.[54] This reference to governmental approval for communal cultivation came as a surprise to James E. Peaker, Dominion Lands agent at Yorkton.[55] He did not know of the 'Sifton concessions.' Verigin then made a personal visit to the deputy minister of the Interior, but he could not locate the Sifton letter either.[56] Finally, a copy was found in the Immigration office in Winnipeg. Orders were then issued that no more homestead 'entries' be cancelled for lack of cultivation.[57]

When officials studied the concessions made by Sifton, who in April 1905 had been replaced as minister of the Interior by the less sympathetic Frank Oliver, they felt that it would be difficult to honour them. Applications for homesteads from other people were coming in and in order to refuse them officials had to show that the existing entries could not be cancelled, that is, that the legal requirements for maintaining the existing entries were being fulfilled. To do this on the basis of the Sifton concessions would require taking the total number of acres cultivated by the Doukhobors and dividing it by the total number of Doukhobors for whom entries had been made. This calculation would indicate whether the amount of cultivation was sufficient to meet the legal requirements, but it would be an unusual procedure. Officials were also concerned that if the arrangement was taken to include the issuing of patents, then 'patents will be issued for homesteads upon which there will be not a stroke of work done.'[58] The officials were willing to respect the proposal made early in 1901 by the then-commissioner for Dominion Lands, J.G. Turriff, to the effect that the residence requirement could be waived but not the cultivation requirement. In other words, they were willing to let the Doukhobors live in villages but they wanted to some cultivation on every homestead.

The question of whether the department would permit the Doukhobors to practise communal cultivation in accordance with the Sifton concessions became a major issue. Several investigations were conducted. The first was done in summer 1905 by C.W. Speers, the general colonization agent, on instructions from Frank Oliver, the new minister of the Interior. Speers travelled to the Doukhobor villages and suspected initially that there were some irregularities, that Verigin, through the arrangement for making entries on a proxy basis, had entered the names of people who did not exist. Speers also said that in his view Verigin and the Doukhobor committee had too much control over the people: 'The individual homesteader has never been impressed with his rights as a settler nor his independence as an individual.'[59] Speers recognized that the people probably had a 'right to cultivate in block' but recommended that there be another more thorough investigation of their work on the land.

This led to a second investigation, begun in October 1905. Under the directions of one Mr McNab, a homestead inspector, local land agents were instructed to 'lay aside whatever work you have on hand' and to make an investigation 'so that not only the privileges of the homesteaders in question may be maintained, but also that the right of the applicants for cancellation shall receive due consideration.'[60] McNab submitted his report in February 1906. His view was moderate. He had found some 114 irregularities but he did not attribute these to deceitfulness. He had words of praise for the Doukhobors but he was not sympathetic to their communalism:

We would respectfully suggest that no drastic method of procedure be pursued, but rather a line of action be taken in the light of the fact that these people have become anxious to attach themselves to particular locations – that they are among the very best material out of which to make good citizens – that they are superior to most of the foreigners finding homes in our land in intelligence, industry, aspirations and ambitions as evidenced by enterprises undertaken and work accomplished – and finally that they are rapidly absorbing Canadian sentiments.

It might here be suggested that the regulations re cultivation might be so amended as to assist in the development of individuality of action. If it were required that after a sufficient amount of 'en bloc' cultivation had been done in the neighbourhood of the Village to maintain its inhabitants, that improvements be then made upon each individual homestead ... curiosity would then impel them to discover the possessor of each parcel.

If the suggestion that upon each individual homestead some improvements be required, were acted upon it would encourage those who have the inclination to leave the Community ...[61]

Clearly, McNab did not favour a permanent communalism but neither did he wish to forcibly end the communal cultivation practices. The new minister, Frank Oliver, would have preferred stronger recommendations. On 7 March 1906, Oliver ordered that the homestead entries be 'respected for the time being' but that those entries marked by irregularities be cancelled immediately. More serious was his statement that 'no promise of patent can be made nor can patent be issued unless the requirements of the Dominion Lands Act have been fulfilled.'[62] It soon became evident that Oliver's 'requirements' included naturalization for each homesteader and cultivation on each homestead.[63] He had long been critical of communal settlements and would soon issue a drastic reinterpretation of Sifton's promise.[64]

Oliver's 7 March instructions were followed by some minor disputes regarding the cancellation of entries that appeared to be irregular. Peter Verigin argued that the entries were not irregular but that some of the men had been away from the community working on the railroad at the time when Speers and McNab made their investigations and that the mothers had answered falsely because they had feared that the officials were actually trying to make a list of young men who could then be forced into military service.[65]

The more serious shift in direction came after the next commission of inquiry. This inquiry began in August 1906 and was led by Rev. John McDougall, a Protestant clergyman who had earlier served the government in negotiations with the Indians and who, like Oliver, came from Alberta. The McDougall commission was instructed to tour the Doukhobor villages, take a general census, list the homestead entries, identify the locations of the homesteads, inspect areas under cultivation, note the amount of stock and machinery held by the Doukhobors, and discuss with them 'their experience with and attitude towards this country, the Government and things in general.'[66] The commission was also to make recommendations on which a final solution of Doukhobor land issues could be based.[67]

The McDougall commission did its work in detail. It used McNab's

1905 findings but was more negative in its judgments. McDougall wrote that the Doukhobor reserves were 'a most serious block and impediment to the natural and righteous growth of the country' and that the government in allowing the Doukhobors to have these lands was committing a 'serious injustice to the general public.'[68] He stated that of their 421,155 acres, the community Doukhobors had cultivated only 42,523 acres to date.[69] He did not acknowledge that this was adequate. The law at this time required only that a settler cultivate at least 15 of the 160 acres on a homestead in order to retain his claim.

McDougall was particularly critical of the Doukhobors' communism. He attributed this system not so much to the Doukhobor background as to the leadership of Peter Verigin, stating that 'all influences traditional and sectarian have been brought to bear on this people for the purpose of securing an abject communism under and subject to an absolute one man power.'[70] McDougall referred to Doukhobor illiteracy, superstition, and reverence in matters of faith as making it easy for Verigin to control the people. The results of this communism were, he said, 'extreme passivity and general lethargy ... a childishness in the performing of all labour.' He continued: 'No matter how small the task, yet a number will gather to perform the work therein. Thus energy and talent and time are frittered away.' McDougall stated further that 'the individual having no special interest in the land or its product becomes extremely unstable.' He praised those who had left the Community and taken individual homesteads like other settlers. McDougall said that the Independent Doukhobors, who numbered 849 in comparison with the 7852 in the Community, were being 'systematically boycotted, and persecuted' by the Community Doukhobors.

McDougall also reported, as one 'effect of this kind of communism,' that the Community Doukhobors were not interested in becoming owners of the land or naturalized as Canadian citizens. In his discussions with them they had readily agreed that the Canadian government was better than the one in Russia. They had no particular complaints. Still, they had insisted that God was their king and that therefore they could not 'join any Government in this world.' They remained firm in this even when McDougall had warned them that unless they naturalized and became citizens they could not secure patents for the homesteads for which they had entered. They had said: 'We do not want to own the land – all we want is to be permitted to make a living thereon.'

The solution that McDougall proposed was simple but drastic. His first recommendation for dealing with the Community Doukhobors was to 'relieve them ... from the necessity of citizenship by cancelling all their entries to homesteads.'[71] In other words, the Doukhobors would lose the land. McDougall also outlined a plan whereby the land located immediately around each village and consisting of '17–20 acres per soul of population' would be formed into new reserves. In this way the outlying areas would be opened to the public while the Doukhobors could still provide for their livelihood. The new reserves would be much smaller and they would not become the property of the Doukhobors. They would be held for them 'during the Government's pleasure.'

McDougall also proposed that if the government accepted his recommendations, then, before implementing them, the Doukhobors should be given a three-month grace period. During this time, instead of opening the cancelled entries to the public, the Doukhobors would be able to reclaim them. But such new Doukhobor entries should be accepted only if the individual Doukhobor would indicate his willingness to cultivate his particular homestead and to take up residence on it or else to reside in a village not more than three miles away, and to become naturalized.

With McDougall's recommendations in hand the government would soon withdraw its earlier arrangements for accommodating Doukhobor communalism. McDougall not only disagreed with the Doukhobors but seemingly failed to understand their views. He saw the role of Peter Verigin only in negative terms, even though Verigin had led the Doukhobors in making homestead entries, in building a general prosperity, and in gaining social stability. McDougall recognized that Sifton had given them the privilege of cultivating their land communally but he recommended, in effect, that this concession be severely curtailed.

RATIONALIZING AND IMPLEMENTING A RESTRICTIVE POLICY

The minister of the Interior, Frank Oliver, now prepared an elaborate memorandum to gain Cabinet approval for McDougall's recommendations.[72] Oliver's reasoning began with the fact that a 'large proportion of the homesteads held under entry by Doukhobors were not being cultivated.' As a result they had become the object of public concern. Other people were asking about the land, creating public pressure that Oliver described in the following way:

Increasingly numerous and persistent demands have been made for the cancellation of those entries so that the land might be entered for by other settlers ... The demand came not only from people who desired to acquire the land as homesteads, but also from people concerned in the business interest whose success depends on the settlement and cultivation of the adjacent land.

A considerable number of persons who desired to homestead on these lands have unlawfully entered into occupation by squatting on them ... and hoping that if they were in occupation when the entries were cancelled they would thus secure a prior right to entry ...

As a result of developments during the season of 1905 it became apparent that something must be done to satisfy public opinion on the one had and to protect the legitimate interests of the Doukhobors on the other.[73]

After stating that something had to be done to satisfy public opinion, Oliver discussed the Sifton concessions and the communal arrangement whereby the Doukhobor entries had been made. He interpreted these in a most novel and restrictive way: 'The Doukhobors have since assumed that the entries so made by the community on behalf of the community, and the letter of the Minister permitting cultivation in common were sufficient protection to them in the exclusive occupation of the area at first set apart as their reserves, and afterwards entered for as homesteads, without compliance with the terms of the Homestead Act. This, of course, is not the case. The affidavit which an applicant for homestead entry must take explicitly provides that the entry must be for the sole use and benefit of the entrant.'[74]

Oliver was right about the affidavit for making homestead entries. In taking it an applicant stated that the homestead 'is made for my exclusive use and benefit, and ... for the purpose of actual settlement.' The Doukhobors had been concerned about the inappropriateness of these words at the time when they had made the entries. Their friend Herbert Archer had requested different forms but the commissioner for Dominion Lands, J.G. Turriff, had rejected the request.[75] (Early in the 1880s a Mennonite request for a more suitably worded form had been approved.)[76]

Oliver argued further that the Sifton concessions were only for a temporary period and that the Doukhobors had mistakenly assumed that they allowed for a permanent arrangement:

It would appear that they have also assumed that the permission of the Minister to cultivate in common was without restriction as to time ... that it was given to permit the perpetuation of community conditions.

The provisions of the Land Act are clear that ... there must be ... cultivation on individual holdings for individual use and benefit in order to maintain entry and to secure patent. While the Minister had power to hold in abeyance the effect of these provisions he could not vary them; and as the statute was not amended to meet the case it would seem that the permission was given to encourage and facilitate individual cultivation and ownership, not to permit it to be avoided.

... the Minister's permission to cultivate in common was a sufficient protection for Doukhobor entries ... not sufficient to entitle him to patent.[77]

It has to be admitted that Sifton's letter does not refer to patents, but there is nothing in that letter to suggest that the privilege of communal cultivation was for a temporary period only. To argue that it was, is to imply that Sifton either deliberately deceived the Doukhobors or unwittingly went beyond his legal authority.

Oliver also interpreted Sifton's communalism in terms of villages rather than in terms of the community as a whole. Sifton had stated: 'The land around the village itself may be cultivated and the work which otherwise would be required on each individual homestead may be done altogether around the village.'[78] Oliver now held that Sifton's concession required 'that the homesteads of the village must be located around the village in which the homesteaders reside.' He stated that the Sifton concession 'debars from protection all entries made by residents of one village in the area around another village and also those whose entries were at first in the vicinity of the village of their residence but who have since removed to some other village, as well as those at an unreasonable distance from the village in which the homesteader resides.'[79] It is probably true that the Doukhobor committee that made the homestead entries did not always ensure that the homestead of a particular person was near the village where he resided. Also, some people had relocated to other villages. But to argue that this violated the Sifton concessions was a basic reinterpretation. At the 10 February 1903 meeting, when the entry procedures were finalized with J.S. Crerar and Hugh Harley, no such restrictions were mentioned; at least none are recorded.

Further, Oliver interpreted terms that Sifton had used to illustrate the privilege in such a way that they would serve to limit the privilege. Sifton had said:'If, for instance, a village wants fifty homesteads around the village, I will be satisfied if the amount of improvements required for each quarter-section is done around the village, only for the whole fifty. This would enable all those in the village to live together and to work together in and around the village without being compelled to go a long way out to their individual homesteads.' Oliver now argued:

Mr. Sifton's letter contemplates that there may be up to fifty homesteads around each village. Throughout the greater number of townships in which Doukhobor entries have been made ... There ... [are] 105 quarter-sections available for homesteading within three miles of each village, or twice as many homesteads as a village of 50 homesteads would be entitled to ... It would therefore seem fair ... that entries held on homesteads more than three miles distant from the village of the residence of the homesteader could not be held in compliance with the most liberal possible construction of Mr. Sifton's letter.[80]

Also, in accordance with McDougall's recommendation for a system of small reserves, Oliver's memorandum to the Cabinet stated that land around each village, 'not exceeding in total area 15 acres to each resident of the village ... but in no case exceeding a distance of three miles from the village,' should be held for the Community Doukhobors 'during the pleasure of the Government.' In setting forth the rationale for these new reserves, Oliver stated that 'whatever their religious beliefs and however much these have prevented them from conforming to the terms of the Lands Act they are at least a peaceable self-supporting people whom it would not be sound public policy under any circumstances to reduce to the condition of paupers by depriving them of their homes and the land which they hold under cultivation.'[81]

To further rationalize the cancellations Oliver referred to the failure of the Doukhobors to apply for patents. He noted that 'the Dominion Lands Act provides that if at the end of five years from the date of entry patent is not applied for the entry may be cancelled.'[82] In fact, it was not yet five years from the time that the Doukhobor entries had been made. But Oliver cannot be faulted for concluding that the Doukhobors were not intending to apply for patents.

The government now proceeded quickly. Oliver's submission to the Cabinet was dated 1 December 1906. On 17 December McDougall was given another assignment. Now he was to serve as 'Commissioner for the investigation and adjustment of land claims' for Doukhobor lands.[83] To do this he was empowered to recommend the cancellation of homestead entries and the Dominion Lands agents would then act on his recommendations. He was also authorized to receive applications for re-entry from the Doukhobors, to issue receipts if homestead fees were paid, and to administer the naturalization oath.[84]

To carry out his new task McDougall made two tours of the Doukhobor settlements in 1907. The first took place in January and its purpose was to identify those entries that would be recommended for cancellation. At the same time a lengthy notice was sent to each

Doukhobor village setting forth the government's new policy.[85] Distributed in English and Russian, the notice stated, among other things, that the government had hoped that every man would cultivate his own land for his own use and become a citizen. Because individuals had not done these things, the government would now cancel all entries except those held by people who (a) lived either on their individual homesteads or in a village within three miles of their homesteads, (b) cultivated their own land for their own use, and (c) had already become Canadian citizens or British subjects or were intending to seek such status.

The notice also stated that for those who did not meet these criteria the government would hold reserves of land at its pleasure around each village up to an amount of fifteen acres for each person in the village so that these Doukhobors could continue to live there and not become destitute. Further, the government would give the Doukhobors a three-month grace period during which they could individually apply for 're-entry' and thus obtain individual homesteads. The notice also stated that 'the Government ... will protect them as it has hitherto done in their religious beliefs, but it cannot longer give them privileges in regard to land which it does not give to other people.'

Understandably, when the Community Doukhobors learned of this plan, they protested. On 10 February 1907 they made a lengthy 'Petition To The Minister Of The Interior And All People In Canada From The Christian Community of Universal Brotherhood, The Doukhobors of Canada.'[86] In this petition they set forth a number of arguments. They said that the charge that they had not cultivated the land was untrue. To support their contention they pointed to the McNab investigation of 1905 and to the 150,000 bushels of wheat and 100,000 bushels of oats that they had sold. They asked: 'If we do not cultivate the land where do these crops come from?' They also emphasized their strong commitment to farming as a way of life: 'We prefer this work as being the most regular, the most honest, the most lawful and the most fundamental.' When they first arrived they had had no horses. Therefore, they said, 'we, and our wives, harnessed ourselves to the plough and thus we tilled the soil.'

The Doukhobors, in this petition, also suggested that much of the animosity against them came from local business people who were unhappy that they had set up stores and factories of their own. They also explained why they would not take the oath of allegiance by pointing to their history in Russia and certain teachings of Jesus set forth in the Bible. They said: 'John McDougall assures us that the Government will protect us, as it is said in the circular letter, in the free exercise of our faith, as heretofore: but he insists at the same time on the necessity of taking the oath of allegiance.' To the Doukhobors, mindful of Jesus' teaching against taking oaths, this was a contradiction.[87]

Soon after sending this petition, a delegation of Community Doukhobors travelled to Ottawa and met with the minister, Frank Oliver. Their lengthy exchange was candid, but Oliver remained firm. The Doukhobors pointed out that 'Mr. Sifton ... in the new agreement said nothing about naturalization. He said that in three years the land would be ours.'[88] Oliver replied that the Doukhobors had 'mis-read' Sifton's letter. He emphasized that he could not treat the Doukhobors differently from other people or provide a special law for them. Regarding Sifton's letter, he made the amazing claim that 'the whole intent of that letter was to get you to take the land individually, as the law required.'[89]

The Doukhobors explained that in the early years some of their people had wasted energies on religious pilgrimages while others had to work on the railway, but that now they had steam-engines, large ploughs, and were making rapid progress in cultivating the land. In conclusion they stated:

We will ask you very earnestly as we know we cannot do anything against you. You have the power. You are the Government. We have very kind and friendly wishes to you and are asking you to take our condition before your attention and let us have the land we have entered for, and we hope that you will never be disappointed that the Doukhobors will do any harm to you. This year we have decided not to go out to work at all but to put all our force into cultivation, and we will do all we have promised and cultivate the land we have under entry, except land not fit for cultivation, like sloughs, and sand. All the Doukhobors say we hope the Canadian Government will continue ... to protect us in our religion.[90]

Oliver replied: 'The giving of public land is not a matter of religion but of law and fair play ... I have to deal with all the people in the same way.'[91]

After this exchange between the Community Doukhobors and the government, James Mavor tried to intervene on their behalf. He sent letters to several government officials including Prime Minister Laurier. He reviewed the early negotiations, Sifton's letter, and the current situation. In one memorandum he charged that Oliver, by asserting that the object of Sifton's letter had been to get the Doukhobors to take the land individually, 'suggests that Mr. Sifton intended deliberately to deceive the Doukhobors and to prepare the way for the expropriation of their lands by himself or his successor, by affording a technical pretext.'[92] Mavor did not believe that Sifton was 'capable of doing anything of the kind.' He submitted that in implementing Oliver's plan, the government was guilty of a 'very serious breach of faith.'

Despite these strong appeals, Oliver's plan was being implemented. McDougall visited the villages and recommended that 2503 homestead entries be cancelled. A total of 8175 Doukhobors, steadfast in their communal orientation, chose not to accept the terms of the government for 're-entering' on homesteads. For these Doukhobors the government created small new reserves on the basis of fifteen acres per person. This took up 768 quarter-sections that the government then held for these Doukhobors at its 'pleasure.' Another 384 quarter-sections were held as homesteads by individual Doukhobors who either had already been independent or were willing to accept Oliver's new 're-entry' terms. A total of 1605 homesteads, representing just over 250,000 acres, which had earlier been 'entered' for by the Doukhobors, now became available to the public.[93] When officials began to accept applications for these lands from the public on 1 June 1907, the demand was so great that in some areas additional police detachments had to be called to the offices to maintain order.[94] Nevertheless, on 1 August 1907 there were still 394 homesteads that had not been claimed.[95]

The Community Doukhobors, seeing that the land was being taken up by others, became dispirited and discouraged. A few now made another pilgrimage across the prairie.[96] Others attempted to relocate so that their new small reserves would be as close together as possible, but Oliver discouraged this movement. The majority, it appears, tilled what land they had will all possible diligence and lived with unusual frugality in order to save money to find another place to live.[97] Peter Verigin had already been looking for a new place and in spring 1908 he purchased several thousand acres in British Columbia. The migration to British Columbia was a gradual one, but by 1912, about 5000 Doukhobors had moved.[98] This still left a significant number in Saskatchewan; but the continuing exodus also involved a reduction in the reserves there because the government held closely to its formula of allowing no more than fifteen acres per person.[99]

By 1918 'the government's pleasure' in holding the small reserves was coming to an end. It decided to sell them. Naturally, the remaining Doukhobors living on them were interested. But the government's opposition to communal arrangements was still so strong that it passed an order-in-council, on 6 July 1918, barring the Community from purchasing the land. The purchase had to be made by individual heads of families in the amount of fifteen acres per family member and the purchaser could not transfer the land to the Community until he had gained title to it by completing payment.[100] In spite of these restrictive terms the Doukhobors bought the land. After making several payments they arranged for a loan from the Sun Life Insurance Company and paid the government in full. Owning this land strengthened the Community in Saskatchewan. But by this time the number of Doukhobors in Saskatchewan who were still committed to communalism had dropped. Some had become independent; many had moved to British Columbia.

Clearly, the Doukhobors, in this communal landholding effort, experienced a profound change in government policy. At first the government seemed willing to accommodate their communalism. It reserved large areas of land for the Doukhobors. It allowed them to settle in villages. It made arrangements with the railway companies so that they could have both the even- and odd-numbered sections in most of the reserved areas, and it permitted them to register their homestead entries in a communal way. The government even allowed for communal cultivation by waiving the normal requirement that each individual homestead be cultivated. Altogether, it was a broad range of accommodations, more extensive than that arranged for the Mennonites. But the government's initial accommodating stance did not last.

One reason for the change in government policy relates to new economic and agricultural developments on the prairies. In the 1890s, when the Doukhobors first came, the government was very eager to attract settlers. During the depression of the 1880s many Canadians had left for the United States. Canada's wheat exports had fallen drastically.[101] Clifford Sifton, who in 1896 became minister of the Interior in the Laurier government, was determined to attract more immigrants to the west and introduced, among other things, a greater flexibility in land settlement policies.[102] By 1905, however, the situation had changed. Immigration was reaching record levels: 146,266 people came in 1905 and 189,064 in 1906. Most immigrants, as well as many land-hungry people from other parts of Canada, made their way to the prairies. Land quickly became scarce with the result that homestead regulations were applied more strictly: for example, if residence and cultivation requirements were not met then the 'entries' could be cancelled. Around 1905 approximately 15,000 entries, made before 1902 under more flexible policies, were cancelled.[103] This made nearly 2.5 million acres available for new settlers. Obviously, then, the greater strictness applied to the Doukhobors was in keeping with a general trend.

Second, a different social perception of immigrant groups had evolved. Earlier, the main object was to persuade such groups to come to Canada. Now there was a growing concern about integrating them. Frank Oliver, in his career as an Alberta journalist, had called for integration. Another advocate was J.S. Woodsworth, who wrote in 1909: 'First of all, they [the new settlers] must in some way be unified. Language, nationality, race, temperament, training are all dividing walls that must be broken down. Poor distribution may do much. There is a very natural tendency for people of the same nationality to settle in large colonies ... Such colonies are really bits of Russia or Austria or Germany transplanted to Canada. Not only are they less open to Canadian ideas, but closely united, they can control the entire community ... It would seem a wise policy to scatter the foreign communities among the Canadian, in this way facilitating the process of assimilation.'[104]

Third, there was the increased political pressure, resulting in part from population growth in the west and the new concern for integrating the immigrant groups. Also, the Doukhobors were an easy target because almost 90 per cent of their land was still not cultivated, even though they had cultivated more than the minimum amount required. Furthermore, the uncultivated land lay in vast untouched areas, not interspersed with individual farms as elsewhere. Also, the pilgrimages, though involving only a small minority of the Doukhobors, had aroused public antipathy. Finally, Doukhobor unwillingness to accept Canadian citizenship would have been difficult for many people to understand. That there was considerable political pressure is evident not only from several of the communications of the period but also in the eagerness of the new settlers to register claims for Doukhobor land when it became available to the public.

Fourth, the institutional arrangements were inadequate; the early negotiations with the Doukhobors were vague on several key points. The concessions outlined by Sifton on 15 February 1902 suggested that the Doukhobors were to be allowed to keep the land on a communal basis permanently, but this view was not explicitly stated. Nor was it stated that the Doukhobors were exempted from the requirement of accepting Canadian citizenship, which involved taking the oath of allegiance. By themselves these and other ambiguities need not have been serious. Some of the arrangements for the early Mennonite settlers were not clear either. But in the social and political environment that emerged in the Doukhobors' first decade in Canada, the ambiguities in the arrangements became serious problems. As suggested in the preceding chapter, Canada's institutions were not well suited for people who wished to live as communities, differently and separately from the larger society.

Fifth, the encounter between Canadians and the Doukhobor immigrants also revealed a fundamentally different interpretation of the principle of freedom for religion. The Doukhobors took a broad view. For them, religion was inseparable from their way of life. It was a basic reason for their initial request for reserves, for their desire to live in villages and to cultivate the land communally, for their resistance to the idea of making individual homestead entries, and for their refusal to take the oath of allegiance to become Canadian citizens. They described the religious basis of their way of life in their petition of 28 January 1907: 'Christ in his teaching called and calls the whole of mankind up to such a union as children of the same Father, and such a life as described in the Gospel ... those who followed with Faith Christ's doctrine also put it into practise: they brought their riches and all their material wealth to the apostles and called that common property. Our life in common is exclusively based on that principle.'[105]

The government, however, preferred a narrower view of religion. It assured the Doukhobors that it would continue to protect them in their religious beliefs but claimed that the landholding question was not a matter of religion. Some of the government's representatives had little respect for the Doukhobor approach. John McDougall, himself a clergyman, saw their religion as encouraging a subservient attitude among the people and thereby making possible both their communalism in general and the rule of Peter Verigin in particular.[106] C.W. Speers stated: 'The individual homesteader has never been impressed with his rights as a settler nor his independence as an individual.'[107]

For the Doukhobors there were to be more traumatic encounters. Those involving education are described in chapter six. But late in the 1930s, in British Columbia, they also lost a multimillion-dollar industry of orchards and a factory producing jam for a national market, partly because government officials refused to give their communal enterprise access to the financial assistance programs set up to deal with the effects of the economic depression.[108] Their way of life, which had met so much resistance in Russia, was not well received in Canada either.

4 The Hutterite Colonies

HUTTERITE COMMUNALISM

The Hutterites have been remarkably consistent in their communalism. They came to Canada in 1918. They obtained land by purchasing it, rather than by homesteading. And they set up small colonies of about fifteen families each, rather than large exclusive reserves with many villages. In 1988 there were approximately 70 Hutterite colonies in Manitoba, 122 in Alberta, and 48 in Saskatchewan.

These colonies are relatively autonomous and independent of each other but within each colony there is a highly integrated community. Each family occupies separate living quarters but meals are eaten in a communal dining hall. The property is owned collectively and no one receives wages but the needs of the people are provided for and all are treated alike. In nearly all instances a colony is a large farm. There is a division of labour and a specialization in skills but the people all work for the benefit of the colony as a whole.

The Hutterite pursuit of communalism in this form has a long history and deep religious roots (see chapter 1). Paul Gross, a twentieth-century Hutterite leader, has written: 'It is not an invention or a social system devised by the Hutterites, nor is it always to their personal liking to live this life. In this they have no choice. They have to live by the command of the Holy Spirit, as we are exhorted by the apostle Peter.'[1] Gross explains further that Hutterites claim to follow the example of the early Christian church as described in the following passage of the Bible: 'The company of those who believed were of one heart and soul, and no one said that any of the things he possessed was his own, but they had everything in common ... There was not a needy person among them.'[2] The Hutterites see communal property as a sign of obedience to God and private property as a reflection of greed, vanity, and pride.[3] On a few occasions in their long history they have abandoned the practice of holding their property in common but each time, they say, 'a restirring of Christian conscience has revived it.'[4]

Although they came to Canada only in 1918, the Hutterites had entered into negotiations with Canadian authorities earlier. In 1899 a deputy minister of the Interior stated that 'there will be no interference with their living as a commonwealth if they desire to do so.' And in 1918, when they sought confirmation of the earlier arrangements, the deputy minister, W.W. Cory, sent a telegram stating: 'Agreeable also to granting of requests as to community life and holding of property in common, but matter is one of provincial control. Do not anticipate slightest difficulty.'[5]

During their first two decades in Canada there were no restrictions on Hutterite communalism, but in the 1940s public feelings against them became strong. Initially this change may have been a result of the atmosphere of the Second World War, but the antipathy that continued can also be attributed to the nativist concern for Anglo-Saxon institutions and social homogeneity and to the social and economic forces that so changed rural life in the 1950s and 1960s. Whatever the source, these pressures prompted the governments of each prairie province to restrict the rights of the Hutterites to hold land communally.

A 'GENTLEMAN'S AGREEMENT' IN MANITOBA

When the Hutterites arrived in Manitoba in the fall of 1918, their reception was mixed. The federal government was eager to have them but locally there were protests.[6] Before long, however, the Hutterites were well accepted. People noted that, unlike some other immigrant groups, they accepted English schools. Even the secretary of the Great War Veterans' Association visited a colony in 1919 and was 'relieved to find that the Hutterians had no political connections with Germany.' He was impressed also with the organization of their colony life.[7] In the 1930s the Hutterites became popular with local authorities because, unlike many other people affected by the depression, their self-sufficient economies enabled them to pay their taxes. Municipalities began to compete with each other in efforts to attract Hutterite colonies to their areas.

By the mid 1940s, however, a more negative public attitude had developed. Critics referred to Hutterite effects on rural communities.

The Hutterites had their own schools and did not send their children to the established public schools. They did not participate in the social activities of communities. And they sometimes made bulk purchases in larger centres, thus bypassing local businesses. Rural communities were already experiencing a decline because of improved transportation methods and other trends, but the Hutterites, being conspicuous, could easily be blamed. One critic wrote about 'being deprived of certain rights, such as community life, by the encroachment of Hutterite colonies.'[8]

The pressure continued and in April 1947 the Manitoba government appointed a legislative committee to investigate the concerns and to recommend a solution. The committee received a number of submissions. Some charged that the Hutterite children were getting an inadequate education. Others asked that the government require the colonies to give a share of their assets to any member who might want to leave. One brief came from the Municipality of Cartier, which had 10 Hutterite colonies owning 20 per cent of the land and making up 40 per cent of the population. The Cartier brief asked that 'the present Hutterite colonies within the municipality be restricted from further formation of new colonies in this municipality.'[9]

The committee also received submissions in defence of the Hutterites from the Civil Liberties Association of Manitoba, the Manitoba Conference of the United Church, and other groups and individuals. These pointed to positive elements in the Hutterite education system, to the Hutterite practice of caring for their own sick and aged without public assistance, and to the fact that they were 'peaceful industrious law-abiding people and seldom appear in either the civil or criminal courts.' In its report the committee recommended against restricting the right of Hutterites to purchase land: 'This Committee hesitates to make any recommendation to the effect that anything be done by legislation or otherwise which will interfere with what may be termed one of the basic fundamental rights of every person – the right to purchase land in Manitoba where and when he pleases.'[10] The committee was more sympathetic to the idea of a requirement whereby any person leaving a colony would be given 'his or her equitable share of colony assets.' It recommended that the legislature at its next session appoint a committee to study this issue.

This recommendation was accepted and a new committee was formed to consider such legislation. The new committee began work in summer 1948 and again heard a number of submissions. One organization, the

Community Welfare Association, had been formed especially to bring the Hutterite problem to the attention of both the public and the government. It favoured legislation requiring a colony to give a share of its assets to a member who might wish to leave. This procedure, it argued, would be in the interests of 'inmates of Hutterite colonies,' whose participation in the larger society was now being impeded by the Hutterite system.[11] The association's brief argued that the Hutterites remained ignorant of the larger society, that the children did not have the privilege of having their faculties developed, and that the general inadequacy of Hutterite education was preventing them from fulfilling their duties to their fellow citizens. The brief noted, however, that even if such legislation were enacted it would not bring about a speedy assimilation of the Hutterites or relieve the concerns of the rural communities where the colonies were located. The association urged that the right of the colonies to obtain land be restricted.

The strongest defence of the Hutterites was made by their solicitor, E.A. Fletcher.[12] He reviewed the long history of Hutterite communalism and the seriousness with which the people, as adults, took the vows of membership. He pointed out that the complete renunciation of personal property was a very basic part of these vows and that to require the colonies to give a share of their assets to a departing member would be like saying to a Hutterite: 'In spite of your solemn undertaking upon joining your church, and in spite of your contract under seal, you can leave the community and claim compensation for work done while a member of the community.' Fletcher continued: 'If the Legislature desires to destroy these religious communities, this is the way to do it. They would then become merely secular organizations which it has herein been pointed out do not last.'

Fletcher argued that the Hutterian Brethren were 'a just and good people' who could 'safely be relied upon to treat an erring brother justly' and urged that the legislation being considered not be enacted. He said that communal property was 'an essential element of Hutterian Brethren faith and doctrine' and that it was not 'within the province of the Legislature to restrain or control religion [sic] practices.' One unsolicited brief in favour of the Hutterites came from a Winnipeg businessman who said: 'A friend of mine joined the Sisters of the Holy Name. She put in $100,000 and she takes a vow of communal poverty. If she leaves she takes nothing.' He urged that the legislature not compel colonies to give a share of their assets to individuals who left.

When a motion calling for the legislation was brought to the floor of the legislature later in 1948 it was defeated. For some years thereafter 'the Hutterite problem' remained quiet. By 1954, however, when the complaints had become quite strong again, the Union of Manitoba Municipalities, at its annual convention, called on the government to introduce measures to restrict the amount of land that any one colony could have and to specify also that no new colony could be set up unless the location was at least a certain distance from existing colonies.[13] The government did not immediately act on these recommendations so the pressure became stronger. Eventually, the union proposed that if the government would not act then it would try to make its own agreement with the Hutterites. Premier Campbell of the ruling Liberals favoured this approach. Indeed, he called in the Hutterite leaders and said that if they did not make an agreement with the union then he would have to deal with the matter through legislation.[14]

This left the Hutterites with little choice. So, on 12 April 1957, an agreement was reached between the Union of Manitoba Municipalities and the Hutterian Brethren of Manitoba.[15] In the following years it was often referred to as a 'gentleman's agreement' because it was not a formal law; but, in effect, the Hutterites had acceded to virtually all the demands of the municipalities. They promised, among other things, to limit the holdings of new colonies to 5120 acres, to place no more than two colonies into any one municipality without specific permission from that municipality, and to ensure that the land of any new colony would be at least ten miles from the land of any existing colony.

This arrangement was relatively satisfactory, but some problems continued. On one occasion, a few months after the agreement was signed, the Hutterites entered into negotiations to purchase a particular piece of land. It met all the terms of the agreement but the municipality still wanted the provincial government to intervene and block the sale.[16] The government did not do so. Other difficulties came from the fact that the land of a particular colony was not always in one block. Pieces of land might be somewhat scattered. This made the provision in the agreement stipulating that the land of a new colony be at least ten miles from the land of an existing colony more restrictive than it first appeared. Despite its restricting effect, the Hutterites respected the agreement.

In 1969, however, the Hutterites made it known that they would no longer consider themselves bound by the agreement.[17] Little became of their new position until 1971 when the government wanted to sell an abandoned air base and a Hutterite colony made the highest bid. The Union of Manitoba Municipalities asked the government not to sell it to the colony because it would be in violation of the agreement. If necessary, the union announced, it would take legal action to force the Hutterites to comply with the agreement. However, Manitoba's new premier, Ed Schreyer of the New Democratic Party, who seems to have had a personal sympathy for the Hutterites, now declared that the agreement was discriminatory and therefore invalid.[18] The Manitoba Human Rights Commission supported this position, stating that it viewed the agreement as 'a gross violation of the spirit and intent of the Human Rights Act.'[19] In the end the Union of Municipalities did not proceed with legal action. In the following years the Manitoba government, regardless of which political party was in power, held that the Hutterites 'are people the same as anyone else and are entitled to the same rights, privileges and restrictions.'[20] Despite this policy, there continued to be calls for restrictions at annual meetings of the Union of Manitoba Municipalities but these did not receive majority support.[21]

Aside from these concerns about the expansion of the Hutterite colonies, the question of whether individuals leaving a colony were entitled to a share of its assets reappeared. In the mid 1960s several members of one colony became involved with an organization known as the Radio Church of God. They renounced the religious beliefs and practices of the Hutterites and, when numerous efforts to persuade them to reconsider their position failed, they were expelled from both the Hutterian Brethren church and from the colony. They then asked for their share of the colony's assets. The colony refused. Eventually the matter was brought to the courts and after several appeals it was heard by the Supreme Court of Canada. It became known as the *Hofer* case. In 1970 the Supreme Court ruled in favour of the colony.[22]

The reasoning of the court on the *Hofer* case is significant. Justice Ritchie ruled that the property of the colony was not held in trust for the individual members but for the colony as a whole, in conformity with the principle of communal property fundamental to the Hutterite religion, and that the several members were validly expelled from both the church and the colony. An important element in his reasoning was a broad view of the role of religion and of the authority of a church. He saw membership in the colony as inseparable from membership in the church, not only because of the articles of association, which were accepted voluntarily and individually when the people, as adults, formally became members of a colony, but also because of the nature of colony life. Moreover, he did not want to interfere with the right of the church to determine who should be its members. He explained his position in the following way:

In my view, adherence to the Hutterite faith was a prerequisite to membership in the Colony which by its very nature was required to be composed exclusively of Hutterian Brethren and their families. I am also of opinion that the decision as to whether or not any individual was a Hutterian Brethren so as to be entitled to continue as a member of the community was a decision which could only be made by the Hutterite Church. In the present case, as I have indicated, the decision to expel the appellants from the Colony was made by the church, but it had the effect of making appellants ineligible for continued membership in the Colony ...

There is no doubt that the Hutterian way of life is not that of the vast majority of Canadians, but it makes manifest a form of religious philosophy to which any Canadian can subscribe and it appears to me that if any individual either through birth within the community or by choice wishes to subscribe to such a rigid form of life and to subject himself to the harsh disciplines of the Hutterian Church, he is free to do so. I can see nothing contrary to public policy in the continued existence of these communities living as they do in accordance with their own rules and beliefs.

Justices Cartwright, Hall, and Pigeon also wrote judgments on the *Hofer* case. Cartwright, though agreeing with Ritchie, spoke further about the principle of freedom of religion. The appellants had argued that the contract embodied in the articles of association, which a person would accept on formally joining a colony and in which he would renounce all claims to private property, was contrary to public policy inasmuch as it reduced the appellants to a condition of serfdom. Cartwright held that this did not violate the principle of freedom for religion. He explained: 'One of the liberties chiefly prized by a normal man is the liberty to bind himself. Unless the members are free to enter into contracts of the sort set out in the articles of association, it is difficult to see how the Hutterian Brethren could carry on the form of religious life which they believe to be the right one ... The appellants ... remain free to change their religion but they have contracted that if they do so and leave the Colony, voluntarily or by expulsion, they will not demand any of its assets.' Justice Hall also agreed with Ritchie but he wanted to register the view that the powers of a church should not be seen in terms so broad as to be virtually unlimited. In circumstances involving minors or others under disability, he said, public policy would limit the way in which a church might deal with them.

The one dissenting judgment in the *Hofer* case came from Justice Pigeon. His view of religion and of the authority of a church was significantly more narrow. He stated that 'freedom of religion includes the right for each individual to change his religion at will.' Churches were free to make rules and regulations, he said, but 'freedom of religion means that they cannot make rules having the effect of depriving their members of this fundamental freedom.' In his view this was precisely what these Hutterites were attempting to do. Pigeon rejected the decision of the lower courts: 'The decision in the Courts below proceeds on the assumption that religion extends to whatever a particular congregation may choose to include in it and that the religious authority is coextensive with such definition. This is contrary to the proper legal conception of religion whereby its scope is limited to what is commonly so considered and the extent of religious authority is limited to what is consistent with freedom of religion as properly understood, that is freedom for the individual not only to adopt a religion but also to abandon it at will.' Pigeon pointed out that it was 'as nearly impossible as can be' for people in a Hutterite colony to do otherwise than to embrace its religious teachings, that they had no right at any time in their lives to leave the colony without abandoning everything, even the clothes on their backs. In his view, this high cost of changing their religion meant, effectively, that they were deprived of freedom of religion.

Despite Pigeon's strong reasons, his was only a dissenting judgment. The majority of the court in the *Hofer* case ruled in favour of the colony. In 1971 the issue was raised again, when J.R. Boyce, a member of the Manitoba legislature, introduced a bill 'which would require a colony to take money from its communal assets and pay it to any Hutterite who leaves the colony.'[23] Like the earlier attempts, this one was rejected by the legislature.

In Manitoba, then, there had been numerous attempts to impose restrictions on the Hutterites but the only ones ever implemented were those in the 'gentleman's agreement' between the Union of Manitoba Municipalities and the Hutterian Brethren, and it remained operative only from 1957 until the early 1970s.

STATUTORY RESTRICTIONS IN ALBERTA

When the Hutterites moved to Canada in 1918, nine of the first fifteen colonies were set up in Alberta. This relative concentration in Alberta has continued and may help to explain the more elaborate and firm methods used in that province to regulate the expansion of the Hutterites.

As in Manitoba, the Hutterites in Alberta encountered some opposition in the early years but during the depression of the 1930s they became more popular. Indeed, the desire of local authorities to attract more colonies was quite strong. One telegram sent by a Calgary businessman to Prime Minister R.B. Bennett requested the admission of more Hutterites: 'Owing to prevailing conditions due to several years' of losses the entry of Rockport Colony would be of great benefit to vendors, their creditors and all other persons concerned in this district. Anything you may do to avoid further delay will be greatly and personally appreciated.'[24]

With the outbreak of the Second World War, however, this hospitable public attitude changed. The Hutterites were not serving in the military, although they participated in the Alternative Service Program. Farming had become profitable again and farmers who wanted to expand their holdings had to compete with the Hutterites who also wanted more land. In addition, critics charged that the Hutterites were contributing little to the social and economic life of the rural communities. Before long, there was strong criticism. According to one account, 'the Canadian Legion, farmers groups and mass meetings of protest in some Alberta towns pressured the Alberta government to enact the Land Sales Prohibition Act in 1942.'[25]

This first measure to restrict the growth of the Hutterite colonies was a simple prohibition on land sales to 'enemy aliens and Hutterites.' When Solon Low, speaking for the Social Credit government, introduced it in the legislature on 11 March 1942, he said its purpose was 'to allay public feeling which has been aroused to the point of threatened violence in some instances.' He spoke positively of the Hutterites and said that the act was 'not a persecuting measure but one adopted to meet a situation which has developed since the war started.' He saw it as 'a temporary expedient until an orderly arrangement can be worked out.'[26]

One year later, in March 1943, the act was amended so that it covered not only sales of land but leases as well.[27] Later that year, however, the federal government formally disallowed the act 'because it infringed on the exclusive jurisdiction of the federal government to legislate in the area of rights and obligations of enemy aliens.'[28] This set-back was quickly remedied. In 1944 the legislature simply passed a new Land Sales Prohibition Act that referred to Hutterites but not to enemy aliens. A 1945 amendment stipulated that the act should remain in force until one year after the war.[29] Another amendment, in 1946, extended the act 'until the first day of May, 1947.'[30] Before it expired, however, a legislative committee was appointed to study the Hutterite problem and to make recommendations about 'whether the said Act should be continued in force, and if so, whether it should be modified or amended in any way.'[31]

This legislative committee was the first of several that would study the problem in the following decades. It heard briefs from a number of individuals and organizations, including Alberta Farmers' Union locals, municipalities, school trustee associations, Canadian Legion locals, and various citizens' groups. Members of the committee also accepted an invitation to visit a colony and observe Hutterite life at first hand. The arguments against the Hutterites dealt with a number of concerns but most were focused on their expansion. A lengthy brief from the Alberta Farmers' Union noted that the Hutterites already owned one-sixth of the land in the Warner municipality and one-tenth of that in the Sugar City municipality. It urged that the Hutterites go outside Alberta if they needed more land.[32] The brief attributed their capacity to expand to their position during the war: 'While Canadian boys were fighting and dying for the very existence of our Nation, the Brethren have been able to save sufficient profits to enable them to establish at least one colony for each one now in existence ... The Hutterites can pay more for land than any of our young men who expect to live by Canadian standards ... thus making it impossible for the veterans to become established on any land that they, the Hutterites, may desire.'[33]

The Farmers' Union brief also charged that the Hutterites were depriving their own children of culture, beauty, and refinement. It urged that a group that denies its posterity 'the right to live as free individuals and Canadian citizens' should not be given any special privileges.[34] The brief also stated: 'What will become of our schools, hospitals, parks, playgrounds, swimming pools, rinks, churches – all the things which mark our modern civilization – if the Brethren be permitted to continue their expansion?' It argued that a dispersion of the colonies would lead them to associate more closely with their Canadian neighbours and eventually to assimilate.

The main statement in defence of the Hutterites was made by their lawyer, L.S. Turcotte.[35] His lengthy brief argued that the Hutterites obeyed laws and paid taxes; that none could be found in jails or asylums; that they cared for their weak and aged; that they accepted no Old Age Pensions and only one colony accepted Family Allowances; that none was a public charge in hospitals; that even during the depression they went without governmental assistance; that during the 1930s many organizations had asked for more Hutterites; that during the war Hutterites had purchased nearly half a million dollars of bonds of the interest-free variety lest they make money out of the war; that their young men had performed alternative service in labour camps as prescribed by Selective Service Regulations; that if the reason for preventing them from buying land lay in their pacifism then Mennonites, Moravians, Seventh Day Adventists, and Jehovah's Witnesses should also be subject to such restrictions; that the concern about their expansion was greatly exaggerated because they had only 275 square miles out of Alberta's 67,621 square miles of occupied farm land and only 33 colonies out of Alberta's 99,732 farms; that most of the colonies were located on the outer edge of settled areas; that teachers in charge of Hutterite schools spoke well of their elementary school education; that immediate neighbours were not complaining; that with regard to the charge that they were competing with war veterans for land, they would suggest a system whereby when they would make an offer on a particular piece of land, then that piece of land should be offered for sale under the Veterans' Land Act for sixty or ninety days during which a veteran would have priority; and that Alberta's recently enacted Bill of Rights provided 'that every citizen of Alberta shall be free to acquire land ... so long as he conforms to the laws.'

Despite this strong representation on behalf of the Hutterites, the committee found that 'the conditions which prompted the passing of the Land Sales Prohibition Act still exist and that the communal form of living will continue to be a matter of concern to the people of Alberta unless regulations can be applied which will, in the public interest, control the expansion or increase of communal groups.'[36] Accordingly, the committee recommended that the government continue with some restrictions on Hutterite landholding to prevent a concentration of colonies in any one area. The legislature then passed the Communal Property Act.[37] It came into force on 1 May 1947 and stipulated that no colony could purchase land within forty miles of any land held by another colony or increase its holdings beyond ten sections or 6,400 acres. Also, before a colony could make a purchase, the land would have to be offered for sale under the provisions of the Veterans' Land Act for a period of sixty days. Clearly, the new law, though no longer a complete prohibition, was still very restrictive. The forty-mile limit virtually ruled out further expansion in the area south of Calgary. The Hutterites would have to look elsewhere. Some moved farther north. Others turned to Saskatchewan, where as yet there were no restrictions. Some moved to northern parts of the United States. South Dakota was somewhat attractive because it had enacted legislation in 1935 in order to facilitate Hutterite settlement. Mexico was also considered as a possible site for further expansion.

In 1951 the Alberta restrictions were eased somewhat, perhaps because of the return to peacetime conditions. Now the province was divided into three zones according to the productivity of the land. Hutterite colonies in the zone with the poorest land would be allowed to have 24 sections, those with the medium-quality land 16 sections, and those in the zone with the best land would remain under the 10-section restriction.[38] The restrictions were also loosened in relation to unofficial leases, hire agreements, and other arrangements, but the Hutterites gained very little land by these methods.[39] They faced a serious land shortage.

Despite these restrictive provisions, by the late 1950s public criticism of the Hutterites again reached a level where it seemed necessary for the government to act. Accordingly, in 1958, the government set up another committee, 'to determine whether or not the provisions of the Communal Property Act ... are necessary and in the best interests of our agricultural industry ...' and to study 'any other matter relevant to the orderly and harmonious integration of members of the Hutterian Church into local communities.'[40] Like the 1947 committee, the one of 1958 heard a variety of briefs and the Farmers' Union locals were again prominent in calling for further restrictions. The Warner local charged that the Hutterites were 'attempting to establish a country of their own within a country. If they are allowed to do so, they can eliminate personal contact of their members and hold them in ignorance which is the foundation and success of the communal system.'[41] The New Dayton Farmers' Union local stated that without restrictions the Hutterites would soon displace several thousand farm families in the larger Lethbridge area, resulting in the loss of potential markets for automobiles, radios, television sets, appliances, dry goods, foodstuffs, and advertising revenue.[42]

As might be expected, the committee concluded that 'some form of regulation governing the acquisition of lands by Hutterites for the purpose of establishing communal settlements is necessary and in the interests of the agricultural industry as a whole.[43] On the matter of integrating the Hutterites into the larger society, the committee was somewhat more innovative:

Throughout this report the committee has endeavoured to emphasize that the assimilation of a religious sect exhibiting such strong social cohesion as the Hutterian Brethren will take time and patience.

Official restrictions placed upon these people over the centuries would seem to indicate that the process of integration has been retarded rather than advanced by such measures. In the opinion of the Committee then, the solution of the problems that have arisen in the province over the past years lies in other approaches. The appointment of a Board with discretionary powers and also acting in a consultative and advisory capacity would appear to be the answer.[44]

The committee's recommendation for a board was passed into law in 1960. It was known as the Communal Property Control Board. Any Hutterite colony that wanted either to increase its holdings or to establish a new colony was now required to submit an application to the board. The board then had to determine two things: first, whether the proposed land acquisition met the criteria of the zoning system adopted in 1951 that limited colony size to 10, 16, and 24 sections, depending on the zone in which they were located; and second, whether the proposed acquisition was 'in the public interest.' Although the board had a broad discretionary power to determine 'the public interest,' it set up guidelines prescribing that there should be no more than two colonies in an average-sized municipality; that colonies should be at least fifteen miles apart; and that no more than 5 per cent of the assessable land in any municipality should be under communal ownership.[45]

Public hearings and cabinet-level decisions also found their way into the new law even though they had not been recommended by the committee. Now when the Hutterites applied to the board for permission to set up a new colony, the board had to hold public hearings but the final decision would be made, not by the board, but by the provincial cabinet. These two procedural conditions had the effect of politicizing this already contentious matter. The public hearings became focal points for bitter charges against the Hutterites. In one instance, where Hutterites had applied to buy a ranch, some '300 people from the area warned that they were prepared to "break civil laws ... if necessary" if the application was granted.'[46] In 1962 the requirement that there be public hearings was abolished but the role of the cabinet remained. Of this, a later government study observed: 'As long as the Cabinet had the power to approve or disapprove new colonies certain segments of the public which opposed the establishment of new colonies on emotional rather than factual grounds were likely to continue to attempt to influence the Cabinet's decision by bringing the pressure of public opinion to bear on the government. Under such conditions, it was extremely difficult to determine what course of action was "in the public interest.'"[47] The later study also noted that the recommendation of the 1958 Hutterite Investigation Committee that the board 'play a public relations role' had never been implemented. It stated that if the board had been allowed to work effectively in accordance with this recommendation then 'much of the public misunderstanding of the Hutterian Brethren could have been dispelled and the problem overcome.'[48]

In a different development, in the mid 1960s, the legality of the Communal Property Act was challenged by several people who had made land sales to Hutterites and who were prosecuted for violating that act. In their defence they sought a declaration that the act was 'ultra vires,' meaning outside the jurisdiction of the province because it dealt with religion. The case, which became known as the *Walter* case, was eventually appealed to the Supreme Court of Canada, which ruled in 1968 that the law dealt not with religion but with property and was therefore within the jurisdiction of the legislature of Alberta.[49] In the judgment of the court, Justice Martland noted the argument that the act, 'in its pith and substance,' deals with religion by quoting from Justice Johnson of the Appellate Division of the Supreme Court of Alberta, who had said in his reasons: 'If a bylaw which prevents the distribution of religious tracts (the *Saumur* case) was an interference with religion, I find it difficult to say that legislation which is aimed at the restriction of new and existing colonies and the holding of land in common as practised by these colonies when living in such colonies and holding land in that manner are the principal tenets of Hutterian faith, does not also deal with religion.' After thus describing this position, Justice Martland rejected it and ruled as follows: 'The legislation in question ... does not forbid the existence of Hutterite colonies ... [and] is not directed at Hutterite religious belief or worship, or at the profession of such belief. It is directed at the practice of holding large areas of Alberta land as communal property, whether such practice stems from religious belief or not ... The fact that a religious group upholds tenets which leads to certain economic views in relation to land-holding does not mean that ... legislation which may run counter to such views, can be said in consequence, to be legislation in respect of religion and not in respect of property.'

Although the legality of the Communal Property Act was thus confirmed, other developments late in the 1960s contributed to a more accommodating atmosphere. The two major daily newspapers in the province, the *Calgary Herald* and the *Edmonton Journal,* became more sympathetic to the Hutterites. Intolerance of ethnic groups became generally disreputable. One scholar has observed that 'there has been a growing understanding and appreciation ... of pacifism and of the communal values which the Hutterites profess as the effects of the bomb and of the excessive individualism and anomie of industrial society have become clearer.'[50] Also, the Hutterites began to participate more in the life of the communities in which they lived. They began to vote, to participate in agricultural marketing associations, and to attend annual ratepayers' meetings. They also made contributions to local charities and provided free labour in the construction of community halls and hockey arenas even though they would never use them.[51]

This change in atmosphere prepared the way for the next step early in the 1970s. Public figures began to question the need for the controls. Some felt that the controls were incompatible with the spirit of Alberta's Bill of Rights. The Progressive Conservative party, led by a sympathetic Peter Lougheed, was elected to office. So, late in 1971, the operation of the board was suspended and in May 1972 a Select Committee of the Legislative Assembly was established to once again study the matter. Like the committees of 1947 and 1958, it heard many briefs. Most of these asked for continued restrictions. But the committee concluded that many of the criticisms grew out of other rural problems and that upon close examination, the Hutterites were not the true cause of the difficulties.[52]

The 1972 committee dissociated itself from the objective of integrating the Hutterites that the 1958 committee had been asked to look into. Instead, it favoured 'a policy of cooperation and co-existence.' It stated: 'The Hutterite colonies in Alberta make an important contribution to the Agricultural industry of our Province.' Unlike the 1958 committee, this one found that restrictions were not 'in the interests of the agricultural industry as a whole.' The committee concluded 'that the Hutterite colonies presently established in Alberta have had no disproportionate adverse effect on local communities ... that the time has come to repeal the present restrictive legislation ... although there is a definite need for a liaison function to promote understanding and co-operation, to advise the Hutterites, and to advise the government if any unforeseen difficulties occur.'[53]

In accordance with the committee's recommendation, a liaison officer was then appointed. In addition, the Hutterites set up a province-wide Committee of Elders to advise individual colonies on possible land acquisitions. Assisted by the liaison officer, this committee considers questions such as: Will children from an already struggling school be displaced? How many other farm families will be bought out and removed from the community? Will the geography of the proposed acquisition cause other farmers to be 'boxed-in'? Is there already a heavy concentration of Hutterite colonies in the area? The objective, said Rev. Isaac Wurz in 1988, is to minimize the disturbance to the existing community. The Committee of Elders also examines the viability of the proposed colony so as to protect Hutterite interests. Sometimes colonies are advised not to proceed with their plans.[54]

Despite this procedure, the Alberta Association of Municipal Districts has continued to receive calls at its annual meetings for firmer restrictions on Hutterite land purchases. In response, a 'dialogue group' organized by the Farmer's Advocate of Alberta, has met once each year since the early 1980s. The group includes representatives from rural municipalities, urban municipalities, school trustee associations, chambers of commerce, a number of Hutterites, and other interested people. The dialogue allows people to express their views and to receive information. The group has not expressed serious concern about Hutterite actions but the encounters probably reinforce the internal controls that the Hutterites have placed on themselves. At the same time, it helps outsiders to understand Hutterite concerns.[55]

VARIOUS RESTRICTIONS IN SASKATCHEWAN

The Hutterites first came to Saskatchewan from Alberta in 1958 when restrictions there made it necessary for them to look elsewhere for land. The reception in Saskatchewan was not particularly hospitable, however. Local groups immediately began to press the government for restrictive legislation. But the CCF (Co-operative Commonwealth Federation) government of Saskatchewan was cautious. It wanted to deal with the situation in a way that would prevent the growth of strong anti-Hutterite feelings. It also wanted to respect the 1943 Bill of Rights, which guaranteed the right to acquire land by purchase or lease or occupancy without discrimination.[56] As a first step, the provincial government asked the Saskatchewan Branch of the Canadian Mental Health Association to study the attitudes of the public towards the Hutterite settlements.

The study found that the public attitude was mixed. According to one summary: 'A considerable number of people were concerned about the effect of Hutterite settlement on local community life – particularly on the local economy – but many others seem to feel that the Hutterites might make a considerable contribution to community welfare through exemplification of advanced farming techniques. Similarly local citizens disapproved of Hutterite isolation and pacifism but admired their religious conviction and industry.'[57] The study concluded that no serious problem existed at the time and that future difficulties could be kept to a minimum by disseminating accurate information about the Hutterites. Much of the opposition to the Hutterites was based on inaccurate information, the study concluded.

The findings of the study did not lead to substantial action. No 'information service' was set up although some articles about Hutterites were published in local newspapers. For a time thereafter the matter was quiet. By 1956, however, public criticisms were becoming strong again. They pointed to the Hutterites' social isolation and commercial practices and expressed 'concern for the economic future of the local communities.' Organizations like the Canadian Legion and the Saskatchewan Association of Rural Municipalities (SARM) became vehicles for pressing the government to bring in restrictive legislation. The SARM, at its 1956 annual meeting, passed a resolution stating:

Whereas the Provincial Government has no legislation in force restricting the settlement of Hutterite colonies, and
whereas the colonies are of no asset to the community because they will not take part in any community affairs or activities, nor will they, if at all possible, patronize local businesses as it is their policy to endeavour to purchase requirements at wholesale prices, and
whereas several colonies have established themselves in the southwest part of the province and are endeavouring to gradually increase their holdings thus creating the danger of forcing or crowding out the small farmer;
Be it Resolved Therefore, that the Provincial Government be asked to enact legislation similar to that in force in Alberta, that the holding of colonies be limited to 10,000 acres in the better farming areas and 15,000 acres in the poorer farming areas and that the colonies be 100 miles apart. [Resolution no. 72][58]

The government did not take immediate action on the resolution of the SARM. However, public criticism was so strong that it had to do something. In its search for alternatives, it set up a Provincial Committee on Hutterite Settlement, under the chairmanship of the Hon. John H. Sturdy with representation from the government's adult education staff. This suggested that education would be used as a means of dealing with the problem. At its first meeting the committee decided that more information was needed about the Hutterite settlements before starting a program. Accordingly, another study was undertaken.

This second study, completed in 1957, confirmed that the anti-Hutterite sentiments had become quite widespread in those areas where the colonies were located and that, although not many persons were actively anti-Hutterite, 'a few determined individuals could carry the bulk of the population along if they set out to exploit the feeling.'[59] Regarding the substance of the complaints, the report said that the majority were unfounded and that 'people are using the colonies as scapegoats upon which to project the tensions and anxieties caused by changing conditions in rural Saskatchewan.' The study recommended: (i) the establishment of a provincial government committee on Hutterites to 'formulate, direct and co-ordinate provincial programming' with regard to Hutterite settlement; (ii) a more intensive study of Hutterite/community relations with the objective of developing ways of integrating the two social systems into one complementary system; and (iii) the establishment of joint committees at the local level, involving Hutterites and representatives from the community, so as to combat misconceptions of Hutterite life and to promote colony/community co-operation.[60]

The government acted quickly on the first two recommendations. However, as the study called for in the second recommendation got under way late in 1957, a significant change occurred. Officials became persuaded that setting up local joint committees and pursuing colony/community co-operation were not timely objectives, that instead the government should aim for 'the development of a dispersed Hutterite settlement pattern which would free local communities from the ever present fear of overcrowding.'[61] Initial investigations also indicated that 'there was a possibility for voluntary dispersal of colonies if Hutterite confidence could be gained and their search for suitable sites facilitated.'

With these new objectives, the government's committee sought to become well informed about suitable settlement sites, to convince the Hutterites of 'the fairness and sincerity of the government,' and to inform the public of its plans so as to allay anxiety. A field-worker went out to visit the Hutterites. He sought to gain their confidence, to learn of their projections for expansion, and to encourage them not only to consider the suggestions of the government's committee for new colony sites but to go to the committee first whenever they wanted to set up new colonies. If they would commit themselves to such a practice, then, noted the clever field-worker, 'Hutterite morality could be brought to bear on the problem of finding mutually satisfactory sites.'[62]

After a number of visits the field-worker was able to get one colony to make such a commitment. This colony was then used to encourage others. Eventually, on 22 August 1958, an agreement was signed with one group of Saskatchewan Hutterites known as the Lehrer-Leut. The agreement was for an initial five-year period with the understanding that it would probably be renewed thereafter. For the second five-year period, the other main group of Saskatchewan Hutterites, known as the Darius-Leut, also signed but only after the government threatened to bring in legislation if they refused.[63] Like the agreement in Manitoba, this one was referred to as a 'gentleman's agreement.' It had few details. It emphasized the consultative dimension of the new relationship between the colonies and the government but the colonies did commit themselves to checking with the government's Hutterite committee before setting up a new colony and to working with that committee in seeking mutually satisfactory sites.

Of greater significance was the government's statement of 'Policy and Procedures – Hutterite Colonies.'[64] It stipulated that a new colony should be at least thirty-five miles from an existing one, that none should be larger that 10,000 acres, and that the needs of nearby farm families should be given priority. By way of procedures, the government's committee, when informed of the Hutterites' intention to set up a new colony, would have its field-worker investigate the situation by interviewing the local councils, school officials, and business and farm people. He would then submit a detailed report to the committee. The committee would then make a decision and communicate it to the Hutterites.

This arrangement, although operative for many years, was not without difficulties. The Hutterites found the procedure very time-consuming. The government's committee, which included three cabinet ministers, would usually take more than six months from the time that the Hutterites first indicated their interest in a particular site to decide the issue.[65] During this time the price of the land would often rise substantially.[66] Sometimes the government deliberately kept the procedures moving slowly. One civil servant reported that applications were 'intentionally held up, on occasion, because of political queries or in the hope that a delay will result in Colony indecision with respect to proposed purchases.'[67]

As a result of these and other difficulties the Hutterites refused, in

1968, to sign a renewal of the agreement.[68] This did not mean that they would proceed without consideration for the public's concern. Indeed, the government now issued guide-lines very similar to those in its earlier policy statement. The guide-lines suggested that the size of a colony be limited; that the land of any one colony be in one block; that new colonies be at least thirty-five miles from existing colonies; and that the Hutterites await government approval before purchasing land. The Hutterites tried to co-operate and to follow these guide-lines and the government's Hutterite committee continued to function.[69]

In 1977, however, a dispute arose. A Hutterite colony at Waldeck, Saskatchewan, had reached the size of nearly 150 people when it was customary to draw lots and have some of the people set up a new colony.[70] Some land had become available near Vanguard so the Hutterites took 'options' on it, thus indicating their interest in purchasing it. The land, which was not in a single block, amounted to over 6000 acres and spanned the rural municipalities of Whiska Creek, Glenbain, and Auvergne. On 27 October 1977 Rev. Michael Entz, who was to be the leader of the new colony, sent a notice to the government to indicate their intention to purchase the land. The liaison officer for the cabinet's Hutterite committee, Michael Czornobay, then set out to investigate the situation.[71] On 10 November 1977 he met with the Council of the Rural Municipality of Whiska Creek where he found strong opposition to the Hutterites. When asked whether anything could be done, he reportedly replied that the council could meet with planners of the Municipal Affairs Department and draw up by-laws to restrict construction within the municipality. On the same day Czornobay also attended a meeting of ratepayers where he learned of more anti-Hutterite feelings.

On 14 November 1977, when provincial planners met with the Council of Whiska Creek, interim by-law zoning restrictions were drawn up and enacted.[72] On 25 November the Hutterites, having received no request from the government that they not purchase the land, proceeded to make the purchase. Then, on 28 November the Hutterites received a registered letter from the Whiska Creek municipality informing them of a requirement that they would have to obtain building permits before they could construct buildings.[73] When the Hutterites attempted to obtain these permits, they were refused on the ground that the new interim zoning by-laws allowed for no communal buildings and stipulated that only two family dwellings could be built on any one quarter-section.[74] Rev. Michael Entz then exclaimed that 'the controls are absolutely intended to try and stop us from living our lifestyle.'[75] The

Whiska Creek authorities were reported to have said: 'Hutterites should live like everyone else, one dwelling per quarter section of land ... [in] the traditional Prairie settlement pattern.'[76]

After the Hutterites were refused in four attempts to obtain building permits, they proceeded to build anyway.[77] The Whiska Creek municipality then laid charges. In the ensuing trial the reeve of the municipality, Henry Godenir, told the court that the controls were set up because of a concern about large farms generally and that they were not aimed at Hutterites specifically.[78] The lawyer for the municipality argued that 'if rural municipalities do not have the power to zone, they are emasculated.'[79] Other municipalities appear to have supported Whiska Creek financially and the SARM, at its annual meeting, passed a resolution indicating support 'for all municipalities in their efforts to obtain financial assistance to uphold their zoning by-laws.'[80]

The Hutterites, for their part, argued that the by-laws were directed at them and that they were discriminatory on the basis of religion and were therefore in violation of the provincial Bill of Rights. They felt, too, that the provincial officials had helped the municipality to draw up the by-laws in an effort to establish generally firmer control over the Hutterites. The lawyer for the Hutterites, when he cross-examined the provincial officials, found considerable evidence to support this view.[81] On 27 June 1979, Judge Fielding rendered his decision. He held that the by-laws were null and void on the basis of a technicality but added: 'If ... it were necessary to do so, I would find that the municipality did not pass the resolution in good faith since it did so for the purpose of discriminating against people because they were Hutterites.'[82]

During the course of these proceedings, the government appears to have become somewhat more understanding of the difficulties that the Hutterites faced. The minister of Municipal Affairs indicated a willingness to remove the thirty-five-mile limit from the guide-lines and to simplify the general procedures so that they could be completed more quickly. There was understanding also of the Hutterites' desire to have the procedures carried out with less publicity. One municipal official acknowledged that 'prices rise when their interests are known.'[83] Moreover, the Hutterites were willing to work with the government to avoid problems and to try to maintain good public relations.[84]

Despite this ruling in favour of the Hutterites, a few years later there was another encounter with municipal by-laws. Early in the 1980s the Rural Municipality of Eagle Creek passed zoning by-laws that allowed the construction of buildings on agricultural land only if they were 'accessory or incidental' to the agricultural use of the land. On this basis, the municipality refused to issue building permits to Hutterites who, as part of their effort to set up a new colony in the area, wanted to construct a school, a church, a community kitchen, a laundry, and a slaughter-house. The Hutterites then appealed, first to the Zoning Appeals Board, then to the Provincial Planning Appeals Board, and finally to the Saskatchewan Court of Appeal, which ruled in their favour. In giving its reasons, on 8 February 1983, the Appeal Court referred to 'common law and statutory protection in relation to religious and racial discrimina-tion.' It quoted from the Ritchie judgment in the *Hofer* case and mentioned also the Canadian Charter of Rights and Freedoms. The court then stated: 'Our law does not permit municipal bylaws to be used as instruments of intolerance or oppression. All citizens must have equal opportunity to live the life they can and want to live, without being hindered by discriminatory practices, as long as their actions are in keeping with their obligations as responsible members of society. It is not the function of municipal councils through the medium of zoning bylaws, or otherwise, to strive to forestall the practises of a particular religious faith.'[85]

Nearly two years later the same parties were before the same court again. This time the Hutterites had been refused permits to construct four multi-family residences on their lands. The municipal zoning by-law permitted only two single-family dwellings on any one agricultural hold-ing, unless additional dwellings were 'accessory or incidental' to the farming operations. The court now rendered only a brief judgment and did not explicitly discuss the question of religious freedom. However, it referred to its 1983 judgment and then stated that the particular life-style of the Hutterites included living in residential structures of the type proposed, that this was not unique to this colony but integral to the life-style of Hutterites generally, and that therefore the living quarters proposed were 'incidental to their farming operations.'[86]

The concern about the Hutterites appeared again, albeit in a different form. In October 1987 the SARM submitted a brief to the provincial cabinet warning that 'a storm cloud of public resentment is building against the Hutterite sect due to accelerated expansion and concentra-tion of Hutterite colonies.' The SARM stated that the earlier idea of maintaining at least '35 miles between colony headquarters' was not being followed and that to 'enable our cultures to live in harmony' a required '35 to 50 mile distance between colonies' should be placed in legislation.[87]

SARM representatives were not optimistic that the government would bring in such legislation but they hoped that their expression of concern might make the provincial Hutterite committee, which now included four Hutterites, two SARM representatives, three ministers from the government, one school trustee, and several other people, more active in addressing these matters.[88]

Obviously, despite the restrictions imposed by each province, the Hutterites have survived. The liberties given to them were broad enough so that they could continue to hold land in a communal manner. But those liberties were not secure. They changed a number of times and were most vulnerable to public pressure. The Hutterites were exposed to intense public criticism and lived with much uncertainty.

Many of the reasons for public feelings against the Hutterites seem to relate to broader social and economic changes. Rural communities were being depopulated. New farm technology meant that fewer workers were needed. Better roads meant that local stores were passed by as people travelled to larger centres. Country schools were closed and children were bused to towns. In this context, a Hutterite colony, buying up a sizeable block of land, was one more factor contributing to the decline in the traditional life of a rural community. But because a Hutterite colony was so conspicuous and because of a lingering nativist sentiment, it often became the focus of the concern.

Because these social and economic trends affected each of the prairie provinces, it is not surprising that the provincial governments, even though they represented four different political parties, responded to the situation in broadly similar ways. All, for a time, limited the size of the colonies and stipulated that there had to be a certain minimum distance between them. Alberta, which had the largest number of Hutterites, used legislation. The other two provinces used less formal means but both pressured the Hutterites by threatening to enact legislation. The results were virtually the same, though it must be noted that Manitoba was more lenient, calling only for a ten-mile distance between the colonies. In the 1970s and 1980s there was a dismantling of the restrictions under such politically different leaders as Ed Schreyer in Manitoba and Peter Lougheed in Alberta. This again suggests that the reasons for reducing restrictions lay more in broad sociological trends than in the virtues of any one political party.

The Hutterite encounters are significant also for what they reveal about how the concept of freedom for religion was perceived. In

Chapter 3, about Doukhobor communal landholding, we saw a federal minister, Frank Oliver, claiming that freedom from religion meant little more than freedom to believe and to worship. In the Hutterite experience discussed in this chapter, there seems to be an awareness that religion is broader, that it can, at least for some people, be inseparable from a way of life. Lawyers for the Hutterites used such an argument repeatedly, and governments seemed to recognize that although they could impose restrictions on the Hutterites, they could not make it impossible for them to continue in their way of life without violating the principle of religious freedom. This is probably a key reason why the Social Credit governments in Alberta did not completely give in to the anti-Hutterite pressure that was so strong in that province from the 1940s to the 1960s.

Admittedly, the exact breadth of the concept of freedom of religion is not defined. In the *Walter* case, the Supreme Court said that Alberta's Communal Property Act, with its restrictions on Hutterite landholding rights, dealt not with religion but with property and that it was therefore within provincial jurisdiction. Also, in the *Hofer* case, Justice Pigeon set forth a narrow view of freedom for religion. But his was only a dissenting judgment. The majority in that case held that the colony way of life was inseparable from its religion. This view is reflected also in the more recent judgments of the Saskatchewan courts.

In addition to the recognition that freedom of religion includes considerably more than freedom to believe and to worship, the encounters also reveal that giving freedom to the communities can mean allowing the freedom of individuals within them to be restricted. Critics pointed to this dilemma repeatedly. The Alberta Farmers' Union said that the Hutterites, by their communal and separate way of life, were denying their children the right to live as free individuals and Canadian citizens. And the Community Welfare Association of Manitoba said that Hutterite children were denied the privilege of having their faculties developed and learning the things necessary to fulfil their duties to their fellow citizens. The conflict between freedom for individuals and that for groups was central also in the *Hofer* case. One scholar attributes the persistent criticism about restrictions on individual freedom to the 'tradition of agrarian radicalism and ... egalitarian and individualistic values.'[89]

Why were the Hutterites given such freedoms when the Doukhobors, in the century's first decade, were not? Obviously the contexts were different but it should also be noted that the freedom that the Doukhobors needed for their way of life was broader. The Hutterite colonies were much smaller and more like other large farms than were the Doukhobor blocks of land. The Hutterites worked all their land just as other farmers did. They had English-language schools. And they accepted Canadian citizenship. For these and other reasons the Hutterite way of life represented less of a departure from the Canadian norm than did the early Doukhobor way of life.

PART THREE

Schools

The approach of Mennonites, Hutterites, and Doukhobors to the education of their children is a second area that reflects their desire to live as communities somewhat separately from the larger society.

However, on schooling as on land-holding, these groups have not been entirely of one mind. Some people from these groups, wanting a very complete separation, have said of public schools: that they supported militarism; that they nurtured competitiveness and profit seeking and a readiness to exploit other people; that they did not support the spirit of co-operation and concern for the welfare of others; that they made people less willing to accept the burdens of daily toil; and that they made it difficult to continue seeing religious and secular truth as parts of one whole.

Other people from these groups, favouring a measure of integration with the larger society, have accepted public schools and then supplemented them with evening and weekend classes in order to teach their religion, their language, and other aspects of their way of life. These people have also encouraged individuals from their own ranks to take the necessary training and become teachers in the public schools in their communities. They have also become involved with local school-boards. By these methods, these more integrated people have influenced the public schools that their children attended.

Understandably, those who accepted the public education system, albeit with supplementary classes of their own, have had few difficulties with governments. But those who wanted to live more separately, in communities unto themselves, have challenged the political system and thereby tested the limits of liberty. These more difficult encounters are the subjects of the following three chapters.

The first involves the Mennonites who came from Russia to the Canadian prairies in the 1870s. They had long had their own schools. Indeed, one reason for leaving Russia was the increased government control over private schools there. In their early negotiations with the government of Canada, these Mennonites received assurances of broad educational freedoms, and for several decades they operated their own schools with little governmental interference. Gradually, however, the governments of Manitoba and Saskatchewan began to promote public education; around the time of the First World War, they ruled that virtually all instruction had to be in the English language and in public schools. Some Mennonites accepted this ruling but others refused. For the latter it was a traumatic encounter. Thousands of dollars were exacted in fines. A few Mennonites were imprisoned. Eventually, about 6000 emigrated to Latin America.

A second encounter involves the Doukhobors. Soon after their arrival on the prairies in 1899 they established a few schools of their own, but these did not function on a regular basis. Formal education was not deeply rooted in the history of the Doukhobors, partly because their religious emphasis on 'the God within' made formal learning less important and partly because of their experience in Russia, where many schools had been dominated by the Russian Orthodox church. Thus, when the government of Saskatchewan began to promote public schools the Community Doukhobors remained hesitant for a number of years. However, the Independent Doukhobors, who had become more integrated with Canadian society, accepted the public schools. Eventually the other Saskatchewan Doukhobors followed. In British Columbia the difficulties were more serious. There the Community Doukhobors' resistance continued longer; even after they accepted the public schools, the Sons of Freedom Doukhobors remained adamant. A bitter confrontation resulted. Eventually the British Columbia government removed Doukhobor children from their homes and held them in a dormitory school surrounded by a barbed-wire fence. In 1959, after this situation had continued for about six years, the Doukhobor parents agreed to send their children to public schools. The government then returned the children to the parents.

A third encounter involves the Hutterites. These people were accommodated more easily. They had a historic interest in formal education. They were prepared to accept English as the language of instruction and a measure of government control over their schools. There were a few difficulties when they first came to Canada but before long there were public schools on each colony. Other children were not prohibited but in reality only Hutterite children attended. Because of this exclusive enrolment, and because of the supplementary classes each morning and evening, the schools were and remain somewhat like private Hutterite schools, despite their official status as public schools. Occasionally, there has been pressure to force Hutterite children to attend public schools outside their colonies but this idea has never been implemented.

5 Mennonite School Controversies in Manitoba and Saskatchewan, 1874–1925

MENNONITE SCHOOLS AND GOVERNMENT ACCOMMODATION

Mennonites had always held that a measure of schooling was important. Their children had to have the ability to read the Bible. They also needed sufficient writing and arithmetic skills to operate farms. However, most Mennonite schools, until the middle of the nineteenth century, did not provide more than this basic schooling for the Mennonite way of life.

For the Mennonites in Russia the privilege of operating their own schools in the German language changed in the 1870s. The government then announced that it would take over the direction of the schools and that Russian would become the official language of instruction. The change was part of a new policy directed at the many colonies of foreigners. The Russian government recognized that some might oppose the policy so it gave the colonists ten years either to adjust or to emigrate. During this time, some Mennonites negotiated compromises with the government. Others explored emigration possibilities.

Those seeking emigration approached the authorities for Canada to ask for the freedom to operate their own schools. The initial responses were favourable, and in 1873, when four members of the larger delegation to North America chose Canada, they received an apparently firm assurance of this freedom. On 25 July 1873, John Lowe of the Department of Agriculture, which was responsible for immigration at the time, gave the Mennonites an elaborate letter, which stated in paragraph 10: 'The fullest privilege of exercising their religious principles is by law afforded to the Mennonites without any kind of molestation or restriction whatever, and the same privilege extends to the education of their children in schools.'[1] On 13 August 1873 this letter was embodied in an order-in-council and the paragraph on education, now slightly modified, stated that the Mennonites had 'the fullest privilege of exercising their religious principles, and educating their children in schools, as provided by law.'[2]

The substance of this promise was not unusual. Most schools at the time were operated by religious groups. French-Catholic schools had long served the French-Canadian settlers at St Boniface, as well as Métis and Indian people throughout the west. Anglican schools and those of other religious groups were each serving their own people. It was assumed, writes W.L. Morton, 'that the education of the young was an office of religion, that church and school should be inseparable.'[3] Thus, for the government to assure the Mennonites that they could have their own schools was not to promise something unusual.

FREEDOM AND ITS WITHDRAWAL IN MANITOBA

Although the provinces were virtually autonomous in matters of education, the Manitoba Act passed by the federal Parliament in 1870 stated that the provincial legislature could not pass any laws that would 'prejudicially affect any right or privileges with respect to denomination-al schools which any class of persons have by law or practice in the Province at the union.'[4] This sanction for the existing denominational education structure was reflected also in the province's first School Act, passed in 1871. This act created a Board of Education and divided the province into twelve Protestant and twelve Catholic school districts. Further, the board was divided into Protestant and Catholic sections equal in size and with an equal amount of money to supervise and assist the schools in their respective districts.

The act, however, did not authorize the board to set up schools by itself. A request was to come from local residents. Nor did the act set out any particular language requirements, although it may have been assumed that Protestant schools would use English and Catholic ones French. There were no limits on religious instruction. And attendance was not compulsory.[5] Because of its minimal character, the act would not necessarily affect the new Mennonite settlers.

When the Mennonites arrived they began to operate their own schools just as they had in Russia.[6] However, in 1877, the Protestant section of the Board of Education sought to organize the Mennonite village schools into official governmentally recognized district schools. The board offered a grant of $80 to $100 per year per school and some of the pioneering Mennonites, being in need of funds, were interested. The board's offer was accompanied by strong assurances that Mennonite freedoms would not be affected, that they could continue to use their own language and curriculum, and also their own teachers.[7] Recognition appeared to involve little more than the registration of Mennonite villages as school districts.[8] After some discussion two Mennonite bishops agreed, in fall 1878, to have some thirty-six village schools registered in this way. Probably an equal number remained unregistered.[9]

Before long it became apparent that the province's Board of Education was interested in more than just giving money. It wanted a measure of control. The first indication came in 1879 when the board attempted to examine and classify teachers. This disturbed the Mennonites and when one bishop expressed his concern, an official said: 'Well, you don't think that the government will give its money to men who are cowherds in summer and school teachers in winter.'[10] When the seriousness of the Mennonite concerns became apparent, the board modified its position but the episode prompted many Mennonites to withdraw their schools from the provincial arrangement.[11] Some Mennonites, however, did not fear government involvement and remained with the provincially approved schools in the expectation that doing so would provide their people with the skills necessary for communicating with the larger Canadian society.

This division among the Mennonites was to become deeper. Some of those who favoured the district schools sought to promote their acceptance among the other Mennonites. In this they were helped by the municipal system of local government introduced into the Mennonite areas early in the 1880s.[12] The legislation for the municipal system provided that when the ratepayers in any locality petitioned for the formation of a school district, then the municipality would raise the necessary funds by levying taxes on property. Because there was no exemption for supporters of private schools, they had to pay for both types of school. To the conservative Mennonites, these developments appeared to violate the terms on which they had come to Canada. They had assumed a greater internal autonomy. They raised the issue with federal authorities but the deputy minister of Justice held that the provincial legislature was within its jurisdiction in giving such authority to municipalities.[13]

Mennonites who favoured the district schools continued their efforts and made contacts with Mennonites in the United States who had a more advanced education. They also received encouragement from George Bryce, chairman of the provincial Board of Education. He said that 'they should improve the schooling of their children in order to give them a better chance in the competitive society in which they would have to make a living.'[14] By 1889 they had a teacher-training school in the town of Gretna. Though modest and in frequent difficulty, it served for several decades.[15]

Alongside these changes among the Mennonites, there were significant developments in the larger Manitoba society. Many new settlers were arriving, including a number of English Protestants from Ontario. These carried 'a deep-set conviction ... that Manitoba must be made British and that a "national" school system should be the agent to accomplish this task.'[16] Their most immediate concern was with the right of the French Catholics to have their own schools. Encouraged by political developments in Ontario, they supported a campaign that led the Manitoba legislature, in 1890, to pass a School Act that, in section 179, stated simply: 'In cases where ... Catholic school districts have been established ... such Catholic school districts shall ... cease to exist.'[17] This was a drastic change. The denominational schools were to be replaced with one integrated public school system administered by a Department of Education whose minister would be responsible to the legislature.

Nearly a decade of political and legal controversy followed. The French Catholics were not the only ones affected. Anglicans protested, too. At one point the federal government attempted, unsuccessfully, to bring in remedial legislation, pursuant to section 93 of the British North America Act. Eventually, in 1897, a compromise was negotiated that allowed for a bilingual public school system. The arrangement provided that 'when ten of the pupils in any school speak French or any language other than English as their native language, the teaching of such pupils shall be conducted in French, or such other language, and English upon a bilingual system.'[18] In addition, if a significant number of local people requested it, then a Catholic teacher was to be hired. Also, schools could arrange to have religious classes for a small portion of each school day.

Strangely, this arrangement, which did not completely satisfy either the French Catholics or the English Protestants, was relatively well suited to the Mennonites. The conservative Mennonites, like the Reinlaender Mennonite church, who wanted no government involvement in the education of their children, were left alone. They could continue with their private schools where German was the only language and where much of the curriculum had a religious orientation even though, if they lived in an area that had been organized into a public school district, they also had to pay taxes to support the public schools.

Meanwhile, the less conservative Mennonites could now participate in a strengthened public school system and instead of a French/English bilingualism, they could opt for a German/English bilingualism. In this way their children would learn to communicate with the larger society while retaining the German language and remaining close to their traditions. These Mennonites now set out with renewed energy and government encouragement to strengthen their small teacher-training school at Gretna. Already in 1891 the government's new Department of Education had helped them to recruit H.H. Ewert, a well-educated Mennonite from Kansas, to serve as principal of the school. At the same time, the government appointed him as a school inspector in order to promote public schools among the Mennonites.

Things moved slowly but the number of public schools in Mennonite areas gradually increased. The teachers, though helped by the five-week training courses at Gretna, did not suddenly become fluent in English. Still, some English was being taught.[19] A 1911 inspector's report stated that the year marked 'an era of progress' which should be 'very gratifying to the Department of Education' and that this was due to the 'excellent work done by the teachers' who represent 'a new force of educational missionaries.'[20] C.B. Sissons, who was generally critically of the bilingual system, was to write later that 'by 1914 most of the Mennonites in Manitoba ... were maintaining some of the best schools of the Province.'[21] A 1916 Department of Education report also spoke highly of them in comparison to French, Polish, and Ruthenian bilingual schools.[22]

Despite the bilingual system's good record among the Mennonites, others began to criticize it strongly. Many Manitobans claimed that it did not adequately integrate the various immigrant groups or effectively promote a British orientation. According to the *Manitoba Free Press*, which actively campaigned against the bilingual system, 'the schools were in effect perpetuating immigrant tongues without adding English to them.'[23] Critics also pointed to the serious administrative difficulties. Providing teachers trained in English and the various other subjects was difficult enough, but whenever a group would request instruction in a second language within the terms of the law, then the Department of Education had to provide teachers and curriculum materials in that language, too. Because a number of groups had made such requests the department had set up special schools to train teachers in different languages. Moreover, the second language to be used in a particular school could easily change as a result of the relocation of one family. In some schools the minimum number of ten children needed to request a second language was met by more than one ethnic group. R.S. Thornton of the Education Department said: 'Each district becomes in succession a storm centre and peace returns because one or the other section is driven out of the settlements. In most cases the English people are driven out of the settlement and those who cannot afford to move have to stay and endure conditions.'[24] Since attendance was not compulsory, these controversies led many parents to withdraw their children from school.

As a result of the growing call for changes, the Liberal party of Manitoba, at its convention on 26 March 1914, 'demanded national schools, obligatory teaching of English in all public schools and compulsory school attendance.'[25] In the provincial election of August 1915, the Liberals, led by T.C. Norris, came to power and in the Speech from the Throne that followed, the government announced that a 'proper elementary education' would be made compulsory, though it would allow this to be attained either 'by attendance at the public schools or by such substitute within the choice of parents or of guardians as shall attain that end.'[26] These words suggested flexibility but in reality the new government was to become very firm. In January 1916 the new minister of Education, R.S. Thornton, spoke in the legislature saying:

We are building for the Canada of tomorrow, and our common school is one of the most important factors in the work. In this Dominion we are building up, under the British flag, a new nationality. We come from many lands and cast in our lot, and from these various factors there must evolve a new nationality which shall be simply Canadian and British ... There should be one common school ... There should be one standard of teacher eligible to teach in all the schools of the province. There should be a normal training to which all teachers should measure up. There should be a school inspector, eligible to inspect every school under the government ... A grave injustice is being done to the children who do not receive a satisfactory education in English. Without that knowledge they grow up under a continuous handicap. We wish to give them the same consideration that is accorded to our own children, to fit them to earn their way through life and to take their places as citizens of our Canadian nationality.[27]

The Mennonites in the bilingual public system had been aware for some time that the political trends were not in their favour. They now appealed to Valentine Winkler, the member of the legislative assembly from their area, who also served as minister of Agriculture in the new cabinet. The first meeting with him took place in the fall of 1915. He assured the Mennonites that 'their schools would not be affected by the new legislation if they operated them privately.'[28] This was not the answer that these Mennonites had hoped for. They did not want to revert to private status.

Soon thereafter the new legislation was announced. It was categorical. Instead of only requiring the effective teaching of English, it would now be the only language of instruction. The Mennonites appealed to Winkler again. In a January 1916 meeting they made a strong plea for the continuation of the bilingual system. They wanted their children to learn the English language, but German was important, too. They said that all their religious and devotional literature was in German, and their children needed to know it in order to have a religious life in common with their parents, and that it was helpful also for communicating among themselves and for maintaining a sense of their tradition. They also said that they would cover all costs related to training the teachers necessary for the bilingual system. And in order to solve the general difficulties of administering the bilingual system, they suggested that the law be changed so that a clear majority of the ratepayers in any district would have to support a request for instruction in a second language rather than just the parents of ten children.[29]

Winkler could not respond definitively to the concerns of the Mennonite leaders, but he arranged for them, in the spring of 1916, to meet with the premier and the minister of Education. For this meeting their delegation included representatives from most of the Mennonite groups in Manitoba except the conservative Reinlaender Mennonite church. According to one account, 'they contended that the norms of their education could not be established by outsiders because Mennonites considered themselves responsible to God alone in this matter, that instruction in religion and the German language were indispensable ingredients in the right instruction of the children and that education provided continuity of spiritual fellowship between the generations.'[30] They also pointed to the promises on the basis of which they had come to Canada and indicated that they might consider emigrating to another country rather than surrender their values.

When the government refused to change its policy, the Mennonites held a number of church meetings to search for a proper course of action. Before long a large majority of the Mennonite public schools reverted to private status.[31] Even H.H. Ewert, who had done so much to help the Mennonites fit into the provincial education system, supported the change to private status. This, however, was financially burdensome. Private schools had to be supported directly by the people who, in most instances, also had to pay taxes for public schools. Moreover, there was uncertainty about the private schools. The government now had the authority to determine, at any time and for any reason, that the private schools were not providing 'a proper elementary education.'

For a time the government regarded the Mennonite schools as 'a rather minor problem.'[32] But the return of public schools to private status was not welcomed even though many of these schools continued to teach and to use the English language. The Mennonites understood the reversion to be within the provisions of the law but according to the government's perception, 'a campaign was inaugurated to destroy our public school system in the rural districts. Meetings were held, urging the ratepayers to give up the government grants and run the schools as private schools.'[33] Accordingly, the government took decisive action. As local trustees of public schools resigned, it appointed official trustees who would then hire teachers and keep the schools open as public schools. Some twenty-nine schools were saved for the public system in this way.[34] But their official status was different from the reality. One teacher wrote: 'When I hoisted the flag on the first of September, there wasn't a child in school. The old people got together, fixed up a log cabin and hired a private teacher for the 45 children in the district. They paid him the same salary I was getting – $80 a month. But I stuck to it and hoisted the flag every one of the 202 days but I did not have one pupil.'[35]

When parents in these districts refused to send their children to the public schools the government launched prosecutions. Most of the sentences were in the form of fines but some people were imprisoned for brief periods.[36] One case reached the Manitoba Court of Appeal. It involved one John Hildebrand, charged with violating the compulsory attendance provisions by not sending his daughter to public school or making other 'satisfactory provisions' for her education. He based his defence on the promise made by the federal government at the time when the Mennonites had come to Canada, set forth in the letter of 25 July 1873. The court, however, was not persuaded. It referred to the paragraph in the letter that spelled out the privilege of operating Mennonite schools, and also to the paragraph's slightly amended words in the order-in-council of 13 August 1873. The court then ruled that the position in the letter 'must be taken as merged' in that of the order-in-council but that neither was of any effect because of Manitoba's constitutional authority to make laws in relation to education. The judgment stated:

This province came into being on May 12, 1870 by virtue of the Manitoba Act, ch. 3, 33 Vict., confirmed by the Imperial Act, ch. 28, 34 S. 35 Vict. By sec. 22 of that Act it is provided that 'In and for the Province, the said Legislature may exclusively make Laws in relation to Education.' Nothing can be plainer. The Dominion of Parliament itself could and can pass no legislation affecting education in this province, save in the circumstances indicated in subsecs. 2 and 3 of sec. 22, which have absolutely no application here. And if that cannot be done by a statute of Canada how is it possible that it could be accomplished by an order of the Governor-General in Council or by the letter of an official of a department of the Dominion Government?[37]

An attempt was made to have the case heard by the Privy Council in London, to which some Canadian cases could be appealed at that time, but the council refused to grant leave to appeal.[38]

In light of this apparent defeat, many Mennonites decided to comply with the new law. But the more conservative groups like the Reinlaender Mennonite church, also known as the Old Colony Mennonite church were still largely unaffected. Throughout the several decades when the other Mennonites had been in the public school system, the conservatives had continued to operate their own schools without any government involvement. As a result they had remained on the sideline of the controversies. Now Education Minister Thornton was determined to bring them into the public system as well. The legislation was amended to give the Department of Education the authority to create school districts without petition from local residents. Districts were then mapped out and the construction of school buildings begun. When people refused to sell land for school sites, the government expropriated it. When local merchants refused to sell building materials, they were brought in from Winnipeg, with the additional cost charged to the district.[39] And because local people were unwilling to serve as trustees, an official trustee was appointed by the government. It was a harsh confrontation accompanied again by fines and some prison sentences.

In response, the Reinlaender Mennonite church, probably with the assistance of their lawyer, J.B. McLaren, prepared an elaborate submission to the members of the legislative assembly.[40] They expressed

gratitude for the protection given by federal and provincial governments through the years and assured the legislators of their loyalty and
their prayers. They then reviewed the privileges given to them by the
government at the time of their immigration and stated: 'Believing then
as we do now that the word of the Government is inviolate because the
Government is ordained of God, we started our own schools.' They
described their schools, which now numbered twenty-two, and emphasized that the curriculum was well suited to their particular way of life.
They said their children were taught to be loyal to governments, to live
in harmony with nature, to do physical work, to live in community, to be
co-operative, to help the needy, and to live peacefully with all. They said
they felt conscience bound to teach their children 'religious and secular
truth as part of one whole, that they may be holy and good and loyal and
diligent and unselfish and co-operative in all their relations to God and
to their fellow men.' They noted that their way of life had been blessed
with prosperity and said they felt that this had benefited Canada as well.
In conclusion, they requested that the government, before breaking the
promise of 1873, make a broad investigation. They said: 'We would ask
you to kindly make an independent and unprejudiced investigation into
the social, economical and moral conditions of our community and base
your opinion of us and our school system on the facts as you find them ...
one favour we would ask of you ... that is not to examine the details of our
school system ... and condemn it because it differs in some respects from
that of the state school, without considering the results we obtain
through our schools.'

The gracefully worded submission reflected a different purpose of
education. These Mennonite schools were to prepare their children for
life in their communities. In contrast, the *Manitoba Free Press*, which
published the Mennonite brief, outlined its view that state schools were
symbols of a new freedom. The *Free Press* held that the modern
democratic state 'cannot agree that the parents have the sole right of
determining what kind of education their children shall receive ... a
doctrine which in its practical working means every time absolute clerical
control of education. The children are the children of the state of which
they are destined to be citizens; and it is the duty of the state that they are
properly educated.'[41] The government followed the *Free Press* philosophy and continued to implement its schools policy.

When the conservative Mennonites found that their appeals were
being rejected, they began to explore the possibility of immigrating to
another country. They now sent delegates to other parts of the western

hemisphere the way they had once sent them from Russia to North America. This development raised the concern of some observers. William Jennings O'Neill, a Winnipeg businessman who had had considerable contact with these Mennonites, wrote lengthy letters to the provincial education minister, Thornton, and also to Prime Minister Borden in Ottawa.[42] He argued that the Mennonites were conscientious, law-abiding, hard-working people with good morals, and that they had been generous during the war by buying Victory Bonds and contributing to the Red Cross and to other funds. He held that in a free country, inhabited by so many different kinds of people, governments should be tolerant. He referred to the arrangements made in the 1870s at the time when the Mennonites had come, stating: 'Whether this treaty was a good one or not for the government to make, I respectfully submit is not for us to say. It is law, and it is the majesty of that law which we have to respect.' He concluded the letter to Borden by saying: 'I trust that the Government may deem it expedient to take some action ... in regard to the ... rights that were guaranteed to the Mennonites in 1874.'[43]

The appeals of Jennings O'Neill were in vain. The governments continued in their course and the conservative Mennonites continued in their efforts to find a new homeland. Eventually, the Reinlaender Mennonite church was able to make satisfactory arrangements with the government of Mexico, while another group reached agreement with Paraguay. During the decade of the 1920s about 6000 Mennonites left Canada for Latin America.[44]

FREEDOM AND ITS WITHDRAWAL IN SASKATCHEWAN

The development of the education structure in Saskatchewan was similar to that in Manitoba, although the institutionalization of a Protestant/Catholic dualism was more limited and the idea of a bilingual system was not seriously pursued.

The earliest schools in the area were set up by church groups before the North-West Territories Act was passed in 1875. That act, in its references to education, provided, first, that a majority of the ratepayers of any area could 'establish such schools therein as they may think fit, and make the necessary assessment and collection of taxes therefor' and, second, that the minority of ratepayers in an area, whether Protestant or Catholic, could establish separate schools and pay taxes only for those.[45] In 1884, 'An Ordinance Providing for the Organization of Schools in the North-West Territories' established a Board of Education with Protestant and Catholic sections and authorized each section to supervise its respective schools, to prescribe the curriculum and textbooks, and to regulate the training and licensing of teachers. There were no restrictions on religious instruction nor was any particular language prescribed.

These early provisions suggested a dualistic denominational school system, but in 1892 there was a consolidation. The Board of Education, with its two sections, was replaced by a Council of Public Instruction consisting of the Territorial Executive Committee, which was somewhat like a cabinet, and four non-voting advisers, two of whom would be Protestant and two Catholic. This council 'assumed control of the administration of all schools in receipt of public funds, public and separate, in the matter of inspection, the certification of teachers, and the authorizing of textbooks.'[46] With this act the 'management of the schools had been virtually taken over by the State.' There could be religious instruction, if locally requested, but it was limited to the last half-hour of the school day. The French language could be used only in the first grade.[47] Separate schools were allowed but because they were subject to the same restrictions, little was gained by having them and few were established.

With the move to provincial status for both Saskatchewan and Alberta in 1905, there was further debate about provisions for education. The central question was between protection for the French-Catholic minorities and provincial autonomy. The differences in the federal Parliament were intense. Clifford Sifton, who favoured stronger provincial autonomy, resigned from Laurier's Cabinet and other members defected from the party, while Roman Catholic parliamentarians joined forces to protect their minorities in the west. In the end, the Saskatchewan Act provided only that no 'law shall prejudicially affect any right or privilege with respect to separate schools which any class of persons have at the date of the passing of this Act.'[48] In this way the very limited rights of the separate schools would not increase. Saskatchewan would have an integrated public school system with little room for minorities who preferred a different arrangement.

While this education structure restricted the French Catholics, it did not raise particular concern for Saskatchewan Mennonites. Some Mennonites, who had recently emigrated from the United States and Europe and who had not settled on the Hague and Swift Current reserves, were prepared to accept the public schools though they still wanted to use the provisions that allowed for the teaching of religion and the German language in the half-hour at the end of a school day. These 'more integrationist' Mennonites also set up a teacher-training school, suitably called the German-English Academy, to train their own people as teachers for the public schools in their areas.[49] Meanwhile, the more conservative Mennonites in the reserves could still operate their private schools.

The conservative Mennonites, meaning primarily the Reinlaender Mennonite church, had set up private village schools as soon as they had arrived in the area. But in the century's first decade there were problems. Some church members who had moved to nearby towns to start businesses had begun to send their children to public schools. Largely because of this step, they had been excommunicated. As a result, other members of the church no longer made purchases in their stores. This action had serious economic consequences for these new Mennonite businessmen. They now complained to the government. J.J. Friesen, writing to the minister of Education, J.A. Calder, on 1 October 1908, stated:

No doubt at this time you are fully aware of the undesirable condition of our schools and church governments. As I am one of the ex-communicated Mennonites I think it very necessary to tell you briefly my experience in this matter and hope that it might help to stir up the Government of Saskatchewan without any more delay. I lived in Warman until last spring and my business connections were principally with the members of the so-called Old Colony Church; and as I had two boys of school age I was sending them to the public school in Warman, which the leaders of the aforesaid church, as soon as they found out about it, forbade me to do ... As soon as the leaders of the Old Colony Church got notice of my steps they excommunicated me and forbade all the members to have any more dealings with me. The consequence was that I had to give up my home, my business, and everything for the sake of giving my children a better education; and this in the land of the free. Now my dear Mr. Calder, don't you think that the existing conditions are an insult to our liberal constitution?[50]

The province's Liberal government was not sure how to respond. It considered threatening the conservative Mennonites with the possibility of forcing public school districts into their communities and with the withdrawal of the right of their clergy to solemnize marriages.[51] However, before acting it sent out a commission of inquiry. The commission held hearings in the public school building in the town of

Warman on 28 and 29 December 1908 and heard testimony from about a dozen of the excommunicated people as well as from two leaders of the Reinlaender Mennonite church.[52]

The stories of those who had been excommunicated were similar to that of Friesen quoted above. There were charges of oppression and church leaders had to provide an explanation. The reasons of Bishop Jacob Wiens emerged gradually in the exchange of questions and answers, made through an interpreter.

Q Do I understand you to say that the Word of God teaches you not to send your children to the public school?

A Yes, because God's Word says about Moses: 'What I instruct you today thou shalt take to heart, and instruct thy children ...' Out of that, he says, we take that we want to teach God's Word. That is why we left Russia and so forth, that we wanted to teach God's Word in the schools and so forth, which privilege has been granted to us from the High Government.[53]

The questioning then turned to the process and the power of excommunication.

Q Who has the power to excommunicate?

A The whole community. The whole congregation has that power. He says it is first presented to the congregation ... they pass a resolution that a certain member be excommunicated.

Q Would the member himself know anything about it before the meeting?

A Yes, he is invited to come and attend and speak for himself.

Q Can the bishop excommunicate?

A Not alone.

After this, the questioning turned to the case of one particular person.

Q Was he excommunicated because he sent his children to the public school?

A He says, because he was disobedient ...

Q He would not send his children to your schools? Is that right?

A No, he didn't want to.

Q Is that the only thing he was disobedient in?

A And then we wanted to talk to him and we asked him to come and he would not come. And then he has sent notice that we can excommunicate him 50 or 75 times and he would not come.

Q In order to prevent excommunication a man would have to promise not to send his children to the public school?

A Yes, the congregation takes that view.
Q And that is your view?
A Yes, since we understand that out of the Scripture.

The next questions dealt with the effects of the excommunication.

Q Do you tell your brethren not to buy anything from a man who is excommunicated? ... Do you tell them that God's Word teaches that they must not have any business dealings with a man?
A Yes, he teaches it that way.
Q Suppose a member of your Church does buy something in the store of a man who is excommunicated what would happen to him: what would you do?
A He says as far as he remembers they have not excommunicated anybody on that account.

The questioning then turned to the significance of the federal government's 1873 promise that the Mennonites would be free to exercise their religious principles and to operate their own schools without any kind of molestation or restriction whatever.

Q Ask him if he is not violating the principle of that when he ... restricts others in the exercise of their own opinions?
A He says, 'We can't understand any different according to the Word of God, and we are trying to abide by what we believe.'

Another minister of the church, Rev. John Wall, explained, under questioning: 'We don't avoid ... people who don't belong to our church and send their children to the district schools ... only ... those of ours who don't wish to keep the vow which they once made to us.' The vow he referred to was made by people as adults when they were formally received into the church. It was, among other things, a vow of loyalty to the church and once made, the church would not release a person from it. At one point a commissioner asked: 'Which would you rather do: give up your rights to solemnize marriage or let your people send their children to the public school?' At another point the commissioner explained that 'boycotting is a criminal offence, and we pride ourselves on this being a free country, and while those of your people who want to send their children to the private schools may not necessarily be interfered with, still you should not interfere with those who want to send their children to the public schools, and it may be necessary to take some steps ... and making it understood that you must accord religious liberty and freedom to your fellowmen.'

Because Bishop Wiens had said that he could not speak on certain issues without first consulting the membership of the church, the commissioners encouraged him to call a meeting of the membership. The bishop did so and on 21 January 1909 he reported on it to the provincial government stating, after a lengthy and gracious salutation:

We feel ourselves forced not to accept the claims made upon us by our rebelling brethren.

This was unanimously decided and voted on at the meeting, which was promised you in Warman, which was held on the 19th instant, and at which more than 300 brethren were present ...

We cannot accept this claim without transgressing God's word and commandments ... we would ask you kindly not to consider us disobedient and troublesome people. No, we wish to obey you in everything insofar as Jesus teaches us in Matthew 22, 21. Render, therefore, unto the King the things that are the King's and unto God the things that are God's. We trust and hope that you will not deprive us of this right.[54]

The work of the commission appears not to have resulted in a policy change. However, in the following years it was observed that the church had become reluctant to excommunicate people for sending their children to a public school.[55] And the government, for its part, did not press the matter further. Education Minister Calder wrote, on 3 October 1910, that the commission's report had convinced them that 'even if it were possible to establish public schools among these people they would not send their children as their religious beliefs prohibit them from doing so.'[56] Perhaps, then, the encounter had encouraged a coexistence.

Meanwhile, the pressure to promote the public schools as a way of integrating the different immigrant groups increased. The 1913 annual report of the Department of Education concluded that 'every effort should be made to furnish the child with such ideas and trend of action as will assist in making him an intelligent and patriotic citizen.'[57] In 1915 E.H. Oliver, principal of the Presbyterian Theological College in Saskatoon and vice-president of the Saskatchewan Public Education League, said:

The problem that confronts us is one that involves almost the dearest possession in a man's life, his language; and, I fear, the question is not entirely free from religious associations. Let us in our discussions not seek to wound. But let us remember that the greatest wound of all would be a wound to Canada, her national life. We are citizens of no mean country. Let us seek her good. Let us approach this language question with an eye single to the good of the future *Canadian* citizenship of this Province ... Are we to be a homogeneous people on these plains or are we to repeat the tragic sufferings of polyglot Austria? This question must be solved in our elementary schools. And we must solve it now. A few years and it may be too late.[58]

Oliver surveyed the situation of schools in several immigrant settlements including thirty-two private Mennonite schools with 800 children. These, he said, 'are receiving what no stretch of imagination can designate as an adequate education ... are learning nothing of our literature, our history, or our language.'[59] He then asked: 'Can this state of things be allowed to continue? ... What is the function of a school?' He answered: 'I venture to state that the function of our schools must not be to make Mennonites, nor Protestants, nor Roman Catholics, but Canadian citizens.'

Some public school districts had already been organized on the fringes of the Mennonite reserves.[60] Those Mennonites who lived in these districts were subject to compulsory attendance legislation. When they failed to comply, the government initiated prosecutions. But these had little effect. Early in 1916, Premier Scott, who was also the minister of Education, recounted: 'In one instance the parent of Mennonite children was taken before Court three times, convicted, and fined under our law, but it did not change his ways ... They have religious convictions about the matter.'[61] The premier was ambivalent about the use of force. Late in 1915 he said: 'Jail may prove to be the only and the necessary remedy – not for the delinquent parents but for the heads of the church who coerce the parents.'[62] Soon thereafter, he said: 'I doubt if the Mennonite problem will be best settled by an application of coercive methods.'[63]

The ambivalence of Premier Scott notwithstanding, the trend was toward firmer action. In December 1916, W.S. Cram, school inspector in the Swift Current area, expressed his view that it 'would not only be to the best interests of the newer generation of children on the reserve but to the best interests of the state as a whole, that steps be taken toward organizing school districts amongst these people.'[64] He hoped for 'a more drastic compulsory system of education.'

These hopes for greater firmness became law on 1 May 1917 with the new School Attendance Act. It made attendance compulsory for all children between the ages of 7 and 14 years. The head of the provincial police was made the chief attendance officer.[65] The act stated further that 'all schools shall be taught in the English language,' although a language other than English could be taught between the hours of three and four in the afternoon.[66] Private schools were not explicitly ruled out but the government had the authority to set up public school districts, without a request from the local people, and to appoint an official trustee for the schools if people in the district were unwilling to serve in that capacity. The government could also expropriate land for school sites if people did not want to sell it.[67]

The new approach would have profound implications for the conservative Mennonites. W.M. Martin, who succeeded Scott as both premier and education minister in the province's Liberal government, set forth his view of their situation in a speech in the legislature:

The Mennonite question is one by itself. The Mennonites are the only people who do not want their children to learn English. A distinction must be made between the old colony Mennonites and the more progressive class ... the old colony Mennonites ... before they came, they sent ... representatives over to Canada to see the government and in 1873 an agreement was made with the dominion government under which they were exempted from military service and given certain privileges in regard to religion and education.

While the situation is very unfortunate I have never been able to see how we could allow them to continue to have schools where they learn nothing but their own language, the Bible and the Catechism. It was unfortunate that these people came here deceived by some document that they had from the Dominion government ... whoever comes here must be given to understand that they must adopt our public school system and see to it that their children are given a proper appreciation of Canadian institutions. (Cheers.) Some months ago the government determined that the only course we could pursue with respect to the Mennonite problem was to establish schools among them.[68]

Premier Martin also communicated the government's position to Bishop Jacob Wiens. Martin had personally visited some of the Mennonite schools in the summer of 1917; on 23 April 1918 he wrote to Bishop Wiens:

After seeing the schools that were being conducted in the Mennonite Colonies I came to the conclusion that it was high time that some improvement should take place; and I now desire to advise you that it is the intention of the Department of Education to enforce the provisions of the School Attendance Act insofar as they can be enforced among your people. The teachers you employ in your schools are not in many instances qualified to teach and have no standing insofar as the law is concerned. No instruction in English is being given. If you desire to retain your private schools you must have these schools conducted according to the standards of efficiency of the public schools and the teachers employed by you must be recognized by the Department of Education and the authorized text books of the Department of Education must also be used. I shall be glad to hear from you to the effect that you intend to act along these lines.[69]

The Reinlaender Mennonite church responded by sending a delegation to Ottawa claiming that the action of the provincial government was an invasion of the rights guaranteed to them by the federal government in the 25 July 1873 letter. But the federal government refused to intervene. The solicitor-general, Arthur Meighen, discussed the matter in Cabinet and then replied that 'the Government does not feel that it would be justified in interfering with the course outlined by the Prime Minister of Saskatchewan ..., nor in contesting the validity of the view which the Government of Saskatchewan evidently holds that the exercise of the privilege guaranteed your community in Clause 10 ... is not inconsistent with the fullest provision on the part of that Government of the essential elements of education for all children in your community.'[70]

If the Saskatchewan government was becoming more firm, so too was public opinion, no doubt affected by the war. The provincial Liberal party, at its convention in Moose Jaw in March 1917, passed a resolution emphasizing the need to ensure that every child obtains a thorough knowledge of the English language.[71] The Saskatchewan Association of Municipalities expressed a similar view. The Council of the Rural Municipality of Warman, which included most of the Hague reserve, urged 'the Government to continue to enforce the School Regulations in the Province and to carry out, without fear or favour, the promise to see that properly qualified teachers are placed in every private school in the Province, and to insist that the English language be used in these schools in accordance with regulations laid down in the School Acts.'[72] A citizens' meeting in Swift Current similarly resolved that 'the children of these people must be educated up to our standards of British and Canadian citizenship, so that they may, in the future, voluntarily relinquish their claims to an unjust exemption.'[73] The provincial school trustee's association called for 'national schools and one language.'[74]

Empowered with the School Attendance Act and a largely supportive public, the government now set out to organize school districts in the Mennonite areas.[75] However, instead of local people offering to serve as trustees, the government had to appoint official trustees. Instead of land for school sites being willingly sold, it had to be expropriated.[76] Teachers were sent out but sometimes no students attended.[77] The Mennonites would not give in. In summer 1919, Premier Martin visited Rev. Abram Wiebe, bishop of the group at Swift Current, and tried in vain to gain his co-operation.[78] The premier, however, was not to be deterred. He said: 'I presume that by the application of constant pressure, ultimately we will have a much better attendance.'[79]

The 'constant pressure' that the premier referred to was applied through prosecutions and fines under the School Attendance Act. More areas had now been organized as school districts and the pressure could be applied more widely. By mid May 1918 there had been some fifty prosecutions.[80] At one point the government imprisoned eleven men for a period of ten days but then decided against this course lest those imprisoned 'pose as martyrs for their religion.'[81] Instead, the government would seize their goods and chattels. In fall 1919, when eight ratepayers in the Flora school district near Swift Current had not paid the fines, the government seized 'three horses, a hog, and five cured hams' and sold them at a public auction in Wymark. When the total proceeds, $129.50, were not sufficient, the police made another seizure of 'five cows, two heifers and two horses.'[82] So determined was the government that for the period 1920–1 Saskatchewan Mennonites in eleven districts paid over $26,000 in fines and court costs under the School Attendance Act.[83] This was a substantial amount. At that time, $5000 was enough to build and furnish a new one-room school, complete with a residence for the teacher. For the Mennonites, economically, it was becoming very difficult.

Not everyone supported the severe measures. In 1916 the deputy minister of Education wrote: 'Those who shout on Saskatchewan platforms about Canadian citizenship being endangered because 800 children in Saskatchewan are being educated in Mennonite schools are hysterical fools.'[84] In March 1917, when Henry Vogt, a Mennonite lawyer near Swift Current, learned of the plan to use coercive measures against the conservative Mennonites, he proposed that the government entrust this matter to a special mediating committee 'composed of men that know these people not only in a business way but also know their church principles, morals etc., in every way.'[85] Some time later, in 1918, W.S. Cram, the school inspector in the Swift Current area, suggested to

Premier Martin that perhaps the Mennonite private schools could be allowed to operate under 'some form of licence system' for a time because people who had been left to themselves for so long would not change quickly.[86] The premier replied: 'I question very much whether any law with respect to private schools would simplify our difficulties among the Old Colony people.'[87]

On 22 November 1919, W.W. Cooper, a businessman in Swift Current, reported that a Mennonite delegation to South America had just returned and that it now seemed likely that a sizeable emigration would take place. Cooper noted further that 'there are a number of families being reduced to destitution through the fines being imposed upon them.' Accordingly, he urged that the government consider 'that the School Attendance Act be not forced for a period of about two years ... to give the families that leave the country an opportunity to get away.'[88] The government did consider such a suspension but several months later the premier wrote: 'I do not see how we would be justified in stopping the operation of the Act.'[89]

On 13 April 1920, Johann F. Peters, a leader of the Reinlaender Mennonite church in the Hague area, appealed to the premier:

We cannot send our children to public schools because it is contrary to our religious belief, it is against the laws of God according to our faith, we have to trespass the promise given our God and Redeemer at the time of baptism ... Is the Premier's intention to force us to disobey God's commandments ... in that case our Redeemer would say: 'If you are trespassing my commandments and not remain true unto them, you will become unworthy of me, ...' If you knew how hard it is to be a true Mennonite ... there is much distress amongst our people ... If you had been here and seen the conditions you would not have had the heart to exact money from these poor people. I beg you, Honourable Sir, to be good enough to grant us two years time to leave this country if you consider us a bad class people, we believe that we are worthy of such a privilege at least.[90]

Again, the premier refused. He affirmed the intention of the government to enforce the School Attendance Act among all classes of people. He also stated that he did not want to interfere with their religion but that 'the sending of children to school where they will acquire a proper education cannot in any way interfere with your religion.'[91]

On 29 May 1920, Henry Vogt appealed to the premier again. He had had further discussions with the conservative Mennonite leaders and had come to the conclusion that they would not object to teaching the

English language but that they opposed the school system that the government was attempting to force upon them. They feared that it would eventually have the effect of changing the church, even on the very basic issue of military service. Vogt suggested that if the government would offer an arrangement whereby these Mennonites could retain their private schools but teach English within them, then the emigration plans would be set aside.[92] Once again the premier refused. He was convinced that no mutually satisfactory compromise was possible. He emphasized that the government had 'no desire to interfere with their religion.' In his words: 'All that we desire is that they should give their children an education that will properly fit them for citizenship in this country.'[93]

On 30 June 1920 Vogt wrote one more letter to the premier. He reported that one of the Mennonite leaders had come to him and emphasized that they had 'absolutely nothing against the English language and were willing to take it into their schools.' However, they did not want to hand over control of the schools to the government. The government's school system, they felt, was for one thing 'too militaristic and for another not good enough to raise Christians.' They would also want to 'train their own teachers from their own boys' and 'keep up their own tongue.'[94] Vogt thought that this approach was reasonable and suggested that the government call on H.H. Ewert, the Mennonite educator in Manitoba, to help set up a mutually satisfactory arrangement. The premier, however, was not to be persuaded. He replied: 'Our school law provides for the teaching of religion for one half-hour a day ... this will not satisfy them ... I do not believe it is possible to get an agreement with them to the effect that they will use the text books which are authorized in this Province.'[95]

By now the conservative Mennonites were seriously exploring emigration possibilities. This action brought forth more appeals. In November 1921, A.J.E. Summer of Saskatoon, who, as a real estate agent, was involved in Mennonite land transactions, also appealed to the premier:

This movement, if allowed to take place will be a serious economic loss to the West, and in a lesser degree to the Dominion as a whole ... An extensive trip of inspection ... has prompted me to ask whether it is necessary that thousands of the best farmers Canada possesses should be allowed to leave in this manner.

Twenty-five years in the history of the nation are nothing but that time would suffice to prove that the present matters of contention would solve themselves.

I suggest that even at this late date an effort be made to avert this migration.[96]

The premier replied: 'I have exhausted every means at my disposal to arrive at some reasonable compromise with the leaders of these people. I think ... all classes of people ... should abide by all laws and ... give their children an education such as our schools provide.'[97] Summer tried again: 'I believe the reason that negotiations have failed is primarily due to lack of sympathy and failure to appreciate the deadly earnestness of these people by your colleagues and officials.' The imposition of fines and seizure of goods, he said, had resulted in situations where families were stripped and left to starve except for their neighbours' assistance. He agreed that the School Attendance Act was for the good of the country but he argued that 'there are ... broader and underlying principles to be considered in this question, and the policy adopted has been wrong.'[98] Summer's efforts proved futile.

The Mennonites also made several appeals on their own. On 7 January 1922, the Reinlaender Mennonite church at Swift Current sent a 'Petition to the Honourable Members of the Legislative Assembly of the Province of Saskatchewan' that stated in part:

Consider in what serious a position we are put by having enforced the School Attendance Act upon many of us, notwithstanding the facts that we have been granted by the Dominion government the privilege of not being restricted in educating our children ...

If these enforcements of the said Act could be suspended for several or for a few years only, it would be worth much thankfulness to us ...

We are preparing, as our Forefathers have done centuries ago, to migrate, not for the sake of the language but for the sake of our religious grounds to which we all have professed before God and many witnesses to be true ...

It is with grief and sorrow that we prepare to migrate to a new home, but we are hopeful, as we have found and got promised what we desire, but to carry out such an undertaking it takes time and money, and to get the latter we have to sell out, which also takes time, and for this reason we humbly pray once more, like children to their fathers, and please do not reject our prayers when we petition you to suspend the enforcements of said Act for a sufficient time to carry out this problem.[99]

On 12 February 1923, the Reinlaender church in the Hague area made a similar request of the minister of Education. In a lengthy letter, Rev. John P. Wall described the situation in the following way:

There are many who are weakened so much in financial respect through the many, many prosecutions that it is a very great loss to the country, specially to the District. Since they have been unable to do their farming according to the usual good methods.

Yes many of them could not support themselves any more, and would be in need and misery if they had not been supported by others.

But the Credit is exhausted, and paying the School Fines will eventually cease. And when the Farmers are deprived of their working stock, they cannot do their farming, as much as they want to do it.

The misery is very much larger, than what I think, you believe.

Therefore ... If you cannot keep the exemption that was granted to our people please give us a few years in which to settle our affairs, we pray ...

Would you not be inclined to show sympathy as well as the Russian Government did, who granted sufficient time in which they were free to carry out their move?[100]

In addition to these letters there were some personal visits. But they accomplished little. The minister of Education, Mr Latta, replied to Rev. John P. Wall: 'You have my sincerest sympathy in the condition in which your people are placed in relation to the compulsory school attendance law ... [but] the law is on the statute book and ... the Legislature of the province is supreme in these matters. I am powerless to do anything outside of that which the law says I should do.'[101]

These words of sympathy from the minister were not completely without significance. In the fall of 1921, A.W. Ball, the deputy minister, had ordered a suspension, albeit a temporary one, of the prosecutions in the Hague area. Soon thereafter he wrote that while most people do not need to be prosecuted more than once, 'with the Mennonites it is a case of repetition, which I personally very much regret but which, under our school attendance law, cannot be avoided.'[102] He had also noted that if the Mennonites would be exempted from the School Attendance Act, 'it will produce a storm of opposition from many parts of the country.' Also, in the fall of 1923, he prepared a memorandum for Mr Latta, the minister, suggesting that in the six years that the School Attendance Act had been in force there had been 'no appreciable headway in the direction of getting into our schools the children of the Old Colony Mennonites.' In light of this, he felt, the government would now be 'amply justified in attempting to compromise with the Mennonite leaders.' No government, he argued, 'has yet been successful in applying methods of compulsion and punishment in the case of "conscientious objectors."'[103] The compromise that he proposed was to permit them to attend a traditional Mennonite school in the afternoons 'on the understanding that the children attended regularly an "English" school in the mornings.' He concluded the memorandum by noting that 'some of the Mennonite families have been reduced to a condition of privation by the continual fines. Considerations of humanity almost compel an attempt at compromise.'

Newspapers, too, carried an occasional expression of sympathy for the Mennonites. One person, J.N. Doerr, who had taught in a public school near a Mennonite colony, wrote that the public schools were superior 'in those many things which are considered necessary for man's equipment in this materialistic age,' but that Mennonite private schools would probably be superior 'so far as the science of human relations is concerned.' Doerr praised the Mennonites for not contributing to the prison population and for their ability as farmers. He condemned the intolerance of the public and called on the government to work out a compromise so that the Mennonites would not emigrate.[104]

Despite these expressions of sympathy, the position of the government did not change. Nor was there any suspension of the prosecutions except for the brief 1922 pause in the Hague area. The problem was 'resolved' when the Mennonites emigrated. Those who stayed in Canada eventually complied with the law.

Clearly, the Mennonite school encounter was traumatic. But it did not stand in isolation. There were broader developments. One was the fervour of the First World War. Canada, with a population of under 8 million, provided nearly 750,000 servicemen. Of these 66,695 died and 138,950 were wounded. Because comparatively few Quebecers joined the military, people elsewhere in Canada must have felt their own involvement and sacrifice intensely. Also, because Canada's war effort was for the British Empire, it fueled English Canada's nativism and the conviction that non-English groups should be integrated and made to appreciate British institutions. This conviction led to many unusual measures. Mennonites were particularly susceptible because they did not serve in the military and because they spoke German, the language of the enemy.

However, quite aside from the war, there was a lengthy and multifaceted social transformation under way. One aspect of this transformation is that the larger society's view of minority groups changed. Until the end of the nineteenth century a primary concern was to attract settlers. To achieve this goal, Canada was quite ready to assure minority groups that they would be allowed to continue in their particular ways of life. However, early in the twentieth century when the prairies were more fully populated, the concern, understandably, was with integrating the various groups into one society.

But it was not only a matter of integrating the different ethnic groups. It was also a case of rejecting a religiously based pluralism and replacing it with a Protestant and more secular dominance. Thomas Berger has written that it was 'a matter of conflicting views about industrialization and modernization and about the kind of citizenry necessary to uphold the institutions of democracy. Protestants wanted state schools, in which the government, not the church, would appoint teachers and prescribe the curriculum. They regarded state schools as the means of inculcating in the rising generations the values of democracy. Separate schools were, to them, an impediment to progress.'[105]

In the new framework, institutions based on religious tradition and ethnicity had little room. According to W.L. Morton, the Mennonite village and the Catholic parish, which had long served as institutions of local government, were replaced with municipalities that flourished in 'the atmosphere of secular and utilitarian democracy, not that of traditional, religious custom.'[106] E.K. Francis has said: 'It is not accidental that the Liberal party was the first power group in the Province which adopted a platform directly aiming at the assimilation of minority groups.'[107]

One aspect of this new framework was a much narrower view of religion and religious freedom. In the 1870s, religious freedom was broad. It included the freedom of a religious group to operate its own schools. At that time virtually all religious groups did so. However, around 1920, when the conservative Mennonites continued to claim this broader freedom, believing that it was inseparable from their religiously based way of life, they were clearly out of step. The *Manitoba Free Press* now argued that despite the coercive methods used to force the Mennonites to accept the public schools, 'there never was any attempt made to interfere with religion.'[108] And W.M. Martin, the premier of Saskatchewan, wrote to one Mennonite leader that 'sending ... children to school where they will acquire proper education cannot in any way interfere with your religion.'[109] In a letter to Henry Vogt, the lawyer who tried so hard to negotiate a compromise, the premier wrote that there was no intent to interfere with religion, adding: 'All that we desire is that they should give their children an education that will properly fit them for citizenship in this country.'[110]

This broader social transformation also brought out the tension between freedom for individuals and freedom for groups. In 1908 in

Saskatchewan, when several business people suffered economically because they had been excommunicated from the church for sending their children to public schools, they called on the government to compel the church to give individuals within the church the freedom to send their children to public schools. The argument appeared again in 1916 when Manitoba's minister of Education said: 'A grave injustice is being done to the children who do not receive a satisfactory education ... to fit them to earn their way through life and to take their place as citizens of our new Canadian nationality.'[111] Clearly, there was a problem. The liberty of individuals was being restricted. But the change, which restricted the power of the group over its individuals, did not simply give more freedom to those individuals. It increased the power of the state over them. Education, instead of serving the church community and its desired way of life, now had to give greater attention to the interests of the state and the larger society.

Related to this development is the question of who carries responsibility for educating children. The Mennonites felt that they, as parents and church, had to retain control, that the education of their children was a sacred responsibility which they could not neglect 'without culpable consequences.'[112] In one petition they said: 'Your Petitioners cannot delegate to others the all-important responsibility of educating their children, convinced as they are that instruction in other than religious schools would result in weakening and even loss of faith.'[113] In sharp contrast stood the view of the *Manitoba Free Press* that 'the children are children of the state, of which they are destined to be citizens, and it is the duty of the state that they are properly educated.'[114]

Also to be noted is the way in which the promise made to the Mennonites in 1873 was set aside. In Manitoba the promise was formally overruled in a court decision. In Saskatchewan it was Premier Martin's political decision. One interpretation of this development, which is significant conceptually, even if not practically, relates to 'minimum standards.' When the Saskatchewan Mennonites appealed to the federal government, the solicitor-general, Arthur Meighen, responded by stating that the provincial government, when it insisted on providing 'the essential elements of education' for the Mennonite children, was not acting in violation of that promise.[115] This could mean that the federal government felt that the Saskatchewan government was pressing for no more than adherence to minimal standards and that, even though such pressure interfered with Mennonite school practices, it was not incompatible with a proper interpretation of the earlier promises.

E.K. Francis, and analyst of the situation, denies that this logic was operative in the realities of the time. He notes that some of the conservative Mennonites declared themselves ready to raise the educational standards of their schools in substantial ways, to intensify the training of their teachers, to facilitate inspection by the Department of Education, to teach the English language, and to 'place our schools beyond just criticism,' as long as they could keep them under church control. Their proposals were rejected and Francis states that 'it was no more a question of educational standards which prompted the authorities to destroy the Mennonite private grade schools once and for all, and to replace them with English public schools. It was part of a consistent national policy aimed at the assimilation of ethnics to safeguard national unity and cultural uniformity. In this policy the school figured prominently as the most effective means to wean the children of immigrants away from the traditions of their group and to indoctrinate them with the ideals and values of the dominant majority.'[116]

This broader social transformation was bound to have a substantial effect on the Mennonite communities. With the war, that effect was all the more drastic.

6 Doukhobor School Controversies in Saskatchewan and British Columbia

THE DOUKHOBOR VIEW AND THE SASKATCHEWAN EXPERIENCE

Doukhobors, like Mennonites, were concerned that the public schools would lead their children away from their community life and religious ideals. Also like Mennonites, there were not all of one mind. Some Doukhobors saw positive elements in the public schools and wanted to rely on supplementary classes to teach their own language and other values of their tradition. Other Doukhobors, however, resisted the public schools strongly and they, like the conservative Mennonites, encountered the opposition of determined governments. But unlike the Mennonites, the Doukhobors did not emigrate. They stayed. And the conflict, which became quite bitter at times, continued intermittently for half a century.

Historically, Doukhobors had not emphasized formal education. Perhaps their view of 'the God within' made it less important. Also, in Russia the involvement of the Russian Orthodox church in the schools there, dampened the interest of the Doukhobors in those schools. Nevertheless, according to one historian, 'careful attention was paid [by the Doukhobors] to the religious and vocational instruction of children. Parents were responsible for the proper upbringing of their children. It was their responsibility to see that their children learned the psalms, the law of God. Within the *Mir* each commune member believed that he was obliged to teach something useful to each child in the village.'[1]

A Doukhobor spokesperson, quoted in 1923, indicated that educational practices should be oriented towards the community with its religious ideals and practical needs. He said: 'To us education means being a good Doukhobor. That is, to love all living things and to do no evil, not to shoot, not to eat meat, not to smoke, not to drink liquor. We teach these things to our children. And more, too. The mothers teach their daughters to bake and to cook and to spin and to embroider, and the fathers teach their sons to be handy with an axe, a carving knife, a plough, a team of horses. Such things are useful and good, and the other things that you educated people speak of ... you can have them.'[2]

Did this modest support for education include literacy? Peter V. Verigin wrote in the mid 1890s that literacy was 'a hindrance and a brake to man's development; that is the development of knowledge of truth.' He had, after careful consideration, come to the conclusion that 'it would be better if there were no literacy.'[3]

This ambiguity may be one reason why education was not dealt with in a clear way in the negotiations for Doukhobor immigration to Canada. At one point in those negotiations, James Mavor, who met with Canadian officials on behalf of the Doukhobors, wrote to Leo Tolstoy and asked 'if they would send their children to non-sectarian common schools and if they would object to the compulsory education.'[4] Tolstoy replied that they 'would send their children to the common school if the children would not be obliged to receive religious training.'[5] Kropotkin, too, was optimistic. He wrote: 'In ten years they all will speak English.'[6] Vladimir Tchertkoff, who worked on behalf of the Doukhobors in both Russia and England, also wrote to Mavor and stated that the matter of education 'must be left to the Doukhobortsi themselves to be consulted. They are quite willing that their children be educated, but have not wished them to be taught the superstitions of the Greek church.'[7]

While the preparations for the migration to Canada were under way, Verigin, still in Siberian exile, wrote another letter on the subject. This time he encouraged the people to accept the schools of their new homeland:

I am told that education is absolutely compulsory in North America. That is for the best, because simple literacy is necessary as an aid to life; for example, so that one should know how to read and write. One must not understand that literacy will positively enlighten a man, yet again I repeat it can only be an aid, and a person reading books may gather information; and in such manner his mind may become developed. In general, I think if God wishes that our people should establish themselves in America, then simple literacy (reading, writing and arithmetic) is absolutely necessary.[8]

When the Doukhobors first settled in Canada, several Tolstoyans and

Quakers came and set up schools in their villages. Two Quaker women from Ontario, Eliza Varney and Nellie Baker, came in 1899, the same year that the Doukhobors arrived.[9] Immigration officials gave them a tent for holding classes and within one month forty-six pupils were enrolled. Herbert Archer, the generally helpful English Tolstoyan, also assisted with teaching. And Michael Sherbinin, a Russian nobleman and former diplomat, fluent in twelve languages, began educational work in the Prince Albert colony on the North Saskatchewan River.[10]

Generally, the Doukhobors welcomed these efforts but there were misgivings. Perhaps the Quakers were proceeding too quickly. They took a few Doukhobors to Philadelphia for schooling. They also had plans to build a school 'to train Doukhobor girls to become teachers.'[11] Moreover, despite their helpfulness, the Quakers disagreed with the Doukhobors on the issue of communal property, which was a point of controversy at the time. One Quaker, Joseph Elkinton, wrote of the Doukhobors: 'They do not wish strangers to indoctrinate them with new interpretations, as they have suffered so much to maintain their own.'[12]

The misgivings about the Quaker education efforts became stronger in 1903 after Peter V. Verigin, released from exile in Russia, had assumed leadership responsibilities in Canada. In the summer of that year, when the Quakers were making plans to expand their work, he thanked them but said that the Doukhobors no longer desired charity, that they would provide for their own education by building schools and choosing teachers from among themselves.[13] Soon thereafter a number of village schools were built but their performance was uneven. By 1908, some villages were without schools altogether. According to one Doukhobor, Verigin was not pursuing the matter seriously on the ground that 'a true Christian should have only Christ for a teacher.'[14] A Quaker observer wrote later that Verigin had feared that 'if their children were educated then he would be unable to dominate them along communalistic lines.'[15] In spite of Verigin's opposition, the Quaker education efforts did not stop completely. In the Prince Albert colony, where the influences of Verigin and the Christian Community of Universal Brotherhood (CCUB) was weak, the Quaker work continued. There it included a boarding-school that operated for nearly a decade until around 1912, when public schools became more common.

Public schools came into the Doukhobor settlements gradually. The policy of the Saskatchewan government was that they be set up on the basis of requests from local people. The CCUB Doukhobors, usually referred to as Community Doukhobors, did not make such requests for a time but the Independent Doukhobors soon indicated interest. However, some of their early contacts were not endearing. In the Devil's Lake area, near Yorkton, where a number of Independent Doukhobors had settled, the non-Doukhobor people had already formed a school district in 1899. When these residents discovered that the boundaries of the district included several Doukhobor villages, they wrote a letter to the attorney-general stating: 'We should like to know if we shall have to provide accommodation for the Doukhobor children ... We are not anxious to have them at our school, as they are not, in our opinion, a desirable class for our children to come in contact with.'[16] While objecting to having Doukhobor children in the public school, these non-Doukhobors wanted, nevertheless, to collect taxes from the Doukhobors for the school. The Doukhobors then complained to officials.[17] Finally, in 1903, a settlement was reached whereby the Doukhobor children were accepted at the school along with the Doukhobor tax monies.

The gradual acceptance of public schools by the Independent Doukhobors was helped by the efforts of Herbert Archer, the Tolstoyan. In February 1907, when he was working near Yorkton, he assisted them in submitting a petition to the Department of Education for the formation of the Bear's Head School District: 'We, the Doukhobors living in the Swan River Valley, not members of the Doukhobor Community hereby petition to have School Districts formed in our several localities. There are not among us men able to write English and so form Districts according to law; we also do not desire that we wait until the Doukhobor Community organize Districts so that our children may learn English and appoint a Commissioner to manage same.'[18] Soon several school districts were established. Archer then took formal teacher training, received a certificate, and taught in the public schools. He continued to be instrumental in the formation and operation of new districts for several years among both Doukhobors and non-Doukhobors. Often he served as secretary-treasurer of the new districts.

In addition to the work of Archer there were some direct efforts by the government. In 1908, Joseph Megas, a supervisor of schools, organized two school districts among Doukhobors in the Prince Albert colony. In his report for 1910 he wrote: 'Even the reluctant phlegmatic Doukhobors have awakened and school districts are being organized in their ... settlements at their own request.'[19] By 1912 most children of Independent Doukhobors were attending public schools. Also in that year one young Doukhobor, who had studied in Quaker schools in the United

States, received a certificate to teach in Saskatchewan's public schools. In 1932 the Independent Doukhobors in the Prince Albert colony could boast 'nine public schools, almost entirely under the supervision of Doukhobor trustees and teachers ... 13 qualified teachers, four doctors, one practising lawyer, about 12 university students, and approximately 30 high school students.'[20]

If the Independent Doukhobors accepted the public schools quickly and completely, the Community Doukhobors were more cautious. However, many of these moved to British Columbia after 1909 and most of those who remained in Saskatchewan gradually accepted public schools before the government forced them to do so. An early indication of their interest is evident in a 1911 dispute when a petition for a school district around the town of Verigin was filed with the provincial Department of Education. At first the local member of the legislative assembly, J.K. Johnston, opposed the petition. But then a leader of the Saskatchewan Community Doukhobors, M.W. Cazakoff, wrote to the department: 'Mr. J.K. Johnston ... has been of the opinion, all along, that this school was unnecessary. He being unmarried, and having no children is trying to deprive our children of an education. Then too, he would be liable to extra taxes, and this he would rather not pay.'[21] The dispute became quite intense, involving not only the views of Johnston but those of other local people, too. By 1913, however, through the appointment of an official trustee, the problem was resolved and the school constructed.

Cazakoff's support for the public schools was clear but not unqualified. Some Community Doukhobors did not send their children to the public school and when the official trustee indicated his intention to force them to do so, Cazakoff appealed to Saskatchewan's deputy minister of Education: 'I do not think it advisable for the government or any school trustees to enforce the compulsory education on the children of the Doukhobors ... and I might say to you friendly, that if the government enforced compulsory education on the Doukhobors, it would only make trouble for the government as well as the Doukhobors, and would bring no beneficial results.'[22]

Cazakoff's appeal was successful. Attendance was not forced but the voluntary attendance of Doukhobor children increased to such an extent that even the School Attendance Act of 1917, which made attendance compulsory, caused few difficulties. Later in the decade, when Premier Martin spoke in the Saskatchewan legislature, he boasted: 'There is not a solitary Doukhobor child in this province attending any school where there is anything but the English language taught.'[23] The premier may have overstated the situation but there was widespread Doukhobor support for public schools. This stance was strengthened further after 1927 when Peter V. Verigin's son, Peter P. Verigin, assumed leadership of the Community, Verigin senior having been killed in a British Columbia train explosion in 1924. At first Peter P. Verigin attempted to set up a private Doukhobor school system but when this failed, he made a general commitment on behalf of all Doukhobors to support the public schools.

Nevertheless, some Doukhobor opposition to public schools remained. It came from the radicalism that had been evident earlier: in the occasional pilgrimage-like wanderings across the prairie; in the brief refusal to use animals for farm work; and in the 1918 burning of Peter Verigin's elaborate house in the town of Verigin. That burning had been meant to free the senior Verigin from encroaching worldliness and materialism.[24] It was a religious act and these Doukhobors, who later became known as Sons of Freedom, gathered around the fire, undressed, and sang hymns. Now, late in the 1920s, they began to see the younger Verigin's commitment to the public schools as another departure from true Doukhoborism. In June 1928 they issued a manifesto to the other Doukhobors and identified the public school as the cause of wars, revolutions, and other calamities plaguing the world:

The cause of all this is the SCHOOL with its wrong orientation, thrusting sadism upon the youthful generation. Especially when a person partakes of higher education, or attends military academies, does he become a truely insane animal. Sometimes, through oversight on the part of a common soldier to salute a general or a lesser officer, the unfortunate is beaten half to death or oftentimes to death.

The clergy, upon graduation from the institutes of higher learning, i.e. the universities, under pretext of religion and fanaticism, inveigle the unwary, bless them in the churches and then send the young people off to war, to kill their own brothers and themselves in the name of their fatherland.[25]

They pointed to such educated individuals as G.B. Shaw, Tolstoy, Tagore, and Gandhi, and said that they had 'received enlightenment through Spiritual Regeneration,' not through public schools.[26] Along with this manifesto, they withdrew their children from public schools.

The emergence of this Doukhobor radicalism, late in the 1920s, coincided with an increasingly antipathetic social atmosphere, in part reflected in the 1929 election of J.T.M. Anderson as Saskatchewan's premier. In his earlier position as director of Education among New Canadians, Anderson had followed the policy that every child should have 'an adequate knowledge of the English language and the training necessary for good Canadian citizenship.'[27] Now, when the radical Doukhobors withdrew their children from public schools the provincial government began to prosecute them. Several school buildings were burned down.[28] By mid July 1929 a dozen school buildings in Doukhobor areas had been destroyed by fire. A considerable amount of ccub property was also destroyed.[29] In addition, several nude demonstrations took place in towns near Doukhobor settlements. A total of fifty-five men and women were convicted and imprisoned, albeit only for brief periods.[30]

When Premier Anderson threatened to hold the ccub liable for all damage to public property, the Community Doukhobors protested strongly. One Doukhobor said: 'British Justice ... holds a man innocent until he is proven guilty; there is no ... evidence to even suggest that Doukhobors of our Community ... had anything to do with the burning of schools.'[31] Anderson denied that he was accusing the Community Doukhobors of burning the schools, but then added: 'If you and your leader are prepared to acknowledge loyalty to our Sovereign and our Country – if you both are prepared to endorse our public school system; if you are prepared to give allegiance to what the Union Jack stands for, then there is no cause for further argument or discussion.'[32] To this the Doukhobors replied: 'State patriotism affects our religious feelings and our contemplation of the world as a universal brother-hood and the equality of all men upon the face of the earth.'[33]

For various reasons the confrontation subsided. According to one account, 'the moderation exercised by Saskatchewan civil servants and judges seemed to placate the fears of the Sons of Freedom.'[34] Judges in nudity trials granted short sentences and the police offered a reward for information leading to the capture and conviction of school arsonists. This last aspect was significant strategically in that it provided an incentive for other Doukhobors to oppose the extremists. Another factor in the decline of the confrontation was that when the imprisoned Sons of Freedom were released, they were expelled from the ccub. Consequently, they were forced to depend on support from friends and relatives. Many then modified their views. Others moved to British Columbia where they found more support for their orientation.

FORCED SCHOOLING IN BRITISH COLUMBIA

1909–1913: Acceptance, Rejection, and a Commission of Inquiry
The story of the Doukhobors and public schools in British Columbia is
complex. Virtually all the Doukhobors who moved there belonged to the
Christian Community of Universal Brotherhood. As such they had both
a stronger communalism and a greater hesitancy about the larger
society. The approach of the provincial government was different, too.
British Columbia had had a public school system since the 1870s. It even
had an attendance requirement, though it applied only to children aged
7–12, and only if they lived within three miles of a school accessible by
public roads.[35] Also, the system operated under a central Council of
Public Instruction with relatively little scope for local boards. This
circumstance tended to bring school issues into the arena of provincial
politics even though it might have been possible to resolve them locally.[36]

The Doukhobors' first contact with British Columbia's school system
came soon after they arrived in 1909.[37] By 1910, some who lived close to
public schools discovered that their children were expected to attend.
They then complied without complaint. In 1911 the school district of
Grand Forks built the Carson school near Doukhobor lands to accommodate more Doukhobor children. Soon thereafter the Doukhobors,
who were quickly becoming established in their new settlements, built a
school right on their land near Brilliant. It opened in 1912 as an official
public school with an all-Doukhobor board and an enrolment of
forty-eight pupils.[38] The teacher, Beulah Clarke Darlington, spoke
highly of the Doukhobors and of the experience in general. In a letter to
a local newspaper she stated: 'It is a relief to find people with no pretense
who are willing to work with their hands, and who show, by the
wonderful development of that country, that they are capable of
working with their brains as well; who are content with simple pleasures
and who keep a right outlook on life because they are not striving after
wealth or trying to attain a position in society which is worthless when
procured.'[39] The Doukhobors were very pleased with Darlington as a
teacher. They planned to expand class-room facilities for the coming
year and encouraged Darlington to bring some of her friends also to
serve as teachers.

Then, suddenly, there was an interruption. The schoolchildren were
withdrawn, not to return until four years later. A major reason was the
arrest of five Doukhobors who had been sentenced to three months in

prison for failing to register a death.[40] The chief constable for the Grand Forks area met with Peter V. Verigin and was informed that the Doukhobors, at a large meeting, had decided not to register births, deaths, and marriages even though the law required it.[41] When the constable reported this information to the attorney-general he was told: 'You may inform Mr. Verigin ... that the laws of British Columbia must be obeyed ... and ... will be strictly carried out, without any favour being shown to him and members of his Society.'[42] The Doukhobors then sent a letter, dated 16 July 1912, addressed to 'The Government of British Columbia,' to explain their position. They said: 'We believe that the favourable adorable power is ruling all the world and endeavour to be written in eternal life book, and propose ourselves obligation to live quietly and to employ honest labour on the earth, so as to get substance. All the human race registration we calculate unnecessary. We can say, briefly, our religion confines on two commandments to be gentle and to employ agriculture.'[43]

The public, which at first had welcomed the Doukhobors for contributing to the economic development of the area, now became more critical. Newspapers pointed out that they were not taking the oath and that they were not co-operating fully with the 1911 census.[44] Local citizens expressed concern that the Doukhobors were becoming numerous, that they might 'swamp the community,' and 'that it would be impossible for them to be assimilated.'[45] In response, the Conservative government led by Premier Richard McBride appointed a royal commission to make a broad inquiry. The person chosen for the task was William Blackmore, a newspaper editor from the nearby town of Nelson.

When Blackmore came to the Doukhobor community, later in 1912, he was welcomed in an elaborate way. The Doukhobors showed him their orchards, sawmills, and other prospering enterprises, and talked of their plans for further development. They also invited him to their religious assembly, where the children sang for him. In one such ceremony, a young boy stepped forward and said: 'We've been attending school during the eleven weeks it was in session, but we no longer wish to go to school again, because the teacher, though very kind, belonged to the people who had put our friends in prison.'[46] Blackmore stayed with the Doukhobors for almost four months and held long public hearings. He also made a trip to their settlements on the prairies. At the end he produced a report that was extensive and remarkably sympathetic to the Doukhobors but it did not relieve them from the responsibility of abiding by the established laws of the province.

Regarding their refusal to register births, deaths, and marriages, Blackmore stated: 'They will not register because they desire to remain unmolested in their communal life. They want no interference, as they call it, which means no intrusion of any kind. They claim that birth and death are the acts of God, and call for no cognizance on the part of man; and as to marriage, they take the high ground that it is purely a matter between the contracting parties.'[47] Blackmore also found that the Doukhobors feared that registration would somehow lead to military service. In their own words they said: 'The registration intimately ... tied ... with religious faith ... we wish to be citizens of all the world, and do not wish to register our children in the Royal Crown Government books ... We are not refusing to give knowledge of increase or decrease of our Doukhobor Community people in ten or five years once. But to enter in your register books we will never do it. Because we calculate we are already registered in the Book of Life before Him the Founder, which is called Eternity.'[48]

Regarding public schools, Blackmore found that the Doukhobors were concerned that 'education was likely to make the children discontented with the life of cultivation of the soil followed by their parents,' and 'separate the children from their parents and from the customs and habits of the Community.' He reported further that the women had said that 'among them crime was unknown, and that, whereas among educated people poverty existed, no Doukhobor ever suffered for want of food or clothing; so ... while the laws spoken of were needed for other people, they did not think they were required among the Doukhobors.'

In a statement of their own, the Doukhobors listed three reasons for their objection to the public schools:

1) The school education teaches and prepares the people, that is children, to military service, where shed harmless blood of the people altogether uselessly. The most well educated people consider this dreadfully sinful such business as war, lawful. We consider this great sin.

2) The school teaching at the present time had reached only to expedience for the easy profit, thieves, cheaters, and to large exploitation working-class laborious on the earth. And we ourselves belong to working-class people and we try by the path of honest labour, so we may reap the necessary maintenance, and to this we adopt our children to learn at wide school of Eternal Nature.

3) The school teaching separates all the people on the earth. Just as soon as the person reached read and write education, then, within a short time leaves his parents and relations and undertakes unreturnable journey on all kinds of speculation, depravity and murder life. And never think of this duty, respecting his parents and elder-ones, but he looks opposite, turning themselves, enslaving of the people, for theirs own licentious and insatiableness gluttony ... educated people, swallow down all the national peoples ... the people suffer from not having land even a piece of daily bread ... we distinctly understand instruction of Christ, we holding on to Community life and we calculate all the people on earth are our brothers.[49]

These three objections – that education in public schools leads to militarism, that it is not practical, and that it alienates people from one another, thus militating against community life – were to be referred to again and again in the following half-century as the controversy continued.[50]

In his report, Blackmore spoke positively of how the Doukhobors themselves provided for the education of their children:

It must not, however, be supposed that, because this misguided people refuse elementary education for their children, they do not give them the best home training.

The children are intelligent, respective, and observant. The home life is almost ideal. They are taught all the cardinal virtues with which most of us, as children, we acquainted, but which are now too often regarded as old-fashioned – such as obedience, reverence, industry, and thrift; and it is not a little to the credit of their parents to find that the chief objection that they entertain to education is the fear that secular teaching may undermine the religious spirit.[51]

Blackmore also praised their capability as agriculturalists, their irrigation system, their large orchards, and the other enterprises that they, as the Christian Community of Universal Brotherhood, had collectively developed. Blackmore stated:

It is not out of place at this point to comment on the wonderful success that has attended the fruit-growing operations of the Doukhobors. To them it was a new industry. They had never been engaged in it before coming to British Columbia. Yet, today, if you were to go through their orchards, you would find that they are the cleanest, the best-kept, the heaviest-cropped of any in the district ...

In addition ... the Doukhobors have manifested a spirit of enterprise at

Brilliant by putting in a splendid concrete reservoir capable of holding 1,000,000 gallons of water, and from this reservoir the water is being piped all over the Settlement. It is to be used both for domestic purposes and irrigation.

The reservoir will be supplied partially from a creek in the mountains, and partially by an immense pumping plant which the Doukhobors have erected ... on the banks of the Kootenay River. This is the largest pumping plant in British Columbia ...

Besides the farming industry, the Doukhobors have established sawmills on all their properties, which are used chiefly to convert the timber into building material ...They have also a good brick-making works at Grand Forks, which is producing a high-class brick, commanding a ready sale. This brick is being used in the new Government Buildings at Grand Forks, which is a fair testimony as to its quality.[52]

While recommending that the Doukhobors should be required to obey provincial laws, Blackmore cautioned against 'drastic steps ... to force their immediate compliance,' stating that 'persecution is fuel to the flames of fanaticism. Withdraw the fuel, and the fire will die out.' He suggested a policy of 'patience with the people' and 'pressure on their leaders' and that, 'if it is found necessary to resort to prosecution and conviction ensues, it is desirable that the punishment should take the form of fines rather than imprisonment.' Prison sentences, he felt, might nurture a martyrdom complex. He also recommended that to facilitate the registration of births, deaths, and marriages, a member of the Doukhobor Community be appointed as a sub-registrar. And to facilitate matters in the schools he said that 'Russian teachers could be employed in conjunction with Canadian teachers, and that the curriculum be modified so as to include only elementary subjects.' He also suggested that a permanent Doukhobor agent be appointed to serve somewhat like an Indian agent.

Most of Blackmore's observations and recommendations were such that a mutually satisfactory compromise might have developed. But the Doukhobors' disposition towards a compromise was drastically set back because, at the very end of the report, Blackmore recommended that their exemption from military service be cancelled.[53] This suggestion was most upsetting to the Doukhobors. They had questioned Blackmore about the possibility of war between Britain and Germany, about the probability of Canadian involvement, and about the status of their exemption. Now they felt confirmed in their suspicion that there was a connection between registration, school attendance, and military service.

1914–1927: Pressing Community Doukhobors to Accept Schools
While Blackmore's final recommendation disappointed the Doukhobors, the generally moderate tone of his report disappointed the authorities.[54] Supported by local citizens, officials soon discarded his counsel for patience. They rejected a Doukhobor offer that for vital statistics, they check the Community's records.[55] The public wanted compliance with the existing law; to gain evidence for prosecutions they exhumed bodies and raided a village.[56] Naturally, this approach was upsetting to the Doukhobors. Regarding the schools, the Doukhobors were now also concerned about a recently introduced program of military drills and rifle shooting. The Department of Education had started the program in order to foster 'the spirit of patriotism in the boys, leading them to realize that the first duty of every citizen is to be prepared to defend his country.'[57]

Early in 1914, when Doukhobor children were still not in school, the government prepared itself for an unusual course of action. It enacted the Community Regulation Act, which made the Doukhobor Community, that is, the CCUB, liable for an infraction committed by any member.[58] The act referred particularly to infractions relating to vital statistics, school attendance, and the Health Act. It authorized officials to seize, without warrant, the goods and chattels of the Community in order to cover fines not paid by individuals. In one sense, holding the Community liable was understandable. The Doukhobors, as individuals, had little property while as a Community they had a sizeable amount. Nevertheless, as a form of collective punishment this law was a departure from Canada's tradition of justice. More seriously, the law defined a Community member as any person who, on the oath of one witness, had been found on or about Community lands. This meant that even if the Community expelled trouble-making individuals, which it did on occasion, it could still be liable for the actions of such individuals. Obviously, the Community was extremely vulnerable.

As the authorities became more threatening, some Doukhobors, apparently against the advice of Peter V. Verigin, responded with a threat of their own. They sent a long list of grievances to Attorney-General Bowser and then said: 'The [Community] Doukhobors, of whom there are six thousand members, are planning beforehand in this case, to all take off what clothes still remaining on them after the plunder they have been subjected to in Saskatchewan, take them and throw them into the faces of your officials in Nelson and Grand Forks, and leave themselves stark naked on the very street of the town. This will be a good illustration to show the attitude taken by the government officials in regards to Doukhobors.'[59] The attorney-general replied that if the clothes came off the law against indecent exposure would be enforced.[60]

As the confrontation became increasingly intense several non-Doukhobors tried to intervene. Blackmore continued to counsel moderation in the columns of his newspaper.[61] A lawyer from the town of Nelson wrote to the attorney-general: 'I contend that the Grand Forks people are not playing the game square as far as these people are concerned. They welcomed them to their midst and took their money for the land, and now, when they have made a success of agriculture in that district, they want to drive them out.'[62] A CPR superintendent urged the government to seek a compromise so as to avoid 'injury to the religious convictions of the Doukhobors.' A.E. Miller, inspector of schools, was cautious, too. He predicted that 'any attempt to enforce attendance will be met with opposition.' Others, however, supported the action of the government. A group of Quakers from Pennsylvania who had earlier supported the Doukhobors now said: 'The sooner the Commune is broken up, the sooner will be real progress amongst these simple, misled people.'[63]

For a time the trends pointed towards a harsh confrontation. A.E. Miller was instructed to warn the Doukhobors that 'the refusal to comply with the requirements as to education would mean the breaking up of their community.' In August 1915 the attorney-general issued instructions to enforce the Community Regulations Act.[64] At that point, however, certain technical obstacles were noticed. The property, until 1917, was registered in the name of Peter V. Verigin, not in the name of the Community. Also, school attendance was compulsory only if people lived within three miles of a school, accessible by a public road. Most roads in the Doukhobor settlements were private.[65]

Before these legalities could be tested a compromise was reached. On 20 September 1915 the attorney-general promised a delegation of Doukhobors that no military training would be forced upon their children and that they would be excused from religious exercises.[66] The Doukhobors in turn promised that their children would return to both the Carson and the Brilliant public schools. As a result, a period of co-operation followed. The Doukhobors built nine additional public schools although these were administered not by local boards but by an official trustee appointed by the government. At one point, in the 1920–1 school year, the enrolment rose to 414, which was more than 80 per cent of those eligible, although attendance was little more than 50 per cent. Inspector Miller, following a policy of caution and patience, did not press for full attendance.

This co-operation lasted for several years, but soon after the First World War there were strains related to the Doukhobors' exemption from military service and to their prosperity. In February 1919 a meeting of returned soldiers in Nelson demanded that all Doukhobors be deported to Russia and that their lands be given to veterans. A meeting of citizens declared its support for the veterans and at one point twelve ex-soldiers went to Verigin to force their demands upon him. Apparently Verigin then signed an agreement to turn over the Doukhobor lands to the Soldiers' Settlement Board but a few days later he wired Arthur Meighen, the minister of the Interior, that he had signed under duress.[67] Meighen, the Conservative who according to George Woodcock 'consistently proved fairer to the Doukhobors than his Liberal predecessor Frank Oliver,' ruled that the Soldiers' Settlement Board had no right to carry out expropriations.[68]

The soldiers' claim to the land was thus nullified but the general criticism of the Doukhobors continued, leading some Doukhobors to withdraw their children from school. However, a 1920 amendment to the Public Schools Act broadened the compulsory attendance provisions and authorized the construction of schools on the lands of the Doukhobor Community and at its expense.[69] Also, Inspector A.E. Miller, under whose patient supervision things had worked reasonably well, was replaced by E.G. Daniels, who began to press for better attendance. In December 1922, the Grand Forks school board took legal action against eight cases of truancy. Fines were imposed and when they were not paid, some CCUB property, meaning Doukhobor Community property, was seized. However, before it could be sold, Community officials intervened and paid the fines.

In April 1923, Inspector Daniels pressed further. Fines of $50 each were levied on six parents. When they were slow in paying, a large truck, used by the Community for farm work, was seized. Again the Community paid the fines. But soon after, in May 1923, a school building was destroyed by fire.[70] In the months that followed a total of nine schools in the Brilliant area were destroyed, the burnings in each case coinciding with an attempt on the part of the police to seize property in payment of fines.

The burning of schools was a relatively new type of action on the part of the Doukhobors. There were some acts of civil disobedience in their history, and a few times some Doukhobors had destroyed property as a way of witnessing against materialism. However, this more widespread destruction of property was a departure from their tradition. It also created a new dynamic among the Doukhobors. Those who committed these acts were a very small minority. Verigin and other Community leaders publicly declared that the Community as a whole had nothing to do with the burnings and that many of their children were still attending school. At one inquiry a teacher of a burned school testified that the Community Doukhobors had, 'instead of burning schools, been guarding them and that the destruction has been the work of a small but fanatical element among them.'[71] The authorities, however, did little to apprehend the guilty individuals. Instead, they followed the orientation of the Community Regulation Act and held the Doukhobor Community liable for the depredations.

While dissociating themselves from the acts of destruction, the Doukhobor Community leaders also charged that School Inspector Daniels was using undue compulsion in pressing for attendance. They warned that if the prosecutions continued, they would not be able to guarantee the safety of other schools. In a letter to the minister of Education, dated 17 May 1923, the Doukhobors said:

It is apparent that the government is only seeking an excuse to create a quarrel with the Doukhobors, on the basis of the school issue.

Doukhobors are fanatics – so the English say, but what can we term the action of Mr. Daniels? This is more than fanaticism. What compels them to take such measures when the school question is so favourable, and the people are living peacefully, working and cultivating their own holdings ... You are only expert at ruining peaceful residents and plundering the proletariat ...

There is a saying: 'One fool can roll a stone off a mountain top into a river, but ten wise men, try as they may cannot take it up again". Mr. Daniels rolled this stone down, although it's not yet of very large proportions. He too must salvage it from the nether regions before it is too late.[72]

The tension continued and in April 1924 Verigin's own house was destroyed. He then appealed to the premier for protection and offered to provide the names of the twenty to thirty arsonists. To his surprise, there was little interest in his offer.[73] The government, instead of seeking to apprehend the guilty individuals, levied special taxes on the Doukhober Community in order to pay for destroyed property. On 24 October 1924, in an even more drastic event, Peter V. Verigin was killed in a train explosion, along with eight other people. The reason for the accident was never established. Many blamed the 'fanatical' Doukhobors but some Doukhobors thought that the Canadian government had killed him just as Russian governments had exiled their earlier leaders.[74]

It was a traumatic time for the Doukhobors. The authorities continued to enforce the law with prosecutions, fines, and the seizure of Community property. Before long most of the Doukhobor children who had been in school were withdrawn. In April 1925, a police inspector, 10 deputies, and 100 citizens forced their way into Community warehouses and seized $20,000 worth of goods, according to the Community's estimate.[75] This response was unusually severe. But then, suddenly, things changed. Peter P. Verigin, the new Doukhobor leader, who would soon be coming from Russia, sent word that 'all children should be sent to school and no protests held until he arrived.'[76] The Doukhobors complied and a three-year calm followed.

In summer 1925 the Doukhobor Community built five new schools and in the next few years it erected several more. When Peter P. Verigin arrived in September 1927 he said he wanted the Doukhobors to have the best possible education while retaining their religious faith. He also had plans to set up private Doukhobor schools. To assist in this matter he had brought along Paul Biriukov, a friend of Tolstoy. Provincial authorities, however, turned down the private school proposal so the effort was redirected into Russian-language classes after regular school hours, and into choirs and other cultural activities.[77] Peter P. Verigin's acceptance of public schools settled the question for a majority of the Community Doukhobors. Those who were not persuaded gradually became known as the Sons of Freedom.

1927–1959: Forcing School on the 'Sons of Freedom' Doukhobors
When Peter P. Verigin arrived in 1927, the Sons of Freedom numbered only a few hundred. Indeed, they were not a fully distinct group. However, their activities and their numbers were about to increase. In January 1929, when most Doukhobor children were in school, this group withdrew its children and announced that they would not be returning.[78] This event resulted in ten arrests, which in turn led to a nude demonstration. Verigin who, in an earlier appeal for unity, had described the Sons of Freedom as 'the ringing bells who cleared the way for the movement' now disowned and denounced them.[79] In a press release to newspapers dated 6 February 1929, he stated: 'Please take notice that the Christian Community of Universal Brotherhood, Limited, had nothing to do and will never have any connection with these people and with their dirty insolent violence, and all their stupid, childish actions, such as unclothing to the skin ... these persons do not belong to the membership of the Community. The Community is not

taking any responsibility for their actions materially or morally and moreover the Community refuses to consider such persons as brothers and to have any connections with them.'[80]

In March 1929, the Sons of Freedom issued a letter addressed to 'the Executives of all Countries: Judges, Government Inspectors, Police and all other servants of man-made laws,' which stated:

The time has come to reveal ... why we reject the Government schools and their orders. We are conscious of our history, and denote it by saying that Christ was the first Doukhobor. We are the direct Spiritual descendants of the Apostles of Christ and his followers, the so-called Christian martyrs of this time. It was the same kind of Government as the Canadian, that crucified Christ two thousand years ago ... Take our Government school education; people are so hypnotized by it that they do not see that its results are demoralizing. The present Government schools are nurseries of militarism and capitalism ... If there are men to be found among educated people like George B. Shaw, Tolstoy, Tagore, Gandhi, and many others, these men received enlightenment through Spiritual Regeneration, heeding the voice of Christ, and if such men are to be given honour, it was not attained by college education. Our whole history is marked by cruel persecutions by the churches, governments and capitalists. These persecutions are on account of our loyalty to Christ's teaching and our uncompromising refusal to submit to any Authority but God's.[81]

In summer 1929 there were numerous acts of property destruction. In most instances it was property used by the Community Doukhobors. On 29 June three schools that the Community Doukhobors had built in 1925 were burned. In August three more schools, a flour mill, and a warehouse belonging to the group were destroyed.[82] When two men were arrested, demonstrations involving nudity followed. As a result fifty-five men and forty-nine women were convicted for indecent exposure. Their sentence was six months at the Oakalla Prison Farm in New Westminster. It was the first mass imprisonment. Some of the prisoners' children were held in custodial care by the province until the parents were released.[83]

In February 1930 those who had been imprisoned were released but they now found that they were no longer accepted as members of the Doukhobor Community. They were expelled. But some Doukhobors in the 'branch communes,' especially in the poorer ones, welcomed them. This action led Verigin to withdraw all loyal Community Doukhobors from those areas, thus creating a more complete separation between the

Sons of Freedom and the Community Doukhobors. This separation, however, did not prevent the acts of property destruction. However, to the consternation of the Community Doukhobors, the police were still not eager to apprehend the guilty individuals or to protect the community's property. Peter P. Verigin now complained: 'The police are standing and looking ... what is the use of building schools when they are burning and dynamiting them faster than we can build them.'[84] The Community Doukhobors wanted the Sons of Freedom removed from their property and offered to pay the cost of a government investigation into the problems. The government instead continued with its policy of holding the Community liable for the destruction of property while arresting individuals who participated in nude demonstrations.

The provincial authorities were strengthened when the federal government, in August 1931, changed the Criminal Code so as to provide 'a mandatory penalty of three years' imprisonment for nudity in a public place.'[85] Because prison terms longer than two years are served in federal penitentiaries, the three-year penalty brought some financial relief to the provincial government. It also helped provincial politicians to project an image of 'getting tough' on the Doukhobors. However, lengthening the prison term was not effective as a deterrent to the nudity problem. The demonstrators wanted to make a religious witness, and the longer imprisonment could only enhance the martyrdom they sought.[86] Instead of the demonstrations diminishing, they became larger. One participant later spoke of them in this way: 'You see the (zealots) refused to pay their taxes, refused to comply with the ownership regulations; they just refused ... and had written a kind of appeal to everyone to the effect that the time had arrived when we must take this ownership from Caesar and give it back to God ... It was a wonderful sight. I doubt if this planet had ever seen anything like it ... It was a protest against land ownership and all ownership – against the Caesar's injustice that he has taken the cosmic property into his own hands.'[87]

In spring 1932, in a second mass imprisonment, approximately 600 men and women were convicted for nudity and given three-year prison sentences, to be served on Pier's Island, forty miles from Victoria, where special facilities had been erected. As the train carrying the convicts departed from the Kootenay Valley, the Doukhobors sang the hymns of their martyred forefathers. For them it was a spiritual pilgrimage.[88]

No less significant than the imprisonment of the parents was the placement of their 365 children in orphanages and industrial schools in

Vancouver and Victoria. Clearly, the children had to be cared for while their parents were in prison but the authorities also hoped that by exposing the children to a new environment their attitudes would change. It turned out that the children did not stay the full term. After one year, when a delegation of Independent and Community Doukhobors approached authorities with an offer of taking the Sons of Freedom children into their homes, it was accepted on the condition that they would attend public school. When the parents were released, between October 1934 and July 1935, the children were reunited with them. But it appears that few attitudes had changed. A 1947 study found 'that some of these children are actively participating in the quasi-anarchistic activities of the present day.'[89]

In the following years the school situation continued to be a public concern. An inspectors' report for 1935/6 stated: 'In the community schools and in those schools in which there is a major proportion of Doukhobors, no great progress has been made in Canadianizing this people. The persistence of the Doukhobors in maintaining their identity as such and in resisting Canadian influence is as strong as ever. While the children seem to be happy at school, they quit at the earliest possible date and at the present time there are many of school age who, supported by their parents, are defiantly absenting themselves from school.'[90]

In 1939 the British Columbia Teachers' Federation suggested that real Canadian homes 'radiating the best in our Canadian mode of life' be placed among the Doukhobors in order to help them to establish intimate contacts with 'lovable Canadians' and thus overcome their prejudice. Two years later, the Teachers' Federation stated that 'the supervision and administration of all Doukhobor schools should be vested in a single official, a trained and experienced educator of vision, initiative and wide sympathies, whose contacts with the Doukhobors will justify affection and confidence, and that it would be part of wisdom to entrust such a man with authority to adjust the curriculum.'[91] Some years later the federation recommended that teachers for the schools among the Doukhobors be chosen with special care, that they be given a wide liberty to adapt the curriculum to the needs of the Doukhobors, and that attendance be enforced consistently but only with fines and not with prison sentences.

For most of the Second World War period, 1939–45, the Sons of Freedom were relatively quiet. The attacks on the property of the Doukhobor Community ceased in 1938 when that body went into formal bankruptcy, having suffered from the depression, poor management, and government unwillingness to let the Community benefit from programs set up to assist industries affected by the depression.[92] With this collapse, the Christian Community of Universal Brotherhood (CCUB) was renamed the Union of Spiritual Communities of Christ (USCC). But the war and the disappearance of much Community Doukhobor property as a target did not keep the Sons of Freedom quiet for long. In 1944, there was a demonstration in which 'women's clothes and jewelry were burnt as symbols of the vanity of modern civilization.'[93] Soon after, the house of John J. Verigin, who had succeeded Peter P. Verigin as leader of the Community Doukhobors, was burned. From then until 1947 there were over 100 acts of destruction. Most of these were directed against other Doukhobors as a protest against their prosperity and materialism but some involved public property, including a CPR station, a bridge, and schools.[94] The USCC condemned the destruction and John J. Verigin publicly asked for police protection for his followers.

To deal with the continuing problem, the government of British Columbia, in September 1947, appointed Judge H. Sullivan to conduct an inquiry. In the public hearings that followed, one person confessed to having committed twenty-five acts of vandalism in the preceding twelve years, the largest being the 1943 burning of the $400,000 jam factory at Brilliant, long owned by the Community Doukhobors but taken over by the government in 1939. This person explained: 'I believe that this was necessary to wake up our brothers from materialism, which is the main source of patriotism.'[95] One person wrote to Sullivan that 'schools, forced upon the Doukhobors by the government, were destroyed by fire because schools are propagators of a false conception of civilization, patronizing the beast, militarism.'[96] Others came to the hearings and created 'an epidemic of true and false confessions, of accusations and counter-accusations that brought an atmosphere of pseudo-religious hysteria into the courtrooms.'[97] After four months of hearings Judge Sullivan was exasperated. He felt it was useless to continue 'until the crazy people are put in the mental asylum and the criminals locked up in the penitentiary.'[98] As for Doukhobor children, they should be educated with a view toward assimilation, he said. His brief recommendations did not, however, lead to a program of action.

Meanwhile, the nude demonstrations and acts of property destruction continued. In summer 1950, over 400 Sons of Freedom were in jail for nudity and arson.[99] By now another commission was at work. The president of the University of British Columbia had agreed, at the request of the attorney-general, to assemble a group of social scientists for a more thorough study. Chaired by anthropologist H.B. Hawthorn, the study lasted two years and involved twelve researchers. Their lengthy report, like the Blackmore report of 1912, showed considerable sympathy and respect for the Doukhobors but called also for compliance with the laws. As a matter of strategy, it recommended 'a balance of pressures and inducements.'[100] Claudia Lewis, one of the social scientists engaged in the study, advised against removing children from their parents. Instead, schooling should be made more acceptable to the Doukhobors. She suggested that Doukhobors be included on local boards, that the practices of saluting the flag and singing patriotic songs be discontinued, that some teaching of the Russian language and music be included, that the reading program be modified to include excerpts from Tolstoy, and that some aspects of the social studies program be changed, too. Notwithstanding these proposals for change, the report did not rule out prosecution as a way of dealing with cases of habitual truancy.

As with the moderate Blackmore report of 1912, the Hawthorn report was not followed, at least not immediately. The government that had commissioned the study was defeated in the 1952 election. The Social Credit party that came to power was in a minority situation at first, so in 1953 it went back to the people to get a majority. In doing so, 'getting tough with the Doukhobors' became a priority.[101] The Social Credit party received the desired majority and, on 9 September 1953, 148 Doukhobor adults were arrested and imprisoned for parading nude near a school. They were taken to Vancouver in a train that had been especially prepared for them. There, the next day, a court was convened in a community hall and all those arrested were sentenced to three years at the Oakalla prison.[102]

In addition, 104 children were loaded into buses and taken to New Denver, an old mining town, where the buildings of an old sanitorium served as their dormitory. The dormitory was surrounded by a high wire fence and the government invoked the Children's Protection Act to make them wards of the Provincial Superintendent of Child Welfare. Occasional police raids on Sons of Freedom settlements brought in more children. In one such raid, seventy police officers entered the small village of Krestova before dawn and seized forty children.[103] According to one mother's account:

On January 18th [1955] at eight o'clock, in the morning my little son awoke me and come to lie down beside me as though he knew it would be the last time. Then all of a sudden we heard a loud banging on the door, we thought it would break. Three RCMP officers came in and went straight to the bed waving the clubs in their hands in front of me and my child, and they said: 'How old is the boy?' We told them he is only six years old. The boy started to cry and begged us not to take him, but they said: 'Get him dressed or we'll take him in his underwear.' So, I dressed my little son for the last time, and he was taken from us who is not even school age. Only a mother who has gone through the same thing will know what it means to have the dearest ones taken from her.[104]

A total of 170 children passed through the institution in its six-year history. They attended the regular public school in the town of New Denver, while evening and weekends were spent in the dormitory. Parents were allowed to visit their children two Sundays per month but they had to procure special passes. In protest most chose to see their children through the fence outside.

Understandably, the New Denver project attracted considerable controversy. Civil libertarians protested the brutality of a government that would separate children from parents in this way. Journalists wrote numerous stories about it. One reported on the death of a Doukhobor woman found hanging from a beam in her home. A nearby note from her nine-year-old daughter at New Denver said: 'Mommy, I am lonesome for you – come and visit me. I love you. Goodbye.'[105]

The government also publicized its point of view. It stated that it was 'the birthright and privilege of every Canadian child to receive an education' and that because the Sons of Freedom refused to send their children to school, the government had no alternative. It pointed out also that of the 12,500 Doukhobors in the province only about 2500 belonged to the Sons of Freedom group and that of these only about forty-six families continued to refuse to send their children to school.[106]

For their part, the Sons of Freedom lodged a complaint with the United Nations under the Genocide Convention, which condemns the forcible transfer of children from one group to another.[107] They also, in 1957, challenged the government's action in the courts, arguing that the question was one of freedom of religion. However, Judge Sidney Smith did not accept that argument. In what became known as the *Perepolkin* case, he said:

I, for my part, cannot feel that in this case there is any religious element involved in the true legal sense. It seems to me that religion is one thing: a code of ethics, another, a code of manners, another. To seek the exact dividing line between them is perhaps perilous but I absolutely reject the contention that any group of tenets that some sect decides to proclaim form part of its religion thereby necessarily takes on a religious colour. I turn to the affidavit relied on by the appellants: ... the objection to public schools is that they interpret history so as to glorify, justify, and tolerate intentional taking of human and animal life or teach or suggest the usefulness of human institutions which have been or can be put to such purposes ... that public schools 'expose their children to materialistic influences and ideals' ... that Doukhobors object to education on secular matters being separated from education on spiritual matters.

This clearly to my mind involves the claim that a religious sect may make rules for the conduct of any part of human activities and that these rules thereby become ... part of that sect's religion. This cannot be so.[108]

At one point during the six-year detention of children some thirty Doukhobor women went to see Dr Campbell, British Columbia's deputy minister of Education. Campbell told them that if they would agree to send their children to school, they would be returned. 'We can't change the laws of the country,' he explained. The Doukhobor women replied: 'We can't change the laws of God either,'[109] The other Doukhobors, even though they had often sought to dissociate themselves from the Sons of Freedom, were sympathetic to them in this situation. They, too, appealed to the government but without success. Eventually, in 1959, when the parents appeared before a judge in Nelson and promised that their children would attend the regular public school, the children were returned to their homes.

This Doukhobor encounter on education stands out for its length and its harshness. Essentially, the British Columbia government forced the Doukhobors to comply with its regulations. Some observers have argued that the government had no alternative, that the ongoing destruction of property, belonging either to the government or to other Doukhobors, reflected a way of life that, though religiously based, was prone to violence and simply could not be accommodated, and that it was natural to look to education – forced if necessary – as a long-term solution.

A closer analysis shows, however, that there could have been significant accommodations at a number of points. The government could have accepted the 1912 Doukhobor offer to take information about vital statistics from the Community's record books and not exhumed bodies. It could have pursued the individual arsonists much more vigorously and focused less on those engaged in nude demonstrations. It could have removed military drills, flag-saluting ceremonies, and other activities from the schools much earlier. It could have incorporated Russian-language classes, Tolstoyan literature, Doukhobor music, and certain Doukhobor concerns about the teaching of history into the curriculum. It could have continued the lenient policy of Inspector A.E. Miller and not pressed for full attendance. It could have followed the moderate course recommended by Blackmore in 1912, by the Teachers' Federation in 1939, and by the Hawthorn Committee in 1952. The government could have given the Doukhobors a broader educational liberty. Repeatedly, it chose not to do so. Ewart P. Reid wrote in 1932 that 'much of the Doukhobor opposition to public schools arose not because of school per se ... but because of the course content and methodology employed. Many of these difficulties arose because of the educational theories and practices ... dividing children into grades, or using military drill ... competitive tests and comparative grading ... teaching history with military and political orientations, and refusing to allow the teaching of Russian did nothing to make schools more palatable, even to the Independent Doukhobors.'[110]

The government's policy of pressing ahead without making accommodations divided the Doukhobors, making their experience similar to that of the Mennonites. Some yielded, albeit reluctantly, while others became more determined in their resistance. Unlike the conservative Mennonites, the Doukhobors did not emigrate, though they did consider this option. Instead, they simply withheld their children from the public schools. Some engaged in nude demonstrations and a small number, probably no more than 200, destroyed buildings and other property.[111] Regarding the underlying reasons for this behaviour, one analyst wrote in 1973 that 'while Freedomite nude parades and destruction of Community property may have been attempts to convert Independents and Community members, incendiary attacks on schools and other non-Doukhobor property were clearly a response to attempts to enforce registration laws and compulsory education ... They reacted ... against what they viewed as an attempt to destroy their way of life and the faith of their children ... also against the Independent and Community members' acceptance of the forces of acculturation.'[112] According to this interpretation the violence was, at least to a large extent, the result of the provincial government's refusal to accommodate a distinctive Doukhobor way of life.

In probing the reasons for the British Columbia government's refusal to accommodate the Doukhobors there, certain similarities to developments affecting Mennonites and Doukhobors on the prairies emerge. Like the early settlers on the prairies there, the Doukhobors of British

Columbia were appreciated for their contribution to the economy when they first arrived.[113] But when the primary concern shifted from the frontier economy to social development there was no longer as much room for non-conforming groups. Also, as on the prairies, when the authorities pressed for social integration they defined religion in narrow terms and liberty on an individual basis. The narrow definition of religion in British Columbia is indicated most clearly in the *Perepolkin* case where it is suggested that the schooling of children is not a religious matter. The individualistic interpretation of liberty was indicated when the government defended the New Denver forced-schooling effort by saying, essentially, that the future liberty of the Doukhobor children required it.

Other explanatory factors lie in characteristics peculiar to British Columbia. Its educational structure was unusually centralized. Local school units had relatively little authority. Hence, developments in one locality could be used by politicians at the provincial level to project a 'get-tough' image. Also, the British Columbia educational system was unusually uniform. Unlike most other provinces, it had never had to accommodate a French-Catholic minority. Further, the approach of holding the Doukhobor Community liable for infractions committed by individuals was most unusual. It meant that law-enforcement agencies could impose fines and other punitive actions against the Community instead of looking for the guilty individuals. Community leaders were willing to help the police in identifying the individuals but the authorities showed little interest in their offers of assistance. The resulting atmosphere was poisonous, both among Doukhobors and between the government and those Doukhobors who wanted to be law abiding. If the Doukhobors could be treated as a community for purposes of liability, should they not also have been treated as a community for purposes of rights?

To say that the government of British Columbia could have been much more accommodating is not to say that accommodation would have solved all the problems. It must be conceded that there were some unusual and difficult elements among the Doukhobors. The actions by some Doukhobors to destroy the property of others, as a way of protesting against materialism and alleged departure from a true Doukhobor way of life, were a serious and persistent problem. It was probably necessary for the government to use some coercive measures in dealing with these developments but if it had granted the Doukhobors a broader educational liberty earlier on, the coercion required would probably have been much less.

7 Hutterite Schools in the Prairie Provinces

THE HUTTERITE APPROACH TO EDUCATION

The Hutterites, like the conservative Mennonites and Doukhobors, have been apprehensive about the regular public schools lest they lead their children away from their own way of life and into the larger society. Yet the Hutterite concern has been more moderate than that of the other two groups. This moderation has helped the Hutterites in making relatively successful arrangements with the governments of the three prairie provinces.

Hutterite concern for appropriate education has a long history. One contemporary scholar has written:

Three hundred years before Froebel introduced the first kindergarten in Europe and James Mill introduced the infant school in London, the Hutterian Brethren had established their *Kleinschule*. Our programs of technical education were preceded with the Brethren's apprenticeship program by four hundred years. The hygienic principles of cleanliness and healthful living were introduced to their schools in the early 16th century at a time when these principles were not accepted generally ... Most Hutterians were literate in a century when illiteracy prevailed; and for those adults who joined the Brotherhood and could not read or write, special adult education classes were established.[1]

According to a sixteenth-century Hutterite leader, schools were to direct the minds of children 'to honour and fear God, so that they may be brought up in the nurture of the Lord.'[2] A more recent leader has written that Hutterites 'are interested in attaining Godliness not ... acumen in making money.'[3] Public schools, they say, promote an exploratory attitude and an intellectual curiosity, encouraging people to question values and to compete and succeed on materialistic terms in the larger world.[4] When a 1974 sociological study asked Hutterite parents to identify the highest good that they hoped their children would achieve in life, they answered: 'That they be honest and faithful Christians and learn to love God and the communal way,' and 'We want our children ... following the footsteps of our Dear Lord and Savior; to give their time and strength, and if need be, their blood and very life.'[5]

In contrast, the larger society tends to hold that the purpose of education is to develop a person's rational powers. 'A person with developed rational powers,' it is said, 'has the means to be aware of all facts of his existence ... He can enrich his emotional life and direct it toward even higher standards of taste and enjoyment ... He can make of himself a free man.'[6] The approach of the Hutterites is concerned not primarily with the potential for rationality but with, as they see it, the need for obedience. They argue that education should reorient the individual's self-regard and nurture a desire to abide by the will of the community.[7] For children to overcome their 'carnal nature' and to learn obedience and faith, they need to receive the spiritual nature and learn the 'wisdom of God,' which, they say, cannot be obtained in public schools because they 'deny the true source of knowledge.'[8]

The Hutterites argue further that modern educational authorities hold an amoral perception of human nature and that this attitude has destroyed 'the organic unity which is necessary for healthy minds.'[9] According to one Hutterite leader, the modern educational 'process has become fragmentalized into various often antagonistic subprocesses, teaching incompatible elements to the growing generation. The result of this fragmentalized educational process is ambiguity, alienation, and often cynicism in the younger generation.'[10] Hutterites argue that 'false theories' about human nature have 'removed an awareness of responsibility from young people.'[11] They believe that the public school system is partly responsible for crime, juvenile delinquency, and alcoholism. When educational authorities say that Hutterite children ought to become more integrated with the larger society, Hutterites reply that their children are already well integrated within themselves and with their own communities and that sending them to public schools would lead to disintegration.

In addition, Hutterites have said that the public schools have militaristic elements; physical drills are too much like military drills and 'there is too much emphasis on war in history text books.'[12] They also say that they do not 'consider the military leaders of the past to be heros' but that 'in school much valuable time is taken studying the lives of mass butchers which time should be given to God, or to the study of righteous men.'[13] In addition, the Hutterites point out that although they may not have the diplomas to prove it, their young men study scientific and technical literature on agriculture and are well-informed farmers, using the latest technology. They add 'It is not a diploma which makes the ground bring forth its fruit, but knowledge and industry!'[14]

In 1899, when the Hutterites inquired about immigrating to Canada, they asked about the possibility of having their own schools. In their petition they stated: 'We would humbly beg for legal right to practice our religious services and principles, without any molestation, or encroachments, and that our children might also be accorded the same, and that we may be allowed to hold independent schools in order to teach them their mother tongue, and that they may not be compelled to attend other schools.'[15] In reply the deputy minister of the Interior, James A. Smart, stated: 'These people will not be molested in any way in the practise of their religious services and principles, as full freedom of religious belief prevails throughout the country. They will also be allowed to establish independent schools for teaching their children if they desire to do so, but they will have to be responsible for their maintenance themselves. The children will not be compelled to attend other schools if their education is properly provided for.'[16]

Despite these negotiations, the Hutterites did not migrate to Canada at the time. As noted in chapter 1, their anxieties in the United States subsided when the Spanish-American War came to an end. However, two decades later, when their non-participation in the American effort in the First World War resulted in severe hardship, they made a hurried move to Canada. At this time their agent, Michael Scott, wrote: 'They are quite willing to conform to the school laws of any province in which they settle.'[17] This willingness to accept public schools was a result not only of the urgency of the immediate situation, but also of the fact that in the intervening two decades the Hutterites had partially accepted American public schools, supplementing them with a system of morning, evening, and weekend classes to teach their own religion and the German language. This pattern would be used in Canada as well.

THE EXPERIENCE IN ALBERTA

When the Hutterites moved to Canada in 1918 a majority settled in

Alberta. Soon after they arrived, government officials went to the colonies to explain the provincial education laws.[18] The Hutterite elders were receptive and before long there were mutually satisfactory arrangements. In most instances, schools were erected on the Hutterite colonies although in a few cases Hutterite children began to attend nearby public schools. By the end of 1918 seven of the nine colonies in the province had erected schools, and non-Hutterite children from neighbouring farms also attended several of these.[19]

This mixture of Hutterites and non-Hutterites did not last, however. The non-Hutterites became uneasy because of the close contact that their children had with Hutterite children. The Hutterites, too, were concerned. Consequently, a more complete separation developed. The Hutterites continued to operate the public schools on their colonies but only Hutterite children attended. Nevertheless, the authorities were generally satisfied. In 1919 one inspector reported:

The people in these colonies appreciate the efforts of the department, in extending educational advantages to their children. They are very prompt in the payment of their taxes, and exert themselves in making comfortable the teacher who serves them ... The teachers in these communities are consistent in their efforts to further the knowledge of the English language ... During the winter evenings the teacher's residence is the meeting place of the younger men of the colony. With the teacher's help they read the current magazines dealing with Agriculture and scientific problems. Encouragement has been given the teachers to foster these meetings, and make them of real value.[20]

In 1920 another inspector reported that there was good co-operation, regular attendance, and that the colony 'displayed a deep interest in the school and inquired closely into the progress the children were making in school, especially in the learning of English.'[21]

Despite this trouble-free beginning, several difficulties appeared. The Department of Education had registered each colony as a school district. This meant that colony land was not usable as a tax base by the non-Hutterite community for its public school. In most instances the non-Hutterites accepted this limitation. But in one case the local member of the legislative assembly argued strongly that 'Hutterites should be assimilated through the existing schools.'[22] In another instance, the Hutterites, instead of defying the surrounding community, set up their own school under the provisions for private schools while continuing to pay taxes for the nearby public school.[23]

Another area of concern related to the character of the teachers. The department required them to have an official teaching certificate and because no Hutterite qualified for such a certificate, the teachers had to come from the outside. Some of these teachers, appointed by the official trustee, had recently returned from service in the First World War and were not sympathetic to the Hutterite way of life.[24] To deal with the problem, the Hutterites decided to try to have some of their own people certified. With this in mind they sent four of their young men to high school. However, only one of the four returned to the colonies to teach. Two returned years later. One never came back. Because of this failure, the plan was discontinued.[25] After this the Hutterites tried to influence the selection of teachers. They set up a committee on each colony and proposed that it work with the official trustee in selecting better-suited teachers. The minister of Education in 1925 responded favourably:

Your petition that the wishes of the various Hutterian communities be given consideration in the appointment of teachers is one which can be readily granted.

As a means of doing so, I would suggest that in each community there be appointed a school committee of three, with one of the members acting as chairman, and that you send to me the names and addresses of the various chairmen of these committees.

When this is done, I will send the names to the School Inspector J. Morgan, B.A. your Official Trustee, instructing him in the appointment of teachers to carry out as far as possible the wishes of the communities as expressed through their school committees.[26]

The economic depression of the 1930s brought out new aspects in the relations between the Hutterites and the larger Canadian society. Not only was the Department of Education continuing to receive favourable reports, but the Hutterites were among the few who were able to pay their taxes. In the Lethbridge School Inspectorate, which had 187 districts, only 3 districts were free of tax arrears. These happened to be on Hutterite colonies.[27] The financial situation led municipalities to compete with each other in attempts to have new colonies locate in their areas. Efforts were also made to bring more Hutterite colonies into the province. In one such effort in 1934, Owen Williams, a school inspector, wrote a testimonial to Premier Brownlee:

As the Official Trustee of these Districts I have been responsible for the selection of teachers and for the maintenance of their schools ... The leaders of these Colonies have always co-operated with the Department of Education in the schools and have invariably supported their teachers.

When the isolation of the children in these schools is considered their attainments in the English branches is all the more remarkable.

... They pay their taxes promptly. In the Hutterite District of the Lethbridge Inspectorate, all obligations to banks, teachers and school supply houses are regularly made at the end of each month.

During the inspection of these schools I have never witnessed mentally deficient children. In fact the Hutterites have the proud boast that since their arrival on this continent only one instance of such is on record.[28]

The financial solvency, which made Hutterites popular during the depression of the 1930s, was not characteristic of all the colonies. One colony, which had been operating a private school while also paying taxes to the nearby public school, found itself in financial difficulty. To deal with this problem, representatives from the colony approached the board of the nearby public school and asked for permission to send their children there. The board then called a public meeting and among the views expressed was that of the schoolteacher. He said:

Personally I am glad to welcome these Hutterite children into my school. I know of no better way to make Canadians out of them. I have not the least doubt that, through association with our own boys and girls, through observation of our ways, our customs and our manner of dress, and by taking part in our games and by learning our songs, they will become quite dissatisfied with the colourless, monotonous life of the colony. These children will be quick to learn and to adopt our way of life, and to discard that which circumstance and accident of birth now forces upon them. It is through the children that we will break up these colonies, these islands of isolation within our midst, and eventually bring about a true assimilation of the Hutterites into Alberta and Canadian society.[29]

When the Hutterites heard that their children would be welcomed with a view to their assimilation, they quietly walked out of the meeting, not to return.

Late in the 1930s the Alberta Department of Education began a process of reorganizing the small school districts into larger school divisions. This gradual process, lasting several decades, had far-reaching implications for rural life. But the effect on the Hutterites was relatively slight. Admittedly, the colonies could not be school districts any more. They were inside the larger divisions now. But most division authorities allowed the Hutterites to continue to have their own schools. Detailed agreements were drawn up with division boards stipulating that the colonies would provide the school buildings, teachers' residences, and various other facilities, while the division would appoint and pay the teachers.[30] The general principle of the division boards was that the operation of the school on the Hutterite colony should not cost the non-Hutterites any more than if the Hutterite children attended the centralized schools of the division.

The good relations between Hutterites and the larger society that prevailed during the years of the depression were not to continue through the following decade. By the end of the Second World War significant portions of the public were hostile toward the Hutterites. In 1947, when a legislative committee investigated the Hutterite situation in order to recommend whether the 1944 Land Sales Prohibition Act should be extended, some of the public criticism was directed also against the Hutterite schools. One of the more elaborate briefs presented to the committee came from the Alberta School Trustees Association: 'Education forms the background of society and conditions the manner in which Governments function. An adequate system of public education is a prerequisite for a successful democracy. It is the catalyst that resolves the composite sects and racial groups in this country into Canadians. In its broad, philosophical aspect it provides the means whereby the individual may obtain a better enjoyment of life and may become more useful citizens who can make some contribution to the country that shelters them.'[31] The association's brief then proceeded to criticize the isolation of the Hutterites:

The tenets of their religion include a belief in the community of goods, that is, that all property is held in common, that they shall not take oaths, and that they shall not vote or hold public office. Hutterites are opposed to higher education because they believe it makes people shirk their share of manual labour. It is a part of their creed that they will not mix with the society in which they are living ... They seek to remain isolated and sufficient unto themselves ...

Not only do the Hutterites isolate themselves, but these barriers have the effect of isolating some parts of the divisions with respect to both normal rural life and the administration of the educational system.[32]

The association also criticized some physical aspects of the Hutterite schools including the lighting and seating arrangements, the ventilation and furniture, and the absence of pictures and other decorations. It charged that the classes in German and religion conducted by the Hutterites after hours had the effect of so exhausting the children that they were not able to work properly in the English school. The association was critical, too, of the fact that the school buildings were used not only for the German school but for church services as well and that for these functions the flag was always taken down. The association concluded: 'The Hutterites have, in effect, arrogated to themselves a special position under School Law. To permit these Colonies to expand or multiply is to aggravate the trouble ... For that reason, the Association supports the extension of the Land Sales Prohibition Act.'[33] Another brief, submitted by the Alberta Farmer's Union, argued that the Hutterites were depriving their children of all culture, beauty, and refinements: 'Music, art, literature and organized sport are as far removed from them as if they lived in darkest Africa ... any Society that must keep its members in ignorance to hold them in subjection ... is not one to be encouraged and given special privileges so that they may continue to deny their posterity the right to live as free individuals and Canadian citizens.'[34]

The defence of the Hutterites was made by L.S. Turcotte, their lawyer. He submitted the testimonial letter, quoted above, written in 1934 by school inspector Owen Williams to Premier Brownlee. He also produced depositions signed by thirteen teachers in charge of Hutterite schools stating that 'Hutterite children are well behaved, possess better than average ability and are receiving a good public school education.'[35] In the end, the legislative committee did not make specific proposals regarding education. Its primary task had been to determine whether the Land Sales Prohibition Act should be continued. Nevertheless, its tone suggested that 'legislation and regulations on education should be more strictly enforced.'[36]

During the 1950s the concern about Hutterite education reappeared on several occasions. At one point in the mid 1950s the school committee of a county with seven Hutterite colonies wanted to set up one centralized school for them.[37] The Hutterite children were to be transported by bus from the different colonies to this one school, which would be equipped with modern teaching aids like motion picture projectors to help give the Hutterite children a 'good' education. The county's school committee worked on this plan for several years but the Hutterites objected strongly. In a lengthy formal response they declared that such a school 'would bring the ultimate abolition of the Hutterite faith; that the radios, televisions, pianos, and movies would expose their children to various influences from the outside world; that it would be undesirable to so remove the children from the setting of the colony with its religious exercises and parental supervision; that the time taken up with transportation was badly needed for their own supplementary classes in religion and the German language; that children were needed closer by so that they could help with farm chores; and that the cost of such a school would probably raise the resentment of county taxpayers against them. They added: 'We are confident you will not disprove as gentlemen who believe in freedom of religion.'[38] The minister of Education, perhaps influenced by the strength of Hutterite opposition, stated that the department 'would hesitate to support an enforced transporting of Hutterite pupils to schools outside their colonies.'[39] With little support from the department and strong resistance from the Hutterites, the proposal was dropped.

Still, the public sentiment against the Hutterites continued. One newspaper early in 1958 called for the dissolution of the colonies and suggested two methods of bringing this about: 'One way is by making it compulsory for the colony to pay a certain sum to any person who wishes to leave the colony and another way is insisting that the children go to division schools rather than to their own school on the colony land.'[40] The agitation was such that in September of that year, when the provincial government set up another committee to investigate the adequacy of the land restrictions, it also asked that educational matters be studied. The order-in-council of 8 September 1958, setting up the committee, stated that its purpose was 'to determine whether or not the existing educational facilities established for Hutterite colonies are satisfactory especially in the matter of instruction in the responsibilities of Canadian citizenship ... [and] any other matter relevant to the orderly and harmonious integration of the Hutterian church into local communities.'[41]

The objective that the Hutterites be integrated into the larger society was supported by a number of the briefs presented to the committee. The Lethbridge school division stated: 'There is no possibility of Canadianizing these people until their education is standardized with ours away from the domination of the elders.'[42] It proposed a centralized Hutterite school built by the division 'so that the full resources of the Division could be brought to bear on the problem.'[43] A United Farmers of Alberta group from New Dayton also saw changes in the educational system as necessary in order to integrate the Hutterites gradually into the social and economic life of the larger society. One University of Alberta professor suggested that Hutterite children be required to attend non-Hutterite schools 'in order to learn about birth control.'[44] At this, one Hutterite in attendance at the committee hearings said, 'And this is what a university education does to you.'[45]

The committee also heard from some who were sympathetic to the Hutterites. R.A. Kimmet, a former school superintendent in an area heavily populated by Hutterites, said that their attendance was good and that the technical education received on the colonies was excellent. He also spoke against the idea of forcing assimilation, saying that Canada had fought wars for the sake of freedom. His statement met with angry shouting.[46] Other supporters asked whether the larger society was indeed that much better and whether the Hutterites were not well within their rights. Still others praised them for being good farmers and good citizens.

Despite these several statements in support of the Hutterites, the report of the committee was clearly in favour of integration: 'The ultimate aim must be to look forward to a time when these people are prepared to enter more fully into the life of the dominant society.'[47] It was sharply critical of the Hutterite German school:

The average child learns by rote many verses of scripture and Hutterian doctrine. No studies designed to develop the intellect are offered or encouraged. This dual system of education has a serious effect on scholarship in the colony public school courses. One or more hours of study per day under the German teacher leaves the pupils with only a limited amount of time and energy to devote to the day school courses. Counter indoctrination by the colony minister, the German teacher and parents further retard the work of the day school.

Pupils are promptly removed from school at the age of fifteen regardless of ability or grade attained.

No loyalty to the country in which they live is acknowledged by the Hutterites, as responsibilities of citizenship are not accepted by those born in the country.[48]

The committee noted that 'the progress of pupils in colony schools from Grade IV up does not compare too favourably with the scholarship in public schools generally.'[49]

Although integration was the goal, it was not to be brought about by drastic methods. The committee recognized that such an approach 'would be strongly opposed by the Brethren and would only lead to them taking advantage of The Department of Education Act ... which makes provision for the establishment of private schools.'[50] The committee suggested a different strategy: 'A more subtle approach, aimed at ultimate integration, might be more effective. The Department of Education could make it possible to secure capable, personable teachers by providing higher salary bonuses. Indoctrination is not recommended but it is felt that Hutterite children would respond well to stimulating teachers with plenty of personality.'[51] The committee also said that the teachers should work under the supervision of a superintendent trained in anthropology who would try gradually to improve Hutterite education. To do this, it recommended the use of correspondence courses, night schools, and extension lectures 'to raise the level of education and pave the way for integration of Hutterite people with the dominant culture of the country.'[52]

In view of the committee's clear desire to promote their integration, the Hutterites made further representations to the government. In one substantial brief, submitted on 29 March 1960, the Hutterites emphasized their desire to have their own schools, arguing that 'parents have a prior right to choose the kind of education that shall be given to their children. It is neither the function of the neighbours or the state to do this, above all, in non-communist countries ... There are no high fences around Hutterite colonies as some would make believe, nor is force applied in any form in preventing children from leaving the colonies if it is their wish.'[53] They also pointed out that, 'in view of the large number of children in the province leaving school with a Grade 9 education only, and unprepared to take up employment in different fields, as contrasted with the Hutterites staying on the farm and furthering their skills in agriculture under parental tutelage, it is a question of fact whether or not the Hutterite children might not be better prepared for the occupation they will follow than many other boys and girls in Alberta. One thing certain is that the Hutterites would not be joining the ranks of the unemployed nor will they be competing for positions in the professions or elsewhere.'[54]

The government did not pursue further the matter of integrating them into the larger society. However, the issue of school-leaving age remained controversial for some time. The Hutterites continued to argue that when their young people left school at age 15 they entered an apprenticeship in one of the several lines of work on the colony, while teenagers in the larger society often remained uncertain and unsettled for several years. To deal with the situation of these non-Hutterite teenagers, the government, in 1966, raised the school-leaving age from

15 to 16.[55] But this created difficulties for the Hutterites. The age of 15 had long been important as a time when their people entered more fully into the colony's work force. According to one Hutterite, the change in this 'threw our system out of kilter.'[56] Also, for the first time, there were attendance problems. Some division school-boards then decided to exempt Hutterite children from attendance when they became 15 years of age. Other boards refused. In 1969, one Rev. Martin Walter of the Spring Point Colony spent ten days in jail after being convicted for refusing to send his 15-year-old son to school.[57]

A new school act in 1970 kept the school-leaving age at 16 but empowered boards, inspectors, and superintendents to exempt children from attendance under certain conditions.[58] This was a partial resolution but some inequities continued. In some areas Hutterites at age 15 were automatically exempted. In other areas there was strong pressure for continued attendance. Some parents were prosecuted. Eventually a compromise, whereby children could discontinue at the age of 15 years on the condition that they remain for the duration of the term they had begun, was widely accepted.

Other concerns were also settled in a compromise. The 1972 legislative committee, although it did not deal with education concerns at length, was oriented less towards integration and more towards coexistence.

THE EXPERIENCE IN MANITOBA

In Manitoba the Hutterite experience was similar. When the Hutterites moved to Canada in 1918, six of the first fifteen colonies were set up in Manitoba and, as in Alberta, the authorities soon helped to organize them into school districts with public schools on the colonies. Also, as in Alberta, organizing these districts required the appointment of an official trustee. The Hutterites could not form a board of trustees because they were neither Canadian citizens nor 'individually registered property owners.'[59] Nevertheless, the official trustee, school inspectors, and attendance officers seem to have discharged their responsibilities well. On 21 February 1921, Education Minister Thornton stated in the legislature:

During September of last year I personally visited the various public schools which had been established in the Hutterite settlement west of Winnipeg. There are now six of them in operation and all the children are attending these public schools. The buildings which have been erected are of the very best type and the members of the community are taking a very justifiable pride in the equipment which they have provided for the children, and in the very evident progress which they are making in education generally and the knowledge of the English language. Today the public school with its regular curriculum and its Canadian teachers is an accepted part of the life of each of the Hutterite communities.[60]

This arrangement whereby public schools were operated on Hutterite colonies worked reasonably well for several decades. In a few instances, when new colonies were set up, the established school districts were unwilling to relinquish taxable land or to allow the Hutterites to have their own school district. As a result the Hutterites sometimes set up private schools while continuing to pay taxes to the district's public school.[61] There were situations, too, where Hutterites mixed with others. In one case several French-Canadian families sent their children to a public school on a Hutterite colony. In another case, Hutterite children attended on off-colony public school together with children from neighbouring farms. These instances were exceptions, however. The most common practice was for the Hutterites to have a public school on a colony, attended by Hutterite children only.[62]

During the Second World War the Hutterites in Manitoba, like those in Alberta, received considerable public criticism. This led, in 1947, to the appointment of a legislative committee to 'obtain information regarding colonies or societies of Hutterites or Hutterian Brethren and to report and make recommendations upon the same.'[63] The education arrangements had not been the main focus of the criticism but neither were they excluded from the committee's broad mandate. One brief, submitted by School Inspector E.D. Parker, stated that 'there is not the same desire for an education on their part. There has never been any particular desire for a higher education, and so the standard in that way is low. The attendance too, to a certain extent, will interfere with that, because of the fact that they require their children to aid them in looking after the babies and looking after the geese, and looking after the various chores about a big farm.'[64] Inspector Parker held that 'it would be better to have the children of the Hutterites and the other children of the surrounding territory all attend the same school.'[65] In contrast, Dr Marcus Bach, a well-known American education expert, said that the Hutterites 'are on the threshold of assimilation' and that it would be better to let the various natural forces take their course than to force the situation.[66]

In its report, the committee did not recommend that the Hutterite children attend the same school as other children. However, it did ask that the Hutterite schools be within the public school system wherever possible, that the standard of education used in other schools be enforced also in the Hutterite schools, that the Hutterite pupils be encouraged to continue attendance at school after the minimum requirements of the School Attendance Act had been met, and that the functions of the school administrator, the school inspector, and the attendance officer be vested in a single official who would then be the main education official for the Hutterites.[67]

The committee of 1947 was followed by another in 1948.[68] The new committee's mandate did not include education matters but its hearing provided another opportunity for people to express their concerns about Hutterite schooling. John Bend of the Community Welfare Association, which had been set up mainly to deal with the concern about Hutterites, said:

God has endowed every child with certain faculties. It is the undeniable right of every child to have the privilege of having these faculties developed. Such an opportunity is provided outside of Hutterite colonies, and so we have teachers, professors, doctors, lawyers, merchants, nurses, music teachers, etc. In Hutterite colonies no such opportunities are afforded. Children born in Hutterite colonies are all destined to be farmers; they have no alternative. Every child has a right to be taught and trained to take his or her place among his fellow citizens. Under the Hutterite way of life this is impossible ... inmates of Hutterite colonies through lack of education and training are prevented from discharging their duties to their fellow citizens and to their country.[69]

Despite this strong criticism, Bend said: 'We at no time have questioned the right of any individual to pursue his own religious thoughts.'[70]

Another person who appeared before the committee was a Mrs Piper who had lived in the area where the Hutterites settled when they first arrived. For a time she had also served as a teacher. In her words: 'When these Hutterites were allowed to immigrate here into Canada, the general idea was that in the years to come, through education and association with us other Canadians, they might in time become true Canadians.'[71] She was concerned that this was not happening and she attributed this failure to the Hutterite communal form of living. With regard to the criticism directed at her that she was attacking their religious system, she said: 'That is entirely untrue. It is not their religious system, it is their communal system.'[72]

Despite these concerns, the 1948 committee did not refer to education matters in its recommendations. However, the recommendations of the 1947 committee were gradually implemented, including the one calling for a consolidation of the three education offices, that is those of administrator, inspector, and attendance officer. The Department of Education acted on it by appointing Bernard Grafton as supervisor of special schools. In the years that followed Grafton came to be highly respected by the Hutterites. He did not seek to create pressures for assimilation. However, he did try 'to raise the existing standards in all grades and extend general interest in education.'[73] He reported to annual school meetings on each colony and usually his recommendations were accepted. The result, according to one account, was that 'the Hutterian public schools operate more efficiently in many ways than some rural schools in Manitoba.'[74]

This happy arrangement continued without serious interruption until 1967, when there were province-wide changes in the school structure. The small school districts were replaced with the larger, more-centralized school divisions. This change was of concern to the Hutterites. On 23 January 1967, before the change took effect, Hutterite leader Rev. Jacob Kleinsasser, together with the Hutterite's lawyer, Roy Baker, met with Education Minister Dr George Johnson 'with a view to getting some special consideration for the Hutterites so far as the proposed consolidation' was concerned.[75] Baker reported on the meeting:

Doctor Johnson indicated that the Hutterites' position, although understood by the Government and appreciated, could not become a political issue and no amendments for the benefit of Hutterites could be made to the Public Schools Act. We have, however, been assured by Doctor Johnson and Mr. Dalton that the Department of Education will assist our office in making representation before the Divisional Boards in order to protect your interests. The Department of Education believes that ... the new Divisional Board will understand and respect the problems of the Hutterites and maintain Public Schools upon the Colonies to service the children of the Hutterian Brethren.[76]

The Hutterites entered into negotiations with the divisional school-boards but it soon became apparent that some of the boards were not interested in allowing the Hutterites to continue to have public schools on their colonies. The Hutterites then prepared an elaborate presentation addressed to 'The Unitary School Divisions of Manitoba.'[77] They reiterated their basic approach to education by referring to 'the obligation of the adults to rear their young as honest, forthright and upstanding citizens devoted to their way of life.' They also referred to a recent professional sociological publication which had said of their educational practices: 'The ultimate goal of education is salvation. In order to achieve this, children are to be kept separated from the world where they would see, hear, and learn all sorts of Godless things, and are disciplined in school and at home.'[78] The Hutterites explained the role of education in their social structure in an elaborate way:

Education for the Hutterian Brethren is the crux of their way of life since perpetuation of Hutterianism depends upon the education of the children. All children between the ages of 6 and 15 under supervision of the German School Teacher, have a daily routine upon a Colony as follows: Morning prayers in the children's dining-room, in conjunction with the partaking of the first meal of the day; thereafter German School classes are conducted for one hour at which time German Education and Language, Religious teachings, Christian Ethics and Citizenship are taught to the children; thereafter the children attend a public school situated upon the Colony which school is maintained for the standard hours with the curriculum approved by the Department of Education taught by qualified public school teachers; for one hour after termination of public school, German school is conducted once again by the German school teacher in the same manner as the German school held prior to the commencement of public school in the morning; at the end of the day the children attend for their evening meal at the children's dining-hall under the supervision of the German school teacher where they partake of their evening meal in conjunction with prayers.[79]

In contemplating the possible attendance of their children at the consolidated schools, the Hutterites said: 'The Children of the Hutterian Brethren, if forced to go to Consolidated Schools, will be *displaced persons*, foreigners, in the midst of children bred in a Society completely and utterly different to theirs. Can we permit an unpleasant meeting between two groups of children, the result of which may cause very serious mental injury to one or other of the two groups' (emphasis in the original).[80] In concluding their presentation the Hutterites expressed the hope 'that the Divisional Boards will continue to see their way clear to maintain upon each of the Colonies a Public School, to service the children of the Hutterian Brethren.'[81]

Soon after this the divisional boards agreed, at least for the 1967/8 school year, that the public schools on the Hutterite colonies would continue to operate.[82] A longer-term commitment, however, was not immediately forthcoming. In May 1968, Dr Johnson, the minister of Education, indicated a willingness to assist the Hutterites in approaching the divisional boards.[83] But some boards were not persuaded even then. Consequently, several Hutterite colonies began to operate their schools on a private basis while continuing with further appeals.[84] In one submission to the department they pointed to the problems that transporting their children to the consolidated schools would create. They said it would 'seriously disrupt a 400 year-old tradition of daily education of our children in their religion and in the German language, which education takes place one hour prior to and one hour after public school. We cannot suffer to permit this education to be terminated or abridged as our children will suffer irreparable damage in their way of life. The long day, resultant from transportation, would not permit them to enjoy the valuable benefit of additional education.'[85]

If the divisional boards would not allow the Hutterites to have public schools on their colonies, then, instead of having their children transported long distances to the consolidated schools, they would operate their schools on a private basis. But the Hutterites pointed out that this too would create difficulties. They said: '(i) qualified teachers will not likely be available for such private schools since teachers are generally required to relinquish pension rights in order to teach in private schools; (ii) teachers in such private schools will be without the valuable assistance of a school superintendent and therefore at a distinct disadvantage; (iii) when qualified teachers are not available, then the Colonies will be forced to retain permit teachers thereby drastically limiting the quality of teaching for their children.'[86]

The Hutterites said that the arrangement that had been used for several decades was effective in preparing their children for the way of life that they would likely follow as adults and that 'it is the obligation of the Department of Education with respect to the education of all children to consider their ultimate welfare and so gear their education with a view to such welfare.'[87] They argued also from the basis of religious freedom: 'According to our way of life, we have ... reared our children within our homes and colonies and ... any infringement on this right would be a denial of the religious and other freedoms granted to us as citizens of Manitoba and Canada.'[88]

Some divisional boards continued to resist the idea of public schools on Hutterite colonies. The possibility of a centralized Hutterite school to which Hutterite children from different colonies would be transported was considered but not implemented.[89] Eventually, the pressure from both the Hutterites and the Department of Education prevailed and all divisions agreed to operate public schools on the Hutterite colonies.[90]

THE EXPERIENCE IN SASKATCHEWAN

Because the Hutterites came to Saskatchewan only in 1952, some thirty years after they had settled in Alberta and Manitoba, their encounter with the provincial government on matters of education was less complex. In Saskatchewan the process of replacing small school districts with larger school divisions, here known as units, was already well under way. As a result the Hutterites had to make arrangements with the unit boards if they were to have schools on their colonies. In most cases the unit boards co-operated. The arrangements usually stipulated that the Hutterites would provide the school building and other facilities and that the unit board would provide the teachers.[91] It was not to cost the unit more to educate a Hutterite child than to educate other children.

The Department of Education was supportive but it did not have the power to force a unit board to make these kinds of arrangements. Although most boards were co-operative, a problem arose in 1962 when the Leader School Unit refused to provide an on-colony school for a particular Hutterite colony. The department urged the unit to reconsider but unit representatives said that there was a school within easy travelling distance, that the per pupil cost of operating an on-colony school for the Hutterites would be high, and that 'the burden of the cost would fall upon the ratepayers of the Unit.'[92] The Hutterites replied that they had agreed to locate in the area 'only after receiving assurances from a provincial Cabinet Minister, and the Leader Unit Board, that an on-colony school would be maintained.'[93] The unit board persisted and eventually the Hutterites, instead of going to the nearby public school, arranged to take the official government correspondence courses under the supervision of an older Hutterite.[94] This measure, however, was a temporary exception. Before long a satisfactory arrangement between the unit board and the colony was worked out.

In general, then, the Saskatchewan Hutterites developed a pattern similar to what their groups had worked out in Manitoba and Alberta. Their schools operated with the curriculum and under the authority of the public school system but were located on the colonies and only Hutterite children attended. This colony atmosphere, plus the various supplementary classes that the Hutterites conducted with their own teachers, proved to be satisfactory to them.

In reviewing these Hutterite encounters on education, it must first be noted that the Hutterites have survived. This distinguishes them from the conservative Mennonites who, after a traumatic encounter, left the country and from those Doukhobors who accepted public schools only after prolonged coercion by the British Columbia government.

One reason for the relative success of the Hutterites is that the liberty they sought was less broad than that sought by the other two groups. There were more accepting of the English language, the need for a formal education, and a measure of governmental control. By accepting these features, the Hutterites charted a course that did not depart as far from the Canadian norm as that pursued by the conservative Mennonites and some Doukhobors. In this sense, the liberty they asked for was less broad and hence easier for governments to accommodate.

Nevertheless, there are noteworthy similarities with the experiences of the Mennonites and the Doukhobors. All three groups were welcomed for their economic contribution and all three eventually faced strong assimilative pressures, as the larger society became impatient with their continuing separateness. Those who argued that the Hutterites, like the other two groups, should assimilate revealed that they had a different view about the purpose of education. Canadians felt that education was to prepare children for life in the larger society, giving them an exploratory mind and the understanding needed to enjoy the wider culture, to participate in the regular political process, and to gain personal economic advancement. In contrast, the Hutterites wanted their children to gain the understanding needed to follow their historic way of life, with its agricultural, communal, and religious dimensions. They felt that the public schools, located on their colonies and supplemented by classes of their own, prepared their children for this way of life, which they would likely follow, better than the regular public schools prepared children in the larger society for their probable futures.

Also evident is a difference in the way freedom, particularly freedom for religion, was understood. The Hutterites saw it in broad terms. For them freedom meant freedom to continue in their communal way of life. Their critics saw it in individual terms. They felt that Hutterite schools kept individual Hutterites ignorant and submissive and that regular public schools would give the Hutterite children the right to have their talents developed and 'the right to live as free individuals and Canadian citizens' without being dominated by Hutterite elders. The critics claimed that they did not intend to interfere with the Hutterite religion but they seemed not to understand that for the Hutterites, their communal way of life and their school system were inseparable from their religion.[95] However, the critics, though strong at times, were not successful. When the Hutterites appealed to 'freedom of religion,' it appears that the authorities felt that their argument had merit.[96] The authorities never articulated precisely what they meant by this concept but it seems that they felt that if they took actions seriously detrimental to the Hutterite way of life, then they would be violating this fundamental principle.

Although the authorities were relatively accommodating about the school arrangements desired by the Hutterites, the accommodations were not secure, nor were they firmly institutionalized. At several points officials seriously considered the possibility of sending Hutterite children to centralized public schools. The uncertainty must have been troubling to the Hutterites but if they had insisted on greater certainty they might have had to settle for a narrower liberty. In Manitoba the minister of Education, while ultimately successful in persuading the larger school units to allow the Hutterites to have on-colony schools, refused to make this arrangement into a statutory right. He pointed out that in order to do so, the issue would have to be opened for debate in the legislature, making it a political issue. As a result, it might not pass a vote, he said.[97]

The minister was probably right, but if the Canadian political system is to be praised for its flexibility and for the relatively broad liberty that it gave to the Hutterites, it must be criticized for leaving that liberty uncertain and vulnerable. Fortunately for the Hutterites, as the arrangement continues to be used for years and decades, it attains a certain security.

PART FOUR

Military Service Exemptions

A third area in which the way of life pursued by Mennonites, Hutterites, and Doukhobors has required special governmental arrangements relates to their desire to be exempted from military service.

In Canada the first promises of military exemption were made late in the eighteenth century, when many people moved from what had become the United States of America to what remained of British North America. In 1792 Upper Canada's lieutenant-governor, John Simcoe, made a promise of military exemption in order to attract certain settlers. And in 1793, when the Assembly of Upper Canada passed a Militia Act, it contained the following:

And be it further enacted, that the persons called Quakers, Mennonists, and Tunkers, who from certain scruples of conscience, decline bearing arms, shall not be compelled to serve in the said Militia, but every person professing that he is one of the people called Quakers, Mennonists, or Tunkers, and producing a certificate of his being a Quaker, Mennonist, or Tunker, signed by any three or more of the people (who are or shall be by them authorized to grant certificates for this or any other purpose of which pastor, minister, or preacher shall be one) shall be excused and exempted from serving in the said Militia, and instead of such service, all and every such person and persons, that shall or may be of the people called Quakers, Mennonists, or Tunkers, shall pay to the lieutenant, the sum of 20 shillings per annum in time of peace, and five pounds per annum in time of actual invasion or insurrection.[1]

This exemption provision was significant but there were two problems. One was the requirement that the people pay a special tax in lieu of militia service. This payment was a financial burden on the pioneers.

Also, paying this extra tax was not easily reconciled with their religious teaching because it seemed to be just another way of supporting the military. Yet, if they refused to pay the tax, as some Quakers did, then their property might be confiscated.[2]

The second problem involved the question of church membership. For both Mennonites and Tunkers (Tunkers later adopted the name Brethren in Christ) formal church membership was open only to adults. This restriction was related to their historic rejection of infant baptism and to their theology of the church as a voluntary association. Now, however, it meant that if their young men had not yet formally joined the church then they might not be entitled to the desired exemption.

To deal with these two problems the groups petitioned the authorities to have the law changed:

We therefore humbly pray the same indulgence may be extended to them that is granted to ourselves, their parents, that is that they may be exempted from serving in the Militia by paying the commutation money until they arrive at the age of twenty-one, or until they be admitted as Church Members.

... And Your Petitioners further pray that your Honourable Body will take into consideration the many difficulties which poor people, with large families have to labour under in new settlements, and if you in your wisdom should deem meet to lessen the burden of our commutation money, Your Petitioners, as in duty bound, shall ever pray.[3]

In 1810 their efforts were rewarded with 'An Act for the Relief of Minors of the Society of Mennonists and Tunkers.'[4] The special tax was removed in 1849, after many more petitions.[5]

During the war of 1812, these provisions for exemption were tested rigorously but it appears that they were generally respected. The historian W.H. Breithaupt states: 'The government, finding them unalterably opposed to carrying arms, required the Mennonite settlers to serve in camps, hospitals, etc., and as teamsters in the transport service, they having to furnish their own horses.'[6] This non-combatant alternative service would become a contentious issue in the world wars of the twentieth century.

New militia acts were passed in 1855 and 1868, each with exemption provisions.[7] The one of 1868, passed by the government of the new Dominion, stated that 'any person bearing a certificate from the Society of Quakers, Mennonists or Tunkers, or any inhabitant of Canada, of any religious denomination, otherwise subject to military duty, but who, from the doctrines of his religion, is averse to bearing arms and refuses personal military service shall be exempt from such service when balloted in time of peace, or war, upon such conditions and under such regulations as the Governor in Council may, from time to time, prescribe.'[8]

In addition to extending eligibility to individuals from other religious groups, this provision is significant also because it served as the basis of the promises of exemption given to the Mennonites who would emigrate from Russia in the 1870s. The negotiations for the 1870s migration began in January 1872 when these Mennonites contacted the British Consulate in Berdjansk, Russia. They asked, even in this first official inquiry, for 'exemption from all military service.'[9] A report of their interest was quickly communicated to Ottawa, where the government, on 26 April 1872, passed an order-in-council that referred to the existing statutory provisions and then stated: 'Any person bearing a Certificate from the Society of Mennonists shall be exempt from Military Service ... upon such conditions and such regulations as the Governor-in-Council may ... prescribe.'[10]

The Mennonites were concerned about this wording. They did not want their exemption to depend on what the governor-in-council might prescribe. When they asked for clarification the government passed another order-in-council, dated 25 September 1872, giving them 'the fullest assurances of absolute immunity from military service.'[11] This order quoted the existing statute and then explained: 'The Mennonites are expressly included, are absolutely free and exempted by the law of Canada from military duty or service, either in time of peace or war' and 'the Governor-in-Council cannot prescribe any conditions or regulations under which, under any circumstances, the persons referred to in the above quoted section can be compelled to render any military service.'

Soon after this assurance was given, the Mennonites in Russia sent ten delegates, together with two Hutterite delegates, to investigate more directly the prospects for settling in Canada and the United States. Only four of the delegates chose Canada but this explicit assurance of complete exemption from military service was a key factor in persuading them to do so.[12] The John Lowe letter of 25 July 1873, which was passed as an order-in-council on 13 August 1873, repeated the promise by stating, in the first of its fifteen paragraphs: 'An entire exemption from military service is by law and Order-in-Council granted to the Denomination of Christians called Mennonites.' Encouraged by these assurances, approximately 7000 Mennonites then emigrated from Russia to Manitoba, Canada.

Several decades later, in 1898, when the Doukhobors of Russia wanted to immigrate to Canada, the government passed an order-in-council with a similar promise.[13] The order noted that 'the Doukhobors would appear to be a most desirable class of settlers to locate upon the vacant Dominion Lands' and that therefore 'it is expedient to give them the fullest assurance of absolute immunity from military service.' The exemption was unconditional but individual Doukhobors would have to produce 'a certificate of membership from the proper authorities of their community.' A few months after this order was passed approximately 7400 Doukhobors arrived in Canada. Another order-in-council, with these same words, was passed for the Hutterites on 12 August 1899.[14] However, as noted in chapter 1, the Hutterites did not immigrate to Canada until two decades later.

These provisions for military exemption were tested severely in the two world wars of the twentieth century.

8 Exemptions in the First World War

DEVELOPMENTS BEFORE THE CONSCRIPTION ACT WAS PASSED

The First World War encounter involved primarily the Mennonites and the Doukhobors because the Hutterites had not yet immigrated to Canada. Mennonites and Doukhobors were not always of one mind but virtually all wanted to be exempted from military service. The exemption issue, however, did not become serious until 1917 when the conscription law was passed.

Officially, Canada became involved in the war with Great Britain's declaration on 4 August 1914. In many parts of Canada this act was greeted with enthusiasm. In Winnipeg, according to the *Free Press*, 'the floodgates of patriotism were thrown open ... last night, and scenes of the wildest enthusiasm were enacted on the main thorough-fares when a *Free Press* "extra" announced shortly after 8 o'clock that war was declared between Great Britain and Germany.'[1] The government, for its part, had been preparing for the possibility of war. It now passed 'scores of Orders-in-Council ... activating the Militia, providing for home defence, taking control of communications networks, establishing censorship of trans-Atlantic cables, and shoring up the credit of the banks against an unanticipated run of their funds.'[2] The most far-reaching action was the introduction of the War Measures Act. With it the government obtained virtually all the authority necessary for pursuing the war effort. No longer would it have to receive parliamentary approval for particular measures.

Despite these steps toward a major war effort, the government was not about to impose conscription. On 22 August 1914, when the Hon. Sam Hughes, minister for the Militia and Defence, proudly reported that

100,000 men had volunteered for overseas service, he stated further: 'I am absolutely opposed to anything that is not voluntary in every sense, and I do not read in the law that I have any authority to ask Parliament to allow troops other than volunteers to leave the country.'[3] Prime Minister Borden, speaking in Halifax in December 1914, said: 'There has not been, there will not be, compulsion or conscription. Freely and voluntarily the manhood of Canada stands ready to fight beyond the seas.'[4]

Although the government was not imposing conscription, many non-governmental organizations were promoting recruitment. There were public meetings, advertisements, and appeals of many kinds. Churches, entertainment centres, and the mails were used to promote enlistment.[5] However, by summer 1915, after one year of these efforts, there were 'rumblings about difficulties in securing men for the army.'[6] The concern became greater after October 1915 when plans called for 250,000 men in the army and greater still after January 1916 when that figure was raised to 500,000.

The complaints dealt not only with the difficulty of recruiting an adequate number but also with the question of fairness. To rely on volunteers it was said, was unfair and undemocratic. It did not distribute the burden equally. One critic, Lt-Col Lorne Mulloy, a Royal Military College instructor, argued that 'voluntarism entailed the right to refuse' and that this undermined 'the basic principle of democracy,' which he defined as 'In Time of War the Eligible Male Citizen Must Fight.'[7] He argued that the system was 'drawing largely from the more efficient and those the country can least afford to spare,' that it did not distinguish between industries, 'drawing alike from the munitions plant and the distillery.' What was needed, according to Mulloy, was an authoritative selection system involving a classification of industries and a registration of all manpower. Those employed in the important industries would then be allowed to stay, while those in less essential industries could be conscripted.

This call for national registration and selective conscription, articulated by Mulloy in March 1916, was heard also from other sources. On 14 April a large delegation from private recruiting organizations met with the prime minister and proposed the registration of all manpower, the classification of industry, and 'some just and comprehensive system of draft.'[8] When the prime minister asked why they considered the existing system as a failure, since substantial numbers were still being recruited, they replied: 'We are getting the wrong men.' Chief Justice T.G.

Mathers of the Manitoba delegation said that the voluntary system was iniquitous because it distributed the burden of sacrifice unequally.

Prime Minister Borden did not promise immediate changes. He was concerned about the effect that conscription might have both on Quebec politically and on the continuing effort to attract immigrants to the west. For the duration of the war the United States would be the main source of immigrants and in a letter soon after the 14 April meeting, Borden wrote: 'American Real Estate men who are actively engaged against the effort of our Immigration Agents have eagerly seized upon the cry of conscription to render our efforts entirely nugatory.'[9]

Despite this reluctance, in August 1916 the government became more involved in the recruitment effort. A National Services Board was set up and R.B. Bennett became its director-general. Its purpose was to determine 'whether the services of any man of military age are more valuable to the State in his present occupation than in military duties ... and either to permit or forbid his enlistment.'[10] To carry out this task, the board first needed extensive information about what the men of military age were doing. To obtain this information it decided to conduct a national registration.

The national registration was a major event. Cards were sent out and distributed through the post offices in all areas of the country. People were to complete them and send them back to Ottawa. It was not compulsory but the government tried 'to create an atmosphere sufficient to induce the people voluntarily to sign the cards.' There were public meetings, advertisements in newspapers, and letters to 150,000 prominent people throughout the country asking them to promote the registration effort. In addition, the first week of January 1917 was designated for the registration effort. When people expressed fear that it would lead to conscription, Borden explained that national registration was necessary in order to systematize and strengthen the voluntary efforts and thus to make conscription itself unnecessary.

The Mennonites and Doukhobors had remained more or less unto themselves until this point, although in 1915 the Mennonites in Ontario had sent a statement describing their theological views on war and military service to the government.[11] Also, in summer 1916, one group of the more 'integrated' western Mennonites (integrated in the sense of having accepted public schools) from Manitoba and Saskatchewan passed a resolution expressing gratitude to the Dominion government not only for not conscripting them but also because the campaigns for voluntary enlistment had not put undue pressure on their people.[12]

Now, in November 1916, with the national registration in mind, the conservative Reinlaender Mennonite church in the west sent a delegation of three bishops to Ottawa to seek further clarification.[13] The government's response was reassuring. Solicitor-General Arthur Meighen wrote: 'I ... beg again to assure you of the determination of the Government to adhere to the full to the obligations of honour incurred by this country at the time of the admission of your people to this country.'[14] As a sign of gratitude for this assurance, the Reinlaender Mennonites sent a cheque of $1383.00 to Meighen with instructions that he use it wherever it was most needed to relieve victims of the war.

The Reinlaender Mennonites understood the assurance to mean that they would not be expected to participate in the national registration either. Thus, in January 1917, when other Canadians were filling in their registration cards, the Reinlaender Mennonites did not do so. One bishop, in a letter dated 4 January 1917 to Prime Minister Borden and Solicitor-General Meighen, stated that in view of the understanding arrived at, at the meeting in November 1916, their group assumed that it would be in order if they would return the cards without filling them in. He added that they desired only to be 'the quiet in the land,' that they did not seek government offices or vote for others who sought them, that instead they sought the welfare of the country by praying to God on its behalf.[15]

The government, however, understood the matter differently. It wanted all Mennonites to register and tried hard to persuade them to do so. The Manitoba representative of the National Services Board called the leaders of the Reinlaender Mennonite Church to Winnipeg and urged them to reconsider their position. The leaders agreed to give the matter further thought and to do so they called a large meeting with representatives from the churches in both Saskatchewan and Manitoba. The result was the same, however. According to a Royal North-West Mounted Police report: 'At a large meeting of Mennonite preachers and Bishops at Rhineland, Manitoba, at which there were about 450 delegates ... it was decided to fill in no National Service cards, regardless of what form such cards should take. However it was decided that the heads of the Church, would, if required, draw up a statement of the male members of the congregation.'[16] Whether this compromise was accepted is not clear.[17] But it appears that the government did not insist on strict compliance. After all, this registration was not compulsory.

The more 'integrated' western Mennonites also feared that the registration might lead to conscription. Accordingly, they, too, sent a delegation to Ottawa.[18] Consisting of five church leaders, this delegation, on 8 January 1917, met with three governmental representatives: the minister of Public Works, Robert Rogers, who was from the west; Col. Clark, under-secretary of state for Internal Affairs; and R.B. Bennett, director-general of National Services. In a written presentation these church leaders reviewed their theological reasons for opposing military service and noted that in the 1870s their predecessors had chosen Canada primarily because of the definite Canadian promise of exemption from military service. They also referred to an address given in 1877 by Lord Dufferin, governor general of Canada, to the early Mennonite settlers in the west. The governor general had reaffirmed their exemption from military service and called them, instead, to a battle against the wilderness, to till the soil and make it productive. He had also invited the Mennonites to participate in the politics of Canada at all levels. The delegation concluded by saying that further assurances of exemption would be appreciated both by their own people and by the many Mennonites still in Russia who would want to immigrate as soon as the war was over.[19]

This delegation, like the earlier one, received a written reply. In a letter of the same day (8 January 1917), R.B. Bennett stated: 'The terms of the Order-in-Council under which the Mennonites settled in Canada, guarantee their freedom from Military Service. Canada will respect to the utmost its obligations under that Order-in-Council.' He stated further: 'Members of the Mennonite communion are requested to fill in correctly and return promptly the National Service Cards, and it is suggested that they should write across the face of each card the word "Mennonite" as indicating their religious faith.' He explained that the information on the cards might be needed for directing people to 'agricultural or industrial work.' Bennett also encouraged the Mennonites to increase their agricultural productivity, 'which while not essential to the success of our cause, is as important as military service, for the reason that armies cannot exist without food.' He also stated that any Mennonite who had joined an overseas battalion under 'misapprehension or otherwise' would be released if he made a request to that effect.[20]

The reference in Bennett's reply to the possibility that Mennonites might be sent to work in agriculture or industry suggests an alternative national service. This possibility was raised on several occasions. Some Mennonites in the west 'signified their willingness to agree to any legislation by which their people shall be required to serve the country in any capacity other than military, at regular soldiers' pay.' S.F. Coffman, the Ontario Mennonite leader, expressed a similar view.[21] Some Canadian Quakers did serve in the Friends Ambulance Units in Italy and France. Also, there was discussion of a forestry service unit but it did not materialize in the First World War.[22] Lacking an alternative national-service program, these Mennonites then chose to express their gratitude for Bennett's assurances by sending $5577.17 to the government to be used for relief purposes, just as the Reinlaender Mennonites had done earlier.[23] In the next year Mennonite support for relief work grew considerably. By the end of 1918, they had donated $150,000 to public relief agencies.[24]

The Doukhobors approached the registration in a similar way. They, too, were apprehensive lest it be a step towards conscription. To resolve their concerns they sent a delegation to Ottawa. In a meeting with Meighen, they said that they were quite willing to sign the cards provided their religion would be respected. They also indicated that in lieu of military service they would be willing to pay a double measure of taxation. They reported that they were supporting the agriculture-production campaign and that they had placed as much of their land as possible under crop. As with the Mennonites, Meighen assured the Doukhobor delegation that there would be no interference with their privileges.[25] Also, like the Mennonites, they then sent a sum of money to be used for the victims of war. In one letter the Society of Independent Doukhobors at Buchanan, Saskatchewan, sent a donation and stated: 'Our faith and conscience will not permit us to take an active part in the strife, but our sympathy and compassion for those who, though innocent and in no wise responsible for the hostilities, have been rendered homeless, indigent and destitute by its progress, bid us to at least share with them the produce of our labor applied to God's soil.'[26]

Throughout the time of the registration the government maintained that it was not a precursor to conscription. However, by March 1917, things were changing. Prime Minister Borden travelled to the Imperial War Conference in London, where the British prime minister, Lloyd George, emphasized that there was a great need for more men.[27] Borden, after visiting the battle fronts in Europe, agreed. In a letter to Archbishop Bruchesi of Montreal, Borden wrote: 'What I saw and learned made me realize how much more critical is the situation of the Allies and how much more uncertain is the ultimate result of the great struggle.' He added that he had had the 'privilege of looking into the eyes of tens of thousands of men at the front who look to us for the effort which will make their sacrifice serve the great purpose for which it was undertaken.'[28] On 18 May 1917, Borden announced in the House of Commons that he would introduce a conscription bill.

This announcement intensified public debate about the issue. Newspapers in English Canada, like the *Globe* in Toronto and the *Free Press* in Winnipeg, promoted it strongly. However, in Quebec anti-conscription parades became common.[29] In the House of Commons, Borden tried to broaden the political support for conscription, first by proposing a coalition government with Laurier and, when this attempt was refused, then by other means. At one point a War-Time Elections Act was passed that enfranchised the mothers, wives, sisters, and daughters of soldiers, while disfranchising naturalized immigrants from enemy countries who had arrived in Canada after 1902, as well as Mennonites, Doukhobors, and conscientious objectors.[30] The debates in the House over the Military Service Act, as the conscription law was formally known, were unusually contentious, but on 29 August 1917 the law was passed.[31]

Clearly, the purpose of the act was to produce more soldiers but it still included certain protections for Mennonites, Doukhobors, and other conscientious objectors. These protections, however, were to prove complex and uncertain. The act itself divided these people into two categories. It had a Schedule of Exceptions, which referred to 'those persons exempted from Military Service by Order-in-Council of August 13, 1873 and by Order-in-Council of December 6, 1898.' Obviously this provision covered the Mennonites who had moved from Russia to Manitoba in the 1870s and the Doukhobors who arrived on the prairies two decades later. These, it would be said, had no duty to perform under the act, meaning neither combatant nor non-combatant service. All that individuals from these groups had to do, theoretically, was to satisfy the selection boards in their respective provinces that they in fact belonged to these groups.

Strangely, and probably unintentionally, the Mennonites of Ontario, who had been given a statutory promise of exemption in 1793, were not covered by the act's Schedule of Exceptions. They would have to cope with a complicated provision for exemptions within the act. This provision allowed exemptions on grounds of conscience and religion, alongside five other grounds such as illness, family hardship, and occupational demand, but all these required personal appearances before tribunals. For exemptions on grounds of conscience and religion, the tribunals were to consider: (a) whether the individual had a personal belief against combatant military service; and (b) whether he belonged to a religious denomination that prohibited such service. However, men so exempted could still be called up for non-combatant military service.

As these provisions were administered in the following fourteen months, enormous confusion resulted. Officials unintentionally gave inaccurate advice both to Mennonites in the west and to those in Ontario.

THE GROUPS IN THE WEST 'EXCEPTED' FROM THE ACT

Uncertainty about the 'Exceptions'
The orders-in-council of 13 August 1873 and 6 December 1898, issued respectively for Mennonites and Doukhobors immigrating from Russia to western Canada and referred to in the 'Schedule of Exceptions,' required a person seeking exemption to produce a certificate signed by the proper authorities of this church or community indicating that he belonged to that group. This procedure gave considerable power to those community leaders. As might have been expected, it raised questions about who the rightful leaders really were and whether they might misuse their authority.

These questions arose quickly among the Doukhobors who by this time were organized in two groups: the Christian Community of Universal Brotherhood (CCUB), whose 8000 people were commonly known as Community Doukhobors; and the Society of Independent Doukhobors, which had 4000 people. Peter V. Verigin was still the leader of the Community Doukhobors at this time and he did not recognize the Independents as Doukhobors. He felt that by leaving the Community and living like other Canadians they had forfeited their privileges. In a letter of early October 1917, addressed to the Hon. Charles J. Doherty, minister of Justice, Verigin explained the Doukhobor situation in the following way: 'One party is still following their previous principles. The principle is not to have firearms, not to eat meat, not to drink wine, not to smoke tobacco, not to belong to any empire in existence, and, therefore, this party carries the name "The Christian Community of Universal Brotherhood," in other words, these people belong to all empires, recognize all people as brothers, and therefore cannot be subject to any one empire.'[32]

Verigin said further that the Community Doukhobors had lost their land in Saskatchewan because they had refused to become British subjects. The 'other party,' he explained, 'accepted the home-steads and became British subjects and now they have firearms in their houses, and shoot wild animals, and fowl, also kill domestic stock and eat meat, drink whisky, smoke and chew tobacco and openly laugh at Doukhobors religion and therefore, the Government of Canada in such a serious question as military service should carefully distinguish between the two parties.' His opinion about what the government ought to do was clear. 'At the present time, I Peter Verigin, the representative of Doukhobor community, do not recognize the second party as Doukhobors and consider that these people must be liable to be conscripted for military service on the same basis as other citizens of Canada.'[33]

The government, however, was not persuaded. In a memorandum dated 18 October 1917, S. Mabor, superintendent of the Department of the Interior, stated that the Independent Doukhobors had become British subjects and had accepted the homesteads on the understanding 'explained to them repeatedly that the exemption in this case held, that they were exempted in good faith and that they could become British subjects and still be exempted from conscription.'[34] Mabor continued: 'In our opinion, the persons who are exempt under the Order-in-Council of 6th Dec. 1898, are those Communist Doukhobors or Independent Doukhobors or other Doukhobors who were members of the Doukhobor sect which migrated to Canada under the guarantee of exemption provided in the said Order-in-Council, and who still retain conscientious objection to military service.'

After this and with the exception of some brief episodes in the summer of 1918, the Doukhobors appear to have encountered few problems during the war. Leaders of both the Christian Community of Universal Brotherhood and the Society of Independent Doukhobors issued certificates to their young men. On the basis of these certificates, the authorities in both Saskatchewan and British Columbia recognized them as being 'excepted' from the act. Between 200 and 300 enlisted voluntarily, but 'there appears to have been no attempt to enforce military service.'[35]

The Mennonites in the west had other questions. After the act was passed, they asked A.L. Haining, the registrar for the Saskatchewan Military District, about what, if anything, they ought to do. Haining, seemingly unaware that they were 'excepted' from the act and needed only to show that they belonged to the group, advised them to register under the act and then to file claims for 'exemption.'[36] This meant that they would have to appear before the tribunals who would then decide whether to relieve any given individual from military service obligations.

Even though Haining's advice was later found to be erroneous, the Mennonites accepted it and publicized it in the October 1917 issue of *Der Mitarbeiter*, a Mennonite periodical in western Canada. Many young Mennonites then followed the procedure but soon there were difficulties. Young men who, though of Mennonite parents, had not yet been baptized and formally joined the church were not being recognized as Mennonites and hence not granted exemptions. After all, as noted above, the tribunals could exempt an individual on grounds of conscience only if he 'belonged' to a religious denomination that prohibited combatant service. Whether these young men really 'belonged' to the church for purposes of the law was a debatable point. Mennonite leaders claimed, however, that they had raised this concern in their meeting in Ottawa on 8 January 1917 and – even though it was not referred to in the written reply from Bennett – had been assured that their young men would also be recognized as Mennonites.

When these problems now appeared, Benjamin Ewert of Manitoba, who had been part of the January delegation, wrote to the prime minister.[37] Referring to that January meeting, he said: 'Your ministers also stated that by the term Mennonite they understood not only the persons who had actually joined the Mennonite Church but also the young people of Mennonite parentage, who may not have yet considered themselves mature enough to join that church.' Ewert continued: 'Our deputation brought this assurance back to our people and their hearts were filled with deep gratitude for the prospects of such liberal treatment by your government.' He then said that some of the local tribunals were not carrying out this policy: 'We may particularly name the one at Winnipeg. Some of our young people who share with us the same religious convictions, but have not yet joined the church – it being customary with us to receive them at the age of 18–24 – have had their exemption claim denied them and ordered to enter the service.' Ewert then asked that the local tribunals be instructed 'to deal with our people in conformity to the promise made to our deputation; i.e. that sons of Mennonite parents, who have not yet actually joined the Mennonite church, shall also be exempt from military service.' Strangely, neither Ewert nor any other wartime Mennonite leader referred to the 1810 Act, which specifically covered the situation of such young men.

Ewert's appeal seems to have resolved the problems in Manitoba, at least for a time. In one part of Alberta, too, the Mennonites were going to the tribunals with letters from their bishop and receiving exempt status without hesitation.[38] In the Swift Current area of Saskatchewan, the tribunal was also quite generous.[39] In other parts of Saskatchewan, however, there were various difficulties relating to the identification of eligible young men. As a result, the Mennonites decided to send another delegation to Ottawa.[40] This delegation met with Col. Machin, Col. Mess, and Mr Justice Duff on 12 April 1918. They raised the particular problem of young Mennonites who had not yet formally joined the church as well as the more general identification problems. They now proposed that every Mennonite of military age be required to have a certificate signed by an ordained Mennonite minister, stating that he is a Mennonite and exempt from all military service; that the certificate be countersigned by another Mennonite person, approved for this purpose by the government; and that all relevant authorities, including the police, be informed of the significance of the latter's signature.[41] The officials responded favourably. The Mennonite delegates understood them to say that 'the children of parents belonging to any communion must be considered as belonging to that communion until by their actions they show a contrary intention.'[42] The officials also, after some consideration, accepted the proposal for having each Mennonite carry a certificate, duly signed and countersigned.[43]

The immediate effect of this Ottawa meeting was positive. In Alberta, some Mennonites had been ordered to report for military duty but now the registrar there 'cancelled all orders to report for duty issued to Mennonites.'[44] In Saskatchewan, too, a different attitude appeared. In mid May 1918, Registrar Haining formally acknowledged that the advice that he had given in the fall of 1917 to the effect that the Mennonites should register and then apply to the tribunals for 'exemption' had been wrong.[45] To rectify the situation, he now stated: 'Whenever a man in whose file appears indication that he is a Mennonite, is about to be ordered to report for duty, the Order will not be sent until an Ordained Minister of the Mennonite Church has been communicated with.' This suggested that if a minister claimed that a given young man was a Mennonite then he would not be called up and hence would not have to go before a tribunal to seek an exemption. As such it gave effect to their 'excepted' status.

The improved conditions did not last, however. In June 1918, three young Mennonites in Manitoba who were ordered to report for military training were taken to an army barracks and held there.[46] Two were released when it was shown that they were church members. The third, Abraham Dyck, who was not yet a church member in the formal sense, was detained for a longer period. To deal with the problem, Mennonite leaders met with appropriate officials in Winnipeg and made an elaborate argument that a person born of Mennonite parents was raised in the atmosphere of the church and was accepted as belonging to the church community even though he had not yet formally become a member of the church through baptism: 'Our church considers its children and young people just as much their own as a baptized member and any protection that our church has sought and obtained against military service, is in all honesty considered as given to their young people or men of military age, irrespective of their being baptized or unbaptized. No assurance meaning less than that could ever have induced us to accept the invitation of the Canadian Government to come and settle in this country.'[47] After this appeal, Abraham Dyck was released and in Manitoba few subsequent problems appeared. The board there now seemed to recognize that the Mennonites were 'excepted' from the act.[48]

Restrictive Developments and Cancellations
While some difficulties were being resolved, others were to become more serious, particularly in Saskatchewan. There, in May 1918, Registrar Haining had indicated a willingness to acknowledge the authority of Mennonite ministers in determining whether a person would be recognized as a Mennonite. However, in June 1918 Mennonites reported that he 'began to question by what authority ministers of the Church became ministers so that they could sign such certificates. If they were ordained from whom did the persons so ordaining obtain the power to ordain? Who appointed the Bishops and presiding Elders, etc.? What right our ministers had to perform marriages and solemnize baptism; what church records were kept.'[49]

In response, Bishop David Toews, a prominent Saskatchewan leader, prepared an affidavit listing fifty-eight 'properly qualified and duly ordained ministers of the denomination of Christians called Mennonites' in fourteen districts of Saskatchewan.[50] He also complied when the authorities requested that they bring in their church records to show that they indeed 'were bona fide Mennonite organizations, and that records were kept by the Church including baptisms, marriages and births, and that these organizations had been in existence for some years.'[51] Toews found this somewhat demanding. He wrote: 'Up to that moment everyone seemed to know who was a Mennonite and who was a Mennonite Minister, Elder or Bishop,' and that 'such vexatious subtleties were not resorted to in the adjoining provinces of Alberta and Manitoba.'[52] Even though the officials of the government were demanding, they insisted that they did not want to 'break faith with the Mennonite community in the matter of military service' nor 'allow small technicalities to stand in the way of seeing that substantial justice is done.'

Moreover, David Toews acknowledged that 'in justice to the Military authorities we must say than when once satisfied as to the standing of the individual conscript among our boys, they have invariably discharged him. But the trouble and inconvenience caused us has been almost intolerable, our boys being in camp and compelled to do work for weeks and in many cases months which our people hold in the greatest abhorrence. Our main trouble, however, has continued to be with the civil authorities who through the Registrar have continued calling up our boys to report for duty.'[53]

The stricter interpretation of the laws is not entirely surprising. In spring 1918, the British and allied forces suffered serious set-backs on the battlefields of Europe. Also, in the October 1917 call-up, 95 per cent had asked for exemptions, usually on the ground that they were needed in their current employment.[54] In light of this and the need for additional soldiers, the government resorted to more drastic measures. On 19 April 1918 it passed an order-in-council, commonly known as the Manpower Bill, which, among other things, cancelled all exemptions for those in class one, that is, those 19–34 years of age, and resulted in the immediate call-up of those aged 19–23 years.[55] The call-up had a serious effect on Canadian farmers and others in need of workers, but such concerns were now to be set aside. Indeed, the tribunals were to be bypassed because 'time does not permit of examination by exemption tribunals of the value of civil life.' Despite the order's far-reaching implications, it specifically excluded the groups mentioned in the act's schedule of Exceptions. But the question of precisely who belonged to these would now be looked at more closely.

In addition to the increased need for soldiers, there was growing public concern about the privileged status of the Mennonites and Doukhobors. There were suspicions that the leaders of these groups were misusing their authority to sign the identification cards.[56] In at least one instance those suspicions were justified. Klaas Peters of Herbert, Saskatchewan, was signing certificates as if he was a Mennonite minister, when in fact he had joined a different church as early as 1902. Admittedly, he had retained strong connections with Mennonites and according to a police report: 'He has been the most prominent colonizer of Mennonites in Canada, having been sent out by the Government on many occasions to bring these people from "Europe and elsewhere" for colonization purposes.'[57] Some Mennonites had now used Peters, against the advice of Mennonite leaders, to intercede on their behalf before local military tribunals and also before officials in Ottawa.[58]

During the summer of 1918 the police investigated the situation. A prosecution followed and late in the fall, after the war ended, Peters was convicted.[59]

The Doukhobors were also faced with questions about the adequacy of the certificates and the authority of the leaders signing them. In July and August 1918 a number of draft-age Independent Doukhobors in Saskatchewan were arrested even though they had certificates signed by officials of the Society of Independent Doukhobors. The certificates were disregarded and, 'in a number of instances, were destroyed' by the police.[60] Some of the men were fined $10 to $50 and then released; others were detained and some were turned over to the military. At the town of Blaine Lake, this detention raised such concern that 'the whole community gathered at Blaine Lake and all their farm work was suspended during that time, despite the fact that the grain had already ripened and was ready for cutting.' The men were released soon after.

At one point the Doukhobors were requested by the police to produce 'certificates of membership signed by ordained ministers.' But Doukhobors had never had ordained ministers. At another point it was 'maintained by the Military Police, and apparently upheld by the trial of the Justice of the Peace, that the Order-in-Council, exempting Doukhobors from Military Service, is applicable only to Community Doukhobors, under the leadership of Peter Verigin.' The Independent Doukhobors then sent a telegram to the Hon. Arthur Meighen in Ottawa.[61] They also sent a delegation to Regina. Authorities quickly recognized that there was a 'misunderstanding on the part of the Military Police' and resolved the matter in favour of all Doukhobors.[62]

A further and more serious sign of increasing strictness appeared in the summer of 1918. Government officials now prescribed a declaration form stipulating that for a Mennonite to be 'excepted' he had to be 'a Mennonite and a member of the denomination of Christians aforesaid and that he is a descendant of one of those Mennonites who came to Canada from Russia subsequent to the order of the Governor-General in Council of 13th August 1873, pursuant to the arrangement thereby sanctioned.'[63] Of particular significance was the requirement that the words 'to Canada from Russia' meant direct travel. This was not a problem for those in Manitoba, or for the Reinlaender Mennonite groups in Saskatchewan, who had come from Russia in the 1870s. However, in Saskatchewan there were many more recent immigrants who could not meet this requirement. Some of these had come around the turn of the century from the United States, having migrated there from Russia in the 1870s. Others had come from Prussia directly.

Especially significant was the fact that the Government of Canada had encouraged these later migrations and had assured the people that in Canada they would be free from military service obligations. Klaas Peters had been asked by the government to carry this message to prospective Mennonite immigrants in Europe. A police report about him stated: 'Sometime about 1895 Klaas Peters was called to Winnipeg by the Government and the railroads and told to colonize Western Canada with these people "from Europe and elsewhere," assurance being given that the agreement of 1873 recognizing their aversion to military service still obtained.'[64] Peters testified to this fact personally and said that without this specific promise many would not have come.[65]

Similarly, David Toews, in a submission outlining the problems, stated: 'Immigration agents of the Canadian Government have gone among our co-religionists in European countries and have held out to them the "treaty" of 1873 as an inducement to emigrate to Canada.'[66] He also referred to the Mennonites who came to Canada from the United States prior to the passing of the Military Service Act of 1917 and said: 'In their cases too authorized representatives of the Canadian Government held out that "treaty" of 1873 to them as an inducement to change their place of abode and which was the only inducement that could have brought such large numbers.'

Canada's welcoming stance had continued into early 1918. By that time the United States was in the war and conscientious objectors there faced a most hostile public. Mennonites and Hutterites in the United States then began to look to Canada for refuge. When they inquired about liability for military service, W.D. Scott, the superintendent of Immigration, wrote (4 February 1918) that anyone who belonged to the Mennonite religious community was covered by the act's Schedule of Exceptions and that newly arriving immigrants would be outside the act also because it applied only to British subjects resident in Canada.[67] The Hutterites were informed at approximately the same time that the promise of exemption set forth in the order-in-council of 1899 would also be honoured.[68]

The possibility of an immigrant from the United States avoiding military service in Canada by virtue of not being a British subject was changed in July 1918 when an agreement was signed with the United States whereby a citizen of one country, who was subject to military service there, and who migrated to the other, would remain liable to such service although he would have sixty days to decide whether to serve in the forces of the country in which he was resident of in those of which he was a citizen.[69] This agreement removed a certain protection for those now leaving the United States. But on 20 August 1918 such people were given a partial protection with an order-in-council that made US citizens resident in Canada not only liable to military service in Canada but eligible also for whatever exemptions Canadian laws might offer.[70] Two months later, however, on 25 October this and other protections were severely curtailed. The government then passed an order-in-council that confirmed a very narrow interpretation of the 'exception' provision and, for all practical purposes, cancelled the 'exemption' provision. The order stated that 'Mennonites in Canada who did not immigrate, or are not descendants of those who did immigrate to Canada pursuant to the arrangement evidenced by the Order-in-Council of August 13, 1873, or, who having so immigrated, or being descendants of the latter, have not continued without interruption to be members of the sect or denomination of Christians called Mennonites, or to reside permanently in Canada, shall not be deemed to be exempted from Military service or within the 7th exception to the Military Service Act of 1917.'[71]

To David Toews, the prominent Mennonite leader in the west, these developments were most disappointing. Many of the people he represented would now be eligible for neither the 'exception' nor the 'exemption.' He had felt for some time that the authorities were trying to restrict the term 'Mennonite' to include only the most conservative ones. In his words: 'what was sought was to restrict the Mennonite church to include only those who had refused in secular affairs to associate themselves with the rest of the community, who refused to patronize the public schools, who refused to use any language other than German in their private schools, who refused to accept Lord Dufferin's invitation to take part in public affairs and help to mould the political future of the country.'[72]

In light of these severe restrictions, as a result of which 'scores' of young Mennonites had been called to report for military service, Toews now made an elaborate appeal to the federal cabinet. With the help of J.E. Doerr, a lawyer in Regina, he prepared a brief of 27 pages supplemented with 21 pages of exhibits.[73] In it, he reviewed the many efforts they had made to obtain protection from military service based on what the Mennonites had understood as government promises. He described the problems with the tribunals and noted that Arthur Meighen had said in the House of Commons: 'The honour of the nation is pledged to these people and they should not have to prove their cases before Tribunals.' He reported that some government officials had advised the Mennonites to seek a resolution of their problems in the courts but that they had refrained from doing so because such action might just aggravate public feeling and because 'our faith rested and continues to rest in the successors in office of those with whom our fathers entered into a solemn contract. It is unthinkable to us that they should violate this contract and we are quite sure that it only requires a thorough presentation of our case.'

Toews proposed that the government set up a commission to investigate the charges of fraud against the Mennonites and, if these were found to be false, that the government then pass legislation so as to make their position unmistakably clear. Specifically, he asked that it 'make the provisions of the Order-in-Council of August 13, 1873 applicable to all Mennonites who have arrived in Canada and whose home previous to that was in Europe, and the descendants of such, whether baptized or unbaptized, irrespective of whether they immigrated into Canada from the United States or from any country of Europe.' Such a ruling would clearly place nearly all Mennonites in the west under the Schedule of Exceptions. If the law could not be made clear in this way, then, he submitted, the government of Canada ought to give them ten years' notice so that they could settle their affairs and look for a different country in which to make their homes. Toews explained: 'Even barbarous Russia gave our fathers such notice as did also Germany and Holland centuries before.' This long brief was dated 4 November 1918. One week later the war came to an end so the government did not deal with it. Thus, the problems were lifted but the questions about the legal status of Mennonites in the west were not clearly answered.

Though the war was over, public antagonism against these groups continued to grow. There were public petitions, resolutions from citizen groups, and strong newspaper editorials. In Winnipeg the *Free Press* stated: 'We do not want in Canada anybody who is not prepared to become a citizen in the full meaning of the word ... People of "peculiar" religions living in colonies and clinging to an alien tongue and to racial habits are from every point of view undesirable ... If this country is not good enough to fight for, it is not good enough to live in.'[74] The *Calgary Eye-Opener* asked: 'Why do they want to impose such a bunch of cattle on us?' The *Globe* in Toronto noted: 'The agitation over the Mennonite invasion is not an isolated protest but the explosion of a feeling that has been developing for years.' One public speaker referred to the admission of Mennonites to the country as 'treason,' saying that Canada was being used 'as a dumping ground for these outlawed parasites from the

States.' Doukhobors, it was said, should be deported 'back to the country from whence they came' and their land should be made available to returning soldiers.[75]

Before long, federal authorities yielded to the pressure and brought in restrictive measures. On 1 May 1919, an order-in-council was passed stating that 'until further ordered, the entry into Canada of immigrants of the Doukhobor, Hutterite and Mennonite class is hereby prohibited.'[76] Fortunately, a few years later this ban was lifted.

PEOPLE IN ONTARIO 'EXEMPTED' FROM THE ACT

Because the Mennonites in Ontario were not covered by the orders-in-council of 1873 and 1898 listed in the Schedule of Exceptions of the Military Service Act, they had to cope with the act's provision for 'exemptions.' This required local tribunals to decide if it would be in the national interest for the applicant to (1) remain in the 'work in which he is habitually engaged'; (2) 'be engaged in other work in which he wishes to be engaged and for which he has special qualifications'; (3) 'continue to be educated or trained'; (4) 'remain where he is since serious hardship would follow upon his departure'; and (5) 'remain, for reasons of ill-health.' The sixth and last ground for an exemption was for conscientious objectors. The act allowed such an exemption on the following conditions: 'That he conscientiously objects to the undertaking of combatant service and is prohibited from so doing by the tenets and articles of faith, in effect on the sixth day of July, 1917, of any organized religious denomination existing and well recognized in Canada at such date, and to which he in good faith belongs.'[77]

The act provided further that a certificate of exemption 'may be conditional as to time or otherwise, and, if granted solely on conscientious grounds, shall state that such exemption is from combatant service only.' (Individuals from religious groups that were not recognized as having a prohibition against military service as one of their basic principles were not eligible for the exemption on conscientious grounds. This exclusion became a serious problem for some individuals. Approximately 130 men were imprisoned. Some were tortured. One died three weeks after being detained.)[78]

To the Mennonites of Ontario, the possibility that their young men might now be required to render non-combatant military service was of serious concern. They sent a delegation to Ottawa that met with Prime Minister Robert Borden and Solicitor-General Arthur Meighen on 11 October 1917. The delegation stated:

We have always maintained that any form of military service is opposed to the spirit and practice of good will to man, and hence our desire to follow only such activities and pursuits in civil life as are in keeping with the doctrine which we believe to be the laws of God and of Christ.

We recognize the good will of the Government in inserting in the Military Service Act a clause granting exemption to all adherents of religious denominations whose articles of faith forbid combatant service, and hereby express our thanks for this gracious consideration, while we also humbly petition that the exemption clause cited may always be so construed as to meet the requirements of the faith and practice of those whom the government has thus graciously favoured, in continuing to them those principles of liberty which have been the occasion of many thanksgivings to God and the constant joy of many humble citizens.[79]

After the meeting these Ontario Mennonite delegates prepared a report for their churches outlining their understanding of the discussions. It included four points:

1 All of our members who are in the age limit liable for military service, when called must apply for exemption according to Government regulations.
2 Physical examination before a medical Board is not required of those who apply for exemption for conscientious reasons.
3 None of our members are expected to vote under the present Election Act. Those who do so forfeit their right of exemption.
4 Non-combatant service will be dealt with later should circumstances require it.[80]

The Mennonite delegates sent a copy of this report to Meighen and he assured them, stating: 'Your understanding of our position as set forth in your letter is fairly correctly expressed.'

The Ontario Mennonites were grateful for this exchange but soon new questions arose. On 13 October 1917 the proclamation calling up men in class one was issued and it deemed these men 'to be soldiers in the military service of Canada save as the said Act otherwise provides.'[81] Also, on 18 October there were newspaper reports indicating that, according to regulations soon to be published, 'a tribunal is not to allow an application for exemption on conscientious grounds unless the applicant signifies in writing his willingness to perform when required non-combatant work or service including service in the army medical corps, the army service corps and mechanical transport.'

The Ontario Mennonites were disturbed about these developments so they prepared another petition (22 October 1917) for the prime minister.[82] They outlined in detail their concern about not being exempted from non-combatant military service, stating: 'In this respect the proclamation seems to us to contravene the articles of faith of our church and its members would thus be made to transgress its principles and practices which have been maintained during the centuries past.' They added: 'We cannot participate in war in any form; that is to aid or abet war whether in combatant or non-combatant capacity.' They also pointed out that their own religious position was identical to that of the Mennonites mentioned in the Schedule of Exceptions who were not liable for non-combatant military service. They reminded the prime minister that in the earlier meeting he had told them that no arrangements for calling them to non-combatant service would be made without first consulting them.

The Ontario Mennonite leaders urged the government to review the situation. They did not want their people to appear before the tribunals and be in a position of either receiving no exemption at all or else having to sign statements indicating a willingness to render non-combatant service. They concluded by assuring the government of their basic desire to respect the laws and the lawmakers, to avoid any 'act that may be construed as insubordination and disloyalty,' and to 'bear our part of the nation's burdens.'

This elaborate and strong appeal brought a most positive response, though it was later found to be erroneous. In a letter dated 3 November 1917, E.L. Newcombe, the deputy minister of Justice, stated: 'Under paragraph 7 of the Schedule of Exceptions to the above Act, Mennonites are excluded from the operation of the Act and have no duty to perform thereunder ... the matter has been thoroughly discussed by the Military Service Council and the opinion now is that if Mennonites should be prosecuted for non-compliance with the Act the answer to the prosecution would be that they are Mennonites and on the proof of that fact, undoubtedly prosecution would be dismissed.'[83]

This favourable position was also referred to in Tribunal Circular no. 11, issued on 5 November 1917 by the Military Service Branch of the Department of Justice. It described the order-in-council of 1873 as granting 'an entire exemption ... to the denomination of Christians called Mennonites,' without limiting it to those who had migrated from Russia to Manitoba in the 1870s.[84] This position was reaffirmed by E.L. Newcombe in a letter dated 6 November 1917. He now also suggested that the Mennonites had been disfranchised in the Wartime Elections

Act on the assumption that they would not be required to render military service.[85]

However favourable, some Ontario Mennonite leaders were not convinced that this positive interpretation, 'excepting' them from the act, would remain operative for long. L.J. Burkholder, moderator of the Mennonite Conference of Ontario, was of the opinion that 'it is a mistake and that the Minister of Justice has confused the issue with the position of the Manitoba Mennonites.'[86] Another Mennonite leader, J.L. Byler, who had, on his own initiative, written a long letter to the prime minister and who had received the same reply, wondered: 'After all my details as to Ontario conditions in the letter to Sir Robert Borden could such a mistake occur? ... While I think it seems too good to be true yet I cannot conceive of such a blunder being made on such a serious question.'[87]

S.F. Coffman, who was appointed by the Mennonites of Ontario to serve as their government correspondent, felt that it was not a mistake. He pointed out that the 1873 order-in-council, made to encourage the Mennonites of Russia to immigrate to Manitoba, was based on Militia Acts that had long exempted the Quakers, Mennonites, and Tunkers of Ontario. He also pointed to words found in the 25 September 1872 order-in-council: 'That the Constitution does not confer upon the Governor General any power to over-ride or set aside, under any circumstances, the plain meaning of statute law.'[88] He reasoned that if the order-in-council has the effect of 'excepting' the Mennonites of Manitoba from the act then surely the statute upon which the order-in-council was based, and which had been worked out for the Quakers, Mennonites, and Tunkers of Ontario years earlier, would have the same effect.

On the assumption that this interpretation was correct and would remain operative, the Mennonites prepared a letter of thanks, dated 20 November 1917. It was addressed to the prime minister and said: 'We cannot adequately express to yourself and to the Government what this interpretation of the regulations of the said Act means to us, nor can we tell you of the joy that it gave to our people, nor the thanksgivings to God which have ascended from hearts and homes and assemblies.' The Mennonites also indicated their desire 'to undertake voluntarily some share in the sacrifices of our fellow-citizens, and by some means, the plans of which are now under consideration, express in a more substantial manner our gratitude to the Government ... [and] our Christian sympathy toward our fellow-citizens and toward humanity.'[89]

This indication of willingness to serve on the part of the Ontario

Mennonites appears, like that of Mennonites in the west, to be a suggestion for an alternative-service program. Coffman favoured it. Among the things he suggested were 'care for disabled soldiers' and contributions for relief work in countries devastated by the war. He said: 'Our taxes are not sufficient as a share of the burden. Others are giving more and we should not give less.'[90] Some months later the Ontario Mennonites and Tunkers formed the Non-Resistant Relief Organization and supported a substantial amount of relief work in the war-ravaged countries.[91]

The letter of thanks of 20 November 1917, though carefully written, was not sent. Before it was ready for mailing, complications appeared in relation to the government's positive interpretation. Many young Mennonites were receiving calls to appear before the tribunals, meaning that instead of being 'excepted' from the Military Service Act, they would have to ask for 'exemptions' from the tribunals, and they might still be called up for non-combatant service. In appearing before the tribunals it soon became evident that they were more inclined to exempt the men on the basis that they were needed on farms than on grounds of conscience. Most Mennonites were farm people and were thus able to obtain exemptions, but they were concerned because this process failed to acknowledge their religious position. Early in November, J.L. Byler from Markham reported that he had asked a local tribunal official 'what they would do with any Mennonite that they deemed was not necessary for the production of food etc.' The official had replied 'that they would likely be called for Army Transport work, etc.'[92] This possibility of non-combatant military service was of concern to the Ontario Mennonites.

Also worrisome were the variations among the tribunals. The tribunal in London continued to hold that Mennonites were 'excepted.'[93] Others granted exemptions but only to church members and not to those young men who, though of Mennonite parents, had not yet, at the time of the hearing, formally joined the church. Some held that to qualify it was necessary for the men to have been church members before 6 July 1917, a date that the act used for other purposes. Still others exempted the men from combatant service but wanted them to sign a statement saying that they were willing to render a non-combatant service, though most Mennonites, it appears, refused to sign such statements, choosing instead to appeal their cases to higher tribunals. Still other tribunals granted exemptions on religious grounds with little hesitation.[94]

In light of these variations and the consequent uncertainties, S.F.

Coffman wrote, on 21 November 1917, that 'there must be a mistake ... since the statement from the Department of Justice clearly says that Mennonites are excluded from the operation of the Military Service Act and have no duty to perform thereunder.'[95] He encouraged all 'young brethren who are not entirely exempted on account of their belonging to the Mennonite church to appeal at once to the next higher tribunal.' He believed this approach to be in keeping with advice received from the Department of Justice.[96] He continued: 'If the Central Appeal Tribunal gives a different verdict ... then it will be necessary for us to appeal to the Government or even to the Crown for a ratification of the privileges which we have heretofore enjoyed.'[97]

This strategy of appealing to higher levels had also been encouraged by W.G. Weichel, a member of Parliament for the Waterloo area. On 8 November 1917 Weichel reported that Arthur Meighen, after hearing of the problems, 'told me that if the Tribunals refuse exemption to your young men who have not as yet been taken into the Mennonite Church as active members, then they should just take the appeal ... I can assure you that from what I can gather from Mr. Meighen that you will not have cause for worry, as the situation is thoroughly understood at Ottawa.'[98]

To this end, Coffman, on 7 December 1917, wrote letters to both the minister of Justice and the central appeal judge:

There has not been a uniform consideration of the said claims for total exemption from all military service, which privilege they have had just reasons to claim as a result of the appeal made by a Committee of our Church to the Government and the decision rendered there upon by the Military Service Council ...

We have taken the liberty of advising our members not totally exempted or who have been exempted for other than religious reasons, to appeal from the decisions from the Local Tribunals, this advice being based on the above mentioned decisions of the Military Service Council.

We trust that these appeals may be granted the same favourable and uniform consideration as has been granted us by the Military Service Council, for which our people have been sincerely grateful.[99]

Coffman also described the Mennonite problems to the district registrar in London, Ontario. In a letter dated 29 January 1918, he reviewed their negotiations with Ottawa and noted especially the promise received on 3 November 1917 that they had no duty to perform under the Military Service Act.[100] He then pointed out that 'the majority of the local tribunals have not taken into consideration the fact that Mennonites are totally exempted and have granted only ... exemption from combatant service.' He concluded: 'Because there has not been a uniform decision on the part of the local tribunals, and because some of the decisions are not clear in stating the extent of exemption granted, and in order to avoid having the names of our brethren placed on the lists as eligible for non-combatant service and considered 'soldiers on leave of absence' which would be in contravention of their principles of faith, we have advised them to appeal to the higher tribunals for total exemption so that they may secure a uniform and complete exemption and be freed from all military obligation.'

While Coffman was making these appeals there were more indications that the promise of a complete exemption, as provided for those 'excepted' from the act, might not be fulfilled. On 2 February 1918, Glyn Osler, registrar for Ontario, replied to one inquiry stating: 'Men exempted on religious grounds are not, as you seem to think entirely exempt from performing any duties under the Act. According to Appendix 4 of the Instructions to Tribunals, the decision in the case of a man exempted for religious belief will read as follows: Exempted from Combatant Service on account of religious belief.'[101] Still, around this same time, a Mennonite minister reporting on one hearing said: 'The judge spoke kindly and firmly, told us he could not grant our desire, but, urged us to appeal at central judge or court, and told us how to do it, and said repeatedly he thinks it will come out all right there.'[102]

Some weeks later, on 27 March 1918, a delegation from the newly formed Non-Resistant Relief Organization met with officials in Ottawa. The main purpose of the meeting was to make arrangements so that monies, which the Ontario Mennonites were in the process of collecting, could be turned over to the government and 'used for relief and charitable purposes only.'[103] During the meeting, however, the delegates also discussed the difficulties regarding exemption from military service. The pointed out that their religious position was not being recognized by the law, that 'no provisions were made under the Exemptions Regulations for correctly stating our faith and the grounds of our claims as opposed to all forms of Military Service, whether combatant or non-combatant.'[104] The delegates described the way the tribunals were dealing with their claims and said that their appeals were not successful. In conclusion they said: 'We could not believe that the Canadian Government had annulled in any degree those religious liberties and immunities which our forefathers enjoyed.'

In response, the two federal representatives present, the Hon. J.A. Calder, minister of Immigration and Colonization, and F.S. Scott, member of Parliament for South Waterloo, gave the delegates 'the fullest assurance' that their concerns would not be disregarded and that 'complete exemption from Military Service would be allowed.'[105] No doubt Calder and Scott hoped this would be true. The reality, however, would be different.

Exemptions Restricted and Cancelled

After March 1918 the problem was not so much with uncertainties as with clear restrictions and cancellations. The order-in-council of 19 April 1918 cancelled all 'exemptions' for men in class one, that is, those 19–34 years of age and without family responsibilities; it placed these under military law, ordered them to register within ten days, and called up those aged 19–23 years for immediate service, bypassing the tribunals. One of the purposes of this so-called Manpower Bill was to recruit the many young men who had earlier been exempted for farm reasons. But those exempted for reasons of conscience were affected in the same way. Accordingly, S.F. Coffman quickly appealed to Calder and Scott. In a letter (22 April) to Calder he asked: 'What application will be made of the provisions for Mennonites as stated in the Man-power Bill? Will it apply to all Mennonites as well as to those other established Churches – Quakers and Tunkers – whose faith was recognized and provided for by the laws of Canada?'[106] He stated further: 'Under the War-Times Elections Act, provisions were made that sons of such persons as were disenfranchised as Conscientious Objectors, who had not attained their majority, were not to be called into service. Will the present Man-Power Bill cancel the provisions of the War-Times Elections Act?' In the letter to Scott, Coffman wrote: 'We do not wish to place ourselves on the list of Excepted classes if it is not the purpose of the Government to class us as such, yet we feel that, owing to our tenets of faith and practices of our Christian principles we belong to such excepted classes.'[107]

In light of the very difficult situation in which this order-in-council placed the Ontario Mennonites, S.F. Coffman concluded that they should simply claim to be under the Schedule of Exceptions of the Military Service Act. Those so 'excepted' were excluded also from this order. Coffman now argued that because 'the name Mennonite is stated in the Order, I believe that we should avail ourselves of the privilege of claiming the exclusion as belonging to all Mennonites.'[108] He had some misgivings about this approach, suspecting that it 'may lead to a definite test,' but he advised the ministers in the churches that the young men should not even register, saying, 'Any of our brethren called to register or report for service should claim to be under the Exception which the Military Service Council decided applied to all Mennonites.'[109]

There were some indications that this might be the right approach. N.W. Rowell, president of the Privy Council, wrote: 'The Mennonites are excluded from the new Act and from all military service,' and 'have no duty to perform and are altogether excluded from the operation of the Military Service Act and also from the new Manpower Bill just passed.'[110] Rowell had raised the matter with Colonel Machin, head of the Military Service Council, who had replied: 'Mennonites are undoubtedly excepted from the Act and have no duty to perform in connection therewith.'[111]

There were other indications, however, that this claim to being in the 'excepted' category was no more acceptable now than it had been earlier. Accordingly, Coffman made a lengthy appeal to Calder. In a letter dated 4 May 1918, Coffman attempted especially to have the government understand and recognize the Mennonite's religious position.[112] He said that they were not trying to avoid danger or hardship or to stay at home for the purpose of economic and material gain. Yet in appearing before the tribunals, he reported, their people had been 'shamefully abused and needlessly exposed to the heartless badgering of some officials who did not know and could not appreciate the faith of our people.' In reality, he said: 'The motive of our appeals for freedom from military service has been to be free to fulfill our obligations of loyalty to God ... We desire to continue the testimony of those who have lived according to these principles and have kept these tenets of faith in the history of the Church.'

Coffman pointed to the problems regarding Mennonite legal status, noting the differences between the situation of the western Mennonites whom the law 'excepted' from all duties on the basis of the 1873 order-in-council, and the situation of the Ontario Mennonites whom the law 'exempted' from combatant service only, even though the latter had been in Canada much longer. There are, he said, 'two laws for the same class of people, and the Statutes are set aside for citizens of long residence and recognized principles, in favor of Orders-in-Council.' He asked whether the Military Service Act and especially the recent so-called Manpower Bill 'have superceeded [sic] the Statutes of Canada which provided freedom from Military Service.' He concluded that 'if such is the case, we trust that some measures may be taken by the Government that will restore and permanently safeguard lawful religious beliefs ... We hope that there may be affixed to the one-hundred years record of liberty for the non-resistant faith the seal of the Government which will perpetuate such liberties forever. If it is lawful to believe the teachings and follow the example of Christ, we pray that it may be permitted us. In full accord with the liberality of the Government toward our people we hope that immediate steps may be taken to prevent any of our brethren from being molested ... under present regulations.'

While making this elaborate appeal, Coffman continued to advise young Mennonite men not to register.[113] The legality of this action was questionable because the order-in-council of 19 April 1918 had prescribed that those in class one and 'not within one of the exceptions in the Schedule to the Act' should report to a registrar's office within ten days. They would then until 'placed on active service be deemed to be on leave of absence without pay.'[114] F.S. Scott, the member of Parliament, appears to have supported Coffman, at least for a time, in advising his people not to register.[115]

At the same time Calder, Scott, and Weichel were exploring a different avenue. They discussed with military authorities the possibility of bypassing the Department of Justice and the tribunals. In mid May, Scott and Weichel had a meeting with the Militia Council. Scott reported on this meeting in a letter to Coffman: 'The Minister of Militia was present and after discussing the whole situation thoroughly, it was arranged that we should secure from your Church the names of Bishops or someone in authority who could issue certificates of membership in your Church. The Officer Commanding the Military District will then be authorized to accept these certificates and allow the men off on leave.'[116]

Requiring men to register in accordance with the 19 April order-in-council and then letting them go on 'leave' was unusual, but that same order-in-council had stipulated, as a way of compensating for bypassing the tribunals, that the minister could grant 'leaves' to people in special circumstances. In the case of the Mennonites, the military authorities had been persuaded to take the view 'that these men would be of little use to them under any circumstances holding the belief which they did and that it was better to leave them at their present occupations.'[117] The arrangement helped many young Mennonites in the remaining months of the war.

It was not, however, a happy solution. The Mennonites were not comfortable with registering as if to serve in the military.[118] They did so trusting that the general officers commanding would, in their discretion, give them 'leave.' In one report to the churches Coffman stated: 'While registering implies an application for service and a leave of absence is a soldier's permit to be absent, the arrangement is the best that the Government is able to make for us under the present military law.'[119] At first the arrangement was restricted to draftees who had formally joined the church by 6 July 1917. When church leaders objected, the arrangement was broadened to include anyone who 'was, prior to July 6, 1917, a regular attendant at the Church, and a bona fide adherent and has since actually joined the Church.' This requirement may have prompted some young men to quickly seek formal church membership.

Even though the Ontario Mennonites and Tunkers now had a way out of military service, thanks to the discretion of military officials, questions about their status under the law, that is the Military Service Act, were not yet fully answered. In an effort to seek clarity, a member of Parliament, W.D. Euler, wrote to the minister of Justice on 29 May 1918:

Legal Officers of the Department of Militia have given opposing views of the matter. One officer, Col. Biggar, holding that the Ontario Mennonites do not come under the Order-in-Council, which places the Mennonites and Doukhobors outside the scope of the Act altogether, while Col. Machin is of the opinion that all Mennonites etc., no matter where found, are included under the Order-in-Council. If the second view is correct they would not be required to register, I presume, but would prove themselves outside the operation of the Act by exhibiting certificates of membership from the heads of the church.

May I suggest that there seems to be no good reason why any distinction should be made among the various classes of Mennonites and other bona fide conscientious objectors ... I would suggest that the Government remove all uncertainty by an amending Order-in-Council which would place *all* Mennonites and other objecting sects outside the operation of the Act. Thus the possession of a membership certificate in said churches, signed by a Bishop or other ecclesiastical head, would be all the protection necessary.[120]

In June 1918 this legal question was clarified. The central appeal judge ruled that 'Tunkers and Ontario Mennonites are not excepted from the Military Service act.'[121] This is not what the Mennonites had hoped but neither was it a surprise. It meant that they had to cope with the provision for 'exemptions,' and because the possibility of obtaining 'exemptions' had been cancelled for a certain age category by the order-in-council of 19 April, those so affected now had no other recourse than to follow the uncomfortable procedure of registering and then relying on the mercy of the military authorities to give them 'leave.'

Though extremely helpful, this procedure was not without problems. Some officials questioned the authority of the ministers and bishops who signed the certificates, as well as the eligibility of young men who had only recently become church members. As a result of these questions a number of young men were temporarily detained in military camps.[122] The Ontario registrar suggested to S.F. Coffman that the Mennonites and Tunkers consider 'a compromise on the subject of non-combatant service with Hospital Corps or other non-combatant units.' He said: 'You should find some better use for your young men than having them sent to prison.'[123] Despite these difficulties, the special arrangement, supported by senior militia officials, continued to function.[124]

On 25 October 1918, two weeks before the war ended, the government passed a most restrictive order-in-council. It not only reaffirmed that Ontario Mennonites were not 'excepted' from the Military Service Act, but stated that they were not eligible for the 'exemptions' under the act either.[125] Fortunately for these Mennonites, the special arrangement whereby they registered with the military authorities who then gave them 'leaves' continued to operate and was not affected by this change in the law.

Obviously this encounter with military service exemptions was marked by many difficulties. What had begun as a broad liberty ended up very narrow, at least in the legal sense. Still, it appears that few young men from these groups were forced into military service, though some were held at military camps before their eligibility for exemption was established.

The legal narrowing occurred in both the west and Ontario. In the west, the Mennonites who had immigrated from the United States and Europe around the turn of the century on the basis of assurances that the order-in-council of 1873 covered them were told, near the end of the war, that it did not cover them. Thus, they were left only with the 'exemption' provision with which the Ontario Mennonites were wrestling. The latter, whose assurances of exemption dated back to the 1790s, found, to their consternation, that under the Military Service Act of 1917 they were liable for non-combatant service. Moreover, their eligibility for this 'incomplete exemption' was cancelled, first for a certain age category in April 1918, and then comprehensively in October. Fortunately this period was so near the end of the war that it had little practical effect.

One reason for the narrowing of this liberty relates to the social pressures aroused by the war. Canada, with a population of under 8 million, provided nearly 750,000 military service personnel of whom 66,695 died and 138,000 were wounded (see chapter 5). The Canadian people will have felt their involvement and sacrifice keenly. Moreover, the whole British-oriented way of life seemed to be at stake and military leaders were urgently calling for more soldiers. In light of this, it is not surprising that the Canadian public became critical of those who did not manifest a British orientation and who stayed home and appeared to benefit from the wartime economy. Moreover, Mennonites spoke German, the language of the enemy, and the conservative Mennonites refused public schools. Also, during the First World War, there was no alternative national-service program in which people from these kinds of groups could demonstrate that they, too, were willing to serve. Whether they would have participated in such a program if there had been one cannot be taken for granted, though they did give substantial sums for relief work, purchased a considerable sum of government bonds, and indicated a willingness to do more.

A second reason for the problems in obtaining the desired exemption relates to the complex structure of the law and its confused administration. The law itself unintentionally divided the people into two categories. Those 'excepted' from the Military Service Act were liable for neither combatant nor non-combatant service, but those who had to cope with the 'exemption' provision within the act could be lawfully called up for non-combatant service. A number of senior officials did not understand this duality in the law so they gave legally inaccurate directives, telling Mennonites in Ontario that they were 'excepted' from the act and those in the west that they should apply to the tribunals for 'exemptions' under the act. Both directives were eventually found to be wrong, but in the meantime there was much confusion. The local tribunals also differed in their interpretation of the law.

On the question of what it meant to 'belong' to one of these religious groups for the purposes of the law, which was vital for people in both legal categories, there was much uncertainty, too. Did 'belonging' mean formal church membership and, if so, did it have to be before a certain date? Or could it also include young men who had regularly attended church but who had not yet reached the age when it was customary to formally join? There were also questions about the leaders who certified that the young men 'belonged.' Were these leaders duly authorized? Were they misusing their power? Clearly, the question-filled structure of the law made it vulnerable to pressures and different interpretations.

All these factors could have quashed this liberty but they did not do so. Why not? One reason lies in the flexibility of the system, illustrated most vividly in Ontario after April 1918. It was clear then that the Mennonites there were not 'excepted' from the act and that the 'exemptions' for a certain age group were cancelled. Several parliamentarians, particularly J.A. Calder and F.S. Scott, then bypassed the Department of Justice, approached the military authorities, and persuaded them to give 'leaves of absence' to those who, after being sent into the military, would present a certificate indicating that they belonged to the Mennonite church. The fact that this arrangement worked reflects a remarkable flexibility, particularly on the part of the authorities but also on the part of the Mennonites.

In addition, there were certain favourable elements in the political culture. Despite all the problems, the hostile voices in the west at the end of the war, and the harsh treatment of conscientious objectors from other church groups, there were sympathetic elements, too. These were evident at the Cabinet level in Borden, Meighen, and Calder, in several members of Parliament such as F.S. Scott, W.D. Euler, and W.G. Weichel, and in officials such as R.B. Bennett and E.L. Newcombe. This sympathy may have been prompted by the character of these groups or perhaps by the principle of conscientious objection, which had a long history also in Britain. In several instances, the sympathy seems to be related to the importance of honouring historic promises. Borden and Meighen said as much. The military authorities seem to have responded to the argument that people from these particular groups would not make good soldiers anyway. Though the reasons varied, all these factors combined to create a sympathetic effect.

The persistence and good faith of the Mennonites also helped. They did not simply protest. They did not want to defy the government. They wanted solutions that would be acceptable to both sides. Their attitude toward government is reflected in the words of Bishop David Toews: 'Our faith rested and continues to rest in the successors in office of those with whom our fathers entered into a solemn contract. It is unthinkable to us that they should violate this contract and we are quite sure that it only requires a thorough presentation of our case.'[126] These attitudes on the part of the Mennonites, the flexibility in the political system, and the elements of sympathy in the culture help to explain why this particular liberty received a measure of respect, even in a time of severe stress.

9 Exemptions in the Second World War

ASSURANCES OF EXEMPTION, THE CONSCRIPTION LAW, AND
NATIONAL REGISTRATION

The situation in the Second World War was different from that in the First World War. The Hutterites were now established in Canada although their total population was still only about 5000. The Mennonite numbers, augmented by 21,000 immigrants from Russia in the 1920s, were approximately 106,000. And nearly 17,000 Canadians identified themselves as Doukhobors.[1] In addition to being larger, the groups were now more diverse in their attitudes and social structures and also more dispersed geographically. Still, a substantial majority of their people sought and obtained exemption from military service, albeit under problem-filled procedures. Approximately 7500 of those exempted participated in a civilian alternative-service program. This program was begun at the initiative of Mennonite leaders but most Doukhobors, seeing it as a compromise, opposed it.

The beginning of the Second World War encounter must be traced to certain early efforts by these groups to obtain assurances of their exempt status. One question of concern to Mennonites was whether the restrictive order-in-council of 25 October 1918 was permanently binding. They were quickly assured that it was not, because it had been made under the authority of the War Measures Act, which itself was no longer in force.[2] A second and more complex question involved the status of the Mennonites who had come from Russia in the 1920s.[3] Did the exemption promised in the order-in-council of 1873 cover them, too? In 1924 the acting deputy minister of Justice, W. Stuart Edwards, answered this question by stating that that promise 'should legally be held not to apply to persons of the Mennonite class who may now be seeking entry to Canada from southern Russia.'[4] He argued: 'More than half a century has elapsed and conditions have changed so much that I do not think it could reasonably be held that the Government is now inviting immigrations upon the terms then stipulated.' In his view the 1873 order-in-council still had 'legal effect to grant immunity from military service ... to Mennonites who belong to or are descended from the immigration of 1873.' Later immigrants, he said, would be covered by the section in the existing Militia Act that exempted 'persons who from the doctrines of their religion are averse to bearing arms or rendering personal military service.' This statement was reassuring but there was concern that the 'Russlaender,' as the newly arriving Mennonite immigrants were known, would be treated differently from the 'Kanadier,' as the Mennonites of the earlier migration from Russia were known.

In 1936 F.C. Blair, the assistant deputy minister for Immigration, responded to a further request for clarification by stating that 'all exemption from military service that now exists or has existed ... is by Statute not by Order-in-Council,' that the governor-in-council cannot 'grant exemption to persons who are not entitled to it by Statute,' that the order-in-council of 1873 merely confirmed that the Mennonites then immigrating came within the statutory provisions, and that the provisions in the existing statute, as quoted above, covered all current concerns.[5] This response was reassuring, too, but it raised the question of whether the 1873 order-in-council had any significance at all. That question, however, was not pursued at this time. Hutterites and Doukhobors, it was said, would also have to base their claim to exemption on the statutory provisions, meaning the Militia Act, not on the earlier orders-in-council.[6]

While these groups were seeking assurance of exemption from military service, Hitler's armies were advancing in Europe. As a result, Britain, on 3 September 1939, declared war. Canada followed suit on 9 September but conscription was not imposed until almost one year later. In June 1940, after France had fallen and Britain was threatened, Mackenzie King wrote in his diary: 'I see wherein now there is a real possibility of invasion of our shores, an effort will be made to seize this country as a prize of war.'[7] Soon after, on 18 June, the government introduced the National Resources Mobilization Act (NRMA). It was passed three days later and authorized the government to take almost any action it 'deemed necessary or expedient for securing the public safety, the defence of Canada, the maintenance of public order, or the efficient prosecution of the war, or for maintaining supplies or services essential to the life of the community.'

Significantly, the NRMA did not authorize conscription for service overseas, only for 'home defence'.[8] But this would create a large pool of trained soldiers who could then be encouraged, in various ways, to volunteer for overseas service. By not forcing overseas service Mackenzie King hoped to avoid the national division that had been aroused in the First World War. Mackenzie King also had words of reassurance for the religious groups who had communicated with him in recent weeks regarding exemption concerns.[9] He now said: 'The government has no desire and no intention to disturb the existing rights to exemption from bearing arms which are enjoyed by members of certain religious groups in Canada as for example the Mennonites. We are determined to respect these rights to the full.'[10]

This assurance of exemption did not, however, apply to the national registration scheduled for 19–21 August 1940. The registration was to provide the government with information regarding people's occupational skills, physical condition, educational background, language facility, domestic responsibilities, and other factors, so that it could conscript the appropriate ones. But the Mennonites, Hutterites, and Doukhobors feared that if they participated in the registration then they might later be conscripted. As a result, they sought more assurances. The Hutterites were quickly satisfied, following an exchange in July 1940.[11] The Mennonites in the west, under the leadership of David Toews, proposed that the word 'Mennonite' be written onto their registration cards, following the practice in the First World War.[12] The cards did not ask for a person's religious affiliation but Toews felt that this would make it easier for the officials to identify the Mennonites. James Gardiner, the minister responsible for the newly created Department of National War Services, supported the idea and agreed to advise the registrars accordingly. However, when the registration took place many registrars did not write the word 'Mennonite' onto the cards and, indeed, refused to permit Mennonite registrants to write the word onto the cards themselves. Later an official conceded: 'It may be that in the hurry of events here that we overlooked instructing the Registrars.'[13] It was an unfortunate oversight. The National War Services Regulations, announced on 27 August 1940, referred, among other things, to 'persons whose registration cards disclose that they represent themselves to be ... Mennonites.'[14] Later in the war, when there was so much difficulty obtaining military exemption, David Toews saw this oversight in the registration process as part of the problem.[15]

The Mennonites in Ontario were more successful. In the summer of 1940 they were forming the Conference of Historic Peace Churches (CHPC), together with the Friends (Quakers), Brethren in Christ (Tunkers), and other groups.[16] They co-operated with the government's registration program but after consulting the authorities they also did a registration of their own using CHPC registration cards.[17] This process helped them later in obtaining exemption from military service. Unlike many of the Mennonites in the west, members of the Ontario groups would not have to appear individually before the boards to testify about their personal 'conscientious objections.'

The Doukhobors were no less concerned about military exemption and about the implications of the registration process. Already in September 1939, Doukhobors in Saskatchewan had set up 'a joint committee ... for the purpose of assuring the Doukhobor people the protection against military service afforded them by law.'[18] This joint committee, representing the Independent Doukhobors and a more orthodox group known as Named Doukhobors, now sent a delegation to Ottawa for the purpose 'of arranging with the government, as we did in the last war, to handle our own registration in the forthcoming registration of man power in Canada for war purposes.'[19] British Columbia Doukhobors were invited to join the delegation but they 'could not settle their differences' sufficiently.[20]

The delegation consisted of only two people, P.G. Makaroff and Wasyl Novokshonoff. The first meeting in Ottawa took place on 4 July 1940 with the minister, James Gardiner, and senior officials of the National War Services Department. These, however, showed little interest in an arrangement whereby the Doukhobors would opt out of the government's registration system and set up their own. But the Doukhobor delegates, instead of accepting a negative response, made another appeal, this time in writing.[21] They repeated their desire to register their own people and stated that they wanted to do so in a manner acceptable to the government. They explained that if the government insisted on registering the Doukhobors, then the fears of their people about conscription would increase and many might then withhold all co-operation. As Doukhobor leaders, they said, they wanted to spare the government such troubles. They also said that in the First World War many of their people would certainly have refused to comply if a separate registration arrangement had not been allowed. But such arrangements had been made and as a result 'the best of relationship was preserved between the government and our people throughout the course of the war.' They indicated that even though they represented only the Doukhobors of Saskatchewan, they felt confident that any system that they would be able to negotiate would be acceptable to Doukhobors elsewhere, too.

The government still feared that if deviations were allowed, they might lead to chaos. It tried again to reassure the Doukhobors that their participation in the government's registration process would not commit them to military service.[22] However, after another submission from the Doukhobors, the deputy minister, T.C. Davis, and the minister agreed to a 'simple system ... whereby the Doukhobors would make their own registration, or, in other words, fitting their own registration into our system.'[23] The Doukhobors then set up their own system and registered over 11,000 individuals.[24]

Though relatively successful, some Doukhobors did not want to co-operate even with their own registration. A Doukhobor leader in Saskatchewan then received a telegram from T.C. Davis explaining that the information was needed because 'if your people in future ask to perform useful services not connected with war and independent of military control then we would need the list of persons to be asked to render such service. We would only ask those in same classes as other citizens who are rendering military service.'[25] This satisfied the Saskatchewan Doukhobors but many in British Columbia remained hesitant.[26] But when officials emphasized again that the registration 'had no connection whatsoever with military service of any kind,' many Doukhobors 'were more or less reluctantly prevailed upon to register.' However, the Sons of Freedom, numbering about 2000, refused to register even then.[27] According to an RCMP report, these people 'agitated among the other Douk groups,' claiming that 'the government could not be trusted, that registration was for military purposes.'

The authorities then prosecuted some of the Sons of Freedom Doukhobors. On 7 September 1940 'four men were sentenced to three months in jail for failing to register.' However, 'provincial police had to use tear gas to disperse the ensuing demonstration.'[28] For some time after this the government acted with restraint. Instead of prosecuting them it used 'economic pressure in a general way' by refusing licences for cars and ration books for sugar to those who had not registered. It appears that the Sons of Freedom accepted this pressure quietly, perhaps as a reasonable price for not registering.[29]

Not all Mennonites co-operated with the registration either. Several families near Waldheim, Saskatchewan, refused. As a result, fourteen people were jailed; when they were released and still refused to register they were jailed again. Their argument was that national registration would identify them with war. Interestingly, they also attempted to pay the government for the food they were given in jail and for the costs incurred in their arrests. They said: 'We have never taken anything from our dear Government for which we did not pay. No relief, no land, nothing – the Bible says we shall work with our own hands and earn our own bread.'[30]

Despite these instances of opposition, most people in these groups co-operated with the national registration effort, albeit on the basis of modifications and special arrangements.

MILITARY EXEMPTION REGULATIONS AND NEGOTIATIONS
FOR ALTERNATIVE SERVICE

After the national registration, officials prepared for calling the men to report for military training. The National war Services Regulations, published on 27 August 1940, organized the country into thirteen administrative divisions, most of which coincided with provincial boundaries.[31] Each division would have a National War Services Board that would judge all claims to exemption, referred to in the regulations as 'indefinite postponement of military training.' Each division would also have a registrar to issue orders to the men in accordance with the directives of the boards.

Significantly, the regulations for exemption were similar to the First World War provisions in that there were two categories. The first referred to Mennonites and Doukhobors; the second to conscientious objectors. Eligibility in the first category was limited to those who had immigrated to Canada pursuant to the orders-in-council of 1873 and 1898 and their descendants, if they had 'continued without interruption to be members' of the denomination of Mennonites or the community of Doukhobors and had 'resided without interruption in Canada.' This category was broad enough to cover all Doukhobors; however, for Mennonites it covered only those who had come from Russia in the 1870s (sometimes called Kanadier), not those who had come from Russia in the 1920s (sometimes called Russlaender) or those who had come from Pennsylvania, most of whom now lived in Ontario. Those not covered by the orders-in-council would have to seek exemption under the second category: conscientious objectors. Strangely, the Hutterites were not referred to in the first category either. The order-in-council issued for them in 1899 had been forgotten. The deputy minister of Justice, while preparing the regulations, had stated: 'I am not aware of any special immigration arrangements having been made with the Hutterites.'[32] As a result, the Hutterites would also come under the second category.

This conscientious-objector category, as defined by the regulations, had more than a 'membership criterion.' It also had a 'personal belief' criterion. It provided that a person could be exempted if he 'conscientiously objects to the bearing of arms or the undertaking of combatant service and is prohibited from [doing so] ... by the tenets and articles of faith in effect on the first day of September 1939, of any organized religious denomination' to which he belongs. Four months later, in December 1940, this statement was changed so that, although a person still had to belong to a religious denomination, it was no longer required that that denomination prohibit military service.[33] This broader definition, requested particularly by pacifists from the United Church, opened the way for people from other churches. Mennonite leaders had also encouraged it. A further broadening came later. An order-in-council of 22 April 1942 stated simply: 'Any man who claims that he conscientiously objects to bearing arms or to undertaking combatant service may ... apply.'[34] In other words, anyone could seek conscientious-objector status regardless of whether he belonged to a religious denomination.

Although the 27 August 1940 regulations provided two military exemption categories, they also stipulated that people exempted in either category could be compelled to render a non-combatant service under military or civilian auspices. This touched an issue that was divisive among Mennonites. Those Mennonites who had left Russia in the 1870s, meaning the Kanadier, had always felt somewhat critical of those who had stayed, meaning the Russlaender, many of whom had come to Canada in the 1920s, for accepting an alternative national service in Russia. Starting early in the 1880s the young Mennonite men in Russia had done forestry work and during the First World War they had had a special medical corps on Russia's front lines. The Mennonites there had formed 'complete hospital units, including stretcher bearers who gathered the wounded on the battlefield, complete hospital trains transporting them back to hospitals at Ekaterinoslav and Moscow, also fully manned by Mennonites.' About 8000 Mennonites had served in the medical corps while 4000 had continued in forestry work. Some 120 of those in the medical corps had lost their lives in the war. And, as with the forestry work, almost the entire cost was met by the Mennonite communities.[35]

Despite this impressive Russlaender record, many Mennonites in Canada saw such forms of service as too closely linked to the military. This difference in views was of concern to leaders such as David Toews of Saskatchewan. Accordingly, he invited representatives of all Mennonite groups to a conference in Winkler, Manitoba, in May 1939.[36] Nearly all came. Hutterites too were represented. However, the desired unity was not achieved. The Kanadier Mennonites remained unwilling to offer an alternative service to the government and many of the Mennonites in Ontario who had come from Pennsylvania were also hesitant.

In the following year, however, many things changed. With the outbreak of war in the fall of 1939, all the Mennonite groups increased their relief efforts. Large amounts of food and clothing were gathered and sent overseas, together with personnel to facilitate the distribution.[37] In June 1940, when the National Resources Mobilization Act was passed by Parliament, David Toews travelled to Ottawa to, among other things, 'offer the help of his people in any way that would be consistent with their principles which are opposed to taking part in war in any way.'[38] In Ontario the emerging Conference of Historic Peace Churches (CHPC) included the Quakers, who intended to propose 'a project of non-military national service' to the government.[39] Before long, the other groups in the CHPC were supportive, too.

By October 1940 the CHPC had formulated a more detailed alternative service proposal. Entitled 'Canadian Fellowship Service,' it was 'not alone an expression of appreciation to our government, but much more, an acknowledgment of our Christian duty to God and to our fellow-men.'[40] The work was to be 'strictly non-military in character' and for the general welfare of the public. Envisioned was work on roads, forests, farms, industries, ambulance and first-aid, as well as relief and reconstruction in Canada and perhaps also abroad. The proposal was communicated to officials in Ottawa by letter on 16 October 1940.

While the groups in Ontario were coming together, in the west the differences between the Russlaender Mennonites and the Kanadier Mennonites continued. When the Kanadier Mennonites saw that the National War Services Regulations, announced on 27 August 1940, referred specifically to their 1873 order-in-council they felt that they might yet be completely exempted. They were strengthened in this view in a 28 September meeting with National War Service officials in

Winnipeg.[41] As a result, they decided to continue in their position of not offering an alternative service to the government. However, if the government would require such a service, then they would consider it, if it was under civilian supervision.

The Russlaender Mennonites, unlike the Kanadier, did not believe that they would be exempted from alternative service, nor did they seek such an exemption. They felt that by proposing a program, rather than waiting for the government to set one up, they could influence the kind of service they would render. They also felt that the public had to be shown that Mennonites, too, were sacrificing for the country in this time of crisis. One strong proponent of this view was B.B. Janz from Alberta, where public antipathies were such that in June 1940 two Mennonite churches were burned down.[42] The Kanadier, being more concentrated, at least in southern Manitoba, may not have felt the public criticism quite as sharply though it also was evident there. Whatever the exact reasons, the Russlaender and Kanadier Mennonites in the west formally parted ways on 22 October 1940.[43]

The Russlaender then moved forward and formulated an alternative-service plan that was broadly similar to Ontario's 'Canadian Fellowship Service.' They indicated a willingness to do farm, forestry, first aid, and other work. They asked that all service be under civilian authority. They also asked that their men be exempted on the basis of lists prepared by church leaders without having to appear individually before the National War Services Boards. They also wanted their men to work in groups in order to facilitate spiritual supervision.[44]

The similarity of this western Mennonite position with that of the Ontario Mennonites would help them to present the case to the government more persuasively. This was important because government officials at first resisted the idea of a civilian-based alternative-service program. Already in September 1940, T.C. Davis, one of two deputy ministers for National War Services, had responded to Bishop David Toews with the counter-suggestion that all the Mennonite young men in any province be sent to one military training camp to be trained 'in some military non-combatant service – such as first aid to the wounded.'[45] The instruction would be given by military officers but it would be completely separate from the training for combatant service. Alternatively, the Mennonites could go to military camps and simply do maintenance work and other activities without taking training of any kind. Davis indicated that they could even be housed separately.[46]

Mennonite leaders, however, wanted a separate civilian-based program. With their newly broadened support they now sent a delegation of eight members to Ottawa, four from the west and four from Ontario, including one representative from the Quakers and one from the Brethren in Christ church.[47] The delegation met with T.C. Davis and L.R. Lafleche, the two deputy ministers of National War Services, on 12 and 13 November and again on 22 November 1940. They repeated that the work would have to be of a non-military nature, under civilian supervision, for the benefit of the country, and that they wanted their men to serve in groups.[48] The deputy ministers resisted the idea. They said that the number of men going into such a program would be small, that the transportation costs would be high, and that some organizations in Canada were saying that 'no provision should be made for conscientious objectors.' They suggested that the delegation give further consideration to non-combatant service under military control, adding that the men in such a program need not wear the uniform.[49]

The Mennonite delegates then pointed out that the National War Services Regulations referred to the possibility of doing non-combatant service under civilian authority. They said that most of their young men would not respond favourably to the idea of working in military camps even if they did not have to wear a uniform. They restated their interest in work 'of an agricultural or forestry nature combining if possible reforestation, setting up of nurseries as needed, land reclamation and farm improvement.' They would prefer that the work be done on government-owned land under the supervision of the appropriate government departments. They also suggested that first-aid courses be given in order to train the men to serve 'in the event of epidemics or other emergency resulting from the war.'

The two deputy ministers were still not persuaded. They said it would be difficult to arrange for work under civilian control. They pressed again for non-combatant service in the army. One of the delegates, B.B. Janz of Alberta, was willing to consider ambulance work under military supervision but the others stood firm.[50] At one point Lafleche attempted to frighten the delegates, saying : 'What'll you do if we shoot you?' At this Jacob H. Janzen, who had lived through the revolution in Russia, replied forcefully: 'Listen, Major General, I want to tell you something. You can't scare us like that. I've looked down too many rifle barrels in my time to be scared in that way. This thing is in our blood for 400 years and you can't take it away from us like you'd crack a piece of kindling over your knee. I was before a firing squad twice. We believe in this.'[51] Lafleche then adjourned the meeting, stating that he would be making recommendations to the minister, the Hon. James G. Gardiner, and that a decision on the matter would probably be made quite soon.

Because the delegates were sceptical of Lafleche, they decided to try to meet directly with Gardiner who, it turned out, was remarkably sympathetic. When E.J. Swalm introduced himself as bishop of the Brethren in Christ church, once known as Tunkers, Gardiner happily recounted some connections that he had had with Tunkers years earlier. On the matter of alternative service they said: 'While it is true that some of our members of military age, in Alberta, would be prepared under certain circumstances, to undertake ambulance work under military supervision, we feel that the larger number of our men are strongly averse to undertaking any form of service under military authority. These men, however, are ready to render constructive service under civilian authority.'[52] They referred to the detailed proposals they had submitted to the deputy ministers and said they hoped that their concerns would be respected. Gardiner listened sympathetically and then reassured them: 'There's one hundred and one things that you fellows can do without fighting; we'll see that you get them.'[53]

Gardiner's response, together with other factors now prodding the government to authorize alternative forms of service, moved things forward.[54] On 24 December 1940, when amendments to the National War Services Regulations were announced, they included provisions that allowed for three forms of alternative-service involvement including (1) training and service under military auspices but without the requirement to bear arms; (2) training for stretcher-bearing, ambulance and first-aid work; and (3) service of a completely civilian nature.[55] This last category suggested the type of program that most of the Mennonites had been looking for. But there would yet be many problems, both with obtaining exemption from military service and with alternative-service arrangements.

THE EARLY PERIOD: PROBLEMS WITH MILITARY EXEMPTION AND ALTERNATIVE SERVICE

With the regulations amended, there was now a framework that allowed for both military exemption and alternative service but numerous problems soon arose because of incomplete practical arrangements and because of a questionable orientation on the part of some officials. On 7 January 1941, Deputy Minister Lafleche sent out a Circular Memorandum communicating the three alternative-service options to the National War Services Boards across the country.[56] But he did not encourage the boards to utilize these options extensively. In his view, 'many members of the Mennonite faith would be prepared to take ordinary military training.' He also advised the boards, regarding option one, that they not direct a man to a military training centre for non-combatant training or service without first checking to ensure that adequate practical arrangements had been made. He also informed the boards that although they remained autonomous in the sense that their rulings could not be appealed to a higher body, they could 'rehear' cases if that seemed appropriate.

Lafleche then began to work on the necessary practical arrangements. Interestingly, he first approached the Department of National Defence stating: 'I can see no reason why their services should not be placed at the disposal of your Department should you so desire and as long as National Defence would put them to work under the conditions specified in the Regulations.'[57] The Department of National Defence, however, rejected the offer stating that it was poorly equipped for using the large number who it expected would now opt for alternative service.[58] More favourable responses came from the Department of Mines and Resources, particularly its National Parks Bureau.[59] Several provincial governments were also willing to co-operate. This interest, however, involved primarily the third alternative, that of civilian service. This particular alternative had been underscored also by representations of Mennonites in Ontario and Kanadier Mennonites in the west. These groups had sent delegations to Ottawa in January and February 1941 to re-emphasize their opposition to any form of service under military supervision.[60] Perhaps there were still apprehensions that the government might have listened too much to some Russlaender Mennonites.

Finally, in spring 1941 alternative-service work-camps were set up in the Banff, Jasper, Prince Albert, and Riding Mountain national parks. The men would clear away dead timber, build trails and roads, work on insect control, construct drainage facilities, and undertake other projects.[61] Several road construction projects were set up outside national parks. One, under an agreement with the government of Saskatchewan, involved work on a highway near Lac La Ronge in the north and nearly all the men sent there would be Doukhobors. The other, under an agreement with the government of Ontario, was for the construction of a portion of the Trans-Canada Highway, north of Sault Ste Marie. The men sent to this project would come primarily from Ontario.

These alternative-service projects were publicly announced on 29

May 1941 and soon nearly 1000 conscientious objectors were on their way. They would serve only four months, which was the training time then required of recruits in the military.[62] Nevertheless it was a significant step. Accordingly, Mennonite leaders in the west now sent a letter to the minister expressing their desire to co-operate and their gratitude that the government was respecting 'the principle of religious liberty and that promises once given are kept to the utmost.'[63] The Kanadier Mennonites now also participated in the program. Their representatives had been told in the February 1941 meetings in Ottawa that despite their order-in-council of 1873, 'it is impossible at this time to dismiss you from all service because of the agitation amongst the people.' Also, their young men would have to appear personally before the boards. This was different from the assurance given to Kanadier leaders at the 28 September 1940 meeting with the National War Services Board in Winnipeg. It suggested that instead of having to meet only a 'membership criterion,' as the regulations seemed to imply, the Kanadier Mennonites would now also have to meet a 'personal belief criterion.' Though disappointed, the Kanadier leaders accepted the situation. Before long they were co-operating with the Russlaender and other Mennonites in providing spiritual supervision for the men in the alternative-service camps.[64]

Though virtually all Mennonites were willing to participate in the alternative-service program, there were administrative and other problems. In Ontario in spring 1941, several young men who claimed to be conscientious objectors enlisted in a field ambulance unit on the assurance that they would not be required to take any training involving rifle drill.[65] After enlisting they discovered that the required training involved rifle drill after all. As a result, the CHPC appealed to ottawa where Lafleche explained: "No recruiting officer has authority to promise to any recruit exemption from basic drill.' He pointed out that a member of an ambulance corps would normally not be required to use weapons but that a situation could arise in which he would be ordered to do so and that it was necessary, therefore, to take basic training including rifle drill.

Lafleche's explanation identified a basic problem – one that would appear again – with the second alternative-service option. The regulations referred to training in ambulance and first aid but they did not state explicitly that this service, and the training for it, were to be of a completely non-combatant nature. To deal with the immediate problem of the several young men in Ontario, Lafleche suggested that the delegation ask the board to rehear their cases and that they also approach the officer commanding the unit to which they had been assigned. Soon after the men were released. With this minor exception, the men in Ontario had virtually no difficulties. CHPC representatives simply brought the names, gathered in their own registration effort, to the registrars who then gave them the desired 'postponement.' The men did not have to appear personally before the boards as the regulations suggested.[66] In effect, they were exempted on the basis of a 'membership criterion' only.

In Alberta the problems involved both alternative service and military exemption. On 10 June 1941, the Alberta board sent out letters announcing that it would 'meet for the purpose of disposing of claims of Mennonites and other Conscientious Objectors' at the court-houses in four cities on certain dates in the second half of June.[67] The announcement also stated: 'If you do not take military training you will be required to perform equivalent service in the National Parks.' To B.B. Janz, the prominent Alberta Mennonite, this was an inadequate form of alternative service. He had understood, after his elaborate representations both in Ottawa and before the board in Edmonton, that Mennonite men would have an opportunity to do ambulance and first-aid work 'for the wounded and sick soldiers.'[68] He now appealed to the minister, J.G. Gardiner, but was told that the necessary practical arrangements for such a service had not been made.

When the Alberta hearings took place the military exemption problems became evident, too. Janz now wrote: the 'situation has turned to the worst.'[69] Out of 'approximately 180 applications as Mennonites or other C.O.'s only 17 were granted a postponement on these grounds.'[70] The board had ordered the rest to take basic military training with the understanding that they could then go into non-combatant military service. Horace Harvey, chairman of the board in Alberta, explained that many of them 'when told that if they would take two months of basic training they could then elect to enter a non-combatant unit, consented to take military training.'

Harvey's approach, like that of Davis and Lafleche in the Ottawa negotiations in November 1940, blurred a distinction that was important to Mennonite leaders. Admittedly, non-combatant service was preferable to combatant service, but the fact that it still involved rifle training and the possibility, in exceptional situations, of being required to use the weapons made it unacceptable. B.B. Janz, greatly disturbed by Harvey's direction, now appealed to the minister, the newly installed J.T.

Thorson.[71] Janz stated that the service to the wounded and sick that they had offered was an expression of the Christian idea of love and mercy and that what the government was now proposing was entirely different. He said: 'The idea there is to work for destruction. We always have been opposed to do that.'

Janz also criticized the board on the matter of military exemption, saying that it had rejected 'the young men, no matter how good they expressed themselves.' He had had a long discussion with the board and especially with Harvey, its chairman, but these talks had only deepened his disappointment. He reported that the board 'felt bound to do so in promoting the war effort,' adding, 'they gave me to understand, that only the people with the Order-in-Council of 1873 may have exemption, but we other people through c.o.'s have to do non-combatant service and if the young man cannot agree then the Board has to overrule him.'

In replying to Janz, T.C. Davis stated simply: 'The Board decides each case on its merits.' With regard to the possibility of organizing a separate ambulance corps for the conscientious objectors, Davis said the time was not yet ripe for that.[72] Janz was deeply disappointed. The authorities were refusing to let them do ambulance and first-aid work as an alternative service but pressuring them to serve as regular non-combatants. In another letter he wrote: 'After the hearing of the boys in June we are witnessing the collapse of the whole situation for our c.o.'s: No ambulance work at all, but a very strong pressure to work in the army for destruction as non-combatants, including 2 months full military training with arms.'[73] In addition to Janz's strong appeals, the Ontario CHPC delegation, which was meeting with Davis and Lafleche around this time, discussed the problems in Alberta as well. Davis and Lafleche advised the CHPC delegation to suggest to the Alberta Mennonite leaders that they ask the board there to rehear the cases. The board in Alberta agreed and soon a majority of the men were redirected to the alternative-service projects in the national parks.[74] Still, some problems with obtaining military exemption in Alberta were to reappear.

In Saskatchewan there were similar problems. Unfortunately they proved more intractable. In spring 1941, board chairman J.F.L. Embury reported that they 'had allotted a great number of these people to undergo military training in a camp apart from arms drill, preparing them to be stretcher bearers and to do first-aid work.'[75] Such an activity would be in accord with option two in the alternative-service regulations, but, as noted above, there were no facilities for training that did not involve the use of arms. Soon after, the Saskatchewan board was informed 'by people in higher authority that this was not to be done.' The men were then sent to work in the national parks, under civilian supervision.

In fall 1941, Embury made another attempt. He now recognized that the training would involve weapons but he felt that the Mennonites should accept it if they were assured that after two months of such training they would be permitted to choose 'some arm of the Service, where they do not have to bear arms to take life.'[76] After proposing this course of action to the Mennonites, Embury reported: 'The matter has been so well explained to them ... that nearly all of the Mennonite young men have fallen in line with this.' Later he admitted that the options he had in mind were only 'more or less non-combatant' and that the consent of the Mennonites had been 'preceded by a certain amount of persuasion.'[77] Nevertheless, he felt confident that the plan was sound.

Significantly, the Department of National Defence was not interested. In a response dated 26 November 1941, an official of that department explained: 'There is no conditional service in the army ... all personnel therein must be subject to transfer from one arm to another in the interest of the service.'[78] The official stated further: 'No branches or units of a modern army can be considered as entirely non-combatant. Modern warfare makes all branches the object of direct attack, and, therefore, all units must be responsible for their own defence. They are trained to bear arms with the idea that these weapons will some day have to be used by the men so trained.' The Defence Department did not want to work with a person whose enlistment was conditional. It was of the view that 'the manner of dealing with Mennonites, Doukhobors and Conscientious Objectors should be a matter for the civil authority.'

In Manitoba, too, there were problems with military exemption. Here the board seemed to be particularly concerned with the personal-belief criterion. Officials felt that instead of speaking their own minds the young Mennonites were being pressured by their church leaders. This concern surfaced in December 1940. At a three-day sitting in the town of Morden, almost all the 498 Mennonites with whom the board dealt had claimed to have 'conscientious objections' to military service. A local physician found this incredible. In a letter to the *Winnipeg Free Press* he said it was 'impossible to escape the conviction that there has occurred in the Morden courthouse ... the worst demonstration of mass perjury that has ever taken place in that building.'[79] He continued: 'I have no quarrel with the Mennonite young people ... but I am forced to believe that they are very unfortunate in their church leadership.'

Later, in May 1941, when the Manitoba board opened a session in the town of Steinbach, heavily populated by Kanadier Mennonites, the board chairman, J.E. Adamson, urged them to reconsider their views.[80] In a lengthy speech he said that no one in Canada wanted war but that war was necessary to defend freedom and avoid the 'slavery of body and mind' now being threatened. He urged the Mennonites to help their country in its 'hour of trial' saying: 'Every man and every woman in this country is either for Canada or for Hitler.' He commended them for their desire not to take life but in his view: 'Canada's part in this war is to save lives, to save the lives of women and children ... no true Christian can say he would stand by and see a murderer take the life of a child rather than take the murderer's life.'

Adamson continued by pointing to the agreement of 1873 and said that the conditions of war had changed completely, that now everyone had to be involved and that 'agreement or no agreement, the Mennonites can no more escape taking part in this mobilization than a box of matches can escape in a burning building.' He explained that in the modern army only one in four was actually engaged in fighting and then asked: 'Why should your young men not go and serve in transport corps or ambulance corps or as mechanics?' He noted that 'a considerable number' of young Mennonites had enlisted and expressed his belief that many more would do so if the Mennonite leaders would not try so hard to influence them. He concluded by saying: 'To you Bishops, preachers, elders and fathers, I say, do not attempt to influence your young men. Leave them free ... it is their conscience, and not yours ... And to you young men, I say ... speak the truth. Do not say anything that you do not really, sincerely believe. Remember it is your conscience. Remember too that it is your country.' Before proceeding with the hearing Adamson said that he and his colleague wanted only 'to find the truth and to carry out the true spirit and intention' of the regulations.

The problems were not long in coming. In early July 1941 three Kanadier Mennonite bishops from Manitoba wrote to the minister, J.T. Thorson. They spoke appreciatively of the alternative-service arrangements but said: 'We are greatly worried about a number of Mennonite boys, who did not pass their examination before the judge and will now be asked to take military training.'[81] The bishops referred to the exemption promised in the order-in-council of 1873 and said that the boys on whose behalf they were appealing were descendants of those who had come to Canada pursuant to that order and that these boys were true to the Mennonite faith. They said they did not speak on behalf of boys who were not true to the Mennonite faith.

The bishops' appeal, however, did not receive a favourable response. Judge Adamson reported to the minister that a number of men whose applications had been rejected by the board had then gone into military service and were doing well, while one, whose application for conscientious-objector status had been granted, had enlisted voluntarily one week later.[82] In Adamson's view, the only way to prevent some with conscientious objections from being called as recruits would be to allow every claim. If that were done, said Adamson, 'many who are not sincere would avoid the service.' To deal with the situation of those who had been called but who were refusing to report, perhaps for reasons of conscience, he proposed that the officers commanding at the military training centres be authorized to exempt such men from training exercises involving the use of arms and that instead they be assigned to do 'labor and fatigue work about the camp' perhaps without a uniform. In this way a possible injustice to these men could be avoided, he said. Lafleche, however, rejected Adamson's proposal, stating that the Department of National War Services could not instruct the Department of National Defence on how to deal with men at the training centres.[83]

The authorities in Manitoba then began to prosecute those Mennonites whose applications for exemption had been rejected and who refused to go into the military. Early in October 1941, six cases were heard in the town of Gretna and the magistrate imposed sentences of twelve months with hard labour and a fine of $200. Adamson said he was 'glad to see a substantial sentence,' one that would serve as an incentive for others to comply with the orders.[84] He continued to be critical of the church leaders, arguing that although they might counsel the young men in preparation for their appearance before the board, they had no right 'to advise these young men to disregard the orders calling them up after the Board has made its decision.' The possibility of prosecuting the bishops was considered but not pursued.

In Saskatchewan there were difficulties, too. In mid December 1941, the board there disposed of '126 applications for exemption on the grounds of conscientious objection' by ordering 70 to take military training and 52 to go into civilian labour alternative. Four were found unfit for any service.[85] In January 1942 a number of Mennonites from the Hepburn area of Saskatchewan appeared before the board and indicated that although they objected to bearing arms, they were willing to serve in a non-combatant way.[86] The board turned them down for conscientious-objectors status and ordered them to report for military training after which they could go into a 'non-combatant' branch of the military. However, this training involved the use of arms, so the men refused to take it. They said that they would rather go to jail. When the board remained adamant the Mennonites went to their member of Parliament, Walter Tucker. He now appealed to Embury not to take action against these men until authorities in Ottawa had had a chance to review the situation. Tucker stated: 'I cannot think that the Government would want to treat Mennonites, who are willing to cooperate to the extent that these are, in this way, when they take no steps against the Sons of Freedom in British Columbia, who have not even registered and seem entirely unwilling to cooperate in any way.'[87]

Embury replied: 'We are not prepared to deviate one inch from our findings.'[88] Embury was greatly concerned with what he felt was the generally patriotic attitude of the Mennonites:

Some schools have been carrying on all across this Province and Alberta and Manitoba openly teaching High German, and turning out students intended to be preachers, some of whom, openly in effect, say they are not interested if Hitler wins this War or not − as they will leave it to Providence ... it is to us nothing more or less than an utterly traitorous doctrine which has not even the remotest connection with religious doctrine .

Some of our public Schools have been used to instil into the minds of the young people at a tender age that they should never engage in war, regardless of the circumstances. How then is it possible when this kind of thing goes on, to create a nation able to defend itself ...

Tucker then carried the appeal further. In letters to the minister, J.T. Thorson, he argued that Embury, by basing his decisions on such concerns, was deviating from the law and that the government should not allow him to do so. However, Tucker supported Embury's call that the Department of National Defence be instructed to arrange for a service that would be completely non-combatant.

Embury himself made another attempt to have such a service set up. In a series of memoranda in mid January 1942 he criticized the practice of assigning Mennonites to the national parks, saying that it 'produces no noticeable public benefit, annoys the old Soldier, is of no value as a War Effort; and is unsuited to the many educated Mennonites, who have expressed to our Board their desire to serve the country in any dangerous war service except that involving the actual taking of life.'[89] He asked again that arrangements be made for a truly non-combatant form of service. Once again, however, the plan was rejected by the Department of National Defence.[90]

The many difficulties in the west had prompted Mennonite leaders there to write to the minister, J.T. Thorson, in October and to the prime minister in November.[91] Now, in January 1942, they decided to travel to Ottawa in person. For this David Toews from Saskatchewan and C.F. Klassen from Manitoba were joined by J.B. Martin and J. Harold Sherk from Ontario. They met with Thorson and his deputy L.R. Lafleche and presented a lengthy statement.[92] They reported that in Saskatchewan their people had been told by the board 'that they must accept two months of basic military training, after which they may elect some type of non-combatant service.' They said, 'thirty or more young men' who had recently been dealt with in this way and who were now receiving orders to report were 'unable to accept military training because of religious convictions.' As a result they were again asking the board for an 'indefinite postponement.' In Manitoba, they said, about 800 Mennonites had applied for 'indefinite postponement.' Of these, 260 had been sent to the civilian alternative-service camps. Another 20 had been ordered to report for military training, with the assurance that after two months of basic training they could elect some form of non-combatant service. Eleven of these 20 had refused to comply and had then been penalized with jail sentences and fines. The remaining – approximately 520 – had not yet received any instructions.

After describing the situation, the delegates asked that the boards be instructed 'to give affect to the letter and intentions of the Regulations' so that those with conscientious objections to military service would be allowed to serve in a different way. They also wanted the department in Ottawa to ask the boards in Manitoba and Saskatchewan to respond favourably to the requests for 'rehearings' made by those whose applications for postponement had been rejected. In addition they asked for clemency on behalf of those in prison who were 'steadfastly professing their conscientious objection.'

The appeal accomplished little. Thorson told them that already on 3 December 1941 he had sent 'clear instructions' to the divisional boards that no form of non-combatant military service was available in which there was absolute assurance that combatant duties would never have to be performed. He said there were only two forms of service: 'military service in its various forms, all of which require basic military training,' and 'alternative (civilian) service in camps now operated by the Department of Mines and Resources.'[93] The officials also stated that 'the Department favours clemency very much' for those imprisoned and that they wanted the boards to deal fairly with all concerned but that the boards were 'autonomous and supreme' so the department could not force them to change their decisions.

The problems continued. On 2 April 1942, David Toews wrote to Embury again because 'a number' of Mennonites receiving calls to report for military training were coming to him for advice on what to do. This placed him in a difficult position, he said. On the one hand, if he advised them not to report then he would be violating the law. On the other hand, if he advised them to obey the law and report for military training then he would be violating one of the most basic tenets of their religion. He knew that the authorities were already suspicious that he was exercising too much influence. Thus he wrote to Embury: 'I am worried about what to advise them,'[94]

Toews also wrote to Thorson in Ottawa. In a letter on 8 April 1942 he said: 'I shall not repeat our grievances, because at our last interview you would not accept our statements.' However, he emphasized: 'Our young men are quite in earnest in asserting their conviction that they oppose military training on conscientious grounds and although a number of them may be induced by threats to do military training, the majority of our young men will remain firm in the conviction that they must obey God more than man and many will do this at any risk of the consequences.'[95] He pointed out that of the five provinces in which there were Mennonites, it was only in Manitoba and Saskatchewan that 'our young men are required to do military training with the promise that they will be assigned to non-combatant service in the army after two months of military training.' In other provinces, he said, 'young Mennonites are not even required to appear before the Board.'

These military exemption problems were not resolved but in the spring of 1942, the first step toward a more diversified alternative-service program was taken. The call for a diversified program came from a number of sources: from well-educated conscientious objectors including some from other Protestant denominations who felt there were ways of rendering a better service; from certain church leaders; and from parliamentarians such as John Diefenbaker. Most important was the emerging recognition that the conscientious objectors could make a vital contribution in alleviating the country's labour needs.

THE LATER YEARS: ALTERNATIVE SERVICE DIVERSIFIED / MILITARY
EXEMPTION PROBLEMS CONTINUE

The first step in the gradual diversification of the alternative-service program came in spring 1942 when 1000 conscientious objectors were sent as 'fire rangers' to the forests of British Columbia.[96] These forests, it was feared, were in danger of sabotage action, following the Japanese attack on Pearl Harbor. There were other alternative-service changes, too. Those alternative-service workers sent out now, instead of serving only four months, had to stay for the duration of the war. Also, over the course of the next year, many of the conscientious objectors who had not yet been called up would be given alternative-service assignments.[97] The Mennonites did not oppose these changes. They had always said that they did not want to avoid sacrifice and service. Nevertheless, their men in the camps would now need more support in terms of clothing and footwear. Regular clergy visits would also become more important. In addition, with more of the young men away in the camps, there would be labour shortages on Mennonite farms. This led to requests for 'leaves' from those already in the camps and to requests for 'postponements' from those not yet called up.

The government recognized the need for farm work. Indeed, it called for an increase in agricultural production. Accordingly, it approved the principle of farm leaves and farm postponements. In reality, however, these were not easily obtained. On 27 April 1942 David Toews from Saskatchewan wrote to the minister and explained that a number of young men in the camps were urgently needed for spring work on their farms. He said: 'These farms cannot be cultivated unless these boys are permitted to come home for farming operations in the spring.'[98] The reply from Ottawa was not favourable, however. Lafleche wrote that it was difficult to grant leaves 'in view of the very great urgency of providing men for the protection and conservation of British Columbia forests.'[99] He also reminded Toews of an earlier comment by Mennonite leaders that their communities 'would go to great lengths to assist the parents of young Mennonite men sent to alternative service work camps.'

The Kanadier Mennonites of southern Manitoba were also concerned. On 4 June 1942 they held a general meeting, attended by over 100 ministers, and agreed to send an urgent appeal to Minister Thorson, saying: 'We face a very serious situation ... The operation of many farms will cease, sugarbeet growing must vanish, and dairy farming cannot be maintained.' They added: 'Under such circumstances many of the boys will not answer the call for service.' They asked that the four-month system be reinstated and that it operate on a rotation basis.[100] This request was rejected. However, the need for farm labour was genuine. A number of young Mennonites who had been given 'leaves' did not return to their alternative-service assignments as the regulations required.[101]

The government did take some accommodating measures. Specifically, it delayed issuing the orders to send the men to the alternative-service camps until late in the fall after much of the farm work was completed. Clearly, this delay was helpful to the particular people involved, but from the perspective of those already in the camps for the duration, who were not even allowed to go home on leave, it was a serious inequity. It also prompted Adamson to complain to Ottawa that a majority of those to whom the board had granted conscientious-objector status were not yet sent out on alternative-service assignments. One Kanadier Mennonite bishop, J.J. Froese, proposed again that the alternative-service workers be sent out on a rotating basis. This would help to address the farm-labour shortage and also treat the men who had been exempted from military service in a more equitable way. But the rotation idea was again rejected.[102] Obviously, the alternative-service program, though perceived in a more positive light than before, was still accompanied by problems.

Meanwhile, the difficulties in obtaining exemption from military service continued. Some of the boards, according to David Toews, were 'mere recruiting offices.'[103] He felt that they sometimes made up their minds to turn down applications for conscientious-objector status even before the hearings took place.[104] In a 1 June 1942 letter to the Thorson, he described the situation in Saskatchewan and said that a number of the men whose applications had been rejected had received calls to report for military training but were refusing to go. As a result, they 'now stand in danger of being arrested' said Toews.[105]

When the appeal to Thorson seemed to avail little, Toews sought the advice of F.C. Blair, director of Immigration, with whom he had long had contact on immigration matters.[106] In a 'private and confidential' letter to Blair he said that they found it 'absolutely useless' to appeal to the deputy minister, General Lafleche, and that the minister, J.T. Thorson, seemed unwilling to believe that there were problems. He noted that in the other provinces the situation was almost trouble-free, but that in Manitoba and Saskatchewan there were serious difficulties. According to his account, 'our boys are not recognized as Mennonites nor as conscientious objectors. I claim that ministers who have known the boys from their youth on know more about their convictions than a biased Board could know after they have examined them for five or ten minutes.' He then cited several incidents:

A young Mennonite ... came before the Board and one of the questions was: 'Did you go to school' Answer: 'Yes.' Question: 'Did you ever have a scrap in school?' Answer: 'Yes.' – 'Well, you are not a conscientious objector, your application is not accepted, get out!!!'

Another boy came before the Board. 'Are you a Mennonite and a Conscientious Objector?' Answer: 'Yes.' – 'Why is it that you are asking for postponement?' Answer: 'Besides being a Mennonite and a Conscientious Objector, I am a farmer and I am the only one working on the farm.' Answer: 'I do not care a hoot about your farm, we want you, your application is not accepted, get out!!!'

Soon thereafter, in responding to a letter from Thorson, Toews wrote: 'If only some of the young men, as you state in your letter, were not recognized as conscientious objectors, I do not think that I would have taken the liberty to write to you, but if almost all of our young men are not given recognition as having conscientious scruples about military service, I believe some consideration should be given to this fact.'[107] He said that surely the purpose of the regulations was to provide justice for all, including conscientious objectors. In his view the boards in Manitoba and Saskatchewan were not pursuing that purpose.

At Mennonite church conferences in the summer of 1942 there were reports from all five provinces where Mennonites resided.[108] From Ontario there were no complaints. In British Columbia the registrar had recently talked of the difference between the Kanadier Mennonites who came to Canada pursuant to the 1873 order-in-council and those who came in the 1920s, but no problems had yet appeared. In Alberta, the only concerns were about obtaining farm leaves. In Saskatchewan and Manitoba, however, the military exemption problems remained very serious. Consequently, it was decided to send another delegation to Ottawa to describe the situation to officials personally.

The delegation to Ottawa was small, consisting only of David Toews and C.F. Klassen. They met with Thorson and Lafleche on 28 September 1942 and presented a lengthy statement.[109] They began with a word of gratitude for the alternative-service arrangements. They referred also to reports indicating that government officials were well satisfied with the work of their young men. Then they explained the military exemption problems:

In November 1940 we pointed out to Mr. Justice Davis and Major General LaFleche our doubt as to whether justice could be expected if the War Services Boards were given full authority to decide whether a young man is a Mennonite or a conscientious objector, because in some cases these Boards have not the information to enable them to give a just verdict as to the honest or dishonest claim of young men being examined. We could not understand why the National War Services Board should be given such far reaching authority to decide whether a young man is an honest conscientious objector. We submit that the leaders of the churches know more about the stand of the young men than these Boards, and should at least be regarded as witnesses and their testimony should receive some consideration. We also could not understand why the decision of the Boards should be final and without the possibility of an appeal.

They reported that a number of their young men were receiving calls for military training and that some obeyed the call but that most did not because, in the words of the delegates, 'they knew their scruples re military training better than any other person.' Along with their refusal, these young men sent letters of explanation to the boards in which they reaffirmed their willingness to render an alternative service. Nevertheless, reported Toews and Klassen, 'one after another of these men was called before a Police Magistrate and sentenced to very severe penalties. Eleven young men persisted in their stand and went to goal.' On appeal to the minister of Justice, the men had been released after serving five months in jail. Later, however, another eight young Mennonites had been sentenced to jail, some to twelve months with hard labour. in conclusion the delegates stated:

Conditions are becoming unbearable in Manitoba and Saskatchewan ... Is it just to put men in gaol who are ready and willing to do the other work provided by our Government? Why is the testimony of the ministers given no consideration? Why are Mennonites examined and cross-examined by lawyers as though there is an attempt to hide the truth? Have we not established a reputation for honesty and truthfulness?

We humbly submit, that justice demands that the situation be changed so that there is a possibility of an appeal for those who are refused recognition as Mennonites or conscientious objectors. [Emphasis in the original.]

The possibility of setting up a higher body to which the decisions of the boards could be appealed had already been raised in the House of Commons.[110] Two prominent members of Parliament from Saskatchewan, John Diefenbaker and T.C. Douglas, favoured it but the government opposed it on the ground that the many appeals in the First World War had made that recruitment process very complex and inefficient. The minister also questioned whether the situation was really serious because he knew that many Mennonites seemed to be serving well in the army. Toews and Klassen agreed that a number of people of Mennonite background were willing to render military service but that they were appealing only on behalf of those who were sincere and conscientious followers of the historic Mennonite position. They left with a feeling that the officials were not willing to help.[111]

When the problems continued, David Toews wrote directly to Prime Minister Mackenzie King on 24 October 1942.[112] He reviewed the 400-year Mennonite history of refusing to participate in war, even at the cost of persecution, and then argued that it was wrong that 'now the National War Services Board, composed of a judge, a lawyer, a military man and another person are given the right to decide as to whether our boys have conscientious scruples about going to war and shedding human blood.' He pointed out that in Ontario, Alberta, and British Columbia the Mennonites were having no significant difficulties but that in Manitoba and Saskatchewan there were problems. Here, he said, 'our young men ... are being sent to jail for not being willing to deny the faith of their fathers.' He referred to the various assurances of exemption given before the war and said: 'Now we are told that only those who came to Canada pursuant to the Order-in-Council of 1873 are free from military service.' He pointed out that there was no appeal from the decisions of the boards and that numerous petitions to the Department of National War Services brought little satisfaction. He suggested that the prime minister put some of the questions before the Supreme Court. He emphasized again that Mennonites were willing to serve the country but that they could not bear arms.

The prime minister replied by saying that he was asking the minister of National War Services to look into these concerns.[113] Instead of an improvement, however, church leaders from Manitoba soon reported that the situation was deteriorating further, that more young men were being imprisoned, and that the board seemed caught up in the fervour of the war.[114] They did not know what further steps to take. On 2 February 1943, C.F. Klassen wrote to the minister of Labour, Humphrey Mitchell, who was now responsible for the administration of the regulations, and asked him to 'grant an interview to a small group of Mennonite delegates from the western provinces in order to place before you our need and submit plans and suggestions how best to overcome those difficulties which now confront us.'[115] He described the problems and said that the boards were not capable of deciding fairly the question of 'who is a Mennonite or conscientious objector.' That question, he argued, should be lodged with 'a body which is thoroughly familiar with the young man in question and the Mennonite Church.' He pointed to the Militia Act of 1927, which provided exemption for 'persons who, from the doctrines of their religion, are averse to bearing arms or rendering personal military service.' Because of this provision, he reasoned, no board 'may lawfully compel a Mennonite or Conscientious Objector to bear arms or undergo military training.' He described the prevailing situation in the following way: 'If the Board refuses to recognize the Mennonite status of a certain young man and sends him a "call for military training" notice, and the young man for conscience sake refuses to answer the call, then he is ... sentenced to imprisonment and at the expiration of the prison term, ordered to be turned over by the Police to the nearest military training centre, where he is to be kept until he consents to become a member of the army.' Klassen also referred to the different forms of alternative service that the Mennonites had first offered in 1940 and noted with regret that to date the government had accepted only a narrow range of such services.

The minister of Labour was not persuaded. He rejected the request for a meeting and made a strong defence of the boards:

The Associate Director of Selective Service (Military) ... advises that there are some persons of the Mennonite denomination who do not come under the protection of the agreement made with the Dominion Government at the time of their immigration to Canada, and of this latter group some have been unable to establish to the satisfaction of the Board that they are conscientious objectors. The Board's decision in each case constitutes a finding of fact based upon the evidence submitted to it. The Chairman of each Board is a Superior Court Judge and the Boards, as constituted, are competent to arrive at fair decisions ... Applicants should be prepared to abide by the Board's decision.[116]

Regarding the suggestion for a more diversified use of alternative-service workers, the minister reported that that matter was being studied 'with a view to enabling conscientious objectors to take employment in agriculture or ... essential industry.

This last comment was significant. A major diversification in the alternative-service program was indeed under consideration. Already in 1942, responsibility for the National War Services Regulations had been transferred to the Department of Labour to ensure 'the most effective use of manpower in the war effort.' With that the regulations had been renamed the National Selective Service Mobilization Regulations. In January 1943, when a delegation from the CHPC of Ontario met the deputy minister of Labour, Arthur MacNamara, he asked for their opinion as to the practicality of having alternative-service men employed in private industry, including agriculture, lumbering, and coal-mining.[117] The delegates generally favoured a diversified program to 'enable each person to make the largest possible contribution to the good of Canada and of all mankind.'[118] However, they felt that to make a specific response they would need to consult with their people. MacNamara encouraged them to do so and then to submit a reply.

The CHPC response was one of caution. There were concerns about assigning men individually to private industry: the disparity in earnings between alternative-service workers and those doing the work as a normal occupation might lead to disaffection; the industries to which men might be assigned could have 'greater war significance' than the work performed to date; and individual assignments would make it more difficult to provide religious guidance.[119] The CHPC favoured group assignments and agricultural work on government-owned land so that the work would clearly be for public, rather than for private, benefit.

After initiating these discussions with the CHPC of Ontario, the minister of Labour also sought the opinion of Walter Tucker, the member of Parliament from a Saskatchewan constituency with many Mennonites. The minister now described the plan in a more detailed way:

When a man is postponed from military service as a conscientious objector his name will be turned over to the Selective Service Officers who will have the authority to direct the man either to the performance of Alternative Service in camp as at present, or to take specified employment on the farm or in industry at a wage rate which, if in agriculture, will be fixed by the Department, or if in other employment at the going wage rate. In either case, there will be a contract of employment which will limit the remuneration which the man himself will receive to $25.00 per month plus board and lodging, and the balance of the wages will be paid into the Crown.

Men now performing alternative service at camps would be similarly subject to the direction of the Selective Service Officer, and may be retained in camp service or directed to outside employment on the terms which I have outlined.

I would assume that if a man were needed on the home farm, he would be directed to employment on such farm. Otherwise, he would be directed to take employment elsewhere.[120]

With these details in hand, Tucker sought the view of several western Mennonite leaders. Generally, these were supportive. The possibility of having the young men back on their own farms was very attractive. B.B. Janz of Alberta was supportive, too, but he and C.F. Klassen felt that the plan was still too restrictive.[121] They continued to hope for arrangements whereby Mennonites could form a medical corps unit.

Formal authorization for the new arrangements was made by order-in-council on 7 April 1943.[122] This order noted that hitherto alternative service had been done mainly in the national parks and in the forests of British Columbia but that it was now 'expedient to make such persons available for work in agriculture and industry.' Mennonite leaders were concerned about how this would be implemented so they again travelled to Ottawa and raised the question of which industries their men might be assigned to.[123] When MacNamara, the deputy minister of Labour, responded by inviting them to draw up a list of those which they would find acceptable, they submitted the following statement: 'Industries and Occupations which are approved by the Historic Peace Churches as fields of service for Conscientious Objectors – Agriculture, Experimental Farms, Feed Mills, Food Processing, Meat Packing, Cheese-masking, Creameries and Dairies, Canning Factories, Teaching, Hospital Service, Medical and Dental Services.'[124] Soon they received a reply from MacNamara, stating: 'In regard to the industries and occupations suggested, we will work along this line.'[125]

Implementing the new plan was a major task. The alternative-service program now became a branch of the Employment Service of the Department of Labour. There was a chief alternative-service officer and additional alternative-service officers in Ontario and the four western provinces where most of the conscientious objectors lived.[126] These officers then went to the registration files in their respective divisions and gathered information on each conscientious objector. Their first task was to find alternative-service assignments for those who had appeared before the boards and received the desired exemption but who had never been sent to an alternative-service project. These men were now interviewed and if they already were in 'essential work,' be it in agriculture or in industry, then they were simply asked to accept the alternative-service contract whereby part of their earnings would be given to the Canadian Red Cross Society. Those not yet in 'essential work' were reassigned, again subject to their acceptance of the alternative-service contract.[127] Those who, like Jehovah's Witnesses, were not willing to accept the contract were sent to the alternative-service camps in the national parks.

The second task of the new alternative-service officers was to determine whether those currently in the camps were qualified for 'essential work' elsewhere. If so, and if they were willing to accept the contracts, then they were reassigned. As a result, a majority of the Mennonite men ended up on farms, in some cases on their own family farms, at least for the summers, though some were given lumbering and other assignments for the winter seasons. Before long the work in the national parks was reduced to a secondary part in the total alternative-service program.[128]

Alongside this major diversification there was another noteworthy, though small, development. In September 1943, the government finally agreed to allow men to enlist for medical corps work with a complete assurance that they would never have to bear arms.[129] B.B. Janz and others had long pressed for medical corps work, arguing especially for a separate Mennonite medical corps unit. They believed this would attract some of their young men who were going into regular military service at a rate of 50 per cent in some areas.[130] The arrangement that now had governmental approval did not allow for a separate medical corps unit. It provided only that the men could serve individually in the regular medical corps. Nevertheless, the Russlaender Mennonites endorsed the arrangement.[131] However, the Kanadier Mennonites from the west and the Mennonites in Ontario opposed it, claiming that any service under military auspices was unacceptable.[132] By the end of the war only 227 men had served in this capacity.[133] At least one was killed in action.[134]

The Mennonites were generally satisfied with the new alternative-service arrangements but their problems with obtaining military exemption continued, at least for a time. In May 1943, C.F. Klassen wrote to MacNamara about eighteen men whom the board had not recognized as conscientious objectors.[135] They had then been ordered to report for military training and when they had refused, they had been arrested and sentenced to jail, in some instances for twelve months with hard labour. In addition, some were to be 'handed over, in Police custody, to Military Authorities' on termination of these jail terms. Klassen recognized that a number of Mennonites were joining the military forces voluntarily but felt very confident that these eighteen were sincere in their 'conscientious objection.' He again raised the issue about the authority of the boards: 'The leaders of the various churches are worried and uneasy over the fact that the Board has the authority to judge who is a Mennonite and who is not, as they know neither the young men nor the Mennonite Church, and the Board does not take into consideration the reference given by the leading Minister of the congregation.'

MacNamara checked with the board in Winnipeg and then replied stating that he had been assured by the chairman that each of these cases had been given 'very thoughtful consideration' but that the board had simply not been satisfied that these men really had 'conscientious objections.'[136] He noted that these men were from the Russlaender Mennonites who, he understood, tended to enlist anyway. He reported also that the board had given him an 'assurance that everyone of these men will be re-heard before they are prosecuted a second time should they default when re-called for service on their release from gaol.'

In Alberta there were problems now, too, perhaps in part because of an ambivalence among the Mennonites. Judge Harvey wrote to B.B. Janz, on 9 February 1943, that the board had heard 'many cases of Mennonites' recently with the result that 'members of the Board have become pretty well satisfied that if the young men are left to themselves there will be very little difficulty in getting them to take military training in many cases as their conscientious objections are not their own but those of their parents or elders. As you pointed out to me nearly as many young Mennonites are in the army as are in the alternative service and I have no doubt that the army will use every endeavour to see that they are not called on to do anything that will be prejudicial to their conscience.'[137]

Clearly, the board had become impatient. One victim of that impatience was Sam Martin. He first appeared before the board on 20 February 1943 but instead of giving him an 'indefinite postponement' as a conscientious objector, the board gave him a temporary postponement because his services as a mechanic were needed by the local farming community.[138] Then, in March 1944, the board decided not to grant another temporary postponement. He was then ordered to report for military training. He refused and as a result he ended up spending the next nineteen months in detention, some in a provincial jail and some in a military jail. There were periods of solitary confinement, limited food, and other serious deprivations. Despite numerous appeals from church leaders, he was not released until well after the war ended.[139]

In Manitoba the situation also remained difficult. On 27 August 1943 C.F. Klassen reported that 'in June and part of July Just. Adamson gave us a breathing spell. But lately things again are becoming unbearable. One of our boys after expiration of his jail sentence was taken to the military barracks, where he refused to be examined by a military doctor, then was sent to Winnipeg and sentenced to one year with hard labour. We have three similar cases ... In B.C. it is the same. Just. Manson became a very hard man who lately does not want to give any consideration to applications from c.o.s'[140] In early September, Klassen travelled to Ottawa and presented the problems to Major-General Riley, director of Mobilization. Riley acknowledged the problems and promised to try to improve the situation. A helpful step came on 1 December 1943 when an order was issued whereby the commanding officer of an army unit could, at his discretion, recommend discharges for men who he believed would not make good soldiers. This, it was felt, would deal with 'a great many of these Conscientious Objectors who have been already called into the Army and are of no use to the Forces.'[141] Around this time, Kanadier Mennonite leaders in southern Manitoba reported that the board now seemed less determined to send men to prison but it was 'increasingly harder to get releases from prison.' One year later, in January 1945, they stated: 'It is much easier to get the c.o. stand now. There are only a few boys in prison ... The prison terms are usually of two months duration.'[142] Perhaps the order of 1 December 1943 and the increased recognition that people seeking conscientious-objector status could make an important contribution to the country's labour needs helped to ease the situation.

The Hutterites, who were a very small group in comparison to the Mennonites, did not encounter significant difficulty in obtaining exemption from military service and in the alternative-service program. Early in 1943, Alberta's Judge Harvey reported: 'We have had no difficulty with the Hutterites. Their conscientious scruples have been recognized and in all cases they have been given the privilege of alternative service. They usually take their examination and ... they want to take the alternative service without objection.'[143] There was, however, some public criticism that the Hutterites were not doing 'their share' for the war effort. Specifically, their land purchases were seen as indications that they had a surplus of labour on their colonies and that even if they did not serve in the military, they should at least make a larger contribution to the alternative-service program. The record itself raised questions. In Alberta, a total of 220 Hutterites had been granted 'postponements' as conscientious objectors since the beginning of the war, but a substantial majority of these had not been given any alternative-service work.[144] They had been allowed to stay on the colonies. In Manitoba 129 men had been postponed as conscientious objectors and again only a minority had been assigned to alternative-service projects.[145] Even Mennonites complained that Hutterites were 'treated too leniently.'

The new alternative-service arrangements of 1943 were an occasion for renewed efforts to utilize the Hutterite labour resources. Some of the postponed men, it was recognized, should remain on the colonies but come under the new alternative-service contract arrangement. However, this arrangement had to be modified. A Hutterite alternative-service worker on a colony could not simply agree to give a portion of his monthly earning to the Red Cross because Hutterites did not have any individual earnings.[146] Also, when some Hutterite alternative-service workers were assigned to other farmers, Hutterite elders expressed concern about 'the degree of independence' that some of these men tended to develop.[147] Others simply left such assignments.[148] These acts resulted in a number of prosecutions.

The Hutterites preferred to work in the camps where they could be together and under a Hutterite minister. Authorities co-operated, and in the winter of 1943–4, about 100 Hutterites served in the Kananaskis camp in Alberta, cutting timber for 'pit props' in the coal-mines.[149] Also successful was an arrangement, in summer 1944, whereby about 80 Hutterites from both Alberta and Manitoba were sent to Fort William to load grain into the ships.[150] Here, too, they lived and worked together under the supervision of two Hutterite ministers, and their work was described as 'excellent.'[151] In addition, authorities made a more careful investigation of the colonies and found that there was relatively little surplus labour and that the men were well occupied with agricultural production.[152] Noting this, L.E. Westman, chief alternative service officer, came to the view that officials should leave things alone and not spend too much energy in 'pushing c.o.'s about.'[153]

THE DOUKHOBOR ENCOUNTER WITH MILITARY EXEMPTION AND ALTERNATIVE SERVICE

The Doukhobor experience with military exemption and alternative service had a character of its own. In 1940 the Doukhobors conducted their own registration. And in 1941 they argued that their young men should not have to appear personally before the boards. They said that they had been promised exemption in the 1898 order-in-council and that it should not be necessary for them to seek it again from the National War Services Boards.[154] Their attitude was similar to that of the Kanadier Mennonites, who had the 1873 order-in-council. For the Doukhobors, however, the government granted the request, at least for a time. General Lafleche agreed to rely on the Doukhobor registration process and advised the boards that they could 'grant the Doukhobor postponement from military service without requiring his appearance,' that they should simply assign the Doukhobor men to alternative-service projects and inform them accordingly.[155]

But assigning the Doukhobors to alternative-service projects was not that simple. Most Doukhobors were unwilling to render an alternative service. Initially there had been words of support. In June 1940, when their representatives negotiated the special registration arrangements, the Doukhobors expressed a desire to make contributions for refugee relief work. In September 1940, one of their leaders, P.G. Makaroff, wrote: 'It is just possible that our privilege may be in danger unless we do something to allay the criticism and ill feeling ... Those in authority would welcome some voluntary effort on the part of our people ... Such a gesture could take the form of some construction work having nothing to do with war, or some project in the way of improving our National Parks perhaps ... we should be giving some thought to some such effort.'[156] This support reflected a minority view, however. In February 1941, after Mennonite leaders had negotiated a civilian alternative-service program, the Doukhobors held a conference in Saskatoon and sent a statement to Ottawa indicating their assumption that they were exempted from 'direct or indirect war service.'[157]

Government officials, however, wanted Doukhobor participation in the alternative-service program. Recognizing that there might be difficulties in British Columbia, they set out to get things under way in Saskatchewan first.[158] The government planned a road-building project in co-operation with the provincial government. Officials met with Saskatchewan Doukhobor leaders in April 1941 and described the project, explaining that service in one form or another would be required of the Doukhobors.[159] These Doukhobor leaders accepted the project but when the 'orders to report' were issued to the 117 Saskatchewan Doukhobors in the first age category, only 42 reported.[160] Arrangements at the camp had been made for about 120, so those in the next category were also called. As a result, the number who participated in the first four-month assignment rose to about 70.

To deal with those who refused, the authorities quickly launched prosecutions, believing that not to do so would jeopardize the co-operation of those who had reported. The chairman of the war services board in Saskatchewan, J.F.L. Embury, even proposed that the men be sent to an internment camp perhaps for the duration of the war.[161] This proposal, however, was not accepted, but nearly 100 Doukhobors spent four months in prison in Prince Albert.[162] Also, four Doukhobor leaders were arrested for encouraging the young men not to co-operate with the alternative-service program. In the words of a Doukhobor report, they were 'actively engaged in defending our religious ideals and rights.'[163] One man received a one-year prison sentence.

Obviously, the Doukhobors were divided. They held numerous meetings to discuss the issues.[164] The Society of Independent Doukhobors passed a resolution on 10 June 1941 stating that the project 'is not in any sense incompatible with our religious convictions and does not violate our exemption from military service.'[165] Some of the men in the camp sent positive reports back to their communities.[166] But other Doukhobors rejected the alternative-service program as an indirect form of military service.[167] They applauded those who went to prison and criticized the leaders who had negotiated the road-building project for 'playing politics' and compromising their historic position.[168]

In the fall of 1941 those who had been in the alternative-service program for four months returned to their homes. Officials considered making another call-up but it became apparent that it would not be any more successful than the first, so they decided to leave the Doukhobors alone.[169] There were further discussions in 1942 and one group of Doukhobors, near Langham, Saskatchewan, now pledged themselves to 'donate two thousand bushels of wheat to the Canadian government to alleviate suffering.' However, the likelihood of compliance with the alternative-service program remained low so, rather than lose their labour in agriculture and other productive activities in another mass imprisonment, officials decided not to take enforcement measures.[170]

The Doukhobors in British Columbia opposed the alternative-service program more categorically. The 1941 imprisonment of Doukhobors in Saskatchewan had increased their apprehension and the Sons of Freedom in British Columbia soon began to express their opposition through demonstrations.[171] The RCMP reported that if 'orders to report' were issued, the Sons of Freedom 'would refuse and ... if arrest followed then mass demonstrations, nude parades, etc. would be organized until all were in custody.'[171] Government officials were not sure how to deal with the situation. At a June 1941 meeting federal and provincial officials recommended the internment of the Sons of Freedom on the assumption that it would then be possible to make satisfactory arrangements with the other Doukhobors.[173] This recommendation, however, was not implemented. As in Saskatchewan, officials came to the view that 'the wisest thing to do was to do nothing at all.'

In 1942 there were further discussions about bringing the BC Doukhobors into the alternative-service program. The intent now was to have them cut timber on the Queen Charlotte Islands.[174] The chairman of the BC war services board believed that 'by some tactful handling the young men ... could be brought to accept alternative service.'[175] However, when the police investigated the situation they reported: 'Conditions among the B.C. Doukhobors are as satisfactory as can be expected ... no trouble is anticipated until such time as alternative service is enforced on them.'[176] Accordingly, the BC Doukhobors, like those in Saskatchewan, were again left alone. Officials also reasoned that because they had been disfranchised it was in order to exempt them from the obligation to render a national service as well.[177]

In 1943 a more concerted effort began to register those who had not yet been registered (meaning the Sons of Freedom), to have all Doukhobors seek military exemption on an individual basis before the boards, and to bring those so exempted into the alternative-service program. Orders to report for medical examination, normally the first step in reporting for military training, were sent out early that year to young Doukhobors in both Saskatchewan and British Columbia.[178] The words on the form stated explicitly: 'You have been called out to undergo military training and in accordance with the National Selective Service Mobilization Regulations, are hereby notified to present yourself for medical examination.'[179] Officials explained that despite these words, Doukhobor rights to exemption from military service would be respected, that the Doukhobors were merely to take the medical examinations and thus be ready for alternative-service assignments. The board chairmen in both provinces said that they intended to prosecute any who refused to take the medical examinations.[180]

Some Doukhobors in Saskatchewan now appealed to the prime minister, pointing out that the words on the form violated the promise of exemption given to them in 1898.[181] At several meetings, officials were able to persuade some Doukhobors 'that this medical call in no way jeopardizes their immunity from military service.'[182] Others, however, refused to co-operate. Some returned the notices with a 'polite explanation' of their position. The RCMP, for their part, did not want to launch prosecutions lest they arouse strong resistance and precipitate demonstrations.[183] The question was not resolved until late in 1944 when officials stopped pressing the Doukhobors for medical examinations.

Aside from the issue of whether to insist that Doukhobors take the 'medicals,' officials had to arrange for alternative-service work that the

Doukhobors would accept. In Saskatchewan, at least some of the Doukhobors 'expressed their willingness to perform some service.'[184] Of the possibilities suggested, they preferred cutting wood in the bush for greatly needed fuel. This, then, became a winter assignment, while in the summer they would be transferred from one farm to another as needed. But considerable flexibility was required, particularly in relation to the alternative-service contract and the payment of money to the Red Cross. One group of Doukhobors near Langham, Saskatchewan, wrote: 'We are willing to pay in cash ... but we refuse to sign any contracts.' There were further discussions with officials but eventually the government accepted the arrangement, believing that even partial co-operation was 'a better service to the nation' than a situation where, by attempting to force compliance, a significant portion of the group would go to jail.[185]

Officials for British Columbia would eventually demonstrate a similar flexibility but not before seriously pursuing other options. The situation there was more complex. The Sons of Freedom Doukhobors had never registered and those belonging to the Union of Spiritual Communities of Christ (USCC) were more hesitant about alternative service.[186] Some officials raised the possibility of using force to obtain compliance with both registration and alternative service. Again the RCMP were cautious. They reported, early in 1943, that most Doukhobors were already employed in useful work and that 'forcible induction into Alternative Service Camps would result in considerable opposition.'[187] Other officials, however, including A.M. Mansion, chairman of the War Services Board in British Columbia, and Maj.-Gen. H.J. Riley of the Mobilization Section in the Labour Department, saw it as 'most unwise that one section of the population should be allowed to ignore the regulations.'[188] In mid May, L.E. Westman, the chief alternative service officer, suggested that a way be found to bring the Doukhobors under the alternative-service program without requiring them to register.[189] Advocating a policy of expediency, Westman suggested that the government try simply to get the best possible labour result from the Doukhobors.[190] He said: 'It might be possible by giving a blanket guarantee of freedom from Military service to definite groups and by keeping Boards from harassing them individually ... to make an arrangement whereby they would register in some kind of mass manner and accept a form of Alternative Service.'

Manson opposed this course. He suggested that officials be sent out to the Doukhobor settlements to 'proceed with tact, but firmness, to register all unregistered persons' and that the board then deal with them individually to determine whether they were sincere in their faith and entitled to exemption.[191] This process, he felt, would make them into a law-abiding people rather than a law-defying people. Westman now agreed to support Mansion's approach so he recommended to the minister that the male Doukhobors of callable age be brought to a nearby registration office, by the police if necessary, that the board be 'very generous in granting postponement to these men,' and that they then be required to render an alternative service, 'probably in camps cutting wood or pit props.'[192]

When the Doukhobors learned of these plans they sent their leaders to Ottawa to learn more details and to express their concerns. Late in October, representatives of the small moderate group known as the Named Doukhobors met with MacNamara, the deputy minister, and were told that the government was prepared to forgo the medicals but that the Doukhobors would have to obey the other regulations and that, if postponed on grounds of conscience, they would have to render an alternative service.[193] Officials also suggested that they apply for postponement as essential workers in farming or lumbering because they would then probably be left alone in their present positions and not be sent to alternative-service camps. The delegates accepted the information and said that before making any commitment they would have to consult with their people.

In mid November 1943 a larger delegation consisting of representatives of both the Independent Doukhobors and the more orthodox USCC travelled to Ottawa but the discussions were similar. Officials said that those not yet registered would have to do so, that the boards would deal generously with their applications for postponement, meaning military exemption, but that the government wanted them 'to make a contribution to the welfare of Canada.' Officials explained that those postponed could accept employment in one of the work-camps at a rate of $15 per month or else stay in their present work and agree to make monthly payments to the Red Cross or to the government. They also offered to consult with a Doukhobor advisory committee in working out the details if the Doukhobors wished to set up such a committee.[194]

The Doukhobors were not persuaded. But neither did they wish to appear defiant. Before leaving Ottawa, the USCC delegates prepared the following statement for the officials: 'Our refusal of medical examination and alternative service does not mean we won't do anything for the country we live in, or rather that we are not doing anything nor have we any idea to fight the Government. It would be a most unfortunate day for us to see jails filled with Doukhobors, where they would become a burden upon the government instead of an asset through their working capacity. However ... the Doukhobors will abide by their principles of religion notwithstanding any consequences.'[195] They added that if they had to make financial contributions they would want to make them not individually but from the community as a whole. Their preference was to simply have their people 'continue to contribute to the country's welfare by their hard work.' However, they said they would be willing to put the government's proposals before their people, preferably in the presence of government officials who could then explain them directly.[196]

Preparations were then made for such a mass meeting. It was scheduled for 12 December 1943. In the meantime, there were meetings and discussions among the Doukhobors by themselves. The members of the USCC met on 5 December 1943 and adopted a lengthy resolution stating: 'We refuse military service on religious principles, and not on the grounds of being essential farm workers.'[197] They reaffirmed their commitment to 'Toil and Peaceful Life' and referred also to the biblical command: 'Render unto Caesar the things that are Caesar's and unto God the things that are God's.' They explained: 'Everything demanded of us which is not contradictory to the Law of God and to the Faith of Jesus, we will accept, fulfill and execute not through fear but by conscientious guidance.' More specifically, they rejected the idea of making financial contributions, saying that these 'Would be looked on as a way to purchase our freedom.' They saw these as an indirect participation in war. They also indicated that they felt betrayed by the national registration of 1940. They had co-operated with that only after receiving assurances that it would not lead to military service. Now, however, some of their people who had registered were receiving the 'Orders – Medical,' which they saw as the first step to military service.

On 12 December, when the meeting with government officials was to take place, Maj. L.B. Cowell, regional director of Selective Service, and several other officials came to the Doukhobor settlement and found a gathering of 3500 Doukhobors. It was a Sunday afternoon. The crowd sang hymns and the officials were welcomed by a young people's choir. The main spokesman for the Doukhobors was John J. Verigin. He introduced the officials and then, in a gracious but clear manner, informed them that the Doukhobors had had meetings among themselves and that they had decided not to accept the government's proposals. He then addressed the large gathering, read the resolution that the USCC had adopted at the earlier meeting, and asked the people to express their view. They responded in a way that led Major Cowell to say later: 'Thirty-five hundred people can make NO sound pretty loud.'[198] Despite the negative answer, a number of Doukhobor leaders made short speeches and according to an RCMP report: 'All these speeches had a conciliatory tone.'[199] That evening, however, the $400,000 jam factory, once the glory of the Community Doukhobors but taken over by the government in 1939, was burned down, presumably by the Sons of Freedom.

Cowell was not to be deterred. In his report to MacNamara, he said: 'We held a meeting for four hours avoiding arguments and leaving with a firm note that the Government intended to put your formula into effect.'[200] Cowell was prepared to use force if necessary. Manson was of the same view.[201] They recognized that there might be 'bombings and fires' but they planned to quietly move a battalion of troops into the area to protect factories, electricity installations, and other things. In addition, they would have enough police support so that those Doukhobors who refused to comply could be arrested and charged according to the regulations. They made detailed plans with officers of the Pacific Command, but on 4 February 1944 the Cabinet War Committee in Ottawa rejected the plans.[202] That committee had noted the concern of the RCMP that the action would entail 'a serious diversion of enforcement personnel from other essential wartime duties.' It had also concluded that 'no substantial effect could be anticipated from the Doukhobors so drafted for alternative service.'

With Cabinet rejection of the plan to use military and police force to obtain compliance, officials now sought an alternative policy. The Doukhobors also indicated a desire to discuss the matter further. In January 1944, John J. Verigin stated, in a newspaper article, that he recognized that the Doukhobors 'must make certain contributions to the nation's labour supply and charities.'[203] He also visited officials in Vancouver to explore the possibility of resolving the impasse. Leaders of the Named Doukhobors indicated a similar concern.[204] However, the Sons of Freedom expressed their view in other ways. They held meetings where they disrobed, sang psalms, prayed, and burned their non-Doukhobor clothes as if to renounce worldliness.[205] On 28 January, when Verigin was conferring with officials in Vancouver, they gathered at his home and burned some things there. Early in February a group of several hundred Sons of Freedom began a long march through the

Doukhobor areas, inviting people to put their government documents, including registration cards, birth certificates, ration-books, and money, into a box that would then be given to the government.[206] In addition, two schools and a CPR station were burned, presumably by the Sons of Freedom.[207] Leaders of the USCC denounced these acts strongly.[208] Nevertheless, a number of young men from the USCC left their jobs, attended these gatherings, and became generally sympathetic to the Sons of Freedom.[209]

The demonstrations subsided by the end of February 1944, but they had the effect of increasing public pressure on the government. One official said that at this time 'strong letters of protest began to arrive in great volume.'[210] The Canadian Legion sent a letter to MacNamara stating that the Doukhobors knew that they had won this round and that the government's failure to act was encouraging them in their defiance and lawlessness.[211] The legion said further that the government should not bow to the fears of the West Kootenay Power and Light Company which had argued against firm action on the ground that it might cause many of their badly needed Doukhobor workmen to leave their jobs. The legion warned also of vigilante action. In fact, some action of that nature did take place.[212]

The government, however, was cautious. In a report of 15 March 1944 to the minister of Justice, Louis St Laurent, the RCMP reviewed the developments, noted that many of the men of military age were already usefully employed, and then stated: 'The question arises if it is of any practical value to the country to enforce the National Selective Service Mobilization Regulations among them, when the majority, if not all, are already engaged in such work as farming, mining, dam construction, logging and railway maintenance, which work is generally regarded as being in the national interest ... If it is intended ... to compel them to do what they are already doing voluntarily, these religious fanatics will, it is believed, continue to protest by all possible means.'[213]

Officials in Ottawa tended to favour this policy of leaving the Doukhobors alone so as not to disturb the work they were already doing. However, officials in British Columbia took a different view. Manson and Cowell argued that the Doukhobors should somehow be brought under the law. Manson said: 'The present situation is absolutely indefensible from the Government's standpoint.'[214] He criticized the government for being dishonest and for encouraging the Doukhobors in the view that they did not have to abide by the laws. He felt that 75 per cent of the men would readily respond to firm but tactful action and that once these complied the others might follow. Late in May he proposed to go to the Doukhobor settlements to see if something could be arranged. However, MacNamara in Ottawa did not permit him to go.[215]

The alternative-service officer for the British Columbia division, C.S. Henley, wanted to try a different approach. H.R. MacMillan, an employer in the logging industry, which was deemed essential, had indicated a need for several hundred workers. Henley now felt that the registered Doukhobors should be encouraged to take on this work, that the board should then officially declare them 'postponed' (meaning exempted from military service) even without a personal appearance before the board, and that he should then try to arrange alternative-service contracts with them so that they would pay a small amount to the Red Cross each month.[216] From the legal point of view the procedure was unusual, but at least the Doukhobors would be abiding by the law.

Even more unusual was the approach being followed by the National Selective Service Office under the direction of one Mr McKinstry. That office was issuing work permits and helping Doukhobors to take work in the most needed areas without regard to whether they were registered or whether the board had given them a 'postponement' from military training. In this way, at least some Doukhobor workmen were being directed to essential jobs. McKinstry did not want this process disturbed with Henley's talk about alternative-service contracts.[217] When the issue was raised in Ottawa, the initial response of L.E. Westman, the chief alternative service officer, favoured McKinstry's approach over Henley's.[218] He recognized that McKinstry's actions were 'entirely illogical from the angle of the regulations' but praised them for bringing employers and Doukhobors together.[219] McKinstry, he said, 'has simply done the practical, expedient thing ... and has not quibbled about the technical position of a Doukhobor with respect to Mobilization matters.'

Henley was not persuaded.[220] He questioned an approach that so completely bypassed certain parts of the regulations even though he recognized that enforcing them might just fill up the jails. Other officials also had concerns, and in July 1944, MacNamara, the federal deputy minister of Labour, authorized Manson in British Columbia to visit the Doukhobor settlements to explore the feasibility of a compromise approach. Westman now also supported this approach, although he was still sensitive to the labour situation, saying: 'The last thing that anyone wants is for Doukhobor labour to become unavailable.' He suggested that the registered male Doukhobors of military age – about 1000 – be given a 'blanket' postponement, that they be informed of their liability for alternative service, that they be given work permits so they could take jobs, and that the alternative-service officer then try, gradually, to make arrangements whereby they would pay something to the Red Cross. Westman was still not optimistic. He argued that if the plan failed it would be some time before that would be discovered and that 'the position of the government would be better in the meantime.'[221]

Manson then travelled to the Doukhobor settlements, together with another official, F.W. Smelts. They met with employers and local officials and, most important, with leaders of both the Named and the USCC Doukhobors, although not with the Sons of Freedom.[222] They were received sympathetically. John Verigin invited them to meet with the supreme council of the USCC and Manson reported that the Doukhobor leaders were 'cordial and sincere and anxious for a solution of their problem with the Government.' They were sympathetic to the idea of making deductions for the Red Cross from the earnings of the conscientious objectors. P.K. Reibin of the Named Doukhobors suggested that they make these deductions in the same way that income tax was being deducted.

Manson now felt optimistic. He prepared a form letter, to be sent to all registered Doukhobors, in which he, as chairman of the war services board, informed them that they were now classified as conscientious objectors. This meant that they would not have to take the medical examinations or appear before the board. The letter also informed them that deductions for the Red Cross would be made from their monthly wage. Manson also proposed that John DeVoin, a constable of the British Columbia Police who had an unusual familiarity with the Doukhobors, be requested to serve as a special alternative-service officer for them.[223] The necessary authorization was soon given and DeVoin began working in October 1944, although Westman in Ottawa still counselled caution, saying: 'If he [Manson] does postpone a thousand men quickly, it does not follow that we [Alternative Service] will do anything in a great rush.'[224] He did not want to disturb the labour situation.

DeVoin's work soon showed signs of success. He received the names of the postponed men from the board, sought them out, and with various explanations tried to make arrangements so that they would contribute money to the Red Cross on a regular basis.[225] Some were willing to sign alternative-service contracts. Others refused but were willing to make the payments if they were billed by the Treasury office. Also, for those who were unemployed DeVoin tried to find jobs. Significantly, Doukhobor leaders encouraged their people to co-operate with this new approach. The executive committee of the USCC issued a statement on 14 October 1944 explaining that in December 1943 they had decided against making voluntary contributions because that would have appeared as 'our bribe out of military obligations' but that the new arrangement was a 'form of levy or tax' that people should pay in accordance with the rule 'Caesar's unto Caesar.'[226] P.K. Reiben of the Named Doukhobors issued a similar statement. On 2 November 1944 DeVoin reported: 'By the first of the year we will have a majority of these people paying to the Canadian Red Cross Society.'[227]

The arrangement did not resolve all the problems. The Sons of Freedom, with some exceptions, remained outside of it. And in spring 1945, when employers were particularly sensitive about anything that might disturb their Doukhobor workmen, they asked that the deductions not be made too categorically. One fruit grower reported that the man in his orchard would not make payments of any kind, saying: 'He considers paying money to anything connected with the War is taking part in the War.'[228]

The arrangement was much more lenient than that for Mennonites but it brought many Doukhobors into the parameters of the law. The public was pleased that the government was doing something constructive.[229] And officials, both in British Columbia and in Ottawa, found it acceptable.[230]

In concluding this long and involved survey, it must be said that in effect the Canadian government gave the Doukhobors a very broad liberty. For the most part they were given exemptions from military service without personal hearings before the boards, and, except for a brief period at the end of the war, they were also exempted from the alternative-service program. In contrast, the Mennonites on the prairies received military exemption only after personal appearances, and some not even then, and virtually all of them participated in the alternative-service program. In between were the Mennonites in Ontario who participated in the alternative-service program but did not have to make personal appearances before the boards in order to obtain military exemption.

The difficulties of the prairie Mennonites in obtaining exemption from military service, which appear to have involved the Russlaender Mennonites somewhat more than the Kanadier Mennonites, were probably a result of a number of factors.[231] In some cases the refusals will have been valid. Not all Mennonites had 'conscientious objections' to military service. Moreover, because the question involved a subjective matter it was inherently difficult to judge. In response to the difficulties, Mennonite leaders argued unsuccessfully for two corrective measures. Their request for an appeal body empowered to review the decisions of the boards was rejected because of the extensive complications experienced with the First World War appeal system. Their other request, that the word of church leaders who had long known the young men be taken into account, was also rejected. What the prairie Mennonites were asking for with this request was operative both for the Mennonites in Ontario and for the Doukhobors in the west in the sense that their young men were exempted because they belonged to those groups, not on the basis of personal appearances before the boards.

Another reason for the military exemption difficulties relates to what appears as a bias on the part of certain judges. This bias is suggested particularly by the determination of Judge Embury in Saskatchewan and Judge Adamson in Manitoba to persuade Mennonites to take military training, after which, they were told, they could go into regular non-combatant service under military auspices. In this capacity they could still be called on, in exceptional situations, to use weapons but it was not likely. Judge Harvey even made the dubious claim that military commanders would not give Mennonites in the military the kind of assignments that would require them to violate their religious beliefs. In a sense, what these judges were pursuing was similar to what the two deputy ministers, Davis and Lefleche, had attempted in the 1940 negotiations with Mennonite leaders. At that time, Davis and Lafleche objected to the idea of setting up a civilian-based service program. They wanted, instead, to have conscientious objectors serve in some capacity under military auspices. Mennonite leaders resisted this option both in their meetings with the deputy ministers in 1940 and in their oft-stated concern about the rulings of the judges in the years that followed. The church leaders had a point. The evidence of inconsiderate treatment on the part of certain judges is too strong to be discounted. But the fact that a significant portion of the Mennonites, estimated at 37 per cent, served in the military, makes it understandable that judges would be somewhat sceptical about Mennonite claims.[232]

If the government system can be criticized for allowing abuses, it must also be credited with a remarkable flexibility and responsiveness, at least toward these groups. (Jehovah's Witnesses had a different experience.)[233] The responsiveness toward these groups is indicated at a number of points. In June 1940 when the prime minister introduced the National Resources Mobilization Act, he committed the government to honouring the historic promises of military exemption given to certain religious groups. In August 1940, after Doukhobor leaders had made strong and persistent requests to register their own people, a system for doing so was approved; without it, most Doukhobors would probably not have become registered. For most of the war years, the Doukhobors were virtually exempted from the alternative-service program simply because they did not want to participate. The government could have prosecuted them but it recognized that such an action would probably result in mass protests and in the loss of Doukhobor labour. Because labourers were greatly needed, officials decided to leave them undisturbed in their regular work. These policies may have been based on expediency but they also reflect a remarkable systemic flexibility.

The appearance of the alternative-service program is itself an indication of the system's responsiveness and flexibility. The program began because of the determination of Mennonite leaders who eventually prevailed over reluctant senior officials. Once accepted, the program grew substantially even if not smoothly. A total of 10,867 conscientious objectors participated in it.[234] Their regular payments to the Canadian Red Cross Society, as required by the alternative-service program, totalled $2,327,163.12. They planted over 20 million trees in British Columbia alone. Senior officials praised the alternative-service workers as orderly, decent, and hard working. The British Columbia minister of Lands wrote, in January 1943:

It is a notable fact, that no sooner were a few of these alternative service workers in camps in the Province, then a wide variety of interests were inquiring as to the possibility of securing their services. We have been approached by various mills, logging operators, the E. and N. Railway, by C.A. Cotterell, General Superintendent of the Canadian Pacific Railway in Vancouver, by the Lumber and Shingle Manufacturers' Association, the British Columbia Loggers' association, and even by taxi firms. The services of these men were urgently requested for harvesting crops in the Fraser Valley and for harvesting the fruit crop in the Okanagan. It was proposed that they should be returned to the Prairies for the harvest there, and most of them being farmers, we had urgent requests for harvest leaves. These representations have been progressively urgent and pressing as the employment situation has become more aggravated during recent months.[235]

There is little doubt that the value of the alternative-service program helped to prevent the emergence of widespread public feelings against conscientious objectors. It must also be noted that Canada was not quite as fully involved in the Second World War as it had been in the First World War, that the Canadian public was now less fervent in its support, and that eligibility for conscientious-objector status was no longer so restricted to certain groups.[236]

In summary, then, the social climate, the contribution of the conscientious objectors through the alternative-service program, the government's commitment to honour the historic promises of exemption, the persistent lobbying by leaders of these groups, and the flexibility of the political system all help to explain why, despite numerous problems, these groups were permitted to enjoy a relatively broad freedom during the Second World War.

PART FIVE

The Welfare State

Mennonites, Hutterites, and Doukhobors have long sought to take care of the material needs of their people. However, the more conservative groups among them have seen this task as so inseparable from their faith that certain problems arose when the state became more active in providing for the welfare of people.

These problems arose, in one case, in relation to the Canada Pension Plan (CPP) and the effort of certain Mennonites and all Hutterites to gain exemption from it. Both groups argued that they could not, without violating their faith, transfer the task of caring for the material needs of their people to the government. The Hutterites also pointed out that by participating in the CPP, their people would have individual accounts, in violation of their principle of not owning private property. The second case, which involved only the Hutterites, centred on the question of how to apply the Income Tax Act to their situation. If the colonies were treated as corporations, then the tax burden would be extremely high, but the personal income tax provisions were not suited either, because the Hutterites did not have individual incomes.

These two cases are the subjects of the next two chapters but other problematic 'welfare-state' measures must also be noted. First is the Family Allowance program. When it began in 1945, many people in these groups did not accept the allowances. A group of western Mennonite leaders, meeting on 20 March 1945, concluded: 'If the government is called upon to help with the raising of our children, will it not later be entitled to more support from these same children? ... The majority of the elders do not think our people should take this allowance.'[1] Doukhobors also held meetings to discuss the question and, according to one report, 'a large number ... felt that in accepting such payments, they would be incurring a liability to conform to demands of the state that might not be agreeable to them.'[2] Despite such reservations about accepting the benefits, there were no questions about paying the taxes to operate such programs. Most saw the payment of taxes as a religious duty. (Participation in the CPP, these groups would point out later, involved insurance premiums, not regular taxes.) Years later, when the majority in these groups had accepted Family Allowances, the Hutterites still had concerns because the cheques were issued in the names of individuals. They asked that the cheques be issued to the colony instead. These requests were turned down, so the individual Hutterite recipients simply signed the cheques and turned them over to the colony treasurer.[3]

Second is the difficulty of the Hutterites in qualifying for benefits from various government programs such as the Farm Credit Corporation, the Prairie Farm Rehabilitation Act, the Grain Stabilization Program, and the Hog Stabilization Program. Eligibility for benefits under these and similar programs is determined by criteria based on individual family farms or corporations, not on the communal style of the Hutterites. In the 1950s, when numerous marketing boards were set up (for milk, eggs, chickens, hogs, and other farm products) to limit the amount that farmers could produce in order to maintain certain price levels, the Hutterites again suffered discrimination. The boards tended to set the quotas for each farm operation on the basis of the family-farm concept, not on the basis of the communal pattern of the Hutterite colonies. This, together with other factors affecting the farming economy, made things 'exceedingly difficult' for the colonies. As a result, they began to manufacture farm equipment such as hog-pens, hog feeders, heat-exchangers, alfalfa pelletizing machines, prefabricated windows, and roof trusses. Other people beginning such 'light manufacturing' activities would have received grants from the Department of Regional Industrial Expansion (DRIE), but the Hutterites had difficulty in getting grants because DRIE's regulations regarding the employment of unemployed workers were difficult to incorporate into the Hutterite communal style.[4]

Third, a number of domestic programs presented similar difficulties. Early in the 1980s a government home ownership program offered grants of $3000 to help people to become home owners. A number of Hutterite colonies applied but were rejected because their concept of ownership was different and because 'the individuals involved did not own the land' on which the home was being built.[5] In another case there was a program whereby people could obtain funding to remove urea formaldehyde insulation from their homes. The Hutterites, like other Canadians, had used this insulation in their homes before it was found to be a health hazard. But they had difficulty in establishing their eligibility for these grants to cover removal costs, again because 'there is no individual ownership.'[6] In Manitoba, in the mid 1980s, the provincial government set up a Child Related Income Support Program but eligibility was to depend on the income level of the parents or guardians. Once again, the fact that the Hutterites did not have individual incomes complicated their eligibility.[7]

These examples serve to illustrate the inequities that the Hutterites suffer. They pay taxes for these various programs to the same degree that other taxpayers do, but they cannot always obtain the benefits. Their communal life-style does not 'fit the mould' for which these programs are designed. Fortunately, most of these inequities are not so serious as to threaten the existence of the Hutterites. Also, in some instances, government officials have found ways of overcoming the obstacles. Nevertheless, a measure of unfairness exists, at least for the Hutterites who, like other Canadians, have become interested in the benefits of such programs. Some conservative Mennonites continue to refuse the benefits. They want simply to live on their own.

10 Mennonites, Hutterites, and the Canada Pension Plan

The Canada Pension Plan (CPP), which came into force in 1966, was an unusual social-welfare program. It was an insurance plan. The federal government hailed it as 'an important milestone in Canadian social development.' It was to help people to 'make financial provision for their retirement and to protect themselves and their dependents or survivors against loss of income in the event of disability and death.'[1] Every employed individual would contribute 1.8 per cent of his or her earnings to the plan. Employers would pay an equal portion. Self-employed people would also be required to contribute. The monies would be paid alongside income tax payments. Every participant would have a social insurance number. Later these monies would be paid back in the form of a pension.

A majority of the Mennonites in Canada accepted the CPP but the Amish and Old Order Mennonite groups of Ontario and the Hutterites in the west did not.[2] They held that their religion required them to care for the material needs of their people, which they had done for centuries. To participate in the CPP, they felt, would mean delegating this task to the government. It would weaken the bonds of their communities and represent a marked departure from the way of life they believed to be right for them.

Accordingly, when the CPP was introduced in 1966, these Ontario groups asked for an exemption. (The Hutterites were not yet affected because until 1968 they did not pay income tax.) The Ontario groups made their first appeal in April 1966 when they met with Joseph W. Willard, deputy minister of National Health and Welfare, and submitted a letter addressed to the minister, the Hon. Allan J. MacEachen.[3] In it they assured the government of their basic appreciation, support, and loyalty, but said: 'We believe that when the laws of the land conflict with the teaching of the New Testament we must obey God rather than man.' They said that when their forefathers had come from Pennsylvania late in the 1700s and early in the 1800s, 'they were ... promised the free practice of their own religious beliefs under the British Crown.' The letter concluded: 'We, as a group, have instructed our people not to apply for Children's Allowance or Old Age Pension. We believe it to be our Christian duty and privilege to take care of our own people as a brotherhood. We therefore appeal to you, Honourable Minister, to make it possible for us to be exempt from the "Canada Pension Plan" and allow us to continue as at present.'

The minister of National Health and Welfare acknowledged the letter but informed the Mennonites that their concern related to that part of the CPP that was under the jurisdiction of the minister of National Revenue, Edgar Benson. Benson replied on 4 August 1966 to Elven Shantz, an official of the Mennonite Central Committee Ontario, who was assisting the Old Order groups.[4] Benson reported that the government had studied the matter in considerable depth but could not accede to the request. He explained:

The Plan is compulsory because Parliament has decided that the cost of protection against the risks mentioned must be shared by all. Further, it is only through the compulsory principle that the contributions of the employer can be brought into the scheme.

I am sure you will appreciate that each service made available by the Government through a social insurance program, such as the Canada Pension Plan, must be considered as part of the total social service structure in this country, financed collectively on the basis of the social insurance principle. To exempt your Orders from the Canada Pension Plan would serve to undermine the basic principle upon which the plan is founded, namely, the principle of universality.

The Mennonites were disappointed. Elven Shantz wrote: 'I am very sorry that a Canadian Government is taking such an inflexible stand on this request.'[5] Shantz then attempted to find a solution through a provision in the act for exempting religious orders such as those in the Catholic church. In section 6(2) (e) under the general title of 'Excepted Employment,' The Act referred to 'employment of a member of a religious order who has taken a vow of perpetual poverty and whose remuneration is paid either directly or by him to the order.'[6] Shantz now wondered whether the Old Order Mennonite groups might also qualify under this provision. However, they did have private property and Benson quickly rejected the possibility.[7]

The Mennonites then appealed directly to Prime Minister Lester Pearson.[8] In a long letter (27 October 1966), they reviewed developments in the history of religious freedom since the sixteenth century, noting that William of Orange had been a pioneer in promoting tolerance, first in the Netherlands and later in England. They also referred to William Penn under whose leadership many people, including Mennonites, had come to America and enjoyed a broad religious freedom. They explained how after the War of Independence, their ancestors, along with others, had immigrated to Canada 'to again be under the British Crown, which by this time had become synonymous with religious freedom in theory and practice.' They noted that even during the two world wars the government of Canada had upheld the tradition of religious freedom and exempted the Mennonites from military service. They asked whether that tradition, which had also been emphasized in the Bill of Rights enacted by Parliament in 1960, was now coming to an end and whether the government was now assuming the right to force 'social legislation' on all Canadians, regardless of their religious beliefs. They pointed to the fact that in the United States their people were being exempted from such legislation and then asked the prime minister to grant their request.

The prime minister was not persuaded. In a reply on 10 November 1966, he reported that he had discussed the matter with the ministers involved: 'I sincerely regret that for the reasons stated in Mr. Benson's letter of August 4, 1966, it is not considered advisable to introduce amending legislation to exempt from the Plan certain classes of our society, thus endangering the basic principle on which the Plan was premised, that is, the participation of every working person in Canada between the ages of 18 and 70.'[9]

The Mennonites were 'deeply disappointed' at this reply. Along with their lengthy October submission Shantz had asked for a meeting with the prime minister 'to discuss ... the religious beliefs of the Old Order brethren on this specific legislation as well as any future compulsory social legislation.'[10] The request for a meeting had not been granted so they now wrote: 'We had no opportunity to meet the reasons your ministers gave you.'[11] While assuring the prime minister of their respect and loyalty they set out to explore other avenues because 'we believe as Canadian citizens we have a right to live and worship as we interpret the Bible.'

These 'other avenues' referred to legal action. The Mennonites now sought a legal opinion 'as to the possible success of ... challenging the Canada Pension Plan in the courts as infringing the freedom of religion clause of the Canadian Bill of Rights.'[12] They approached a Kitchener law firm, where J.E. Lang then studied the question. He identified the key questions as 'whether in the view of the Mennonites the plan is of a religious nature and secondly whether the right of freedom of religion protects this view.'[13] He then reasoned that 'the Mennonite considers it his moral obligation to care for the aged' and offered the opinion that 'the Plan does not interfere with the moral obligation of the Mennonite and that the requirement of a contribution is like a tax and certainly is not in itself or in the view of the Mennonites of a religious nature.' On this basis he advised them that they 'would probably not be successful in court action.' In summary, Lang wrote:

It is the opinion of this writer that the argument that the Canada Pension Plan infringes on the Freedom of the Mennonite to practice his religion would fail in the Supreme Court of Canada. My reason is that the Canada Pension Plan is social legislation directed at all Canadians; it is not legislation directed at a particular religion or religious belief. Further it is my opinion that such legislation is not basically different from Tax legislation or other social legislation. To say that a group could avoid such a law on the grounds that it prevented them from freely practising their religion would put the Government of Canada in the inequitable position of being unable to affect any legislation for fear of offending some groups.

This contention, that the CPP premiums were like a tax, was to appear again. The Mennonites disagreed.

Some months later the Kitchener Chamber of Commerce became involved. On 13 April 1967 the chamber held a special meeting with representatives of the Mennonites. As on previous occasions Elven Shantz was their spokesman. During the discussions it was decided to propose a compromise to the government. The Mennonites would agree to pay the premiums if the government would agree to use these monies not for the CPP but for a welfare program selected with the approval of the Mennonites.[14] This would demonstrate that the Mennonite concern was not simply one of withholding money or opposing social-welfare programs.

Both Shantz and the president of the Board of Trade wrote letters to the prime minister describing the proposal. Shantz wrote: 'We are prepared to meet our financial responsibilities under the Canada Pension Plan Act; however, we wish ... that consideration be given to our request that all contributions remitted by members of our Orders be directed to a welfare programme to which we may give conscientious approval.'[15] The president of the Kitchener-Waterloo Board of Trade wrote: 'Sympathetic and concerned as we are with the problems of these fine people in this modern age of the "Welfare State," we feel that the new submission offers a reasonable solution to the present impasse, and we hope that you, in consultation with your Ministers, may find it possible to accede to this proposal on their behalf.'[16]

Because the proposal was a compromise it is not surprising that some Mennonites had reservations about it. One elder, S.M. Horst, wrote: 'It does not seem right to suggest an alternative to a thing that was unscriptural from the root up ... if they need more money and tax us in a straight and scriptural way we will endeavor to pay as long as our dollars last ... [However] giving the money so as not to offend them ... we are not letting the truth shine out as we should that way.'[17] Government officials also had difficulty with the proposal. The prime minister wrote back stating that he had reviewed it with Benson and that, 'unfortunately, the present legislation does not provide for allowing amounts paid out of the Plan to be paid to other than the contributor or his beneficiary.'[18]

Despite these repeated refusals, the Mennonites persisted. They now set out to gather information on the way the problems had been resolved in the United States with the intent of making another proposal. They suggested to Benson, the minister of national revenue, that 'any legal action which may come about as a result of our members not wishing to pay their premiums toward the Plan be deferred until further representations have been made to your office.'[19] The minister refused this request: 'The law as presently legislated must be enforced ... any authorization in favour of a particular group which would serve to circumvent the due processes of law would be an abuse of the office which I hold.'[20]

GOVERNMENT SEIZES ASSETS AND MENNONITES MAKE FURTHER APPEALS

In the spring of 1967, while other Canadians were paying both their income tax and their CPP premiums for 1966, these Mennonites paid only their income tax. Elven Shantz, their spokesman, wrote to the government on 23 February 1967 and reported that some thirty-seven leaders of the Old Order groups had met and decided to ask their members to send in their income tax returns as usual but that instead of including the portion for the CPP they should enclose a letter addressed 'To Whom It May Concern,' stating:

I am a member of the Old Order Mennonite Church. We believe that the needs and losses of the brotherhood should be taken care of first by the individual, then the family, then the Church, as we are taught by the Holy Scriptures. Our forefathers have established the system in the church long before the Dominion of Canada was formed, and we cannot conscientiously participate in a compulsory social insurance system.

While it is our desire to extend love and mercy to every man in need regardless of religion or creed, we are very conscientious as stewards over the material things the Lord has entrusted to us.

I am therefore not including the Pension deduction payment with my income tax return.[21]

The Department of Revenue soon responded with letters informing the people of their legal obligation to pay. The Mennonites, however, were firm. In response many used another form letter:

The claim which you request is the portion to be paid to the Canada Pension Plan, which we cannot pay since it conflicts with our faith, since this portion is designated to an insurance fund.

I therefore beg you to review the situation, as I consider the necessity of giving heed to my religious conscience and the unity of our brotherhood.[22]

One Mennonite replied to the letter from the Department of Revenue in the following way: 'I have paid my income tax, the amount you requested [is] ... to be held in a separate fund which we look at as an insurance fund. We are historically opposed to all types of insurance on religious and Biblical grounds. I can therefore not send you the money.'[23] Another Mennonite was informed that not only was his income tax overdue but that he also needed to get a Social Insurance Number.[24] He refused to get the Social Insurance Number and in reply to the request for income tax he used a form letter that stated: 'We respectfully beg to advise that our income tax was paid in full. Therefore your claim must be attributed to the portion to be paid to the Canada Pension Plan which we cannot pay since it conflicts with our faith.'[25]

The Department of Revenue, in the face of the Mennonite refusal to pay the premiums voluntarily, began to seize the money. In mid August 1967 the department went to Silverwood Dairies Ltd in Kitchener, to which many of the Mennonites were selling their milk, and issued 'Demand on Third Party' notices for the milk cheques. The company was then obligated to turn the cheques over to the department instead of to the Mennonite farmers.[26] This action raised considerable public concern and a newspaper reported that Benson, the minister of Revenue, had said: 'The Old Order and Amish Mennonites of the Kitchener district will have to contribute to the Canada Pension Plan or the government will continue to seize their milk cheques or other income'; that 'he will not consider the Mennonite argument that payment was against their religious convictions'; and that 'they'll get their pension cheques when they become eligible – it is quite possible for them to turn those cheques over to a charity or any cause they think proper.'[27]

The Mennonites were not sure what further steps to take. Some talked of migrating to South America or to the Caribbean.[28] One Mennonite wrote to the *Kitchener-Waterloo Record*: 'We are refusing to accept baby bonuses, old age pensions, and milk subsidies, and saving the government at least ten times as much as our pension payment would amount to ... Seizing our milk cheques takes an ironical turn when we consider that for conscience sake we have refused thousands of dollars of milk subsidies which we could have had for the asking.'[29] This same person, David Wagler, replied to a notice from the Department of Revenue, stating:

I regret very much to inform you that I cannot conscientiously pay you the money which you are requesting. We have never taken part in any kind of life insurance as we feel to do so would be putting our trust in man instead of in God

...

You have called this a tax, but Mr. Benson recently made the statement publicly that every Canadian with a certain minimum income will have to pay into the Pension Plan, and will receive when eligible at the age of 65, a pension check as per the Plan.

Please allow me to state that this does not sound like a tax to me, but a compulsory insurance plan, and until I will be able to understand it differently I cannot pay this amount voluntarily.[30]

On 7 September 1967, Wagler received a reply: 'An examination of your 1966 Income Tax Return reveals that you have been properly assessed with the amount in question. It is therefore requested that you forward payment ... Whether or not you apply for benefits to which you are or will be entitled is a matter for you alone to decide.'[31]

The Department of Revenue continued to send out letters requesting payment and the Mennonites continued to refuse. While further exchanges were taking place, the Kitchener Chamber of Commerce became more deeply involved. During the summer of 1967 it conducted a survey of the Mennonites in the Kitchener area and found that 'members of the orders in this area alone are saving the Canadian tax payer approximately $400,000 per annum by declining to apply for family allowance and old age security benefits that they have contributed to through normal taxation and that they are entitled to by law.'[32] This, the chamber said, represented '4 or 5 times the amount they are being told they must contribute to the Canada Pension Plan.'

With this information the Chamber of Commerce appealed to Benson again, asking that these groups be exempted. In a brief dated 11 October 1967, it made the following points: '(a) The convictions of the Old Order are substantiated by their actions, (b) the welfare of these people has never been a local or national problem, (c) migration of long established settlers is not an acceptable solution to the problem, (d) amendment to the Act to exempt these people would affect a saving rather than an expense to the Treasury, (e) a precedent has been set by the United States Internal Revenue Service with regard to the exemption of Mennonite and Amish people in that country, (f) no other group desirous of opting out of the Canada Pension Plan can meet these qualifications.'[33] The brief concluded: 'The Kitchener Chamber of Commerce has committed itself to support of the Old Order plea for exemption from both contributions to and benefits arising out of the Canada Pension Plan.'

The brief was presented to the minister of Revenue and other officials in Ottawa on 16 October 1967. In the same meeting the Mennonites submitted a lengthy brief of their own.[34] In it the Mennonites reaffirmed their loyalty to Canada and their gratitude for its long history of good governments. They then set out, in a fairly elaborate way, their understanding of the proper functions of government and of the church: 'We view the government as ordained of God' and 'We respect government, regularly pray for those in authority and obey it up to the point when its demands conflict with our Christian faith and life.' They explained that joining the church was done voluntarily by adults and that for them it was a serious and sacred matter involving not only 'agreement to a set of theological beliefs but ... also promising to live according to a well defined way of life.' they stated further:

> The church we believe is a genuine brotherhood in which individual members obligate themselves to help one another in time of need and to be willing to submit to the discipline and counsel of the total brotherhood ...
> This is our substitute for insurance systems and other forms of social security programs. It is our understanding of the way we think God means for Christian people to provide for each others need ...
> We see the social security programs as a direct threat to our religion. To be forced to accept such programs is to be compelled to substitute a government welfare program for a church centered program.
> We fear that such publicly sponsored programs will over a period of time, divert the loyalties of our people away from the church and toward dependence upon government.

They then asked again that the government 'respectfully consider the possibility of exempting those with religious scruples from coverage under the Canada Pension Plan by amending the present act.'

At the meeting where the briefs from the Mennonites and the Chamber of Commerce were presented, Benson acknowledged that 'we would not need the Canada Pension Plan if all the people of Canada would live like the Mennonites.'[35] He indicated that he was not happy with the seizure of milk cheques but that he could not change the law. He then indicated a willingness to consider amending the act and promised his personal support for an effort to that effect. He explained that a change in the act required the consent of the provinces and said that he would present the issue to a forthcoming federal/provincial conference scheduled to consider revisions in the CPP. The Mennonites, for their part, although still unwilling to pay the premiums voluntarily, agreed not to protest the seizures for the time being on the understanding that Benson would personally work towards changing the law so that they would eventually become exempted.[36]

The government continued to seize the monies. The Mennonites received letters notifying them of the amounts owing and requesting information about where they sold their farm products or in which banks they held their accounts. Most Mennonites, it appears, now gave such information to the government; however, they wanted it understood that they were not consenting to the seizures. David Wagler, in informing the department of the bank where he held his account, stated:

Please do not construe this to mean that I give my consent to your seizing of our property. Of course I realize that all of our earthly property is subject to seizure or theft and that the law does empower you to seize it.

If you believe the Bible as I assume you do, then please note that Romans 13:3 tells us that the governments are to be a terror not to good works but to the evil.

... we have not done anything evil to incur the displeasure of the government. Because we have carried out the Biblical injunctions of caring for our own and not depending on the government to take care of our old people, babies and needy, we are now being coerced into accepting a form of life insurance.[37]

Despite the commitment made by Benson in fall 1967 that he would personally work to have the act amended and that he would bring the matter before a federal/provincial conference, there was little action. One year later the Mennonites had still not received word as to when such a federal/provincial conference would take place. Meanwhile, the seizure of monies continued and so did public interest in the problem. One official noted that the Department of Revenue had received 'a great number of letters from persons living in the Kitchener-Waterloo area requesting that some action be taken to relieve the Mennonites from contributing to the Canada Pension Plan.'[38]

In 1968 a new government, under the leadership of Pierre-Elliot Trudeau, was elected and in January 1969 the Mennonites met with John Munro, the minister of National Health and Welfare in the new government.[39] He renewed the promise of contacting the provincial governments to seek their opinion about amending the act.[40] The Mennonites also had contact with Max Saltsman, an NDP member of Parliament for a constituency near Kitchener with a number of Old Order Mennonites in it. Saltsman now introduced a Private Member's Bill to amend the act so as to exempt groups like the Mennonites.[41] Despite these efforts there was no movement. The new minister of National Revenue, Jean-Pierre Côté, recognized that the seizure of monies had 'created some unfavourable publicity in the press' but felt that this was not a serious problem.[42] Indeed, Côté was opposed to changing the law.

THE HUTTERITES JOIN THE EFFORT TO SEEK EXEMPTION

Early in 1969 the Hutterites in the west also began to seek an exemption from the CPP. By this time they had, after years of negotiations, concluded an agreement to pay income tax. In these negotiations, they had expressed concern about the implications of such an agreement for the CPP. After all, CPP pensions were tied by statute to income tax payments. At first, revenue Department officials in Winnipeg had told representatives of the Hutterites that 'in view of their vow of perpetual poverty and the fact that no cash income is received by any one of them, they are exempt.'[43] Later, as the negotiations for the tax agreement reached a more final state, officials in Ottawa said that they could not exclude the CPP.[44]

The possible CPP implications made the Hutterites uncomfortable about signing the income tax agreement. They were settling the income tax issue on a 'deemed individual income' basis, that is, in their calculations they would divide the total income of a colony by the number of members, make deductions comparable to those of other Canadians, and then pay tax accordingly. This arrangement carried the appearance of an individual income but the Hutterites emphasized that it was 'for income tax purposes only' as 'a concession on our part in the spirit of public cooperation.' They did not want it carried over to the Pension Plan or other issues. Yet the officials with whom they were finalizing the tax agreement could assure them only that it was 'without prejudice to the rights of the Colonies to contest their liability to pay into the Canada Pension Fund.'[45] And if it would be held that they were liable under the CPP, then, said the officials, they could still approach the government 'in order to obtain a revision in Legislation' of the CPP.[46] In light of this response, two of the three Hutterite groups signed the tax agreement and in November 1968 immediately instructed their lawyers to work on the pension-plan issue.[47]

The Hutterite effort to gain exemption from the CPP began with a claim that they qualified under section 6(1) (e) which, as noted above, exempted members of religious orders. The Hutterites argued that their situation was similar to that of Roman Catholic orders because they, too, had vows to the effect that they would receive no personal income; they, too, were members of a religious community; and any earnings resulting from their labours went to that community for it to allocate as it saw fit. In a formal appeal to the minister of National Revenue early in 1969, they explained: 'The accumulation of benefits under the Canada Pension Plan for a Member of the Church is contrary to the teachings ... and tenets of the Church and could not be accepted by the Appellant.'[48] They also argued, using words from section 6(1) (e), that the 'appellant is engaged in employment as a Member of a religious order who has taken a vow of perpetual poverty and whose remuneration is paid either directly or by him to the order.'

The appeal was not successful. The minister of National Revenue replied by pointing out that the Hutterites, in the agreement settling the income tax question, had been treated as self-employed persons, that the Canada Pension Act covered all self-employed persons, and that because of the statutory connection with the Income Tax Act they were now obliged to pay CPP pensions.[49] This response from the federal government was particularly disconcerting to the Hutterites. The concession they had made in the tax agreement, 'in the spirit of public cooperation,' was now being used against them in their CPP concerns.

The Hutterites then, in August 1969, prepared a more elaborate statement.[50] They described their communal way of life and their religious beliefs against private property. They reviewed their history of four and one-half centuries and pointed out that in the negotiations with the Canadian government in 1899, they had received a letter from James A. Smart, then deputy minister of the Interior, stating: 'There will be no interference with their living as a Commonwealth if they desire to do so.' The 1899 letter had said further: 'The members of the Society in question may rest assured that the statements made above are of as full value to them as they could be made by an Order of the Governor in Council or any document of that nature.' The Hutterites now said that they understood this to be 'a continuing moral commitment, entitling them to the privilege of exemption from the Canada Pension Plan which interferes with their living as a commonwealth.' They referred to the situation of Hutterites in the United States where, by amending the legislation, their 'religious principles have been recognized and protected.' In summary they said:

The Hutterian Brethren Church of Canada submits that as a result of the administrative convenience which required that contributions to the Canada Pension Plan be collected by the Department of National Revenue, discrimination against its Members has occurred. This discrimination results in a direct interference with the beliefs of the Hutterian Religion by imposing individual interests on the Hutterites by law. It is a discrimination which the Hutterites feel the Government of Canada specifically agreed to avoid in inviting them to this country.

The principle of excluding from application of the Canada Pension Plan those persons who have taken a vow of perpetual poverty has been accepted by the legislation (Section 6[1][e]). The results of a tax settlement reached in good faith ... should not result in discrimination in the application of this principle. The Hutterian Brethren thus request that the provisions of the Canada Pension Plan be revised so that the definition of self-employed persons provides an exception

for Members, of a religious or apostolic order, association or corporation whose
vows of perpetual poverty or other tenets exclude them from contribution to the
Canada Pension Plan.[51]

A member of Parliament from Manitoba, Mark Smerchanski, whose
constituency contained a number of Hutterite colonies, now wrote to the
minister of National Health and Welfare expressing his belief that 'the
Department of National Revenue has arbitrarily taken the position that
the Hutterian colonies automatically come under the Canada Pension
Plan as being self-employed' and that 'this is not in accordance with
Section 6(1) (e) of the Canada Pension Plan.'[52] He stated: 'I strongly
suggest Mr. Minister, that these people be exempt from the Canada
Pension Plan because this is a religious group who are competent and
able to care for their aged. The caring for their older people is one of the
basic concepts of their religion.'

The government now needed to respond both to the Hutterites on the
prairies and to the Mennonites in Ontario, as well as to members of
Parliament Mark Smerchanski from Manitoba and Max Saltsman from
Ontario. The public, at least in the Kitchener area, also felt that the
government should be more accommodating. In the words of John
Monro, minister of National Health and Welfare: 'The matter of
exemption ... has boiled down to a policy decision.'[53] It would have to be
brought before the Cabinet.

THE CABINET CONSIDERS THE MATTER

In preparation for Cabinet consideration, W.J. Trudeau, director of the
CPP in the Department of National Health and Welfare, wrote a
background document stating: 'Our view is that no amendment to the
legislation should be considered which would have the effect of
exempting ... groups or individuals from the requirement to make
contributions to the Canada Pension Plan.'[54] Another 'Memorandum to
the Cabinet,' signed by the minister of Revenue, Jean-Pierre Côté,
argued that if such groups were exempted then their young people
would be less inclined to leave since they would have nothing waiting for
them on the outside.[55] The leaders of these groups, the memorandum
said, 'strive continuously to maintain their communities against "worldly
temptations," even to the point of objecting to high school education.
This raises the question of whether the weight of government legislation
should be employed in a way which would help to keep members of some

religious sects economically dependent on their sects.' Côté's memorandum expressed the concern, too, that if these religious groups were to be exempted, then various other groups might also want to be exempted and, if such requests were granted, then the principle of universality would be seriously undermined.

A 'Supplementary Memorandum to the Cabinet,' dated 14 November 1969, reviewed the experience in the United States.[56] There, these religious groups, after several years of negotiations, had been exempted from the Social Security Act. However, the memorandum pointed out, in the United States the principle of universality had never been held up as an ideal.

Early in 1970 the Cabinet considered the issue and decided against granting an exemption. The minister of National Revenue, Jean-Pierre Côté, then wrote to the Mennonites and Hutterites and explained the decision of the Cabinet in identical letters.[57] He noted that the matter had been under review since April 1966, that various ways had been studied in an attempt to resolve the problem 'in a manner that would avoid any charge of discrimination from other groups.' He said that the situation in the United States had also been studied and that it had been found that 'the amending legislation enacted by the American authorities was unquestionably discriminatory and justifiable solely on the grounds that their Act, from its inception, did not purport universal coverage and that even today permits some optional coverage.' The decision of the Cabinet, Côté said, was based on a desire 'not to deviate from the basic principle of compulsory coverage of every individual between the ages of 18–70, self-employed or engaged in pensionable employment in Canada.' He explained: 'It was concluded that universal coverage is the fairest and most acceptable principle that can be followed in the legislating of a government sponsored insurance plan.' He noted, in conclusion, 'the sincere reluctance with which each member of Cabinet reached the decision that the principle of universality of coverage must not be violated.'

Several days later, on 20 March 1970 before the decision of the Cabinet was known, representatives of the Mennonite Central Committee Canada (MCCC) met with Prime Minister Trudeau. They raised this issue among others. In response Trudeau said:

The plan being universal, we didn't feel we could make exceptions, because they would amount to forms of discrimination in a negative sense ... we did consider it at great length ... we had considered it in Cabinet and we discussed it both in

Committee and in full Cabinet ... but the possibility of opting out of this particular form of quasi taxation – if I can call it that – we felt that if we conceded that, there would be a case for too many other groups in this and other areas saying that we don't agree with this particular policy which was adopted by the government on behalf of the majority, therefore we would like to opt out too – I do assure you we have given this deep consideration and in the cases of where we have universal plans for Social Security, we do not find it possible to make exceptions for one group without having to make exceptions for many, in which case we no longer have any universal plan.[58]

Further in this discussion with the prime minister, Newton Gingrich of MCCC acknowledged that some of the reasons for the refusal were understandable, but asked whether the religious dimension of the situation did not make a difference. He requested an explanation of religious freedom. Trudeau replied:

Religious freedom exists, I take it, when people are free in their conscience and they can exercise their beliefs freely within the country, belong to a church of their choice, and so on. But, in some cases, if the morals which flow from their metaphysics – if I can put it that way – are not morals accepted by the community in which they live, it is unfair to say that preventing those moral precepts from applying is an attack on religious freedom ... And in this particular case, the morals of this small minority are in direct conflict with the scheme of social welfare which the governments of today have adopted in order to serve the communities better. And therefore, while they may continue practicing ... believing the same kinds of faith, but in this particular case there is no practical way of not to be bound by the ethic or the morals of the policies ... [sic] when the government adopts laws which are good for the majority, I don't think that freedom of religion permits people from opting out.

To the Mennonites this view of religious freedom seemed narrow. It gave people the freedom to believe and to worship as they wished but for those who felt that their religion led to a way of life different from that of the larger society it offered little protection.

Despite this clear and firm refusal, both the Mennonites and the Hutterites continued their effort to obtain an exemption. On 20 April 1970, the Hutterites sent letters to the two ministers, John Munro and Jean-Pierre Côté, stating: 'Our members are very keenly disappointed that we should be placed in the same category as other sects ... The vow of perpetual poverty taken by our members clearly distincts [sic] us ...

and to our firm point of view clearly entitles us to exemption under provisions of the Canada Pension Plan along with other Religious Orders with the vow of perpetual poverty.'[59] The Hutterites continued: 'We view and hold the Understanding of Agreement reached with your Department to tax our members on an individual basis a concession on our part in the spirit of public cooperation and tolerance only. It was our firm conviction that this would not interfere nor undermine our religious beliefs or way of life as it now threatens to do. We therefore urge you and your government very strongly for immediate reconsideration of the cabinet's decision.'

The request for reconsideration availed little. A reply from Munro, dated 16 June 1970, stated: 'While I fully appreciate the concern that your group feels over the decision made by Cabinet . I assure you that it was made in full light of the facts and must, regretfully, stand.'[60] The Hutterites then came back to the argument that they were a religious order whose members had taken a vow of poverty and who therefore were entitled to an exemption 'under the existing CPP provisions for exempting religious orders.'[61] In order to now establish their eligibility under these provisions, they asked for a change in that part of their recently negotiated tax agreement which referred to them as 'self-employed' individuals. If this could be changed, then they would not be treated as 'self-employed' under the CPP either. As a result, they felt, they would then qualify under the provision for exempting religious orders.

The Hutterites now stated that in the negotiations for the tax agreement, they had felt quite uncomfortable with being classified as 'self-employed' individuals. They said it was not an accurate reflection of what they really were. However, in the interest of reaching a settlement, and because they had believed that the classification would not affect their way of life, they had consented to it. In asking that this classification be changed, they were not asking to withdraw from the agreement to pay taxes, only for a change in the way they were classified in that agreement: 'As a result of that agreement the Hutterian Brethren agreed, for purposes of the Income Tax Act, to allow the profits of the community to be divided equally on certain established principles between members of each community and tax would be paid by the community on the calculation so reached. As a result of this arrangement, the individual Hutterites were treated as self-employed for purposes of the Canada Pension Plan. The result of this treatment is that payment into the Canada Pension Plan is required.'[62] They explained their predicament further: 'If it were not for the tax settlement, which for purposes of the Income Tax Act, treats the Members of the Hutterian Colony as self-employed ... the Members of the Hutterian Colony would be employed by the Colony in all senses. The attribution for tax purposes is simply a mathematical calculation made by accountants ... returns for the colony are made collectively and no amount is received or otherwise charged to each Member internally.'

They concluded:

It is, therefore, submitted that the section of the Agreement of Settlement entered into between two of the Hutterian Brethren Groups, and the Department of National Revenue relating to taxation, does not accurately reflect the factual ... situation insofar as it treats the members of the Hutterian Brethren Church of Canada as self-employed ... It is submitted that in the light of the case and the strong religious conviction of the Hutterian Brethren, that without amending the law the agreement of settlement should be amended to reflect the fact that for purposes of the Canada Pension Plan, the employment of the Hutterites is as a Member of a religious order who has taken a vow of perpetual poverty and whose remuneration is paid either directly or by him to the Order.

The petition of the Hutterites did gain some sympathy among officials in Ottawa.[63] However, instead of a change in the tax agreement with the Hutterites, there was now a breakthrough for change in the CPP legislation. It came late in 1971, following further meetings of the Mennonites of Ontario with the new Revenue minister, Herb Gray. The critical meeting took place on 7 December 1971. Gray listened to their submissions at length and then said that he deeply appreciated the position of the Old Order people and that it might be possible to bring the matter to the Cabinet for reconsideration even without first consulting the provinces.[64] The Mennonites were impressed, saying that Gray was 'the first person to give serious consideration to the religious aspect of the problem.'[65] Two weeks later the government announced that it would amend the CPP Act to accommodate both the Amish and Old Order Mennonites of Ontario and the Hutterites in the west. It would exempt self-employed members of religious sects where 'it is established that the compulsory feature of the Plan is in conflict with the religious tenets of the sect' and where 'the religious sect meets certain criteria.'[66] The announcement stated: 'A sect seeking exemption under this amendment would be required to establish that it has been in existence for a number of years, has established tenets and teachings in opposition to the receipt of benefits from a private or public insurance scheme which makes payment in the event of death or retirement and has, as a practice, made provision for its dependent members which is reasonable in view of their general level of living. Where a sect qualifies for exemption each individual member of the sect would be required to apply for exemption.' The press release also noted: 'Similar exempting provisions have been a part of the United States Social Security legislation for many years.'

DEBATING THE PROMISED AMENDMENT IN PARLIAMENT

Even though the government, in December 1971, made a commitment to amend the CPP Act so that the Hutterites and Old Order Mennonite groups could be exempted, it was another three years before the amending bill was passed by the House of Commons. In May 1973 an amending bill was approved by the Cabinet. On 4 June it was brought into the House of Commons as Bill C-190 and the debate began on 20 July 1973. More than a dozen members participated. Most were with the Progressive Conservative party, the official opposition, although several members of the New Democratic Party also spoke. A survey of their speeches reflects the various perspectives from which the issue was perceived.

The first member to speak on the bill was Stan Schumacher, a Progressive Conservative from an Alberta constituency. He opposed the amendment because of the special privilege that it conveyed: 'Any piece of legislation that is of general application should be applicable to everybody ... I really do not see why those of us who do not support the Canada Pension Plan cannot be exempt from it if various other groups and organizations can be, as proposed by this legislation.'[67] He also held that the premiums were 'a form of taxation' and that 'if the proposed amendment is carried, the Mennonites and Hutterian Brethren will not be contributing to the general welfare of Canada in the way I believe the majority of the people of Canada expect them to.' He expressed sympathy for the principle of conscientious objection but felt that that principle was not at issue here. Another Progressive Conservative speaker, Perrin Beatty who represented an Ontario constituency with 'perhaps a greater proportion of people who will be affected by this bill than any other constituency in Canada,' supported it strongly and said it was 'basic to the principle of freedom for religion.'[68] Douglas Roche of the same party but from an Alberta constituency also supported the bill for reasons of religious freedom.[69]

New Democrat Stanley Knowles from Winnipeg saw the question as a clash between two important principles: that of freedom for religion and that of universality in social-welfare programs.[70] He referred to the persuasive efforts of his colleague Max Saltsman and said: 'Despite my tendency to put the greater weight with ... [the] principle of universality, I am not opposed to this bill.' Fred McCain, however, was not persuaded to depart from the principle of universality. He also said that the people might eventually need the help of the CPP even though now they did not think so.[71] Thomas Barnet of British Columbia also remained unconvinced. He questioned the distinction that had been made between CPP premiums and ordinary taxes and expressed concern about 'the provision for opting out,' fearing that it 'embarks us upon a slippery path.'[72]

The strongest opposition came from Jack Horner, then with the Progressive Conservative party, representing a rural Alberta constituency.[73] He held that CPP premiums were like a tax and that no exceptions should be made in the obligation to pay them. He argued that taxes were necessary for the common good and referred to one study of the Hutterites that stated: 'No loyalty to the country in which they live is acknowledged by the Hutterites ... responsibilities of citizenship are not accepted even by those born in the country.' He said that ordinary farmers had great difficulty competing with Hutterites and that many of these farmers would also like to be exempted from the Pension Plan, albeit for other reasons. Why should the requests of others not be granted, he asked, because 'giving everybody equal treatment is what democracy is all about, not the granting of privileges to some and the withholding of privileges from others.'

Heath MacQuarrie, a Progressive Conservative representing a Maritime constituency after living in Manitoba for many years, spoke at some length in favour of the bill.[74] Referring to the Mennonites and the Hutterites, he said: 'These remarkable people have been able to carry through that familial affection and have been able to make adequate provision for an extended family. They have been able to retain their values, their moral code and at the same time be productive citizens ... They work the soil of Canada and make it produce. They bring forth good crops from the providence which has been given to all of us.' He also pointed out that these groups were conscientious objectors in times of war and said: 'I think in countries that are thoughtfully democratic we recognize that even the right to bear arms need not be forced upon people.' He concluded by saying: 'I know how long these people have pled their case, how carefully and thoughtfully they have put it forward, and I would like them to know that I am delighted that they have been given this measure of adjustment, this reasonable acceptance of their reasonable proposition.'

Max Saltsman of the New Democratic Party, who represented an Ontario constituency, had introduced a private member's bill with objectives similar to this government bill in every session of Parliament in the preceding four years.[75] He now reviewed some of the background developments, including the willingness of the Mennonites to pay an amount equivalent to the Pension Plan premiums to a charity or even to a government social-welfare program. He described this as 'the Mennonite test,' because it demonstrated that 'their objection is one of principle and not of pocketbook.' He was confident that few other groups would meet this standard and that, therefore, to pass this bill would not 'open the flood-gates' for others to gain exemption.

Saltsman also challenged the view that passing this bill would undermine the principle of universality in social legislation. In his words:

I suggest that universality can in fact be strengthened by making certain well-defined exemptions. Of course, if there were widespread exemptions universality would be destroyed. The great criticism against universality is ... that when you force all people into the same position or pattern, while there is a kind of equity in doing that there is also the possibility of some injustice being created in the process. If an exemption can be made in a specific, proven, well documented instance, then universality is strengthened because the small element of injustice that might be present is removed. I suggest that by granting this exemption from the Canada Pension Plan ... the universality of the plan will be strengthened. There is no danger to the plan.

He explained and supported the position of the Mennonites and Hutterites in holding that the CPP was an insurance program. If it were an ordinary social-welfare program then he would be opposed to granting exemptions, he said. Saltsman also pointed out that when these groups had moved to Canada there had been a promise that they would be allowed to live according to the teachings of their religion, differently from the people around them and, in his view: 'To the extent that it is possible for a changing society to honour that kind of guarantee we should do so.'

Another supporter of the bill was Tory Jake Epp, representing a

Manitoba constituency with a number of Hutterite colonies. He began his speech by challenging the statement made by Jack Horner that the Hutterian people were not loyal citizens.[76] He explained that their first loyalty was to their religious precepts but that this 'does not mean that they are not loyal citizens.' He also challenged the argument of universality by pointing out that the CPP had never been universal because from the beginning it had 'clearly exempted groups of people who are members of religious orders and who took the vow of perpetual poverty.' He felt that the Hutterites should have been exempted under these existing provisions and that the amending legislation was simply a way of ensuring it.

Epp's most basic argument was based on the principle of freedom for religion. He referred to the provisions for freedom of religion in the Canadian Bill of Rights and in the promises which Canada had given to these groups when they had immigrated. He then pointed out that an individual participating in the CPP would build up a 'personal equity' and that this violated the basic tenets of the Hutterite religion. He also pointed out that the Hutterites took responsibility for their own people and said: 'I do not believe that ... we must provide them with security by legislation.'

Another supporter was Bill Jarvis, a Progressive Conservative member for a southern Ontario constituency with many Old Order Mennonites.[77] He expressed gratitude for the opportunity to speak in favour of the bill: 'From time to time, and probably on too rare occasions, we in this House have the opportunity of expressing that which is in the hearts and consciences of one of our minority groups ... I suggest to Your Honour that Bill C-190 affords us such an opportunity.' He said the desire of these groups to be exempted was not based on pecuniary gain, pointing out that they were already paying for a variety of welfare programs, provincial and federal, from which they were not accepting benefits. He was disappointed that it had taken the government so long to bring the bill before the House and expressed 'doubt that we would even have this legislation now had it not been for the minority position of the government resulting from the election last October.'

The debate in the House of Commons ended with some brief remarks by the Hon. Marc Lalonde, minister of National Health and Welfare.[78] He referred to the commitment made in December 1971: 'The government believed then, as it does now, that the Canada Pension Plan, in its present form, places an unintended penalty on these groups for the practice of their own particular religions.' The bill then went to the

Health, Welfare, and Social Affairs Committee.[79] Some details received closer attention there and the Mennonite groups were invited to appear before the committee but few new arguments were made. In spring 1974, in a new session of Parliament, the provision came before the House of Commons again. Jack Horner made one further effort to stop it.[80] However, on 7 November 1974, when the provision came as part of Bill c-22, it was finally passed.

Soon after, forms were prepared whereby individuals in these groups could apply for exemption. On the application forms they would indicate that in keeping with the established tenets and teachings of the group to which they belonged, they were 'opposed to acceptance of the benefits of any private or public insurance program which makes payments in the event of death, disability, old age or retirement.'[81] The application forms were countersigned by an authorized spokesman of the group. The authorized spokesman was required, in turn, to provide documentary evidence to show that the group was indeed opposed to acceptance of benefits from insurance programs, that it made reasonable provision for its dependent members, and that it had been in existence and had held to these positions on 1 January 1966 when the cpp first took effect.[82] The arrangements were satisfactory. The exemption was secure.

Obviously the government had changed its approach. It now granted these separate groups a liberty sufficiently broad so that they could continue in their way of life. The process whereby this change came about is noteworthy because the question hinged on legislation, not just on the interpretation of legislation. Hence, it involved politicians, not just civil servants, and thus it contributed to a particular articulation of the issues. For the most part the contest was between the principle of universality in social-welfare legislation and a broad view of freedom for religion. Messrs Benson, Pearson, Côté, Trudeau, and others all held that the principle of universality could not be compromised. The implication, though not articulated until Trudeau did so, was that freedom for religion meant little more than freedom of belief and worship; certainly it could not protect a group if it wished to follow a way of life different from that of the larger society. The Conservative members of Parliament who supported the amendment probably reflected a lesser emphasis on the principle of universality and a broader view of freedom for religion.

Some mps perceived the issue differently. Jean-Pierre Côté, minister of

Revenue at the time, argued that to grant the desired exemption would leave individuals within these groups more dependent on the groups and thus serve as a disincentive for those who might wish to leave. In other words, it would sacrifice the liberty of the individual for the liberty of the group, which is a problem that has been discussed in preceding chapters. Tory MP Jack Horner argued against granting the exemption. He held that CPP premiums were like taxes, necessary for the common good.

NDP MP Max Saltsman supported both the exemption and the principle of universality. In his view, they were not incompatible. He argued 'that universality can in fact be strengthened by making certain well-defined exemptions.' When the amending bill was introduced, its provisions for the exemptions were indeed 'well-defined.' The bill restricted eligibility to groups that had been in existence for some time, whose religion had prohibited participation in insurance plans before the CPP came into force, and that provided for their dependent members by other means.

These groups based their appeals not so much on broad principles of political theory as on the fact that, historically, British and Canadian governments had given them a broad liberty. The Mennonites referred to William of Orange and William Penn and reminded the government that when their people had first come to Upper Canada they had been assured of freedom to practise their religion. The Hutterites quoted an 1899 letter in which the Canadian government stated: 'There will be no interference with their living as a commonwealth'. They also pointed to the promise of freedom for religion set forth in the 1960 Canadian Bill of Rights. Underlying their arguments was an unshakeable conviction that their way of life was right for them and that the Canadian government had a moral obligation to let them to follow it. Undoubtedly, this conviction helped them to persist.

In their efforts to persuade the government these groups relied most on direct appeal. They appealed to the ministers of National Revenue and National Health and Welfare and also to the prime minister. When these overtures were rejected they made further appeals. In March 1970 when Jean-Pierre Coté, then minister of National Revenue, explained that the Cabinet had considered the matter at length and had decided not to exempt them, the Hutterites made another appeal within a few days. Both Mennonites and Hutterites were extremely persistent. And they did not refrain from publicity. Indeed, the Ontario groups, enjoying a relatively good public image, co-operated willingly with newspaper reporters. They saw this co-operation as part of their effort to have the government change its views.[83] They also received significant support from the Kitchener Chamber of Commerce, from members of the public who wrote letters to the government on their behalf, and from member of Parliament Max Saltsman. In 1971, after Herb Gray had become minister of National Revenue, they also found sympathy in that strategic portfolio. These factors contributed to the eventual success of the cause. (It may be noteworthy that both Saltsman and Gray had personal roots in a minority religion.)

That this encountor ended successfully for these groups is indicative of the significant flexibility in the Canadian political system. But the process, marked by so many refusals, even from the highest political levels, reveals an uncertainty and a reluctance that do not reflect positively on the readiness of Canada to accommodate such groups.

11 The Hutterites and the Income Tax System

THE PROBLEM AND INITIAL ATTEMPTS AT A RESOLUTION

Canada's income tax system also had to be modified in order to accommodate the Hutterites. Their communal way of life did not fit well into the personal income tax category because they did not have personal incomes; nor did it fit into the corporation category because their colonies were not commercial corporations organized primarily for making a profit.

The problem lay dormant until around 1960. In the 1940s and 1950s tax officials occasionally took samples of the earnings of colonies to determine what the effect would be 'if they attempted to collect taxes from them by distributing the income to the members on a pro rata basis.'[1] They found that the amount of revenue to be gained was insignificant. Officials were helped in maintaining this view when many colonies adopted the practice of filing statements that they calculated on the basis of the personal income tax laws, listing their total income, the expenses incurred in earning that income, and the statutory exemptions and deductions that would be available for their people. After doing so it was evident that 'there is no tax to pay.'[2] The 1959 Alberta Hutterite Investigation Committee came to the same conclusion.[3] Also, the Hutterites had not, until this point, accepted Family Allowances and Old Age Pensions. E.A. Fletcher of Winnipeg, who had served as the Hutterites' lawyer since they came to Canada in 1918, advised them that by refusing these benefits they would help to remove the suspicion that they were getting something for nothing.[4] Meanwhile, the Hutterites were punctual in paying their other taxes.

Though satisfactory to officials, the arrangement whereby the Hutterites were outside the income tax system did not have legal sanction. This circumstance left them vulnerable to critics who argued that the colonies were highly competitive commercial enterprises, that they created difficulty for other farmers, and that they should be taxed as corporations. Some of their defenders held that the colonies were 'exempt ... because they were associations organized and operated exclusively for a purpose other than profit and no part of their profits was available for the personal benefit of any member of the association.'[5] They also pointed out that Hutterite land supported two to three times as many people as that of other farmers and that the tax calculations the Hutterites were making were fair and reasonable.[6]

Despite the arguments in their favour, around 1960 some western members of Parliament, elected in the 1958 Conservative landslide, were making 'vigorous representations' to the minister of National Revenue about 'the privileged status of the Hutterites.' Accordingly, in December 1960, the minister, the Hon. George Nowlan, announced that 'the members of the Hutterite community in Canada and their corporations or colonies are properly liable to income tax and should comply with all the requirements of the Income Tax Act ... In the calculation of the profits of the colonies or corporations, deductions will only be allowed for disbursements actually made for salaries and wages and the other expenses permitted by the Income Tax Act ... In other words, the Hutterite Colonies and their members will be treated for income tax purposes in exactly the same way as other taxpayers.'[7] Not all the implications of this announcement were immediately clear, although they pointed towards corporation tax. Of special concern was the reference to salaries and wages. Clearly, the Hutterite colonies paid no salaries and wages to their people. Yet much money was used for providing food, shelter, and clothing for them. Were it not for their communalism this money would surely be paid out in the form of salaries. Not it appeared that the tax department would assess them on a corporation tax basis and not allow these expenditures as deductions.

If the implications of the announcement were not immediately clear, neither was the government's determination to implement it. The file 'remained in abeyance until subsequent to the Federal Election of 1962.'[8] However, there were discussions among officials and with Hutterite leaders. Also, lawyers for the Hutterites made representations about the problems involved. Still, the idea of taxing Hutterites on a corporation-tax basis persisted and officials became interested in preparing a test case in order to let a court decide whether this process would be legal. With this possibility in mind, officials began to make assessments of two colonies.

Lawyers for the Hutterites, however, opposed the test-case method. So, early in 1963 when the assessments were made, they filed formal objections, which led to further reviews of the minister's initial directive and of the situation in general. But in May 1965, under the new Liberal government, the minister formally disallowed the objections in a further effort to bring a test case before the courts.[9] Lawyers for the Hutterites then made additional representations and proposed that they work towards a negotiated settlement. They wanted to avoid the delay and the risks of lengthy court proceedings, even though they felt optimistic about the final outcome. They also pointed out that a negotiated settlement might be in the government's interest because a court ruling, even if it was favourable to the government, might have far-reaching implications for the tax status of religious institutions.[10] Eventually, the merits of this position were recognized by Revenue officials. They now agreed to negotiate.

At first, when the effort to find a negotiated settlement got under way, officials of the Department of Revenue defended the position in the minister's 1960 announcement that the department would not allow deductions for the expenditures on food, clothing, shelter for Hutterite members, because these amounts were not paid out in the form of salaries.[11] To overcome this serious problem it was proposed that the by-laws of the incorporated colonies be amended so that a colony would agree to pay a certain amount to its individual members, provided that the members agree beforehand to give back the full amount of that remuneration to the church. It was described as follows: 'The effect ... will be that, for tax purposes, the Colonies have paid the Members remuneration which will be deductible to the Colony in computing its income and, at the same time the Members will have, by prior arrangement, donated the monies to the Church. There will be no physical receipt or handling of money by the Members since the Colonies will pay over the monies directly to the Church on behalf of the Members.'[12]

The Hutterite colonies had strong reservations about this proposal. Its suggestion of private property was too explicit. The government was not enthusiastic about it either.[13] Instead, in the face of new political pressure, it considered once again the possibility of seeking a court judgment in a test case. But once again Hutterite lawyers intervened.[14] They asked for a further effort to find a negotiated settlement.

A COMPROMISE AGREEMENT WITH SOME HUTTERITES

This further effort at negotiation proved fruitful. Hutterite lawyers began by exploring an arrangement based on a 'deemed individual income' concept. This had some individualistic dimensions but these were not as explicit as those in the earlier proposal. The colonies would divide their total income by the number of their adult members, calculate their liability on the basis of the personal income tax schedule, use the available deductions, and pay tax accordingly.

The new proposal was discussed at an Alberta meeting on 29 June 1966 attended by forty-five Hutterite leaders from all three provinces.[15] They were told that the Hutterites in the United States paid taxes on such a basis. Their lawyers, who also attended, advised them that if they rejected this proposal then the federal government might insist on taking the whole problem to court. In a significant decision, the leaders then accepted the plan.[16] They also selected a delegation to go to Ottawa to discuss a settlement on these terms with the minister. The Ottawa meeting took place early in July 1966 and the minister took the view 'that he had no interest in persecuting or attacking the Hutterites but was only interested in ensuring that the law which he was charged with administering was enforced ... in view of the willingness of the Hutterites to pay tax on an individual basis, he was prepared to accept a form of settlement if it could be justified on a legal basis.'[17]

The minister's reference to the need for a firm legal basis for whatever settlement was made had been a basic concern ever since the department first raised the matter in 1960. Indeed, it was the lack of a firm legal basis for the earlier practices that had left the Hutterites vulnerable to criticism. In order to make a settlement on this basis now, it was necessary to set forth the legal arguments as to why it would not be proper to tax the Hutterite colonies on a corporation basis. This became the task of lawyer James Robb.[18]

In an elaborate memorandum Robb said that the Hutterite way of life 'has caused difficulty to several generations of lawyers ... [and that] the principle of community of property [does] not have any real Anglo-American judicial parallel.' Robb explained that the concept of incorporation was not a true reflection of Hutterite life and that the 'corporate entities ... are artificial impositions on the traditional way of life of a Hutterite colony.' They had incorporated, he said, in order 'to simplify the acquisition of property and its transfer.' Earlier, when they had bought land, they had often purchased it in the name of a senior member who had then 'held it for the colony in a form of undefined trusteeship.' When such 'trustees' had died there had been a variety of legal complications. Because of these complications the Hutterite colonies had been advised to become officially incorporated. These reasons for incorporating, said Robb, gave support to his argument 'that the corporate form utilized by the Hutterites were forms of convenience imposed upon them by legal circumstances over which they had no control and which forms bear little or no relation to the actual Hutterite way of life.'

In developing the argument further Robb referred to the judgment in the case of *Barrickman Hutterian Mutual Corporation v. Nault et al.* (1939), SCR 223, in which Chief Justice Duff had stated: 'The Corporation (which takes the place of the former trustees) is simply the legal instrumentality by which this autonomous community of farmers manages under the law its affairs and those of its members (according to the plan of the community of property).' Robb concluded by stating:

The purpose for which the corporations were created was not to carry on a business but ... to replace trustees. The individual members of the Colonies have not the right to benefit by ownership in the land because of their religious commitment. They do have, however, the right to benefit from working the assets of each colony and directing the disposition of these assets. Such disposition does not take place in the formal corporate sense by way of dividends, wages or otherwise but in the application of the assets, usually for the establishment of another Colony. Under these circumstances, it is submitted that the corporations involved are not the persons beneficially interested in the property and that in the first instance the persons interested are the individual members of the Colonies themselves.

Relying on these arguments Robb proposed that 'the corporate entities ... be recognized as mere representatives of the Members of the Hutterite Colonies themselves,' and that the tax assessments be calculated in terms of the situation of the individual Hutterites. To tax them as corporations, he said, would constitute a persecution of the Hutterites who, because of their religious principles, cannot give salaries to their members and thus qualify for the normal deductions.

The arguments set forth in the lengthy memorandum against taxing the colonies as corporations were well received by officials of the government. They were willing now to negotiate an agreement.[19] However, several significant questions remained. One involved the relationship of the tax settlement to the Canada Pension Plan (CPP). The

Hutterites did not want to participate in the CPP. Earlier in the negotiations a government official in Winnipeg had assured Roy Baker, a lawyer for the Hutterites, that 'under the Canada Pension Plan, the Hutterites ... in view of their vow of perpetual poverty and the fact that no cash income is received, by any one of them, they are exempt.'[20] As the negotiations progressed, however, the officials in Ottawa said that they could not exclude the CPP from the tax agreement, the legal situation being such 'that if a person is subject to tax that person is subject to liability for the Canada Pension Fund.'[21] Officials assured the Hutterites, however, that the agreement would not 'affect the possibility of the Colonies approaching the Government in order to obtain a revision in Legislation' of the CPP.[22] Most of the Hutterites wanted to settle the tax issue despite this uncertainty about the CPP involvement. They would have their lawyers work on the CPP concern as soon as the tax issue was 'squared away.'[23]

Another significant question was, who would sign the tax agreement for the Hutterites. When this issue was first raised, in March 1967, government officials asked that a signature be obtained from every colony. Lawyers for the Hutterites stated that arranging this matter would be very complex. The officials then conceded that it would be adequate to have a signature from each of the three Hutterite groups, these being the Schmiede-Leut group (most of whose colonies were located in Manitoba), the Lehrer-Leut group (with colonies in Saskatchewan and southern Alberta), and the Darius-Leut group (whose colonies were in Saskatchewan and central Alberta).[24] Now, however, the Darius-Leut group hesitated about signing even though earlier all three groups had approved of the approach. After some discussion the other two groups agreed to sign anyway.[25]

On 6 November 1968, the minister of Revenue, the Hon. Jean-Pierre Côté, released a statement announcing that 'an understanding has been reached with representatives of the Hutterian Brethren Colonies.'[26] The colonies would not be considered as corporations. They would pay tax on a 'deemed individual income' basis by taking a colony's total income, dividing it by the number of adult members, and making the appropriate exemptions and deductions. The two Hutterite groups who agreed to this procedure did so reluctantly – 'in the spirit of public cooperation' and 'for income tax purposes only' they said.

OTHER HUTTERITES CHALLENGE THE AGREEMENT IN COURT

Even though the agreement was signed by only two of the three

Hutterite groups, the government proceeded to make assessments, on the basis of the agreement, for all the Hutterites.[27] However, the Darius-Leut group, instead of responding by paying the taxes as assessed, set out to have the assessments declared illegal.

At first, the Darius-Leut counter-efforts were not successful. When the case came before the Tax Review Board, Darius-Leut representatives argued that they should not be taxed because they did not receive any income. They said that the assets were owned by the Hutterian Brethren church and were merely used by the members. In their words: 'No individual member nor any person living in the Hutterian way of life derives any income or equities, or profit sharing or interest in any way whatsoever of the Assets of the Hutterian Brethren Church, whether it be monetary or a physical Asset or dividends.'[28] The Darius-Leut Hutterites also referred to the vow taken by every individual upon joining the Hutterian Brethren church. The vow consisted of an affirmative answer to the question: 'Do you desire thus to consecrate, give and sacrifice, yourself, with soul and body and all your possessions to the Lord in heaven and to be obedient unto Christ and his Church?' Without an affirmative answer to this question, an applicant would not be accepted for membership.[29]

The government, in its response, argued that the Hutterites had very large farming operations, 'that each member shares in the distribution of profits or benefits according to his needs or in equal measure with his fellow members,' and that a colony's 'income was divided between the members in nature or otherwise.'[30] The government argued further that the Hutterites were part of Canadian society and should support it with taxes: 'If a human being owes his life spiritually to God, materially he owes his wisdom, his activity, his work, his revenue not only to himself or to a group but to the Canadian society as a whole. The income tax is one way ... to partake of the wealth of each for the good of all.'[31]

The Tax Review Board, on 16 February 1972, ruled in favour of the government.[32] The Hutterites then appealed to the Federal Court Trial Division and when the ruling there was handed down on 19 November 1973 it again favoured the government. Justice Urie of the Trial Division made an elaborate judgment that bears noting because later the Appeal Division would reject it. Urie began by identifying three key elements in the Hutterite argument: first, they did not receive any 'income' as defined by the Income Tax Act; second, even if found to receive taxable income, they could not be taxed on it because they gave it all to their religious order in keeping with their 'vow of perpetual poverty'; and third, taxing the Hutterites would violate the provisions protecting freedom of religion in the Canadian Bill of Rights.[33]

After identifying these arguments, Justice Urie refuted each of them. Regarding the first he held that the Hutterites were indeed earning income and were therefore taxable on that income even though they were not receiving it individually: 'The business of farming was carried on by the Plaintiffs in common with other members of their respective colonies under an agreement which operated as a disposition or assignment of the income earned by the Plaintiffs from such business, which income was for the common use and benefit of each member and therefore, the Plaintiffs were required to declare their aliquot share notwithstanding that it had not been withdrawn by them.'

In explaining this position – that the Hutterites were indeed receiving taxable income – Justice Urie referred to the rulings of the Supreme Court in the *Barrickman* and *Hofer* cases, in 1939 and 1970 respectively, both of which had been significant for the Hutterites. In the *Barrickman* case the question had been whether a certain incorporated colony was a 'farmer' so as to qualify for benefits under the Farmer's Creditors Arrangement Act, 1934. In judging that case, Chief Justice Duff had noted that the act whereby the colony in question had been incorporated in Manitoba had clearly stated that the objects of the colony were both to 'carry on the Christian religion' and 'to carry on farming.' He had then ruled: 'The members of the corporations are farmers ... the Corporation being the depository of the title to all the property and all the revenues of the community, which it holds and administers for their benefit ... I can see no impropriety in designating it as a "farmer" as a "person" whose principle occupation is farming.'[34]

The ruling in the *Barrickman* case, that the Hutterites were farmers, gave considerable support to Justice Urie in finding now that the Hutterites were liable to taxation. However, it was more difficult to reconcile this with the *Hofer* case, described in chapter 4 above, where several Hutterites had left and had then sought to obtain a share of the assets of the colony. They had asked for a declaration to wind up the affairs of the colony and to have the assets distributed equally. The case eventually came to the Supreme Court, which ruled that 'notwithstanding the fact that the Interlake Colony was a prosperous farming community, it cannot be said to have been a commercial enterprise in the sense that any of its members was entitled to participate in its profits. The Colony was merely an arm of the Church and the overriding consideration governing the rights of all the Brethren was the fulfillment of their concept of Christianity. To the Hutterian Brethren the activities of the community were evidence of the living Church.'³⁵ The Supreme Court, in the *Hofer* case, ruled against the claims of those individual Hutterites who wanted to have the assets of the colony divided up. The court interpreted the economic and commercial aspects of the colony to be secondary and derivative from the religious aspects, which were held to be primary.

The ruling in the *Hofer* case seemed to support, at least in part, the current claim of the Darius-Leut Hutterites that their colonies were primarily religious institutions and that therefore they should not be taxed. However, Justice Urie distinguished the *Hofer* case from the current one by noting that, in the former, Justice Ritchie had said that a colony was not a commercial enterprise 'in the sense that any of its members were entitled to participate in its profits.' Justice Urie now interpreted this to mean that 'an enterprise can be commercial and yet exclude the right of shareholders and others to participate in its profits.'³⁶ On this basis Urie held that the Hutterite colonies were commercial enterprises and that the Hutterites were earning incomes. He ruled that they were taxable on these incomes even though they had 'contracted themselves out of the right to receive the share of the net profits to which they would have been otherwise entitled.'

The second argument of the Hutterites, namely that they were members of a religious order who had taken a vow of poverty, was set aside more easily. Justice Urie referred again to the distinction, evident in the constitution of the Hutterian Brethren church and in the incorporating statutes of the colonies, between the religious and the farming aspects of Hutterite life. He then stated: 'When an organization has both charitable and non-charitable objects it is deemed not to be a charitable entity for purposes of taxation.' Further, he said: 'I find that the main purpose for which the colony, as distinct from the Church, is constituted, both originally and at present, is farming, which farming is not just for the purpose of providing food for each member and his family but for profit.' He then concluded: 'Since the objects or purposes of each colony are not exclusively religious they cannot be, in my opinion, "religious orders."'

The third argument of the Hutterites was that the taxes were in conflict with the provisions of the Bill of Rights ensuring freedom of religion. Justice Urie said that this argument 'would seem to be based upon the view that if the Hutterites are forced to pay tax on income earned, it means that, in some mysterious way, they are being forced to accept income which their religious beliefs do not permit them to accept.' Urie set this aside with the statement: 'The application of the Income Tax Act in no way imposes any obligation upon the Hutterites to accept income. All that has been done is to enact legislation within the powers of the Parliament of Canada requiring the taxing authorities to tax the income earned by all Canadians including the Hutterites. This does not mean that there has been any deprivation of his freedom to practice the religion of his choice in the manner required by his Church.' Justice Urie also noted that the traditional teachings of the Hutterite religion called for the payment of taxes except when they were demanded specifically for war purposes.

Despite this elaborate ruling rejecting their case, the Darius-Leut Hutterites pressed on to the Federal Court, Appeal Division. This persistence led to a major turning point: the ruling on appeal favoured the Hutterites.[37] Justice Thurlow rendered his judgment and held that the Hutterites did not have a taxable income. He said that the assessments 'treat the appellant as having been entitled to a share of the profits of the farming operation and they have been upheld on the view that the individual members of the communities ... can be regarded as having been engaged in farming and entitled to an aliquot share of the profits of the operation.'[38] He then stated: 'I am unable to share this view. ... Neither the farming operations nor the profits therefrom are, in any relevant sense, those of the individual members of the communities.' He explained: 'Each appellant devotes his time and efforts to working on the farm of the community of which he is a member, but he owns nothing, he is entitled under the arrangements to nothing, and he gets nothing ... but subsistence.' Thurlow also referred to the *Hofer* case and, instead of distinguishing it from the current case as Justice Urie of the Trial Division had done, he found support for his ruling in its interpretation of a colony as being primarily of a religious character.

Justice Thurlow of the Federal Court, Appeal Division, was joined by Justice Ryan in rendering the judgment of the court. Justice Ryan's reasons were similar to those of Thurlow. He challenged the judgment of Justice Urie of the Trial Division and specifically the assertion that the earnings of the colonies could be said to be those of the individual members and that even though the earnings were 'assigned' to the colony they were to be used for the benefit of the members. Justice Ryan said: 'I am not in accord with this interpretation ... Apart from the support, maintenance and other benefits they were to receive ... the appellants agreed not to charge for their services; in other words, for these services they were to receive the stipulated benefits, nothing else. I therefore do not see what they had to assign.'

After the Federal Court, Appeal Division, had ruled in favour of the Hutterites, the government launched an appeal to the Supreme Court of Canada. However, on 11 February 1976 the Supreme Court dismissed the appeal stating simply: 'We agree with the judgement of the Federal Court of Appeal.'[39]

This turn of events in 1976 had very serious implications for the government and also for the Schmiede-Leut and Lehrer-Leut Hutterites who had been faithfully paying taxes on the 'deemed individual income' basis since 1969. It appeared that they would not have had to do so. In effect the agreement that they had signed in 1968, after long and arduous negotiations, was no longer valid. One official from the Department of Revenue was quoted as saying: 'We are bound [by the Supreme Court] to withdraw from the agreement [with the Lehrer-Leut and the Schmiede-Leut].'[40] Before long, however, the government had decided that it would try to retain the principles of the 1968 agreement by amending the Income Tax Act and continue to tax the Schmiede-Leut and the Lehrer-Leut Hutterites on that basis, while proceeding against the Darius-Leut colonies on a corporation tax basis.

COURT RULINGS IN FAVOUR OF THE GOVERNMENT

The government then retained the basic principles of the 1968 agreement by placing them in the Income Tax Act through an amendment early in 1977.[41] As a result, the Schmiede-Leut and the Lehrer-Leut groups continued paying taxes on approximately the same basis as they had since 1968.

For the Darius-Leut group, however, another chapter of conflict began. The government now took steps to assess this group on a corporation tax basis. But the group found this was no more acceptable than the 'deemed individual income' concept in the 1968 agreement. Moreover, if the corporation assessments were upheld then the group's tax burden would be extremely high. The colonies might become bankrupt. Accordingly, the Darius-Leut appealed the new assessment to the Federal Court, Trial Division. There Justice Mahoney delivered a judgment, in December 1978, in favour of the government, ruling that the colonies could be assessed as corporations.[42] He dealt once again with the question of whether the colonies were indeed commercial enterprises and acknowledged that none of the members were 'entitled to participate in its profits' but held that each colony 'was a commercial farming enterprise, employing up to date farming equipment and techniques and purchasing and marketing with a view to maximum profits.'

Justice Mahoney also ruled against the claim that the assessment interfered with the Hutterites' freedom of religion: 'There is no evidence whatever that the assessments in any way affect the ability of an individual member to practice his religion as he chooses. Two of the witnesses, Bishop John K. Wurz and Reverend John K. Hofer, said their sole objection to paying income tax was a matter of conscience: part of it ... goes to war and preparation for war. The requirement that a corporation of which he is a member, pay tax which may be used for a purpose to which he, in good conscience, is opposed can, in no way, be considered as impinging on an individual's freedom of religion.' Justice Mahoney also set aside the claim that the Hutterite colonies were charitable institutions and as such exempt from taxes. To qualify as a charitable institution it was necessary to establish that no part of the income was used for the personal benefit of a member. Justice Mahoney found that even though individual Hutterites were not receiving salaries, the income of a colony was nevertheless 'applied for their personal benefit.' He also pointed out that most of their activities, which might normally be regarded as charitable, were internal and therefore lacked the element of 'public benefit' necessary to be considered charitable in the legal sense.

The judgment of the Federal Court, Trial Division, had serious implications for the eighty-eight colonies of the Darius-Leut Hutterites. All would be bound by this judgment and the total sum that the government now had a legal right to collect was said to be approximately $37 million.[43] Instead of attempting to pay, the Hutterites appealed to the Federal Court, Appeal Division. But, in December 1979, that court also ruled in favour of the government.[44] There were three judges but they dealt with only two questions. One was whether the activities of a colony were of a commercial nature. This they answered in the affirmative. Justice Pratte noted that one of the main activities of the colonies was to farm and that this was done for profit. As such, he held that it was a commercial activity even though it was 'carried on by persons believing farming to be the only activity compatible with a truly religious life and intending to use their income to assist their co-religionists.' Justice Ryan, in support of this view, stated: 'The business purpose of the corporation was not merely an aspect of a single overriding religious purpose . The motivation of the individuals who farmed may well have been religious. But the farming itself was conducted by the corporation as a business.'

The second question that the Federal Court, Appeal Division, addressed was whether the colonies, in the computation of their income, could deduct the market value of the labour donated by their members. This, the judges answered in the negative. Justice Heald stated that 'the appellant,' meaning the colony, 'would not be entitled to deduct from its net profit the fair market value of donated labour.' Justice Pratte said of a colony: 'It has acquired no property from its members and has not received anything from them by way of gift.' In summary, the Federal Court, Appeal Division, held that the colonies could be taxed on a corporation tax basis.

The ruling of the Appeal Division was a most serious blow to the Darius-Leut Hutterites. If the government would now require them to pay taxes on a corporation basis, then many of their colonies might go bankrupt. They considered the possibility of appealing the matter to the Supreme Court but after exploring this possibility, they decided not to.[45] Instead, they became persuaded in 1980 that they should attempt to negotiate a settlement on a 'deemed personal income' basis, similar to that agreed to by the Schmiede-Leut and the Lehrer-Leut in 1968; since 1977 this category had been part of the Income Tax Act. Officials from the Department of Revenue proved accommodating even though they now had the legal right to extract considerably more revenue from the colonies. The negotiations, which involved the difficult question of how the tax arrears were to be calculated, took about one year. Early in 1981, a settlement was reached.[46]

This encounter, aside from revealing certain questionable pursuits by the Darius-Leut Hutterites, shows again that Canada's institutional framework is not well suited for communal groups. As James Robb said about the Hutterites: 'Their way of life has caused difficulty to several generations of lawyers ... the principle of community of property ... [does] not have any real, Anglo-American judicial parallel.'

Second, the encounter shows that even though the institutional framework was not well suited for such communal groups, the system itself was flexible and the officials accommodating. Accommodation was evident in the decades before 1960, when officials, having concluded that there was virtually no revenue to be gained, allowed the Hutterites to remain outside the income tax system. It was evident again in 1968 when they agreed to an unusual method for taxing the Hutterites. It was demonstrated also around 1980, when it became clear that the government had the legal authority to impose the extremely burdensome corporation tax on the Hutterites. That the government then refrained from doing so reflects a substantial desire to allow the Hutterites to continue in their way of life.

Third, even though there was flexibility and a sympathetic disposition, the encounter clearly indicates that the state does set limits on freedom for religion. It did not exempt the Hutterites from the obligation to pay taxes. The Darius-Leut group tried to obtain such an exemption. It argued that its farming activities were an integral part of the Hutterite way of life, that the primary characteristic of this way of life was religious, and that therefore the group should not be taxed. The courts, however, in holding that the group was liable for income tax, ruled that the farming activities were not of a religious nature, notwithstanding that the motivation might be religious and that the income might be used to help co-religionists. In this way, the state reserved for itself the right to set limits on freedom of religion.

Fourth, many of the Hutterites also demonstrated a significant acceptance and trust of the political system. This response is particularly true of the Lehrer-Leur and Schmiede-Leut groups, which in 1968 signed the agreement to participate in the larger society's income tax system. They accepted the idea of a 'deemed individual income' as a concession 'in the spirit of public cooperation and tolerance' even though they would have preferred an arrangement that did not make any reference to an individual income.[47] By signing, these groups also made themselves subject to the CPP, but they trusted that it would be possible to negotiate an exemption later on.

This trust and flexibility on the part of the Hutterites, together with the flexibility and sympathetic disposition on the part of the government, helps to explain why a mutually satisfactory resolution was achieved.

PART SIX

Conclusion

The aim of this final part is to summarize the limits of the liberties given to the Mennonites, Hutterites, and Doukhobors, to identify the various factors that help to explain these limits, and to explore the implications of the Canadian Charter of Rights and Freedoms adopted in 1982.

It must be acknowledged that these groups were given a relatively broad liberty. The survival of the Hutterite way of life is sufficient testimony of that. Nevertheless, there were significant limitations, and the liberties given were not secure. The limitations were soon discovered by the Doukhobors in their communal landholding effort and by both Mennonites and Doukhobors in relation to the schooling of their children. So firm were these limitations and so deep were the convictions of these groups that no compromise was reached. In the case of the Mennonites, approximately 6000 members immigrated to Latin America in the 1920s; in the case of the Doukhobors, governments resorted to harsh and coercive measures over the course of half a century.

Some of the reasons for these limitations may relate to the contexts in which the encounters took place, like, for example, the unsympathetic atmosphere after the First World War that affected the Mennonite school controversy. But particular historical contexts are not the only factor underlying these limitations. The 'unsuccessful' groups wanted a very broad liberty. To illustrate, on schooling, the Hutterites accepted both a degree of governmental control and the English language but the conservative Mennonites opposed governmental control over the schooling of their children. The Mennonites wanted to continue with their own schools and their own curriculum, in the pattern they had followed for generations. The Doukhobors, in resisting the public schools, did not even have a school system of their own as an alternative.

Similarly, concerning landholding, the Doukhobor effort, when compared to that of the Mennonites who preceded them and the Hutterites who came later, also required a broader liberty. The Mennonites had accepted private property within their blocks of land and the Hutterites, though strictly communal, had much smaller blocks and hence represented a smaller deviation from the Canadian norm. Clearly, for governments to have accommodated the desires of all these groups would have represented a very broad liberty. It appears, then, that there are certain limits, however vaguely defined, that persist despite varying historical contexts.

In addition to being limited, the liberties given to these groups were uncertain and insecure. The right of the Hutterites to obtain land for starting new colonies was subject to various restrictions for many years. Indeed, for a brief period in the 1940s, the Alberta government prohibited it categorically. On schooling, the Hutterites, who had long had 'public' schools on their colonies, were under strong pressure to send their children to the consolidated town schools when these were set up in the 1950s and 1960s. Fortunately for the Hutterites, certain sympathetic officials were able to make arrangements so that they could continue with their 'on-colony' schools but these arrangements were not written into law. Similarly, the exemption from the Canada Pension Plan (CPP) was granted only after these groups had spent years making petitions. Even the exemption from military service, which had historic legal authorization, came to be interpreted in increasingly narrow ways under the pressures of war. Clearly, the liberties were not firm and secure. Nevertheless, with some exceptions, they were not completely extinguished. On many issues, when these groups persisted, governments eventually made arrangements that allowed these groups to continue in their particular way of life, at least to a significant degree.

12 Contributing Factors in Past and Future

FRONTIER SETTLEMENT AND THE EMERGENCE OF 'LIBERAL' VALUES

There can be little doubt that one reason why Mennonites, Hutterites, and Doukhobors were initially promised broad liberties was that they immigrated in periods when governments in Canada wanted to attract agricultural settlers to frontier areas. Late in the eighteenth century the frontier was in Upper Canada and when Mennonites and others from Pennsylvania asked for an exemption from militia duties, the lieutenant-governor of Upper Canada reported to the colonial secretary in London that 'there is every prospect of very great migrations taking place ... and I have not hesitated to promise ... exemption from militia duties.'[1] In 1793, when the Legislative Assembly of the time passed a Militia Act, it included an exemption provision for Quakers, Mennonites, and Tunkers.[2]

Late in the nineteenth century the frontier was on the prairies of western Canada and the attraction of settlers was one of the strongest concerns of the new Dominion. Thus, when the government in the 1870s learned of the interest of the Mennonites in Russia, it invited a delegation to visit Canada and passed orders-in-council promising this group exemption from military service, educational freedoms, and blocks of land.[3] Similarly, orders-in-council passed in 1898 and 1899 for Doukhobors and Hutterites respectively referred to them as 'a most desirable class of settlers' and then stated that 'it is expedient to give [them] ... the fullest assurances of absolute immunity from military service.'[4]

Despite these early accommodations, it was not long before different values emerged. These are evident already in the homestead system set up for the western prairies soon after Confederation. Instead of simply giving large parcels of land to religious groups or commercial companies who could then settle people in a manner of their choosing, the government divided the land into small units that individuals could obtain almost free of charge on the condition that they reside on them and cultivate them. It was an elaborate scheme reflecting egalitarian and individualistic values. To a large extent it was borrowed from the United States; in Canada its strongest promoters were the Clear Grits.[5] Fortunately for the Mennonites and Doukhobors, large areas of the country were still vacant when they arrived, so the government could make many of the modifications that they requested.

Also indicative of different values are the changes of the 1870s and 1880s in Manitoba's basic institutions, resulting, in large part, from the influx of Protestant settlers from Ontario. The system of representation that had carefully reflected the French-Catholic and English-Protestant communities was replaced by one based on representation by population. The French language, which had earlier enjoyed equal status in the courts and the legislature, was restricted. And in local government, the role of church parishes was replaced by the municipal system that, according to W.L. Morton, flourished in 'the atmosphere of secular and utilitarian democracy not in that of traditional, religious custom.'[6]

Gradually, these 'liberal' values also affected the education system. It had once been assumed that each religious group would operate schools for its own people. Even the early efforts of the government had been intended primarily to support the schools operated by Protestant and Catholic churches. But the newly arriving Ontario Protestant settlers wanted 'free, secular public schools.'[7] They felt that 'Manitoba must be made British and that a "national" school system should be the agent to accomplish the task.'[8] They did not change the system immediately, but before long they constituted a firm majority and late in the 1880s they gained a certain fervour. According to Morton: 'In 1889 and 1890 the majority of the electorate and the legislature ... were determined to abolish the ... system of denominational schools and replace it with a system of "national" schools on the American model.'[9]

The change was profound. In some respects it was part of a broader social transformation. Morton has written:

It was ... an age of nationalism, democracy, and public education. The new industrialism required national markets, the new industrial society hastened the spread of democracy, and the machine age demanded general literacy. All these factors made for elimination of differences between peoples and classes, and for assimilation to a common standard. Nowhere was this more true than in the United States, which had become a melting pot of peoples ... as English Canadians aspired to emulate the great material achievements of the Republic, they assumed they must imitate the ... social policies also. But the same factors were at work in Europe as well.[10]

The similarity of these developments in English Canada to those in the United States may be due to more than a desire for material achievements. K.D. McRae has argued that English Canada, in its political culture, shares many of the values of Lockean liberalism that are so strong in the United States. These values include individualism, egalitarianism, integration, participation, and majoritarianism. As these values became more influential, their disharmony with the separate communal life desired by the groups discussed in this book became more apparent.

The disharmony did not affect these groups immediately. The 1890 abolition of the denominational school system in Manitoba still allowed the conservative Mennonites to operate private schools, with their own curriculum and in the German language. And the less conservative Mennonites were pleased that the public schools allowed for a German-English bilingualism and for some teaching of religion. However, after the turn of the century, in the Doukhobor land controversy, the effect of the new values was more direct. Both the government and the surrounding population had become increasingly critical of Doukhobor communalism. Some of the criticism is understandable in light of the large portions of the reserve that were still not cultivated, but there was also a strong bias towards individualism and assimilation. In 1905, one official said of the Doukhobors: 'The individual homesteader has never been impressed with his rights as a settler nor his independence as an individual.'[11] In 1906, the special commissioner, Rev. John McDougall, made similar criticisms in an even stronger way. Another official stated: 'Doukhobors will need a constant watching until schools and contact with other settlers will transform them and make them think in the same way as an ordinary man does.'[12] There was an assumption that the Doukhobors should be assimilated. And the regular homestead laws, to which the government would soon require firm adherence, were to serve this end.[13]

The new and less accommodating values are evident also in the government's 1907 statement, announcing its repossession of Doukhobor land: 'The Government is ... very sorry to see that ... the large majority of the Doukhobors still cultivate their land in common and refuse to become citizens of this country ... The law is that a man must cultivate his own land or he cannot hold it ... The majority of the people say that the Doukhobors must not be allowed to hold land without cultivation any longer, the Government must obey.'[14] Aside from the question of how the government's simple assertion about what the law required can be reconciled with the Sifton concessions, this statement is noteworthy for the majoritarian assumptions that it reveals. Government, it seems, was to serve the interests of the majority without too many qualifications to accommodate minorities.[15] This view had been an important factor in the transformation of the Manitoba institutions referred to above and would continue to have effect.

If the western Mennonites in the 1890s escaped the full effect of the changing values, they were to meet them a quarter-century later. The governments of both Saskatchewan and Manitoba had encouraged people to accept public schools for some time but now they forced these schools upon the public. In 1915, E.H. Oliver, vice-president of the Saskatchewan Public Education League, urged that such efforts be carried forward 'with an eye single to the good of the future Canadian citizenship.' The function of schools, he said, 'must not be to make Mennonites, nor Protestants, nor Roman Catholics, but Canadian citizens.'[16] In 1916, the Manitoba minister of Education stated: 'We are building for the Canada of tomorrow, and our common school is one of the most important factors in the work. In this Dominion we are building up, under the British flag, a new nationality ... A grave injustice is being done to the children who do not receive a satisfactory education in English.'[17] In 1918, the premier of Saskatchewan stated: 'Whoever comes here must be given to understand that they must adopt our public school system and see to it that their children are given a proper appreciation of Canadian institutions.'[18]

The atmosphere of the First World War accounts for the harshness of the Mennonite school encounter but not for the basic difference in values. The Mennonites said they felt constrained by their religion not to delegate to the government the task of educating their children. They argued that their schools were well suited to their communal religious life in rural areas. They pleaded with the authorities to evaluate them by that standard, not by the standard of how well they prepared children for the larger society. But the governments involved did not do so. Their course was similar to that of the influential *Manitoba Free Press*, which argued that 'children are the children of the state of which they are destined to be citizens' and that the modern state is obligated to ensure that they receive an education to suit them for this purpose.[19]

In Saskatchewan, one school superintendent called for 'a more drastic compulsory system of education' with the argument that it 'would not only be to the best interests of the newer generation of children on the reserve but to the best interests of the state as a whole.[20] The differences were sharp and the 1873 promises of educational freedom were of little value. In Manitoba a court ruled that the federal government, in making those promises, had gone beyond its constitutional authority. And in Saskatchewan the premier said: 'It was unfortunate that they came here deceived by some document that they had from the Dominion government.'[21] There were prosecutions and fines for a number of years. Eventually 6000 Mennonites moved to Latin America in order to continue in their desired way of life.

The values of the larger society are evident also in the long education controversies of the Doukhobors in British Columbia. The Doukhobors argued that the education received in public schools alienated children from their communities; that it encouraged a view of life based on expediency, which in turn led to a readiness to exploit people; and that it nurtured militarism. The larger society, it appears, did not understand these arguments. For about half a century it worked at getting the Doukhobors to accept the public schools, sometimes with moderation and patience, at other times with coercion on a broad scale. But the direction wavered little. It was towards assimilation. One observer has written: 'From the time the Doukhobors arrived in British Columbia the government attempted to enforce uniform educational regulations.'[22]

The clash of values is evident also in the Hutterite land and education controversies in the middle decades of the century. On one occasion, in the mid 1930s, when it appeared that some Hutterite children might attend a nearby public school, the teacher there favoured this arrangement, saying: 'It is through the children that we will break up these colonies, these islands of isolation within our midst, and eventually bring about a true assimilation of the Hutterites into Alberta and Canadian society.'[23] In 1959, an Alberta government committee stated: 'The ultimate aim must be to look forward to a time when these people are prepared to enter more fully into the life of the dominant society.'[24] Clearly, the integrationist and majoritarian values were not in harmony with the idea of permitting these groups to live more communally, separate from the larger society.

The principle of individual liberty was also problematic. It must be conceded that some liberties given to these groups involved restrictions on the liberties of individuals within them. The dominant society had difficulty with these restrictions. In the Doukhobor land controversy, one government representative stated: 'All influences traditional and sectarian have been brought to bear on this people for the purpose of securing an abject communism under and subject to an absolute one man power.'[25] In the Mennonite school controversy in Saskatchewan, parents who had become business people and who sent their children to public schools were excommunicated from the church and hence shunned in social and economic matters by other church members. Because this response had serious implications for their businesses they called on the government to intervene. They argued that they were victims of a form of tyranny that stood as 'an insult to our liberal constitution.'[26]

The restrictions on children were also criticized. Indeed, in every school controversy the argument appeared that liberty for the children meant that the government should force them to attend public schools. There was little appreciation for the view that doing so simply took the children out of one way of life and placed them in another. Similarly, in the Hutterite land controversies, the Alberta Farmers' Union argued that Hutterites should not be allowed to expand because they were denying their people 'the right to live as free individuals and Canadian citizens.'[27] On the issue of exemption from military service, J.E. Adamson urged Mennonite parents and church leaders not to influence their young men: 'It is their conscience, and not yours.'[28] In the CPP controversy one government representative argued that to exempt these groups would strengthen the power of the groups over their individual members and make it less likely that individuals would leave. It would remove a source of security waiting for them on the outside.

This question of individual liberty is a significant problem. But these groups saw it from a different perspective. To them it was a choice between two ways of life: their religiously sanctioned communal way of life and that of the larger society with its liberal values. These groups did not claim that their way of life allowed for greater individual liberty, as defined by the larger society, but they felt that it enhanced the well-being of people in other ways and that it was right for them.

THE CONCEPT OF FREEDOM FOR RELIGION

If some liberal values were antipathetic to the idea of groups living unto themselves in a communal manner, the concept of freedom for religion seems to have had both negative and positive implications. Indeed, the experience of these groups suggests that the concept has two interpretations in Canada: a narrow one referring to an individual's freedom in matters of belief and worship and a broader one referring to the freedom of a group to pursue a particular way of life.

The narrow interpretation is evident in a number of the encounters between these groups and Canada's federal and provincial governments. The Doukhobors, in their land controversy, based their communal practices on their religion but the government refused to acknowledge that any question of religion was involved. In the 1907 announcement for repossession of the land, the government stated that it would continue to 'protect them as it has hitherto done in their religious beliefs.'[29] The Doukhobors then made a lengthy appeal. They reviewed the situation and asked the government to reconsider: 'We hope the Canadian government will continue ... to protect us in our religion,' but the Minister, Frank Oliver, replied: 'The giving of public land is not a matter of religion.'[30]

Similarly, the conservative Mennonites in their school controversies emphasized that it was their religion that constrained them to stay with their own educational practices. However, Premier Martin of Saskatchewan replied: 'The sending of children to school where they will acquire a proper education cannot in any way interfere with your religion.'[31] And the *Manitoba Free Press*, in reviewing this traumatic encounter, stated: 'There never was any attempt made to interfere with religion.'[32] Also, in the Doukhobor school controversy, when they claimed that the government, by forcing their children to attend public school, was violating their religion, Judge Sidney Smith stated: 'I ... cannot feel that in this case there is any religious element involved in the true legal sense.'[33]

Especially significant are the words of then prime minster Pierre-Elliot Trudeau in the CPP controversy. After many unsuccessful appeals, one Mennonite leader asked Trudeau to explain his view of freedom for religion. His answer reflected the view that freedom for religion included freedom in matters of belief and church affiliation, but if people's religion led them to practices prohibited by the larger society, then such a prohibition could not be considered as a violation of the principle of freedom for religion. In the abstract it is not an unreasonable approach. But in the context, where the practice at issue was quite harmless, it amounted to a narrow interpretation.

Even though the narrow view was well articulated, the broad view is evident, too. The most formal and official expression of this broader view was made by the Supreme Court in its 1970 judgment in the *Hofer* case. The question in this case was whether a Hutterite colony was obligated to give shares of its assets to individuals who, after renouncing Hutterite beliefs and practices, had been expelled from both the colony and the church. The court ruled that the colony was not obligated to do so. Justice Ritchie, in the judgment for the court, held that the Hutterite practice of holding property in common was inseparable from the Hutterite religion and that to interfere with that practice in the way that the appellants in this case requested would seriously threaten this religion and would be unwarranted. More specifically, Justice Ritchie held (i) that the property belonged to the colony, in accordance with the Hutterite religion, and was not held in trust for the individual members; (ii) that the church and the colony were so integrally related to one another that 'adherence to the Hutterite faith was a prerequisite to membership in the Colony'; and (iii) that the Hutterian Brethren church alone had the authority to decide whether any given individual was a Hutterite so as to be entitled to continue as a member of a colony. He concluded with the following words: 'It appears to me that if any individual either through birth within the community or by choice wishes to subscribe to such a rigid form of life and to subject himself to the harsh disciplines of the Hutterian Church, he is free to do so. I can see nothing contrary to public policy in the continued existence of these communities living as they do in accordance with their own rules and beliefs.'[34]

The broad and narrow views differ significantly. The Hutterite landholding pattern was regarded as part of the religion, but earlier the landholding practices of Doukhobors and the educational practices of both Doukhobors and Mennonites had been held as not related to religion. Also, the Hutterian Brethren church was said to have the authority to decide who was a member of its church so as to be entitled to membership in a colony, but during the two world wars Mennonite church leaders had been challenged when they claimed the right to decide who was a Mennonite so as to be entitled to military exemption.

If the judgment of Justice Ritchie implied a broad view, it must be noted that the court was not unanimous. Justice Hall supported the decision but wanted to set limits on the authority of the church, especially in circumstances relating to minors or others under disability. Justice Pigeon dissented more strongly. He held, basically, that 'freedom of religion includes the right for each individual to change his religion at will.'[35] In his view the Hutterites were violating this precept. He said that anyone growing up in a Hutterite colony would naturally accept its teachings and enter into the official contract at the customary time in young adulthood, but that such an individual should have the freedom to leave at any time in his life without having to abandon all the fruits of his labours. In Pigeon's words: 'The proper legal conception of religion ... is limited to what is commonly so considered and the extent of religious authority is limited to what is consistent with freedom of religion as properly understood, that is freedom for the individual not only to adopt a religion but also to abandon it at will.'[36]

The views of Justice Pigeon would lead to results similar to those of Trudeau but in a sense both were overruled, the former in the court, and the latter by colleagues in Parliament. Parliament eventually amended the CPP Act and the argument that appeared most often in the speeches favouring the CPP amendment was that of freedom for religion. In other words, members of Parliament felt that freedom for religion meant that the Amish and Old Order Mennonites in Ontario and the Hutterites in the west should be permitted to continue in their way of life, without the interference of the CPP. But the members of Parliament did not define freedom for religion in a precise way, which may be significant. Perhaps the broad view is more of a sentiment than a clearly defined principle.

This suggestion of a sentiment rather than a precise principle favouring the broad view would appear to be supported by developments in other encounters. In the Hutterite tax controversy, the government, in the end, could have been much more severe. It had received the authority through certain court rulings to impose corporation taxes on the colonies. However, such a move would probably have bankrupted many colonies. So the government used the more modest personal income tax schedule instead. The reason for the government's restraint appears to be little else than a desire to allow the Hutterites to continue in their way of life. Similarly, in the land controversies, when Alberta's 1944 Land Sales Prohibition Act was reviewed in 1947 many of the submissions called for its continuation. However, L.S. Turcotte, a lawyer representing the Hutterites, made a broad appeal to the concept of freedom for religion. It appears to have had some effect. The new law, while still restrictive, no longer contained the categorical prohibition. In Manitoba in 1948, when a legislative committee studied the question of whether a colony should be required to give a share of its assets to an individual who wanted to leave, E.A. Fletcher, a lawyer representing the Hutterites, made a lengthy presentation arguing that such legislation would destroy the Hutterites' way of life. Again it appears to have been effective. In the mid 1950s, when one Alberta school division wanted to set up a centralized school for the Hutterites, the Hutterites again made a lengthy submission, describing how this process would undermine their way of life. The Hutterites concluded with an appeal to the board members 'as gentlemen who believe in freedom of religion.'[37] Again, the board was persuaded not to proceed with its plans. Even in the *Hofer* case referred to above, Justice Ritchie seems to base his judgment not on a precise principle but on something more vague. In his words: 'I can see nothing contrary to public policy in the continued existence of these communities living as they do in accordance with their own rules and beliefs.'[38]

If there is an imprecise but significant sentiment favouring a broad interpretation of freedom for religion, it was not sufficiently strong to support the Doukhobors in either their land problems early in the century or their lengthy school problems in British Columbia later on. Nor did it help the conservative Mennonites in their school problems. However, these particular pursuits deviated further from the Canadian norm than did those of the Hutterites. The Hutterites accepted much of the government's curriculum, including the English language. Their schools were officially in the public system. And their landholdings were not nearly as large as those of the Doukhobors. It may have been easier to accommodate the Hutterites.

It would seem, then, that there is a sentiment in Canada's political culture favouring a broad interpretation of freedom for religion. It may be a reflection of the larger efforts in Canadian history to accommodate religious groups – efforts that are represented by the Quebec Act of 1774, the British North America Act of 1867, the early dualistic institutions on the prairies, and the separate Roman Catholic school systems that continue to function in a number of Canadian provinces.

PROMISES, PERSISTENCE, AND FLEXIBILITY

If sentiment favouring a broad interpretation of freedom for religion is one factor making a degree of accommodation for these groups possible, at least three other factors must also be noted. One is the desire of Canada's governments to honour the promises made to these groups at the time when they immigrated. This is particularly evident in relation to military exemption. Early in the First World War, when one delegation of western Mennonites went to Ottawa and met with Prime Minister Borden and Solicitor-General Arthur Meighen, they were assured 'of the determination of the Government to adhere to the full to the obligations of honour incurred by this country at the time of the admission of your people.'[39] There were a number of other such affirmations in the First World War, to both Mennonite and Doukhobor delegations. Even when there were serious problems in interpreting the exact meaning of the earlier promises, officials assured David Toews, the prominent Mennonite leader in the west, that they did not want to 'break faith with the Mennonite community' or 'allow small technicalities to stand in the way of seeing that substantial justice is done.'[40]

The early promises were significant also in the Second World War. On numerous occasions in the early stages, these groups asked for and received assurances that these promises would be respected. In June 1940 when Prime Minister Mackenzie King introduced the National Resources Mobilization Act into the House of Commons he confirmed the desire of the government to respect 'the existing rights to exemption ... enjoyed by members of certain religious groups.'[41] In August 1940 when the recruitment regulations were announced they explicitly referred to the orders-in-council of 1873 and 1898 for the Mennonites and Doukhobors respectively. People not covered by these orders could apply for conscientious-objector status. Later, when the National War Services Boards administered the regulations, there were numerous difficulties, but they continued to acknowledge those early orders-in-council.

The early promises figured also in the Mennonite landholding concerns late in the 1800s and again in the CPP controversy almost a century later. In the latter, the Amish and Old Order Mennonite groups in Ontario referred to an early unwritten promise assuring them of freedom to live according to their religion. Max Saltsman, their strongest supporter in Parliament, referred to it among his various arguments: 'To the extent that it is possible for a changing society to honour that kind of guarantee we should do so.'[42] Similarly, the Hutterites, in this encounter, pointed to a clause in an 1899 letter from the deputy minister of the Interior in which they were assured that 'there will be no interference with their living as a Commonwealth if they desire to do so.'[43]

Admittedly, in some encounters the early promises were not upheld. The conservative Mennonites discovered around 1920 that the promise of educational freedom given by the federal government in 1873 could be overruled by provincial authorities. And the Doukhobors in their land controversy found that promises given in writing by one minister, Clifford Sifton, could be reinterpreted so as to be of little effect by his successor. Despite these exceptions, the desire to honour earlier promises was a factor that favoured the accommodations.

A second factor that made some accommodation possible was the political approach of these groups. For the most part they were not anarchists. Usually they tried to make arrangements that would be satisfactory not only to themselves but also to the government. Also, they worked with great persistence and through diverse channels in order to make the necessary arrangements. During the wars, when there were so many difficulties, leaders like David Toews and S.F. Coffman wrote innumerable petitions. These were directed to government representatives at all levels and were made both in writing and in personal meetings. In the CPP controversy, the petitions began in 1966 soon after the plan was enacted and continued until late in 1971 when the government finally agreed to amend the act. In some instances the courts were used. Often the groups were helped by members of Parliament.

Also significant is that these groups were prepared to compromise and to make adjustments. For the Hutterites, in the tax controversy, the idea of a 'deemed individual income' carried the suggestion of individual income and as such was not in harmony with their principle of holding all property in common. Nevertheless, they agreed to it as 'a concession on our part in the spirit of public cooperation and tolerance.'[44] The alternative-service program in the Second World War was a compromise, too, at least in the perspective of some. One reason why the Mennonites wanted it was their expectation that – during the course of the war – public pressure would make it difficult for the government to exempt them from military service if they could not demonstrate that they too were rendering a national service. Neither of these compromises had the full support of everyone in these groups. Some Hutterites refused for years to accept the tax agreement and many Doukhobors resisted the alternative-service program. However, most people accepted these compromises and as such they facilitated a significant measure of mutual accommodation.

A third factor that made a degree of accommodation possible is the flexibility of the Canadian political system. In the CPP controversy, the position of the government was held firmly, having been explained several times by its highest representatives. Nevertheless, there was a capacity for change. The system responded to the persistence of these groups, to the efforts of some members of Parliament, and to the petitions of some elements in the public.

The system's flexibility is evident also in the First World War when the Ontario Mennonites found that the provisions for exemption on which they had long relied were first restricted and then removed altogether. Members of Parliament F.S. Scott and W.G. Weichel and Immigration Minister J.A. Calder were able to work out an informal arrangement whereby the young Mennonite men could receive 'leaves of absence' from the military commanders.

In the 1960s, the Hutterites in Manitoba, after considerable pleading, were assured that they could continue with their on-colony schools, and that they would not have to send their children to the consolidated town schools. They then asked the minister of Education to make this a statutory right. But he refused, saying that he did not want to let it become a political issue. He probably had a point. A public debate in the Legislative Assembly would likely have resulted in a narrower liberty than that which the government could give informally by executive action.[45]

This flexibility, which so helped these groups, has also been noted by W.L. Morton. Writing in 1975, he referred to 'the extreme flexibility of the Canadian state, both in its several parts and its functioning, and in its relations with the society of groups which it serves and from which it derives its being.'[46] In Morton's view, 'in Canada, society is sovereign, and the state is the agent, not the master of society.'

Clearly, from the perspective of these groups, flexibility was not an unmixed blessing. Its 'shadow side' was that some of the liberties, which were very important to these groups, were not firm and secure. But, on the whole, the flexibility probably resulted in a fuller accommodation of the way of life desired by these groups than would have been the case if they had received only those liberties that could be given in a secure way.

It can be concluded, then, that the flexibility of the Canadian political system, the willingness of these groups to make some compromises, the desire of the government to respect at least some of the early agreements, and the sentiment favouring a broad view of freedom for religion all help to explain why these groups were given a significant measure of liberty despite the substantial body of unsympathetic values in the larger society.

THE IMPLICATIONS OF THE CHARTER

Would the Canadian Charter of Rights and Freedoms, adopted in 1982, have led to a different result? Will it lead to different liberties for these or other groups in the future? All the encounters described in the preceding chapters, with one small exception, took place before the charter was adopted but its implications need to be explored.[47]

The charter may not be the determining factor for all the liberties desired by the Mennonites, Hutterites, Doukhobors, or comparable groups. In the CPP controversy the Amish and Old Order Mennonites received a legal opinion that the Canadian Bill of Rights would not help them. Nevertheless, they persisted and eventually their request for an exemption was granted, by Parliament. In regard to the Hutterite income tax problems, several court rulings against the Darius-Leut Hutterites gave the government the legal authority to impose corporation taxes but the government refrained. It chose a more moderate course and levied taxes on a 'deemed individual income' basis. These outcomes suggest that factors other than court rulings, even if based on the charter, will remain important in working out the liberties desired by special groups.

While bills of rights may not determine such liberties, some of the bills enacted at the provincial level in the decades before the charter supported certain liberties desired by these groups. In the early 1970s when Alberta's newly elected premier, Peter Lougheed, moved to terminate the legislative restrictions on Hutterite landholding, he referred to the provincial Bill of Rights. In Manitoba, at approximately the same time, Premier Ed Schreyer took a similar action, with the support of that province's Human Rights Commission. In 1978, a group of conservative Mennonites, known as Holdeman Mennonites, at Linden, Alberta, received permission to operate a private school because of the provision for freedom of religion in that province's Bill of Rights.[48] In that case, a provincial court judge had become convinced that for the Holdeman Mennonites, the task of educating their children in a particular way was a deeply held religious concern; that the state, while also having a legitimate interest in the education of children, would infringe upon their religious freedom if it forced them to send their children to public schools; and that such an infringement was not warranted in this case because the children were receiving a satisfactory education in the private school. He also noted that the Holdeman Mennonites had tried to conform to the law by seeking authorization to operate their school and that their requests had been refused without regard to the quality of education offered there.

These instances suggest that bills of rights, of which the charter is now the most fundamental, may favour these special groups. However, there are significant arguments that the charter will have the opposite effect, that it represents a liberal individualistic regime that will serve to weaken the rights of groups, not to strengthen them. F.L. Morton has written that 'the political theory implicit in those sections of the Charter championed by its civil libertarian supporters ... is a very liberal and very American view of political life ... it does not fit comfortably with the Canadian political experience. As Hartz, Horowitz, Grant and others have all said in different ways, Canada has retained a sense of collective good.'[49] This contention that the charter favours individual rights over those of groups is partially supported by the December 1988 ruling of the Supreme Court of Canada against provisions in a Quebec law (Bill 101) that prohibited the use of languages other than French in certain settings.[50] The court's decision aroused widespread controversy in Quebec so the provincial government quickly passed legislation ensuring a clearly predominant place for the French language. Together with this legislation, the Quebec government invoked the charter's 'notwithstanding' clause to ensure that this new legislation would not be overruled by the Supreme Court on the grounds that it violated the charter. This action was strongly criticized elsewhere in Canada, but Quebec Premier Robert Bourassa explained: 'When a choice had to be made between individual rights and collective rights, I arbitrated in favour of collective rights by agreeing to invoke the notwithstanding clause.'[51] His object was to protect the collective rights of French-speaking Quebecers which, he felt, had been threatened by the charter-based decision of the Supreme Court.

The Charter's tendency to favour individual rights, suggested by these developments, may not be encouraging to the groups examined in this book. But other rulings must also be considered, particularly five that relate to the charter's section 2(a) provision for freedom of religion, some of which were influenced by the section 27 emphasis on preserving and enhancing the multicultural heritage of Canadians. First is the 1984 ruling by the Ontario Court of Appeal in *R. v. Videoflicks Ltd. et al.* At issue was Ontario's Retail Business Holidays Act that required the closing of retail stores on Sundays. This restriction was burdensome for those business people who, because of their religion, had to close their stores also on another day of the week. In the decision, Judge Tarnopolsky referred to section 2(a) of the charter:

Freedom of religion goes beyond the ability to hold certain beliefs without coercion and restraint and entails more than the ability to profess those beliefs openly. In my view, freedom of religion also includes the right to observe the essential practices demanded by the tenets of one's religion and, in determining what those essential practices are in any given case, the analysis must proceed not from the majority's perspective of the concept of religion but in terms of the role that the practices and beliefs assume in the religion of the individual or group concerned.[52]

The judge also referred to section 27 of the charter: 'Religion is one of the dominant aspects of a culture which it is intended to preserve and enhance.'[53] Both these quotations suggest a fairly broad view of religion.

Second is the 1985 ruling by the Supreme Court of Canada in the case of *R. v. Big M Drug Mart*. In this case the court held that the federal Lord's Day Act violated the charter's provisions for freedom of religion because, quite aside from its effect, its purpose was to require everyone to observe a sectarian, namely Christian, sabbath. Chief Justice Dickson stated:

The essence of the concept of freedom of religion is the right to entertain such religious beliefs as a person chooses, the right to declare religious beliefs openly and without fear of hindrance or reprisal, and the right to manifest religious belief by worship and practise or by teaching and dissemination. But the concept means more than that ...

What may appear good and true to a majoritarian religious group, or to the state acting at their behest, may not, for religious reasons, be imposed upon citizens who take a contrary view. The Charter safeguards religious minorities from the threat of 'the tyranny of the majority' ...

In proclaiming the standards of the Christian faith, the Act creates a climate hostile to, and gives the appearance of discrimination against non-Christian Canadians. It takes religious values rooted in Christian morality and using the force of the state, translates them into a positive law binding on believers and non-believers alike. The theological content of the legislation remains as a subtle and constant reminder to religious minorities within the country of their differences with, and alienation from, the dominant religious culture.[54]

Because of this, the chief justice added, the act 'is contrary to the expressed provisions of s. 27,' which, as noted, calls for 'the preservation and enhancement of the multicultural heritage of Canadians.' He continued: 'Equally protected, and for the same reasons, are expressions and manifestations of religious non-belief and refusals to participate in religious practise.'[55]

Third is the 1986 case of *Edwards Books and Art Ltd. et al. v. The Queen*, in which the Supreme Court of Canada upheld Ontario's Retail Business Holidays Act even though, subject to some exceptions, it prohibited retail stores from being open on Sundays and on certain holidays.[56] The court acknowledged that this act infringed in a significant way on the freedom of business people, if they were Jews or Seventh Day Adventists, in the sense that it pressured them to remain open on their own sabbaths in order not to lose business to their competitors. However, the court ruled that the purpose of this law, unlike that of the federal Lord's Day Act, was secular, even though its requirements coincided with those of certain religions, and that its unfortunate discriminatory effects were justified under section 1 of the charter by the social importance of having a common pause day. Section 1 of the charter states that the freedoms set forth in the charter are subject to such limits as can be demonstrably justified in a free and democratic society.

Fourth is the 1986 Alberta case of *Jones v. The Queen*.[57] It involved a minister who educated his children and approximately twenty others in the basement of his church. This, in itself, was not necessarily problematic. The problem was that Jones, the minister, refused to seek either government authorization for his private school or formal exemption from the requirement that his children attend a regular public school. As a result he violated the provincial School Act. But Jones felt that 'requesting the state for permission to do what he is authorized by God to do would ... violate his religious convictions.' The Supreme Court, ruling in 1986, agreed 'that the effect of the *School Act* does constitute some interference with the appellant's freedom of religion' as protected in section 2(a) of the charter but it maintained that 'the state, too, has an interest in the education of its citizens.' The court continued: 'Those who administer the province's educational requirements may not do so in a manner that unreasonably infringes on the right of parents to teach their children in accordance with their religious convictions. The interference must be demonstrably justified.' Having said this, the judges ruled that the infringement on Jones's freedom of religion, represented by the School Act, was justified in terms of section 1 of the charter.

Fifth is the 1989 ruling in *Zylberberg v. Sudbury Board of Education* by the Ontario Court of Appeal against the provision in section 28 of Ontario's Education Act prescribing that religious exercises be held at either the opening or the closing of each school day. The act stated that Christian 'or other suitable' materials were to be used for these exercises but the

Sudbury Board had utilized only those from the Christian religion. The act also exempted students whose parents requested that they not participate in these exercises. In ruling against these provisions the court stated: 'While the majoritian view may be that s. 28 confers freedom of choice on the minority, the reality is that it imposes on religious minorities a compulsion to conform to the religious practises of the majority ... The peer pressure and the class-room norms to which children are acutely sensitive, in our opinion, are real and pervasive and operate to compel members of religious minorities to conform with majority religious practises.'[58] This, the court continued, 'is also inconsistent with the multicultural nature of our society as recognized by s. 27 of the Charter.'[59]

These five judgments, some of which are quoted in a number of other rulings, could be analysed at length. From the perspective of the groups examined in this book three characteristics stand out. One is that freedom of religion, at least when supported by the call to preserve multiculturalism, is significantly broader than freedom to believe and to worship. The rulings indicate that it relates to the education of one's children, the desire not to do business on certain days, and to the culture of a group. The groups considered in this book would like it to also cover particular concerns relating to property holding, schooling, military exemption, and various other matters. Whether the courts will extend it as far as these groups would wish remains to be seen, but that possibility has not been excluded, at least not by these rulings.

A second principle indicated by these rulings is that it is legitimate for the state to restrict an individual's freedom of religion in order to achieve other objectives. This principle is obviously in tension with the first but it is important. It will be recalled from preceding discussions that giving liberties to special groups sometimes meant restricting the liberties of individuals within them. In the *Jones* case, the court restricted the religious freedom of Jones because of the state's interest in the education of the children. In the *Edwards Books* case, the restrictions were justified because of the social importance of having a common pause day. Whether the court would restrict the freedom of individuals on the grounds that such restrictions were necessary in order for the group, to which the individuals belong, to continue to function also remains to be seen. That is what happened in the *Hofer* case, on which the Supreme Court ruled in 1970. But, as noted, the charter may have a more individualistic orientation.

A third characteristic of these rulings is that they reject the primacy of the Christian religion. This is indicated by the rulings against the Lords Day Act and against school opening exercises consisting of Christian prayers and readings. Significantly, in each of the three relevant cases, namely the *Big M Drug Mart*, *Videoflick*, and *Zylberberg* cases, the courts supported their ruling by referring to section 27, which states that the charter is to be interpreted so as to preserve and enhance the multicultural heritage of Canadians. But some observers say that the reality goes farther, that the courts, in their eagerness to avoid discrimination against people who adhere either to no religion or to a minority religion, are causing the removal of all religious references, however vague and general, from Canada's public life and that the result will be a more secularized society.[60] If such a result occurs, would it, in turn, weaken the willingness of Canadian society to accommodate religious groups such as those examined in this book? The movement toward a more secular society that took place around the turn of the century (see the conclusion to chapter 5) was not helpful to these groups.

There are, then, a number of questions that arise: Will the fairly broad view of religion, evident in some of these court rulings, be sufficient to cover the concerns of such groups? Will the courts allow certain restrictions on the freedom of individuals if they are needed for such groups to continue? And how will increased secularization of society affect the willingness of that society to accommodate special religious groups? Also at issue are the promises made to these groups at the time of their immigration. Would section 26, which states that the charter 'shall not be construed as denying the existence of any other rights and freedoms that exist in Canada,' serve to uphold those early promises? A final question is whether the charter, by being virtually supreme, will deprive the political system of the flexibility of which Morton wrote so strikingly and which helped these special groups at a number of points.

The full implications of the charter are not yet known but this survey suggests that for groups such as Mennonites, Hutterites, and Doukhobors it may have both positive and negative consequences. Of course, the liberties desired by such groups need not be determined by the charter alone. But it is not guaranteed that the future for such groups will be better than the past.

Notes

PART ONE   Introduction

1 Thomas Berger, *Fragile Freedoms: Human Rights and Dissent in Canada* (Toronto: Clark Irwin and Company Ltd 1981)
2 Kenneth D. McRae, ed., *Consociational Democracy: Political Accommodation in Segmented Societies* (Toronto: McClelland and Stewart 1974; Carleton Library no. 79). See also McRae, *Conflict and Compromise in Multilingual Societies: Switzerland*, and *Conflict and Compromise in Multilingual Societies: Belgium* (Waterloo: Wilfrid Laurier University Press 1983 and 1986 respectively).
3 McRae, *Consociational Democracy*, 300. See also McRae, 'The Structure of Canadian History,' in *The Founding of New Societies: Studies in the History of the United States, Latin America, South Africa, Canada, and Australia*, ed. Louis Hartz (New York: Harcourt, Brace and World Inc. 1964).
4 Statistics Canada, *Census of Canada 1941*, and *Census of Canada 1981*. The 1941 census included Hutterites in the Mennonite category for a total of approximately 111,000. But the Hutterites numbered 5000 at this time. See Victor Peters, *All Things Common: The Hutterian Way of Life* (Minneapolis: University of Minnesota Press 1967), 207.
5 The claim of 30,000 Doukhobors comes from Koozma Tarasoff, *Plakun Trava: The Doukhobors* (Grand Forks, BC: Mir Publication Society 1982), xi.

CHAPTER 1   The Background of Mennonites, Hutterites, and Doukhobors

1 C. Henry Smith, *Smith's Story of the Mennonites*, 5th ed., revised and enlarged by Cornelius Krahn (Newton, KS: Faith and Life Press 1981)

2 Hans J. Hillerbrand, 'The Anabaptist View of the State,' *The Mennonite Quarterly Review* 30 (April 1958): 98

3 Smith, *Smith's Story of the Mennonites*, 79

4 Frank H. Epp, *Mennonites in Canada 1786–1920: The History of a Separate People* (Toronto: Macmillan 1974), 42

5 Smith, *Smith's Story of the Mennonites*, 177

6 David G. Rempel, 'The Mennonite Migration to New Russia, 1788–1870,' *Mennonite Quarterly Review* 9 (April 1935): 75

7 E.K. Francis, *In Search of Utopia: The Mennonites of Manitoba* (Altona, Man.: D.W. Friesen and Sons Ltd 1955), 31

8 Epp, *Mennonites in Canada 1786–1920*, 177

9 Ibid., 183ff. For the immigration in the 1920s, see Epp, *Mennonites in Canada 1920–1940: A People's Struggle for Survival* (Toronto: Macmillan 1982), 139ff.

10 The Bible, Acts of the Apostles, 2: 44

11 John A. Hostetler, *Hutterite Society* (Baltimore: Johns Hopkins University Press 1974), 30

12 Ibid., 29

13 Victor Peters, 'The Hutterians: History and Communal Organization of a Rural Group,' in *Historical Essays on the Prairie Provinces*, ed. Donald Swainson (Toronto: McClelland and Stewart 1970; Carleton Library no. 53, 133

14 Hostetler, *Hutterite Society*, 131

15 Ibid., 130. See also 'An Account, by Jakob Waldner, Diary of a Conscientious Objector in World War I,' Theron Schlabach, trans. Ilse Reist and Elizabeth Bender, *The Mennonite Quarterly Review* 48 (January 1974): 73

16 Peters, *All Things Common*, 46

17 Tarasoff, *Plakun Trava*, 1

18 Quoted in Aylmer Maude, *A Peculiar People: The Doukhobors* (New York: AMS Press Inc. 1970; reprinted from a 1904 edition), 16

19 Quoted in George Woodcock and Ivan Avakumovic, *The Doukhobors* (Toronto: McClelland and Stewart 1977; Carleton Library no. 108), 29

20 Maude, *A Peculiar People*, 133

21 Tarasoff, *Plakun Trava*, 10

22 Ibid., 11

23 Maude, *A Peculiar People*, 26

24 Ibid.

25 Tarasoff, *Plakun Trava*, 21

26 Ibid., 34

27 Quoted in Epp, *Mennonites in Canada 1786–1920*, 99

28 Quoted in ibid., 100.

29 Order-in-council, no. 827B, 26 April 1872, National Archives of Canada, Record Group 2, 1 (hereafter NA, RG), vol. 108. For more information about these negotiations see Adolf Ens, 'Mennonite Relations with Governments: Western Canada 1870–1925,' PhD diss., University of Ottawa 1979

30 Order-in-council, no. 1043D, 25 September 1872, NA, RG 2, 1

31 Francis, *In Search of Utopia*, 43

32 The full text of the letter is printed in ibid., 44.

33 Order-in-council no. 957, 13 August 1873, NA, RG 2, 1, vol. 83

34 Tarasoff, *Plakun Trava*, 34

35 Order-in-council no. 2747, 6 December 1898, NA, RG 76, vol. 175, part 9 (microfilm reel C7330). The full text of this order is printed in W. Janzen, 'The Limits of Liberty in Canada: The Experience of the Mennonites, Hutterites and Doukhobors,' PhD diss., Carleton University 1981, appendix 4.

36 Quoted in A.M. Willms, 'The Brethren Known as Hutterians,' *Canadian Journal of Economics and Political Science* 24 (August 1958): 391

37 Order-in-council no. 1676, 12 August 1899, NA, RG 76, vol. 176, part 15 (microfilm reel C7330). This order is reprinted in Janzen, 'The Limits of Liberty in Canada,' appendix 5.

38 'A Humble Petition to the Government of the Dominion of Canada' from Christian Waldner and Elias Walter, 5 September 1899, NA, RG 76, vol. 173 (microfilm reel C7330). This petition is reprinted in Janzen, 'The Limits of Liberty in Canada,' appendix 6.

39 J.A. Smart, deputy minister of the Interior, to W.F. McCreary, commissioner of immigration, Winnipeg, 27 October 1899, NA, RG 76, vol. 173 (microfilm reel C7330)

40 W.W. Cory, deputy minister of the Interior, to M. Scott, 7 February 1918, reprinted in A.T.F. Zieglschmid, *Das Klein-Geschichtsbuch der Hutterischen Brueder* (Philadelphia: Carl Schwarz Memorial Foundation 1947), appendix x, 632

41 Epp, *Mennonites in Canada 1786–1920*, 395

42 Orders-in-council, no. 923, 1 May 1919 and no. 1204, 9 June 1919, NA, RG 2, 1. See also Epp, *Mennonites in Canada 1786–1920*, 407.

43 Order-in-council, no. 1181, 2 June 1922, NA, RG 2, 1

44 Order-in-council, no. 418, 17 March 1926, NA, RG 2, 1

45 Berger, *Fragile Freedoms*, 102

46 David Toews, chairman, Canadian Mennonite Board of Colonization, to F.C. Blair, April 26 1923, NA, RG 26, vol. 175, file 58764, part 9. See also

W. Stuart Edwards, acting deputy minister of Justice, to deputy minister of Immigration and Colonization, 18 June 1924, NA, RG 76, vol. 175, file 58764, part 10.

PART TWO   Landholding

1 Epp, *Mennonites in Canada 1786–1920*, 71
2 'A petition of the Mennonites termed "Sommerfelder Gemeinde" to the Dominion Government, Ottawa, Ontario,' signed by H.J. Friesen, bishop, and Johann D. Klassen, secretary of Altona and Rosenfeld, Manitoba, respectively, 28 January 1927, NA, RG 15, vol. 233, no. 3129(5)
3 Deputy minister, Department of the Interior, to J.J. Loewen, Altona, Manitoba, 21 June 1927, ibid.

CHAPTER 2   The Mennonite Reserves

1 Francis, *In Search of Utopia*, 64
2 Chester Martin, *'Dominion Lands' Policy*, edited from the original (published in 1938) by Lewis H. Thomas (Toronto: McClelland and Stewart Ltd 1973; Carleton Library no. 69), 125
3 C.A. Dawson, *Group Settlement: Ethnic Communities in Western Canada* (Toronto: Macmillan 1936), viii. E.K. Francis refers to 'the essentially individualistic property system embodied in the Dominion Lands Act' in *In Search of Utopia*, 64.
4 For developments relating to the Métis, see Berger, *Fragile Freedoms*, 35, 40, and 45. For developments relating to other groups, see Howard Palmer, *Land of the Second Chance: A History of Ethnic Groups in Southern Alberta* (Lethbridge, Alta.: The Lethbridge Herald 1972), 221.
5 Jacob Y. Shantz, *Narrative of a Journey to Manitoba, together with an abstract of the Dominion Lands Act, and an extract from the government pamphlet on Manitoba* (Ottawa: Department of Agriculture 1873), 19
6 Order-in-council. no. 226, 3 March 1873, NA, RG 2, 1
7 Order-in-council, 23 May 1873, NA, RG 2, 1
8 Francis, *In Search of Utopia*, 41
9 Epp, *Mennonites in Canada 1786–1920*, 211, and Ens, 'Mennonite Relations with Governments,' 46
10 Francis, *In Search of Utopia*, 62
11 Order-in-council, no. 397, NA, RG 2, 1, vol. 142
12 John Johnston and eighteen others, a petition to the minister of the Interior, 17 August 1876, NA, RG 15, vol. 236, no. 6411

13 William Hespeler, immigration agent to minister of Agriculture, 5 November 1877, NA, RG 17, I-1, vol. 205, no. 21191

14 A. Belch, Dominion Lands agent, to the surveyor-general, Ottawa, 14 July 1877, NA, RG 15, vol. 232, no. 3129(1)

15 William Pearce, Dominion Lands surveyor, a report, 22 November 1877, ibid.

16 William Hespeler, a report to William Pearce, 15 January 1878, ibid.

17 J.S. Dennis, surveyor-general, to the minister of the Interior, Ottawa, 14 December 1877, ibid.

18 George Newcomb, Dominion Lands agent, Emerson, to Donald Codd, Dominion Lands agent, Winnipeg, 30 April 1878, ibid.

19 Charles Allen, 27 September 1879, ibid.

20 Donald Codd to William Hespeler, 16 September 1879, ibid.

21 L. Russell, surveyor-general, to J.S. Dennis, deputy of the minister of the Interior, 4 October 1879, ibid.

22 Minister of the Interior to the Privy Council, 5 March 1881, ibid.

23 Order-in-council, no. 381, 24 March 1881, NA, RG 2, 1

24 R. Rauscher, Dominion Lands surveyor, to Russell, surveyor-general, 1 September 1881, NA, RG 15, vol. 233, no. 3129(2A)

25 A.H. Whitcher, Dominion Lands agent, to surveyor-general, 17 November 1881, NA, RG 233, no. 3129(2A)

26 L. Russell to D.L. McPherson, acting minister of the Interior, 2 September 1881, ibid. Arrangements to this effect were formalized with an order-in-council on 7 September 1881, NA, RG 15, vol. 233, no. 3129(2).

27 The 9 July 1979 announcement of this planned sale, issued in the German language for the sake of the Mennonites, and made jointly by J.S. Dennis, deputy minister of the Interior, and L. Russell, surveyor-general, was entitled 'Verordnung betreffend der Dominion Laender fuer den Zweck der Canadian Pacific Eisenbahn.' It is in NA, RG 15, vol. 232, no. 3129(1A); see also Ens, 'Mennonite Relations with Governments,' 68.

28 Codd to surveyor-general, 2 April 1880, NA, RG 15, vol. 232, no. 3129(1A)

29 Hespeler to surveyor-general, 14 March 1880, ibid.

30 Order-in-council, 31 January 1881, ibid. This order-in-council authorized a refund of money after the sales had been cancelled.

31 Telegram, Codd to Russell, 25 February 1880, ibid.

32 Ens, 'Mennonite Relations with Governments,' 71f

33 Canada, An Act to amend the Dominion Lands Act, *Statutes of Canada* (1876), c. 19, sec. 9

34 N. Leslie, local land agent, to L. Russell, surveyor-general, 6 June 1881. NA, RG 15, vol. 250, no. 27630 (1); and I. Mueller, Mennonite leader, to L. Russell, 28 November 1881, NA, RG 15, vol. 233, no. 3129(3)

35 A. Belch to J.S. Dennis, surveyor-general, 14 July 1877, NA, RG 15, vol. 237, no. 8974

36 Order-in-council, no. 786, 27 August 1877, ibid. The exchange of correspondence with the Justice Department is in this same file.

37 Donald Codd to surveyor-general, 26 September 1879, NA, RG 15, vol. 232, no. 3129(1)

38 A.M. Burgess, deputy minister of the Interior, to H.H. Smith, commissioner for Dominion Lands, Winnipeg, 13 May 1891, NA, RG 15, vol. 570, no. 179925(1)

39 Order-in-council, no. 1266, 27 June 1898, NA, RG 2, 1, vol. 770

40 Richard John Friesen, 'Old Colony Mennonite Settlements in Saskatchewan: A Study in Settlement Change,' MA thesis, University of Alberta 1975, 68

41 J.B. McLaren to the secretary, Department of the Interior, 21 February 1894, NA, RG 15, vol. 652, no. 270476

42 T. Mayne Daly, minister of the Interior, to A.M. Burgess, 3 November 1894, ibid.

43 J.B. McLaren to Hon. T. Mayne Daly, 2 April 1895, ibid.

44 Order-in-council, no. 188, 23 January 1895, ibid. The land reserved consisted of townships 40 in ranges 3, 4, and 5 and township 41 in range 4.

45 Order-in-council, no. 1627, 24 June 1898, NA, RG 15, vol. 652, no. 270476. The new one was township 41 in range 3.

46 John McTaggart, Dominion Lands agent, Prince Albert, to Messrs McLaren and McLeod, Barristers, Morden, Manitoba, 28 March 1899, NA, RG 15, vol. 652, no. 270476

47 C.W. Speers to James A. Smart, deputy minister of the Interior, 4 April 1899, ibid.; also Huysmans de Deftal, Dominion Lands sub-agent, Duck Lake, to deputy minister of the Interior, 8 April 1899, ibid.

48 James A. Smart, deputy minister, Department of the Interior, to C.W. Speers, general colonization agent, Winnipeg, 7 April 1899, ibid.

49 McLaren, McLeod, and Black, to secretary, Department of the Interior, 12 April 1899, ibid.

50 Memo, Department of the Interior, 6 October 1898, ibid.

51 John R. Hall, secretary, Department of the Interior, to Messrs McLaren, McLeod, and Black, Morden, Manitoba, 24 April 1899, ibid.

52 B.J. Friesen and thirty-four others to the Department of the Interior, 14 August 1899, ibid.

53 G. Turiff, Department of the Interior, Ottawa, to W.F. McCreary, commissioner of Immigration, Winnipeg, 3 August 1899, ibid.

54 C.W. Speers to W.F. McCreary, 26 August 1899, ibid.

55 Speers's misunderstanding about the date of the reserve, which is evident
   in his report of 26 August 1899, was based on a letter written to him by
   James A. Smart, the deputy minister of the Department of the Interior, 20
   April 1899.

56 C.W. Speers to Frank Pedley, superintendent of Immigration, 25 April
   1901, ibid.

57 R.S. Cook to John McTaggart, 7 April 1900. One Mennonite, Abram
   Penner, was persuaded only after the department agreed to pay him
   $50 in compensation for the work that he had done on the land (Abram
   Penner, statement, 1 June 1901, ibid.).

58 Canada, An Act further to amend and to consolidate, as so amended, the
   several Acts respecting the Public Lands of the Dominion therein mentioned, assented to on 23 May 1883, *Statutes of Canada* (1883) c. 17, sec. 32

59 A solemn declaration made by Franz Froese, 6 February 1900. That the
   Mennonites made such a request is evident also in the minister's minutes of his 1894 meeting with the Mennonites, (see Memo, T. Mayne Daly
   to A.M. Burgess, 3 November 1894, NA, RG 15, vol. 652, no. 270476).

60 Order-in-council, no. 441, 6 March 1900, ibid.

61 That there were more than twenty villages is indicated in unpublished
   research done by Leonard Doell of Warman, Saskatchewan.

62 A.M. McLeod to D. Stewart, MP, 6 July 1904, NA, RG 15, vol. 940, no.
   917620(1)

63 Order-in-council, no. 1605, 13 August 1904, ibid.

64 McLaren, McLeod, and Black to Frank Oliver, minister of the Interior, 26
   March 1906, ibid; see also the order-in-council, ibid.

65 Dominion Lands agent, Regina, to the secretary, Department of the Interior, Ottawa, 7 February 1906. ibid.

66 McLaren, McLeod, and Black to the Hon. Frank Oliver, minister of the
   Interior, 26 March 1906, ibid. Oliver, in an earlier career as a journalist, had written critically of government actions in reserving land for Mennonites (*Edmonton Bulletin*, 24 October 1898, 2).

67 P.G. Keyes, secretary, Department of the Interior, to the Dominion Lands
   agent, Regina, 11 April 1906, ibid.

68 'To the Honourable the Minister of the Interior, Ottawa, the Humble
   Petition of the Reinland Mennonite Association .' from Franz Froese,
   agent, and Johann Wiebe, bishop, 12 December 1904, ibid.

69 A. McLeod to Hon. Frank Oliver, 4 July 1906, ibid.

70 McLaren, McLeod, and Black to secretary, Department of the Interior,
   Ottawa, 4 December 1906, ibid.

71 P.G. Keyes to Messrs McLaren, McLeod, and Black, 10 December 1906,

ibid. Also, A. McLeod to Hon. Frank Oliver, 22 February 1907, NA, RG 15, vol. 940, no. 917620(2)

72 McLaren, McLeod, and Black to the Hon. Clifford Sifton, 25 January 1905, NA, RG 15, vol. 940, no. 917620(1); and McLaren, McLeod, and Black to secretary, Department of the Interior, 9 June 1909, NA, RG 15, vol. 940, no. 917620(2)

73 Isaak Mueller to Sir John A. MacDonald, 21 July 1880, NA, RG 15, vol. 232, no. 3129(1)

CHAPTER 3   The Doukhobor Community

1 Woodcock and Avakumovic, *The Doukhobors*, 108
2 Ibid., 29
3 Ibid., 44
4 Ibid., 45
5 Tarasoff, *Plakun Trava*, 11
6 Woodcock and Avakumovic, *The Doukhobors*, 89
7 Ibid., 93
8 Quoted in ibid., 139
9 Tarasoff, *Plakun Trava*, 34
10 James A. Smart, deputy minister of the Department of the Interior, to T.G. Rothwell, also of the department, 16 November 1898, NA, RG 15, vol. 753, file 494483(1)
11 James A. Smart to W.R. Baker, Manitoba and North-Western Railway Company and to T.A. Burrows of the Lake Manitoba Railway and Canal Company, 1 December 1898, ibid.
12 Maude, *A Peculiar People*, 61. Tarasoff suggests that Maude was not sufficiently careful in his negotiations with the Canadian government (see Tarasoff, *Plakun Trava*, 36).
13 Joseph Elkinton, *The Doukhobors* (Philadelphia: Ferris and Leach, Publishers 1903), 190ff; see also Tarasoff, *Plakun Trava*, 42.
14 Quoted in Kathlyn Rose Marie Szalasznyj, 'The Doukhobor Homestead Crisis 1898–1907,' MA thesis, University of Saskatchewan 1977), 89
15 Herbert Archer to the Hon. Clifford Sifton, 21 June 1900, NA, RG 15, vol. 754, file 494483(2)
16 Ibid.
17 'Extract from letter dated June 1, 1900 from H.P. Archer ... to Mr. McCreary, Winnipeg, Manitoba,' NA, RG 15, vol. 753, file 494483(1)
18 Herbert Archer to the Hon. Clifford Sifton, 21 June 1900, NA, RG 15, vol. 754, file 494483(2)

19 Szalasznyj, 'The Doukhobor Homestead Crisis,' 88
20 Ibid., 91
21 Herbert Archer to James A. Smart, 16 June 1900, NA, RG 15, vol. 753, file 494483(1)
22 Szalasznyj, 'The Doukhobor Homestead Crisis,' 91
23 'To the Honourable, The House of Commons of the Dominion of Canada in Parliament ...' signed by William McGillvray and ten others, undated but received in Ottawa by the Department of the Interior on 20 July 1900, NA, RG 15, vol. 754, file no. 494483(2)
24 Letter, William McCreary, commissioner for Immigration, to James A. Smart, 9 June 1900, NA, RG 15, vol. 753, file no. 484483(1)
25 Tarasoff, *Plakun Trava*, 59
26 Ibid., 69
27 As quoted in Maude, *A Peculiar People*, 271
28 Elkinton, *The Doukhobors*, 115
29 Ibid., 120
30 John Bellows, clerk of the committee appointed by the Society of Friends in England for assisting the Doukhobors, 'To the Doukhobors of Canada,' 11 November 1900, NA, RG, B1, vol. 604660
31 This letter is reprinted in Elkinton, *The Doukhobors*, 127.
32 Vassily Potapoff and three others of Village Woscresenovka, 23 March 1901, NA, RG 15, vol. 754, file 494483(2)
33 This matter is referred to in a letter from J. Obed Smith, commissioner for Immigration in Winnipeg to the commissioner of Dominion Lands, Ottawa, 2 January 1902, ibid.
34 Ibid.
35 Woodcock and Avakumovic, *The Doukhobors*, 171
36 This letter is reprinted in 'Doukhobor Claims for Compensation,' *Canadian Slavonic Papers* 1, ed. L.I. Strakhovsky (Toronto: University of Toronto Press 1956).
37 Tarasoff, *Plakun Trava*, 73
38 The pilgrimage may have been prompted also by a letter written by Peter V. Verigin in 1896 while he was still in exile in Russia. It was directed not to the Doukhobors but to a fellow prisoner with whom he was in dialogue about anarchistic ideas. When the Doukhobor settlers became aware of the letter, some were influenced by its extreme contents (ibid., 69).
39 William Blackmore, *Report of the Royal Commission on Matters Relating to the Sect of Doukhobors in British Columbia, 1912* (Victoria: Government of British Columbia, Sessional Papers 1913) 22

40 Quoted in Woodcock and Avakumovic, *The Doukhobors*, 185
41 Blackmore, *Report of the Royal Commission*, 23
42 J.S. Crerar to the commissioner of Immigration, Winnipeg, 8 January 1903, NA, RG 15, vol. 755, file 494483(3)
43 J.S. Crerar to J.O. Smith, 12 February 1903, ibid.
44 H. Harley to J.O. Smith, 14 February 1903, ibid.
45 P.G. Keyes, secretary of the Department of the Interior to J.O. Smith, 6 March 1903, ibid.
46 Quoted in Szalasznyj, 'The Doukhobor Homestead Crisis,' 134
47 Szalasznyj, ibid., 135
48 Ibid., 136ff
49 Tarasoff, *Plakun Trava*, 81
50 E. Challen Clark, JP, to the Hon. Clifford Sifton, 26 November 1904, NA, RG 15, vol. 755, file 494483(4). See also Tarasoff, *Plakun Trava*, 83.
51 Tarasoff, *Plakun Trava*, 82
52 H.H. Brown to the secretary of the Department of the Interior, 7 January 1905, NA, RG 15, vol. 755, file 494483(4)
53 Peter Verigin to Alex Moffat, acting commissioner of Immigration, 21 February 1905, ibid.
54 Ibid.
55 James E. Peaker to the secretary, Department of the Interior, Ottawa, 13 March 1905, ibid.
56 J.O. Smith to W.W. Cory, deputy minister of the Interior, 4 April 1905, ibid.
57 Szalasznyj, 'The Doukhobor Homestead Crisis,' 166
58 F. Roy Dixon to J.W. Greenway, commissioner of Dominion Lands, 6 June 1905, NA, RG 15, vol. 755, file 494483(4)
59 C.W. Speers, general colonization agent, to Hon. Frank Oliver, 7 September 1905, ibid.
60 P.G. Keyes, secretary, Department of the Interior, to Thomas Young, 11 October 1905, ibid.
61 McNab, homestead inspector, Report to the secretary, Department of the Interior, Ottawa, 24 February 1906, ibid.
62 Frank Oliver to J.W. Greenway, 7 March 1906, ibid.
63 W.W. Cory, deputy minister of the Department of the Interior, to Mr Greenway, 12 March 1906, ibid.
64 In 1898, Oliver, as an Alberta journalist, had written critically of the government's decision to reserve a block of land for Mennonites; see *Edmonton Bulletin*, 24 October 1898,2.
65 Peter Verigin to the minister, Department of the Interior, 24 July 1906, NA, RG 15, vol. 755, file 494483(5)

66 John McDougall, 'General Report Doukhobor Commission,' to the Hon. the minister of the Interior, 25 November 1906, NA, RG 15, vol. 755, file no. 494483(6)

67 Szalasznyj, 'The Doukhobor Homestead Crisis,' 182

68 These statements appear not in the main body of McDougall's report, but in a statement entitled 'The General Settlement Attitude towards the Doukhobors in the Northwest,' addressed to the Hon. Frank Oliver by John McDougall, dated 12 December 1906, NA, RG 15, vol. 755, file 494483(6).

69 Ibid. McDougall's figures included the land at Prince Albert.

70 John McDougall, 'General Report Doukhobor Commission'

71 Ibid.

72 Frank Oliver, minister of the Interior, 'Memorandum for Information of Council,' 1 December 1906, NA, RG 15, vol. 755, file no. 494483(6)

73 Ibid.

74 Ibid.

75 Szalasznyj, 'The Doukhobor Homestead crisis,' 133

76 Leslie to Russell, 6 June 1881, NA, RG, vol. 250, no. 27630(1) 76

77 Oliver, 'Memorandum for Information of Council'

78 'Doukhobor Claims for Compensation,' *Canadian Slavonic Papers* I, 53

79 Oliver, 'Memorandum for Information of Council'

80 Ibid.

81 Ibid.

82 Ibid. This cancellation procedure is provided for in section 7 of the 1891 amendments to the Dominion Lands Act.

83 W.W. Cory, deputy minister of the Department of the Interior, to John McDougall, 17 December 1906, NA, RG 15, vol. 755, file 484483(5)

84 P.G. Keyes, secretary to the Department of the Interior, to John McDougall, 28 December 1906, ibid.

85 'To the Elders and People of the Village ...,' in English and in Russian, NA, RG 15, vol. 757, file 494483(10)

86 'Petition To The Minister Of The Interior And All People In Canada From The Christian Community of Universal Brotherhood, The Doukhobors of Canada,' 28 January 1907, NA, RG 15, vol. 757, file 494483(7)

87 This teaching of Jesus appears in the Bible, The Gospel of Matthew, 5:34–37

88 'Report of an Interview between the Honourable Frank Oliver, Minister of the Interior, and certain representatives of the Doukhobors, on Monday, the 25th February, 1907,' NA, RG 15, vol. 755, file 494483(6)

89 Ibid.
90 Ibid.
91 Ibid.
92 James Mavor, 'Memorandum upon Doukhobor Affairs,' 15 April 1907, NA, RG 15, Vol. 755, file 494483(6)
93 John McDougall to Frank Oliver, 14 May 1907, NA, RG 15, vol. 756, file 494483(7)
94 John McDougall to Frank Oliver, 19 June 1907, ibid.
95 'Statement re Disposition of 'Doukhobor Homesteads,' 1 August 1907, a collection of materials entitled 'Reports And Maps Relating To Lands Held Under Homestead Entry By Doukhobors And The Disposition of Same,' Saskatchewan Archives Board, 1x/13, Saskatoon, Saskatchewan
96 Woodcock and Avakumovic, *The Doukhobors*, 223
97 Szalasznyj, 'The Doukhobor Homestead Crisis,' 224
98 Woodcock and Avakumovic, *The Doukhobors*, 229
99 Ibid., 228
100 Anderson, Rose and Company, Barristers and Solicitors, to the Hon. Frank Oliver, 5 May 1919, NA, RG 15, vol. 758, vile 494483(15)
101 Szalasznyj, 'The Doukhobor Homestead Crisis,' 20
102 Ibid., 22
103 Ibid., 163
104 J.S. Woodsworth, *Stranger within Our Gates* (Toronto: University of Toronto Press 1972; first ed. 1909), 234
105 'Petition To The Minister of The Interior And All People In Canada From The Christian Community of Universal Brotherhood, The Doukhobors of Canada,' 28 January 1907, NA, RG 15, vol. 757, file 494483(7)
106 John McDougall, 'General Report Doukhobor Commission,' 61
107 C.W. Speers to Hon. Frank Oliver, 7 September 1905
108 Tarasoff, *Plakun Trava*, 152

CHAPTER 4   The Hutterite Colonies

1 Paul S. Gross, *The Hutterite Way: The Inside Story of the Life, Customs, Religion and Traditions of the Hutterites* (Saskatoon: Freeman Publishing Company Ltd 1965), 28
2 The Bible, The Acts of the Apostles, 5: 32–34
3 Hostetter, *Hutterite Society*, 146
4 David Flint, *The Hutterites: A Study in Prejudice* (Toronto: Oxford University Press 1975), 50

5 W.W. Cory, deputy minister of the Interior, to Michael Scott, 7 February 1918, quoted in Zeiglschmid, *Das Klein-Geschichtsbuch*, appendix x, 632

6 Peters, *All Things Common*, 48

7 Ibid.

8 Manitoba legislature, 'Meeting of Select Special Committee of Manitoba Legislature On Hutterite Legislation,' Winnipeg, 23 July 1948, 10

9 Manitoba legislature, 'Report to the Honourable the Legislative Assembly of Manitoba of the Select Special Committee appointed to obtain information regarding colonies or societies of Hutterites or Hutterian Brethren and to report and make recommendations upon the same,' Winnipeg, 1948, 22 (hereafter known as 'Report to the Honourable the Legislative Assembly ...')

10 Ibid., 27

11 Manitoba, 'Meeting of Select Special Committee,' 8

12 Ibid., 26ff

13 Peters, *All Things Common*, 59

14 Rev. Jacob Kleinsasser, leader of Manitoba Hutterites, Crystal Springs Hutterite Colony, St Agathe, Manitoba, interview with William Janzen, 7 June 1978

15 'Agreement ... between: Union of Manitoba Municipalities ... and the Hutterian Brethren of Manitoba,' Manitoba Archives, ME 15 C 2

16 Peters, *All Things Common*, 60

17 Ian A. Hunter, *Civil Liberties and Human Rights: A Canadian Sourcebook* (Ottawa: Carleton University, Department of Law 1972), 190

18 Rev. Jacob Kleinsasser, interview with Janzen

19 Hunter, *Civil Liberties*, 190

20 As reported in Alberta, Legislative Assembly, Select Committee of the Assembly, *Report on Communal Property* (1972), 11

21 Blaine G. Burton, letter to the editor, *Grainews*, Winnipeg, 9 February 1984, 8

22 *Hofer v. Hofer et al.* (1970), 13 DLR (3d) 1

23 Toronto *Globe and Mail*, 'Hutterite Colonies Threaten to Leave over Manitoba Bill,' 22 June 1971, reprinted in Hunter, *Civil Liberties*, 187

24 Quoted in Peters, *All Things Common*, 53

25 Alberta, *Report on Communal Property* (1972), 6. See also Howard Palmer, 'Ethnic Relations in Wartime: Nationalism and European Minorities in Alberta during the Second World War,' *Canadian Ethnic Studies* 14, no. 3 (1982): 1–23.

26 Quoted in Edwin A. Pitt, 'The Hutterian Brethren in Alberta,' MA thesis, University of Alberta 1949, 115; see also Peters, *All Things Common*, 54.

27 Pitt, 'The Hutterian Brethren in Alberta'
28 Morris Davis and Joseph F. Krauter, *The Other Canadians: Profiles of Six Minorities* (Agincourt, Ont.: Methuen Publications 1971), 94
29 Alberta, An Act to amend the Land Sales Prohibition Act, assented to on 28 March 1945, *Statutes of Alberta* (1945), c. 59, quoted in Pitt, 'The Hutterian Brethren in Alberta,' appendix
30 Alberta, An Act to amend the Land Sales Prohibition Act, assented to on 27 March 1946, *Statutes of Alberta* (1946), c. 54, quoted in Pitt, ibid.
31 Alberta, order-in-council, 18 January 1947, quoted in Pitt, ibid.
32 Pitt, 'The Hutterian Brethern in Alberta,' 120
33 Quoted in ibid., 119
34 Ibid., 122
35 The brief by Turcotte is reprinted in Zieglschmid, *Das Klein-Geschichtsbuch*, appendix.
36 Quoted in Alberta, *Report on Communal Property* (1972), 6
37 The Communal Property Act, *Statutes of Alberta*, 1947, c. 16
38 This change was made by order-in-council, no. 841/51, 12 June 1951. Alberta, *Report of the Hutterite Investigation Committee*, (Edmonton: September 1959), appendix D
39 Alberta, *Report of the Hutterite Investigation Committee* (1959), 16; and *Report on Communal Property* (1972), 7
40 Alberta, *Report of the Hutterite Investigation Committee* (1959), appendix A
41 Quoted in William G. Loatsch, 'Hutterite Colonization in Alberta,' *Journal of Geography* 70 (September 1971): 351
42 Ibid., 352
43 Alberta, *Report of the Hutterite Investigation Committee* (1959), 45
44 Ibid.
45 Howard Palmer, 'The Hutterite Land Expansion Controversy in Alberta,' *Western Canada Journal of Anthropology* 2 (July 1971); 31
46 Ibid.
47 Alberta, *Report on Communal Property* (1972), 7
48 Ibid., 8
49 *Walter et al. v. Attorney-General of Alberta* (1968), 3 DLR (3d)1
50 Palmer, 'The Hutterite Land Expansion Controversy,' 41
51 Alberta, *Report on Communal Property* (1972), 8
52 Ibid., 33
53 Ibid., 10
54 Telephone interviews by William Janzen, 25 February 1988, with Rev. Isaac Wurz, Old Elm Hutterite Colony, Box 220, Magrath, Alberta,

and Ken Hoeppner, Alberta's Hutterite liaison officer. See also Alberta, Special Advisory Committee on Communal Property and Land Use, *A Report to the Minister of Municipal Affairs*, October 1974.

55 Telephone interview by William Janzen, 25 February 1988, with Helmut P. Entrup, farmer's advocate of Alberta, Edmonton

56 Ray. H. Woollam, group resources consultant, Department of Municipal Affairs, Government of Saskatchewan, 'The Treatment of Hutterian Brethren by Provincial and Federal Governments – A Summary,' October 1963, 12

57 Vernon Searl, Department of Municipal Affairs, Government of Saskatchewan, Regina, 'Final Report: The Hutterite Program' (1958), 1

58 Quoted in ibid., 2

59 Quoted in Alberta, *Report on Communal Property* (1972), 11, where it is attributed to Saskatchewan, 'Report on Relations of South-Western Saskatchewan Communities with Hutterite Colonies,' unpublished manuscript (1957)

60 Searl, 'Final Report'

61 Ibid., 6

62 Ibid., 19

63 Hunter, *Civil Liberties*, 188

64 Saskatchewan, 'Policy and Procedures – Hutterite Colonies' in ibid.

65 Ibid. See also Saskatoon *Star Phoenix*, 28 July 1978

66 Toronto *Globe and Mail*, 16 October 1978, 4

67 Woollam, 'The Treatment of Hutterian Brethren,' 13

68 *Western Producer*, Saskatoon, 15 February 1979, 33

69 Ibid.

70 Toronto *Globe and Mail*, 16 October 1958, 4

71 Saskatoon *Star Phoenix*, 1 June 1979, 30

72 Ibid., and *Western Producer*, 15 February 1979

73 Toronto *Globe and Mail*, 16 and 26 October 1978, and *Western Producer*, 15 February 1979

74 *Western Producer*, 15 February 1979

75 *Ottawa Citizen*, 22 July 1978

76 Toronto *Globe and Mail*, 16 October 1978

77 Ibid.

78 *Western Producer*, 15 February 1979

79 Toronto *Globe and Mail*, 16 October 1978

80 Ibid., and *Western Producer*, 22 March 1978

81 *Western Producer*, 15 February 1979; and Saskatoon *Star Phoenix*,

8 and 16 February 1979, and 1 June 1979

82 *Henry Godenir v. Vanguard Hutterian Brethren Inc.*, Provincial Court, Swift Current, Saskatchewan. The judgment was written by Judge G.K. Fielding, 27 June 1979. It was upheld on appeal. See *R. v. Vanguard Hutterian Brethren Inc.* (1979), 6 WWR 335.

83 *Western Producer*, 4 January 1979

84 Ibid., 15 February 1979. The desire for good public relations was indicated also by George Janzen, Herbert, Saskatchewan, in a telephone interview with William Janzen on 5 April 1981. George Janzen served for a time as a teacher on a Hutterite colony.

85 *Hutterian Brethren Church of Eagle Creek Inc. v. Eagle Creek, Rural Municipality of, No. 376* (1983), 21 Saskatchewan Law Reports 361; 144 DLR (3rd) 685

86 *Hutterian Brethren Church of Eagle Creek Inc. v. Eagle Creek* (1984), 35 Saskatchewan Law Reports [SCR] 293

87 The Saskatchewan Association of Rural Municipalities, Regina, 'Submission to the Cabinet of the Provincial Government,' October 1987

88 Telephone interview by William Janzen with Bernard Kirwan, reeve of the Rural Municipality of Gull Lake and vice-president of the Saskatchewan Association of Rural Municipalities, 17 February 1988

89 Palmer, 'The Hutterite Land Expansion Controversy,' 38

CHAPTER 5   Mennonite School Controversies in Manitoba and Saskatchewan, 1874–1925

1 Quoted in Epp, *Mennonites in Canada 1786–1920*, 338

2 Ibid.

3 W.L. Morton, *Manitoba: A History* (Toronto: University of Toronto Press 1967), 186

4 Quoted in C.B. Sissons, *Church and State in Canadian Education: An Historical Study* (Toronto: Ryerson Press 1959), 173

5 Ibid., 175

6 Peter D. Zacharias, *Reinland: An Experience in Community* (Altona, Man.: D.W. Friesen and Sons Ltd 1976) 247

7 Ens, 'Mennonite Relations with Governments,' 106

8 Francis, *In Search of Utopia*, 165

9 The 1878 report of school inspector W.D. Pinkham, as found in John Bergen, 'A Historical Study of Education in the Municipality of Rhineland,' MEd thesis, University of Manitoba 1959, 43

10 Epp, *Mennonites in Canada 1786–1920*, 340

11 Francis, *In Search of Utopia*, 212
12 Ens, 'Mennonite Relations with Governments,' 113
13 Francis, *In Search of Utopia*, 167
14 Ibid.
15 Henry J. Gerbrandt, *Adventure in Faith: The Background in Europe and the Development in Canada of the Bergthaler Mennonite Church of Manitoba* (Altona, Man.: D.W. Friesen and Sons Ltd 1970), 254
16 Morton, *Manitoba: A History*, 245
17 Quoted in Sissons, *Church and State in Canadian Education*, 181. For an extensive discussion of these developments, see Lovell Clark, *The Manitoba School Question: Majority Rule or Minority Rights* (Toronto: Copp Clark Publishing Company 1968).
18 Sissons, *Church and State in Canadian Education*, 194
19 H.H. Ewert, 'Report of 1892' as found in J.F. Galbraith, *The Mennonites in Manitoba, 1874–1900: A Review of Their Progress and Their Present Prosperity* (Morden, Man.: The Chronicle Press 1900), 22
20 A. Weidenhammer, 'Annual Report to the Department of Education, 1911,' as found in Bergen, 'A Historical Study,' 53. Weidenhammer changed his name to Willows around the time of the First World War.
21 Sissons, *Church and State in Canadian Education*, 203
22 C.B. Sissons, *Bi-lingual Schools in Canada* (Toronto: J.M. Dent and Sons, Ltd 1917), 144
23 Quoted in Morton, *Manitoba: A History*, 351
24 Quoted in Francis, *In Search of Utopia*, 182
25 Ibid., 179
26 Quoted in Morton, *Manitoba: A History*, 350
27 Quoted in Bergen, 'A Historical Study,' 256
28 A. Willows, 'A History of the Mennonites, Particularly in Manitoba,' MA thesis, University of Manitoba 1924, 74
29 'To the Honourable Valentine Winkler ... From the Mennonite School Commission of Southern Manitoba ... Presented ... January 7th, 1916,' Manitoba Archives, ME-14 B45
30 Epp, *Mennonites in Canada 1786–1920*, 355
31 Ibid., 357, and A. Willows, 'A History of the Mennonites,' 75
32 Francis, *In Search of Utopia*, 182
33 R.S. Thornton, quoted in I.I. Friesen, 'The Mennonites of Western Canada with Special Reference to Education,' MEd thesis, University of Saskatchewan 1934, 116
34 Ens, 'Mennonite Relations with Governments,' 214

35 Quoted in C.A. Dawson, *Group Settlement: Ethnic Communities in Western Canada* (Toronto: Macmillan of Canada Ltd 1936), 105

36 Dawson, ibid., 105; Francis, *In Search of Utopia*, 185; Ens, 'Mennonite Relations with Governments,' 212

37 *Rex v. Hildebrand*; *Rex v. Doerksen* (1919), 3 WWR 289

38 Francis, *In Search of Utopia*, 185

39 R.S. Thornton, quoted in Friesen, 'Mennonites in Western Canada,' 117

40 'Memorandum re Mennonite Schools ... To the Honourable Members of the Legislative Assembly of Manitoba,' February 1919, by Johann J. Friesen, bishop, and Franz F. Froese, overseer, on behalf of the Reinland Mennonite church, Manitoba Archives ME-14 C45

41 Quoted in Francis, *In Search of Utopia*, 179

42 William Jennings O'Neill, *Manitoba Free Press*, 24 July 1919

43 O'Neill to the Hon. Robert Borden, prime minister, 6 August 1919, NA, Borden Papers, MG 26, H, RLB, 1167, 121189

44 Francis, *In Search of Utopia*, 187

45 George M. Weir, *The Separate School Question in Canada* (Toronto: Ryerson Press 1934), 63

46 Sissons, *Church and State in Canadian Education*, 256

47 Weir, *The Separate School Question*, 65

48 Canada, The Saskatchewan Act, *Statutes*, 4–5 Edward VII, c. 3

49 Frank H. Epp, *Eduation with a Plus: The Story of Rosthern Junior College* (Waterloo: Conrad Press 1975), 36

50 Quoted in ibid., 36

51 'Memorandum for Mr. Calder,' 2 September 1908, Saskatchewan Archives Board (hereafter SAB), Calder Papers

52 J.A. Calder to His Honour The Lieutenant Governor, 15 December 1908, SAB, Calder Papers

53 'Proceedings of Commission of Inquiry at Warman, December 28–29, 1908,' SAB, RC M28, 61. The reference to the Bible here is to Deuteronomy, 6:4.

54 Rev. Jacob Wiens, bishop, to the Government of Saskatchewan, Regina, 21 January 1909, Scott Papers, SAB, 12d, 118G.

55 E.H. Oliver, *The Country School in Non-English Speaking Communities in Saskatchewan* (Regina: Saskatchewan Public Education League 1915), 7

56 J.A. Calder to Mr Barrett, 3 October 1910, SAB, Calder Papers, no. 2801.

57 Oliver, *The Country School*, 3

58 Ibid., 6

59 Ibid., 8

60 'Report re Organization Work in Mennonites Districts, in German Paro-

chial Schools and in Hungarian and Roumanian Settlements,' SAB, Martin Papers, no. 17329–35

61 Quoted in Weir, *The Separate School Question*, 258

62 W. Scott to J.W. Brady, Esq., Radisson, Saskatchewan, 8 September 1915, SAB, Scott Papers, no. 34643

63 Quoted in Weir, *The Separate School Question*, 266

64 W.S. Cram to deputy minister, Department of Education, Regina, 15 December 1916, SAB, Martin Papers, no. 18836

65 John E. Lyons, 'History of Doukhobor Schooling in Saskatchewan and British Columbia 1899–1939,' MA thesis, University of Calgary 1973, 72

66 J.T.M. Anderson, *The Education of the New Canadian: A Treatise on Canada's Greatest Educational Problem* (Toronto: J.M. Dent and Sons Ltd 1918), 103

67 'Memorandum for Mr. Martin,' R.F. Blacklock, deputy minister of Education, 7 December 1917, SAB, Martin Papers, no. 19863

68 Premier W.M. Martin, notes from a speech in the Saskatchewan legislature, 19 December 1918, ibid., no. 18478

69 Premier W.M. Martin to Rev. Jacob Wiens, Hague, Saskatchewan, 23 April 1918, NA, MG 26, H,RLB, 1167, no. 121123

70 Arthur Meighen to Rev. J.P. Wall, Hague, Saskatchewan, 14 May 1918, NA, Borden Papers, ibid., no. 121124

71 *Regina Morning Leader*, 2 September 1918, 4, quoted in Ens, 'Mennonite Relations with Governments,' 225

72 Rural Municipality of Warman no. 374, Warman, Saskatchewan, 15 February 1918, SAB, Martin Papers, no. 19878

73 *The Canadian Annual Review*, 1918, 427, quoted in Ens, 'Mennonite Relations with Governments,' 226

74 Sissons, *Church and State in Canadian Education*, 293

75 *The Canadian Annual Review*, 1920, 756

76 W.S. Cram, inspector of schools, report, 'New Public School Districts – Mennonite Reserve South of Swift Current,' 14 August 1919, SAB, Martin Papers, no. 18889

77 W.S. Cram to W.M. Martin, premier and minister of Education, Regina, 24 November 1919, ibid., no. 18908

78 Ens, 'Mennonite Relations with Governments,' 235

79 Premier W.M. Martin to W.S. Cram, inspector of schools, Swift Current, Saskatchewan, 18 August 1919, SAB, Martin Papers, no. 18892

80 Ens, 'Mennonite Relations with governments,' 236

81 Ibid., 237

82 Ibid., 253

83 Adolf Ens, 'The Public School Crisis among Mennonites in Saskatchewan 1916–1925,' *Mennonite Images: Historical,Cultural, and Literary Essays Dealing with Mennonite Issues*, ed. Harry Loewen (Winnipeg: Hyperion Press 1980), 80

84 Ibid., 76

85 Henry Vogt to Professor H.V. Meyer, referred to in Meyer to R.F. Blacklock, acting deputy minister of Education, 17 March 1917, SAB, Martin Papers, no. 17324

86 W.S. Cram to W.M. Martin, minister of Education, Regina, 18 November 1919, ibid., no. 18904

87 W.M. Martin to W.S. Cram, inspector of schools, Swift Current, Saskatchewan, 21 November 1919, ibid., no. 18906

88 W.W. Cooper to Premier W.M. Martin, Regina, Saskatchewan, 22 November 1919, ibid., no. 18912

89 Premier Martin to J.P. Murphy, Esq., 430 Eleventh Street, Saskatoon, Saskatchewan, 22 March 1920, ibid., no. 18933

90 Johann F. Peters, Hague, Saskatchewan, to Premier Martin, Regina, 13 April 1920 (trans. from German by N. Goldsmith), ibid., no. 18941

91 Premier Martin to Johann F. Peters, Esq., Box 143, Hague, Saskatchewan, 10 May 1920, ibid., no. 18947

92 H. Vogt, to Premier Martin, Regina, 29 May 1920, ibid., no. 18955

93 Premier W.M. Martin to H. Vogt, Neville, Saskatchewan, 7 June 1920, ibid., no. 18956

94 H. Vogt, to Premier Martin, Regina, 30 June 1920, ibid., no. 18957

95 W.M. Martin to H. Vogt, 3 July 1920, ibid., no. 18959

96 A.J.E. Summer, of the R.M. Buchanan Company Ltd of Saskatoon, to W.M. Martin, premier of Saskatchewan, 29 November 1921, ibid., no. 18991

97 Premier Martin to A.J.E. Summer, 2 December 1921, ibid., no. 18993

98 A.J.E. Summer to W.M. Martin, premier of Saskatchewan, 9 December 1921, ibid., no. 18994

99 'Petition to the Honourable Members of the LegislativeAssembly of the Province of Saskatchewan' from Bishop Abraham Wiebe and six ministers, dated 7 January 1922 at the Village of Schoenfeld, near Wymark, Saskatchewan, SAB, Latta Papers

100 Rev. John P. Wall of Hague, to the minister of Education, Regina, 12 February 1923, ibid.

101 Minister of Education to Rev. J.P. Wall, 19 February 1923, ibid.

102 A.W. Ball to G.C. Thomson, barrister, Swift Current, 29 November 1921, ibid.

103 'Memorandum for Mr. Latta,' Regina, 21 August 1923, by A.W. Ball, ibid.
104 *Regina Morning Leader*, Regina, Saskatchewan, 14 October 1922
105 Berger, *Fragile Freedoms*, 67
106 Morton, *Manitoba: A History*, 187
107 Francis, *In Search of Utopia*, 179
108 Quoted in E.K. Francis, 'The Mennonite School Problem in Manitoba
    1874–1919,' *Mennonite Quarterly Review* 27 (July 1953): 235
109 Premier Martin to Johann F. Peters, 10 May 1920, SAB, Martin Papers,
    no. 18947
110 Premier Martin to H. Vogt, 7 June 1920, ibid., no. 18956
111 Quoted in Bergen, 'A Historical Study,' 256
112 Quoted in Friesen, 'The Mennonites of Western Canada ...,' 127
113 Ibid., 126
114 Quoted in Francis, *In Search of Utopia*, 179
115 A. Meighen to J.P. Wall, Hague, Saskatchewan, 14 May 1918, Borden
    Papers, no. 121124
116 Francis, *In Search of Utopia*, 186

CHAPTER 6 Doukhobor School Controversies in Saskatchewan and
British Columbia

1 John Edward Lyons, 'A History of Doukhobor Schooling in Saskatchewan
   and British Columbia, 1899–1939,' MA thesis, University of Calgary
   1973, 49. *Mir* is the name for a traditional Russian peasant commune.
2 Maurice Gershen Hindus, 'Bookless Philosophers,' *The Century Magazine*,
   January 1923, 105, quoted in ibid.
3 Peter V. Verigin, quoted in J.F.C. Wright, *Slava Bohu: The Story of the
   Doukhobors* (New York: Farrar and Rinehart, Inc. 1940), 101
4 James Mavor to Leo Tolstoy, 26 July 1928, quoted in Lyons, 'A History of
   Doukhobor Schooling,' 24
5 Leo Tolstoy to James Mavor, 16 August 1898, quoted in ibid.
6 Peter Kropotkin to James Mavor, 31 August 1898, quoted in ibid., 25
7 Vladimir Tchertkoff to James Mavor, 27 August 1898, quoted in ibid.
8 Peter Verigin to 'all the brothers and sisters,' 27 November 1898, quoted
   in Wright, *Slavu Bohu*, 132
9 Elkinton, *The Doukhobors*, 82ff
10 Quoted in Lyons, 'A History of Doukhobor Schooling,' 53
11 Ibid., 57
12 Elkinton, *The Doukhobors*, 89
13 Quoted in Lyons, 'A History of Doukhobor Schooling,' 57

14 Quoted in ibid., 58

15 William Harvey to Ewart Reid, 16 March 1932, quoted in Ewart Reid, 'The Doukhobors in Canada,' MA thesis, McGill University 1932, 117

16 H.W. Peel, secretary-treasurer to attorney-general of Northwest Territories, 16 January 1900, quoted in Lyons, 'A History of Doukhobor Schooling,' 62

17 Lyons, 'A History of Doukhobor Schooling'

18 Quoted in John Lyons, 'The (Almost) Quiet Evolution: Doukhobor Schooling in Saskatchewan,' *Canadian Ethnic Studies* 8, no. 1 (1976): 25

19 Saskatchewan, 'Annual Report of the Department of Education, 1910,' quoted in Lyons, 'A History of Doukhobor Schooling,' 75

20 'An open letter to all our neighbours, peaceful citizens, and our Democratic Government of Canada,' signed by the president and secretary of the Society of Independent Doukhobors, *Blaine Lake Echo*, 13 April 1932, quoted in C.A. Dawson, *Group Settlement: Ethnic Communities in Western Canada* (Toronto: Macmillan Company of Canada Ltd 1936), 69

21 M.W. Cazakoff to D.P. McColl, 5 July 1911, quoted in Lyons, 'The (Almost) Quiet Evolution,' 28

22 M.W. Cazakoff to A.M. Mall, deputy minister of Education, 14 July 1913, Quoted in ibid., 28

23 W.M. Martin, premier, in the Saskatchewan legislative assembly, SAB, Martin Papers, no. 18478

24 Woodcock and Avakumovic, *The Doukhobors*, 311

25 'Open Letter from the Sons of Freedom, 1928,' quoted in Harry B. Hawthorn, ed., *The Doukhobors of British Columbia* (Vancouver: University of British Columbia 1955), 261

26 Koozma J. Tarasoff, 'In Search of Brotherhood: The History of the Doukhobors,' manuscript, 1963, 588, in Library of the University of Victoria

27 *The Canadian Annual Review, 1919*, 552; see also Anderson, *The Education of the New Canadian.*

28 Lyons, 'The (Almost) Quiet Evolution,' 32

29 Ibid.

30 Lyons, 'A History of Doukhobor Schooling,' 101

31 Quoted in Tarasoff, 'In Search of Brotherhood,' 600

32 Ibid.

33 Ibid.

34 Lyons, 'The (Almost) Quiet Evolution,' 33

35 Lyons, 'A History of Doukhobor Schooling,' 114

36 F. Henry Johnson, 'The Doukhobors of British Columbia: The History of

a Sectarian Problem in Education,' *Queen's Quarterly* 70 (Winter 1964): 528

37 In 1909 only about 800 Doukhobors migrated to British Columbia. By 1912, however, there were 4000 (Blackmore, *Report of the Royal Commission*, 35).

38 Tarasoff, 'In Search of Brotherhood,' 433

39 Beulah Clarke Darlington, letter to the editor, *Nelson Daily News*, 27 March 1914, quoted in Tarasoff, ibid., 434

40 Ibid.

41 Blackmore, *Report of the Royal Commission*, 34

42 Quoted in ibid.

43 Ibid.

44 Lyons, 'A History of Doukhobor Schooling,' 118

45 Blackmore, *Report of the Royal Commission*, 64

46 Quoted in Tarasoff, 'In Search of Brotherhood,' 438

47 Blackmore, *Report of the Royal Commission*, 54

48 Quoted in ibid., 51

49 Quoted in ibid., 52

50 Woodcock and Avakumovic, *The Doukhobors*, 247

51 Blackmore, *Report of the Royal Commission*, 23

52 Ibid., 32

53 Ibid., 66

54 Lyons, 'A History of Doukhobor Schooling,' 123

55 Tarasoff, *Plakun Trava*, 125

56 Ibid., 121

57 Lyons, 'A History of Doukhobor Schooling,' 124

58 Tarasoff, 'In Search of Brotherhood,' 457

59 Ibid., 458; see also Woodcock and Avakumovic, *The Doukhobors*, 250.

60 Tarasoff, 'In Search of Brotherhood,' 458

61 Woodcock and Avakumovic, *The Doukhobors*, 249

62 Quoted in Tarasoff, 'In Search of Brotherhood,' 459

63 Quoted in Tarasoff, *Plakun Trava*, 126

64 Tarasoff, 'In Search of Brotherhood,' 460

65 Tarasoff, *Plakun Trava*, 126

66 Ibid.

67 Woodcock and Avakumovic, *The Doukhobors*, 253

68 Ibid., 254

69 Tarasoff, *Plakun Trava*, 128

70 Woodcock and Avakumovic, *The Doukhobors*, 255

71 Quoted in Tarasoff, 'In Search of Brotherhood,' 471

72 Quoted in ibid., 470
73 C.B. Sissons, 'What Can We Do with the Doukhobors?' *The Canadian Forum* 4, no. 46 (July 1924): 229
74 'The Doukhobor Question and a Suggested Answer,' *The b.c. Teacher*, June 1939, quoted in Lyons, 'A History of Doukhobor Schooling,' 137
75 Lyons, 'A History of Doukhobor Schooling,' 146
76 Ibid., 147
77 Mary Ashworth, *The Forces which Shaped Them: A History of the Education of Minority Group Children in British Columbia* (Vancouver: New Star Books Ltd 1979), 147
78 Lyons, 'A History of Doukhobor Schooling,' 157
79 Ibid., 149
80 Quoted in Tarasoff, 'In Search of Brotherhood,' 589
81 Quoted in ibid., 588
82 Ibid., 590
83 Ibid., 591ff
84 Quoted in ibid., 594
85 Woodcock and Avakumovic, *The Doukhobors*, 316
86 Tarasoff, 'In Search of Brotherhood,' 599
87 Quoted in ibid., 605
88 Ibid., 607
89 R.H.C. Hooper, 'Custodial Care of Doukhobor Children in British Columbia 1929 to 1935,' ma thesis, University of British Columbia 1947, 109–10
90 Quoted in Ashworth, *The Forces which Shaped Them*, 154
91 Quoted in ibid., 156
92 Brian Juriloff, 'A Legal History of the Christian Community of Universal Brotherhood 1899–1942,' unpublished paper written for Prof. Douglas Sanders, Law School, University of British Columbia 1978; see also Tarasoff, *Plakun Trava*, 152.
93 Woodcock and Avakumovic, *The Doukhobors*, 321
94 Ibid., 328
95 Tarasoff, *Plakun Trava*, 134
96 Quoted in Ashworth, *The Forces which Shaped Them*, 157
97 Woodcock and Avakumovic, *The Doukhobors*, 326
98 Tarasoff, *Plakun Trava*, 134; see also Johnson, 'The Doukhobors of British Columbia,' 536.
99 Tarasoff, *Plakun Trava*, 171
100 Hawthorn, *The Doukhobors of British Columbia*, 9, 246, 248
101 Johnson, 'The Doukhobors of British Columbia,' 538

102 Woodcock and Avakumovic, *The Doukhobors*, 341
103 Sidney Katz, 'The Lost Children of British Columbia,' *Maclean's* magazine, 11 May 1957
104 Mrs A. Perepolkin, quoted in Margaret Hill, 'The Detention of Freedomite Children, 1953–59,' *Canadian Ethnic Studies* 18, no. 3 (1986): 54
105 Quoted in Ashworth, *The Forces which Shaped Them*, 165
106 Ibid., 166
107 Johnson, 'The Doukhobors of British Columbia,' 540
108 *Perepolkin v. Superintendent of Child Welfare* (1957), 23 WWR 592
109 Quoted in Katz, 'The Lost Children'
110 Ewart P. Reid, 'The Doukhobors in Canada,' MA thesis, McGill University 1932, 190
111 Woodcock and Avakumovic, *The Doukhobors*, 333
112 Lyons, 'A History of Doukhobors Schooling,' 186
113 Tarasoff, *Plakun Trava*, 104

CHAPTER 7   Hutterite Schools in the Prairie Provinces

1 William D. Knill, 'The Hutterites: Cultural Transmission in a Closed Society,' *Alberta Historical Review* 16 (Summer 1968): 2
2 Ibid., 3
3 Gross, *The Hutterite Way*, 50
4 Peters, *All Things Common*, 137
5 Hostetler, *Hutterite Society*, 201
6 Ibid., 202, quoting from *The Central Purposes of American Education* (Washington, DC: Educational Policies Commission, National Educational Association 1961), 8
7 Knill, 'The Hutterites,' 10
8 Gross, *The Hutterite Way*, 51
9 Ibid., 52
10 Quoted in Robert J. MacDonald, 'Hutterite Education in Alberta: A Test Case in Assimilation, 1920–70,' *Canadian Ethnic Studies* 8, no. 1 (1976): 11
11 Gross, *The Hutterite Way*, 50
12 Lee Emerson Deets, *The Hutterites: A Study in Social Cohesion* (Philadelphia: Porcupine Press 1975), 41
13 Gross, *The Hutterite Way*, 56
14 Ibid.
15 'A Petition from The Hutterites,' 5 September 1899, NA, RG 76, vol. 173 (microfilm reel C7330)

16 J.A. Smart, deputy minister, Department of the Interior, to W.F. McCreary, commissioner of Immigration, Winnipeg, 27 October 1899, NA, RG 76, vol. 173, (microfilm reel c7330). The letter is also quoted in Peters *All Things Common*, 47.

17 Willms, 'The Brethren Known as Hutterians,' *Canadian Journal of Economics and Political Science* 24 (August 1958): 401

18 Alberta, *Report on Communal Property* (1972), 5

19 William D. Knill, 'Hutterite Education: A Descriptive Study on the Hutterian Colonies within Warner County No. 5, Alberta, Canada,' MA thesis, Montana State University 1958, 80

20 Inspector Williams of Cardston, Alberta, quoted in Knill, ibid., appendix F, 179

21 Quoted in MacDonald, 'Hutterite Education in Alberta,' 13

22 Alberta, *Report on Communal Property* (1972), 5

23 Knill, 'Hutterite Education,' 82

24 Ibid., 178

25 Ibid., 84

26 Parren Baker, minister of Education, to the Hutterian Brethren church, 8 July 1925, Quoted in ibid., appendix D, 171

27 Alberta, *Report on Communal Property* (1972), 5

28 Owen Williams, inspector of schools, to the Hon. J.E. Brownlee, 12 January 1934, quoted in appendix of Zieglschmid, *Das Klein-Geschichtsbuch*, 649; see also Knill, 'Hutterite Education,' 162.

29 E.A. Pitt, quoted in Flint, *The Hutterites: A Study in Prejudice*, 108

30 'Copy of Type of Agreement between a Divisional Board and Hutterite Colony,' Knill, 'Hutterite Education,' appendix G, 182

31 'Brief: Submitted to the Committee of the Legislative Assembly of the Province of Alberta appointed to obtain information regarding Colonies or Societies of Hutterian Brethren,' Alberta School Trustees' Association, February 1947, Archives of Alberta, accession 18.60, p. 2

32 Ibid.

33 Ibid., 11

34 Quoted in Pitt, 'The Hutterian Brethren of Alberta,' 122

35 Ibid., 130

36 MacDonald, 'Hutterite Education in Alberta,' 15

37 Knill, 'Hutterite Education,' 88

38 'A Petition Presented to the Warner County No. 5 School Committee,' 9 April 1956, by Rev. John Wipf and the ministers of six other Hutterite colonies, reprinted in ibid., appendix C, 167

39 The Hon. A.O. Aalborg, minister of Education, 6 May 1958, quoted in ibid., 90

40 *Claresholm Local Press*, 17 March 1958, quoted in ibid. 79
41 Alberta, *Report of the Hutterite Investigation Committee* (1959), 24
42 Quoted in MacDonald, 'Hutterite Education in Alberta,' 16
43 Ibid.
44 C.F. Bentley, professor of soil science, University of Alberta, quoted in ibid.
45 Quoted in ibid.
46 Ibid.
47 Alberta, *Report of the Hutterite Investigation Committee* (1959), 26
48 Ibid., 27
49 Ibid., 29
50 Quoted in ibid., 35
51 Quoted in Ibid., 42
52 Ibid., 43
53 'Submission To The Agricultural Committee of The Legislature of the Province of Alberta On Behalf of Alberta's 51 Hutterite Colonies of The Darius-Leut And Lehrer-Leut Groups,' 29 March 1960, Archives of Alberta, accession 73.219, p. 19
54 Ibid., 18
55 Alberta, *Report on Communal Property* (1972), 9
56 Quoted in MacDonald, 'Hutterite Education in Alberta,' 19
57 Alberta, *Report on Communal Property* (1972), 9
58 Ibid.
59 Peters, *All Things Common*, 139
60 Quoted in a night letter from Alexander Adams to F.C. Blair, secretary for the Department of Immigration, 23 March 1921, NA, RG 76, vol. 175, file 58764
61 Peters, *All Things Common*, 139
62 Ibid., 142
63 Manitoba, 'Report to the Honourable the Legislative Assembly,' 2
64 Quoted in ibid., 14
65 Ibid., 16
66 Ibid.
67 Ibid., 26
68 Manitoba, 'Meeting of Select Special Committee'
69 Quoted in ibid., 8
70 Quoted in ibid., 77
71 Quoted in ibid., 16
72 Quoted in ibid., 14
73 Peters, *All Things Common*, 140
74 Quoted in ibid.

75 'Re: Consolidation of School District Referendum March 10, 1967' by Roy H.C. Baker, of Fletcher, Baker & Wolchock, Barristers and Attorneys-at-Law, 7 March 1967, found in the files of Rev. Jacob Kleinsasser, Crystal Springs Hutterite Colony, Ste Agathe, Manitoba (hereafter referred to as the Kleinsasser files)

76 Ibid.

77 'To: The Unitary School Divisions of Manitoba, Regarding the Education of the Children of the Hutterian Brethren,' by Fletcher, Baker & Wolchock, Counsel for the Hutterian Brethren of Manitoba, undated, but probably submitted in June 1967, the Kleinsasser files

78 Ibid., 2; the quotation comes from John A. Hostetler.

79 Ibid., 3

80 Ibid., 7

81 Ibid., 8

82 S.R. Wolchock of Fletcher, Baker & Wolchock, 'Re: Consolidation of Public Schools and Sales Tax,' 22 August 1967,the Kleinsasser files

83 S.R. Wolchock of Fletcher, Baker & Wolchock, 'Re: Education of the Children of the Hutterian Brethren,' 30 May 1968, ibid.

84 S.R. Wolchock of Fletcher, Baker & Wolchock to the Hon. Dr George Johnson, minister of Education, 18 September 1968, ibid.

85 'To The Honourable Minister of Education of The Province of Manitoba, The Honourable Mr. Saul Miller' from Rev. Joseph Kleinsasser, et al., 5 November 1969, ibid.

86 Ibid., 2

87 Ibid.

88 Ibid., 1

89 Clement LeClaire, secretary-treasurer of the Red River School Divison No. 17 to Rev. Jacob Kleinsasser, Crystal Springs Colony, 16 October 1970, ibid.

90 Interview by William Janzen with Rev. Jacob Kleinsasser, leader of Manitoba Hutterites, at the Crystal Springs Hutterite Colony near Ste Agathe, Manitoba, on 7 June 1978

91 Woollam, 'The Treatment of Hutterian Brethren, 5

92 Ibid.

93 Ibid., 8

94 Ibid.

95 Manitoba, 'Meeting of Select Special Committee,' 77 and 14

96 'A Petition Presented ot the Warner County No. 5 School Committee,' 9 April 1956, by Rev. John Wipf; and 'To The Hon. Minister of Education of The Prov. of Manitoba' from Rev. Joseph Kleinsasser

97 Michael F.C. Radcliffe, from Baker, Zivot and Company to William Janzen, 28 September 1988, author's files

PART FOUR Military Service Exemptions

1 George III, c. 1 (1793), quoted in Epp, *Mennonites in Canada 1786–1920*, 100

2 Epp, *Mennonites in Canada 1786–1920*, 101; see also A.G. Dorland, *The Quakers in Canada: A History* (Toronto: Ryerson Press 1968), 317.

3 Alexander Fraser, *Eighth Report of the Bureau of Archives* (Toronto: King's Printer 1911), quoted in Epp, *Mennonites in Canada 1786–1920*, 103

4 50 George III, c. 11 (1810), quoted in Epp, *Mennonites in Canada 1786–1920*

5 Epp, *Mennonites in Canada 1786–1920*, 106

6 W.H. Breithaupt, 'First Settlements of Pennsylvania Mennonites in Upper Canada,' Ontario Historical Society, *Papers and Records* 23 (Toronto 1926); see also Epp, *Mennonites in Canada 1786–1920*, 104.

7 These were, respectively, 18 Victoria, c. 77, passed by the Assembly of the United Province of Canada; and 31 Victoria, c. 40, passed by the Federal Parliament of the Dominion of Canada. See also *Revised Statutes of Canada* (1886), c. 1; *Statutes of Canada* (1904), c. 23; and *Revised Statutes of Canada* (1906), c. 41.

8 *Statutes of Canada* (1868), c. 40, sec. 17

9 Epp, *Mennonites in Canada 1786–1920*, 185

10 Order-in-council, no. 827B, 26 April 1872, NA, RG 2, 1

11 Order-in-council, no. 1043D, 25 September 1872, ibid.

12 Francis, *In Search of Utopia*, 43

13 Order-in-council, no. 2747, 6 December 1898, NA, RG 76, vol. 175, part 9

14 Order-in-council, no. 1676, 12 August 1899, NA, RG 76. vol.176, part 15

CHAPTER 8 Exemptions in the First World War

1 *Winnipeg Free Press*, 4 August 1914

2 Robert Craig Brown and Ramsay Cook, *Canada 1896–1921: A Nation Transformed* (Toronto: McClelland and Stewart; reprinted 1976 from 1974 original), 213

3 Quoted in John Lewis, 'Canada at War,' in *Canada in the Great World War*, vol. II: *Various Authorities* (Toronto: United Publisher of Canada 1918), 32

4 Quoted in Brown and Cook, *Canada 1896–1921*, 212

5 Charles Hanbury-Williams, 'Creating the Canadian Army,' in *Canada in the Great World War*, 73

6 J.L. Granatstein and J.M. Hitsman, *Broken Promises: A History of Conscription in Canada* (Toronto: Oxford University Press 1977), 34

7 Ibid., 37

8 Ibid., 38

9 Ibid., 40

10 Ibid., 43

11 L.J. Burkholder, ed., *A Brief History of the Mennonites in Ontario* (Toronto: Mennonite Conference of Ontario 1935), 262. This book was reprinted in 1986 by the Ontario Mennonite Historical Society, Waterloo, Ont.

12 Ens, 'Mennonite Relations with Governments,' 281

13 The three bishops were Johann J.S. Friesen, Abram Doerksen, and Jacob Wiens of Manitoba, Swift Current, Saskatchewan, and Hague, Saskatchewan, respectively. See Johann J.S. Friesen to Robert L. Borden, and Arthur Meighen, Borden Papers, NA, MG 26, H. vol. 214, no. 121078.

14 Solicitor-General Arthur Meighen to Rev. Jacob Wiens, 29 January 1917, ibid., no. 121093

15 Johann J.S. Friesen to Robert L. Borden and Arthur Meighen, 4 January 1917, ibid.

16 'Report re distribution of National Service Cards' by Cpl C.T. Hildyard, Rosthern Detachment RNWMP, 4 April 1917, Borden Papers, NA, MG 26, H, 1(c), vol. 214

17 Ens, 'Mennonite Relations with Governments,' 285

18 These five church leaders included David Toews and Klaas Peters from Saskatchewan and Heinrich Doerksen, Abraham Doerksen, and Benjamin Ewert from Manitoba; *Der Mitarbeiter* (Gretna, Manitoba), January 1917. (This monthly periodical served many of the Mennonites in western Canada at that time.)

19 'A Petition of the Mennonite Delegation to the Government at Ottawa, in regard to military service,' 8 January 1917, Mennonite Heritage Centre Archives (MHCA), Winnipeg, vol. 1321, file 929. The 1877 address by Lord Dufferin is in the same file. It is also reprinted in William Schroeder, *The Bergthal Colony*, rev. ed. (Winnipeg: CMBC Publications 1986).

20 R.B. Bennett, 'Written Reply to the Petition of the Mennonite Delegation,' Ottawa, 8 January 1917, MHCA, vol. 1321, file 929

21 The view of the western Mennonites is set forth in Circular no. 5, issued by the Military Service Branch of the Department of Justice to all Registrars on 29 August 1918, NA, RG 24, vol. 115, file HQ 7168-1-1. The view of S.F. Coffman is described in a letter from him to Daniel Kauffman,

dated 12 July 1917, quoted in John S. Weber, 'History of S.F. Coffman, 1872–1954: The Mennonite Churchman,' MA thesis, University of Waterloo 1975, 41.

22 Thomas P. Socknat, *Witness against War: Pacifism in Canada 1900–1945* (Toronto: University of Toronto Press 1987), 75. See also 'Memorandum on the Treatment of Conscientious Objectors in Canada,' dated 10 October 1918, Department of National Defence, Directorate of History (hereafter DND, D. Hist.), file 934.009 D322.

23 R.B. Bennett to Abraham Doerksen, 28 May 1917, MHCA, vol. 542, file 3

24 Ens, 'Mennonite Relations with Governments,' 310. Ens explains that Manitoba Mennonites also purchased Victory Bonds valued at $600,000–$700,000 but only after the government agreed to use an amount equal to what they would buy for relief purposes.

25 *Ottawa Citizen*, 15 January 1917; see also NA, RG 15, vol. 758, file 494483(14).

26 *Regina Leader*, 1 March 1917; see also NA, RG 15, vol. 758, file 494483(14).

27 Granatstein and Hitsman, *Broken Promises*, 62

28 Quoted in Col. G.W.L. Nicholson, *Canadian Expeditionary Force 1914–1919* (Ottawa: Queen's Printer 1964), 342

29 Ross Munro, 'Conscription in Canada,' *Canada in the Great World War*, 95

30 The War-Time Elections Act (1917), *Statutes of Canada* (1917), c. 39. It is reproduced in C.P. Stacey, *Historical Documents of Canada* v (Toronto: Macmillan 1972), 591.

31 The Military Service Act (1917), *Statutes of Canada* (1917), c. 19. A portion of the act is reproduced in Stacey, ibid.

32 As reported in the *Regina Post*, 12 October 1917, NA, RG 15, vol. 758, file 494483(14)

33 Ibid.

34 S. Mabor, superintendent of the Department of the Interior, to the deputy minister of that department, 18 October 1917, ibid.

35 The enlistment of 200 or 300 is referred to by S. Mabor in the memorandum, ibid., and the quotation that 'there appears to have been no attempt to enforce military service' comes from Woodcock and Avakumovic, *The Doukhobors*, 252.

36 'Petition to His Excellency, the Governor-General of Canada in Council,' 4 November 1918, signed by the solicitor for the Mennonites, J.E. Doerr, NA, RG 2, 3, vol. 199, PC no. 2897 (hereafter referred to as 'Petition to His Excellency ...')

37 Benjamin Ewert to Sir Robert L. Borden, 17 November 1917, MHCA, vol. 542, file 3

38 *Der Mitarbeiter*, December 1917
39 Klaas Peters to Benjamin Ewert, 23 January 1918, MHCA, vol. 542, file 3
40 David Toews to Benjamin Ewert, 26 March 1918, MHCC, vol. 542, file 4
41 Submission from David Toews et al. to Col. Machin, 12 April 1918, ibid.
42 'Petition to His Excellency ...,' 13
43 That the arrangement was accepted is stated in the 'Petition to His Excellency ...' 14 and exhibit D; that it was not immediately accepted is reported in a letter from David Toews to Benjamin Ewert, 1 May 1918, MHCA, vol. 542, file 4.
44 J.M. Carson, registrar, Province of Alberta, to David Toews, 3 May 1918, in the 'Petition to His Excellency ...' exhibit J
45 'Petition to His Excellency ...,' 17
46 *Der Mitarbeiter*, June 1918
47 A submission from the bishops of Sommerfeld and Bergthal congregations in Manitoba, 11 June 1918, MHCA, vol. 542, file 3
48 Epp, *Mennonites In Canada 1786–1920*, 382
49 'Petition to His Excellency ...,' exhibit B
50 Ibid., exhibit E
51 J.E. Doerr to David Toews, 28 June 1918, ibid., exhibit H
52 'Petition to His Excellency ...,' 14
53 Ibid., 17
54 Socknat, *Witness against War*, 75
55 Order-in-council, no. 919, 19 April 1918, reprinted in Stacey, *Historical Documents*, 580
56 Epp, *Mennonites in Canada 1786–1920*, ch. 16
57 Augustus M. Pearman, provincial constable to Capt. F.R. Glover, chief inspector, Dominion Police, MSA, Vancouver, 5 June 1918, and chief inspector Civil Section, CMPC, to assistant provost marshal, MD no. 12, Regina, 're Klaas Peters, alleged Mennonite Minister,' 23 October 1918, NA, RG 24, vol. 115, files 7168-1-2
58 A resolution at one Mennonite conference stated: 'We,the Mennonites of the Rosthern District, urgently request the Mennonites of the Herbert and Rush Lake districts, to separate themselves in their dealings with the authorities regarding our position in Military matters, from those who are not of our faith' (12 July 1918, ibid.).
59 Kirk Barons, 'An Examination of the Mennonite and Hutterite Immigration Crisis 1918–19, in the Provinces of Western Canada,' major essay for history course 433, Carleton University 1974
60 'Facts Communicated By A Deputation of the Society of Independent Doukhobors,' NA, RG 24, vol. 6613, file HQ 8498-1-1

61 Telegram, P.G. Makaroff to Arthur Meighen, 17 August 1918, in ibid.

62 Colonel, provost marshall, to adjutant-general, 30 August 1918, ibid.

63 'Petition to His Excellency ...' This government action relates also to the enforcement of a long-dormant regulation that required immigrants to Canada to come directly from their native country. It was used to bar the immigration of some, who, though they had lived in the United States for awhile, were still citizens of Russia (see Barons, 'An Examination of the Mennonite and Hutterite Immigration Crisis,' and Willms, 'The Brethren Known as Hutterians,' 393).

64 J.H. Reid, chief inspector, Civil Section CMPC, Regina, to the provost marshal, director of contracts, Ottawa, 15 October 1918, NA, RG 24, vol. 115, files 7168-1-2

65 Klaas Peters to Benjamin Ewert, 1 February 1918, MHCA, vol. 542, file 3

66 'Petition to His Excellency ...,' 20

67 W.D. Scott, superintendent of Immigration, Department of the Interior, 4 February 1918, NA Department of Colonization and Immigration files 58764 1

68 Willms, 'The Brethren Known as Hutterians,' 392

69 Treaty between the United States and Canada, NA, RG 24, vol. 115, HQ 7168-1-1

70 'Petition to His Excellency ...,' 25

71 Order-in-council, no. 2622, 25 October 1918, NA, RG 2, 1; also in RG 76, vol. 176, part 15

72 'Petition to His Excellency ...,' 14

73 Ibid.

74 Quoted in Barons, 'An Examination of the Mennonite and Hutterite Immigration Crisis,' 15

75 *Daily News*, Nelson, British Columbia, 14 February 1919

76 Order-in-council, no. 923, 1 May 1919; another order-in-council, no. 1204, with almost identical words, was passed on 9 June 1919 (NA, RG 2 and 1).

77 The Military Service Act, 1917, *Statutes of Canada* (1917), c. 19. A portion of this act is reprinted in Stacey, *Historical Documents of Canada*, vol. v.

78 Socknat, *Witness against War*, 80–4. Those tortured included Jehovah's Witnesses, then known as International Bible Students. The person who died three weeks after being detained was David Wells, a Pentecostal. Tunkers, though referred to already in the 1793 statute, had recently changed their name to Brethren in Christ and were not recognized until later in the war as a religious denomination that prohibited military service. Their young men experienced serious difficulty.

79 S.F. Coffman, 'Mennonites and Military Service,' ed. L.J. Burkholder, *Brief History of the Mennonites in Ontario*, 264. In spring 1917, the Mennonites of Ontario had asked the law firm of McCullough and Button of Stouffville, Ontario to inquire about their status. A reply from the office of the minister of Militia and Defence stated: 'No proposal has been made to treat Mennonites in Ontario any differently than Mennonites in Western Canada.' See McCullough and Button to the minister of the Militia, 9 March 1917, NA, RG 24, vol. 115, HQ 7168-1-1, and letter from E. Bristol, private secretary to the minister of Militia and Defence, to McCullough and Button, 24 May 1917 (Waterloo, Ont., Conrad Grebel College Archives, Military Problems Committee files [hereafter referred to as CGCA, MPC files] XV-11.2.2).

80 Coffman, ibid., 265

81 'Non Resistant Groups in World War I,' an unpublished paper probably written by S.F. Coffman, CGCA, MPC files, XV-11.4.7

82 Ibid.

83 E.L. Newcombe, deputy minister of Justice, to S.F. Coffman, 3 November 1917, CGCA, MPC files

84 Tribunal Circular no. 11, issued by the Military Service Council under the Military Service Branch of the Department of Justice, 5 November 1917, ibid., XV-11.4.6

85 E.L. Newcombe, the deputy minister of Justice, to Messrs McCullough and Button, barristers, Stouffville, Ontario, 6 November 1917, CGCA, MPC files

86 Reported in a letter from J.L. Byler to S.F. Coffman, 5 November 1917, ibid.

87 Ibid.

88 S.F. Coffman to L.J. Burkholder, November 1917; and S.F. Coffman to Asa Bearss and Fred Elliot, 6 November 1917, ibid.

89 The draft of the letter of thanks addressed to the prime minister is dated 20 November 1917. The names of eight Mennonite leaders appear as planned signatories (ibid.).

90 S.F. Coffman to L.J. Burkholder, 13 November 1917, ibid. This suggestion is significant for understanding the discussions about an alternative-service program in the Second World War in which S.F. Coffman played a significant role.

91 S.F. Coffman, 'The Non-Resistant Relief Organization,' ed. Burkholder, *A Brief History of the Mennonites in Ontario*, 273ff

92 J.L. Byler to S.F. Coffman, 5 November 1917, CGCA, MPC files

93 W.E. Wismer, deputy registrar, London, Ontario, to Local Tribunal, 263, Milverton, Ontario, 10 November 1917, ibid.

94 The difficulties are described in various letters, including: (1) J.L. Byler, from Markham, to S.F. Coffman, 5 November 1917; (2) Osias Cressman, from New Hamburg, to S.F. Coffman, 19 November 1917; (3) Asa Bearss, from Ridgeway, to S.F. Coffman, 3 December 1917; (4) Jonas Snider, from Waterloo, to L.J. Burkholder, 20 November 1917; (5) Osias Cressman, in reference to the tribunals at Drumbo and Preston, to S.F. Coffman, 28 November 1917; (6) an unsigned letter, from Waterloo, to the Hon. Arthur Meighen, 26 November 1917 (CGCA, MPC files). The fact that the tribunals dealt with the Mennonite cases in many different ways is also referred to in Burkholder, ed., *A Brief History of the Mennonites in Ontario*, 267.

95 S.F. Coffman to Osias Cressman, 21 November 1917, CGCA, MPC files

96 S.F. Coffman to Osias Cressman, 29 and 30 November 1917, ibid.

97 S.F. Coffman to David Bergey, 22 December 1917, ibid.

98 W.G. Weichel to D. Bergey, 8 November 1917, ibid.

99 S.F. Coffman to the Hon. Charles J. Doherty, minister of Justice, 7 December 1917, and to His Honour Chief Justice Duff, central appeal judge, 7 December 1917, ibid.

100 S.F. Coffman to W.E. Wismer, registrar under Military Service Act, 1917, London, Ontario, 29 January 1938, ibid.

101 Glyn Osler to L.J. Burkholder, 2 February 1918, ibid.

102 John Ebersole to S.F. Coffman, 14 February 1918, ibid.

103 S.F. Coffman to the prime minister, the Right Honourable Sir Robert Borden, 20 February 1918, ibid.

104 A four-point statement from the Non-Resistant Relief Organization to the government, entitled, 'The Conflicting Points Between the Faith Of The Non-Resistant Churches And The Military Service Act,' ibid., sv-11.4.7

105 'Report of Committee' by delegates S.F. Coffman, Thomas Reeser, and D.W. Heise, CGCA, MPC files. This meeting is also referred to in J.S. Hartzler, *Mennonites in the World War or Non-Resistance under Test* (Scottdale, PA: Mennonite Publishing House 1924), 84.

106 S.F. Coffman, secretary of the Non-Resistant Relief Organization, to Hon. J.A. Calder, minister of Immigration and Colonization, 22 April 1918, CGCA, MPC files

107 S.F. Coffman to F.S. Scott, member of Parliament, 22 April 1918, ibid.

108 S.F. Coffman to the 'Brethren' (Meaning various ministers and members of the Non-Resistant Relief Organization), 20 April 1918, ibid.

109 S.F. Coffman to the 'Brethren,' 22 April 1918, ibid.

110 This information had come from N.W. Rowell to J.L. Byler of Markham, who in turn passed it on to S.F. Coffman. Coffman referred to it in letters dated 23 April 1918 to Osias Cressman and John Ebersole, ibid.

111 Quoted in a letter written by J.L. Byler to S.F. Coffman, 1 May 1918, ibid.
112 S.F. Coffman, secretary of the Non-Resistant Relief Organization, to the Hon. J.A. Calder, minister of Immigration and Colonization, 4 May 1918, ibid.
113 That Coffman was continuing to give this advice is indicated in a letter from John R. Ebersole to S.F. Coffman, 18 May 1918, ibid.
114 The order-in-council of 19 April 1918 is printed in Stacey, *Historical Documents*, 580.
115 Indicated in a quotation from Scott that appears in a letter written by S.F. Coffman to the 'Brethren,' 23 May 1918, CGCA, MPC files
116 F.S. Scott to S.F. Coffman, 17 May 1918, ibid.
117 F.S. Scott to S.F. Coffman, 15 June 1918, ibid.
118 S.F. Coffman to John R. Ebersole, 21 May 1918, ibid.
119 S.F. Coffman to the bishops and ministers of the Mennonite and Tunker churches, 14 June 1918, ibid.
120 W.D. Euler to the Honourable Minister of Justice, 29 May 1918, ibid.
121 Ontario registrar to Bishop S.F. Coffman, 27 June 1918, ibid.
122 There is no exact information about the number and duration of these detentions. However the problem is referred to in at least twelve letters to and from S.F. Coffman in May, June, July, August, and October 1918, ibid.
123 Ontario registrar to Bishop S.F. Coffman, 27 June 1918, ibid.
124 Major deputy assistant adjutant-general for the acting adjutant-general to Capt. Tyndale, secretary, Military Service Sub-Committee, 5 November 1918, ibid.
125 Order-in-council no. 2622, 25 October 1918, NA, RG 2.1
126 'Petition to His Excellency ...'

CHAPTER 9 Exemptions from the Second World War

1 The population figures for Mennonites and Doukhobors come from Statistics Canada, Census of Canada, 1941, vol. 1, ch. 10. The figure for the Hutterites comes from Peters, *All Things Common*, 207. The census in 1941 did not have a separate category for Hutterites; they were included in the Mennonite category. I have adjusted the Mennonite figure accordingly.
2 F.C. Blair to Heinrich Friesen, bishop of the Sommerfelder congregation, Altona, Manitoba, 25 April 1923, NA, RG 76, vol. 175, file 58764, part 10
3 In order to admit these Mennonites, the 1919 prohibition against further

Mennonite immigration had to be lifted (done by order-in-council PC 1181, 2 June 1922); see Frank H. Epp in *Mennonites in Canada 1920–1940: A People's Struggle for Survival* (Toronto: Macmillan 1982), 155ff.

4   W. Stuart Edwards, acting deputy minister of Justice to the deputy minister of Immigration and Colonization, 18 June 1924, NA, vol. 175, file 58764, part 10

5   F.C. Blair, acting deputy minister of Immigration to Rev. David Toews, Rosthern, Saskatchewan, 2 November 1936, NA, RG 76, vol. 176, file 58764, part 14

6   Deputy minister to Hon. Mr Forke, 15 March 1927, and F.C. Blair to John Shukin, Verigin, Saskatchewan, 20 June 1934, NA, RG 76, vol. 176, file 58764

7   Quoted in Granatstein and Hitsman, *Broken Promises*, 141

8   Government of Canada, *Statutes of Canada*, 1940, c. XIII, 43–4. Late in the war some men were conscripted for overseas service.

9   Doukhobor leaders had met with Mackenzie King during an election campaign visit to Prince Albert, Saskatchewan, in February 1940; according to a Doukhobor report, 'he practically assured our representatives that the Government would keep up its agreement with Doukhobors in regard to exemption from military service' (quoted in a letter from P.K. Reibin to P.G. Makaroff, 24 June 1940, in P.G. Makaroff Papers, Saskatchewan Archives Board (SAB), Saskatoon, I-18). Hutterite contact is indicated in a letter dated 13 July 1940 from Rev. John P. Entz to F.C. Blair, (NA, RG 76, vol. 176, part 14). And David Toews, the Mennonite leader, travelled to Ottawa and met with the prime minister at the time when the legislation was introduced (see the *Free Press Prairie Farmer*, 19 June 1940).

10   House of Commons, *Debates*, 18 June 1940, 904

11   Letter, Rev. John P. Entz to F.C. Blair, 13 July 1940, and telegram to director of Immigration Branch, 21 August 1940, NA, RG 76, vol. 176, parts 14 and 15

12   David Toews to Mr Justice T.C. Davis, 19 August 1940, MHCA, vol. 1321, file 929

13   T.C. Davis to David Toews, 22 August 1940, ibid.

14   National War Services Regulations, 1940 (Recruits), *The Canada Gazette* 74, no. 23, 27 August 1940, sec. 17(2)

15   A report on the military situation written in German by David Toews, June 1942, Rosthern, Saskatchewan, MHCA, vol. 1320, file 940

16   Two other groups, albeit very small ones, included in the Conference of Historic Peace Churches (CHPC) were the Old Order German Baptists

and the Church of the Brethren (see E.J. Swalm, 'The Organization of the Conference of Historic Peace Churches,' unpublished paper, CGCA file XV-11.1.1).

17 Minutes of CHPC meeting, 26 January 1941, CGCA file XV-11.1.10. Many of the CHPC registration cards are in CGCA files XV-11.1.10, 11, 12.

18 P.G. Makaroff to John A. Shukin, 5 October 1939, in P.G. Makaroff Papers, SAB, I-18

19 P.G. Makaroff to M.G. Popoff, 21 June 1940, ibid.

20 P.G. Makaroff to Peter K. Reibin, 21 June 1940, and P.K. Reibin to P.G. Makaroff, 24 June 1940, ibid.

21 W.G. Novokshonoff and P.G. Makaroff to the Hon. James G. Gardiner, July 9, 1940, ibid.

22 James G. Gardiner to P.G. Makaroff, 9 July 1940, ibid.

23 T.C. Davis to P.G. Makaroff, 12 July 1940, ibid.

24 RCMP, 'Memorandum Re: Doukhobors,' for minister of National Defence, 8 March 1943, NA, RG 24, vol. 6521, file H.Q. 420-18-28. See other letters of summer 1940 in SAB, P.G. Makaroff Papers.

25 T.C. Davis to P.G. Makaroff, 17 August 1940, SAB, P.G. Makaroff Papers

26 Tarasoff, 'In Search of Brotherhood,' 671

27 RCMP Intelligence Section, 'Conditions among Doukhobors in British Columbia,' 26 April 1941, NA, RG 24, vol. 6521, file H.Q. 420-18-28

28 A Canadian Press newspaper story, Vancouver, 16 December 1943

29 RCMP, 'Memorandum Re: Doukhobors,' for the minister of National Defence, 8 March 1943, NA, RG 24, vol. 6521, file H.Q. 20-18-28; see also Hawthorn, *The Doukhobors of British Columbia*, 59.

30 A Canadian Press newspaper story, Regina, 6 March 1941

31 National War Services Regulations, 1940 (Recruits), *The Canada Gazette* 74, no. 23, 27 August 1940

32 W. Stuart Edwards, deputy minister of Justice to deputy minister of National War Services, 23 July 1940, NA, RG 27, vol. 991, file 2-101-1

33 Order-in-council, no. 7215, 24 December 1940

34 Order-in-council, no. 1822, 18 March 1941, amended on 22 April 1942, reprinted in J.A. Toews, *Alternative Service in Canada during World War II* (Winnipeg: Publication Committee of the Canadian Conference of the Mennonite Brethren Church 1959), 118

35 Smith, *Smith's Story of the Mennonites*, 299 and 311. See also C.F. Klassen to the Hon. Humphrey Mitchell, minister of Labour, 2 February 1943, Mennonite Brethren Bible College Archives (MBBCA), B.B. Janz Papers, Winnipeg, vol. 38–9.

36 David P. Reimer, *Experiences of the Mennonites of Canada during the Second*

World War, 1939–1945 (Steinbach, Man.: Derksen Printers Ltd, undated), 37

37 Frank H. Epp, *Mennonite Exodus: The Rescue and Resettlement of Russian Mennonites since the Communist Revolution* (Altona, Man.: D.W. Friesen and Sons Ltd 1962), 332ff

38 *Free Press Prairie Farmer,* 19 June 1940

39 Toews, *Alternative Service,* 31

40 Minutes of the third session of the CHPC, 8 October 1940, CGCA file XV-11.1.10. Apparently the formulation was largely the work of the aged S.F. Coffman. See also David Fransen, 'Canadian Mennonites and Conscientious Objection in World War II,' MA thesis, University of Waterloo 1977), 48

41 See the German report of this meeting, entitled 'Mitteilungen von der Board of National war Service in Canada,' 28 September 1940, MHCA, vol. 1321, file 928. An English version of that same report, though undated, is entitled 'The following are explanations which have been given to us by the Board of National War Services,' NA, RG 27, vol. 991, file 2-101-1

42 Letter, B.B. Janz to J.G. Gardiner, 13 June 1941, MBBCA, B.B. Janz Papers, vol. 38–9. For a fuller account of these developments, see also Fransen, 'Canadian Mennonites and Conscientious Objection,' and Kenneth Reddig, 'Manitoba Mennonites and the Winnipeg Mobilization Board in World War II,' MA thesis, University of Manitoba 1989.

43 Reimer, *Experiences of the Mennonites of Canada,* 76

44 B.B. Janz to Justice H. Harvey, chairman of the Board of National War Services, Edmonton, 7 November 1940, MBBCA, B.B. Janz Papers, vol. 42

45 T.C. Davis to David Toews, 9 September 1940, MHCA, vol. 1321, file 924

46 T.C. Davis to David Toews, 19 October 1940, ibid., file 929

47 The eight-member delegation included six Mennonites: David Toews, B.B. Janz, C.F. Klassen, and J. Gerbrandt from the west, and J.B. Martin and J.H. Janzen from Ontario. E.J. Swalm represented the Brethren in Christ church and Fred Haslam the Quakers.

48 See David Toews, B.B. Janz, C.F. Klassen, and J.J. Gerbrandt to T.C. Davis, 12 November 1940; and David Toews, B.B. Janz, J. Gerbrandt, C.F. Klassen, E.J. Swalm, J.B. Martin, Fred Haslam, and J.H. Janzen to T.C. Davis and L.R. Lafleche, 13 November 1940, MHCA, vol. 1321, file 928. For a fuller account of these negotiations, see Fransen, 'Canadian Mennonites and Conscientious Objection.'

49 Ottawa delegates report, 14 November 1940, CGCA, file XV-11.1.10

50 B.B. Janz to L.R. Lafleche, 19 November 1940, NA, RG 27, vol. 986, file 1

51 Quoted in Fransen, 'Canadian Mennonites and Conscientious Objection,' 102
52 E.J. Swalm, J.B. Martin, Fred Haslam, J.H. Janzen, B.B. Janz, C.F. Klassen, J.H. Sherk to J.G. Gardiner, 22 November 1940, MHCA, vol. 1321, file 928
53 Fransen, 'Canadian Mennonites and Conscientious Objection,' 102
54 Socknat, *Witness against War*, 235. There was substantial public concern, particularly in Manitoba, that Mennonites should be required to do something by way of a national service.
55 Order-in-council, no. 7215, 24 December 1940, published in *The Canada Gazette* 74, no. 64, 7 January 1941. Soon after, T.C. Davis wrote to B.B. Janz: 'I think you will find that the Order-in-Council is pretty well in line with the recommendations which your bodies made to us and the only point of deviation is that the case of each individual must be considered on its own merits ... we could not consent to having them treated in bulk on certificate of their membership in the Church' (Davis to Janz, 23 January 1941, MBBCA, B.B. Janz Papers, vol. 38–9).
56 Circular memorandum 120, 7 January 1941, NA, RG 27, vol. 991, file 2.101.2, part 3
57 L.R. Lafleche to Brigadier Cassels, deputy adjutant-general, Department of National Defence, 7 January 1941, NA, RG 27, vol. 991, file 2-101-2
58 Brigadier Cassels, 22 January 1941, quoted in a memorandum to the minister, from Lafleche, 25 January 1941, ibid.
59 'Report On Work Done by Conscientious Objectors (Mennonites, Doukhobors And Other Sects) Under Director of Department of Mines and Resources From June to November 15th, 1941,' NA, RG 27, vol. 986, file 1
60 Regarding the Ontario delegation, see 'Report of Ottawa Delegation,' 29 January 1941, MHCA, vol. 1320, file 915. The Kanadier Mennonite delegation, which was in Ottawa in mid February, is referred to in Reimer, *Experiences of the Mennonites in Canada*, 26.
61 'Report On Work Done by Conscientious Objectors,' 15 November 1941
62 Ibid.
63 A letter signed by David Toews and twelve others Mennonite leaders from western Canada to the Hon. James G. Gardiner, 11 June 1941, NA, RG 27, vol. 986, file 1
64 Jack Hoeppner, *Search For Renewal: The Story of the Rudnerweider/EMMC*, (Winnipeg: Evangelical Mennonite Mission Conference 1987), 133
65 'Report of Delegation to Ottawa,' 5 July 1941. Members of the delegation were J.B. Martin, J.H. Janzen, and J. Harold Sherk (MHCA, vol. 1321, file 915).

66 The situation in Ontario is described by David Toews in an untitled general report dated June 1942 (MHCA, vol. 1320, file 940). It is also referred to in numerous documents of the CHPC. See also N.N. Driedger, *The Leamington United Mennonite Church: Establishment and Development 1925–1972* (Altona, Man.: D.W. Friesen and Sons 1972), 66ff.

67 Letters sent out by Registrar J.P. McIsaac, Administrative Division 'N,' Department of National War Services. The letters do not carry a date but B.B. Janz's letter of 13 June 1941 to the board in Alberta suggests that they were sent out on 10 June 1941 (MBBCA, B.B. Janz Papers, vol 42).

68 B.B. Janz to Hon. J.G. Gardiner, 13 June 1941, NA, RG 27, vol. 986, file 1. See also J.T. Thorson, minister of National War Services, to B.B. Janz, 18 June 1941, MBBCA, B.B. Janz Papers, vol. 38–9.

69 B.B. Janz to Hon. J.T. Thorson, 28 June 1941, MBBCA, B.B. Janz Papers, vol. 38–9

70 'Report of Delegation to Ottawa,' 5 July 1941. Members of the delegation were J.B. Martin, J.H. Janzen, J. Harold Sherk (MHCA, vol. 1320, file 915).

71 B.B. Janz to Hon. J.T. Thorson, 28 June 1941, B.B. Janz Papers, MBBCA, vol. 38–9

72 T.C. Davis to B.B. Janz, 2 July 1941, ibid.

73 B.B. Janz to L.R. Lafleche, 15 July 1941, ibid.

74 The divisional registrar sent out announcements of new hearings, stating: 'The Board considers that you should have the right to a reconsideration of your claim' (ibid., vol. 42). The result of these second hearings is referred to, albeit loosely, in a letter from B.B. Janz to H. Harvey, dated 14 August 1941 (ibid.). In the following weeks many, perhaps a third of those who applied for conscientious objector status, were nevertheless sent to military camps (indicated in 'Memorandum' for Mr Smart from G. Rattray, 3 September 1941, NA, RG 27, vol. 1501, file 2.N.101.7).

75 'Memorandum Re: Mennonite Camps – Bishop Toews, Rosthern,' signed by J.F.L. Embury, chairman, National War Services Board, Division 'M,' 31 July 1941, MHCA, vol. 1321, file 922. See also Saskatoon *Star Phoenix*, 16 January 1941.

76 'Memorandum for War Services Board Division "M"' attached to a letter of 19 November 1941 from J.F.L. Embury to Brigadier W.W. Foster, NA, RG 39, vol. 41, file 49810

77 J.F.L. Embury to Brigadier Foster, 19 November 1941, ibid.

78 Memorandum to the district officer commanding, Military District 12, from B.W. Browne, 26 November 1941, DND. D. Hist., file 326.009 D102

79 *Winnipeg Free Press*, 26 December 1940
80 Adamson's speech of 7 May 1941 was reprinted by Lafleche in circular memorandum no. 239, 23 May 1941, NA, RG 27, vol. 997, file 2.106.213.
81 P.A. Toews, David Schulz, and J.F. Barkman to Hon. J.T. Thorson, 9 July 1941, NA, RG 27, vol. 986, file 1. On 25 August 1941, Adamson wrote to Thorson that he had rejected 200 applicants for conscientious-objector status (ibid.).
82 Hon. J.T. Thorson from J.E. Adamson, 11 August 1941, ibid. See also Reddig, 'Manitoba Mennonites,' 109.
83 L.R. Lafleche to Mr Justice Adamson, 25 August 1941, NA, RG 27, vol. 986, file 1
84 L.R. Lafleche, memorandum to the minister, 6 November 1941, ibid.
85 Memorandum, 'Conscientious Objectors' by A.S. Redford, Lt-Col DOC's Representative, Military District 12, 19 December 1941, DND, D. Hist., file 326.009 D102
86 Several letters from the young men indicating this view are in NA, RG 27, vol. 986, file 1.
87 Walter Tucker, member of Parliament, to Embury, 10 January 1942, ibid.
88 J.F.L. Embury to Walter Tucker, 12 January 1942, ibid.
89 Three memoranda from Embury, all dated 13 January 1942, addressed to the departments of National War Services, National Defence, and Mines and Resources, NA, RG 27, vol. 986, file 1
90 Memorandum, 'Alternative Service for Mennonites and other Conscientious Objectors,' by B.W. Browne, adjutant general, Department of National Defence, 27 January 1942, DND, D. Hist., file 168.009 (D71)
91 David Toews, C.F. Klassen, and J.H. Enns to Hon. J.T. Thorson, 20 October 1941; and David Toews to the Rt Hon. W.L.M. King, 3 November 1941, NA, RG 27, vol. 986, file 1. See also MHCA, vol. 1321, file 929.
92 J. Harold Sherk, J.B. Martin, David Toews, and C.F. Klassen to the Hon. J.T. Thorson, 9 January 1942, NA, RG 27, vol. 986, file 1
93 'Report of Delegation to Ottawa,' 13 January 1942, MHCA, vol. 1322, file 930
94 David Toews to J.F.L. Embury, 2 April 1942, MHCA, vol. 1320, file 914. Embury was strongly suspicious of Toews. In a 22 May 1942 letter to Toews, Embury said: 'You appear to exercise a dominating influence in the part of the Country concerning which we are most dissatisfied. We are convinced that the younger people would gladly co-operate with the Government and are only prevented by superior influence ... There are a number of defaulters around your North Country who will have to

be dealt with ... and you can rest assured that as soon as we can get around to it that they will be proceeded against according to law, and if there is any attempt at improper influence ... you may rest assured that the authorities will know how to deal with it' (MHCA, vol. 1320, file 914).

95 David Toews to the Hon. J.T. Thorson, 8 April 1942, NA, RG 27, vol. 986, file 1; also in MHCA, vol. 1322, file 930

96 T.A. Crerar to the Hon. A. Wells Gray, minister of Lands, British Columbia, 3 February 1942, reprinted in Toews, *Alternative Service*, 121

97 Circular Memorandum no. 500, 7 April 1942. The authority for ordering the men to serve for the duration was provided by order-in-council no. 2451, 30 March 1942, NA, RG 39, vol. 41, file 49810. The government expected that this condition would reduce the number of people seeking conscientious-objector status (see memorandum to L.R. Lafleche from T.C. Davis, 4 November 1941, ibid.). The government's expectation appears to have been correct. A submission made by Mennonite leaders stated: 'Since the order has been enforced that men have to stay in for the duration ... Many of our young men have volunteered, and joined the Army, a number are overseas' (statement to Hon. J.T. Thorson from bishops Peter A. Toews and J.F. Barkman, 6 May 1942, NA, RG 27, vol. 986, file 1).

98 David Toews to Hon. J.T. Thorson, 27 April 1942, NA, RG 27, vol. 991, file 2-101-1; also in MHCA, vol. 1322, file 930

99 L.R. Lafleche to David Toews, 29 April 1942, MHCA, vol. 1322, file 930

100 Bishop Peter A. Toews and eight other bishops to Hon. J.T. Thorson, 9 June 1942, NA, RG 27, vol. 986, file 1

101 This is evident from numerous communications, including a letter from J.T. Thorson to Bishop Peter A. Toews, 17 June 1942; circular memorandum no. 594, dated 3 June 1942, NA, RG 27, vol. 991, file 2-101-1; and other letters in NA, RG 27, vol. 993, file 2-11-9, part 11.

102 J.T. Thorson to H.W. Winkler, MP, 20 August 1942, NA, RG 27, vol. 991, file 2-101-1

103 David Toews to Hon. J.T. Thorson, 23 June 1942, MHCA, vol. 1322, file 930

104 An untitled report, written in German, dated June 1942, Rosthern, Saskatchewan, MHCA, vol. 1320, file 940

105 David Toews to the Hon. J.T. Thorson, 1 June 1942, NA, RG 27, vol. 986, file 1; also in MHCA, vol. 1322, file 930. See also the letter from Toews to Thorson dated 16 April 1942 in the same file.

106 David Toews to F.C. Blair, director, Immigration Branch, Department of Mines and Resources, 13 July 1942, MHCA, vol. 1322, file 930

107 David Toews to the Hon. J.T. Thorson, 14 July 1942, ibid.
108 'Protokoll der Sitzung des Zentralkomittes in der Dienstfrage fuer West-canada,' 30 July 1942, ibid.
109 David Toews and C.F. Klassen to the Hon. J.T. Thorson, 28 September 1942, NA, RG 27, vol. 991, file 2-101-1; also CGCA, file XV-11.1.2
110 House of Commons, *Debates*, 18 May 1942
111 Reported in 'Protokoll der Sitzung des Mennonitischen Zentralkomittees in der Dienstfrage,' 12 December 1942, MHCA, vol. 1322, file 930
112 David Toews to the Right Hon. W.L.M. King, 24 October 1942, ibid.
113 W.L. Mackenzie King to David Toews, 29 October 1942, CGCA, file XV-11.1.11
114 'Protokoll der Sitzung des Mennonitischen Zentralkomittees in der Dienstfrage,' 12 December 1942, MHCA, vol. 1322, file 930
115 C.F. Klassen to the Hon. Humphrey Mitchell, minister of Labour, 2 February 1943, NA, RG 27, vol. 991, file 2-101-1; also in B.B. Janz Papers, MBBCA, vol. 38–9
116 Humphrey Mitchell to C.F. Klassen, 13 February 1943, MBBCA, B.B. Janz Papers, vol. 38–9
117 Report, Delegation to Ottawa, 7 and 8 January 1943, CGCA, file XV-11.1.11
118 'Memorandum'; presented by CHPC delegation on 7 and 8 January 1943 to officials in Ottawa, including J.M. Wardle, director, Survey and Engineering; A. de Gaspe Tache, supervisor of Mobilization; and A. MacNamara, director of National Selective Service and deputy minister of Labour (ibid.)
119 J.B. Martin to Humphrey Mitchell, minister of Labour. The letter appears to be in draft form but it does indicate their views (ibid., XV-11.1.1).
120 Humphrey Mitchell to Walter Tucker, MP, 10 March 1943, MBBCA, B.B. Janz Papers, vol. 38–9
121 B.B. Janz to Walter Tucker, MP, 23 March 1943, ibid.
122 Order-in-council, PC 2821, 7 April 1943
123 Report of delegation to Ottawa, 27–29 April 1943. The delegates were E.J. Swalm, J.B. Martin, C.F. Klassen, and J. Harold Sherk (CGCA, file XV-11.1.11).
124 'Memorandum,' E.J. Swalm, J.B. Martin, C.F. Klassen, and J. Harold Sherk to Hon. Humphrey Mitchell, minister of Labour, and Arthur MacNamara, director of National Selective Service, ibid.
125 A. MacNamara to E.J. Swalm, J.B. Martin, J. Harold Sherk, and C.F. Klassen, 29 April 1943, ibid.
126 Toews, *Alternative Service*, 55
127 'Statement for the attention of men postponed as Mennonites, Doukho-

bors or Conscientious Objectors under Order-in-Council P.C. 2821, May 1, 1943,' from L.E. Westman, chief alternative service officer, 16 June 1943, Ottawa, MHCA, vol. 1323, file 937; see also J.A. Toews, *Alternative Service*, 90, 91.

128 On 1 December 1945, 6655 men were employed in agriculture and 1412 in essential industries (Toews, *Alternative Service*, 90, 92).

129 Order-in-Council, PC 7251, 16 September 1943

130 B.B. Janz to H. Harvey, chairman of the Board in Alberta, 21 January 1943, MBBCA, vol. 42. In this letter Janz appealed once more for special medical corps work, saying that about 50 per cent of the men in his area, largely populated by Russlaender Mennonites, had enlisted voluntarily even though they would have preferred to go into truly non-combatant medical corps work.

131 David Fransen, 'The Debate on Alternative Service during World War II,' paper presented to the Institute of Anabaptist-Mennonite Studies at Conrad Grebel College, Waterloo, Ontario, October 1975, p. 25, CGCA

132 Reimer, *Experiences of the Mennonites of Canada*, 123. The Kanadier Mennonites wrote to Ottawa stating: 'It is against our conscience to be a member of the Army, to be under military law, and take military obligations (P.A. Toews, D. Schulz, and J. Barkman to L.E. Westman, 3 November 1943, NA, RG 27, vol. 991, file 2-101-1). An Ontario Mennonite leader wrote: 'We have always held the position that we cannot do any kind of service, either non-combatant or combatant in the army or under military direction (Elven Shantz to pastors of churches, MHCA, vol. 1320, file 915).

133 Toews, *Alternative Service*, 95

134 Driedger, *The Leamington united Mennonite Church*, 71

135 C.F. Klassen to Arthur MacNamara, director of National Selective Service, 12 May 1943, MBBCA, B.B. Janz Papers, vol. 38–9

136 Arthur MacNamara to C.F. Klassen, 4 June 1943, ibid.

137 H. Harvey to B.B. Janz, 9 February 1943, ibid., vol. 42

138 Horace Harvey, chairman Mobilization Board, Alberta, to A. MacNamara, deputy minister of Labour, 12 May 1944, CGCA, file xv-11.4.9

139 William Janzen and Frances Greaser, *Sam Martin Went to Prison: A Story of Conscientious Objection in Canada and Canadian Military Service* (Winnipeg: Kindred Press 1990)

140 C.F. Klassen to J.B. Martin and J.H. Sherk, 27 August 1943, CGCA

141 C.S. Henley to L.E. Westman, 15 December 1943, NA, RG 27, vol. 991, file 2-101-2, part 2

142 Reimer, *Experiences of Mennonites in Canada*, 127 and 132

143 Harvey to A. MacNamara, 30 March 1943, NA, RG 27, vol. 133, file 601.3-6-2
144 'Hutterites in Alberta,' four-page memorandum signed by L.E. Westman. It is not dated but appears to have been written in 1944 (ibid.).
145 A. MacNamara to Senator John T. Haig, 15 August 1944, ibid.
146 L.E. Westman to A. MacNamara, 29 November 1943, ibid.
147 L.E. Westman to A. MacNamara, 31 May 1944, ibid.
148 A memorandum of three pages, with no title, author, or date, ibid.
149 Memorandum, L.E. Westman to A. MacNamara, 25 February 1944, ibid. This memo refers to '85 additional Hutterites' being sent to this camp. A 16 February 1944 memorandum from Westman to MacNamara says that 15 to 25 had been working at this camp for some time.
150 Letters and memoranda: E.N. Griggs to A. MacNamara, 9 August 1944; L.E. Westman to A. MacNamara, 17 August 1944; M.P. Blair to E.N. Griggs, 18 August 1944; and L.E. Westman to A. MacNamara, 5 September 1944, ibid.
151 Senator W.A. Buchanan to A. MacNamara, 16 January 1945, ibid.
152 L.E. Westman to A. MacNamara, 16 February 1944, ibid.
153 L.E. Westman to A. MacNamara, 17 August 1944, ibid.
154 H.A. Pearson to T.C. Davis, 1 April 1941, NA, RG 27, vol. 1500, file 2-M-101-2
155 Circular memorandum no. 229, issued 17 May 1941 by L.R. Lafleche, NA, RG 27, vol. 997, file 2-106-213
156 P.G. Makaroff to John J. Anatooshkin, 5 September 1940, SAB, P.G. Makaroff Papers, I-18
157 Mike Khadiken to the Rt Hon. W.L. Mackenzie King, 23 June 1941, NA, RG 27, vol. 986, file 1
158 RCMP, 'Memorandum re: Doukhobors' to the minister of National Defence, 8 March 1943, NA, RG 24, vol. 6521, file H.Q. 420-18-28
159 'Editorial,' *Blaine Lake Echo*, 8 October 1941. See also *Mir: A Doukhobor Youth Publication*, January 1975, 13, and May 1975, 14. For reference to a road-building project in British Columbia, see memorandum, L.R. Lafleche to the minister, 7 May 1941 NA, RG 27, vol. 991, file 2-101-1).
160 'Report on Work Done by Conscientious Objectors,' 15 November 1941
161 J.F.L. Embury to T.C. Davis, 3 July 1941, NA, RG 27, vol. 1500, file 2-M-101-2
162 RCMP, 'Memorandum re: Doukhobors.' Other sources report different numbers. The Doukhobor publication *Mir* (January 1975, p. 13) says that 85 served in the alternative service camp and 'about that many' went to jail. A letter from A.C. Stewart, Regina, to National War Services,

Ottawa (18 December 1942) states that 100 were jailed (NA, RG 27, vol. 991, file 2-101-2). A memorandum, H.J. Riley to A. MacNamara (15 January 1943, ibid.), says '106 were sent to gaol.' Koozma Tarasoff says 92 were imprisoned (see *Plakun Trava*, 155). There is also some uncertainty about the length of the prison terms. They may have been longer than four months (see memorandum, A.S. Redford to deputy-adjutant general 'M,' 22 January 1942, DND, D. Hist., file 112.3H1.009 D220).

163 Telegram, Mike Khadiken to the Rt Hon. W.L. Mackenzie King, 23 June 1941, NA, RG 27, vol. 986, file 1. See also *Blaine Lake Echo*, 11 June 1941; and 'Memorandum: Confidential' from H. Darling to F.C. Wilson, registrar in Saskatchewan, 28 April 1941, NA, RG 27, vol. 1500, file 2-M-101-2.

164 'Memorandum: Confidential,' ibid.

165 This resolution, adopted by the Society of Independent Doukhobors at a meeting held at Buchanan, Saskatchewan, on 10 June 1941, is quoted in a newspaper clipping that is not identified but probably comes from the Saskatoon *Star Phoenix*.

166 RCMP, memorandum, Kamsack Detachment, 28 November 1941, NA, RG 27, vol. 1500, file 2-M-101-2

167 *Mir*, May 1975, 14

168 RCMP, memorandum, Kamsack Detachment, 28 November 1941; see also 'Editorial,' *Blaine Lake Echo*, 8 October 1941.

169 RCMP, several memoranda, Radisson Detachment, dated 19 March 1942, 24 April 1942, and 24 August 1942, and one from the Kamsack Detachment dated 24 April 1942, all in NA, RG 27, vol. 1500, file 2-M-101-2

170 Ibid. The reference to the donation in wheat appears in an RCMP report, 24 December 1942.

171 RCMP, 'Memorandum re: Doukhobors'

172 Ibid. A news story, put out by Canadian Press on 16 December 1943, states that in 'February of 1941, the first call-up notices were going out to those who had registered and a mass meeting was called at Brilliant to discuss the situation. It ended with the Doukhobors deciding to disregard the notices.'

173 R.J. Waterous to T.C. Davis, 10 June 1941, NA, RG 27, vol. 986, file 1

174 J.T. Thorson to L.R. Lafleche, 30 May 1942, NA, RG 27, vol. 991, file 2-101-2

175 A.M. Manson, chairman of the National War Services Board in British Columbia, to L.R. Lafleche, 24 June 1942, ibid.

176 RCMP, 'report,' Vancouver Detachment, 11 July 1942, ibid.

177 RCMP, 'Memorandum re: Doukhobors'

178 F.J. Mead, assistant commissioner, RCMP, 'Memorandum' to director of Mobilization, National Selective Service, Department of Labour, Ottawa, 9 March 1943; and F.J. Mead to A. MacNamara, 19 June 1943, NA, RG 27, vol. 991, file 2-101-2

179 James J. Popoff and four others to the Rt Hon. W.L. Mackenzie King, 1 May 1943, ibid., part 2

180 F.J. Mead, 'memorandum' to director of Mobilization, 9 March 1943; A.M. Manson, chairman of the board in British Columbia, to C.S. Henley, alternative service officer, 15 June 1943; and J.F.L. Embury, chairman of the board in Saskatchewan, to Maj.-Gen. H.J. Riley, associate director of Mobilization Section, 29 June 1943, ibid.

181 James J. Popoff and four others to the Rt Hon. W.L. MacKenzie King, 31 May 1943, ibid.

182 Stan Clark, agricultural representative to W.W. Dawson, supervisor of farm labour requirements for Saskatchewan, 31 July 1943, DND, D. Hist., file 326-009 D102

183 H.J. Riley to A. MacNamara, 10 May 1943; and from F.J. Mead to A. MacNamara, 11 June 1943, NA, RG 27, vol. 991, file 2-101-2

184 Memorandum to W.W. Dawson, supervisor of farm labour Requirements, Saskatchewan, 30 June 1943, DND, D. Hist., file 326-009 D102

185 The position of the Doukhobors at Langham is indicated in a letter by John G. Savankoff to National Selective Service, 15 August 1944 (NA, RG 27, vol. 992, file 2-101-2, part 4). The flexibility of officials in accommodating the Doukhobors was demonstrated in 1943 (see letter, G.R. Bickerton to A. MacNamara, 8 September 1943, ibid., part 2). It was demonstrated again in 1944 (see letter, R.S. Hinchey, alternative service officer for Saskatchewan, to L.E. Westman, 28 August 1944, ibid., part 4).

186 RCMP, 'memorandum,' New Denver Sub-Division, 28 May 1943, NA, RG 27, vol. 991, file 2-101-2

187 RCMP, 'Memorandum,' Vancouver Detachment, 27 March 1943, ibid.

188 H.J. Riley to A. MacNamara, 10 May 1943, ibid.

189 L.E. Westman to C.S. Henley, 15 May 1943, ibid.

190 L.E. Westman to Allen Mitchell, 16 July 1943, ibid.

191 A.M. Manson to L.E. Westman, 12 August 1943, ibid.

192 L.E. Westman to Allen Mitchell, 20 August 1943, and L.E. Westman to Humphrey Mitchell, 29 September 1943, ibid.

193 H.T. Pammelt to A. MacNamara, 27 October 1943; see also memorandum, H.J. Riley to F.C. Wilson, 1 November 1943, ibid.

194 'Results of Conference between the Following Representatives of the

Doukhobors and the Director of National Selective Service,' Ottawa, 15 and 16 November, ibid.

195 'Statement of Doukhobor Delegation (Union of Spiritual Community of Christ),' 16 November 1943, ibid.

196 Reported in A. MacNamara to J.E. Adamson, 17 November 1943, ibid.

197 Resolution of mass meeting of members of the Union of Spiritual Communities of Christ, at Brilliant, BC, 5 December 1943, ibid.

198 The events of this meeting are referred to in several memoranda, including C.S. Henley to L.E. Westman, 15 December 1943; RCMP, Vancouver, 20 December 1943; and Maj. J.B. Cowell to A. MacNamara, 13 December 1943, ibid. See also Tarasoff, 'In Search of Brotherhood,' 685; and Woodcock and Avakumovic, *The Doukhobors,* 321.

199 RCMP, 'memorandum,' Vancouver, 20 December 1943, NA, RG 27, vol. 991, file 2-101-2, part 2

200 J.B. Cowell to A. MacNamara, 13 December 1943, ibid.

201 A.M. Manson to A. MacNamara, 31 December 1943, ibid., file 2-101-2, part 3; and J.B. Cowell to A. MacNamara, 29 January 1944, NA, RG 27, vol. 133, file 601.3-6-1 (vol. 4)

202 A.D.P. Heeney to Humphrey Mitchell, 7 February 1944, NA, RG 27, vol. 133, file 601.3-6-1 (vol. 4)

203 *Vancouver Sun,* 'We'll Do Anything but Fight,' 28 January 1944

204 RCMP, 'Memorandum,' Vancouver, 20 December 1943, NA, RG 27, vol. 991, file 2-101-2, part 2

205 Memorandum signed 'G.R.P., GOC in C. Pacific Command' to the secretary, Department of National Defence, 1 March 1944; and 'Report on Doukhobors' from BC Police, 26 February 1944, DND, D. Hist., file 322.009 D420

206 'Summary of Activities in the West Kootenay,' February 1944, ibid.

207 'Doukhobor Depredations in British Columbia,' 10 February 1944, NA, RG 27, vol. 133, file 601.3-6-1 (vol. 4). See also Tarasoff, 'In Search of Brotherhood,' 687ff.

208 J.J. Zoabkoff and J.J. Verigin of the executive committee 'To all Members of the Union of Spiritual Communities of Christ,' 16 February 1944, NA, RG 27, vol. 133, file 601.3-6-1 (vol. 4)

209 British Columbia Police,'report,' 21 February 1944, ibid.; and A.M. Manson to A. MacNamara, 24 July 1944, NA, RG 27, vol. 992, file 2-101-2, part 4

210 S.T. Wood of RCMP, 'report,' to Hon. Louis St Laurent, minister of Justice, 15 March 1944, NA, RG 27, vol. 133, file 601.3-6-1 (vol. 4)

211 R.A.D. West, president, Castlegar-Robson Branch, Canadian Legion, to A. MacNamara, February 1944, ibid.

212 *Vancouver Sun*, 'Castlegar Residents Take Law into Own Hands,' 17 March 1944

213 S.T. Wood of RCMP to Louis St Laurent, 15 March 1944, NA, RG 27, vol. 133, file 601.3-6-1 (vol. 4)

214 A.M. Manson to A. MacNamara, 30 May 1944, ibid.

215 A. MacNamara to A.M. Manson, 6 July 1944, NA, RG 27, vol. 992, file 2-101-2, part 4

216 C.S. Henley to L.E. Westman, 29 June 1944, ibid., part 3

217 Ibid.

218 L.E. Westman to C.S. Henley, 4 July 1944, ibid., part 4

219 L.E. Westman to A. MacNamara, 13 July 1944, ibid.

220 C.S. Henley to L.E. Westman, 7 July 1944, ibid.

221 L.E. Westman to A. MacNamara, 24 July 1944, ibid.

223 A.M. Manson and F.W. Smelts to A. MacNamara, 24 July 1944, NA, RG 27, vol. 133, file 601.3-6-1 (vol. 4)

224 L.E. Westman to C.S. Henley, 24 August 1944, NA, RG 27, vol. 992, file 2-101-2, part 4

225 DeVoin to A.M. Manson, 2 November 1944, ibid.

226 J.J. Verigin, 'To Trustees of the Spiritual Communities of Christ in B.C.' 14 October 1944, ibid.

227 DeVoin to A.M. Manson, 2 November 1944, ibid.

228 R.B. Hughes to H.K. Whimster, farm labour placement officer, 4 June 1945, ibid.

229 DeVoin to L.E. Westman, 28 February 1945, ibid.

230 L.E. Westman to W. MacGillivray, director, Emergency Farm Labour Service, 26 April 1945, ibid. See also letter, A.M. Manson to A. MacNamara, 19 February 1945, NA, RG 27, vol. 133, file 601.3-6-1 (vol. 5)

231 The contention that the difficulties involved the Russlaender Mennonites more than the Kanadier is supported by several earlier references in this book. See also (1) 'MemorandumRe: Mennonite Camps – Bishop Toews, Rosthern,' 31 July 1941, CHCA, vol. 1321, file 922; (2) letter, C.F. Klassen, J.H. Enns, and J.A. Kroeker, to J.E. Adamson, 11 June 1941, NA, RG 27, vol. 986, file 1; and (3) letter, David Toews, C.F. Klassen, and J.H. Enns to T.C. Davis, 25 August 1941, in MBBCA, B.B. Janz Papers.

232 It is estimated that 4500 Mennonites served in the military and 7500 in the Alternative Service Program (see Reddig, 'Manitoba Mennonites and the Winnipeg Mobilization Board,' 102; also Toews, *Alternative Service*, 95).

233 Berger, *Fragile Freedoms*, 170. See also M. James Penton, *Jehovah's Witnesses in Canada: Champions of Free Speech and Worship* (Toronto: Macmillan 1976).

234 A. MacNamara to John G. Rempel, 19 June 1946, NA, RG 27, vol. 991, file 2-101-1
235 Quoted in Toews, *Alternative Service*, 109
236 In the Second World War Canada's population was 11,300,000; 44,893 service personnel died; 53,000 were wounded. In the First World War, the population was 7,879,000; 66,695 died; and 138,000 were wounded (see also Socknat, *Witness against War*, 193).

PART FIVE   The Welfare State

1 Reimer, *Experiences of the Mennonites of Canada*, 135
2 J.F. Mckinnon to J.E. Westman, 17 April 1945, NA, RG 27, vol. 992, file 2.101.2, part 5
3 Michael Radcliffe, legal counsel for Manitoba Hutterites, in House of Commons, 'Minutes of Proceedings and Evidence of the Special Committee on Participation of Visible Minorities in Canadian Society,' chaired by Bob Daudlin, MP, 24 October 1983, issue no. 19, p. 99
4 Ibid. See also documents prepared for a visit to Ottawa in July 1986 in the law offices of Baker, Zivot, and Company (hereafter, the Baker files), 360 Main Street, Winnipeg, Man.
5 House of Commons 'Proceedings of Special Committee on Visible Minorities,' issue 19, p. 98
6 Ibid.
7 D.W.A. Norris, CA to Doug Smith, director of Child Related Income Support Program, 22 June 1984, in the offices of Meyers, Norris, Penny and Co., Chartered Accountants, 160–14th Street, Brandon, Man.

CHAPTER 10   Mennonites, Hutterites, and the Canada Pension Plan

1 Allan J. MacEachen, minister of National Health and Welfare, 'Annual Report: Canada Pension Plan' (Ottawa: Queen's Printer 1967), 7
2 Approximately fifty Mennonite families in northern Alberta also opposed the Canada Pension Plan (CPP). It was one factor that prompted their immigration to Bolivia (Peter Janzen, a teacher in northern Alberta, interviewed by William Janzen, 4 July 1979).
3 Edward Bauman, Joseph N. Jantzi, Noah B. Martin, and others, to the Hon. Allan J. MacEachen, minister of NationalHealth and Welfare, 25 April 1966, Mennonite Central Committee Ontario files (hereafter MCCO), 50 Kent Street, Kitchener, Ont.
4 E.J. Benson, minister of National Revenue, to Elven Shantz, 4 August 1966, MCCO files

5 Elven Shantz to E.J. Benson, 19 August 1966, Private Papers of Elven Shantz, Kitchener, Ont.

6 The Canada Pension Plan Act, 13–14 Elizabeth II, ch. 51

7 E.J. Benson to Elven Shantz, 8 September 1966, MCCO files

8 Elam S. Martin, Edward M. Bauman, Amsey Martin, and Amos Albrecht to the Rt Hon. Lester B. Pearson, prime minister of Canada, 27 october 1966, NA, minister's office files, box 15, file 32-8-2, 'Mennonites (Amish) and Hutterian Colonies re CPP,' 1966–1971

9 Lester B. Pearson to Elven Shantz, 10 November 1966, MCCO files

10 Elven Shantz to Lester B. Pearson, 27 October 1966, NA, ministers office files, box 15, file 32-8-2

11 Elven Shantz to Lester B. Pearson, December 7, 1966, Ibid.

12 James Schofield, of the Kitchener Law Firm of Bray, Schofield, MacKay and Kelly, to Elven Shantz, 6 January 1967, Elven Shantz Private Papers

13 J.E. Lang, 'Memorandum Re: The Canada Pension Plan and Religious Freedom,' to J. Schofield, undated, ibid.

14 Kitchener Chamber of Commerce, 'Minutes of the Special Meeting of the Provincial and Federal Affairs Committee with Representatives from the Old Order Mennonite and Amish,' 13 April 1967, MCCO files

15 Elven Shantz to Lester B. Pearson, 13 April 1967, Elven Shantz Private Papers

16 A.G. Bramford to Lester B. Pearson, 17 April 1967, MCCO files

17 S.M. Horst to 'Kind Friend,' 24 June 1967, ibid.

18 Lester B. Pearson to Elven Shantz, 8 May 1967, ElvenShantz Private Papers

19 Elven Shantz to E.J. Benson, 19 May 1967, MCCO files

20 E.J. Benson to Elven Shantz, 6 June 1967, ibid.

21 Elven Shantz to C.L.R. Gray, Unemployment Insurance Commission, 25 St Clair Avenue, Toronto, 23 February 1967, ibid. The form letter of the same date is in the same files.

22 A form letter addressed to L.B. Ross, Accounts Section for Director Taxation 1. Re: 1966 Assessment, ibid.

23 Amos W. Brubacher to Department of National Revenue (attention: Mr F.B. Bermon), 24 July 1967, ibid.

24 Department of National Revenue, 'Tax Notice,' to Joseph Stoll, 23 June 1967, David Luthy Papers, David Luthy, RR 4, Aylmer, Ont.

25 A form letter addressed to Department of National Revenue, Taxation Division, David Luthy Papers

26 *Kitchener-Waterloo Record*, 14 August 1967

27 *London Free Press*, 18 August 1967

28 Ibid.

29 David Wagler, *Kitchener-Waterloo Record*, 'Letter to the Editor,' 19 August 1967, David Luthy Papers

30 David Wagler to Department of National Revenue, 22 August 1967, ibid.

31 P.J. Fleming, director Taxation Collections, London, to David L. Wagler, 7 September 1967

32 F. Keith Staebler, president, Kitchener Chamber of Commerce to the Hon. E.J. Benson, 11 October 1967, MCCO files

33 Ibid.

34 'The Old Order Mennonite and Amish Basis of Objection to Government Sponsored Social Security Programs,' 16 October 1967, Kitchener, Ont. Elven Shantz Private Papers. The brief was printed in *The Canadian Mennonite*, Altona, Man., 31 October 1967.

35 Minutes of the meeting, 'Representation to Mr. Benson, Minister of National Revenue, The Commonwealth Room, House of Parliament,' 16 October 1967, MCCO files

36 Elven Shantz and Douglas Snyder to Mr Fleming, Department of National Revenue, London, Ontario, 19 October 1967, ibid.

37 David Wagler to P.J. Fleming, Department of National Revenue, London, Ontario, 25 January 1968, David Luthy Papers

38 Memorandum to W.J. Trudeau, 12 February 1969, NA, ministers office files, box 15, file 32-8-2

39 F. Keith Staebler, president, Kitchener Chamber of Commerce, to the Hon. John C. Munro, minister of National Health and Welfare, 14 January 1969, MCCO files

40 Douglas Snyder, executive director, MCCO, to Ed Good, member of provincial parliament, Toronto, 7 May 1969, ibid.

41 Press release, New Democratic Party, 25 April 1969, 'Bill to Amend the Canada Pension Plan – presented by Max Saltsman. (The bill was C-190, first reading, 25 April 1969.)

42 Jean-Pierre Côté, 'Memorandum,' 21 February 1969, NA, ministers office files, box 15, file 32-8-2

43 James A. Robb of Stikeman, Elliott, and Co., Montreal, to Department of Justice, Ottawa (attention: G.W. Ainslie), 6 January 1967, the Baker files

44 James S. Robb to Roy H.C. Baker, 16 January 1967, ibid.

45 Roy Baker to Messrs Stikeman, Elliott and Co. (attention: James A. Robb), 28 March 1968, ibid.

46 James A. Robb to Roy H.C. Baker, 1 April 1968, ibid.

47 Roy Baker to Messrs Stikeman, Elliot and Co. (attention: James A. Robb), 28 March 1968, ibid.

48 That they made the appeal early in 1969 is referred to in a document dated August 1969 and entitled 'Submission on Behalf of the Members of the Hutterian Brethren Church of Canada for Exemption under the Canada Pension Plan,' p. 6, found in the Kleinsasser Papers. The early 1969 submission is probably the one entitled 'Memorandum of Fact and Law to be Attached to and Forming a Part of the Appeal of Jacob Kleinsasser under the Canada Pension Plan Section 28 (1).' It is among the Kleinsasser Papers and is not dated.

49 'Submission on Behalf of the Members of the Hutterian Brethren Church of Canada for Exemption under the Canada Pension Plan,' ibid.

50 Ibid.

51 Ibid.

52 Mark G. Smerchanski, MP, to the Hon. John Munro, 10 October 1969, NA, ministers office files, box 15, file 32-3-2

53 Ian Howard, executive assistant to the minister of National Health and Welfare, 'Memorandum,' to J.A. Blais, director-general, Income Security, 30 April 1969, ibid.

54 W.J. Trudeau, director, Canada Pension Plan, 'Memorandum,' to J.A. Blais, director-general, Income Security, 21 April 1969, ibid.

55 Jean-Pierre Côté, minister of National Revenue, 'Memorandum to the Cabinet, Canada Pension Plan Exemption from Coverage on Religious Groups,' 14 November 1969, ibid.

56 Supplementary memorandum to the Cabinet, Canada Pension Plan, Exemption from Coverage on Religious Grounds, signed by Jean-Pierre Côté, minister of National Revenue, 14 November 1969, ibid.

57 Letters, Jean-Pierre Côté, to Elven Shantz, Kitchener, Ontario, and to James A. Robb, Montreal, 16 March 1970, MCCO files and the Kleinsasser Papers, respectively

58 Transcription of meeting between MCCC delegation and Prime Minister Trudeau, Winnipeg, 20 March 1970, MCCC files, Winnipeg, MB

59 Rev. Jacob J. Waldner, for the Hutterian Brethren Church Lehrer-Leut group, to the Hon. Jean-Pierre Côté, minister of National Revenue, with copies to John Munro, H.A. (Bud) Olson, and Mark Smerchanski, 20 April 1970, NA, ministers office files, box 15, file 32-8-2. The further efforts of the Mennonites are indicated in a letter from Elven Shantz to Jean-Pierre Côté, 12 May 1970 (see Hunter, *Civil Liberties and Human Rights*, 203).

60 John Munro to Rev. Jacob J. Waldner, 16 June 1970, NA, ministers office files, box 15, file 32-8-2

61 'Submission on Behalf of the Members of the Hutterian Brethren Church of Canada Relating to Exemption under the Terms of the Canada Pension Plan,' 13 July 1970, the Kleinsasser Papers

62 Ibid.

63 James A. Robb to Roy H.C. Baker, 14 September 1971, the Baker files

64 Memo of the meeting with the Hon. Herb Gray, Parliament Buildings, Ottawa, Tuesday, 7 December 1971, MCCO files

65 Ibid.

66 Press release, Department of National Revenue, 'Proposed Announcement re Exemption from Canada Pension Plan Coverage on Religious Grounds,' for release 24 December 1971, the David Luthy Papers

67 House of Commons, *Debates*, 20 July 1973, 5847

68 Ibid., 5848

69 Ibid., 5851

70 Ibid., 5850

71 Ibid.

72 Ibid., 14 September 1973, 6603

73 Ibid., 13 September 1973, 6505

74 Ibid., 14 September 1973, 6599

75 Ibid., 6602

76 Ibid., 18 September 1973, 6675

77 Ibid., 6677

78 Ibid

79 House of Commons, *Proceedings of the Standing Committee on Health, Welfare and Social Affairs*, 20 September 1973 and 18 October 1973

80 House of Commons, *Debates*, 18 April 1974, 1544

81 Form CPT 16, Department of National Revenue, Taxation, entitled 'Application for Exemption from Coverage under the Canada Pension Plan on Account of Religious Beliefs'

82 Form CPT 17, Department of National Revenue, Taxation, entitled 'Certification by an Authorized Spokesman of a Religious Sect Concerning Exemption from Coverage under the Canada Pension Plan'

83 *The Canadian Mennonite* 16, no. 11, 12 March 1968, quoted in Hunter, *Civil Liberties*, 197

CHAPTER 11 The Hutterites and the Income Tax System

1 Roy Baker, House of Commons, 'Proceedings of the Special Committee on Visible Minorities,' 24 October 1983, issue 19, p. 7

2 *Calgary Albertan*, 'Hutterites and Income Taxes,' an editorial, 11 December 1958

3 Alberta, *Report of the Hutterite Investigation Committee* (1959)

4 James A. Robb, of the law firm of Stikeman, Elliot, and Co., Montreal, to Roy H.C. Baker, of Baker, Zivot and Co., Winnipeg, 16 January 1967; also other letters, the Baker files

5 The Hon. John R. Garland, minister of National Revenue, to Ray Woollam, 26 September 1963, quoted in 'Treatment of Hutterian Brethren by Provincial and Federal Governments – A Summary,' a report prepared by Ray Woollam for the minister of the Department of Municipal Affairs, Regina, Saskatchewan, October 1963

6 *Calgary Albertan*, 'Hutterites and Income taxes,' an editorial, 11 December 1958

7 Quoted in Woollam, 'Treatment of Hutterian Brethren'

8 'Memorandum re Implementation of Settlement, the Hutterian Brethren Church,' 31 March 1967, the Baker files

9 Ibid.

10 James A. Robb to E.A. Fletcher, 11 February 1966, ibid.

11 'Memorandum re the Hutterian Brethren Church,' 14 March 1966, ibid.

12 Ibid.

13 James A. Robb to Roy H.C. Baker, 26 May 1966, ibid.

14 Ibid.

15 Minutes of a meeting of the Hutterian Brethren Church of Canada, held at the Hutterville Colony at Magrath, Alberta, 29 June 1966, ibid.

16 Ibid.

17 James A. Robb to Rev. Jacob Kleinsasser, 14 July 1966, ibid.

18 'Submission of Fact and Law for Purposes of Settlement Hutterian Brethren Church of Canada, Test Case Appeals, Rock Lake and Hutterville Hutterian Brethren,' 26 September 1966, ibid.

19 James A. Robb to Roy H. Baker, 12 October 1966, ibid.

20 James A. Robb to Department of Justice (attention: G.W. Ainslie), 6 January 1967, ibid.

21 James A. Robb to Roy H.C. Baker, 16 January 1967, ibid.

22 James A. Robb to Roy H.C. Baker, 1 April 1968, ibid.

23 Roy Baker to Messrs Stikeman, Elliot, and Co. (attention: James A. Robb), 28 March 1968, ibid.

24 James A. Robb to Roy H.C. Baker, 21 March 1967, ibid.

25 Roy Baker to Messrs. Stikeman, Elliot, and Co. (attention: James A. Robb), 8 January 1968, ibid.

26 'Statement by the Honourable Jean-Pierre Côté, Minister of National Revenue, re the Application of the Income Tax Act to Hutterian Brethren Colonies in Canada,' 6 November 1968, ibid.

27 John R.V. Palmer, special assistant to the minister of National Revenue, to Roy H.C. Baker, 25 July 1973, ibid.

28 'Notice of Appeal of Judgement of Tax Review Board between John K. Hofer, Peter S. Tschetter, Jacob K. Wipf, Joseph K. Wipf, and John K. Wurz, and the Minister of National Revenue, Ottawa, February 16, 1972,' Federal Court Registry Files, Ottawa

29 Quoted in ibid.

30 Ibid.

31 Ibid.

32 *Rev. J.K. Hofer et al. v. Minister of National Revenue* (1972), Dominion Tax Cases 1248; Canadian Tax Cases 2275

33 *Wipf et al. v. The Queen*, 73 Dominion Tax Cases 5558; (1973), Canadian Tax Cases 761

34 *Barrickman Hutterian Mutual Corporation v. Nault et al.* (1939), SCR 223

35 *Hofer et al. v. Hofer et al* (1970), SCR 958

36 *Wipf et al. v. The Queen* (1973), Dominion Tax Cases 5558; Canadian Tax Cases 761

37 *Wipf et al. v. The Queen* (1975), Dominion Tax Cases 5034

38 Ibid.

39 *The Queen v. Joseph K. Wipf et al.* (1976), Canadian Tax Cases 57

40 *Lethbridge Herald*, 28 October 1976

41 The plan of the government to amend the Income Tax Act is indicated in notes on a telephone call of 23 March 1976 from Roy Baker to Jim Gourlay, head of Special Investigation, Department of National Revenue. It was a 'conference telephone call' and seven Hutterite leaders and several accountants participated in the conference, too. The transcript of the telephone conference is in the Baker files.

42 *Hutterian Brethren Church v. The Queen* (1979), Dominion Tax Cases 5052

43 *Ottawa Citizen*, 13 December 1978

44 *Hutterian Brethren Church of Wilson v. The Queen*, Federal Court Appeal Division, judgment delivered on 3 December 1979; (1980), Canada Tax Cases 1.

45 As told to William Janzen by David Morris, chartered accountant of Mayers, Norris, Penny and Co., Brandon, Man., in a telephone interview 11 December 1980. (Norris has done accounting work for the Hutterites for many years.)

46 David Norris, in a telephone interview with William Janzen on 22 June 1981

47 Rev. Jacob J. Waldner to the Hon. Jean-Pierre Côté, minister of National Revenue, 20 April 1970, NA, minister's office files, box 15, file 32-8-2

CHAPTER 12   Contributing Factors in Past and Future

1 Quoted in Epp, *Mennonites in Canada 1786–1920*, 99
2 33 George III, c. 1 (1793); see also Epp, *Mennonites in Canada 1786–1920*, 100.
3 Orders-in-council no. 827B, 26 April 1872; no. 1043D, 25 September, 1872; and no. 957, 13 August 1873; NA, RG 2,1, vol. 83
4 Orders-in-council no. 2747, 6 December 1898; and no. 1676, 12 August 1899; NA, RG 76, vol. 175 and vol. 176
5 Martin, *'Dominion Lands' Policy*, 137
6 Morton, *Manitoba: A History*, 187. See also Janice Staples, 'Consociationalism at Provincial Level: The Erosion of Dualism in Manitoba 1870–1890,' in McRae, *Consociational Democracy*, 288ff.
7 Morton, *Manitoba: A History*, 157
8 Ibid., 245
9 Ibid., 247
10 Ibid., 228
11 C.W. Speers, general colonization agent, to Hon. Frank Oliver, 7 September 1905, NA, RG 15, vol. 755 file 494483(4)
12 Michael White, quoted in Szalasznyj, 'The Doukhobor Homestead Crisis,' 236
13 Szalasznyj writes: 'Land policy ... became an instrument of assimilation' (ibid., 238).
14 Minister of the Interior, circular to Doukhobor Elders and People, February 1907, NA, RG 15, vol. 757, file no. 494483(10)
15 Kenneth D. McRae, 'Epilogue,' *Consociational Democracy: Political Accommodation in Segmented Societies*, ed. McRae (Toronto: McClelland and Stewart 1974: Carleton Library no. 79), 300
16 Oliver, *The Country School*, 8
17 Quoted in Bergen, 'A Historical Study,' 256
18 W.M. Martin, notes from a speech in the Saskatchewan Legislature, 19 December 1918, SAB, Martin Papers, no. 18478
19 Quoted in Francis, *In Search of Utopia*, 179
20 W.S. Cram to deputy minister, Department of Education, Regina, 15 December 1916, SAB, Martin Papers, no. 18836
21 W.M. Martin, notes from a speech in the Saskatchewan Legislature, 19 December 1918, SAB, Martin papers, no. 18478
22 Lyons, 'A History of Doukhobor Schooling,' 191
23 Quoted in Flint, *The Hutterites: A Study in Prejudice*, 108

24 Alberta, *Report of the Hutterite Investigation Committee* (1959), 26
25 John McDougall, 'General Report Doukhobor Commission,' 25 November 1906, NA, RG 15, vol. 755, file no. 494483(6)
26 Quoted in Epp, *Education with a Plus*, 36
27 Quoted in Pitt 'The Hutterian Brethren in Alberta,' 122
28 Circular Memorandum, no. 239, 23 May 1941, NA, RG 27, vol. 997, file 2.106.213
29 'To the Elders and People,' February 1907, NA, RG 15, vol. 757, file 494483(10)
30 'Report of an Interview between the Honourable Frank Oliver, Minister of the Interior, and certain representatives of the Doukhobors,' 25 February 1907, NA, RG 15, vol. 755, file 494483(6)
31 Premier Martin to Johann F. Peters, Hague, Saskatchewan, 10 May 1920, SAB, Martin Papers, no. 18947
32 Quoted in Francis, 'The Mennonite School Problem in Manitoba 1874–1919,' *Mennonite Quarterly Review* 27 (July 1953): 235
33 *Perepolkin v. Superintendent of Child Welfare* (1957), 23 WWR 592
34 *Hofer v. Hofer et al.* (1970), 13 DLR (3d) 1
35 Ibid.
36 Ibid.
37 'A Petition Presented to the Warner County No. 5 School Committee,' 9 April 1956, by Rev. John Wipf et al., reprinted in Knill 'Hutterite Education,' 1958, appendix C
38 *Hofer v. Hofer et al.* (1970), 13 DLR (3d) 1
39 Solicitor-General Arthur Meighen to Rev. Jacob Wiens, 29 January 1917, Borden Papers, NA, RG 26, H vol. 214 no. 121093
40 'Petition to His Excellency, the Governor-General of Canada in Council' 4 November 1918, signed for David Toews and the Mennonites by J.E. Doerr, NA, RG 2,3, vol. 199, PC no 2897
41 House of Commons, *Debates*, 18 June 1940, 904
42 Ibid. 18 April 1974, 1544
43 James A. Smart, deputy minister of the Interior, to W.F. McCreary, commissioner of Immigration, 27 October 1899, NA, RG 76, vol. 173
44 Rev. Jacob J. Waldner, for the Hutterian Brethren church Lehrer-Leut group, to Hon. Jean-Pierre Côté, minister of National Revenue, 20 April 1970, NA, ministers office files, box 15, file 32-8-2
45 Michael F.C. Radcliffe, from Baker, Zivot and Company, to William Janzen, 28 September 1988, author's files
46 W.L. Morton, 'The Historical Phenomenon of Minorities: The Canadian Experience,' *Canadian Ethnic Studies* 13, no. 3 (1981): 34

47 The exception is referred to near the end of chapter 4 where the Saskatchewan Court of Appeal referred to the charter in cases relating to Hutterite land.

48 *R. v. Wiebe* (1978), 3 Western Weekly Reports 36

49 F.L. Morton, 'Group Rights versus Individual Rights in the Charter: The Special Cases of Natives and the Quebecois,' *Minorities and the Canadian State*, ed. by Neil Nevitte and Allan Kornberg (Oakville, Ont.: Mosaic Press 1985), 81

50 *Ford v. Quebec* (1988), 2 SCR 712

51 Quoted by Daniel Drolet, in *Ottawa Citizen*, 24 December 1988

52 *Regina v. Videoflicks Ltd. et al.* (1984), 14 DLR (4th) 35

53 Ibid., 43

54 *R. v. Big M Drug Mart* (1985), 3 WWR 517–18

55 Ibid., 519, 526

56 *Edwards Books & Art Ltd. v. The Queen: R. v. Nortown Foods Ltd.* (1986), 35 DLR (4th) 1

57 *Jones v. The Queen* (1986), 28 CCC (3d) 513 (SCC)

58 *Zylberberg v. Sudbury Board of Education* (1989), 52 DLR (4th) 591

59 Ibid., 593

60 William To-Tang Wan, 'The Impact of the Canadian Charter of Rights and Freedoms on Religious Freedom,' PhD diss., University of Ottawa 1989, 490

Index